RISE OF THE LABOR MOVEMENT IN LOS ANGELES

PUBLICATIONS OF THE
INSTITUTE OF INDUSTRIAL RELATIONS
UNIVERSITY OF CALIFORNIA

RISE OF
THE LABOR MOVEMENT
IN LOS ANGELES

By

GRACE HEILMAN STIMSON

UNIVERSITY OF CALIFORNIA PRESS
BERKELEY AND LOS ANGELES
1955

UNIVERSITY OF CALIFORNIA PRESS

BERKELEY AND LOS ANGELES

CALIFORNIA

◇

CAMBRIDGE UNIVERSITY PRESS

LONDON, ENGLAND

2298

PRINTED IN THE UNITED STATES OF AMERICA

BY THE UNIVERSITY OF CALIFORNIA PRINTING DEPARTMENT

TO

CLAUDE WILLIAM STIMSON

FOREWORD

WITH THIS VOLUME, *Rise of the Labor Movement in Los Angeles,* the Institute of Industrial Relations, Southern Division, has expanded its research program to include a unique and important approach to labor-management relations. We are here presenting a history of the origin and early development of trade-unions in the southern California community. The significance of such historical research is succinctly pointed out by Provost Gordon S. Watkins, of the University of California at Riverside, in his introduction.

A primary objective of the Institute, as established on former Governor Earl Warren's recommendation, is to promote the more effective use of the human and economic resources of the community by bringing about a better understanding of the problems in the relationships between labor and management. A basic requirement for such understanding is a knowledge of how present institutions emerged and grew. One of these institutions, about which little has been recorded until the publication of this volume, is the organized labor movement.

This book is the beginning of a study which has no real conclusion. Although it is hoped that this first volume will be followed by one or several others which will record the history of labor in Los Angeles to the present day, scenes are unfolding and unknown actors are appearing with every new year. It will be noted that many organizations—newspapers, labor unions, and employers' associations—which are part of this history, are still in existence. Their names have remained the same, but their attitudes may have changed, just as the character of the labor movement as a whole has changed in the intervening years.

The guiding spirit for this study was Provost Watkins. The John Randolph Haynes and Dora Haynes Foundation initiated the investigation and furnished the financial support for the undertaking. The Institute is deeply grateful to Dr. Watkins and the Haynes Foundation for making many research materials available and for the grant which made it possible to transfer Dr. Stimson and Miss Eleanor Gold to the Institute staff for completion of this work. Dr. Stimson's laborious unearthing of primary sources, her patient documentation, and her skillful weaving of these materials into an integrated and illuminating story represent a masterful exercise in historical research.

Until this publication, the principal source of information about organized labor in the state has been Professor Ira B. Cross's *A History of the Labor Movement in California.* That study was primarily concerned with developments in northern California. Students of industrial relations have long recognized the marked differences between trade-unions and labor-management relations north and south of the Tehachapi, but no previous effort has been made to portray these developments in southern California. The Los Angeles labor movement, as a significant factor in the economy, is customarily thought of as evolving out of the Great Depression and World War II. Dr. Stimson's research shows that its slow growth and its maturing character had their origin in the period around the beginning of the twentieth century. This history provides a perspective from which the past and the present may be more clearly viewed.

EDGAR L. WARREN, *Director*
Southern Division
Los Angeles, California

INTRODUCTION

THE IMPORTANCE of regional and local research studies in the fields of economics, government, and sociology is now generally recognized by social scientists. Such investigations fill in the essential details undiscovered in broader inquiries, and provide a valuable perspective on problems within the framework of their immediate social environment. This is one of the principal reasons for the present study, *Rise of the Labor Movement in Los Angeles,* by Dr. Grace Heilman Stimson, Research Associate in the Institute of Industrial Relations at the University of California's Los Angeles campus. Further justification, perhaps an even more convincing one, is the significant part which Los Angeles has played in the development of labor-management relations in the United States. Few cities, outside of Detroit and Indianapolis, have commanded more widespread attention on the part of those interested in the relative positions of labor and capital in the American economy.

Los Angeles has been the focal point of national attention in matters of employer-employee relations because, almost from the inception of its industrial life, this city has been known as one of the citadels of the open shop and the center of what is generally characterized by champions of the open shop as "industrial freedom." These terms are subject to a wide range of definition, but their connotation traditionally implies the right of the employer to hire workers regardless of membership or nonmembership in a labor organization, and the corresponding right of the workers to sell their labor under the same conditions.

An historical study of labor relations in this city reveals the multiple facets of a dynamic, rapidly changing economy. Here, as in so many regions of the United States, an emerging industrialism encroached persistently upon the domain of a basically agricultural economy. Here, too, are evident the significant processes of economic change and the varying fortunes incident to the business cycle, the net result of which is an economic system alternately enjoying the fruits of business expansion or helplessly idle in the doldrums of recession and depression. The speculative fever has often run high in this community. In response to the magnet of promised fortune, and sensitive to the disillusionments of business reverses, population has ebbed and flowed, always leaving a residue of humanity larger than subsisted here before—a population whose composition, as Dr. Stimson so clearly points out, has greatly influenced the progress of the labor movement.

In Los Angeles, unionism has displayed the characteristics commonly associated with it in the more industrialized centers of American civilization. Here organized labor's ideals, aspirations, and programs of action, as well as its abject defeats and its encouraging triumphs, have revealed the essence of a movement in search of an improved standard of living for the mass. The program for improvement has run the gamut of industrial and political reform. Conservatism, reformism, and radicalism have, each in its turn and time, dominated unionism here as in other segments of the American economy. The pendulum has characteristically moved from economic action to political action and back again, never quite coming to a dead stop at the center of compromise. No less important have been divergencies of opinion concerning the structure and functions of unionism, one faction favoring industrial unionism, the other regarding craft unionism as the more effective weapon of advance.

Dr. Stimson's detailed analysis shows clearly that Los Angeles has been from the early period of its economic life a frontier of union expansion, an often neglected, if not completely forgotten and forsaken frontier. Until recently, labor carried on its struggle for recognition and power without adequate financial resources—one compelling reason for the tragedy of defeat which so frequently has marked the labor movement here. Furthermore, the forces opposed to organized labor have been powerful, influential, and exceedingly effective, politically and economically. To combat such forces, there emerged in Los Angeles vigorous, sometimes militant, leaders of the working class. Dr. Stimson introduces her readers to men like Arthur Vinette, Jonathan Bailey, Frank Colver, and Isaac Kinley—mere names to most of us until we read her story of their vital part in labor's struggle for power. One also meets national leaders who carved important niches for themselves in labor's hall of fame—Andrew Furuseth, T. V. Powderly, Samuel Gompers, Eugene V. Debs, and Daniel DeLeon.

It is doubtful if any other American city has presented so able an array of militant, uncompromising opponents of unionism and so fervent a championship of the open shop. The magnitude of the influence and power of a single metropolitan newspaper is one of the striking features in the annals of the labor movement in this city. The fixed and firm convictions of General Harrison Gray Otis, implemented through an uncompromising policy of antagonism to union domination, made the Los Angeles *Times* an historic instrument in molding labor-management relations in this city for generations. General Otis' vigorous spirit still pervades the attitude, policies, and actions of those who see in organized labor a monopoly that threatens the national economy. In the combination of industrial power that adopted the policy of the open shop, organized labor often met its nemesis.

Originally sponsored and financed by the John Randolph Haynes and Dora Haynes Foundation, the study has continued under the direction of the Institute of Industrial Relations, University of California, Los Angeles. The Institute, like the Foundation, is dedicated to impartial, objective inquiry. Dr. Stimson has rigorously adhered to this ideal. With tireless energy, she has explored hitherto unknown sources of information, collected and processed a myriad of facts, and organized voluminous materials into a balanced study. Her analysis has been made with meticulous care, and her deductions have been drawn with a high regard for the canons of genuine scholarship. Yet she has told the story of labor in Los Angeles in a manner that should command the interest of both the specialist and the lay reader. To her difficult task she has brought the insight and perspective of the trained historian.

This study is designed principally to provide valuable supplements to the economic, political, and social history of California. But its further purpose is to discover in the past a prelude to the present and a constructive guide to the intelligent solution of the complex problems of human relations in contemporary industry.

GORDON S. WATKINS
Provost of Riverside Campus
University of California

Riverside, California
June, 1953

ACKNOWLEDGMENTS

I AM deeply indebted to the John Randolph Haynes and Dora Haynes Foundation, Los Angeles, and to the Institute of Industrial Relations, University of California, Los Angeles, for their joint sponsorship of this history of organized labor in Los Angeles. The following individuals associated with the two institutions deserve a full measure of gratitude for their consistent encouragement and help: Miss Anne M. Mumford, formerly Executive Secretary of the Haynes Foundation; Dr. Gordon S. Watkins, Provost of the University of California, Riverside Campus, and trustee of the Haynes Foundation; Mr. Edgar L. Warren, Director of the Institute of Industrial Relations; and Dr. Irving Bernstein, Research Associate at the Institute of Industrial Relations.

I wish also to express my appreciation to the Institute's reading committee, consisting of Professors John W. Caughey of the History Department, Wayne L. McNaughton of the School of Business Administration, and Warren C. Scoville of the Economics Department, for their careful review of the manuscript and their helpful suggestions for its improvement.

Professor Arthur C. Bining of the History Department, University of Pennsylvania, and Dr. Dora Mae Clark, Professor of Political Science and American History, Wilson College, Chambersburg, Pennsylvania, gave me unusually valuable advice in matters of style, organization, and content of this volume.

Many members of the staff of the Institute of Industrial Relations showed great interest in and gave much needed help to the preparation of this volume. Deserving special mention are Mr. Robert Thomason, Librarian; Mrs. Nancy Taylor, Administrative Assistant; Mrs. Anne Cook, Editor; and Miss Louise Margolis, Mrs. Carol Sadler, and Mrs. Lois M. Hurwitz, secretaries.

Four individuals who at one time or another served as research assistants on this project merit high commendation for their conscientious and intelligent work both in gathering the data and in editing the manuscript. They are Mrs. Roberta S. Greenwood, Miss Eleanor Gold, Miss Alice Robinson, and Miss Tasile Carter.

There are many people, both in and out of the labor movement, upon whom I frequently and freely called for assistance. Too numerous to mention by name, they generously provided information not elsewhere available, which found its way into the completed manuscript.

I am particularly grateful to Dr. Ira B. Cross, Professor Emeritus of the University of California, Berkeley, both for his pioneer work in a related field, *A History of the Labor Movement in California,* which served as a valuable starting point for my own researches, and for his personal helpfulness.

Newspaper files used extensively in the research were made available by the Los Angeles Public Library and the office of the Los Angeles City Clerk. The staffs of the Huntington Library, San Marino, California; the Los Angeles County Museum Library; the Bancroft Library, Berkeley, California; and the Library of the University of Michigan, Ann Arbor, were also of great assistance. Of particular value was the personal attention of Miss Agnes Inglis, formerly curator of the Labadie Collection in the University of Michigan Library. The Huntington Library has granted me permission to quote from and cite original materials in its collection.

Of greatest usefulness in supplying material representing labor's point of view were the minutes of Los Angeles Typographical Union No. 174, from its founding in 1875 throughout the period under discussion. I am exceedingly grateful to the union for permission to examine these files. The International Typographical Union, as well, contributed pertinent information through its research director, Mr. Clark B. Hicks. Mr. W. J. Bassett, secretary of the Los Angeles Central Labor Council, was generous in allowing me to consult the Council's minutes, extant from the year 1909. The original material contained in the files of these three labor organizations was invaluable.

GRACE HEILMAN STIMSON

Los Angeles, California
June, 1953

CONTENTS

TABLES

I. ANTECEDENTS OF THE LABOR MOVEMENT

THE LOS ANGELES area has been blessed with a benign climate, rich natural resources, and extraordinary economic opportunities. Its great promise has made it, through decades past, a mecca for those seeking good health, profitable employment, or financial advancement. Eager newcomers from all strata of life and from all sections of the country, even of the world, have created a complex and volatile society whose uniqueness has long been a commonplace. It is not surprising, then, that the labor movement in Los Angeles has been strikingly unusual. Here the open-shop principle made an early appearance, attracted powerful support, and weakened or disrupted labor organizations whose brief and fumbling early history had ill prepared them for the steady, concerted onslaught of organized capital.

The extremity of labor's hardships in Los Angeles singled out the area, to the minds of many, as one of sharp deviation from the progress made elsewhere with comparatively less strain. For years labor leaders in older, better established communities looked upon Los Angeles as a chronic trouble spot, whether they regarded its problems as challenging or hopeless. In particular they noted a marked contrast between Los Angeles and San Francisco, for despite their common heritage these two Pacific Coast centers evinced no homogeneity with respect to the development of organized labor. San Francisco was one of the earliest closed-shop cities in the United States. The reasons for the divergence between Los Angeles and both San Francisco and eastern labor strongholds are many and complex, some stemming from the history of the state, some from regional development, and some from the city's own growth.

The state of California had a singular history. Geographically separated from the East by mountains, deserts, and vast continental distances, this potential giant of the West developed almost independently and thus faced its own peculiar economic problems. Population was sparse, almost insignificant, before the gold rush, and even the rapid growth after 1849 did not bring the state's cities and towns into competition with commercial and industrial centers in older sections of the country. Los Angeles was particularly backward. Established as a city in 1781, with a nucleus of forty-four settlers, it had achieved a population of only 1,610 by 1850, and 4,385 by 1860.[1] Furthermore, as the western terminus of continental expansion, California, with its frontier civilization, attracted the ambitious and restless and venturesome. The earliest arrivals came not to establish homes but to seek their fortunes in the gold mines. Thus was established a society that was mobile and unstable, but at the same time resourceful and enthusiastic. Immigration from many European countries and from Asia added a dash of cosmopolitanism. An unusual combination of circumstances—the conquest of California and its admission to statehood without the intermediate territorial stage, the discovery of gold, the lure of free lands, and the unprecedented influx of thousands of adventurers and gold-seekers—created a "new and quickly developed colonial civilization" which "grew up like a gourd in the night."[2]

Such a civilization was not a likely milieu for unionism but instead stimulated utopian attempts to correct social and political wrongs. After a visit to the west coast in the 1880's, the English historian, James Bryce, described the Californians of his day as "impatient, accustomed to blame everything and everybody but themselves for the slow approach of the millennium, ready to try instant, even if perilous, remedies for a present evil."[3] California workers exemplified this tendency in their avid support of demagoguery and of ephemeral reform movements. Throughout their early search for the most effective weapon against current evils—in pragmatic trade-unions, societies for the promotion of special causes, or political labor parties—ran a thread of idealistic hope that fundamental social change could be brought about through agitation. On the same premise American labor went through a similar phase of trying to better working conditions through political means. It was only after such attempts proved more illusory than practical that labor awoke to the need for strong craft organizations as weapons against the tightening grip of industrialism. Political goals eventually yielded to economic objectives, and reform groups gave way to unions which preferred direct bargaining to fruitless agitations, bread and butter to Utopia. Thus the American Federation of Labor, the uncompromising exponent of business unionism, assumed the leadership of the national labor movement. Finally California workingmen reached the same conclusion: that reliance on craft unionism would best serve their purposes.[4]

Although California's frontier community, with its thinly distributed population, its high prices and wages, its immature financial and industrial structure, embraced both north and south, the labor movements of the two areas developed in almost diametrically opposed ways, with only a few points of juncture before 1900. The isolation of Los Angeles from San Francisco was as marked as that of California from the rest of the nation. The feeling that southern California was "a sort of island on land"[5] grew out of geography and climate, but was intensified to a political concept by a number of attempts at state division, one of which failed only because it reached the floor of Congress just as the Civil War started. The resulting mutual disaffection between the two sections of California lingered on and, in the crucial formative period, denied Los Angeles labor the benefit of guidance from San Francisco.[6]

But regional tension alone cannot fully explain the discrepancy between the labor movements of these two Pacific Coast cities. The most compelling reasons for divergence and the most decisive determinants of labor's development in Los Angeles are found, not in the history of the state nor in the cleavage between north and south, but in the forces operating within the Los Angeles area itself. Most of these reasons will emerge in later discussions, but the most obvious early determinant of Los Angeles labor history was the predominantly agricultural economy of the area. Nothing in the limited opportunities afforded by the derided "cow counties" of southern California gave a hint of the area's tremendous potential productive capacity. The few new settlers who straggled into the area, many of them disappointed gold-seekers, roustabouts, or vagrants, scarcely provided the beginnings of the artisan class essential to industrial progress. During the 1850's and 1860's, mechanical industry—though starting in a small way—suffered not only from a lack of skilled workers but also from the prohibitive prices of raw materials, the shortage of capital, a small domestic market, and lower profits than accrued in mining or agriculture. The only enterprises established were those required to meet the immediate needs of the local population, and they were carried on, for the most part, by self-employed craftsmen and did not cover a wide range of occupations.[7] It was thus the type of economy which was primarily responsible for a slow and hesitant start in the development of a Los Angeles labor movement, and this in turn delayed the establishment of a union structure with strength and stability.

Within its limited scope, however, the small Spanish town of Los Angeles enjoyed relative prosperity during the 1850's and supported, among other enterprises, a number of newspapers and job printing concerns. Toward the end of the decade, somewhat surprisingly, the printers employed in these offices got together and formed the first known labor organization in southern California. On September 12, 1859, the National Typographical Union chartered Los Angeles Local No. 44; by November the new union had fourteen members, including C. R. Conway, president, and Alonzo Waite, who together established the *Semi-Weekly Southern News* in January, 1860. The failure to distinguish between proprietors and employees for purposes of union membership extended beyond local boundaries, for Conway was a member of the national union's executive board during the year 1860–1861.[8]

This early organization of printers was in keeping with the traditions of trade-union history, for skilled workers were everywhere the first to form unions. The pioneers of labor organization in the East, as well as in northern California, were newspaper compositors. Since the founding of the Los Angeles Typographical Union followed closely on the heels of the reorganization of both the San Francisco and Sacramento unions, it may well have signified the first impulse from labor organizations in the northern part of the state. Or the Los Angeles union may have been stimulated by the current mild boom, by the arrival of a printer with previous union experience, or by fear of a possible wage cut. But whatever the reasons for its organization, the Los Angeles union did not long survive. A depression beginning in 1859, the same year in which the union was organized, forced many small business concerns in Los Angeles, including printing firms, to close their doors. Los Angeles Typographical Union No. 44 disappeared in 1860, remarkable only as a freakish and ill-timed manifestation of labor organization.[9]

Following this premature organization of the printers, a decade elapsed before other craftsmen felt a similar urge. Changes in the local economy during the 1860's increased both the number and the variety of artisans in Los Angeles. Newcomers interested in launching commercial ventures or in working at trades, in contrast to the adventurers of the previous decade, laid the foundations of a rudimentary industrial structure. The first bank was established in 1865; the volume of real estate transactions increased; and a local building boom took place during 1868–1869. Through this business expansion, however small its scale, an artisan class was slowly being created in Los Angeles.[10] Meanwhile, workers in other parts of the country were vigorously agitating for the eight-hour day and in 1866 organized the National Labor Union to aid their cause. Los Angeles craftsmen, though they were to respond to the first recognizable impact of the national labor movement in the eight-hour agitation, waited to act until San Francisco unionists launched a state movement.[11]

By the 1860's the labor organizations in the northern city, some of them dating from the previous decade, had formed a central body which they called a Trades' Union. This federation, never very stable, seized upon the eight-hour agitation as a possible means of strengthening itself and at the same time of benefiting workingmen. Support of the movement for a shorter working day did, in fact, infuse new life into the Trades' Union, and in 1866 it brought an eight-hour bill before the California Legislature. The measure did not pass because the law-makers believed that by increasing the already high wages it would impede further industrial development. Not deterred by this initial setback, San Francisco workingmen organized eight-hour leagues along craft lines, as well as a state Industrial League, active during the spring and summer of 1867. The League's major objectives were, in addition to the eight-hour day, a mechanics' lien law and prohibition of Chinese immigration and of convict labor. That political ineptitude caused it to fail does not by any means obscure the League's significance in the history of California working-class organization. It represented the first state-wide body of wage earners and, more important, sought for the first time in California to obtain workers' demands through political methods. As an innovator it attracted the publicity which was later to ease the passage of laws providing the desired remedies.[12]

The Industrial League passed into oblivion, but was shortly replaced by the Mechanics' State Council, organized on November 6, 1867, by delegates from eight-hour leagues, meeting in San Francisco. The new organization was dedicated to essentially the same ideals as its prede-cessor, but differed in concentrating on only one of its objectives, the passage of a state eight-hour law. The Mechanics' State Council, in-stantly popular, grew rapidly itself and also stimulated more wide-spread organization of local eight-hour leagues. In advance of the legis-lative session of 1868, the Council prepared bills stipulating the eight-hour working day and appropriate regulation of mechanics' liens. The Council's own prestige, coupled with workingmen's previous agitation through other agencies, won a handy victory for labor in February, 1868, when the Legislature passed both bills. The new eight-hour law stated that eight hours constituted a legal day's labor within the state, except for domestic and agricultural workers, and that employment of a minor for more than eight hours a day was a misdemeanor. The law, however, soon lost its efficacy, for a court decision in October, 1869, reduced it to little more than an enunciation of principle.[13]

Los Angeles mechanics, who had taken no part in the eight-hour agitation during 1867, found the usable weapon of an actual statute more to their liking. Meeting initially on May 29, 1868, to "take into consideration the eight-hour law,"[14] various building trades workers organized a local branch of the Mechanics' State Council and by July were ready to make the following pronouncement in the press:

The Carpenters, Bricklayers, Stone Masons, Plasterers, and Painters of the "Mechanics' League of Los Angeles," hereby notify all employers that from and after the 10th day of August, A. D. 1868, eight hours' labor will constitute a day's work, without reduction of wages from present rates, for all of the above mentioned Trades. By order of the League. Los Angeles, July 10th, 1868.[15]

For a short time, and to a limited extent, the Mechanics' Eight-Hour League of Los Angeles accomplished its objective. By April, 1869, it numbered fifty-two members but with thirty-five additional "co-operative mechanics not actual members" it embraced a total of eighty-seven "journeymen, contractors, and employers in Los Angeles strictly observing the Eight-Hour Law."[16] Although employers were reported so satisfied with the new system that wider adoption seemed inevitable,[17] the League did not long survive. Disintegration set in before the end of 1869, and accomplishments proved not only meager but ephemeral. The League had failed to institute the eight-hour day for any great length of time, but it indirectly served workingmen in another way by arousing public interest in the problems of labor. As a local newspaper pointed out, "California . . . has given no thought whatever to the comfort, interests and elevation of the laborer. . . . The class of laborers so much needed will not come to us if we fail to offer them inducements for the certain improvement of their condition."[18]

Through the decline of their Eight-Hour League, Los Angeles mechanics shared the fate of others in the state; all the trades which had established the shorter working day were forced to relinquish it between 1870 and 1877. In San Francisco this resulted from determined employer resistance and a sudden dislocation of the labor market. Post–Civil War depression, unemployment following completion of the Central Pacific Railroad in 1869, and new rail connections with the East, facilitating travel to California, so increased the labor supply that workingmen were unable to enforce their demands for an eight-hour day. Yet the Mechanics' State Council survived at least nominally until 1877 and, despite the brevity of its effective life, left its mark on the state labor movement. By continuing the Industrial League's policy of unifying the working people of California in a politically-minded organization, it prepared the way for the reform movements of the 1870's, both by labor and other groups.[19]

Neither the Los Angeles Typographical Union of 1859 nor the Mechanics' Eight-Hour League of 1868 entitled the southern city to any claim to real partnership in the state labor movement. But events during the 1870's made Los Angeles workingmen more active organizationally and, moreover, brought them into collaboration with other groups of citizens. In the 1870's Los Angeles began its gradual transition from a slow-moving Spanish backwater to a modern American city. New arrivals increased the population from 5,728 in 1870 to 11,183 in 1880; urban property was improved; great tracts of land were subdivided; and a Chamber of Commerce was organized in 1873. The stimulus behind much of this development was the knowledge that the railroad was coming to Los Angeles from San Francisco. But when the Central Pacific completed the line south in 1876, the effects of the Panic of 1873, together with a serious drought, not only prevented the expected prosperity from materializing but caused a depression which lasted until the close of the decade. Antirailroad sentiment, already traditional in the state, burgeoned into active discontent in southern California, where monopolistic rates created greater hardship. It was thus very easy to blame railroad exactions for the ills of drought and depression. Throughout a long period, hatred of the Southern Pacific Railroad (a subsidiary of Central Pacific) united groups which, normally antagonistic to each other, had found a common enemy.[20] Physical growth and industrial development during the 1870's made public-minded citizens as well as workingmen more aware of inequities springing from political corruption and monopolistic practices, and they embarked on programs directed at the correction of such evils. The movements arising during the early 1870's in the Los Angeles area established a tradition of coöperation between labor and other groups which persisted for several decades and markedly colored certain specific periods in the development of the local labor movement.

Farmers were the first in southern California to implement antimonopolism with organization. There were two reasons for their leadership: previous movements by farmers in both state and nation set an example; and farmers constituted the largest group in the Los Angeles area. The first farmers' club in California had been formed at Sacramento in December, 1871. Responding to this stimulus, farmers in Los Angeles County organized a series of clubs and in July, 1873, consolidated them into the Southern California Farmers' Union. Although ostensibly dedicated to the promotion of irrigation and other agricultural benefits, and the establishment of bureaus of farm information, the Union revealed an underlying motivation when it passed resolutions condemning the rapacity of railroads and those taxation policies disadvantageous to farmers.[21]

The Farmers' Union, however, never had the opportunity to prove its usefulness, for it immediately ran into competition with the Grange, or Patrons of Husbandry, a national nonpolitical secret society organized in Washington, D.C., in 1867. To attract workers other than farmers, the Grange espoused antimonopolism and coöperative enterprises, demanding, in particular, state regulation of freight charges and railroad land holdings. Preoccupation with this issue was so generally recognized that the whole antirailroad agitation of the 1870's became known as the Granger movement.[22] Farmers in Los Angeles County, quick to sense the greater potentialities of a nationwide organization, began to form local units of the Grange in July, 1873, the same month in which the Farmers' Union was organized. The granges in the Los Angeles area became affiliated with the state movement and, growing rapidly, began to absorb the Farmers' Union and eventually supplanted it altogether.[23]

The Granger movement in southern California was a vigorous though short-lived expression of farmers' objectives. By the end of 1873 a district council was supervising fifteen branches in Los Angeles County, considerably more than the average, per county, in the state. The Grangers' Co-operative Association for Southern California, formed early in 1874, was one of the most successful of such enterprises. In 1875 it established in Los Angeles a coöperative store which continued to function at least until 1883. The Granger movement itself had begun to decline in 1875 and gradually died down, as it did elsewhere in the state and country.[24]

Why was this farmers' organization significant to the development of a Los Angeles labor movement? Most important, it championed the attitudes of workingmen on antimonopolism, coöperation, cheap credit, political action, and equalization of taxes on land. The Grangers also nurtured organizational enthusiasm at a time when mechanics and laborers evinced no feeling of unity; established a precedent for subsequent reform efforts; and acquired experience in the techniques of organization. Because it specifically tried to entice workingmen into its ranks, the Grange served as a forerunner to the later Populist movement, which to a far greater extent brought farmers and trade-unionists together behind a joint reform program.[25]

Unrest in the 1870's found a more direct avenue for political expression than farmers' organizations. A series of small independent parties seemed to spring up spontaneously from consciousness of the need for reform. Although never of long duration, these manifestations of discontent kept alive the sentiment of protest first expressed by the farmers. Arising almost simultaneously with the Patrons of Husbandry, one such party in Los Angeles was an urban counterpart of the farmers' movement. A nonpartisan convention in July, 1873, organized the People's Reform Party, which immediately selected nominees for the state Senate and Assembly, the Board of Supervisors, and other county offices. Although lacking thorough organization and experienced leadership, the new party infected the electorate with its own crusading enthusiasm. After only two months of existence, it won a sweeping victory in the September elections.[26]

Similar successes in other communities inspired reform parties throughout the state to consolidate as the People's Independent Party on September 25, 1873. The platform promised reform of politics and civil service, state control of waterways, and anti-Chinese and anti-monopoly legislation. With an eye on wage-earner support, the party also pledged itself to introduce "all reasonable measures of labor reform" and to enforce the eight-hour law "in regard to manufacturing and mechanical pursuits, and upon all public works."[27] As the anti-Chinese and labor planks bid for working-class votes, so the curbing of monopolies was held out as an inducement to farmers.

A Los Angeles County affiliate of the People's Independent Party was formed on November 13, 1873, under the sponsorship, not of workingmen, but of such civic leaders as Colonel J. J. Warner, Judge John S. Thompson, Henry Dockweiler, and Prudent Beaudry. These men were later to evidence their genuine concern for working-class welfare by their adherence to movements originating with labor. In the municipal election on December 1, several of the people's nominees were elected to the City Council, and all three of their candidates for the Board of Education were victorious.[28] The party died out after the election, but the causes which it upheld did not suffer, for new groups appeared to carry forward the standard of reform.

While farmers and citizens were spiritedly, though briefly, engaging in their reform campaigns, workingmen had singled out anti-Chinese agitation as their most appropriate method of tackling the maladjustments of society. Ever since the first employment of coolie labor in the mines during the 1850's, California workers had seen in Chinese competition a threat to their own wage and living standards, despite a considerable body of opinion outside the labor movement which discounted the danger. According to this opposite point of view, as expressed by one of its spokesmen, the Chinese, instead of lowering wage levels and causing unemployment of white workers, usually entered fields where a chronic labor scarcity and/or high wages prevailed, such as mining, laundering, and domestic service. The Chinese themselves tried to distribute immigrants so as to avoid excessive competition and possibly dangerous prejudice. Nevertheless, the anti-Chinese feeling persisted among white workers, and from the beginning,

San Francisco labor organizations actively sought exclusion. Their agitation was the nucleus for the steady growth of anti-Chinese sentiment among laboring people throughout the state. Moreover, they warned fellow workers in the East that the social and economic consequences of unrestricted immigration, if not checked at the starting point, would eventually spread out from the Pacific Coast. In California, as groups other than labor gradually were indoctrinated with antipathy to Orientals, the anti-Chinese cause became a unifying force which transcended regional division and class consciousness.[29]

The volume of Chinese immigration, following an uneven pattern, determined the degree of opposition at different times. It took a sharp upward swing after the Burlingame Treaty of 1869, which permitted free entry without the right of naturalization. Railroad expansion, by dependence on coolie labor, swelled the tide of immigrants and dispersed them more widely throughout the state. When completion of the transcontinental line in 1869 threw many wage earners out of work, labor organizations attributed the resulting unemployment to the Chinese. San Francisco unions, under the leadership of the Mechanics' State Council and the Knights of St. Crispin, an organization of shoemakers, sponsored a state anti-Chinese convention in August, 1870. Because restriction or removal of the Chinese required legislative action, resort to politics was necessary. The 1870 convention thus marked the beginning of a political labor movement that was to last ten years and culminate in the Workingmen's Party of California, established toward the close of the decade. The groundwork for this kind of working-class endeavor had been laid by the Industrial League and the Mechanics' State Council in the late 1860's.[30]

As with other state labor activities, the Chinese question scarcely touched Los Angeles before 1870. In 1860 there were only eleven Asiatics in the whole of Los Angeles County, compared to 2,719 in San Francisco County. By 1870, the number of Chinese in the southern county had increased to 234; San Francisco, however, had over 12,000. Thus, there were too few Orientals in Los Angeles to warrant exclusionist agitation, and the city sent no representatives to the state convention of 1870. The looting of Chinatown in Los Angeles in 1871, accompanied by the massacre of nineteen Chinese, was more the climax of a period of general lawlessness extending from 1850 to 1870 than evidence of strong anti-Chinese sentiment in the city. There was, in fact, no anti-Chinese movement in Los Angeles until 1873, when a new influx of immigrants intensified existing unemployment and led to greater activity throughout the state. Even then only one meeting was

son, formerly active in the Grange, helped to form the characteristic
liaison between farmers and workers. Judge W. C. Wiseman, known
as the "Battle-Axe" of the anti-Chinese campaign, provided a link with
another reform group. The reappearance of men such as these suggests
that the movements of the 1870's were all facets of the same political
philosophy, integrated and summarized by a party in which not only
workingmen but other dissatisfied groups found expression.

Not all Los Angeles citizens were in sympathy with the aspirations
of the workingmen. Alarmed by the excitable reports in the local press of
the riots which followed the July 23 assemblage in San Francisco, some
of them set up a voluntary committee of safety just before the meeting
scheduled for August 3. This precaution amused Moore, who "had no
idea, when a few workingmen got together and devised the little call
and platform ... for a labor meeting, that they were going to cause
such tremulous excitement. . . ." As his real object was presentation of
a people's ticket, Moore concluded that politicians "afraid of losing
their heads" were behind the safety measures.[9] When the meeting took
place, it amply justified Moore's faith in the good behavior of the
workingmen. Judge Thompson, echoing Stephen White's advice of a
year before, advocated dependence on Congress for a solution to the
Chinese problem. G. A. Bunch, a laboring man later prominent in the
Workingmen's Party, stressed the need for peaceable procedures and
for a platform insuring justice to labor with minimum emphasis on
politics. Judge Wiseman, after obliging with a rabid denunciation of
Chinese labor, shifted to the more personal objective of winning subscribers to his newspaper. After deciding to go ahead with preparations
for the approaching county election, the gathering dispersed so quietly
that the committee of safety heard no call for its services.[10]

It was easy, in the camaraderie of an enthusiastic mass meeting, for
a group of political neophytes to adopt resolutions looking toward
formal party organization and entrance into an election only a month
away. But in actual execution of the two primary functions of formulating a platform and nominating a ticket, the Workingmen were beset
by every conceivable difficulty. Lacking time for proper organization,
the amorphous party had to depend upon a rather indeterminate leadership to run its affairs. Petty bickering clouded relationships between
leaders who carried no specific mandate from the group and who tried
haphazardly to get a ticket into the field. Externally, the uncertain
reaction of Democrats and Republicans to the new political venture
added to the confusion, for the Workingmen's inability to produce
qualified candidates of their own on short notice forced them to rely

chiefly on endorsements of major party nominees. This, in turn, alienated laboring men who had hoped for a bona fide workingmen's party.
A final hardship was the unfriendly condescension of the local press.

These handicaps precluded any systematic functioning of the new
party in its first month of existence. During August, 1877, the newspapers listed three different "Workingmen's" tickets, all of them borrowing from major party nominations. Numerous candidates on the
first two tickets, unable to decide whether labor endorsement was a
curse or a blessing, withdrew their names. The third slate, which appeared on August 28, consisted largely of Republicans who allowed
their names to stand, suggesting that their party had finally ventured
to accept working-class support.[11] The notion was strengthened by
James M. Pearson, a labor party member who had appeared on the
first ticket but had subsequently withdrawn because he believed that
"a few wire-pulling politicians have joined our ranks for the purpose
of defeating a few of the Democratic candidates. . . ."[12] Later, other
disgruntled members alleged without contradiction that Republicans
had made financial contributions to the labor campaign.[13]

There were other evidences of friction within the Workingmen's
Party. Edward Evey, a prominent Granger whom the Workingmen
had nominated for assemblyman, and Judge Wiseman, heading the
labor ticket as candidate for state senator, both withdrew their names.
Going beyond such individual defections, discontent within the party
crystallized as early as August 14, 1877, in a factional movement among
those "opposed to the farce being made of their class by Alfred Moore's
meetings."[14] Although unsuccessful in dislodging Moore, the challenge
to his leadership was prophetic of more serious disharmony in the
future.

The Workingmen's Party adopted a platform in almost as random a
way as it chose a ticket. The first set of party principles took the form
of a constitution read at a meeting of "Alfred Moore's Labor Party"
on August 11. An expanded and more explicit constitution, promul-
gated a week later, served as the party platform for the first election.
The tendency of Los Angeles Workingmen to welcome interested outsiders into the party made this document, originating with "mechanics,
farmers, and laboring men," a curious hodgepodge. An initial brief
plank protesting Chinese immigration and labor quickly disposed of
the reason for the party's existence. Then the platform, declaring that
the workingmen would support only Democrats and Republicans with
acceptable records in public service, went on to condemn those "chronic
office-holders" who had favored rich monopolists by levying unequal

and exorbitant taxation on the poor and had greedily filled their own pockets at the expense of the county treasury. The Workingmen, therefore, stressed the need for economy in all branches of the public service. With concern for the proper functioning of the educational system, they proposed to exclude sectarianism from the schoolroom and to insure teachers proper compensation. Touching briefly on national issues, the platform urged control of the railroads and telegraph system by the federal government, and asserted the principles of individual liberty, freedom, and suffrage for all citizens.[15]

This platform was more a working hypothesis for the future than a practical program for the present, since the Workingmen had few nominees of their own and, further, failed to eliminate friction within their ranks. At a meeting on September 1, 1877, just four days before the election, L. E. Page, candidate for assemblyman, with the help of three other Workingmen's nominees, wrested the leadership of the party from Alfred Moore. It is worthy of note that many leaders of the Workingmen's Party were not mechanics or laborers; Page, for example, was a partner in a firm of carriage manufacturers. Plunging into an election without adequate organization and with ticket and platform hastily devised, the labor party could hardly be expected to influence the outcome. Yet the Democrats, perhaps hoping that the emergence of new leadership would destroy the alleged liaison between Workingmen and Republicans, made a last-minute bid for labor votes in an election eve rally, represented as a joint move by themselves and Workingmen. The election results on September 5 were discouraging for the new party. Page received the highest labor vote, 212, as against more than 3,000 for each of the winning candidates for the assembly. He attributed his defeat to a campaign contribution of $25,000 from "Stanford and Company" to stop the Workingmen, and to the infancy of the Los Angeles movement.[16] Page and his cohorts regarded the coup through which he had supplanted Moore on September 1 as the actual beginning of the local Workingmen's Party. This shift in leadership, plus the disastrous election, spelled the end of Moore's organization.

The election results were damaging enough to keep both factions quiescent for several months. Then, in November, 1877, Moore rallied to form the Greenback Labor Club, a new organization which thenceforth claimed his allegiance and embodied his aspirations for personal advancement. But despite the ease with which he attracted new followers, Moore still hankered for reassociation with the Workingmen's Party, which he regarded as his own creation. Under Greenback auspices, he persuaded Denis Kearney, of the San Francisco Workingmen's Party, to include Los Angeles in a speaking tour of the state at the end of 1877. Fearing the possible reinstatement of Moore through this device, Page's faction so manipulated the Kearney meeting as to relegate Moore to the background and dictate the choice of Dr. K. D. Wise and A. J. Norton, both Page supporters, as chairman and secretary.[17]

This meeting had important consequences. With Moore decisively pushed out, the new group of leaders strengthened their grip on the revived Los Angeles movement and represented themselves to local party members as the recipients of Kearney's blessing, an argument of some force in a period before violent anti-Kearneyism rocked the northern party. The Page faction forged a link with its own past and with the whole state movement by organizing as Workingmen's Club No. 1. By the end of 1877, this club, with Page as president, had become in reality the southern branch of the Workingmen's Party of California.[18] Among its leaders was Jesse Butler, poet, jeweler, and agent for a patent medicine known as Spence's Positive and Negative Powders.[19] By his election as secretary of Club No. 1, Butler bowed his way into a political career marred by his inability to compromise and to maintain equable relationships. His first act in a long association with labor reform movements, however, was restrained enough to allay any public suspicion of his party's intentions. In January, 1878, he begged Los Angeles citizens to help workingmen solve the "all-important Labor Question in a peaceable, honorable and rational way," and proposed as a first step the employment of native Americans in preference to Chinese.[20]

Shortly thereafter the reorganized Workingmen were ready to announce their program to a public already partially lulled by Butler's calm statement. Their open meeting on February 2 was attended by approximately one thousand persons, a goodly audience from a city population of perhaps ten thousand. Banners with such mottoes as "Down with Chinese labor," "Equality," and "The Workingmen will see that no more votes are bought," gave advance notice of the party's aims. Proceedings were so harmonious as to suggest that all factionalism had already been submerged and that violent outbreaks were as far from the party's intentions as from the public's desires. Among the speakers were Judge Thompson, who was a convert from the Moore faction, and A. J. Norton, both of whom had previously established themselves as advocates of moderation. Norton, in fact, stressed reliance on the polls as more fruitful than the Kearney type of agitation, and stipulated political education as a prerequisite for intelligent voting. By this slower method, he said, Workingmen would more certainly reach their ultimate goal of cleansing Los Angeles elections of the customary corruption. With unusual acumen, Norton envisioned an objective of organized labor during the next two decades when he urged Workingmen to seek a share in revision of the city charter. Later in the month, party representatives actually did get into the charter a clause requiring that all contracts for public work prohibit the employment of Chinese,[21] thus carrying a step further the accomplishment of the anti-Chinese club in 1876.

In addition to generating good will and harmony, the meeting on February 2, 1878, adopted a platform for the Workingmen's Party of Los Angeles. Modeled to some extent on the constitution of the San Francisco party, this instrument was a broad statement of reform principles which went considerably beyond the demands of a pure and simple labor organization. The straightforward working-class planks demanded government safeguards for labor's rights, and restriction of Chinese immigration, with a corollary suggestion that the public join in resisting any encroachments on civil liberties and the rights of labor. Along with a demand for the curbing of capitalistic influence in government went a request for public improvement programs by state and local authorities to alleviate unemployment. Educational planks promised a free public school system, with free textbooks and compulsory attendance of children between the ages of five and sixteen, as well as a state industrial school system. Antirailroad sentiments found expression in a requirement that any railroad receiving government aid, especially the hated Southern Pacific, be prohibited from employing Chinese. Borrowing from the Greenback Labor Party, the Workingmen called for government issue of paper money and condemned the currency retraction policy as causing the Panic of 1873 and nearly ruining the debtor class. Land planks demanded the limitation of corporate and individual holdings and the assessment of large and small tracts on the same basis. For economy and elimination of corruption in high places, the Workingmen demanded lower salaries for public officials; more stringent laws for punishing malfeasance by public, corporation, and savings bank officers; and a statute proscribing bribery in elections.[22]

This platform well demonstrated the heterogeneity of the Los Angeles Workingmen's Party. By shifting emphasis from the basic Chinese issue to the evils of monopoly, government corruption, and social inequalities, it continued a trend noticeable in Alfred Moore's constitution of 1877. This change brought wide general support, just as the inclusion of land and railroad planks attracted the remnants of the Granger movement. These broader objectives differentiated the southern party from the northern and, combined with more conservative leadership

in the south and less pro- and anti-Kearney factionalism, prolonged
the effectiveness of the Los Angeles movement. Enjoying steady growth
in membership and influence during 1878, it reached the climax of its
power toward the end of the year, whereas in San Francisco and other
centers the decline set in early in the year, chiefly because of intraparty
dissension.[23]

Los Angeles, however, did not entirely escape the friction which
demoralized the party in San Francisco. It was not long before disputes
over two issues broke the new-found serenity of early 1878. The first
stumbling block was the policy of secrecy adhered to by Workingmen's
Club No. 1. In February, A. J. Norton, believing the time had come
for more open procedures, organized a Second Ward Club as a protest
against the policy of Page and Butler. Thereupon Page, acting as
Kearney's representative, reorganized Club No. 1 as the Central Workingmen's Club and, through it, managed to stay in control of the Los
Angeles movement. The Central Club acted as a parent organization,
chartering new branches which adopted its platform and bylaws and
looked to it for guidance. By the fall of 1878, seven clubs had been
formed on either a ward or a language basis: Central, First Ward,
Second Ward, German, Spanish, French, and Irish.[24] These clubs found
a second point of disagreement in the issue of Kearneyism. Although
it is by no means easy to trace their frequent and seemingly irrational
changes in allegiance, it is safe to draw two general conclusions. First,
pro-Kearneyism in Los Angeles was largely a matter of expediency so
long as the direction of the San Francisco movement was in doubt.
Second, the preponderant sentiment in the south was anti-Kearney,
despite a pro-Kearney stand by President Page of the Central Club.
Page, in fact, showed deeper conviction than most of his colleagues by
resigning his position when Kearney was deposed as head of the state
party in April, 1878.[25] After this quietus on the Kearney issue, the Los
Angeles movement became even more independent of San Francisco
than it had been before.

The configuration of the Workingmen's Party may be somewhat
clarified by an inquiry into its nature. It was something of a cross
between a political party and a labor organization, borrowing functions
and methods from both, though obviously it had more in common with
the former. As indicated above, it developed along both ward and
language-group lines with a controlling central club, later replaced by
a county central committee covering groups in neighboring communities. The internal organization of the clubs, on the other hand, gave
them some similarity to labor unions: each one elected a president,

vice-president, secretary, treasurer, and an executive committee. Perhaps the closest analogy to labor organizations lay in the establishment of employment bureaus: the Central Club started one in March, 1878, and appointed a club officer to serve as regular agent; a few months later the German Workingmen's Club provided the same service for its members. The early organizing activities of the Central Club, which sent out representatives to form branch clubs both inside and outside the city, likewise suggested a union enterprise.[26]

With regard to membership and finances, the Workingmen also tended to follow union rather than traditional party procedures. Formal application preceded election to membership. Initiation fees and dues were set up by the state party, but rigid enforcement is doubtful. Although there is evidence that the central committee sometimes audited the books kept by the clubs, the party, in general, conducted its finances in a haphazard way.[27]

Financial ineptitude, in fact, wrecked the party's attempts to establish its own newspaper. On May 20, 1878, the county executive committee began publication of the *Voice of the People,* the first known labor paper in southern California. Preliminary planning had obviously neglected the budget, for within ten days an empty treasury imperiled the weekly journal. The Workingmen temporarily averted suspension by raising $300 at a picnic, but the *Voice of the People* soon succumbed to criticism of its pro-Kearneyism and to party preoccupation with a new journalistic venture.[28] On August 1, the Workingmen purchased the *Daily Star,* oldest newspaper in Los Angeles, and made it the official organ of the party. The editor was Isaac Kinley, a farmer of intellectual bent, whose quiet influence as a reformer was to be felt more than once in the years to come. During the next decade he not only helped to shape the policies of various organizations, but assumed intellectual leadership through editorship of a series of reform journals, of which the *Star* was the first. Kinley came to public notice in January, 1878, when he headed the faculty of an industrial school established in Los Angeles the year before as a substitute for the apprentice system. His interest in the Workingmen's Party stemmed naturally from this introduction to workers' problems, but his able editorship of the *Star* was not enough to save the paper when, within a few months, it ran into financial difficulties. In April, 1879, Kinley retired as editor and by the end of May the *Star* ceased publication. It was never revived.[29]

The first major test of the Workingmen's Party, in the state and in Los Angeles, came with the election on June 19, 1878, of delegates to the State Constitutional Convention. The local contest was marked by

collaboration of Workingmen and farmers, unity within the Workingmen's Party, and Democratic-Republican opposition to the Workingmen through a new nonpartisan organization. The campaign of the
Workingmen, who had dispelled the last traces of Kearney factionalism,
called forth complimentary press notices on procedures, platform, and
candidates. The platform differed little from previous statements of
principle. The candidates were Edward Evey, president of the Anaheim
Workingmen's Club, Judge Thompson, and John P. West, a Compton
farmer. In a notable victory, the Workingmen's Party of Los Angeles
County elected two of these, Evey and West, as delegates to the convention.[30]

The State Constitutional Convention, comprising eighty Non-Parti-
sans, fifty-two Workingmen, ten Republicans, and nine Democrats, met
in Sacramento on September 28, 1878. The delegates of the Workingmen's Party allied themselves with the Granger element and agreed in
advance to a joint program, including some reforms which the convention judged too radical for adoption. Workingmen in Los Angeles
proper exhibited little interest in the proceedings, partly because of
local preoccupations and partly because their own candidate, Judge
Thompson, had failed in the election. West had been nominated by
farmers alone and Evey by a joint convention of farmers and Workingmen. But with the approach of voting day, May 7, 1879, the Los Angeles
party bestirred itself in behalf of the proposed constitution, which was
directed mainly against Chinese and capitalists. Its adoption by a vote
of some 78,000 to 67,000 was regarded as a victory for the Workingmen,
since businessmen, propertied interests, and leading newspapers of the
state had all opposed its passage. That Los Angeles was the only important city to give it a majority was attributed to greater suffering in
the southern part of the state from the exactions of land and railroad
monopolies. The new constitution, however, failed to provide the
hoped-for relief, since it was largely nullified by a conservative supreme
court and legislature and by the rights guaranteed to the Chinese by
federal treaty.[31]

Meanwhile, in the fall of 1878 the Los Angeles Workingmen's Party
had begun to campaign in earnest for the December municipal elections. At the outset a minor victory—election of a Workingman as
county supervisor in September—encouraged the party and strengthened the current belief outside its ranks that it could not fail to win
in the more important contest ahead.[32] Such a reversal from condescension to respect could not have occurred without alterations within the
party. A new slogan, "The Workingmen's Party is the phoenix that has

arisen out of the old parties,"[33] epitomized a changing concept of its function: civic reform and elimination of old-party corruption now seemed more vital, and more likely to bring success at the polls, than solutions for exclusively working-class problems. The continuing leadership of small businessmen rather than of actual workingmen had undoubtedly facilitated the drift away from basic principles. A shift of such magnitude had not been accomplished without intraparty dissension. But now, instead of revolving about the forgotten issue of Kearneyism, this reflected the policies of local leaders. A central committee clique under Jesse Butler, who had profited from Page's retirement in April, 1878, consolidated its control by summarily dismissing outspoken dissenters or reclaiming, with promises of political rewards, those who showed a tendency to waywardness.[34] This gradual accumulation of power led one dispossessed member to charge that the "Central Committee was composed of candidates and a few of their tools."[35] Regardless of what disgruntled Workingmen might think, it was exactly this ruthless policy which created a political machine strong enough to strike the fear of defeat into Republicans and Democrats.

Both platform and ticket for the 1878 elections illustrated the transformation of the Workingmen's Party. The platform, adopted by a mass meeting of all the member clubs in November, was a succinct and practical program:

1. Tax the Chinese to force their removal beyond city limits.
2. Abolish license taxes on businessmen and workingmen having their own shops.
3. Rescind the privileges and condemn the improvements of the Southern Pacific Railroad unless it fulfills its contract with the city.
4. Furnish better city sewage and water supply systems by day labor, working eight hours a day.
5. Insure party control by pledging successful candidates to resign at the request of a majority of Workingmen.[36]

With the supplementary promise that the Workingmen sought office not for their own sake but for the general good, the party reaffirmed its self-imposed obligation to give Los Angeles a clean government. The nominating convention, also held in November, likewise showed the ascendancy of the new leadership by selecting mostly the more recent adherents associated with the so-called Butler ring. A maneuver which further alienated those who distrusted the trend away from bona fide labor politics was the choice of non-Workingmen for leading offices, particularly J. R. Toberman for mayor and J. F. Godfrey for city attorney. This palpable scheme for winning votes, even at the price of party integrity, was harshly criticized by members and outsiders alike.[37]

Nevertheless, the Workingmen's Party was solidly entrenched. Its own vehicle, the *Daily Star,* was being ably edited by Isaac Kinley, and one of the two other daily papers in Los Angeles, the *Express,* unequivocally supported the third party. This forthright aid balanced the sniping of the *Herald* and the complaints of displeased party members. Until the very eve of election the party continued the practice of expelling its more articulate critics, apparently with no fear of an unfavorable public reaction.[38] Its confidence was justified on December 2. Thanks to thorough organization and a well-planned campaign, the Workingmen's Party was literally swept into office. Twelve of the fifteen councilmanic seats, two vacancies on the Board of Education, and all the other city offices were filled by its nominees. Among those elected to the council were four prominent party members, Jesse Butler, S. M. Perry, S. J. Beck, and E. M. Hamilton. By giving the Workingmen substantial majorities, the Los Angeles electorate had indicated its faith in the party as an instrument for reform. As the *Express* jubilantly declared:

> ... The people of Los Angeles have every cause for congratulation. They have demonstrated their freedom from ring control by a most overwhelming majority.... The Workingmen's ticket has won a sweeping victory all along the line.... This result exceeds even the most sanguine expectations indulged in before the election by friends of the movement; it is, in fact, a matter of astonishment to all.... In spite of the most desperate political machinations, in spite of every prejudice which would be excited, in spite of the purchase of votes by coin in hand, the cause of the people of Los Angeles has triumphed against ring rule. Glory enough for one day![39]

As the Los Angeles Workingmen proudly took over the city government early in 1879, they did indeed have a singular opportunity to prove their worthiness of such high praise. Although plagued by disaffection within their ranks and vituperation from without, they had evidenced not only strong internal control but unusual sagacity in discerning and profiting from the public's impatience with machine government. But it soon became obvious that the party's preëlection acumen was no guarantee of wisdom in office. The undercurrent of dissatisfaction among uncompromising party members who denounced the nomination of non-Workingmen was a continuing liability. When the new City Council continued the unpopular policy by appointing a non-Workingman to a minor post, discontent flared up in the first serious challenge to party discipline. In order to make a startling example, the Central Club, coming under control of the dissidents, expelled S. J. Beck, whose prestige as chairman of the county central committee had been enhanced by his capturing the presidency of the

City Council. The dissidents would no doubt have agreed that their party had been helped into office by naming nonmembers on the ticket, but they believed the compromise nullified the victory. These outsiders, they said, had only supported the platform as a political expedient, and some of them were so lacking in sympathy with the Workingmen's original intent that they continued to employ Chinese servants.[40]

Private disregard of the basic tenet that "The Chinese Must Go!" did not postpone Council action on the Chinese plank, but it may well have weakened any determination to substantiate campaign promises. In addition, the careless wording of the platform posed an almost insoluble complication. How could the Council oust the Chinese by imposition of heavy business taxes—which in itself conflicted with federal treaty obligations—and at the same time lift license taxes on other businessmen? And how could it liquidate the heavy city debt without increased revenue from taxes? After long and fruitless controversies, the Council finally managed to pass a licensing ordinance, designed more to balance the budget than to discriminate against Chinese. It taxed all kinds of business, not only those conducted by Chinese, and even increased some levies. There was a storm of objection from all sides. Chinese vegetable peddlers, retaining Stephen M. White as counsel, contested the ordinance in court and won their case. In the face of legal defeat and widespread criticism, the Council was forced to modify the ordinance. Later attempts to tax the Chinese out of the city and simultaneously alleviate the tax burden on small businessmen were no more effective, and this particular dilemma was never resolved. As a last resort the Council turned to a state law of 1876 which required landlords to provide 500 cubic feet of air per lodger. This statute was intended as an anti-Chinese weapon, but the Los Angeles authorities bungled their attempt to implement it locally. Throughout its year in office, the Workingmen's Party in Los Angeles discovered no feasible way of utilizing the power granted to incorporated cities and towns by the new state constitution to remove Chinese within their limits or prescribe the limits within which they might live.[41]

The Council's futility in carrying out campaign promises had lowered the party in public esteem. Other signs of deterioration soon appeared. In May, 1879, two city councilmen elected on the Workingmen's ticket were expelled by the county central committee for disloyalty. In July, one of the ward clubs withdrew from the party.[42] Later the same month another expelled member bitterly attacked the party leaders, particularly Jesse Butler, for mismanagement, unfaithfulness to the Workingmen's ideals, and sacrifice of the party's welfare to personal ambition.

Their overwhelming desire for power, he claimed, had made them promise much more than the city charter permitted them to give; for this reason "the Workingmen's Party has been traveling on the downward grade ever since the city election."[43] It was small wonder that outsiders began to doubt the party's ability to fulfill any of its platform commitments. When the Council undertook to implement the platform recommendation that day labor, with an eight-hour day, supplant the contract system, it was apparent that party disruption had progressed almost beyond redemption. Official negotiations achieved nothing and finally became so embittered that Butler was compelled to resign from the Council in August, 1879. His ouster stirred up yet more trouble within the clubs and prepared the way for complete breakdown of the party.[44]

Preparations for the county elections in 1879 illustrated the weakness of the Workingmen's Party. Farmers shared both in writing the platform and naming a ticket. The platform continued the modification of earlier anticapitalism, and went even further than the city platform by omitting all mention of the Chinese, the eight-hour day, and day labor. The only reminder of working-class origins was a promise that successful candidates would "strive to make labor honorable." Generalizations about implementing the new state constitution and correcting the worst evils of unrestrained monopolism replaced planks promising positive benefits to labor. The nominating convention in June illustrated the dwindling enthusiasm of the party no less than did the compromise of the platform. There was none of the spontaneity of the 1878 campaign. Disagreement intensified into open friction as the French and Spanish Clubs withdrew temporarily in objection to convention procedures and twenty county delegates deserted with greater finality. Only twenty-eight of the original seventy-three delegates remained. Bewildered by the disintegration taking place, the rump convention built a ticket around former party stalwarts in the hope that familiar names would renew public confidence—West for state senator, Butler for assemblyman, Page for county tax collector, Evey for county clerk, and Godfrey for district attorney.[45]

But the Workingmen's Party had spent its force. The withdrawal of Godfrey and others from the ticket showed increasing distrust of the party's stability, and an indifferent campaign spread this sentiment more widely. Although the Workingmen published a daily paper, the *Voice of Labor*, from the end of July until the election on September 3, 1879, they elected only a few of their candidates. It was the Republican Party which carried the day.[46]

With this election the Workingmen's Party lost its strategic position in Los Angeles. Internal dissension and political immaturity, together with recovery from the depression which had bred the party, impaired its usefulness as the hoped-for instrument of reform. Although dispirited participation in the 1879 municipal elections put four Workingmen in the City Council, they were all newcomers to the Workingmen's movement, an additional sign of weakening control. Shortly after this election, the party's prestige suffered further when A. J. Hamilton, elected city tax collector by the Workingmen in 1878, absconded with a sizable portion of the public funds.[47] But far greater damage had already been done by leaders who, while not openly dishonest, had sacrificed ideals to ambition and the general good to personal preferment.

By the middle of 1880, the Workingmen's Party was no longer a political entity anywhere in the state. Its decline invited a contest between the Democratic and Greenback Labor parties for its membership. The latter, organized on a national scale since 1878, advocated the substitution of greenbacks for national bank notes. The election of Workingmen's delegates to the Chicago Greenback Labor convention in April by the San Francisco executive committee, once more under Kearney's domination, alienated the pro-Democratic faction. A decisive split came a month later when Kearney manipulated a state convention of Workingmen into endorsement of Greenbackism. The disaffected Workingmen repudiated Kearney and embraced the Democratic Party, even though the Greenback faction had retained in its platform such demands as the eight-hour day, day labor on public works, regulation of railroad rates, and restrictions on monopolies. This break was the final step in the destruction of the Workingmen's Party of California.[48]

The Los Angeles party was similarly recast, though in a characteristically more orderly fashion. After the 1879 elections the Central Club faced the realities of political deterioration by reorganizing in a different mold and with a new motto, "The Solid West." Its objectives were an appropriate share of state and national recognition for southern California (an outcropping of the old regional antagonism), reduction of immigration from eastern states, and prohibition of Asiatic immigration. But this reorientation did not stay the party's collapse, for Workingmen had already accepted the shift to Greenbackism as inevitable.[49] The initial step was a rally of farmers, Workingmen, and Greenbackers on June 26, 1880, followed on July 3 by another joint meeting to ratify the national Greenback Labor ticket. On this occasion Alfred Moore, founder of the local Greenback movement, had the unusual and gratifying opportunity to welcome into his own organization the much more powerful political party which had repudiated him three years before. He keynoted the meeting by contrasting the two parties: Greenbackers believed the government's financial policy had caused the depression of the 1870's; Workingmen felt that unrestricted Chinese immigration had been responsible.[50]

With the preliminaries completed, the Workingmen were ready to accept new nomenclature and a partially new program, though formal union with the Greenbackers was delayed until the nominating convention of August 10, 1880. The Workingmen's belated adherence to a cheap money doctrine was facilitated by the Greenbackers' supplementation of their monetary policies with demands for establishment of labor bureaus, reservation of public lands for settlers, legislative reduction of working hours, abolition of the contract system for prison labor, and suppression of Chinese immigration. For local purposes, the convention enlarged the Greenback program by restating the Workingmen's planks on monopolies, public lands, rights of labor, irrigation, railroad freights and fares, and misconduct of public officials. Thus the new party gained the prestige of national affiliation while retaining the nucleus, spirit, and intent of the California movement. But in seeking redemption through this political alliance, the Workingmen did not realize that the Greenback Party had passed its zenith. The national Greenback vote dropped from one million in 1878 to three hundred thousand in 1880, a patent demonstration of waning strength caused partly by dissentience over prospective fusion with the Democrats.[51] That California Workingmen and Greenbackers failed to find their 1880 amalgamation mutually beneficial was due not so much to divergent policies as to the fact that both parties were no longer influential or well integrated.

Moreover, the new party neglected to profit from one of its predecessor's errors of judgment. The Workingmen's Party had repeatedly alienated its more single-minded adherents by including endorsements of old-party candidates on its tickets. Although the first Greenback Labor convention recognized the disruptive force of such a policy by resolving to nominate only party members, it did not stick to this decision. The very same convention placed both Republicans and Democrats on the county ticket, along with such Greenbackers as Isaac Kinley, Jesse Butler, and Alfred Moore. Although Butler as a Workingman had earlier sanctioned an identical policy, he withdrew from the ticket because of other-party endorsements, and many others turned against a party so impoverished that it could not name a full slate from its own membership.[52]

Nevertheless, the Greenback Labor Party campaigned vigorously in preparation for the elections on November 2, 1880. Polling a negligible vote, it seemed thereafter to relinquish even the pretense of representing the working class in politics. For example, its municipal ticket for the December, 1880, elections consisted almost exclusively of other-party endorsements.[53] Yet the local party survived well into the 1880's, undergoing various transformations in name and leadership and principle. Like the national movement, it was too ineffectual to attract wide support, but it performed a useful function in keeping open the channel through which the third-party ideas of the 1870's were transmitted to the People's Party of a later period.

The Workingmen's Party of California, though supplanted and absorbed by the Greenback Labor Party, was considerably more useful in bringing working-class complaints before the public than its successor. Chief of these at the time was labor's distress over Chinese competition, a problem whose solution was a primary function of San Francisco labor, whether organized in a political party, anti-Chinese societies, or craft unions. Los Angeles had too few Chinese, either actually or proportionately, for its workingmen to sustain the agitation characteristic of the larger and more industrial northern city. It was really the state Workingmen's Party which compelled the national recognition leading to abrogation of the Burlingame Treaty of 1869 and passage of the Exclusion Act in 1882. The party's southern branch, for a time at least, added its bit to the state program by keeping the issue in the forefront. The value of this preoccupation with the Chinese, though never questioned by workingmen themselves, was problematical from a broader view of the labor movement. It directed potentially constructive energies toward effectuation of a negative policy, and bequeathed to succeeding labor generations a tradition of racial hostility which later heightened resentment among foreign and unskilled groups toward organized labor.[54]

The Workingmen's Party of California, through its control of one-third of the delegates to the State Constitutional Convention of 1878, helped to frame a new instrument of government embodying many of its principles. Although, as noted above, this document was largely nullified by court decisions, it demonstrated the strength of an aroused working class. Republicans and Democrats learned that a third party could have substance and popular appeal, and for a time they showed greater willingness to heed the complaints of those without money or influence.[55]

These achievements must be credited to the state party or, more exactly, to the San Francisco Workingmen's movement. Los Angeles labor, lacking the experience of previous organization and the stimulus of a pressing Chinese problem, was not prepared to make competent use of the general awareness in the late 1870's that social and political reforms were vitally needed. Hence it made but a negligible contribution to the state party, remaining outside the main currents, and even proved unable to survive as a nucleus for reformers within its own area.

And yet the Los Angeles Workingmen's Party compared favorably in many ways with the movement in the north. Its accomplishments have been neglected, if not forgotten, in the quite natural tendency to identify the San Francisco party with the state party. Los Angeles Workingmen, within a month of their initial meeting, entered a ticket in the county elections and thus gained their first political experience a full four weeks before the party was officially organized in San Francisco. In the election of delegates to the State Constitutional Convention in 1878, the Workingmen won as decided a victory in Los Angeles as in San Francisco. In the fall of the same year the Los Angeles party swept the municipal election, a triumph not duplicated by the more spectacular northern party until 1879. Although Los Angeles Workingmen lacked the political sagacity to use their new-found authority advantageously, they had at least given voters an opportunity to express dissatisfaction with the *status quo*. Their record in office, although fumbling and barren of results, was certainly no more reprehensible than that of San Francisco Workingmen, who were "neither better nor worse than the average of politicians," and "as easily controlled as . . . those whom they denounced as the willing and easily purchased tools of the corporations and monopolies."[56] In journalism the Los Angeles party was as competent as its northern counterpart. It not only established several papers of its own, but took over the oldest newspaper in Los Angeles, the *Daily Star*, an achievement possibly unique in labor journalism.

The major difficulties of the Los Angeles movement stemmed from the inadequacies of its leaders or their ambitions for power. But, despite the quarrels which everywhere marred the Workingmen's progress, changes in leadership were effected with less open friction in Los Angeles than in San Francisco. Throughout its career, the Los Angeles party avoided the violence characteristic of the northern city, both in intraparty schism and in anti-Chinese attacks. The San Francisco party teemed with agitators, from radical leaders at the top to noisy partisans at the bottom. There were no ranters, no rioters, no mobs to disturb the calm in Los Angeles, where the real workingmen who formed the core of the party gained the adherence of business and professional groups. Moreover, the obvious conservatism of the Los Angeles party commended it to farmers, who found the Workingmen willing to encompass agricultural grievances in party platforms. This rapport was conspicuous in Los Angeles, where farmers had originated or carried on such reform movements as the Granger agitation and the independent political parties of the earlier 1870's.

The Workingmen's inexperience in organization, which caused them to welcome the aid of farmers, served in another way to distinguish the southern party from the northern. In San Francisco, the Workingmen's movement was an intermediate phase in a long history of striving for better conditions. But in Los Angeles it was preceded only by the transitory Eight-Hour League of 1868 and by a printers' union formed in 1875. This first craft union was to become the nucleus of the labor movement of the future, but between it and the Workingmen's Party there was a wide gulf. The ideals and objectives of the two had so little in common that the Workingmen's Party, presumably without malice, employed nonunion printers in the *Star* office. For most Los Angeles workingmen political organization antedated craft unionism, and future unions, as well as the first central labor body, were to gain something of their character from these political beginnings.

Such influence was to be exerted indirectly. Although a few of the Workingmen's leaders, Isaac Kinley, Jesse Butler, and others, were to speak at craft union meetings, they were not members and made no contributions to the real work of the unions. They found a more congenial home in the Knights of Labor, which first appeared in Los Angeles in the early 1880's; the Anti-Chinese Union of 1885 which, though it coöperated with craft unions, was a spiritual descendant of the Workingmen's Party; the United Labor Party of 1886, which brought together representatives of the Knights of Labor, craft unions, and anti-Chinese groups; and finally in the Populist movement of the 1890's. This was a wholly logical development, for many of these early reformers were not eligible for membership in craft organizations. The fragment of the Workingmen's and Greenback Labor parties which maintained a spasmodic existence during the early 1880's was the link between movements of the 1870's and later outbreaks of the reform spirit. Throughout its formative period, Los Angeles labor was never to be entirely free of the concept of labor in politics.

III. GENESIS OF THE LABOR MOVEMENT

As WE HAVE SEEN, the tendency during the 1870's, in Los Angeles and elsewhere in the state, was for heterogeneous groups to seek reform through political action. Economic conditions following the Panic of 1873 were not conducive to the growth of unions, and it was not until the business revival of the next decade, and the concomitant decline of the Workingmen's Party, that Los Angeles workers turned from politics to the development of craft organizations. There was, however, one exception.

1. THE PRINTERS LEAD THE WAY

The printers became the pioneers of local unionism by organizing in 1875, in the middle of a period when working-class inclinations were tending in a very different direction. The stimulus for the first Los Angeles union came from trade conditions. In 1875 Los Angeles was at the tail end of a rather prosperous period. The optimism attending construction of the railroad south from San Francisco had encouraged the establishment of many new enterprises between 1870 and 1875. Some of these ventures were newspapers. Two of the three leading dailies of the next quarter century were founded in this period: the *Evening Express* in 1871 and the *Herald* in 1873. The *Star, La Cronica,* the *Weekly Mirror,* forerunner of the *Times,* and the *Süd Californische Post* were all published continuously in Los Angeles during these years. Only one important paper succumbed, the *Daily News* in 1872. Therefore, the printers' trade locally seemed stable, even though the temporary decline of the San Francisco Typographical Union reflected a regional dullness. Moreover, the Panic of 1873 did not immediately affect Los Angeles. It was not until the very end of 1875 that the real estate boom accompanying the general prosperity of the early 1870's began to collapse. The printers, then, had ample reason to suppose that good times would continue.[1]

Contributory reasons for the printers' early organization were partly national, partly local, and depended in some degree on the nature of the craft. The International Typographical Union, dating from 1850, was the oldest and one of the hardiest craft organizations in the country. In addition to the security of a strong parent union, the Los Angeles printers had the advantage of a previous local organization. Despite the long interval and no overlapping membership, the 1875 union may have owed something to memories of the experiment in 1859.[2] Furthermore, printers differed sharply from other workers, such as building tradesmen, in the exercise of their craft. Working close together in relatively few shops, they could see their common grievances and talk over the benefits of unionization. Printers were more clearly distinguished from employers than carpenters, for example, who frequently ran small independent establishments of their own or worked on outside building jobs which scattered potential union membership over a wide area.

Formation of the Typographical Union in 1875, following an earlier social gathering, exemplifies the conjecture of Sidney and Beatrice Webb that unionization may result from organization of workers of the same craft for social or beneficial purposes.[3] The city's "first typographical ball," sponsored by the printers on January 22, 1874, attracted prominent citizens who made it a fashionable event in the social season. Some eighteen months later, in August, 1875, the printers employed on the three daily papers, the *Star,* the *Evening Express,* and the *Herald,* decided to form a union. Under the leadership of John W. Paynter they applied to the International Typographical Union and received a charter dated October 1. Formal organization of Local No. 174 was completed on October 24, when the nine charter members admitted six more by election and two by card. By the end of the year, the union had increased to twenty-one active and two honorary members. Strengthening the bond established by national affiliation, it very early appointed a committee on female labor to follow the ITU's program for equalizing women's wages, hours, and working conditions with those of men.[4]

Adversity soon halted the progress of the new union. Contrary to expectations, the period after completion of the Southern Pacific line into Los Angeles in 1876 witnessed an almost immediate deterioration of business conditions. As the printers themselves complained, "The year 1876–'77 was a hard-times year, owing to the lack of sufficient rainfall and the failure of one of the leading banking-houses of Los Angeles. . . ."[5] The Typographical Union discovered that the advantages of national affiliation, an easily organized craft, and an expanded local printing trade could not offset the force of a severe depression. Irregular meetings, fluctuating membership, and arrearages in dues soon convinced the printers that they must "make an effort to quicken the interest in the affairs of the Union, to the end of making it a more live and useful organization."[6]

In 1878 the union made a fresh start by adopting a new constitution, electing new officers, insisting on regular meetings and regular payment of dues, and clarifying relations with the International Typographical

Union. The printers were then ready to essay the enforcement of union principles. Their first venture, in October, 1878, was directed against newspapers employing nonunion as well as union men. Among the offenders was the *Daily Star* which, it will be remembered, had become the official organ of the Workingmen's Party on August 1, 1878. The Workingmen had not initiated the objectionable open-shop policy in the *Star* office, but the printers may have felt that a labor journal would be exceptionally vulnerable to a charge of unfair practices. Accordingly, the first union labor dispute in Los Angeles history centered on the *Daily Star,* the oldest newspaper in the city.[7] The printers' protest revealed their dislike of the labor party's inconsistency:

> Whereas, Since the Daily Star has been the organ of the Workingmen's Party, no Union printer has held a regular situation on said paper, but non-Union printers have held such situations, to the exclusion of Union printers, notwithstanding the declaration of the proprietors of said paper, in their salutation, that among their objects it should be devoted to the elevation of labor; therefore
> *Resolved,* That this Union demand that hereafter Union printers be employed in said office in preference to non-Union men....[8]

The *Star* yielded and employed union printers.[9]

Invigorated by its first demonstration of power, the Typographical Union continued its new aggressiveness for the next year and a half. Early in 1879 it began a dispute with the recently established *Daily Commercial* over the employment of nonunion printers. The ensuing quarrel, covering the four-year life of the newspaper, provided a more adequate test of union ingenuity than the *Star* episode. Trying to duplicate an easy victory, the union first asked the *Commercial,* in April, to institute the closed shop. Receiving no response, it sent a committee in July to acquaint the proprietor with "the sentiments of this Union on the labor question" and "to solicit preference for employment of Union printers at Union prices."[10] A negative answer forced a change in tactics, and the union next invited the *Commercial*'s employees to become members. They were no more tractable than their employer. The union then distributed circulars throughout the city condemning the newspaper as a "rat" office, the first use of this method. After a few months, however, the printers had to concede defeat. In December, 1879, they set aside their closed-shop preference and permitted a member to work in the *Commercial* office.[11]

The union's inability to enforce the closed shop presaged its second relapse. Irregular meetings during 1880, and unfulfilled plans to organize members employed in the several printing offices into chapels—convenient shop subdivisions of the union—were additional signs that the way of the pioneer was not easy. In February, 1881, the printers extended the compromise arrangement with the *Commercial* to all unfair offices, though stipulating that union wages must be paid. To classify all offices for the proper application of this ruling, the union proposed to make a city-wide investigation of prevailing wage scales. Instead of carrying through this plan, it slipped into a period of inactivity lasting fifteen months.[12]

Nevertheless, the printers could take pride in their achievements thus far. In the course of five years darkened by depression, they had firmly established the first Los Angeles union and in 1876–1878 had seen it through a more dangerous crisis than the present one. Typical of the union's courageous history was its willingness to tackle the closed-shop problem when even San Francisco unionists were marking time.[13] Although their union was temporarily enfeebled, the printers knew in 1881 that the depression was over and that business could not be long in reviving.

The Typographical Union responded to improved economic conditions by coming to life again early in 1882. Stimulated by the arrival of three out-of-town printers with union traveling cards, it reorganized in May and immediately set about increasing its membership, regularizing payments of dues, establishing chapels, and formulating a wage scale. A minor altercation between union newspaper compositors and nonunion job printers working together in the same room at the *Times* office was easily settled by admitting the job men to union membership. In September, 1882, the union closed the *Commercial* office to its members; a month later it adopted apprenticeship regulations. These and other efforts to translate principle into reality appealed to printers still outside the fold, and by March, 1883, when the first woman was admitted to the union, the total membership was thirty-one.[14]

In 1883 Los Angeles labor stood on the threshold of organization. Much of its future history was to center in the Typographical Union, whose early origin and immediate preoccupation with the assertion and enforcement of rigid union principles established for the printers a kind of supremacy divorced from numerical strength or popular appeal. The union's determined drive for its own integrity and for absolute control of working conditions made it the potential sustaining force of organized labor in Los Angeles. External forces, too, helped prolong its crucial significance. At the head of those forces was Harrison Gray Otis, proprietor of the Los Angeles *Times* and one of the country's most powerful and articulate antiunion advocates. Because of the juxtaposition of the printers and Otis, the contest between the Typographical Union and the *Times* was the fountainhead of the tremendous open-shop conflict which marked Los Angeles as a continuing trouble spot for labor. As the fight against the *Times* gradually became the concern of all local labor, so the Typographical Union maintained its hegemony even into a period when the multiplicity of unions might otherwise have submerged it.

As it happened, Otis' arrival in Los Angeles was coincidental with the union's reawakening in the early 'eighties. The *Times,* founded on December 4, 1881, was soon purchased by the proprietors of the *Weekly Mirror,* and on August 1, 1882, Otis joined the Times-Mirror establishment as editor of the *Times.* It was a crucial point in the history of Los Angeles when Otis thus began to fulfill a destiny of unprecedented significance to his newspaper, to the city, and to organized labor, both local and national. His close identification with the paper elicited this comparison: "As the *New York Tribune* was Horace Greeley ... so the *Los Angeles Times* was Harrison Gray Otis."[15] Having timed his arrival propitiously, Otis "caught Los Angeles young with the avidity of a mature schoolmaster," and taught his doctrine so thoroughly that the city, sometimes even called "Otistown,"[16] became the home of "True Industrial Freedom"—a motto still serving as the emblem of the *Times*—and eventually a nationwide symbol of the open shop.

It would have been difficult in 1883 to foresee that Otis was going to fashion his newspaper into a bitter and trenchant vehicle of antiunionism. The man's own background was reassuring. At the age of fifteen, when first learning the trade of printer, Otis had quit a job on the Rock Island *Courier* because the proprietor refused to unionize his shop; later, as a journeyman employed in the Government Printing Office, he had joined the Typographical Union in Washington, D.C.[17] Yet Otis had already begun to move away from his youthful prounion ardor when he arrived in Los Angeles. Initially, the *Times* maintained friendly relations with the Typographical Union, even lending its office for meetings after the union's revival in May, 1882. The last meeting held in the *Times* office was in September of the same year, one month after Otis joined the newspaper's staff. It was also in September that the *Times'* job printers were admitted to union membership without opposition from the management, but Otis, still feeling his way, was probably too cautious to raise the union issue in his own establishment so early. The *Times* did, however, begin to make guarded declarations against strikes shortly after Otis entered the company. These signs, pointing to Otis' future harshness toward organized labor, were too faint to be easily recognized, and it was not until after 1890 that local labor correctly appraised his role. Another ten years were to pass before national labor became fully alive to the danger of "the most notorious, most persistent and most unfair enemy of trades unionism on the North American continent."[18]

The minor indications in 1882, that Otis' accession to the editorship of the *Times* would lead to policy changes, were given real meaning in 1883, when the Typographical Union set in motion the events leading to the first strike. In June the union proposed to the management that its members be given preference over nonunion printers in the composing room. The *Times* made no immediate reply, but in reporting a San Francisco printers' strike two months later dramatically denied the right of union members "to coerce either their employers or other workmen" and discredited unionism as "insufferable despotism . . . odious to freemen and injurious . . . to public policy."[19] Here was a clear-cut answer to the Los Angeles union. The sudden and rather unexpected revelation of the *Times'* stand, instead of cowing the local printers, stiffened their determination to defend and promote the principles of unionism. On August 10, 1883, they endorsed the cause of the San Francisco strikers.[20]

Such an audacious contradiction of a *Times* pronouncement apparently convinced Otis that he must check the local union's aggressiveness at the start. On August 17 he discharged A. E. Morrill, his assistant foreman and a union member, for alleged neglect of duty. The immediate walkout of other union printers in the *Times* office in protest against Morrill's dismissal and against Otis' "unpleasantness and overbearing ways"[21] became, with the union's sanction, the first printers' strike in Los Angeles and the first skirmish in an almost endless struggle to unionize the city's leading newspaper. The union, soliciting aid from the San Francisco printers and from a local Knights of Labor Assembly, distributed circulars vindicating its action. Wider publicity came from the friendliness of the *Herald* and the *Express* and of two newer publications, the *Porcupine* and the *Free Lance*.[22] On August 30 the union called out its members working for Bacon and Company, a job printing house which refused to annul its contract with the *Times*. After a few weeks, however, it permitted them to return if they received union wages and did no Times-Mirror work.[23]

Meanwhile, the *Times'* role was not passive. Otis created a bellicose atmosphere by persuading his friend the Chief of Police to deploy members of the force to protect nonunion employees on their way to and from the office. Sober observers derided the precaution as unnecessary in the law-abiding community of Los Angeles and as insulting to an

adversary which had shown no tendency toward violence; in fact it
could have been a tactical move by Otis to overdramatize the incident
and gain public sympathy.[24] Otis also took issue with the union through
the columns of his paper, maintaining that Morrill had indeed been
incompetent and guilty of "objectionable and improper conduct." But
he reserved his real emphasis for a restatement of the stand taken on
the San Francisco printers' strike and on labor conflicts elsewhere: "The
proprietors . . . claim the same right of choosing their employees as is
exercised by employers everywhere, and they do not recognize the right
of persons in their employ to dictate to them the management of the
office."[25] Because Otis stressed this aspect rather than his reasons for the
discharge, the printers were convinced that he had intentionally provoked the quarrel to test the union and had used "neglect of duty" as
justification for a dismissal based solely on Morrill's union membership.
Years later, the printers were to assess the dispute as a deliberate plot
by Otis "to destroy the Typographical Union by causing a strike in the
Times office."[26]

Despite the union's certainty that the bulk of evidence was in its
favor, the officers confessed lack of confidence in its strength and resourcefulness by proffering to the membership, during the strike, a tentative plan to reorganize as a Knights of Labor assembly. At the time,
the national order of Knights was gaining ascendancy, and might well
have impressed the Los Angeles printers as a more valuable ally than
the remote and disinterested International Typographical Union, particularly since a local branch of the Knights had already been established. Such a shift in affiliation would not have been unusual, for many
printers' assemblies were being organized throughout the country in the
early 1880's, and the ITU itself had once considered joining the Knights
of Labor. The local union did not make the change.[27]

The discouragement evinced in the brief look toward the Knights of
Labor led the printers to suggest a compromise early in September,
1883. Otis refused it with the assertion that strikers could be reinstated
only on individual application. But in another month Otis, gradually
losing his nonunion replacements, was likewise ready to make concessions. Finally, when his staff of composing room employees was insufficient to get out the paper, he cajoled the union into helping him.
The arrangement proved satisfactory, and in October, Otis hired a
union foreman when assured he could maintain the open shop. Later
he further conciliated the union by discharging more of his nonunion
men, and by the spring of 1884 the *Times* was completely staffed by
members of the Typographical Union.[28] Although Otis had precipitated

the local walkout at a time when a recent country-wide telegraphers' strike and the San Francisco printers' strike might have predisposed the Los Angeles public to sympathize with any method of deterring union-ism at home, he had rushed into the fray before his physical resources quite matched his ideological readiness. The *Times* still lacked the financial and political security necessary to the implementation of Otis' nascent antiunionism.

One of the printers prominent in the strike negotiations and in sub-sequent union affairs was Frank B. Colver, a very recent arrival in Los Angeles but an old, experienced hand in the Typographical Union. Born at Hudson, New York, in 1833, Colver had had two years of col-lege training before setting out to learn the printing trade at the age of nineteen. Upon completing his apprenticeship in 1855 or 1856, he joined the Typographical Union at Cleveland, Ohio. For the next six years he worked at his trade in the summer and taught school in the winter, traveling about from place to place. After the Civil War, Colver established himself as coproprietor of a newspaper in Sandusky, Ohio. Although engaging in various activities during the next eighteen years, Colver always retained his union membership. Twice he served as local president—in Topeka, Kansas, and in Toledo, Ohio—and once was chosen delegate to the ITU convention. He joined Local No. 174 imme-diately upon arriving in Los Angeles in 1883, helped direct the strike against the *Times,* and became treasurer of the union before the end of the year. Like many craft unionists of the period, Colver belonged to the Knights of Labor. Prevalent uncertainty as to the direction labor should take, and the dual membership of leaders like Colver, explain in part why the Los Angeles Typographical Union could seriously con-sider changing its affiliation from a national craft body to the diffuse and loosely organized Knights of Labor. As a believer in moderation and a union official who never accepted pay for his services, Colver escaped the vituperation which Otis was later wont to level against walking delegates who, he said, squeezed union treasuries to provide fat livings for themselves. Colver's kindliness and genuine concern for the welfare of his fellows endeared him to union members. He died in 1911, a popular and respected man.[29]

By 1884 the Typographical Union was firmly grounded. It had met the first challenge of the *Times* with spirit and had gained useful knowl-edge of its adversary together with the experience of a fullfledged strike. Temporarily, the *Times* was in a pacific mood and accepted, along with the other papers, a new wage scale put into operation on June 15, 1884. In September the union was equally successful in persuading all proprietors to accept a dictum that no newspaper within its jurisdiction could use stereotyped plates, often called "boiler plate,"[30] as news matter.[31] The union's only real trouble during 1884 came not from employer opposition but from the increasing popularity of Los Angeles as a health resort. Too many ill and dying printers were coming to southern California, and during the year the union paid out large sums either to send the invalids back home or to bury those who died. Twice it circularized printers' locals elsewhere, warning the sick to stay away from "this very poor country."[32] The problem recurred constantly in resort areas, and Los Angeles felt its stress more than once.

A business recession during 1884–1885 aggravated the hardships imposed upon the Los Angeles union by ailing printers; it also led to the second local printers' strike. In July, 1885, the *Express*, faced by the necessity for economies, requested a wage reduction from 45 to 40 cents per thousand ems and permission to use "boiler plate." On July 5 the union offered to compromise by granting the use of plates but refusing the wage cut. When the newspaper rejected the proposal, the union called a strike and instituted a boycott. The printers immediately felt their advantage over 1883, for in the interim a number of other unions, a Trades Council, and several additional Knights of Labor assemblies had been organized in Los Angeles. These groups all promised to uphold the boycott, a weapon useful only where there is a body of organized labor. Rather unexpectedly, the *Times* also favored the Typographical Union, partly because it could ridicule a rival newspaper for inability to pay the current rates. The *Express* responded to the charge of inefficient management with the claim, later recognized by a distinction in union wage rates, that it should pay printers less for daywork than the *Times,* a morning paper, paid for nightwork. The *Times* would not grant the validity of this argument, and remained friendly to the union throughout the strike.[33]

The printers issued daily boycotting circulars at first, replacing them on July 11 with a paper called the *Evening Union.* With the subsequent addition of news items and editorials, the printers' journal was ready for conversion when the Trades Council decided that Los Angeles ought to publish a labor paper for the whole Pacific Coast. The *Evening Union* already had the distinction of being the only labor daily on the coast, and its quality and prospects of permanence made the rather grandiose scheme appear feasible. Although the paper was established on a sound financial basis with the formation of the Union Publishing Company at the end of July, 1885, it never became more than a local sheet dedicated primarily to the cause of the printers. The *Times* extended its cordiality to lavish praise of the *Union* and loaned it printing facilities, but categorically denied allegations that it was fostering the labor paper as a rival to the *Express*.[34]

Emboldened by wide local support and especially by the singular aid of the *Times,* the Typographical Union went so far as to threaten the *Express* with political reprisals:

> When the city election takes place this coming fall, if the *Express* does not give in before then, Typographical Union No. 174 will do for the city officers whom the *Express* champions what the New York Typographical Union No. 6 did for those candidates of the New York *Tribune,* a "rat" paper . . . —defeat them.[35]

But the *Express* did not yield, and heavy expenses during the strike forced the printers to make their first overture in September. Meanwhile, a Trades Council committee had also approached the proprietors, but both negotiations were inconclusive. The union then turned the dispute over to the Trades Council, which quickly brought the *Express* to terms. On October 20 the parties compromised the wage issue at 42½ cents per thousand ems and agreed on the use of plates. The union won the closed shop in return for a promise to admit as members the printers currently employed by the newspaper.[36]

The strike was important in several ways to the development of the Los Angeles labor movement. The printers' publication of a strike journal, the first issuance of a labor paper by a Los Angeles craft union,[37] denoted progress in typical trade-union functions. The strike also demonstrated a member union's share in developing a central labor body; the Trades Council mediated a labor dispute for the first time. The inevitability of compromise in most labor controversies was brought home to the printers, as well as the tactical lesson implicit in the *Times'* adaptability to momentary needs. Not only because of journalistic competition did the *Times* champion the Typographical Union throughout the strike. Changes in management during 1884 had brought H. H. Boyce into the company as Otis' partner, but the association was not a happy one. Boyce's ineptitude as business manager had brought the *Times* close to insolvency by the fall of 1885. Otis accused Boyce of designs on the editorial department of the paper and even feared that he might be trying to assume sole proprietorship. Suspicion and ill feeling marred managerial relations until the spring of 1886, when Boyce was forced out of the company.[38] Thus, during the printers' strike against the *Express*, Otis' grip on his business was too precarious to risk antagonizing his employees; his need to consolidate control of the *Times* gave the printers a short reprieve. Except for the identity of the opponent, the 1885 strike was preliminary training for the "Big Strike" of 1890, when came the real break between the *Times* and the Typographical Union.

2. OTHER CRAFTS ORGANIZE

The printers were the only craft in Los Angeles to organize before 1880. The others waited until the depression of the 1870's had come to an end, and began to form unions coincidentally with the Typographical Union's revival after its second period of decline. Recovery from the lean years between 1876 and 1880 was followed in southern California by an expansionist phase lasting for almost a decade, halted only by a brief recession in 1884–1885. Better transportation facilities resulting from extension of railroads and improvement of an ocean harbor led to a remarkable growth of both population and commerce. Manufacturing industries also felt the impact of expansion, though to a lesser degree. Before 1880 there had been little manufacturing, but with a larger local market, improved transportation, solution of credit problems, and development of water power and petroleum, capitalists were tempted more and more to invest in industrial plants. The process was a slow one, however, and received only its first impetus in the confident, enthusiastic years of the early 1880's.[39]

The accelerating tempo of Los Angeles life, spelling profit for workers in plentiful employment and high wages, set the scene for the organization of labor. In San Francisco, similar concomitants of business revival after 1880 brought an immediate response from workers in the renascence of older unions and the organization of many new ones; in the country at large, the year 1881 marked the beginning of a movement which was to culminate in the formation of the American Federation of Labor in 1886. But Los Angeles was still rather an isolated pocket of the nation, insulated against impulses from north and east alike, and the development of its labor movement was subject to little pressure from the outside until a later period.[40]

The building trades were the first to enjoy the fruits of economic progress, and the first to organize after 1880. The painters took the lead in 1881 with a union which, however, did not last very long or prove very aggressive. In October, 1882, the plasterers, in the first recorded strike in Los Angeles history, demanded $5 a day and won because contractors were too busy to afford a prolonged stoppage.[41] Occurring two months after Otis had joined the Times-Mirror establishment, the plasterers' strike brought forth the *Times'* first warning against a prerogative of organized labor:

It is to be hoped...that the temporary demand and the appearance of prosperity will not induce others of our tradesmen to join in a strike, for it is seldom that strikes result as happily as the one just mentioned. Usually they end in the strikers losing a month or so of time, in which all their little accumulations are used up, and in nine cases out of ten they permanently lose good situations.[42]

The Plasterers' Protective Union was formed as a result of the successful strike. About a year later, in October, 1883, the plasterers again struck, this time for reduction of hours from ten to eight with no change in the $5 wage scale. Duplicating their earlier victory, the plasterers were the first craft in Los Angeles to strike for and win demands on the two cardinal issues of wages and hours. With justifiable pride, their union celebrated "a year of great prosperity" by holding its first annual ball on December 31, 1883.[43]

In addition to the printers, painters, and plasterers, only one other group of employees organized before 1884. In February, 1883, retail clerks formed an Early Closing Association and within several weeks had persuaded some thirty merchants, including the well-known J. W. Robinson, B. F. Coulter, and D. Desmond, to close their stores at 6:30 P.M. Having accomplished the immediate objective, the union became inactive.[44] The sum total of all these employee efforts in the early 'eighties was not great, but the ferment of unionization had started to work. It soon spread through an ever-widening segment of the working population.

The year 1884 was a landmark in Los Angeles labor history, for it witnessed the spurt of organization in which the labor movement found its real genesis. In continuation of the 1881–1882 trend, the building trades were again in the fore. On March 11, 1884, eleven carpenters founded Local No. 56, Brotherhood of Carpenters and Joiners of America. This union, later known affectionately as "Old 56," soon gave promise of the phenomenal growth which made it, within the next few years, the largest labor organization in southern California. By April its membership had increased to 225. From the beginning it diverged somewhat from the stricter craft unionism of the printers, for it accepted contractors and builders as active members. Arthur Vinette was the union's first secretary.[45]

The carpenters were stimulated to organize by the interaction of two forces: impaired working conditions during the recession of the mid-'eighties, and the dynamic leadership of the newly-arrived Vinette. Wages of carpenters had sunk to $1.50 for a ten-hour day, and Vinette, who had come to Los Angeles in 1883, decided that unionization was the solution, though unlike Colver he had had no previous union experience. In fact, Vinette tied organization directly to unfavorable working conditions: "An American city had begun to crowd out the historic adobe as well as the rough board shanties. Mechanics flocked in from all parts of the country, wages were lowered, and a pernicious system of piece-work was undermining the carpenters' trade."[46]

Born in Montreal of French-Canadian parents, Vinette had had some college training before learning the trade of ship's carpenter under his father in Troy, New York. After an unsuccessful mining venture in Colorado, Vinette came to Los Angeles where he quickly demonstrated the high quality of his leadership by organizing the carpenters in the Los Angeles area and, a little later, federating all local unions in a central labor body. The many enterprises which won Vinette acclaim as the "most active, prominent, and effective worker in labor circles in southern California in the 1880's and early 1890's" eventually caused his health to fail.[47] When he died in July, 1906, after a long and painful illness, his wife wrote:

Certainly the uplifting of the working classes was his only aim in life.... He was always writing or talking of the better days to come. He certainly had better faith in humanity than I did.... So many times he could not get work ... and many times when he did ... he would come home after working half a day discharged because he was "a d———d labor reformer." We averaged $50 a month and part of that was from rooms in our own house.... It was believed that he had secured graft—a thing utterly impossible in Mr. Vinette.... If he hadn't given himself over to it [trade unionism] so much he would have lived longer.[48]

Like Colver, Vinette was active in the Knights of Labor, but in contrast to the printer, he also embraced such later movements as Nationalism, the People's Party, and Coxey's Army, and in 1904 joined the Socialist Party.[49] Colver's simultaneous membership in a craft union and in the Knights of Labor expressed merely a fairly common indecision of the period, but Vinette's eager participation in various reform movements sprang from deep conviction that fundamental social change was essential to the progressive welfare of the working class. To him unions were necessary for "attending to the need of the hour," but their members should at the same time be "not unmindful of the full measure of justice which shall one day be meted out to all humanity, and which shall usher in the millennium."[50] He forthrightly criticized the social order for imposing upon unions methods he believed inadequate:

I am not sparing of condemnation of all methods pursued heretofore by the laboring man. The wage law of Adam Smith, accepted by society to-day, places them on the market as merchandise, and I certainly recognize their right, by joint action, to create a rise in the article. But I favor labor unions only as expedients for the present to dictate the lowest terms they will accept from other combinations of capital, society, or circumstances.[51]

This was the man who, more than any other, molded the early labor movement in Los Angeles and who was recognized by labor circles in the East, through his writings, as "one of the watchmen detailed to keep the lights burning on the Pacific shore."[52] It was perhaps due to Vinette's philosophy that Los Angeles labor long persisted in an idealistic search for reform through movements extraneous to pragmatic trade-unionism.

By the end of 1884 there were four building-trades unions functioning in Los Angeles. The Plasterers' Protective Association, predating the carpenters' union, was still in existence. The painters, whose earlier union had disappeared, emulated the carpenters by organizing a new union with twenty-five charter members on April 8, 1884. In the absence of a national union of painters, the local group affiliated with the Knights of Labor as Local Assembly No. 3167, in consonance with a country-wide trend. Like the carpenters, the painters admitted contractors to membership. The painters' union was active and prosperous, and within a year had become one of the largest and most influential labor groups in the city. It provided a room called Painters' Hall which all the unions used as headquarters. The fourth building-trades union was the Bricklayers' Protective Association, formed in October, 1884.[53]

Vinette, as the activating spirit of the carpenters' union, was largely responsible for a drive by the building trades in 1884–1885 for shorter working hours. His idealism did not blind him to the need for immediate practical action or to the victories of unionism elsewhere. He took heed of the example offered in San Francisco, where a number of crafts, including the building trades, had won the nine-hour day just before the mid-decade depression; the carpenters had adopted it in May, 1883. A few months after organizing, the Los Angeles carpenters voted to decrease their hours from ten to nine and to establish a minimum daily wage of $3.50, effective August 18, 1884. At the same time they promised contractors and mill owners that acceptance of the scale would guarantee no further demands for a year. Following the lead of the carpenters, the painters announced that as of September 8 they would work only nine hours a day. Although some employers did informally agree to observe the nine-hour day and the carpenters' proposed minimum wage, acceptance was not general or binding enough to bring an unquestioned victory.[54]

Although the carpenters' attempt to establish the nine-hour day in 1884 had fallen short of full realization, Vinette announced in October that the union would enforce an eight-hour day, beginning May 1, 1885. By pointing to employers' noncompliance with the nine-hour rule, Vinette justified the union's violation of its agreement to make no new demands for a year. The carpenters, however, were too hasty, and their new goal was gradually forgotten as they struggled during much of 1885 not only to retain but to extend the nine-hour day. The plasterers had won the eight-hour day in 1883, but they joined with the painters and bricklayers in supporting the carpenters' drive for shorter hours.[55] Early in March, 1885, the carpenters' union published a list of building contractors already observing the nine-hour day, coupled with this political warning to prominent citizens:

> A movement was set on foot some time ago among the labor organizations whereby a record is being kept of all merchants, business men, professional men and others, who, in building or repairing, require ten hours for a day's labor . . . or give out their work to ten-hour contractors (the matter of employing Union or non-Union men being immaterial). Should they notice any decline of patronage, they can draw their own conclusions. And should . . . any of these persons ever get an itching to serve the public officially, they may perhaps find that party ties will not prove strong enough to overcome individual interests.[56]

The union countered the sharp criticism evoked by these threats with a flat statement that the nine-hour day was neither "unreasonable nor communistic," that it would alleviate unemployment, and that it was "in keeping with the spirit of the age."[57] Scrupulously adhering to a program of nonviolence urged by Vinette, the carpenters tried to solidify their bargaining position by increasing their membership and swaying public opinion through open meetings. In the end their strategy was rewarded, for despite the appearance of an employing plasterers' union in June, 1885, and a plan to organize a general contractors' association in July, employers were unable to resist the pressure. By January, 1886, the nine-hour day had been won.[58] Although the boom just then starting contributed to the victory, the building trades, under the leadership of Vinette and his carpenters, had conducted a sustained and orderly campaign in the field of industrial relations.

Quicker but more ephemeral success in the nine-hour drive came in 1885 through favorable municipal legislation. On March 10, City Councilman E. M. Hamilton, with earlier Workingmen's Party affiliations, championed the cause by proposing an ordinance legalizing the nine-hour day for city employees. After prolonged discussion the ordinance was changed to prescribe eight hours as a day's work in deference to state and other laws, and was unanimously carried on April 7 "amid great applause." But toward the end of July the Council found that the new ruling placed too heavy a burden on taxpayers, especially since it failed to put more people to work as had been expected. Some assiduous clerks, now paid for overtime, worked such long hours that they collected pay for sixty working days a month. Although Hamilton strove valiantly to save the ordinance, the Council repealed it on July 28, 1885.[59]

By the end of 1884 there were six unions in Los Angeles; the tailors had formed the Journeymen Tailors' Protective Union in March, 1884. Only three of the six were nationally affiliated: the unions of printers, carpenters, and painters.[60] Although the size of the movement was still small, the pattern of leadership had already been established. For some years the predominant unions were to be those of printers and carpenters: the printers by reason of early organization, affiliation with a particularly strong national body, and insistence on strict craft unionism; the carpenters by force of numbers, primacy among the building trades, and the leadership qualities of Arthur Vinette. It was fitting that these two unions had most to do with the development of the first central labor body in Los Angeles. Vinette spurred its organization by seeing the value of concerted support for the building trades' nine-hour program; the printers, quicker to appreciate hierarchical relationships than other local craftsmen, used every opportunity to foster the growth and prestige of the central body.

3. The First Trades Council

Four of the existing six unions in Los Angeles were organized in 1884, a year of business recession. This was a notable accomplishment in a period when unemployment and wage reductions were affecting workingmen throughout the country. Although workers in California still enjoyed a higher wage level than those in the East (see table 1), they, too, suffered economic hardship. In San Francisco, dissolution of the Trades Assembly in 1884 caused a temporary setback of the labor movement. The slowdown of building operations in Los Angeles during the recession years created unemployment that was aggravated by the accelerated influx of workers seeking to escape distress in the East.[61] Yet Los Angeles crafts, with little previous union experience, organized and campaigned for various benefits—mainly shorter hours and the closed shop—when bad times had silenced San Francisco unions. Moreover, the existing unions combined to form a rudimentary central body.

Although the origins of the first labor council in Los Angeles are obscure, it is clear that the body developed from a movement which began in 1884. In October the following notice was published:

A meeting of the representatives of the various labor unions will be held at Painters' Hall, Nadeau Block, on Wednesday evening next for the purpose of organizing a Trades Assembly.[62]

We do not know what took place at this conference. The unions were
so chary of revealing their proceedings that a second meeting later in
the same month set the press to speculating on the meaning of the secret
conclaves. Most of the conjectures ran to politics: labor was going to
place a ticket in the coming municipal elections, and could command

TABLE 1

COMPARATIVE WAGES, 1885, CALIFORNIA, NEW YORK, AND PENNSYLVANIA

Occupation	Daily wages		
	California	New York	Pennsylvania
Cabinetmaker.....................	$2.50–$3.00	$2.50	$1.67–$3.00
Upholsterer......................	3.00– 5.00	2.95	2.25
Millwright.......................	3.50	3.00	2.50

Occupation	Weekly wages		
	California	New York	
Bricklayer.......................	$30.00	$20.00	
Mason...........................	30.00	18.00	
Plasterer........................	30.00	18.00	
Plumber.........................	24.00	16.00	
Carpenter.......................	24.00	14.00	
Baker...........................	18.00	7.00	
Brewer..........................	12.50	5.00	
Cooper..........................	21.00	12.00	
Teamster........................	15.00	10.00	
Printer..........................	12.50–30.00	13.00	
Tailor...........................	20.00	7.00–12.00	

SOURCE: *Third Biennial Report, 1887–1888*, California Bureau of Labor Statistics (Sacramento, 1888), pp.
139–44.

one thousand votes, including almost four hundred from the carpenters'
union alone; the whole undertaking was a Democratic device to win
labor's support.[63] The only clue to the real purpose behind the conferences comes from a decision of the Typographical Union:

> The business being of a political nature this Union declined to take action upon
> the matter as a Union, but would, as individuals, endeavor to secure for them the
> object desired, viz: To secure the election of such Supervisors as were in favor of the
> nine hour law on county work.[64]

This forthright statement implies that any association which the
unions might have formed had a political end in view. But instead of
organizing a labor party, the unions were following up the nine-hour

agitation of the building trades with a plan to extend that benefit to public work. The move toward centralization must, then, have started with the carpenters and their allies, under Vinette's leadership. The printers, who would not be directly benefited, were willing to support the movement as individuals, but would not commit the entire membership to vote in a specified way. Herewith they established a policy of avoiding political action unless their own immediate and specific objectives demanded it, and they clung to that program with almost undeviating consistency in their early history. The carpenters' urgency to enlist the aid of other unions in a straightforward political campaign suggests an ideological difference between printers and building trades that might become a weakness in so small a labor movement. Notwithstanding the fundamental variations in concept, a central body did emerge from these early conferences, for in the spring of 1885 the Trades Council was meeting regularly every two months, with Arthur Vinette as secretary.

With the continuance of dull trade conditions into 1885, the new Los Angeles Trades Council failed to initiate moves of its own or to integrate the few unions and their rather desultory functions. It seemed content merely to ratify the doings of its members or of outside agencies. It was the Typographical Union, not the Council, which stirred Los Angeles workingmen to press for revision of the state mechanics' lien law through the good offices of Assemblyman Henry T. Hazard. The Council thanked Hazard for his coöperation when amendments adopted in 1885 guaranteed payment to mechanics without manifest injustice to property owners. By the summer of 1885 the Flower Festival Society, an organization quite distinct from the labor movement, had established a home and free employment agency for working women. The Trades Council, whose own plan for a free labor bureau had failed to reach fruition, lauded the women's agency as a worthy enterprise. Again in the role of observer, it boosted the newly organized Anti-Chinese Union[65] by commending to "employers of coolie labor the economic benefits to the community and the prevailing low wages as sufficient reasons for them to make room for unemployed white laborers and keep the dollars at home."[66] In its earliest stages the Trades Council exhibited paternal acquiescence and commendation rather than propulsive force.

Outside Los Angeles, the Council was equally diffident. It sent no delegates to a San Francisco convention held in March, 1885, for the purpose of uniting Pacific Coast labor organizations in a federation designed to bring craft unions closer to the Knights of Labor and the Grangers. The Los Angeles Council expressed agreement with the prospectus by ratifying the convention proceedings, but the opportunity for real integration with a regional movement disappeared when the whole scheme succumbed to the indifference of the key San Francisco unions.[67]

Although the Trades Council had come into being as an indirect product of the building trades' nine-hour drive, the carpenters did not seek the aid of the central body in the continued agitation for shorter hours during 1885. In contrast, the printers gave the Council its first real boost in July of the same year. When the central body emerged as a functioning organization in the spring, the Typographical Union had carefully studied the constitution before committing itself to membership. Upon reassurance that the Council's quasi-political origins would mean no distasteful involvement, the printers elected to affiliate. In a logical sequence, they asked the Trades Council to settle their strike against the *Express*. About this time the Council had eight member unions. The new additions were evidently the Early Closing Association, which had just begun a campaign for shorter store hours, and a cigar makers' local which affiliated with the International Cigar Makers' Union in the fall. A hod carriers' union organized in August, 1885, became the ninth member of the central labor body.[68]

Acting on its own initiative for the first time, the Trades Council summoned a conference of union delegates in the fall of 1885 to select candidates for the City Council and the Board of Education, a political move probably stimulated by the repeal of the eight-hour ordinance in July. But the "labor ticket" of 1885 was nothing more than endorsements of major party candidates. By approving it, the Typographical Union gave substance to its warning, during its recent strike against the *Express,* that political methods might not always remain outside its scope. No clear record of the endorsements remains, but three of the eight new councilmen and all three candidates elected to the Board of Education had supposedly been approved by labor.[69]

Another sign of awakened responsibility was the Trades Council's participation, in November, 1885, in a Pacific Coast anti-Chinese convention called by the San Francisco District Assembly of the Knights of Labor. Delegates were also sent by Carpenters' Union No. 56, Painters' Assembly No. 3167, and the San Pedro branch of the Coast Seamen's Union, established in June, 1885, but not yet identified with the Los Angeles labor movement. The convention, coinciding with the reinvigoration of San Francisco labor and its renewal of anti-Chinese agitation, voted in a spurt of heady enthusiasm to get rid of the Chinese within sixty days. Such impetuosity struck the fear of ensuing violence into the convention's instigators, who had envisioned a peaceful, orderly anti-Chinese campaign. Some of the more conservative unions joined the Knights in withdrawing, and the rump convention dropped the anti-Chinese issue and instead organized a federated trades council of the Pacific Coast, with headquarters in San Francisco. Los Angeles delegates approved the venture, and the Trades Council immediately affiliated with the new regional body. The federation was in running order by January, 1886, with plans for material and social benefits including the eight-hour day and restrictions on convict and Chinese labor, as well as enactment of other labor legislation.[70]

Although growing rapidly at first, the regional federation soon discovered that it could exercise only a very tenuous authority outside the city. The affiliation of Los Angeles labor was never more than nominal, since the distance from headquarters perforce substituted postal communication for close personal association. Thus the only benefits accruing to local labor were psychological: the feeling of isolation weakened, and the prestige of the Trades Council as a recognized subdivision of a regional federation increased.

The composition of the local central body changed but little between the fall of 1885 and the spring of 1886, when Los Angeles stood on the threshold of the great real estate boom of 1886–1887. Printers, tailors, carpenters, painters, hod carriers, and bricklayers were still active, though the plasterers' union and the Early Closing Association had lapsed. The plumbers and gas fitters organized their first "protective association" in March, 1886, but did not join the Trades Council. The cigar makers reorganized as Local No. 225 of their international in April of the same year, and immediately reaffiliated with the central body. The Council thus embraced most of the city's unions, and was just beginning to increase its functions on behalf of Los Angeles workingmen as new economic opportunities unfolded before it in a period of rushing prosperity.[71]

Nevertheless, the Los Angeles labor movement was still far from ready for the rapid expansion of a boom. The Trades Council was not a directive agency in the fullest sense, and the two most influential unions of carpenters and printers employed dissimilar methods and looked toward different goals. The carpenters' membership policy, making no distinction between journeymen and apprentices or between employers and employees, was at variance with the printers' system of grading apprentices below journeymen and of classifying employers as honorary members. Furthermore, the Typographical Union exercised the right to reject unfit or unqualified candidates and frequently suspended or expelled members for infraction of rules or infidelity to

principle. The carpenters preferred the enlisting of popular support
for an immediate gain to the establishment of the strong craft unionism
emphasized by the printers. Instead of concentrating on the closed shop,
they tried to shorten hours, provided membership benefits, and through
the device of open meetings, tackled the tedious but necessary task of
educating public opinion in a community where such a service was
indispensable. The two unions were also in disagreement on the use of
political methods, for the printers, unlike the carpenters, were chary of
committing themselves to a specific political program. Had the central
body been stronger, and the base of unionism broader, the contributions of printers and carpenters would have complemented each other
in the building of a well-rounded labor movement. The lack of a forceful labor council was particularly detrimental in a period when national
unions had not yet reached the zenith of their power, and when the
isolation of Los Angeles permitted only the flimsiest of ties with national
bodies.

Yet considerable progress had been made by Los Angeles labor. The
Trades Council had learned its first lessons, and its few unions stood
ready to aid each other. Several crafts had enjoyed at least partial success in disputes with employers, and none had encountered overwhelming defeat. Most important, the printers' strike in 1885 had developed
an essential community of feeling. Labor was in some measure prepared
for the next phase, when completion of the Santa Fe Railroad in November, 1885, swelled the tide of immigration into southern California
to flood proportions and helped produce the great boom. Participating
first in the state-wide anti-Chinese agitation of 1886 with the Knights
of Labor and other groups, the Trades Council used this peculiar California expression of solidarity as a steppingstone to a wider sphere of
influence.

IV. THE NOBLE ORDER

THE WEAKNESS of the Trades Council, the political tendencies of the labor movement, and the absence of strong ties with national bodies made easier the advent of the Noble Order of the Knights of Labor into Los Angeles. Starting in the early 1880's, at about the same time as the craft unions, the Knights found here a cordial welcome and an opportunity to gain eminence in labor circles. Certain tenets of the national order made it peculiarly adaptable to communities like Los Angeles, where reform notions had, during the 1870's, affected wide segments of the population, where the labor movement was of such recent origin that a purposeful program had not yet been developed, and where the number of workers in one occupation was frequently too small to make unionization feasible.

The Knights vouchsafed to all reformers, of whatever class, participation in a large, national organization dedicated to the creation of a better society. They believed that the substitution of coöperatives for capitalistic enterprises would bring forth a Utopia wherein the real "producers of wealth" would be free of enslavement by the wage system. Educating the public to so sweeping a change was to be accomplished by bringing together all workers, regardless of trade or degree of skill, professional people, employers, and others interested in reforming society or benefiting the downtrodden working class. Decrying the narrow emphasis of craft unionism on wages, hours, and working conditions, the Knights made their unit of organization the "mixed" assembly from which were excluded only lawyers, bankers, gamblers, and liquor dealers.[1] What could appeal more cogently to remnants of the Grangers or the Workingmen's Party, to hangers-on of the Greenback Labor Party, to citizens distressed by current injustices, and to workers impatient, as was Arthur Vinette, for a millennium which craft unionism might never achieve?

Starting as a small secret society in Philadelphia in 1869, the order of Knights of Labor borrowed some of its ideas from the Knights of St. Crispin, a union of shoemakers formed in 1867. As the first craftsmen to feel the impact of the factory system on a large scale, the shoemakers organized secretly to protect journeymen against the competition of unskilled hands on the new shoe machines. The Knights of Labor, some of whose leaders were Crispins, carried adaptation to the machine technique a step further. If new manufacturing methods were to remove all trade distinctions among workers, the logical solution would be "one big union" including all employees. The order of Knights spread slowly at first, partly because of secrecy, and then with increasing momentum as the depression after the Panic of 1873 weakened existing craft unions. The disastrous strikes of 1877 in the East rejuvenated labor's belief in political activity and brought home to workers the value of greater unification. As reliance on politics led to emergence of the Greenback Labor Party (with which the Knights coöperated in many localities), so the need for labor's consolidation redounded to the advantage of the Knights of Labor.[2]

The Knights formed a national body in 1878 with the object of attracting workers in all productive industries and of allotting to them a more equitable share of the wealth they created. To appeal to all groups whom the Knights hoped to embrace, platform recommendations were diversified: bureaus of labor statistics, coöperative enterprises, reservation of public lands for actual settlers, abolition of the contract system on public works, arbitration of labor disputes, health and safety laws for workers, mechanics' lien laws, prohibition of child labor, establishment by government of a national currency, government ownership of railroads and communication systems, and the eight-hour day. Because of labor's failures in the 1877 strikes, the leaders of the Knights further stipulated that the strike should be abjured except as a last resort.[3]

Developments, inside and outside the order, conspired both to render this centralization ineffective and to force the Knights to temporize in the practical application of some of their principles. The nonstrike policy, for example, yielded to the necessities of local assemblies, which frequently found educative or legislative processes too slow and uncertain in the attainment of objectives for which the rank-and-file membership was clamoring. In 1879, Terence V. Powderly succeeded Uriah S. Stephens as Grand Master Workman of the Knights, and was instrumental, two years later, in revoking secrecy as a national policy. Many branches, however, found that community conditions made it expedient to keep their activities under cover. The formation, in 1881, of the Federation of Organized Trades and Labor Unions of the United States and Canada, forerunner of the AFL, forced the Knights into partial amendment of their organizational policies, and they began to encourage craft unions within the order. With local freedom to engage in strikes and boycotts and the decreasing emphasis on secrecy, this change inaugurated a period of tremendously rapid growth: membership in the order increased from some 9,000 in 1878 to over 600,000 in 1886, the peak year. The appeal of the mixed assembly, particularly in small and rural communities where craft unions were not easily sup-

ported, contributed to this phenomenal gain. But the very size of the
organization prevented adequate supervision of the vast membership,
and centralization, never very effectively established, came to have less
and less substance as the number of assemblies, both craft and mixed,
multiplied. Furthermore, the habit of trimming policies to fit the
exigencies of the moment made central control even more lax and
wavering.[4]

The beginnings of the order in California coincided with the period
of rapid national growth. Appearing first in Sacramento and San Francisco in the late 1870's, the movement spread slowly at first. District
Assembly No. 53, with jurisdiction over San Francisco, Oakland, and
San Jose, was organized in 1882 with eight local assemblies. Enough
craft unionists joined the order so that when the state legislature created the California Bureau of Labor Statistics in March, 1883, following
agitation by the San Francisco Trades Assembly, Powderly could claim
for the Knights a share in influencing this important enactment. But it
was not until the depression of 1883–1885 and the decline of the Trades
Assembly that the Knights gained real strength in the state's metropolis.[5]

In the summer of 1882, just before the organization of a district assembly in the San Francisco area, the movement spread to the southern
part of the state with the formation of local groups in Los Angeles,
Anaheim, Santa Ana, Azusa, and other communities. Since California
Knights continued reticent, even after the national order abrogated the
policy of secrecy, obscurity has shrouded the early activities of the Los
Angeles adherents. Their first assembly was a mixed one, No. 2405, and
started off in July, 1882, with ten members. Within a month the local
Greenback Labor Party advised its members to join the Knights of
Labor, and with this fillip Assembly No. 2405 increased to a membership of eighty-seven by July, 1883. But in Los Angeles, as elsewhere,
membership fluctuated sharply because individuals and groups frequently withdrew after their first enthusiastic expectations were not
fulfilled, or were suspended for disregard of rules or policies. Thus,
during its second year, Assembly No. 2405 showed a net gain of only
sixteen members, bringing the total to 103; at the end of its third year,
in July, 1885, it had exactly the same number as the year before, since
gains were offset by losses. Other branches showed a similar growth
pattern. Painters' Assembly No. 3167, organized as the first craft assembly in April, 1884, grew from forty-six members in July to sixty-three a
year later, but it had lost three by withdrawal and fourteen by suspension. A new local assembly of carpenters and woodworkers was formed
during the summer of 1884, probably not long after Carpenters' Union

No. 56. It offered little competition to the latter, for by July, 1885, it had only twenty-one members left after suspending fifteen.[6]

The year 1886 marked the height of the national order, and in Los Angeles it was likewise a period of growth and consolidation. The local Knights were flourishing enough to consider inviting a national officer to speak in the city and to send out an organizer who went as far afield as San Luis Obispo. By July, there were six assemblies of the Knights in Los Angeles with a total of 308 members, functioning under the recently-formed District Assembly No. 140. This was the second district organization in California, following the one formed in the San Francisco area. Only five of the Los Angeles local assemblies are identifiable. Evergreen Assembly No. 7647 (Wage-workers), with William M. Hawkins, member of the Typographical Union, as master workman, had been added to the three existing groups, and the Journeymen Tailors' Protective Society had reorganized as Tailors' Assembly No. 4350, tangible proof of the Knights' appeal to craft unionists.[7]

Fairly substantial numerical growth, as well as the tailors' shift to the Knights, indicated that the order had attained an important status in Los Angeles. Indeed, its local standing was apparent at a much earlier date, when the printers, during their strike against the *Times* in 1883, had appealed for the Knights' support and even considered transformation into a craft assembly. The adherence of prominent craft unionists, like Frank Colver and Arthur Vinette, to the Knights of Labor likewise pointed to the order's influence. Another member of the carpenters' union, C. K. Lamb, was an organizer for the Knights, and W. A. Swain, a later president of the same union, was a member of a mixed assembly.[8] The painters' assembly, though closely integrated with Carpenters' Union No. 56 and the Trades Council, owed its first allegiance to the Knights of Labor. This divided loyalty, both of individuals and groups of workers, lent a certain ambiguity to labor's early development in Los Angeles as well as in other communities.

In illustration, Jonathan D. Bailey, who became a figure of prominence in the Los Angeles labor movement, affiliated with both a craft union and the Knights of Labor. Upon his arrival in Los Angeles in December, 1884, he joined Carpenters' Union No. 56, of which he was later president, and Knights of Labor Assembly No. 2405, which subsequently elected him master workman and organizer. Born in Illinois in 1839, Bailey was raised on a farm in Missouri. At the age of seventeen, after a country-school education, he left home with five dollars in his pocket to learn the carpenter's trade. He continued his studies as he worked, and did some teaching, but a cherished ambition to read law was unrealized because his health had suffered from overwork. Bailey was married in 1866, and established himself as a builder and contractor in Moberly, Missouri. Ruined by the Panic of 1873, he turned from the Democratic Party to groups dedicated to reform, joining both the Greenback Labor Party and the Knights of Labor in 1876. He held several city offices in Moberly before moving farther west in 1880. Sojourning for a few years in Colorado before settling permanently in Los Angeles, he organized the first carpenters' local in the state, became Colorado organizer for the Brotherhood of Carpenters, and was active in the Knights of Labor. Bailey was so firm a believer in the tenets of the Knights that, when the order died out in Los Angeles, he transferred his membership to national headquarters in Washington and continued to pay dues there. He was active in all facets of labor organization in Los Angeles, as well as in such movements as the People's Party, until 1900, when a serious accident forced him to retire to less arduous pursuits. Until his death in 1911, he was proprietor of the Fifth Street Department Store.[9]

Jonathan Bailey, like Arthur Vinette, whom he resembled in many ways, epitomized in his activities and philosophy the Los Angeles labor movement of his time. In him can be found the reliance on craft unionism as a temporary expedient, but at the same time the far deeper faith in education, coöperative enterprises, and industrial and political reform. In common with others, he yearned for a better society, which he believed attainable through the kind of unionism preached by the Knights of Labor. Justice and right, Bailey argued, could prevail only when a coöperative government of and by the whole people controlled all the industries in the nation. Consecrating himself to this conviction, Bailey never relinquished his ideals, and at the age of seventy advocated to the Los Angeles Central Labor Council a system of independent clubs through which workers and other citizens could be educated in labor, economic, and political issues. To him, trade-unionism and politics were so interdependent that their separation was unthinkable. Bailey's logic and fairness were of so high an order that he completely escaped all the bitterness and hate and abuse that clouded the industrial struggle in Los Angeles. He died one of the best-loved union men in the city.[10]

Although leaders like Bailey helped the Knights achieve stature in local labor circles, the order accomplished considerably less than did craft organizations during this formative period. In Los Angeles, as elsewhere, the Knights sometimes appeared to be "in sympathy with everything and involved in nothing."[11] In February, 1885, on the eve of labor's first important anti-Chinese agitation in Los Angeles (see chapter v), Assembly No. 2405 advocated the education of "popular reason and popular conscience" as the best method of winning desired reforms.[12] When the Typographical Union struck against the *Express* a few months later, three local assemblies endorsed the action and promised to support a boycott, though not without this qualification: "While we extend a helping hand . . . we look forward to the day when prejudice and want shall give place to intelligent union and cooperation."[13] Later in 1885, Assembly No. 2405 joined with other labor organizations in favoring a bond issue of $245,000 for municipal improvements, which was subsequently passed.[14] Attitudes like these revealed the local Knights' strict observance of the national principles of coöperation and education, as well as their unwillingness to do anything more specific than commend the acts of others. The state anti-Chinese convention, summoned by the San Francisco District Assembly in November, 1885, presented an opportunity for more active participation, but only the painters' assembly sent delegates—probably because of its close association with Carpenters' Union No. 56 and the Trades Council, both of which were represented.[15]

In their responsibilities on a national level, the Knights were more wide-awake. The Los Angeles assemblies' delegate to the General Assembly of the Knights of Labor, meeting in October, 1885, persuaded that body to make a statistical survey of Chinese in the United States. In 1886, the Los Angeles Knights sent W. L. Wolfe, a painter, to the General Assembly with recommendations which aptly singled out the problems of greatest consequence to the area. This time, consideration of the Chinese issue led to the appointment of a committee on immigration and Chinese labor, of which Wolfe was made chairman. This committee subsequently submitted to the General Executive Board a comprehensive plan for the prohibition of Chinese immigration. A second motion from District Assembly No. 140 proposed that the Knights of Labor hold annual congresses with other labor organizations to promote harmony and concentrate energies. The General Assembly voted this down, but its origin in Los Angeles showed keen perception of the diffusion of effort resulting from simultaneous development of different types of labor organizations. A third suggestion from Los Angeles, looking toward a gradual breakdown of western isolation, evoked a more favorable response when the General Assembly recommended that a lecturer be sent to the Pacific Coast.[16]

These representations to the national order clearly revealed the Knights' understanding of three important local problems: the Chinese, regional isolation, and the need for labor's consolidation. Moreover, Wolfe went to the national convention as a delegate from District Assembly No. 140, not from his own painters' assembly. Thus in clarity of thinking and degree of centralization the Los Angeles Knights had gone beyond the Trades Council, which, in contrast, was an agglomeration of unions without distinct form or planned policy.

Other causes contributed to a prevalent uncertainty in Los Angeles as to whether the Knights of Labor or the Trades Council was the dominant labor organization. Any authority the Council might claim as the official representative body of the craft unions was somewhat diminished by the fact that two of its unions also owed allegiance to the Knights of Labor. The Knights had the advantage of connection with a rapidly growing national order which, during the mid-'eighties, seemed to encompass the future of American labor. The Trades Council had no such link, and not all of its unions had established national ties. The Greenbackers' early recognition of their affinity with the Knights brought politically-minded predecessors of the labor movement, such as Isaac Kinley and E. M. Hamilton, into the order. Kinley was master workman of District Assembly No. 140 in 1886.[17] The Knights thus fell heir, in a measure, to labor's political tradition in Los Angeles, a tradition older than that of craft unionism, if the single instance of the Typographical Union be discounted. Neither the Knights nor the craft unions were entirely willing to disclose their transactions; but the public's greater familiarity with organizations such as the Workingmen's and Greenback Labor parties, with which the Knights had much in common and upon whose membership they drew, added to the notion that the order was more of a spokesman for labor than was the Trades Council. For these reasons the Knights enjoyed an unusual degree of prestige in Los Angeles.

V. UNION AGAINST THE CHINESE

ANTI-CHINESE agitation all but disappeared in Los Angeles after the campaign of the Workingmen's Party in the late 1870's. The party's decline and subsequent amalgamation with the Greenback Labor Party in 1880 meant that no local agency was concerned with the Chinese problem at a time when it was most crucial in the state of California. The Greenbackers, it is true, accepted anti-Chinese agitation as part of their heritage, but the impending disintegration of their party precluded anything more than cursory attention. Knights of Labor and craft unionists were just beginning to organize in the early 'eighties. Hence the only possible exponents of Chinese exclusion were the small and uninfluential third parties which followed in the wake of the Greenback Labor Party. They served to bridge the gap with continuous, if not emphatic, expression of anti-Chinese sentiment.

During the tense early months of 1882 when Congress was debating passage of the Exclusion Act, Los Angeles labor was thus unprepared to share in the state-wide demonstrations to influence legislative action. The San Francisco Trades Assembly, revitalized after the depression of the 1870's, had begun to push an anti-Chinese campaign in 1881. Although not greatly concerned over national trends, San Francisco labor recognized in the Federation of Organized Trades and Labor Unions (created at Pittsburgh in 1881) an opportunity to gain more compelling authority for its own agitation. The San Francisco delegate at the Pittsburgh convention proposed and won adoption of a resolution demanding expulsion of the Chinese. The Federation, forerunner of the AFL, was the first national body to lend its weight to an issue heretofore almost entirely limited to the Pacific Coast. Thus supported, the San Francisco Trades Assembly energetically pursued its objective of Congressional intervention. In April, 1882, it summoned delegates from California, Oregon, and Nevada to a huge anti-Chinese demonstration. The League of Deliverance which emerged boycotted Chinese-made goods and merchants dealing in them, but its continuance became unnecessary when the President signed an exclusion bill on May 6. The new law, which prohibited the immigration of Chinese laborers into the United States for a period of ten years, became effective in August, 1882.[1]

Los Angeles was hardly touched by the fervor animating the northern part of the state. At the behest of the governor, the county committees of the Democratic and Republican parties arranged a Los Angeles mass meeting on March 4, 1882, to urge speedy Congressional action. That

[60]

the function of rallying anti-Chinese opinion was taken over by the two major parties reveals the extent to which an idea originally sponsored by labor had been accepted by the community. Yet there was no urgency to follow up the mass meeting with more specific action. The City Council, after halfheartedly discussing an ordinance excluding Chinese from the city, relegated the matter to its files. Such apathy called forth the contempt of the *Times,* which for several months in the spring of 1882 preached an anti-Chinese doctrine. When passage of the Exclusion Act lessened the need to keep the issue before the public, the *Times* gradually became less vehement. Then, after Otis became a proprietor on August 1, the newspaper abruptly dropped its anti-Chinese policy, and the issue was dead for the next several years.[2]

Obviously the lack of a capable labor organization in Los Angeles was not the only explanation of the city's lethargy. As in earlier periods, the community did not include enough Chinese to call for a really vigorous campaign against them. In 1880, there were only 605 Orientals, or 5.4 per cent of the population, in the city; at the same time, the comparable figure for San Francisco was 21,790, or 9.3 per cent. During the next decade, with the Exclusion Act in operation, the percentage of Orientals in Los Angeles dropped to 3.7, while in San Francisco it decreased only to 8.6. Los Angeles, though smaller than San Francisco, was growing far more rapidly, and in proportion its Chinese problem became less pressing. Many of the southern city's newcomers from the East were devoid of anti-Chinese sentiment and could only with difficulty be aroused to the need for agitation.[3]

Eventually the Exclusion Act proved a disappointment to those who had worked for it, since the wording left loopholes for employers who wanted cheap labor and for the Chinese themselves. Growing discontent up and down the Pacific Coast crystallized by 1885 into a renewal of serious anti-Chinese agitation, often resulting in violence. San Francisco labor, the usual spearhead of such movements, this time lagged behind, largely because the Trades Assembly, dying out during the mid-decade depression, was not replaced by an effective central body until the end of the year. In Los Angeles, where unemployment was increasing with importation of Orientals for construction work on the Santa Fe Railroad, anti-Chinese sentiment revived in the spring of 1885, some six months before the reappearance of agitation in San Francisco.[4]

Although a labor movement had arisen in Los Angeles by 1885, neither the Knights of Labor nor the Trades Council was quite ready to tackle the Chinese problem. Without the self-appointed leadership

of Captain J. F. Janes of San Pedro, Los Angeles might not have preceded San Francisco in the renewal of anti-Chinese agitation. Janes
was an unusual and rather flamboyant character, known in both Los
Angeles and San Pedro for his extraordinary antics. An unfortunate
obscurity has hidden much of his early life; the only event in his pre–
Los Angeles career detailed locally was his participation in a Mexican
filibuster in 1874.[5] Description of him as an "ex-sailor, ex-miner, ex-
explorer, and ex-ward politician"[6] suggests a picturesque past, to which
an episode in 1884 was a fitting addition. In the early 1880's Janes had
published several newspapers, among them the *Shipping Gazette,* in
which he espoused such causes as antimonopolism and anti-Orientalism.
With this entree, association with the straggling third-party movement
was natural, and by 1884 he had established a connection with the
composite so-called Anti-Monopoly–Greenback–Labor Party in Los
Angeles. Omission of his name from the list of accredited delegates to
a county convention in October, because he had refused "to pledge
himself to behave and not to create a disturbance in the body," affronted Janes, and he marched out of the convention "in high dudgeon."
When he later pleaded for admission on grounds that he had "fought
the railroads single-handed" as a staunch antimonopolist, the convention, still distrustful, "summarily fired" him.[7] Following this break,
Janes ran independently for the state assembly, and though failing to
win the election, elicited a friendly comment: "Janes is nothing if not
original, and many a worse man is found under a smoother exterior."[8]

Janes' exploits, together with his publishing and stumping experience, fitted him admirably for making the 1885 anti-Chinese campaign
an example of good showmanship. A colorful orator, he could attract
and hold crowds which would simply have walked away from duller
entreaties. He brought to the movement much the same kind of spontaneity and humor which Alfred Moore provided in the early days
of the Workingmen's Party. When Janes realized that the third parties
stemming from the Greenback movement were not the best vehicles for
promulgation of exclusionist doctrines, he organized, in March, 1885,
a Workingmen's Club known later as Independent Labor Union No. 1
and finally as the Anti-Chinese Union. To bolster its activities, he re-
established the *Shipping Gazette* as an organ for the new movement. A
mass meeting sponsored by the club on March 14 gratified Janes by
voting to boycott those who employed Chinese in any capacity. In spite
of Janes' personal buoyancy and freedom from inhibitions, he was
careful to stress moderation and lawful remedies against the Chinese,
a policy which won public confidence and popularized the movement.

In May, the Anti-Chinese Union adopted a constitution and elected permanent officers. Janes, like Alfred Moore in an earlier period, suffered the indignity of repudiation when George L. Stearns succeeded him as president. The blow to his pride led to abnegation of the movement he had launched, and his later anti-Chinese crusades were to be conducted, like his previous political career, on an independent and individual basis.[9]

Meanwhile, the Anti-Chinese Union had embarked on the preparation of a petition requesting the City Council to remove the Chinese beyond city limits. Needing outside help for an undertaking of this magnitude, the Union dispatched its president to address an open meeting of the carpenters' union, endorsed the printers' strike against the *Express,* obtained the sanction of the Trades Council, and recruited two hundred members to march in the city's July 4th parade. These cordial overtures to labor and the community enabled the Union to gather a total of 1,271 signatures by July, when it presented the memorial to the City Council. But hopes for official condemnation of the Chinese were dashed when the city attorney reported negatively on the constitutionality of the proposed ordinance.[10] Following this reverse, the Anti-Chinese Union virtually disappeared. Apart from the representation of several local unions at the Pacific Coast anti-Chinese convention in November, 1885, there was no further Los Angeles agitation against the Chinese until 1886, when the Trades Council assumed responsibility.

That the Trades Council rather than the Knights of Labor took up the cause was due to the Typographical Union which, after discarding its own half-formulated plan to affiliate with the Knights, was a consistent exponent of craft unionism. The printers' submission of their 1885 strike to the Trades Council's mediation was, for example, a valuable contribution to the centralization of authority. When early in February, 1886, a rumor that an anti-Chinese memorial to Congress was being circulated locally failed to reawaken the Anti-Chinese Union, the Typographical Union instructed its Trades Council delegates "to agitate anti-Chinese measures in that body and favor the calling of a mass meeting at an early date."[11] This suggestion, coming from a craft never threatened by Oriental competition, revealed the printers' desire for conservative sponsorship of an agitation which might easily flare into violence and their hopes of strengthening the Trades Council through management of a popular campaign.

The Council responded immediately to the plea of the printers. At a mass meeting on February 14, 1886, it invited the Knights of Labor,

members of unions "of whatever kind," working people not belonging
to unions, and all "friends of civilization" to join in its first community
undertaking. The Knights were the earliest to promise help, and overwhelming general support was manifest in an attendance of some five
thousand at a second meeting on February 27. Presence of the City
Council gave official sanction. Participation by leaders of the old Workingmen's Party and of the Anti-Chinese Union, as well as by newspaper
proprietors and other prominent citizens, was further reassurance,
though some adherents belittled the Trades Council by regarding the
Knights of Labor as the guiding agency. The *Times'* pro-Chinese stand
was a significant exception to widespread belief that coolie labor constituted a menace not only to the working classes, but to the whole of
society. Otis was conspicuously absent from the meeting, though his
coproprietor, H. H. Boyce, spoke in favor of measures against the Chinese. Their disagreement on this issue was part of the conflict soon to
end in Boyce's ouster from the Times-Mirror establishment. Otis predicated his defense of the Chinese on an argument that exclusionist
agitation, because it did not truly reflect community sentiment, was in
restraint of industrial freedom.[12] His attitude here was a step toward
later advocacy of the open shop.

Despite the *Times'* open disapproval, the February 27 meeting enthusiastically adopted the program put forward by the Trades Council:

1. To discontinue patronage of Chinese vegetable gardens and laundries, and of
   all establishments employing Chinese.
2. To encourage and support non-Orientals engaged in raising produce or operating
   laundries, hotels, restaurants, etc., without Chinese labor.
3. To withhold patronage from individuals employing Chinese, renting or leasing
   property to Chinese, or selling goods manufactured by Chinese.
4. To recommend immediate replacement of all Chinese servants by white help.
5. To request the Board of Supervisors of Los Angeles County to send delegates to
   a state anti-Chinese convention summoned to meet in Sacramento on March 10.
6. To find a legal and peaceful solution to the Chinese question.[13]

The Trades Council, shrewdly realizing that verbal endorsement, no
matter how vociferous, was no guarantee of sustained support, immediately set out on a door-to-door campaign to procure written pledges
to uphold the Chinese boycott. Tangential and unsolicited help came
from Captain Janes, who harangued listeners on his favorite theme at
the old Workingmen's stand in front of the courthouse.[14]

Neither soapbox oratory nor solicitation by a handful of workers
could hold the public's interest for a prolonged period. To prevent a
natural letdown, the Trades Council established anti-Chinese ward
clubs, each responsible for canvassing its own area. This system, remi-

niscent of Workingmen's Party methods, drew into the movement all individuals eager to help, and provided a convenient unit wherein craft unionists, Knights of Labor, former Workingmen, and Green-backers worked together under supervision of a boycott committee responsible to the Trades Council. Jonathan Bailey was prominent, for example, as a club officer and frequent speaker at meetings. As the campaign progressed, club membership grew rapidly and enthusiasm mounted high. More than four thousand citizens had signed the boy-cott pledge by the middle of April, 1886, and many employers had promised to discharge their Chinese help by May 1. With meticulous attention to detail, the Typographical Union refused to continue meet-ing in Painters' Hall because the building's owner employed Chinese; the painters' assembly then procured a new meeting place.[15]

The anti-Chinese campaign of 1886 reached a climax on May 1, which the Trades Council was able to set aside as a half-holiday because of the general popularity of the cause. In choosing this date, Los Angeles labor was in line with California labor, which observed May Day with anti-Chinese demonstrations rather than with the eight-hour agitation which made 1886 the year of "Great Upheaval" elsewhere in the coun-try. In Los Angeles, the day's special feature was another mass meeting, attended by several thousand people. The main speaker was the Rev-erend N. T. Ravelin, state organizer of the Anti-Chinese Non-Partisan Association, an outgrowth of the Sacramento convention in March. Ravelin's address was a recapitulation of the fairly common view that Congressional failure to do more than prohibit further immigration necessitated use of the boycott to remove the Chinese already here. He scored the clergy of the state and especially of Los Angeles for their pro-Chinese attitude, declaring that God, could He be questioned, would certainly commend the expulsion of heathen from a Christian land.[16]

Of far greater pertinence was Ravelin's later report to the state Association. Praising Los Angeles labor for the best anti-Chinese or-ganization on the coast, he explained that the campaign had been conducted under "the direction ... of the Trades Council, an institu-tion closely related to the Knights of Labor, not like the Federated Trades of San Francisco."[17] Here is direct testimony from an eyewitness that the Los Angeles craft union movement was intimately interwoven with the Knights of Labor.

In spite of Ravelin's glowing account, the Los Angeles anti-Chinese campaign died out as speedily as had earlier movements of the same kind. In the first place, advocating the discharge of Chinese employees for whom no replacements were available posed an insoluble problem; and secondly, the refusal of Chinese vegetable peddlers (almost the sole source of supply) to serve families which had dismissed their countrymen caused many people to forget their boycott pledges. Although Ravelin made another appearance on May 7, it was already too late to infuse the movement with new life. The whole fabric of the anti-Chinese organization had disintegrated almost over night, as waning interest caused the Knights of Labor to desert and the ward clubs to disband. Even the Trades Council lost its zeal.[18] The sudden rise and equally abrupt fall of an enthusiasm so compelling that approximately one-tenth of the population attended a mass meeting can only suggest a motivation more emotional than economic. There was no real urgency in Los Angeles for proceeding against the Chinese, and the boom just starting in 1886 quickly diverted labor's attention to craft unionism and its demands, as it absorbed other segments of the population in money-making schemes or plans for the city's development.

Nevertheless, the Trades Council haltingly continued the campaign for a few months. It boycotted several hotels and restaurants which employed Chinese, notably the establishment of J. A. Brown, and expected to reanimate a fullfledged movement when a new Cooks' and Waiters' Union would be ready to assist. But this union, formed on May 21, 1886, with eighty members, was unable to supply the necessary white workers in time to sustain the boycotts. The Council therefore, having depleted its treasury by spending $600 on an apparently futile campaign, became resigned to the hopelessness of its task. It concluded the local anti-Chinese campaign with a few gestures directing union members toward white-labor cigars and shoes, and an unanswered request that the City Council compel Chinese laundries to write receipts in English. The decline of agitation in Los Angeles reflected a regional trend, as Pacific Coast labor temporarily became defeatist when Congress failed to make immigration restriction more effective.[19]

The Cooks' and Waiters' Union survived until November, 1886, when the White Cooks', Waiters' and Employés' Protective Union of the Pacific Coast, formed in San Francisco in 1883, reorganized it as Branch No. 3. This was the first time, barring establishment of the sailors' union in San Pedro, that a San Francisco union helped to organize a particular trade in Los Angeles. The southern branch started with fifty-three charter members, some of them women. Its connection with the parent body was strengthened when five members of the San Francisco union, including the president, installed the local officers.[20]

The agitation of 1886 was barren of progress against the Chinese, but it did serve to focus attention on relations between the Knights of Labor and the Trades Council. Although the latter gained some authority from its supervision of the campaign, it was not yet clear which of the two was going to dominate the Los Angeles labor movement. Some observers were so confused as to believe the Knights were in command of the anti-Chinese campaign, and Ravelin, though understanding the plan of organization, likened the Trades Council to the Knights of Labor. As the anti-Chinese movement faltered to its dispirited end, either the Knights or the Council could have emerged as the authoritative group. The Council paid for its assumption of responsibility by financial exhaustion and open failure; the Knights' organization, on the other hand, was unimpaired by its participation in the campaign.

The question of Trades Council versus Knights of Labor posed in Los Angeles by the 1886 anti-Chinese agitation was not merely local. It was part of the broader conflict between craft unionism and mixed unionism, between practical economics and idealism which confronted workingmen everywhere in the country. Craft unionism received a tremendous boost in 1886 with the formation of the American Federation of Labor as successor to the Federation of Organized Trades and Labor Unions. This young and vigorous rival to the Knights of Labor presented to workers, dismayed by the Knights' unwieldiness and patent inefficiency, the very practical philosophy of business unionism. Because of this, and because of ill-advised and unsuccessful strikes, the national order of Knights began to decline shortly after reaching its highest influence in 1886. For the Los Angeles Trades Council, tending toward craft unionism despite its rather nebulous character, the national situation thus provided a clear opportunity for enforcement of its claims to leadership of the local labor movement.

Locally, the Trades Council had a further advantage over the Knights of Labor in the favorable milieu for the growth of craft unionism soon to be provided by the great boom of 1886–1887. Yet Los Angeles labor was not destined to resolve its uncertainty in any immediate, clean-cut decision. As events of the next few years were to show, instability springing from the confused leadership of the 1880's vastly increased labor's vulnerability to opposition from without, an opposition that was slowly but surely taking form while labor organizations were fumbling their way to a clear definition of policy.

VI. LABOR GROWS WITH LOS ANGELES

THE IMMEDIATE CAUSE of the great real estate boom of 1886–1887 was a rate war between the Southern Pacific and Santa Fe railroads. The former had come to Los Angeles from San Francisco in 1876, and enjoyed an undisturbed monopoly until the fall of 1885, when the Santa Fe brought its first trains into Los Angeles partly on track leased from the Southern Pacific. Although the rate war did not start until the spring of 1887, when the Santa Fe acquired its own roadbed all the way into the city, the Southern Pacific's monopoly was obviously doomed. Its abuse of its advantageous position, however, had created an animosity which embittered the ensuing competition between the two rivals. In addition to cutting individual passenger fares, the railroads held out other inducements, such as low group rates and application of fares to payment for railroad lands. A parallel reduction in freight charges further stimulated immigration by decreasing the cost of living in California and increasing the profits on exported goods.[1]

Cheap railroad rates were not the only stimulus causing people to pull up stakes and move to southern California. Extensive advertisement of the area's attractions—a healthful climate, agricultural advantages, low cost of living, economic opportunities—aroused curiosity and drew large numbers westward. Much of the propaganda emanated from the railroads, anxious to sell their lands and develop the West as a surety of future profits, but boards of trade, chambers of commerce, realty syndicates, and immigration societies helped to spread the news. Travelers' accounts and letters from pleased settlers were an informal addition to the conscious efforts to bring people to the land of golden promise.[2]

In an eager rush to test the verity of the remarkable claims advanced, uncountable thousands of immigrants flocked to southern California during 1886–1887. More than one hundred and thirty thousand of them remained as permanent settlers, and in Los Angeles alone the population increased to an estimated eighty thousand in 1888. Although many of the newcomers departed after the boom collapsed, the city grew faster during the 1880's than in any other decade before 1900. The population climbed from about eleven thousand in 1880 to approximately fifty thousand in 1890. An influx of such proportions had to be accompanied by an equally impressive real estate development. During 1886 the boom was still restrained and conservative, affecting mainly the suburban areas of Los Angeles. But in 1887, as enthusiasm mounted to a feverish pitch and railroad fares dropped to an absurd minimum,[3] unbridled speculation spread to business and residential properties in the city itself. Real estate transactions jumped from $29,000,000 in 1886 to $98,000,000 in 1887. Property assessments in Los Angeles skyrocketed, and the number of personal and business fortunes multiplied.[4]

These spectacular changes revolutionized the character of the city and its surrounding territory. The transition from a pastoral to an agricultural economy, begun in the 1870's, was completed; the culture of the area became predominantly American instead of Spanish; the old apathy and conservatism were swept away in the onrush of people from all sections of the country; development of outlying areas led to improved transportation and commercial facilities; municipal improvements and the enrichment of community life followed the arrival of thousands of new citizens, who added not only numbers but variety and color.

Because this was essentially a land boom, its impact on business was limited. Among the newcomers were many health seekers, small farmers, and retired businessmen uninterested in capitalistic ventures. Commercial expansion was therefore correlated to the agricultural economy and the basic needs of the new population, such as shelter, food, and clothing. Consequently the boom was felt most in building operations and in the establishment of small industries and stores. Apologists for Los Angeles, though granting that theirs was not a manufacturing city, acclaimed with justifiable pride the progress resulting from the boom.[5] Table 2 shows that Los Angeles County still lagged far behind San Francisco County in industrial development, but that it made great strides between 1880 and 1890.

This expansion, providing plentiful jobs at good wages, gave labor an unprecedented opportunity in Los Angeles. Prosperity made employers pliable and, for the most part, willing to grant workers' demands for higher wages or shorter hours or both. Although the Trades Council was financially and physically exhausted after the strenuous anti-Chinese campaign in the spring of 1886, the older unions were ready to grow with the city.

The building trades derived the most substantial benefit. Foremost among them was Carpenters' Union No. 56, which had grown to some eight hundred members by the summer of 1886. As described by Arthur Vinette, "Old 56" was "progressive in thought, conservative in action, generous in assistance to its members, prompt to rally in defense of other Unions and in the building of . . . solidarity . . . among organized workers."[6] These qualities it demonstrated by sending its president,

B. Nelligan, to the 1886 convention of the Brotherhood of Carpenters and Joiners, continuing its open meetings, maintaining a free employment bureau, expanding its benefit program, and organizing a carpenters' local at Pasadena. Absorbing some of the spirit of its Los Angeles progenitor, the Pasadena union followed up its organization

TABLE 2

INDUSTRIALIZATION IN LOS ANGELES AND SAN FRANCISCO COUNTIES, 1870–1890

Year	Number of establishments	Number of employees	Capitalization
1870			
Los Angeles County..............	79	621	$ 648,570
San Francisco County............	1,223	12,377	21,170,956
1880			
Los Angeles County..............	172	706	941,780
San Francisco County............	2,971	28,442	35,368,139
1890			
Los Angeles County..............	820	5,422	7,485,403
San Francisco County............	4,059	48,446	74,834,301

| Year | Percentage increase | | |
	Number of establishments	Number of employees	Capitalization
1870–1880			
Los Angeles County..............	117.7	13.7	45.2
San Francisco County............	142.9	129.8	67.1
1880–1890			
Los Angeles County..............	376.7	668.0	694.8
San Francisco County............	36.6	70.3	111.5

SOURCE: *Ninth Census of the United States, 1870*, Vol. III, *Wealth and Industry*, p. 496; *Tenth Census of the United States, 1880*, Vol. II, *Manufactures in the United States*, pp. 91–2; *Eleventh Census of the United States, 1890*, Vol. XI, *Manufacturing Industries in the United States*, pp. 352, 354.

with a partially successful demand for the nine-hour day. During 1887 the Los Angeles local widened the boundaries of its influence. Nelligan, as state organizer for the Brotherhood, formed many new locals, and in the fall tried to bring P. J. McGuire, secretary of both the national union and the American Federation of Labor, to the city.[7] Although the visit failed to materialize, the proposal was significant as the first attempt to have an outstanding union official come to Los Angeles.

Carpenters' Union No. 56 showed exemplary unselfishness in its local relations with allied crafts, the whole body of organized labor, and the community. This acceptance of responsibility was particularly notable because the carpenters made no demands for higher wages or shorter hours for themselves during the boom period. Acting in lieu of a building-trades organization, the carpenters early in 1887 established a working-card system for allied crafts and expanded their free employment bureau to include all the construction trades. In March they assisted the reorganized plasterers' union in a minor strike over nonpayment of wages and brought the employer to terms. In April, 1887, Local No. 56 incorporated a subsidiary Carpenters' Hall Association to provide suitable headquarters for all the unions. Toward this end it purchased a lot on San Pedro Street for the building, and three more in an outlying district as a speculative enterprise to raise necessary funds. In October the carpenters petitioned the City Council to set up the office of building inspector, which they deemed essential in a fast-growing community. As a temporary expedient the Council gave the fire marshal the appointment and in January, 1888, created the new post.[8]

In contrast to the varied concerns of the carpenters, other building trades concentrated on gains for their own immediate benefit. Painters' Assembly No. 3167, reaching its pinnacle of well-being in the spring of 1887, demanded a wage increase from $3 to $3.50 for the nine-hour day. Opposition came from painting contractors who were still active members of the assembly; they withdrew in protest and prevented the journeymen from winning a complete victory. Stricken by this defection, the painters' assembly started on the gradual decline which was to end with its disbanding several years later. Concurrently, a group of journeymen painters organized Local No. 29 of the national Brotherhood of Painters and Decorators, formed in March, 1887. By the end of May the new union had perfected its organization and existed side by side with the assembly with no external signs of conflict. In September, 1887, the unions of hod carriers, bricklayers, and plumbers all won wage increases, the first by striking and the last two by threatening to strike. Skilled labor was scarce and work was plentiful. The hod carriers' scale rose from $3.50 to $4 a day; the bricklayers', from $5 to $6; and the plumbers', from $4 to $4.50. Of all the building-trades crafts with previous organization, the plasterers made the poorest showing. Their early union had dropped from sight by the fall of 1886, and they had to reorganize twice during 1887.[9]

Several of the building trades organized for the first time during

the boom and made various demands of their employers. The Sheet
Metal Workers' Union was formed in September, 1886, and within a
few days had persuaded thirteen employers to sign a nine-hour agreement. A year later, when the union had over two hundred members,
it established a new scale raising daily wages from $3–$4 to $3.50–$4.50.
Unions of granite cutters and iron molders, organized in May, 1887,
both demanded the nine-hour day in August. The former won an easy
victory with only one employer dissenting, but the molders had more
trouble.[10]

The molders' union, affiliated with the Iron Molders' Union of
North America as Local No. 79, met opposition from the Baker Iron
Works, one of the largest manufacturing establishments in the city.
Seventy of the company's 125 employees, including not only molders
but blacksmiths, patternmakers, car builders, and machinists, struck
on August 15 to gain the nine-hour day with no reduction in wages,
then $3.50 a day. As the only organized craft, the molders sought to
negotiate with the company, but the management at first refused, saying
it would deal with the strikers only as individuals. When the walkout
spread to other foundries, Fred L. Baker, head of the company, participated in a conference between all the affected employers and the strikers
on August 30. The compromise agreed upon bound the employees to
work for thirty days under the old conditions, after which the companies
would institute the nine-hour day for a trial period. If the system
proved satisfactory, they would either revert to the longer day or would
pay for only nine hours' work. Baker accused his men of failing to
keep the agreement and later employed some nonunion workers at
the old rate of 35 cents an hour. But the union men who remained at
work convinced Baker that they could accomplish as much in nine
hours as in ten, and they gradually won their objective.[11]

The printing trades found the boom considerably less of a stimulus
than did the building trades. Only one new union was formed. The
pressmen, after rejecting an invitation to join the local printers' union,
organized their own branch of the ITU in November, 1886. The pressmen's union, however, was little more than a subsidiary of the Typographical Union, to which it deferred as the leader of the printing
trades. The printers themselves drew some advantage from the general
prosperity. By threatening to strike in April, 1886, they forced the
Times to bring its Sunday wage scale up to union standards. Several
months later they demanded an increase in wages from all newspaper
proprietors. Although persuaded to compromise some of the issues, the
union on June 21 established a revised and somewhat higher scale, to
which the *Times* reluctantly agreed.[12]

Having gained the most that was possible in the wage issue, the printers turned to an objective which seemed, in these early years, to be of paramount value to them. The Times-Mirror job office was still open shop and, as part of a growing publishing concern, was a decided obstacle to the union's full control of its jurisdiction. In September, 1886, the printers demanded that the firm employ only union men. Alarmed by the threat of a strike and of pressure from the Trades Council, Otis yielded early in October, reaffirming at the same time his promise to maintain the wage scale. The *Times* could then ill afford to antagonize the union, for it had just installed expensive plant improvements and had recently been awarded a large public printing contract, the county *Great Register* of voters. Unwilling to risk a default on this important job, Otis accepted the lesser evil of keeping peace with the union. Encouraged by a victory won without the aid of the ITU, which had been deaf to hurried appeals for help, the Los Angeles printers barred members from working in any of the smaller unfair offices in town.[13]

It is possible that another coincidental factor influenced Otis to submit to unionization of his job office, for on October 4, 1886, his erstwhile partner, H. H. Boyce, established the Republican *Tribune.* The emergence of this rival to the *Times* was a happy event for organized labor, for the acerbity of the ensuing competition between the two papers temporarily diverted the *Times'* attention from union "iniquities." From the beginning the *Tribune* sought to raise labor in public esteem by giving full and fair publicity to all union activities. Also exceptional were the *Tribune's* own relations with the Typographical Union, for the newspaper voluntarily employed a full staff of union compositors and permitted them to choose their own newsroom foreman. No other Los Angeles newspaper had been so consistently friendly to organized labor, and as a foil to the *Times'* developing animosity it was invaluable to the unions. The printers were quick to express their gratitude to the *Tribune:* "The union not being accustomed to any favors from the press of this city in any respect, any voluntary kindness to it awakens the liveliest feeling of appreciation and remembrance."[14] This amity gave the unions even more than the forthright aid of one friendly newspaper. Not to be outdone in the dissemination of news, other papers took example from the *Tribune* in devoting more space to organized labor, and even the *Times,* a year or so later, ran a labor column for a few months. The wider publicity was a boon to organizations never before assured of a steady news outlet and always apprehensive of prejudiced reporting in the commercial press.

The Typographical Union swept on from its 1886 victories to a series of successful enterprises in 1887. In February, the printers demanded another round of wage increases in all newspaper and job offices. Their threat to strike overcame the opposition of the four daily newspapers and won for them a higher wage scale.[15] The president's annual report on May 1 exulted that the printers had unionized the Times-Mirror job office, "a bone of contention for years," increased their wages by 10 per cent, and filled every job office with union men, all "without the loss of an office" or "without materially affecting the good feeling which . . . at present exists between the Typographical Union and the proprietors."[16] In August, 1887, the union, turning to another project which had periodically caused trouble, persuaded Los Angeles proprietors to enforce the ITU ruling against the use of "boiler plate."[17]

A more important achievement was establishment of the nine-hour day in the fall of 1887. This did not result specifically from local stimuli, but from passage by the International Typographical Union of a nine-hour law. In August the Los Angeles union served notice on proprietors that it would observe the national dictum as of November 1. Although the ITU later left enforcement to the judgment of each affiliate, the local printers voted unanimously to follow the original plan. The nine-hour day went into effect on schedule in Los Angeles. The pressmen's union pledged support to the printers, and on the same date, November 1, won a general wage increase for its own members.[18]

With stability at home assured, the Typographical Union, like the carpenters' local, was able to extend its regional authority. Early in 1886 country printers had been admitted to membership, and later in the year the San Bernardino Typographical Union had acknowledged the leadership of the Los Angeles union by reporting to it just after organization. But the clearest sign of expanding influence was the intervention of the local union in the troubles of the San Diego Typographical Union, which came into conflict with employers soon after organizing in early 1887. During the fight, members of the Printers' Protective Fraternity, a rival of the ITU, were imported into San Diego. This was the first introduction of Fraternity printers to the west coast, and it thoroughly alarmed the Los Angeles union, which spent considerable time and money in a fruitless effort to settle the San Diego dispute. Attention was diverted to the same danger much closer to home when rumor said that a Fraternity branch existed in Pasadena. The Los Angeles union sent off an emergency request to the ITU for a deputy district organizer, and hurriedly investigated the Pasadena rumor. When the ITU failed to send a representative to southern California, the Los Angeles printers organized a union in Pasadena as protection against possible Fraternity inroads.[19]

That the boom was a great impetus to the growth of labor organizations in Los Angeles is manifest from the records of the Typographical Union. During the second half of 1886, seventy-three printers joined the union by card and eight by election. During 1887 those admitted by card and election were, respectively, 267 and 85. Although there were numerous withdrawals, the union's membership was close to two hundred by the fall of 1887. The unusual prosperity of the period was not, however, an unmixed blessing. Although easing relations with employers and permitting both geographical and numerical expansion, it created the same problem encountered by the Typographical Union in 1884. Los Angeles was a health resort for workers as well as for people of means, and the many ailing printers who came to the city for the salubrious climate placed a strain on union finances. Establishment of a funeral fund, with a $75 death benefit, became necessary in October, 1886, and was supplemented by the purchase of a union burial lot early in the following year. By February, 1887, the union's solvency was so imperiled that members were fined $25 for enticing printers to Los Angeles. In the fall, when the benefit fund was depleted, the union abolished official appropriations for sick benefits, hoping that dependence on voluntary contributions would deter malingerers.[20] In 1888 individual hardships occasioned by illness were submerged in the more crucial needs of the many printers thrown out of work by strikes and depression.

Although building trades and printers benefited most from the boom—the former because of the abundance of work in their line and the latter because of their superior organization—other groups of workers also took advantage of the expanding economy. To shorten their excessively long working day, the bakers organized the first Los Angeles union of their craft in August, 1886, and within a few months affiliated with the Journeymen Bakers' National Union as Local No. 45. On November 22 the local members demanded a six-day week; a twelve-hour day except for Saturday, when they would work fifteen hours; weekly instead of monthly payment of wages; and a new wage system paying an extra $5 a week in lieu of the board and lodging usually supplied by the employer. After a two-hour strike all the bakeries, except that of restaurant proprietor J. A. Brown, yielded to the union. Brown's employees defied the union and continued to work for him until March,

1887, when they quit in protest over inferior working conditions. In November, two employers replaced their union help with nonunion bakers willing to work on Sunday. Both were persuaded to reinstate the discharged men and continue the six-day schedule, though one proprietor did not yield until the Trades Council intervened.[21]

The mediation was handled by a special "arbitration" committee set up by the Trades Council in April, 1887, consisting of one representative from each affiliate. If the committee failed to settle a dispute referred to it by the union or unions concerned, it was empowered to pay strikers' benefits of $6 a week for six weeks in walkouts involving more than one trade. The Typographical Union, pleased with the tendency toward greater centralization of the labor movement, endorsed the plan after deleting the last condition.[22]

Like the bakers, the cooks and waiters had uneasy relations with J. A. Brown. Their union, Branch No. 3 of the White Cooks', Waiters' and Employés' Protective Union of the Pacific Coast, joined the Los Angeles Trades Council in January, 1887, and in May set up an employment agency for its members. In August, the union sponsored two successful wage strikes. Brown's waiters won an increase in pay from $40 to $50 a month, and those in another restaurant from $10 to $12 a week. On September 4, Brown's waiters walked out again in a dispute over the employment of a Chinese cook. The difficulty was temporarily adjusted, but several months later Brown reverted to the use of Chinese help. This was not acceptable to a union strongly biased against Orientals, and it imposed a boycott on Brown's restaurant. A picket carrying a banner inscribed with "Boycott! See that white labor is employed" was arrested on a charge of obstructing the sidewalk. The boycott had no noticeable effect on Brown's business. Apart from this trouble, the cooks' and waiters' union flourished. In November, 1887, it reported 170 members, all of whom were employed. The demand for union help outstripped the supply, despite the large numbers of nonunion and Chinese cooks and waiters in the city.[23]

Early in the summer of 1887 three new unions were organized: the Upholsterers' Union, the United Hack Drivers of Los Angeles, and the Teamsters' Association. None of these affiliated with the Trades Council, and only the first was visibly concerned with improvement of working conditions. The upholsterers won higher wages on September 24 by striking; several days later they demanded a second increase, refused by only one shop.[24]

A few groups of unorganized workers made some advances because of the favorable atmosphere. During 1886 and 1887 retail clerks and butchers achieved shorter hours and, from some employers, a Sunday holiday. In March, 1887, post-office clerks, overworked because of the unprecedented increase in the volume of mail, won a pay increase. In July sixty employees of the Los Angeles Cable Railway struck when the company asked them to assume financial responsibility for damage to company property. The drivers and conductors made no wage demands, though they were then earning only $2.16 for a twelve-hour day. When a committee of strikers learned that employees were to be liable only for avoidable accidents, most of the men signed the contract and returned to work, forgoing the unionization which they had contemplated.[25]

Thus, the two boom years in Los Angeles were busy and fruitful ones for labor. It was, however, obvious that a strong central body was lacking. Neither the Knights of Labor nor the Trades Council was more than casually interested in the workers' drive for greater benefits. The order devoted itself mainly to a social program, and even failed to participate in the organization of a California State Assembly in September, 1886.[26] The Council, except for its creation of a rudimentary mediation system, made no effort to unify craft unionists at a time when they might have secured a real foothold. Although the Council numbered fifteen unions early in 1887,[27] it was very far from being truly representative of Los Angeles labor and contributed almost nothing to the improvement of working conditions.

The Council did sponsor one political venture during the boom period, but even in this it shared honors with the Knights of Labor. Early in September, 1886, District Assembly No. 140 of Los Angeles, condemning the dominant political parties for their corruption, their servility to monopolies, and their enmity to organized labor, called upon workers to elect honest and incorruptible men, irrespective of party, to office. Later the same month a workingmen's convention, held in San Francisco under the auspices of the Knights, organized a United Labor Party, which brought together Knights, Grangers, trade-unionists, and Greenbackers in a combined effort to save the state from "boss rule and wholesale corruption." The platform embodied the principles of the Knights of Labor. A full state ticket was nominated, but the party was too weak to make even a fair showing in the election.[28]

Los Angeles workers followed suit in October. A first meeting under the auspices of the Trades Council attempted to endorse Republican or Democratic candidates friendly to labor, but broke up when the delegates' own political preferences prevented their agreement. Several days later a second Council meeting was equally impotent to define labor's policy. Finally, on October 23, a group of assorted Greenbackers, Grangers, and ex-Workingmen, styling themselves a "People's Party," endorsed the state platform and ticket of the United Labor Party, and the county ticket of the Democratic Party. About a month later the Trades Council and most of its affiliated unions decided to support the movement, and a joint convention on December 1 ratified the state platform and ticket of the United Labor Party. The local platform demanded economical municipal administration, the eight-hour day on public works, and just treatment of organized labor. A full municipal ticket, headed by Michael Daly, a hod carrier, and including several members of the printers' and carpenters' unions, was placed in the field. The largest vote polled by any of them was Daly's 219, a poor showing in contrast to the more than two thousand of his successful Democratic competitor. The venture was significant only in continuing the heterogeneous grouping which had existed in the anti-Chinese campaign earlier in 1886; prominent among the party's leaders were Isaac Kinley, district master workman of the Knights, and E. S. Livermore, president of the Trades Council.[29] The United Labor Party in Los Angeles merely emphasized, once again, labor's willingness to cling to the traditional pattern.

The Trades Council came closest to performing a useful function in the fall of 1887, when the turning point of the boom had been passed and unemployment had already set in. Even then it acted only after a constituent union had taken the initiative in protesting a journalistic misrepresentation. When the Boston *Globe* printed an Associated Press report in October that good mechanics were scarce in Los Angeles, Carpenters' Union No. 56 issued a circular of denial. The *Times* upheld the *Globe,* arguing that the city could use more good carpenters, and that labor's policy of limiting hours and fixing wages had dislocated the labor market and discouraged capital investment. The carpenters maintained that the disproportionate ratio of labor and capital flowing into southern California was responsible for the prevailing unemployment.[30]

Labor's response to the *Times'* allegations was immediate and angry. A protest meeting, sponsored by the Trades Council on November 4, brought together representatives of the unions of cigar makers, printers, granite cutters, carpenters, painters, cooks and waiters, sheet-metal workers, plumbers, molders, and the local branch of the Amalgamated Society of Carpenters and Joiners.[31] The Trades Council endorsed the stand taken by the carpenters and urged all its member unions to do the same. The Typographical Union inserted in the official ITU organ a statement that there were already plenty of printers in Los Angeles.[32] Although an external challenge was more effective in unifying labor than a series of victories, the collaboration was of short duration. The furor over the labor supply died down as quickly as it had arisen.

The momentary unity found by Los Angeles labor in the United Labor Party and the labor market controversy did no more than reveal the latent possibilities of a developing labor movement. The expansion of the boom period had come, not from energetic leadership by the Trades Council, but from the initiative and vigor of its member unions, acting for the most part without central guidance. Thus opportunism took the place of the intelligent and positive direction which could have transformed the Los Angeles labor movement from an agglomeration of self-reliant unions into a unified body ready to face the opposition of the years ahead. True, the opposition still lacked clear definition, for the prosperous years of the boom period inclined employers to a tolerant acceptance of unionism and its claims. Only the foundry proprietors, in opposing the nine-hour demand in 1887, had shown any disposition to unite against their employees. Even unionism's inveterate enemy of the future, the Los Angeles *Times,* had been guided by the exigencies of the moment just as much as had labor and management. Although its inclination toward the integration of antiunion forces was implicit, the *Times* had not yet forged the community sentiment which later frustrated organized labor in Los Angeles. Early in 1888 the newspaper reported that local industrial relations were smooth, and even complimented labor for its good sense and conservatism.[33]

The observation that the labor movement had thus far exercised moderation was true. Discounting the negligible influence of propagandists like Alfred Moore and Captain Janes, who were more entertaining than persuasive, Los Angeles labor leaders had been bulwarks of conservatism. Arthur Vinette and Jonathan Bailey, though reformers at heart, were practical unionists who accepted the existing social system as the necessary framework for their activities. Nor did the Knights of Labor, headed by the intellectual Isaac Kinley, endorse any deviation from conservatism. As an educator rather than an agitator, Kinley exercised considerable influence over the labor movement with which he had been associated for almost ten years. His doctrine that the progress of the working class depended upon the growth of intelligence and conservatism[34] contributed to the equable nature of labor manifestations from the regime of the Workingmen's Party through the boom period.

Although their basic conservatism and freedom from strong employer opposition protected Los Angeles workers from dangerous excursions into violence, the local labor movement failed to derive permanent benefit from the expansion of the boom period. There was no directive agency to fabricate actual gains into an enduring basis for further progress. Moreover, the business cycle was turning to the disadvantage of organized labor. The end of the boom was in sight in the last months of 1887; the carpenters' complaint of an oversupply of mechanics in November was the first sign that adversity was impinging upon prosperity. For a while the labor movement was able to coast along on the impetus of the past two years, so that at the end of 1887, the State Labor Commissioner could favorably compare it with San Francisco labor.[35] In a final spurt a few new unions were organized as late as 1888, but the downward trend was imminent and inevitable. After a gradual decline, there was little left in the fall of 1888 to remind labor of its flourishing state a year before. The character of the movement had also changed. The Knights of Labor, overshadowed by the upsurge of craft unionism during 1886–1887, now for a brief period emerged as the dominant organization.

VII. TROUBLE ON THE WATER FRONT

A SAILORS' STRIKE at San Pedro in December, 1887, though apparently unrelated to the Los Angeles labor movement, affected it in two ways. First, by checking the flow of lumber into southern California and thus accelerating the transition from boom to depression, the walkout contributed in part to the cyclical decline of unionism in Los Angeles. Second, it provided a setting for the emergence of the Knights of Labor as the temporary directive agency of the local labor movement. Discarding the national order's antistrike policy and their own local practice of nonintervention, the Knights joined the Coast Seamen's Union and a new longshoremen's association in prosecuting the sailors' strike.

Ever since their participation in the anti-Chinese agitation and the United Labor Party of 1886, the Knights of Labor had passively accepted the dominance of the Trades Council and its affiliated unions. Their gains during the two boom years were largely numerical. District Assembly No. 140, embracing all of southern California, jumped from six local assemblies with about three hundred members in July, 1886, to thirteen local assemblies with a total membership of close to nine hundred a year later. Only one of the new branches was organized in Los Angeles proper. The Knights, though dormant in local affairs, continued their broader interests by again sending W. L. Wolfe as delegate to the General Assembly in 1887.[1]

San Pedro was in the area over which the district assembly had jurisdiction. The sailors, however, had had no dealings with the Knights of Labor until the 1887 strike, for their own Coast Seamen's Union was a vital force not only in the Pacific Coast labor movement but also in the organization of seamen all over the world. Indissolubly linked with the sailors' union is the name of Andrew Furuseth of San Francisco, a giant among west coast labor leaders. Even the Los Angeles *Times* recognized Furuseth's unusual qualities, describing him as "one of the most dangerous" union men because of his "more than ordinary ability."[2] Furuseth became secretary of the Coast Seamen's Union several years after its formation, and in that capacity made invaluable contributions to the welfare of the working classes, particularly in protective legislation for seamen. He was one of the distinguished figures whose unselfish efforts helped create the American labor movement.[3]

The Coast Seamen's Union was organized at San Francisco in 1885, when a wave of unionism sweeping the country coincided with a period of dull shipping and low wages on the water front. When the sailors learned, early in March, that further wage decreases were impending, many of them left their ships in protest and a week later formed the union. Their immediate success in halting the proposed reduction did not bring peace to the water front. The union was a fighting organization, and during the spring and summer of 1885, vigorously campaigned against the shipping of nonunion crews, frequently clashing with the Coasting Boarding Masters' Association, captains, shipowners, and police. The union's forthrightness popularized it among seamen, and by July it claimed a membership of over two thousand. But numerical strength and a combative spirit were not enough to conquer entrenched opposition, and the union failed at this time to establish its own shipping office and coöperative boardinghouse. Encouraged by belligerence in the north, the San Pedro sailors struck successfully in May, 1885, for a wage increase from $30 to $35 a month, and early in June organized a local branch of the union.[4]

The year 1886 was a troubled one for California seamen despite a good beginning. The union's successful demand for further wage increases in March attracted many new members. The employers soon launched a counteroffensive by organizing a Shipowners' Association, which during the summer established its own shipping office and "grade-book" system. Since masters signed only those who shipped through the Association and possessed grade books, obtainable by nonunion men alone, union members were virtually locked out. To maintain its membership, the union secretly issued duplicate cards to sailors who had relinquished their original cards in order to obtain the grade books, but the device did nothing to abate the friction between union and employers.[5]

The unrest crystallized into a strike of all coasting sailors, called by the Coast Seamen's Union on August 25, 1886, to protest the methods of the Shipowners' Association. More than three thousand men, including the members of the San Pedro branch, went out. When the Association refused to arbitrate or to permit joint union-employer control of the shipping office, and the union failed again to establish its own shipping office, the sailors yielded. The union called off the strike at the end of September. Temporarily, sailors' wages dropped sharply, sometimes to $15 a month, and more than half the members deserted the union. Nevertheless, the union persisted in its efforts to keep nonunion men from sailing, with resulting water-front disturbances occasionally leading to violence.[6]

After the strike it took years of struggle to rebuild the Coast Seamen's Union. The major issue in conflicts with employers was not over wages, for the Shipowners' Association usually saw the wisdom of maintaining or exceeding the union scale. Primarily, the union wanted to prevent the shipping of nonunion sailors and to disrupt the alleged combination of shipowners, captains, and boardinghouse masters. This connivance, the sailors claimed, was an evil device to control the water front, and its perpetrators did not balk at shanghaiing men or robbing them of their pay. Although the union eventually forced abolition of the grade-book system, and the Shipowners' Association lapsed after two years, it was not until 1891 that coast seamen were able to set up their own shipping office.[7]

Even before then, the union had proved its worth as a labor organization. In November, 1887, the San Francisco headquarters founded the *Coast Seamen's Journal,* an enduring and creditable addition to labor journalism. At the same time, an official investigation by the California Bureau of Labor Statistics revealed that the union had increased wages and improved working conditions for coasting sailors, though conceding that there were still about five hundred nonunion men eligible for membership. Wages averaged $35 a month with board.[8]

The struggle of the Coast Seamen's Union to reëstablish itself after the disastrous 1886 strike was somewhat mitigated at San Pedro by the building boom in southern California. Lumber for the flourishing construction industry was brought in by boat through San Pedro, and the steady demand for building materials set a high value on the labor of sailors and longshoremen. To avoid delay, ship captains frequently accepted union crews and yielded to their wage demands. The union further strengthened its position by a successful membership drive among nonunionists hired by the Shipowners' Association; by November, 1887, the total enrollment of the San Pedro branch was 228.[9]

As the boom began to decline, the sailors at San Pedro found employers less tractable. In November, 1887, the captain of the *Lucy Matsen* refused to pay the $50-a-month scale asked by the union. The Shipowners' Association thereupon sent Edward H. Carpenter, its San Francisco agent, to San Pedro with a crew for the ship. Carpenter, who had deserted a responsible post in the sailors' union for the employers' association, was a particularly unfortunate choice for this assignment, and the union determined to hamper him at every turn. Failing in his attempt to man the *Lucy Matsen,* Carpenter next planned to ship a nonunion crew at less than union wages on the brig *Discovery.* In great secrecy, he signed men at San Francisco for a term of six months and started to take them to San Pedro by steamer. Alert union delegates in the southern port discovered the plan, met the steamer at Santa Barbara, separated the men from Carpenter, and persuaded them to hold out for union wages. Then, fearing legal action against the men for breach of contract, the unionists brought their new converts to San

Pedro for concealment. Carpenter threatened a conspiracy indictment if the men were not released. Feeling ran high during the controversy, with the San Pedro police and citizens favoring the union. Los Angeles constables had to be called in to arrest six of the unionists on a charge of aiding sailors to escape, for local officers refused to serve warrants on men they believed innocent of wrongdoing. The arrests led to street and water-front brawls, including an assault on Carpenter. Blaming such disturbances on hoodlums rather than on union members, the community showed a tolerance of labor organizations which later was to distinguish it sharply from Los Angeles.[10]

Although winning an acquittal for the six arrested men because of insufficient evidence, the union lost the original issue when the Ship-owners' Association with police aid managed to ship a nonunion crew on the *Discovery* on November 10, 1887. Angered by alleged union intimidation of nonunion crews and the seeming prejudice of local police against the Association, shipowners threatened to boycott both San Pedro and San Diego harbors unless the inhabitants demanded dissolution of the union agencies.[11] Before this reprisal could be effected, more serious trouble broke out. The November episode was a preliminary to the December strike, and clearly indicated how the public and the law enforcement agencies of San Pedro would react to labor troubles.

The shipping of a nonunion crew brought from San Francisco by agents of the Pacific Coast Steamship Company precipitated the strike on December 1, 1887, but underlying causes were more complicated. Members of the Coast Seamen's Union frequently worked as longshoremen for San Pedro lumberyards. The Shipowners' Association wanted to force these sailors working alongshore to go to sea, so as to reduce wages by increasing the labor supply. To this end its San Pedro agent, W. H. Savage, prevailed upon lumberyard proprietors to hire only non-union men and to discharge longshoremen belonging to the union. According to the union, shipowners even employed *provocateurs* to scare sailors into submission. The Coast Seamen's Union regarded these persecutions as part of a broad plan for its destruction; State Labor Commissioner John J. Tobin, who later went to San Pedro to make a personal investigation and report to the governor, concurred. The real object of the strike, then, was protection of the men working alongshore against the machinations of the Shipowners' Association; secondary was the desire to get rid of Savage and establish a union shipping office.[12]

Members of the Coast Seamen's Union working alongshore began the strike and induced some 150 members of the Longshoremen's and Lumbermen's Association, an independent organization formed six months earlier, to join them. At the same time about sixty sailors left their ships. Since some of the strikers belonged to the Knights of Labor, the two San Pedro assemblies, also recently organized, joined the strike. Much confusion arose from overlapping jurisdictions: longshoremen and lumberyard employees belonged both to their own union and to the Knights of Labor, and some sailors working alongshore were Knights as well as members of the Coast Seamen's Union. At first, no one organization attempted to coördinate the participating groups, partly because the strike was unauthorized but also because objectives were different. The Knights, for example, wanted to establish the right of workingmen to belong to the labor organization of their choice.[13]

Within two days 350 men had quit their jobs. The strikers belligerently paraded the streets of San Pedro and threatened to use force against nonunionists hired to replace them. There was little violence, however; two strikers arrested for using threatening language were acquitted. Los Angeles felt the work stoppage almost at once, as lack of materials forced contracting and building to a standstill. Annoyed by the interruption, the Los Angeles Lumber Dealers' Association announced that it would furnish help "at all hazards" to strike-bound lumber vessels. "No such state of affairs will ever again prevail at San Pedro."[14]

Although sailors had really commenced the walkout, the Coast Seamen's Union did not act as an organization in either the inception or the settlement of the strike. The district assembly of the Knights of Labor first instituted official negotiations by sending two members of the executive board, W. L. Wolfe and Robert Adams, to San Pedro to interview Savage. These delegates demanded, as a preliminary to discussion, Savage's acceptance of the principle that workingmen were free to join labor organizations. Savage refused, and in addition argued that he was not obliged to deal at all with the Knights of Labor, since most of the striking sailors had but recently joined the order. The conference availed nothing.[15]

The next step was a meeting between employers and a committee of three Knights and three longshoremen, but it, too, broke up without reaching agreement. The Coast Seamen's Union then invited Savage to attend its meeting on December 3, but he retorted that his association would deal only with individuals, not with labor organizations. After all these attempts proved fruitless, the Knights of Labor distributed handbills in Los Angeles informing the public that it was calling out the rest of its members and that both the Knights and the Coast Seamen's Union sanctioned the strike.[16]

At this juncture, Andrew Furuseth intervened. He wired Arthur

Vinette at Los Angeles, asking him to go to San Pedro and do what he could to effect a settlement. Vinette had acquired some reputation as "a referee in labor troubles, having so acted on a former occasion, and brought it to a successful end."[17] After a thorough investigation, Vinette was convinced that Savage's ultimate aim was destruction of the Coast Seamen's Union, but he believed the plan would fail unless the Shipowners' Association had an ample supply of nonunionists to send to San Pedro. Vinette advocated peaceful measures and planned a fundraising program to aid those out of work. The district and local officers of the Knights of Labor and a committee of coast seamen discussed their grievances with Vinette, and together they prepared a manifesto addressed to Savage. Although the strike was essentially a fight between sailors and shipowners, this document was signed only by the executive board of the Knights and proposed a settlement only on the issue of union membership. Vinette, with two of the Knights, tried to get the statement before the employers, but Savage rejected it and added gratuitously that he would never tolerate a union shipping office. In this, as in his subsequent refusal of Labor Commissioner Tobin's offer to mediate the dispute, Savage spoke for the Shipowners' Association, though the whole membership of that body did not subscribe to his extreme antiunion views.[18]

The Knights of Labor notified Grand Master Workman Powderly of their predicament, and distributed another circular in Los Angeles, warning all workingmen to avoid San Pedro until the strike was over, publicizing Savage's refusal to deal with labor organizations, and reiterating the Knights' willingness to return to work under a guarantee that union membership would not be grounds for discrimination.[19] A spokesman for the seamen's union likewise promised that sailors would end the strike when "the Shipowners' Association will allow men irrespective of race, color, or order to work along shore."[20]

Nevertheless, despite this restatement of the strikers' several aims, resistance was almost at an end. Although preventing a nonunion crew from sailing on December 9, the unionists failed in similar efforts a few days later. Financial assistance provided by the district assembly was inadequate, and on December 15 the Knights, recognizing defeat, called off the strike of longshoremen. Few of the strikers were taken back, though Tobin elicited a promise from Savage that he would try to persuade lumberyards to reëmploy members of the older San Pedro assembly. Tobin's report to the governor emphasized the absence of violence despite bitter feelings, but deemed the strike unauthorized because there had been no previous attempts to negotiate the dispute. Its failure was a serious blow to the Coast Seamen's Union, which had not wanted to strike and which sustained considerable financial loss. Sailors who had gone out lost some $3,000 in wages. More important, the union's prestige declined because of inability to establish its own shipping office and force Savage's dismissal.[21]

The water-front disturbance was unique in the early annals of local labor for several reasons. It was the first sharp conflict in the area between an employers' organization and a labor union. Whatever the superficial contradictions, the real issue was a struggle between the Shipowners' Association and the Coast Seamen's Union for control of the water front. Both organizations were sections of parent bodies in San Francisco, and for the first time a San Francisco union interfered in a labor dispute in the south. Until this time labor in the Los Angeles area had received little help or even encouragement from the stronger San Francisco organizations. Even now the pattern was scarcely altered, for Furuseth's intervention was kept to a minimum.[22] The aloofness of San Francisco labor, originating in geographical and psychological barriers, was to continue with minor exceptions until the turn of the century. The San Pedro strike was also the first in the area to portend the labor disputes of a later day. The disorder and excitement, the taking of sides by the public, the clashes with the police and subsequent arrests, the attempted mediation by an outside labor leader, and the investigation by a government official—all bring to mind the modern counterpart.

The San Pedro strike not only hastened the decline of the Los Angeles labor movement by retarding the building program, but it also affected the interrelationship of the Knights of Labor and the Trades Council. The coincidence of the strike with the collapse of the boom brought into play whatever talents the Knights possessed, as the weakening of craft unionism anticipated complete disintegration of the Trades Council. The Council had no direct concern in the strike, since none of its affiliates was involved. The only link was Vinette's intervention, a measure suggested by the Coast Seamen's Union, not by any local group. The Knights were less able to avoid entanglement. When several of its subsidiaries voted to join the strike, the district assembly realized that withdrawal was almost impossible and accordingly sanctioned their action. The Knights were also preëminent in the negotiations, having originated almost all of the attempts at settlement. With their new role in the sailors' controversy as an introduction, the Knights were to enjoy the kind of prestige ascribed to them in the earlier days of the Los Angeles labor movement. For a portion of the brief period before the establishment of a permanent central labor body in 1890, they accepted the responsibilities of leadership in Los Angeles.

VIII. AFTERMATH OF THE BOOM

THE SAILORS' STRIKE at San Pedro hastened the contraction of building operations which signaled the end of the great boom in Los Angeles. No sharp demarcation was noticeable, though the downward trend was visible during the winter of 1887–1888 in the smaller number of tourists, the decrease in advertising, the drop in real estate investments, the unloading of property by speculators, and the banks' more cautious lending policies. Slowness of the decline, together with a strong agricultural base and a solid underlying business structure, prevented catastrophe for the Los Angeles economy. Prices of real estate did not suddenly plunge, but fell gradually, and building projects not already contracted for were abandoned. Nonspeculators who retained faith in the area's ultimate promise contributed to the stabilization of agriculture and business. The conservatism of banks helped cushion the decline, and stringency in the money market forced economies in the development of natural resources. Although it is true that productive pursuits had been neglected during the frenzy of speculation, the city's physical growth necessitated such permanent improvements as irrigation and sewage systems, street paving, more efficient municipal transportation, and new city and federal buildings. Begun in part before the boom ended, this work provided employment and awakened civic consciousness. Yet the inevitable period of readjustment which followed in the wake of speculation and overexpansion caused hardship, especially among workers.[1]

As the area's economy contracted slowly, so the labor movement shrank almost imperceptibly. There was no specific time when unions stopped growing, when labor ceased making demands. The building trades, first to profit from boom expansion, were the earliest sufferers in a deteriorating labor market. Toward the end of 1887 the bricklayers voluntarily reduced their pay from $6 to $5 for a nine-hour day and, as the depression deepened early in 1888, complained with carpenters, sheet-metal workers, and hod carriers of worsening trade conditions. Moreover, the competition of nonunion workers prevented unions in the construction industry from exercising any control over the labor market. When the plumbers, for example, struck in February, 1888, against a contractor who employed a nonunion man, they merely paved the way for the gradual decline and eventual disintegration of their union. During this period the necessity to fight for retention of previous gains largely precluded demands for new ones. A strike of molders in June against a proposed wage reduction at the Baker Iron Works was successful, but it heralded a change from offensive to defensive tactics.[2]

And yet the building trades did not permit economic distress to smother them completely. Early in 1888 the bricklayers' local affiliated with the Bricklayers' and Masons' International Union, and was rewarded by an immediate membership spurt from one hundred to well over one hundred and fifty. The lathers organized a craft assembly of the Knights of Labor, with forty of the sixty lathers in the city becoming charter members. Paper hangers and decorators organized an affiliate of the National Brotherhood of Painters and Decorators, and several new carpenters' unions were formed in the city and at San Pedro. In March, Los Angeles Carpenters' Union No. 56 sponsored a convention of carpenters' locals in all of southern California for the purpose of forming a league which would restrict encroachments on the trade by unskilled workers, introduce apprenticeship regulations, establish the nine-hour day throughout the area, and equalize dues and benefits. Although unsuccessful, the effort was proof that the carpenters recognized the merits of federation. Another sign of the tendency toward consolidation was the formation of a Los Angeles Building Trades Council in the spring of 1888. Its attempt, however, to negotiate a general wage agreement with contractors failed. The sandstone cutters, now separate from the stonecutters' union, struck in June to increase their daily wages from $4.50 to $5, and won the raise from some employers. But the building trades could not long withstand the hard times. By August, 1888, the carpenters' unions, representing the strongest craft in the construction industry, had all become inactive. The loss by Local No. 56 of every penny of the $900 invested in 1886 in the Carpenters' Hall Association hastened the union's decline, and soon only a score of members remained to hold the charter.[3]

Unions outside the building trades were considerably less active. The cigar makers dealt only with the continuing threat of Chinese competition; in November, 1887, they induced the Trades Council to adopt resolutions urging the purchase of cigars made by white labor. Los Angeles Local No. 45 of the Journeymen Bakers' National Union, somewhat more flourishing than other local labor organizations, was able to send $50 to striking San Francisco bakers early in 1888. During the winter of 1887–1888, Tailors' Assembly No. 4350 attempted to control the market by boycotting local firms which sent their work to San Francisco or employed nonunion labor. Because the district assembly of the Knights of Labor failed to assist in this campaign, whereas the Trades Council proffered aid, the tailors decided on a change of affiliation. Early in 1888 their assembly reverted to its original craft union form independent of the Knights of Labor, and by the middle of 1889 the new organization had joined the Journeymen Tailors' National Union as Local No. 81.[4]

The printers' union, as the oldest and strongest in Los Angeles, best illustrated the declining fortunes of the local labor movement. Its membership dwindled rapidly during 1888, and the union decided not to send a delegate to the June ITU convention. Yet the printers, unwilling to let depression and unemployment halt their customary activities altogether, spent the first half of 1888 in an intensive campaign to enforce the closed shop in job offices. Chief offenders were the Los Angeles Printing Company, the Commercial Printing House, and a weekly newspaper, the *Porcupine*. The Trades Council, the cooks' and waiters' union, and three Knights of Labor assemblies endorsed the series of small strikes and boycotts inaugurated by the Typographical Union, and the pressmen helped with committee work and sympathetic strikes. The Trades Council also made an ineffective attempt to mediate the disputes. The printers themselves asked the ITU for a deputy organizer for southern California, as they had done in a previous crisis, but the request was once again ignored. Finally, despite financial aid from the San Francisco Typographical Union, the Los Angeles printers were unable to continue the struggle and in June admitted defeat.[5]

A summary view of the Los Angeles labor movement in 1888 was provided by the biennial report of State Labor Commissioner John J. Tobin. Although describing the city as "pretty thoroughly organized," Tobin qualified the unions as "insecure" because of the transient population. His register of twenty-one organizations with membership data, compiled from reports sent by the unions themselves, reflected a lingering boom-time strength rather than a realistic up-to-the-minute picture:[6]

Bricklayers	120	Sandstone cutters	20
Carpenters, amalgamated	60	Stonecutters	54
Carpenters and joiners	907	Typographical union	212
Iron molders	50	Pressmen	40
Lathers	75	Bakers	50
Painters	75	Cigar makers	10
Plasterers	150	Cooks and waiters	48
Plasterers' helpers	100	Tailors	87
Plumbers	100	Mixed assembly	153
Plumbers' helpers	40	Wage workers' union	150
Sheet-metal workers	200		
		Total	2,701

Three new organizations formed in the spring of 1888 were not listed by the Commissioner. Retail butchers had organized a protective association in February; thirty-nine musicians had formed an affiliate of the National League of Musicians in April and had soon thereafter established a wage scale; and forty-two clerks in clothing and shoe stores had organized the Los Angeles Salesmen's Association in May.[7] This flurry, however, added no real strength to unionism.

The Knights of Labor, whose membership was not drawn entirely from the working classes, had greater resilience than craft unions in times of economic stress. The Knights' emphasis on political education seemed a valid substitute for a weakening economic program: "The energetic trade-unionist was apt, at ... periods of depression, to turn his attention to special movements which he imagined might remedy the evils responsible for the general decline in business."[8] Los Angeles craft unionists followed this pattern. At a general meeting of local Knights on May 26, 1888, Jonathan Bailey of Carpenters' Union No. 56 presided, and President W. A. Swain of the same union remarked: "At last humanity has come to look upon the Knights of Labor as the labor organization of the world. . . . The workingmen know . . . that the ballot-box is the only weapon whereby they can secure any real redress or permanent triumph."[9] These were strange words to come from the president of a craft union after the heyday of the Knights had passed. They indicated, as little else could, the changing character of leadership in the Los Angeles labor movement. Swain's advocacy of political action was driven home by the guest speaker, William H. Bailey, a national official of the Knights. This was the first time that the city was host to a national figure of any labor group. It is significant that the carpenters' union, unable earlier to bring an officer of the AFL to Los Angeles, gave a resounding welcome to a dignitary of the rival organization.

In addition to pointing up the contrast between Knights of Labor and craft unions, Bailey's visit sharpened labor's interest in national political events and added impetus to a local political movement already under way. In the 1886 campaigns in many sections of the country, Knights of Labor, craft unionists, single taxers, and socialists had combined with some success to support candidates friendly to labor. This was the genesis of the National Union Labor Party. Born in February, 1887, it absorbed the remnants of the Greenback Labor Party and gained the allegiance of farmers' groups, antimonopolists, and Knights of Labor. Reaching out for a still more inclusive membership, the Union Labor Party proposed in 1888 to amalgamate with Henry

George's United Labor Party, but disagreement over the single-tax issue prevented consummation. Both parties nominated presidential candidates, but the United Labor Party withdrew before the election, and the Union Labor Party, now composed largely of farmers, attracted a negligible labor vote.[10]

In Los Angeles, it was the Knights of Labor who launched a political movement in the spring of 1888, when the district assembly invited all labor organizations to participate in a "General Labor Conference." After two secret meetings of the conference, the Los Angeles Union Labor Party was formally organized on June 10, 1888, by such representative workingmen as Arthur Vinette and Jonathan Bailey of Carpenters' Union No. 56, P. S. Dorney of the Knights of Labor, E. S. Livermore of the Typographical Union, and Jesse Butler, a prominent figure in the old Workingmen's Party. The Union Labor Party endorsed the national platform and declared for protective tariffs to benefit labor as well as capital; prohibition of Chinese, convict, and contract labor; legislative representation of labor by workingmen; a lien law to protect the common laborer; equality for women workers; prohibition of child labor and of female labor in certain occupations; employer liability for injuries on the job; repeal of conspiracy and gag laws; nationalization of railroad and telegraph lines; abolition of taxes on legitimate industries; and the establishment in Los Angeles of a nonpolitical police force, with a popularly elected chief.[11]

In order to strengthen their own organization as well as the Union Labor Party, the Knights of Labor supported a strike begun on June 16, 1888, by some four hundred unorganized laborers employed by the Los Angeles Cable Railway Company, which had announced a reduction in wages from $2 to $1.50 a day. The two-day walkout prevented the wage cut and added one hundred and twenty strikers to the Knights of Labor, bringing their total city membership to nearly one thousand. But even this novel concern over the problems of unorganized workers failed to arouse the enthusiasm of the rank and file for the Union Labor Party. Denied permission to hold the picturesque open-air rallies which so easily attracted crowds, the party scarcely survived the summer. The Board of Freeholders ignored the party's one proposal that portions of its platform be incorporated in a revised city charter, and even dropped the anti-Chinese clause inserted in the old charter at the request of the Workingmen's Party.[12]

Although the broad designs of the Union Labor Party were abandoned, its suggestions for charter amendment were taken up by the Labor Conference when it revived in October, 1888. Delegates from twelve labor organizations protested against the charter drawn up by the Board of Freeholders, because it empowered the City Council to levy a license tax on workingmen, designated the contract system for public works, contained no anti-Chinese provision, ignored the state eight-hour law, and included no sanitary or building regulations. Labor's objections were unavailing, and the charter carried.[13]

With visions of a more distinguished future, the Labor Conference then proposed to the unions that it replace the Trades Council as the central labor body of Los Angeles. The Typographical Union favored the change, since the Trades Council was "in a languishing condition and barely able to hold together."[14] But the few surviving unions could rescue neither the Trades Council nor the Labor Conference, and both disappeared in the fall of 1888. Labor in Los Angeles was thus at a low ebb, with all hopes of maintaining a central council dead, many unions disintegrating, and others curtailing their functions. Even the Knights of Labor, who had created the Labor Conference and attempted to assume the responsibilities of the dying Trades Council, became dormant. Early in 1889, Painters' Assembly No. 3167 disbanded after exactly five years of life. The local decline of the Knights reflected a state and national trend, for the noble order was everywhere giving way to growing employer opposition and to the American Federation of Labor.[15]

The difficulties of organized labor reflected the business slump of 1888–1890. The city was caught in the doldrums as the post-boom depression deepened. In January, 1889, Charles Dwight Willard, newspaperman and for many years secretary of the Chamber of Commerce, wrote:

> God help the man who gets out of employment now in this town. The revival which they have all been hoping and waiting for this winter has not come off, and absolute ruin stares a good many people in the face.... The unemployed of the lower classes are very numerous.[16]

In the fall of the year Willard noticed little improvement: "I cannot conscientiously recommend that anyone in need of immediate employment should come here at present. Business of all kinds is horribly dull and every line of labor seems over filled."[17]

Unorganized workers were in a worse plight than those banded together in unions. In January, 1889, when a number of cable railway conductors threatened to strike over the discharge of several fellow workers, the company simply replaced the malcontents. In May, the Cable Railway Company again announced a reduction in laborers' wages, from $2 to $1.75 a day. No labor organization came forward to help, and the protests of Jonathan Bailey and Arthur Vinette were to no avail.[18] When employees of a lumber company struck in August, 1889, against a wage reduction, they lost their jobs to a new gang willing to work for less.[19] In December the gripmen and conductors employed by the Pacific Railway Company, successor to the Cable Railway Company, asked to have their pay increased from 17½ to 22½ cents an hour. They were forced to compromise, and on January 1, 1890, their wages went up to 20 cents, with 22½ cents only for employees of a year's standing. The men then organized a Gripmen's Association and a Conductors' Union and threatened to strike, but in February, 1890, yielded to the company's demand that they disband the unions. A few months later the employees formed a company union called the Gripmen's Benevolent Association.[20]

The inability of labor organizations to alleviate unemployment led to the establishment of a free labor exchange in February, 1889, under the charitable sponsorship of one Barney Fehnemann, who had no apparent connection with the labor movement. Fehnemann charged neither employer nor employee for the services of his bureau, locally reputed the first of its kind in California. The unusual experiment attracted the notice of the State Board of Trade, and early in March caused the San Francisco *Examiner* to establish in the northern city a labor exchange patterned on the Los Angeles venture. Fehnemann soon realized the impossibility of placing all applicants, and therefore sought to arouse the public to the plight of the jobless through a series of mass meetings. Speakers at such gatherings urged the revival of anti-Chinese agitation as a means of removing coolie competition. In April, Mayor Thomas Hazard proposed that the City Council set up and maintain a municipal free employment agency with Fehnemann as manager, but the measure was defeated by the narrow margin of one vote. After this setback Fehnemann's labor bureau passed into oblivion, despite the support and approval of such trade-unions as were still in existence.[21]

As Fehnemann's movement was disintegrating, another outsider stepped forward as a self-appointed spokesman for workingmen. Carl Browne was something of a demagogue, and in this sense carried on the tradition of Alfred Moore and Captain J. F. Janes. Browne, however, had been in closer touch with working-class movements through his association with Denis Kearney in the San Francisco Workingmen's Party, his editorship of the party's official organ, *The Open Letter,* and his activities in the United Labor Party of 1886. He then moved to Los Angeles and in 1888 established a weekly paper, the *Cactus.*[22]

Browne's endeavors differed from Fehnemann's, but were similarly directed toward employment problems. During the spring of 1889, Los Angeles workingmen had petitioned the City Council to employ day rather than contract labor on sewer construction, a continuing part of the municipal improvement program begun during the boom. The Council was helpless, however, for the terms of the bond issue required the contract system. In June, Browne, noting the absence of leadership among the workingmen and their failure to impress the city authorities, took up the day labor cause and tried to bring pressure to bear through a number of meetings open to the public. Unlike Fehnemann, Browne did not evoke the sympathy of organized labor. A group of unions reproved him for his "senseless agitation" and suggested that workingmen might well turn to the ballot box for redress instead of following a charlatan like Browne. Carpenters' Union No. 56, accepting the inevitability of the contract system, petitioned the City Council to prohibit sewer contractors from establishing boarding camps, where employees were overcharged for inferior accommodations. In a more direct attack, workingmen organized an Anti-Sewer Bond Club, which in August helped to defeat a supplementary bond issue specifying the contract system.[23]

Of all the crafts in Los Angeles, the printers best withstood the collapse of the boom and during the latter part of 1888 even seemed to prosper. Failure to unionize the job offices earlier in the year was offset by a victory in August, when the union refused to grant a wage reduction requested by the four daily newspapers. In September, membership began an upward swing. Despite the heavy drain of unemployment relief, union finances were sound, and a new campaign to organize job offices looked promising. General improvement in the printing trade in the fall of 1888 further brightened the union's prospects, and early in 1889 the Commercial Printing House agreed to employ union men.[24]

Then the picture changed swiftly. Recurrent business stagnation after the holiday season dashed the printers' hopes for continuing prosperity, and renewed unemployment plagued them during much of 1889. Two weekly journals, the *Rural Californian* and the *Social World*, broke off relations with the union following a wage disagreement. Some of the union's most prominent members began to desert the distressed city, and those who remained turned to regional and national bodies for help. In January, 1889, the union sent Frank Colver to a district convention of typographical unions held in San Francisco, and a few months later instructed its delegates to the ITU convention to urge permanent status for such regional organizations. The Los Angeles delegate also requested the ITU to provide relief for local unions looked upon as sanitariums by ailing printers, to establish a national strike fund, and to give financial and moral support to the American Federation of Labor. In the fall of 1889 the local Typographical Union had to modify a proposed new wage scale before proprietors would sign annual contracts. At the end of the year, with the *Porcupine* and the Los Angeles Printing Company still resisting unionization, the printers quit the campaign to organize nonunion job offices. However, they kept a nonunion firm from getting the contracts for the county *Great Register* and the *Annual Illustrated Herald,* amended the union constitution to permit the black-listing of any office not paying wages promptly, and shortened the working day to six hours to spread available work.[25]

Immediately after its convention in December, 1888, the American Federation of Labor inaugurated a nationwide drive for the eight-hour day, selecting the carpenters as the first craft to benefit, and May 1, 1890, as the effective date. The period could hardly have been a more trying one for local labor, yet the carpenters responded with gusto and on February 22, 1889, under the leadership of Arthur Vinette, organized the Los Angeles Eight-Hour League. Prevailing unemployment engendered wide sympathy, and for a brief time the League flourished. Some employers did not wait for the appointed time but immediately instituted the eight-hour day with no reduction in wages. The League's major accomplishment—and this was before the San Francisco Eight-Hour League had been organized—was the City Council's passage in April of a public works ordinance establishing the eight-hour day and prohibiting the employment of Chinese. After helping to organize a Pacific Coast Eight-Hour League in June, however, the Los Angeles League had spent its energy. Both the League and its parent organization, Carpenters' Union No. 56, had become so feeble by August, 1889, when it was apparent that the eight-hour ordinance was not being fully enforced, that the Knights of Labor had to shoulder the responsibility for communicating with the City Council.[26]

While the carpenters were busy with their Eight-Hour League during 1889, several other groups of workers evinced a spark of life. In April, Bakers' Union No. 45, composed of German bakers, boycotted a coffeehouse for patronizing J. A. Brown's bakery. This first local use of the secondary boycott—except during anti-Chinese campaigns—was not a successful experiment, for the only outcome was a libel charge against a union member who distributed boycott circulars. Although the suit never came to court, it discouraged the bakers from continuance of their program. Toward the end of 1889, San Francisco Bakers' Union No. 51, one of the many new northern unions, established a Los Angeles branch for American bakers, Local No. 88, but it did not flourish until a later period.[27] In May, 1889, Los Angeles barbers formed a union in the hope of abolishing Sunday work, and a month later the retail clerks reorganized with a similar objective. They were more persuasive than the barbers, for all but two of the city's mercantile firms agreed to close on Sundays.[28]

Heartened by these signs of renewed activity in the spring of 1889, the Typographical Union tried to pull the labor movement together through establishment of a new central body. Obtaining procedural advice from the Federated Trades Council of the Pacific Coast, and letters of encouragement from two San Francisco labor leaders, Alfred Fuhrman[29] and Michael M. McGlynn,[30] the printers called a meeting for May 26. Delegates from ten labor organizations—the Eight-Hour League and the unions of printers (whose secretary presided over the meeting), tailors, cigar makers, carpenters, painters, bricklayers, stone-cutters, cooks and waiters, and bakers—appointed a planning committee, which included the indefatigable Arthur Vinette, and decided to affiliate with the Pacific Coast Council. The Los Angeles Federation of Labor was formally organized on June 23 by the five unions of printers, cigar makers, tailors, carpenters, and bakers, and on July 1 elected as president P. H. Hurley, of the Typographical Union. The reduced representation was an omen of impending failure. Although proposing monthly meetings, the new organization was inactive after August and maintained no semblance of connection with the Pacific Coast body. In December, 1889, the Los Angeles Federation of Labor held its last meeting and adjourned sine die.[31]

The end of the federation's nominal existence marked the lowest point thus far in the fortunes of Los Angeles labor. The illusory strength of the boom period had vanished. Unions were in such straits that they could not sustain a central body, and even the Typographical Union, the hard core of the labor movement, expended no more energy in this direction. Many unionists were leaving town to find work; the giant Carpenters' Union No. 56 was reduced to a shadow; the Eight-Hour League had lapsed; the Knights of Labor discontinued even their social gatherings; and labor's newspaper champion, the *Tribune,* was encountering the financial reverses which were to cause its demise a year later. In October, 1889, State Labor Commissioner John J. Tobin had appointed W. L. Wolfe of the Knights of Labor as his deputy in Los Angeles, but even outside encouragement failed to arouse the dormant labor movement.[32]

The inertia of both craft unions and Knights prompted an outside group to take up the cause of labor in Los Angeles. In 1888 Edward Bellamy had published *Looking Backward,* a romanticized description of a utopian society of 2000 A.D. from which monopolies, competition, and profit-seeking had been eliminated. Bellamy's doctrine of state socialism, with national ownership of all resources and means of production, and of complete political, social, and economic equality was immensely appealing, and his many followers formed the Nationalist Party. The movement was particularly attractive to the people of California; the southern part of the state welcomed Nationalism with a fervor which pointed clearly to the area's well-known readiness to embrace new or unusual doctrines in various fields.[33]

Nationalism gave concrete expression to so many aspirations for reform that it attracted a great variety of adherents. The organizers were chiefly socialists, but the strongest advocates came from professional and literary groups. Although the rank and file of labor were not drawn in in large numbers, many leaders, particularly those already predisposed to basic social change, found great promise in the movement. Arthur Vinette urged collaboration between Nationalists and trade-unionists; Jonathan Bailey and a few Knights of Labor became converts. At the time when Nationalism was sweeping the country, the arrival of W. C. Owen in Los Angeles stimulated development of the local movement. Owen was a San Francisco labor leader who had been active in the International Workingmen's Association during the 1880's and later, after moving to Los Angeles, had assisted Vinette in organizing the Eight-Hour League. In sharp contrast to Owen and other labor leaders was H. Gaylord Wilshire, a wealthy Los Angeles citizen who embraced Nationalism and later devoted himself to the spread of socialist doctrines.[34]

Another early adherent of Nationalism was Lemuel D. Biddle, who arrived in Los Angeles just as the Bellamy doctrine was beginning to take hold. Biddle, born in Philadelphia in 1846, was forced to start work at the age of ten after only three years of formal schooling. Holding varied jobs as tobacco stripper, machinist, and shoemaker, Biddle saw in his poverty-stricken youth grounds for a radical philosophy. Before coming to Los Angeles, he had belonged to the Knights of St. Crispin, a union of shoemakers; the Sovereigns of Industry, an organization growing out of the Patrons of Husbandry in the 1870's and mainly devoted to the establishment of consumers' coöperatives; the Knights of Labor; and the Socialist Labor Party. The last of these had nominated Biddle for governor of Ohio in 1879.[35]

Biddle's arrival in Los Angeles in the later 1880's marked the beginning of a career which greatly enriched both the trade-union and socialist movements. Like Vinette, Biddle demonstrated an unusual aptitude for organization and administration. Beginning in 1890, he held a number of major offices in the Los Angeles labor movement and, as AFL district organizer, established some eighty unions in the area. While busying himself with trade-union affairs, Biddle also found outlets for his reform proclivities. He allied himself with the Nationalists soon after arriving in Los Angeles and retained membership in the Knights of Labor and the Socialist Labor Party. He was frequently nominated for political office on socialist tickets. When several coöperative ventures thrived briefly during the 1890's, Biddle was prominent in their organization and management. An active socialist and labor organizer throughout his life, Biddle often preached his message on Los Angeles street corners, singing appropriate songs when necessary to gather an audience.[36]

Personally Biddle was one of the most loved and respected men in the Los Angeles labor movement. His sense of humor plus an enduring optimism helped to inspire discouraged colleagues during hard times. In a lifetime of devotion to the welfare of humanity, he never failed to respond to a call for aid by an individual or organization. When Biddle died on Labor Day in 1916, at the age of seventy, a long-time friend and associate said of him:

> Lem Biddle was born in Labor, lived in Labor, and died on Labor Day. It is as though he were a man of destiny in the Labor movement.... It was fitting that he should die on Labor Day. When the question of marching on Labor Day arose and it was decided not to march, Lem Biddle said, "I'll march if I have to march alone." He marched, and he marched alone.[37]

As a special token of regard, Biddle's friends inscribed on his tombstone the words "The Grand Old Man of the Los Angeles Labor Movement."[38]

With the signs of craft union failure all about them, Biddle and other labor leaders found it easy to turn to the idealism of the Nationalists. A preliminary meeting at Owen's home in May, 1889, led to the organization a month later of Los Angeles Nationalist Club No. 1, with fifty members. When the start had been made, progress was rapid. By the early summer of 1890, Los Angeles claimed thirty-three of the fifty clubs which had been established in California; one of them was a Workingmen's Nationalist Club. Owen presided over the state convention which, meeting in San Francisco in April, 1890, organized the California Nationalist Party. He also edited the *Weekly Nationalist,* published in Los Angeles as the state official organ from May to November of the same year. A National Co-operative League, a Los Angeles County Co-operative Association, and a Women's Co-operative and Educational Union, all part of the Nationalist program, sprang up in the southern city early in 1890. The women's group planned to establish an industrial exchange and coöperative restaurant, and started to investigate working conditions of women laundry employees.[39]

The Nationalists' most significant contribution in the field of labor was their aid to unorganized workers. On March 2, 1890, Nationalist Club No. 1 publicly charged contractors on city work with violation of the eight-hour ordinance. A week later the City Council, indirectly heeding the reproof, tried to alleviate unemployment by stipulating strict enforcement of the eight-hour law, hiring additional laborers for street repairs at $2 a day, employing only citizens for sewer construction, and prohibiting the use of Chinese labor and Chinese-made materials. Meanwhile, unemployed workingmen had organized informally and on March 10 sent George Feller, later chairman of the Eighth Ward Nationalist Club, to ask the Council for a public works program. But a series of mass meetings and widespread popular sympathy were unavailing, and the unemployed received little practical help from the public authorities. A second attempt to have the city establish a free employment agency failed.[40]

The Nationalists gave more forthright aid by helping the unemployed form a Laborers' Co-operative Construction Company to bid for sewer work, following the suggestion of W. C. Owen. In April, 1890, the new concern, organized as a stock company with fifty members, won a contract for a section of the Flower Street sewer. On May 5 the Co-operative Construction Company began work, strictly observing the eight-hour rule. Although submitting other bids, the company received no more contracts. By July unemployment among unskilled workers had become less critical, and the need for relief measures decreased.[41]

Meanwhile, the Nationalists took up the issue of the shorter working day for carpenters, since the craft unions had been unable to complete the drive begun over a year before. With the assistance of the revived Eight-Hour League and of Carpenters' Union No. 56, the Nationalists won the eight-hour day for the Los Angeles building trades in May, 1890, and sponsored a demonstration on May 10 to celebrate the event. The organizations taking part were the Laborers' Co-operative Construction Company, the Los Angeles County Co-operative Association, and the unions of carpenters, printers, bakers, cigar makers, tailors, bricklayers, stonecutters, molders, painters, plasterers, and barbers. Vic-

tory had been easy, because prevailing unemployment and the absence
of a concomitant demand for higher wages reduced employer opposition
to a minimum. Throughout the nation the results of the eight-hour
drive were disappointing to the AFL, for relatively few cities were able
to make the innovation. In Los Angeles the achievement was short-
lived; during the next few years labor was forced to renew the fight
for the shorter working day.[42]

The Nationalists' career in Los Angeles was now practically concluded. By the latter part of 1890, the movement was declining rapidly
in a pattern now becoming familiar; sustained enthusiasm seemed
impossible for labor and reform groups in Los Angeles. Factionalism
contributed to the demise, as Lemuel Biddle organized a local section
of the Socialist Labor Party which attracted the more radical Nationalists, and the moderate wing eventually found its way into the People's
Party of the early 'nineties.[43] But for a time the Nationalists had controlled the destiny of both organized and unorganized workers in Los
Angeles. As the Knights of Labor intervened in 1888 when unions were
beginning to disintegrate, and as Barney Fehnemann and Carl Browne
tried to help in 1889, so the Nationalists took over in 1890 when disruption was further advanced.

From the vantage point of 1896, Frank Colver looked back upon the
labor movement of the 1880's, which he himself had helped to mold.
To him it was, at best, an ineffectual preparation for the more serious
business of the 1890's, when for the first time Los Angeles labor as a
whole recognized the need for unity. Then it had not only to organize
for protection against a common foe, but, according to Colver, to overcome a prejudice rooted in the general belief that the local trade-union
movement was shot through with radicalism.[44] This suspicion could
have arisen only in the closing years of the 'eighties, for not until then
did rumors of an inarticulate radicalism begin to circulate. Hints of a
local anarchistic society late in 1887, plus the suggestion that single
taxers, socialists, and even more dangerous radicals were behind-the-
scenes agitators in the 1888 political campaign, and finally the more
patent activity of the Nationalists in 1889 and 1890 had partially alienated the public.[45] It is true that the fragments of craft unionism found
their only cohesion through the Nationalist movement in 1890, but
need, rather than widespread conviction, dictated acceptance of the
proffered help. Labor's failure to give wholehearted support to the
allegedly radical Union Labor Party of 1888 was evidence of its essential
conservatism.

Nevertheless, a basically conservative labor movement had become tinged with more or less radical ideas and had thereby increased its vulnerability. Persons like Biddle and Owen were partly responsible for the leftward swing; other stalwarts predisposed to socialism, like Vinette and Bailey, were susceptible to such influence. It cannot be completely coincidental that the known conservative, Isaac Kinley, disappeared from the labor scene at about this time. His withdrawal from the Knights when they reversed the antistrike policy indicated his unwillingness to associate with a movement tending away from his convictions.

More limiting to the development of unionism than the issue of radicalism were certain regional characteristics, the most obvious of which was the tremendous growth in population, particularly in the city of Los Angeles. Between 1870 and 1890 there was almost a tenfold increase, and in the crucial decade of the 1880's, when the organization of workers really began, the population of Los Angeles jumped by 351 per cent. By contrast, the population of San Francisco increased by only 28 per cent during the same ten years.[46] Here was a serious problem of assimilation which might well have confounded labor leaders of far greater sophistication than those who formed the early unions in Los Angeles.

Not only the volume but the character of immigration into southern California presented a grave obstacle to the development of a labor movement. The growing community, with its much advertised mildness of climate and easy living conditions, attracted wealthy folk who wished to retire, sick persons in search of health, farmers seeking a less back-breaking life, small businessmen desirous of establishing themselves, mechanics and unskilled laborers looking for high wages and year-round jobs, and, finally, vagrants escaping rigorous weather in other sections. In all these groups there must have been a sizable proportion predisposed against or neutral to unionism. Even former trade-union members frequently accepted substandard wages in order to remain in a climate suitable for ailing relatives. Furthermore, workers who did join local unions often became a financial liability because of their own illness, or a source of instability because of transience.[47] The super-ficiality of craft union strength during the boom testified to the relevance of these factors.

There were other hindrances impeding the development of a sound union structure in Los Angeles. The economy, predominantly agricultural, did not furnish the most favorable milieu for labor organization. The depression of the mid-'eighties had prevented a substantial growth of unionism at the outset, just as the post-boom depression at the end of the decade wiped out the gains of the intervening years. These cyclical factors, together with the inexperience of local craftsmen, had given Los Angeles labor an inadequate preparation for the future. The few experienced or potential labor leaders coming to Los Angeles during the 1880's commanded attention by their rarity. In contrast, opponents of unionism very early became integrated and articulate through the instrumentality of the *Times* and its editor, Harrison Gray Otis, a man of undeniable force and conviction. Even though the newspaper before 1890 was not consistently antiunion nor completely victorious in its opposition, it had begun to show signs of its owner's fanatical hatred of unions which colored the early portions of Los Angeles labor history.

The circumstances in which union leaders had to operate helped to create the characteristic disunity of Los Angeles labor. Two efforts to develop a central body had failed, and as a result the movement of the 1880's was essentially a collection of individual organizations working opportunistically for their own benefit. Comparable to the absence of unity at home was the lack of strong ties with national labor. A number of local unions, it is true, were affiliated nationally, and during the eight-hour drive there was an attempt to conform to a country-wide movement. Although isolation did not preclude the reflection of national trends in Los Angeles, it did lead to an apparently mutual indifference. Less comprehensible was the failure to establish links with the flourishing San Francisco labor movement. During the 'eighties there was little indication that unionists in the north were even aware of labor struggles to the south.

The subsidence of the boom simply made the disunity of Los Angeles labor more pronounced, the bewildered search for security more apparent. In retrospect, the pattern is clear. Struggling for expression, workers used craft unions, loosely-organized federations, the Knights of Labor, political movements, and, in the end, Nationalism, without finding a wholly satisfactory or sustained outlet. An imperative crisis came in August, 1890, when the printers' strike shocked Los Angeles unions into the realization that the moment for decision was at hand. If the labor movement were to survive, unity and canalization of effort were indispensable.

IX. THE "BIG STRIKE"

THE MOST SIGNIFICANT single event in the history of industrial relations in Los Angeles, before 1910, was the strike of the Typographical Union against the four daily newspapers in August, 1890. It quickly resolved itself into the almost endless controversy between the *Times* and the printers which was to dominate the local labor scene for years to come. Ultimately, as antiunion sentiment crystallized around Harrison Gray Otis, the paper's proprietor, the fight with one employer became a titanic struggle of all organized labor in Los Angeles against a solid phalanx of opposing forces. Led by Otis and the Merchants' and Manufacturers' Association under a banner of "Industrial Freedom," the opposition was instrumental in establishing the open shop in Los Angeles during the first decade of the twentieth century. The strike accordingly led to a situation which, in the end, challenged the resources and ingenuity of the highest authorities in the American labor movement. As an official *Times* publication later said, "Thus was begun the memorable struggle which was to shape the industrial future of a metropolis and to set an example for a whole country."[1]

Although the strike began the consolidation of public antipathy to unionism in Los Angeles, it also taught labor a valuable lesson. As a practical demonstration of the need for unity, it was the catalyst in the emergence of a labor movement guided and centralized by the first effective labor council in the city's history. The Typographical Union, moreover, despite its own incessant struggle, found time to aid in the shaping and evolution of a central body which understood its obligations to local workingmen, to the community, and to organized labor in regional or national federations.

The printers believed that Otis deliberately contrived the 1890 break which resulted in this great trial of unionism. Although restive under relations with the Typographical Union since 1883, when he had been forced to compromise the printers' first strike against the *Times*, Otis had nevertheless kept his antagonism in leash during the intervening years. Pecuniary troubles had dictated the expedience of not translating his philosophy into overt policy during the 1880's; the temporary quiescence of the most articulate adversary of unions in Los Angeles gave labor a brief respite. The reprieve ended in 1890, when the *Times'* prestige and financial security provided Otis with an opportunity to regain full control of his own business, humble the union trying to "dictate" to management, and begin the process of making Los Angeles "the freest city, industrially, within the American Union."[2]

From management's point of view, the moment was well chosen for the opening of a contest with the Typographical Union. A disorganized, barely alive labor movement, with its fortunes at the lowest ebb since 1884, promised a minimum of resistance. All Otis required for thorough control of the situation was the unanimity of newspaper proprietors. Here again circumstances favored him, for the need for retrenchment weaned the others from customary willingness to go along with the union. Even the *Tribune,* in the worst straits financially, was ready to desert its usual friendly policy for collective employer attack. The printers' conjecture that "the proprietors . . . were inveigled into a combination with H. G. Otis"[3] was affirmed by Pauline Jacobson, a San Francisco newspaper correspondent who visited Los Angeles some twenty years later and interviewed both the *Times'* proprietor and a former employee. "Otis' opportunity came in 1890," she wrote. "General H. H. Boyce, proprietor of the *Tribune* and Otis' only feared competitor, was forced to sell out to an Eastern syndicate. These new men Otis enlisted in a 'Newspaper Publishers' Union' to fight the printers' union."[4] The printers themselves, aware in 1890 that "the proprietors had entered into a strong combine to enforce their demands,"[5] saw Otis as the manipulator of a scheme to break the union.

The strike started over wages. In July, 1890, proprietors of the four daily newspapers opened negotiations for pay reductions on the plea that printers alone among Los Angeles craftsmen were still receiving boom rates and that the local scale was twice as high as in comparable eastern cities. To remove these inequalities and to insure continued solvency, Otis and Albert McFarland of the *Times,* James J. Ayers of the *Herald,* H. Z. Osborne of the *Express,* and J. H. Morrow and C. F. Holder of the *Tribune* personally appeared before the union on August 3 with demands for a cut from 50 to 40 cents per thousand ems on morning papers and from 45 to 35 cents per thousand ems on evening papers, and for permission to use stereotyped plates. They would, they said, entertain a counterproposal. Before replying, the printers weighed a disturbing report that the rival Printers' Protective Fraternity[6] in San Diego was ready to ship any needed nonunion replacements to Los Angeles. Nevertheless, by a vote of sixty-seven to ten, the union rejected both demands, refused to offer a compromise, and threatened a walkout unless the proprietors signed an agreement within twenty-four hours of noon on August 4 to continue the old scale for one year.[7]

With the positions of both sides clearly stated, the scene was set for a rudimentary form of collective bargaining, and the printers suggested a conference with the proprietors to "adjudicate" the disagreements.

The employers, however, refused a meeting on the ground that the union had presented them with an ultimatum. The printers had set noon on August 5 as the deadline for the signing of contracts, and four o'clock for a union meeting to take final action. Several hours before the printers convened, Otis closed the *Times* office to union members and the *Herald* put a number of nonunion printers to work.[8] In the graphic words of Pauline Jacobson,

Four o'clock ... was set by the union for their final action. ... Otis had agreed to come before them and state his reasons for a reduction which to the printers seemed unjust in the extreme.

I have it from the little galley boy then, grown to man's estate now. He was at work in the composing-room. Before that time arrived, at half-past one, Otis appeared in the composing-room. Rage was swelling his neck and purpling his face and the veins in his forehead as he raised one fist, bringing it down with full force, shouting:

"Every ———— ———— man get out of here! And get out ———— ———— quick!"

It was a lockout. Otis had prepared for ten days. ... From that time on his hatred of unions grew to such proportions that the mere mention was sufficient to throw him into a passion verging on insanity.[9]

The strike was on. When the union met at the scheduled time, it had no choice but to order a walkout from all four offices, commencing at the close of the meeting in the late afternoon of August 5. The printers' only qualification was a provision that several journals, already in press, might be completed. More than one hundred compositors quit work, but the four newspapers, though badly crippled, were able by exchanging type and hiring all available help to continue publication without a break. For several days the issues were smaller than usual, sometimes delayed, and below standard in content and format.[10]

The printers' strike committee soon discovered that neither the *Tribune* nor the *Express* had the heart for a fight. Morrow of the *Tribune* refused to sign a contract but gave his word to pay the current scale for one year, and Osborne of the *Express,* pleading the interproprietary agreement as his excuse for not signing, emphatically declared: "I will pay Union wages to Union men and do not want any but Union men in my employ." On the other hand, Otis received the union committee's official notification of the strike with a laconic, "Well, gentlemen, all right." His words suggested to the printers the smug self-satisfaction of a man whose long-desired goal of breaking the union was at last within reach, now that the conflict was out in the open. Ayers of the *Herald* stuck with Otis, echoing the *Times'* claim that the union's arbitrary demand for a year's contract was outrageous and the twenty-four–hour ultimatum an insufferable insult.[11]

Although the united proprietary front was not the solid bulwark envisioned by Otis, it held together long enough to give the *Times* an initial advantage over the union. The *Tribune,* from the start the most conciliatory toward the employees, still kept its word to sign no agreement on a yearly basis. Meanwhile, the printers had advised the International Typographical Union of their plan of campaign, receiving in reply a telegram cautioning them that refusal to sign a contract was not legitimate cause for a strike against offices paying the union scale. Recognizing the proprietary firmness at home and the authoritative voice of national headquarters, the local union hastened to make concessions. On August 6 it offered to accept a verbal agreement if the terms of the contract were not altered. The next day, hoping to "break up the combine," it allowed some wage reductions, though insisting on the current rates for straight composition and the employment of only union members.[12]

The union's first withdrawal was sufficient to split the ranks of the employers, though not before one more attempt was made to force down the composition scale. At the instigation of all the proprietors, the *Tribune*'s representative pleaded with the printers for a compromise reduction of 5 cents instead of the 10 cents originally demanded. When the union held firm, the proprietary combine collapsed. On August 8 both the *Tribune* and the *Express* reinstated the strikers and verbally agreed to employ only union men at union rates for the ensuing year. For its part, the union granted both papers the right to reopen wage negotiations before expiration of the agreement.[13]

The printers' concession, far from mollifying Otis, poured fresh fuel onto the controversy, for the *Times* now seized upon the union's willingness to forgo a written contract as an admission of original guilt. It also loosed invective against its former allies, the *Tribune* and the *Express,* charging that their defection from the voluntary employers' association was unethical.[14] Otis was more damning in a letter to his friend H. H. Markham, soon to be elected governor of California:

> Had it not been for the unspeakable cowardice and the inexcusable treachery of our confreres of the Tribune and the Express, we might today be complete masters of the situation, with the strikers minus a foothold in the town. As it is, the Times and the Herald stand together and will fight it out. Principle and manhood require it.[15]

"Fighting it out" meant, for Otis, an unending barrage of accusations against the Typographical Union; the *Herald,* for the time being a willing junior partner, parroted the *Times*' criticisms. The union was chiefly reprehensible, according to Otis, in exercising tyrannical control over its membership. A small group of radicals, he claimed, had overruled the objections of "conservative and fair" printers opposed to the strike. There were individual doubts, it is true, and members who disagreed with the majority were asked by the union officers "to keep silence on the public streets." Yet, in a series of critical votes, the printers showed singular unanimity in endorsing the union's acts, especially those of which the *Times* was most critical. Another favorite complaint was that the union had given only one day's notice before striking. Technically this was correct, but the employer-employee negotiations for several weeks before the union's August 3 meeting, as well as Otis' alleged premeditation in planning to drive the "typos" out of town, nullified the argument. The *Times* repeatedly vilified the union for demanding a written contract, even after the issue was no longer pertinent, yet its proprietor refused to resume negotiations when the printers waived this obstruction. The newspaper was still more inconsistent on the wage question. While asserting that the only possible basis for settlement was reduction of the composition scale, the *Times* advertised for printers at full union rates.[16]

In the face of these contradictions, could the union have come to terms with Otis? Even if the printers had been more conciliatory, for how long could they have maintained peaceable relations with the *Times?* Absolute surrender might have placated Otis, but it would at the same time have destroyed the union as the bargaining representative of journeymen printers. In retrospect the clash seems inevitable, either in 1890 or at a later time, for so long as the union fought for its principles, Otis would have opposed it. The *Times'* excoriation of organized labor in the long years ahead could hardly have arisen from one excessive demand of the union, however objectionable. Nor could such a demand alone have made the *Times* "the most important factor in the creation of an almost universal hatred of unionism among the residents of Southern California."[17] The real conflict went far deeper than disagreement over a wage scale or the form of a contract. It lay rather in Otis' hatred of unionism, so thoroughly ingrained by 1890 that no compromise could have mitigated it.

Having defeated Otis' scheme in part by regaining two of the four offices, the union enthusiastically plunged into the fight against the *Times* and the *Herald.* To obtain funds for maintaining a strike office, aiding needy members, and buying railroad tickets for those leaving town, it levied a 10 per cent assessment on the wages of all printers working more than three days a week. The men employed in the *Times* and *Herald* job offices, though not directly involved in the wage controversy, were called out, and the pressmen were urged to join the strike. The latter, however, refused to walk out unless so instructed by the ITU. Twice before in its history the local union had appealed to the ITU for a deputy organizer for the Los Angeles area, and now at last its request was answered. Immediately after the strike began, national headquarters had ordered its district organizer, J. R. Winders of San Francisco, to help the Los Angeles union. Shortly after his arrival, he appointed as his deputy Virgil E. Fortson, a local printer. The Los Angeles union also began a canvass of the city to arouse sympathy for the locked-out printers and to discourage subscriptions to the two offending papers.[18]

The printers were not without allies. The *Tribune* and the *Express* were, of course, consistently friendly, and two papers not involved in the dispute, the *Weekly Nationalist* and a society journal, Los Angeles *Life,* championed the union. These publications, though granting that printers' wages were still at a boom level, averred that take-home pay had decreased because of changes in the kind of copy; large display advertisements, for example, had been replaced by solid matter much more time-consuming for the compositor. Of even greater value was the offer by a small printing firm of facilities enabling the union to publish its own statement. Thus emerged the *Union Printer,* written, printed, and circulated for several months by strikers. The first issue appeared on August 8 or 9. Since the press of California outside of Los Angeles was almost unanimously with the employers, the strike organ was a useful outlet for the union point of view.[19]

Whatever hopes the union cherished for quick settlement with the *Times* and the *Herald* were nullified by the availability of strikers' replacements from the Printers' Protective Fraternity.[20] This rival of the ITU, partly composed of disaffected or expelled union printers and advocating arbitration instead of strikes, strongly appealed to Otis. Union spokesmen, then and later, contended that Fraternity men were on their way to Los Angeles before the strike had been called; the evidence indicates that Otis had negotiated with the Fraternity before stirring up the local dispute and then simply telegraphed to Kansas City when he needed the men. By August 14 the *Times* was using Fraternity printers, and early in September both the *Times* and the *Herald,* together employing about two-thirds of the printers in Los Angeles, were completely staffed by importations from Kansas City. Thus the *Herald* could afford to ignore union overtures on August 28 for a compromise agreement. About the same time the San Francisco Typographical Union appealed to H. H. Markham to settle the Los Angeles strike, using the argument that Otis, under duress, had granted

Fraternity printers a year's contract at union wages, the very terms he refused his former employees. This duplicity removed any lingering doubt as to Otis' real intentions and made impossible any mediation such as the San Francisco printers suggested.[21]

Despite the obvious accord between Otis and the Fraternity, the Typographical Union was able, in September, to relax its internal discipline. Appeals to sister unions had brought in over $130 in August, more than double the amount collected by the local assessment, and over $600 in September. With the eligibility of some members for ITU strike benefits and the departure of others from the city, union solvency permitted reduction of the assessment from 10 to 5 per cent and abrogation of a rule allowing compositors to work only four days a week. Most of the outside financial help came from San Francisco Typographical Union No. 21. In contrast, nothing but strike benefits came from the ITU, whose indifference to the plight of its Los Angeles branch implied a serious failure to comprehend the deeper meaning of the strike.[22]

Even without substantial aid from the International, the Los Angeles printers won a decisive victory in October, when they broke up the partnership between the *Times* and the *Herald*. At the union's instance, "prominent politicians of both parties" approached the two papers with a plea for settlement of the strike. Otis was as adamant as ever, but this time Ayers was receptive to overtures. Within a week the major points had been settled: the union met Ayers' proviso by sanctioning the use of union-made plates, and the *Herald* agreed to employ only union members in its composing room. The *Herald* was unionized shortly after October 12.[23]

After this agreement was reached and financial problems were eased by outside contributions, the union settled down to the long-run boycott of the *Times* which gave the Los Angeles labor movement its distinctive characteristic. It was an event of some importance in general trade-union history. A boycott is a weapon especially useful against newspapers, whose revenue depends on both advertising and circulation. But printers' unions had resorted to it only sparingly before 1880, because the labor movement lacked the strength to make boycotting effective. The willingness of the Knights of Labor to coöperate with craft unions permitted a greater dependence on this expedient during the 1880's, but the decline of the Knights and their growing estrangement from the craft-union movement again caused less frequent use. The *Times* boycott was an outstanding example of a new reliance on this method, made possible by a reviving labor movement. Realizing that a boycott has little force without a strong body of organized labor, the Los Angeles printers were particularly solicitous about the formation of a new central labor council.[24]

The *Times* resented the boycott more than the strike, which was, it said, a boomerang hurting only the union members who sacrificed good jobs. Although its initial response to the first tentative efforts at boycotting was one of jeering derision, the newspaper soon arrived at a more serious appraisal. First denying the boycott's efficacy by means of circulation figures, which showed only a slight temporary drop in September, the *Times* a little later castigated this union weapon as "a cowardly, mean, un-American, assassin-like method of establishing a petty despotism." Although constantly minimizing the damage to his newspaper, Otis' frequent and virulent attacks on the boycott suggested a higher degree of uneasiness than he openly confessed. The arrival in November, 1890, of Michael M. McGlynn, delegated by the San Francisco Federated Trades to help organize Los Angeles and to give special aid to the printers, was an added irritant, and the outside "professional agitator" became a new butt of the *Times'* abuse.[25]

Before McGlynn's arrival, the Los Angeles printers had been able merely to get the boycott started. Efforts to influence subscribers against the *Times* were sporadic, and the publication of a black list of advertising patrons had been only moderately successful, for most contracts still had some months to run. McGlynn infused the campaign with new life. He reorganized and enlarged the printers' boycott committee and systematized its work. He aroused the labor movement to the urgency of the fight by calling several large rallies in the fall of 1890. To gain greater prestige for the printers' strike organ, he transformed the *Union Printer* into the *Workman* and induced the Council of Labor to sponsor its publication. McGlynn even arranged a meeting with Otis looking toward compromise, but was met, he said, with abuse and profanity and a belligerent determination to drive the "typos" out of town.[26]

McGlynn's twofold task of rebuilding the labor movement in Los Angeles and of helping the printers posed a delicate question of relative emphasis. The Council of Labor tended toward a policy of firmly establishing itself before materially aiding the Typographical Union. Although undoubtedly sound in the long run, this sacrifice of an immediate cause to a distant objective placed a heavy burden on the printers. Their predicament can best be illustrated by the proceedings at a fairly typical union meeting in January, 1891. The election of four new active members and one apprentice member was more than offset by twenty-five withdrawals. Disbursements for the month were $111 in excess of receipts, which totaled $756. Of this amount, $78 came from dues, $34 from the *Workman,* $240 from assessments, and $404 from the San Francisco union. Several months later the Los Angeles printers regretfully decided to forgo representation at the ITU convention—which might have brought additional relief—and voted down a proposal to reduce the assessment from 5 to 2½ per cent. The annual reports in May, 1891, showed a drop in active membership from 142 to 82 during the year past, and expenditures of $8,042 as against $8,032 in receipts, $3,091 of which had come from other unions. Of that amount, the San Francisco Typographical Union alone had contributed over $2,600, only $500 less than it had given to the striking molders of San Francisco during the same period.[27]

The printers' plight worsened as the year progressed. The union's failure to impress municipal authorities with the righteousness of its cause was forcibly demonstrated when the 1891 city printing contract went to the *Times,* the only nonunion daily paper in Los Angeles. Constant bickering between the *Times* and the *Workman,* expressed in claims and counterclaims, statements and rebuttals, intensified the bitterness of the struggle. The union organ charged the *Times* with reducing wage rates and increasing hours so that its compositors averaged less than two-thirds of the daily earnings of union printers. The *Times* tried to create dissension within the union by asserting that many members, now repenting the strike, were dissatisfied with McGlynn's conduct of the boycott and resentful of the heavy assessments. Some justification appeared when forty-one union printers—half the total—requested a special meeting on May 17, 1891, to reorganize and strengthen the campaign against the *Times.* But no satisfactory alternative to McGlynn's program was put forward. When, on June 7, the printers learned that hard times forced discontinuance of help from the San Francisco Typographical Union, they instituted rigid economies in order to keep their union solvent.[28]

All these months the Council of Labor had avoided serious involvement in the printers' dispute. Beyond distributing boycott circulars and inserting paid notices in the *Herald*—both actions designed to decrease patronage of the *Times*—it had made no contribution to the campaign. But in 1891 the Council was rapidly emerging as the directing agency of a growing labor movement and, moreover, achieving a new community status as the representative of organized labor. With the steady enlargement of its sphere coinciding with the patent deterioration of the printers' situation, the Council felt that at last the time had come for straightforward intervention. During the summer of 1891, it drafted a proposition suggesting the arbitration of differences between the Typographical Union and the *Times*. To make the sharpest possible impression on Otis, the Council induced some 120 businessmen to sign this plea for a peaceful settlement; the printers, grateful for the move to end their difficult controversy, voted $40 to defray the expenses of circulating the petition. But when the document was presented to Otis early in September, he declared that submission to an arbitration board would mean the loss of his company's integrity. Had not the striking printers left the *Times* without provocation? And, if the arbitrators decided against Otis, how could he conscientiously discharge his present employees, members of the Printers' Protective Fraternity, who had stood by him in his hour of need? On the basis of such arguments, Otis reiterated that he would never take back the strikers except on terms of his own making, following *individual* applications for reinstatement. In reply, the Council of Labor could only point to the speciousness of Otis' reasoning, in view of his discharge of union printers before the strike vote had been taken and his communication with the Kansas City Fraternity before the local trouble had arisen.[29]

Failure of the Council's proposal, coupled with continuing financial hardship and abandonment of a current enterprise to establish a morning newspaper as a rival to the *Times,* led to new appeals for aid and further economies in the conduct of the boycott. An unwise decision by the printers at this crucial juncture speedily destroyed the recently established rapport with the Council of Labor. The Typographical Union refused to take part in a meeting sponsored by the central body in October, 1891, on the grounds that it was a political convention. The Council, offended by the printers' uncoöperativeness, brusquely reminded them to be more regular in their attendance at stated meetings of the central body, "as their absence is frequently remarked" and as "they need the attention of other workingmen more than any other trade at present." It is little wonder that the printers' appeal for assistance brought in only one local donation, a gift of $5 from the painters' union. So critical had the financial predicament become that McGlynn resigned in November, 1891, and rapidly diminishing funds gave the union no alternative to the acceptance of his resignation.[30]

With local harmony at a low ebb, the printers looked elsewhere for help. They urged McGlynn to put his personal knowledge of their difficulties to good advantage by renewing a plea for aid in San Francisco, and in January, 1892, combined with ten other unions in the state to form the California Federation of Typographical Unions. The new organization, after hearing that $11,500 had thus far been spent in fighting the *Times,* pledged full moral and financial support to its Los Angeles member. Almost at once the promised contributions began to come in, and in March the International Typographical Union, at last awakened to the seriousness of the fight, sent $500 to its Los Angeles branch. With money flowing in, the union was able to discontinue the local assessment which had so overburdened its working members, and therefore to make wage concessions to the friendly papers. In April it reduced composition rates from 50 to 45 cents per thousand ems. Both the *Herald* and the *Express* (the *Tribune* had perished late in 1890) signed a year's contract at the new scale.[31]

Meanwhile the Council of Labor, having recovered from its temporary pique, fell in with a new plan by which the printers hoped to coerce Otis into yielding. If Los Angeles labor could enlist the aid of individuals and groups to whom Otis would listen and could combine such advocacy with an intensified boycott by all local labor organizations in an unbroken front, then the *Times* might be frightened into a settlement with the union. Plans were carefully laid and systematically carried out. The Council first circularized all labor organizations in California, asking them to oppose, openly and vociferously, every political candidate backed by the *Times.* It next approached local and regional Republican committees (the *Times* has always been a Republican paper) with a plea to influence Otis toward greater tolerance of unionism. Finally, the Council aroused its member unions to renewal of the boycott. The results were most encouraging. Practically all the local unions promised full moral support to the printers, some of them going so far as to fine members who patronized *Times* advertisers. Even outside groups, such as the Knights of Labor, the railroad brotherhoods, and the Socialist Labor Party, were persuaded to join in the all-out prosecution of the boycott.[32]

With a solid bulwark behind it, the Typographical Union was ready to act. Realizing that threatened loss of patronage was their most potent weapon against the *Times,* the printers shrewdly chose as their instrument the People's Store, which after temporary desertion had returned as one of the paper's largest advertisers. A secondary boycott supported by the entire body of organized labor against a store whose clientele was largely of the working class was indeed a telling stroke, and the proprietor, D. A. Hamburger, was easily prevailed upon to act as intermediary. Through his persuasiveness Otis agreed for the first time in the history of the strike to have a representative of the Times-Mirror Company sit down at a conference table with delegates from the union. But the negotiations, conducted by Colonel J. A. Woodard for the company, yielded only one small point for the union: regular employment of four union members in the newspaper and job offices. The union, waiving its closed-shop ruling for the *Times,* accepted the offer on April 6, 1892, and on the 7th the Council of Labor officially called off the strike and boycott.[33]

The compromise was a union victory only in the sense that it broke Otis' resolve, reiterated as recently as the fall of 1891, to deal with union members only as individuals. It had not been easy to wring from the *Times* even a limited concession, as the union's conference committee testified:

> After noticing from close observation that the boycott was not having the effect desired and that the *Times* was fast gaining the ground it had lost we concluded to accept the terms offered by the *Times* after having tried for three days and nights to gain more points.[34]

Nor did the ostensibly simple arrangements of the agreement give any indication of the humiliating terms which Otis forced upon the union. He reserved for the Times-Mirror Company full control of conditions of employment, wages, and hours. He refused to discharge his Fraternity printers; he emphasized that his new employees would henceforth be regarded as individuals, not as union members; he demanded that "preliminary to all else, the boycott against patrons of the *Times* must cease and the publication of the boycotter's organ [the *Workman*] must be stopped forthwith"; and, finally, he precluded any resumption of negotiations with the union by stating that "no bargain, contract, writing, verbal promise, conference, parley, publication, overture, agreement with individual, committee or body can be exacted from the *Times* in advance."[35] On April 7, the last issue of the *Workman* heralded the end of the controversy and spoke of concessions by both sides, but it carefully refrained from publishing the precise terms. Three days later the Typographical Union extended the open shop to all printing offices in the city where the union scale was paid and in June returned the $500 to the ITU.[36]

It is not difficult to see why the union finally conceded the major issue of the closed shop. Initially reluctant to do so, it yielded in the end to Woodard's argument that the introduction of only four union men— a device to save Otis' dignity—would lead to gradual unionization of the *Times.* To the printers, an entering wedge was at the moment more valuable than rigid insistence on principle. They could see ahead a bright vision of Los Angeles as a closed-shop town for their craft. To this end a union committee strove for further concessions from the *Times,* but the only gain was the employment of an additional union member. The *Times* was gradually recovering from a temporary setback in circulation and advertising, and was even boasting that it had prospered from the boycott. Any delay, therefore, in accepting the harsh terms offered by Otis would soon mean the end of negotiations. Furthermore, the agreement was effected only after an intensive drive to insure the local support which would force Hamburger to coöperate; abandonment of a project costing so much in time and energy would have alienated other unions as well as Hamburger, whose mediation might at some later time prove useful. Since Hamburger claimed sole credit for the new turn in local industrial relations, his friendship was worth retaining.[37]

Otis' reasons for settling the twenty-month dispute are less clear. The urgent plea of a valued advertiser had, of course, some cogency; Otis may also have been swayed by the recent reduction of union wages, the assistance of the ITU and Pacific Coast unions, the upsurge of local support for the printers, and the awarding of the 1892 city printing contract to the *Express*. Pauline Jacobson put forward a more intriguing hypothesis, based on later interviews with union members and substantiated in part by a union account written only four years after the event. These authorities contended that it was Otis, losing heavily because of the boycott, who intimated his readiness to talk things over with the union. In reality, however, the apparently conciliatory move cloaked a scheme to dupe the union. After concluding the agreement, Otis signed long-term contracts with his advertisers and, thus protected, repudiated the settlement made by his representative. Thus were the printers tricked and defeated by a policy which, if accurately portrayed, was adequate reason for Otis' pretense of making peace with the union.[38]

At the time of the settlement, the printers could not have been aware of such duplicity, if in fact it did exist, particularly since the *Times* temporarily abated its attacks on organized labor. Proceeding on the assumption that Woodard had accurately represented Otis' willingness for ultimate unionization, the printers singled out as their new target the Printers' Protective Fraternity, whose banishment would open up more jobs for union members. Looking for sanction from a higher authority, the Los Angeles union prepared a memorial for the 1892 ITU convention, asked all sister unions to uphold it, and arranged for its presentation by the Sacramento delegate. The document set forth these pertinent complaints: the Fraternity had prolonged the strike against the *Times,* which had cost $16,000; it had reduced wages and increased hours; it was a "scourge" on the Pacific Coast, with branches in San Diego, Santa Barbara, and Los Angeles, and with a recent boast that it would soon invade San Francisco.[39] These representations were so alarming that the ITU was compelled to action; it instituted measures contributing to the ultimate eclipse of the Fraternity, though the Los Angeles union was not to be free of its competition for some years.

After settlement with the *Times,* the local union had leisure to deal with lesser problems, such as the payment of substandard wages in several printing offices. The chief offender was the *Daily Journal,* a paper which printed court news for the city and county. The *Journal* first crossed the union in February, 1892, by failing to pay wages promptly. Union employees walked out, and the office was declared unfair. This decision was not affected when the union opened all shops, since the *Journal* was paying less than the union scale. In the fall, at the printers' request, the Council of Labor circularized all agencies doing campaign printing, urging them not to patronize either the *Journal* office or the Los Angeles Printing Company. The union also published a list of fair printing offices and adopted a label to simplify the distinction between union and nonunion shops. Several of the smaller offices came to terms with the union, but it was not until the *Journal* changed hands in the fall of 1893 that the union saw an opportunity to make headway.[40] Negotiations with the new management of the *Journal,* however, had to be shelved because they coincided with the second and final break between the Typographical Union and the *Times.*

Although a minor difficulty with the *Times* had been easily settled in April, 1893, a feeling of tension developed within the next six months. Otis had reverted to his inimical attacks on unions and had become so outspoken that in September the Council of Labor consulted the Typographical Union about reimposing the boycott. Upon the simultaneous discovery that Otis' union employees were not being paid the wages promised them—for the union had never really accepted Otis' stipulation that wage-setting was an individual affair—the printers voted to strike unless the *Times* would immediately complete unionization. As the only reply to the ultimatum was silence, the union called out its men on September 27 and declared a boycott.[41]

The Council of Labor endorsed the decision and called upon all labor organizations in Los Angeles County to rally behind the printers. The overwhelming response was so gratifying that the Council, wishing to channel the anti-*Times* fervor into one immense and effective stream, organized a joint committee for the *Times* boycott. Established on October 27, 1893, the committee included delegates from sixty-six organizations said to represent 60,000 persons: twenty-two unions of the

Council of Labor, four assemblies of the Knights of Labor, five brother-hoods of railroad men, and thirty-five branches of the County Farmers' Alliance, one of the constituent groups forming the People's Party. Cyren E. Fisk, chairman of this imposing aggregation, said that the unity of feeling among these disparate groups was due to the *Times'* antagonism not only to organized labor but to all who were engaged in productive work.[42]

Fisk was a young labor leader who had plunged into the affairs of the local Typographical Union immediately upon his arrival in Los Angeles in 1892. Born in Michigan in 1869, he joined the printers' union at the age of seventeen and subsequently became president of the Grand Rapids Central Labor Council. In Los Angeles, after selling his interest in the *Farmer and Labor Review,* joint organ of the Farmers' Alliance and the Council of Labor, he engaged in two unsuccessful publishing ventures, *The Masses* and *The Advocate,* neither of which survived for more than a few months. His active participation in the *Times* fight, starting with chairmanship of the joint committee in the fall of 1893, continued for the rest of his stay in Los Angeles. In 1896 he was elected president of the Council of Labor. But, according to a contemporary of some prominence in the labor movement, Fisk's views were too uncompromising and his methods too tactless to win the con-tinued support of the rank and file, and he left Los Angeles in 1902.[43]

The Typographical Union, for its part in the reopened anti-*Times* campaign, again assessed its membership, repeated its appeals for help from Pacific Coast unions, and prepared a second memorial to the ITU urging intensification of the fight against the Printers' Protective Fra-ternity. Response, in terms of financial contributions, was disappoint-ingly meager, and the local union once again found its resources strained. Since it had undertaken to finance the operations of the joint committee, it was soon acutely conscious that the unwieldy body was costing more than it was worth in progress. The printers, though deeply appreciative of labor's consolidation in their behalf, were compelled to forgo the possible advantages of a united effort. In December they voted to assume full responsibility for the boycott, and the joint committee disbanded.[44]

The printers' abnegation of outside help was sheer bravado. Their difficulties were almost insuperable. The Council of Labor had failed them. The joint committee had not justified its expense. Though stronger than ever before, the labor movement was still unequal to the challenge of a renewed boycott against the *Times,* now recognized by all as a common enemy.[45] The printers themselves had little spirit for the reopening of a hard fight. They did not even attempt negotiation with Otis. Only with difficulty did the union maintain its assessment, despite the pressing need for funds. By January, 1894, its treasury was down to $12.[46]

External causes for despair were equally numbing. The union, continuing the canvass for cancellation of *Times* subscriptions and advertising, found that larger advertisers especially were reluctant to withdraw their patronage. The printers knew why they could now make no visible dent on such patrons. In the fall of 1893, shortly after the *Times*-union warfare broke out afresh, a group of Los Angeles businessmen had formed the Merchants' Association (a forerunner of the Merchants' and Manufacturers' Association) with the dual purpose of gaining repeal of a license tax on mercantile establishments and instituting a series of annual carnivals to attract tourists. These publicized reasons, though genuine, cloaked an additional intent of helping the *Times* break the boycott of the Typographical Union. By January, 1894, the printers realized that Otis and his "allies" were in control of the Association and that it would bear losses sustained by any member through a boycott. It was not surprising that members of the new organization could ridicule union efforts to weaken the *Times*' hold on the business community. Some of them, indeed, welcomed the boycott as a test of strength.[47]

In profound discouragement, the Typographical Union, surveying the forces arrayed against it and the collapse of its own allies, went to the extreme of considering the surrender of its charter in January, 1894. In almost two decades of a troubled career, the oldest and most influential union in Los Angeles had never been closer to extinction. But, instead of yielding, the printers chose the harder course and tabled the motion to disband. Within two days they reconvened at the request of thirty-one members, voted a 3 per cent assessment with no time limitation, and prepared to renew the anti-*Times* campaign. In February the union reactivated the boycott, sounded all local organizations once more for aid, and imposed a $5 fine on any member patronizing blacklisted firms. After some hesitation, the boycott was extended to political candidates advertising in the *Times;* the Council of Labor endorsed this measure despite a growing aversion to mixing in politics. The Council also delegated a committee to dissuade advertisers from continuing their patronage of the newspaper. But what really made the printers' fight a communal undertaking was the patient, day-to-day effort of members of many Los Angeles unions to impress the public with the unfairness of the *Times*. The printers took new cheer from the expectation that another morning Republican newspaper, the *Record,* would soon appear as an ally of organized labor, but it was not until 1895 that publication began.[48]

In March, 1894, a separatist movement within the union threatened to cancel some of the gains already being made. The book and job printers organized a Job Printers' Charter League and began publication of the *Charter Advocate* to forward their campaign for a separate union under the ITU. Although avoiding the split and increasing its membership from 101 in April, 1893, to 128 a year later, the Typographical Union had not yet passed the critical stage. During the year ending in April, 1894, expenses exceeded receipts by some $300, and the final balance in the strike fund was less than $40. Many members were in arrears for both dues and assessments. Friendly relations with the *Herald* and the *Express* were balanced by continuing failure to unionize certain job offices.[49]

Yet the report of the boycott committee on May 27, 1894, was confident. The campaign against the *Times* and its advertisers, now in full tide, was going well, as increasing numbers transferred their patronage to other papers. Otis was forced to reduce his advertising rates and to break "that reign of 'silent contempt' which he declared would forever exist against the Union printers."[50] During the Pullman strike Otis' invective was leveled at the American Railway Union, but the end of this great labor upheaval in July, 1894, freed the *Times'* columns for renewed attacks on its boycotters. Meanwhile, with finances improved through generous donations from local unions, the printers were able to vote $50 to the American Railway Union, help a recently organized Newsboys' Union, and pay a $5 fee incident to the Council of Labor's affiliation with the AFL in the summer of 1894. Another service of the Typographical Union to the local trade-union movement was publication of a labor paper. Like the *Workman* of several years before, the *California Federationist,* brought out by the printers in September, 1894, carried the endorsement of the Council. By the end of the year the ITU had approved the publishing venture and tentatively promised it financial aid.[51]

As so frequently happens with a turn for the better, the printers enjoyed further good fortune. In July they had petitioned the California Federation of Typographical Unions for funds and requested the San Francisco Federated Trades to boycott *Times* advertisers in the north. The entreaty to the state organization brought a gift of $100 from the San Francisco union, smaller contributions from other typographical unions, and $10 from the Federation. The San Francisco mission was equally successful, for a *Times* boycott was declared there as well as in Alameda County.[52]

The generous financial response had, however, a darker side. The ITU's district organizer, J. L. Robinette, of Sacramento, proposed to investigate the Los Angeles union because he feared that its assessment, upheld now by only a bare majority, would be discontinued altogether when outside contributions were sufficiently substantial. The local printers, by a vote of sixty-four to five, reproached the International representative with a strong affirmation that their struggle was of vital consequence to all Pacific Coast labor and that they would persevere until the *Times* was unionized. A copy sent to the ITU brought a gift of $100 in September, a warming tribute from national headquarters. Robinette's offer to represent Los Angeles Local No. 174 at the ITU convention in October "for a consideration" was curtly refused, and the San Francisco delegate generously acted for Los Angeles. The convention elected E. A. Parker of San Francisco to succeed Robinette as district organizer, and the new official appointed Cyren E. Fisk as his deputy in southern California.[53]

The local printers had to cope with still another problem arising within the labor movement. They had adopted the union label in 1893 and, along with the Council of Labor and other craftsmen, were anxious to promote the symbol of union manufacture. In their label campaign, the printers met with difficulty from union pressmen, who sometimes carelessly permitted material set up in union offices to be run off on nonunion presses, therefore disqualifying it for bearing the label. This aggravated already strained relations between printers and pressmen. Beginning in 1890, pressmen's unions in the ITU had been withdrawing in order to join the new International Printing Pressmen's Union; repeated efforts by the ITU to regain control had failed. It was not until 1895 that the ITU recognized the jurisdiction of the IPPU. Before settlement of the national issue, the Los Angeles Pressmen's Union, now an affiliate of the IPPU, decided to join the Council of Labor. Its delegates were seated in November, 1894, over the protest of the Typographical Union.[54]

Despite aid from the ITU, coast unions, and local labor organizations, and encouraging reports from the strike committee, a change in the *Herald*'s management caused an abrupt alteration of the printers' policy in the winter of 1894–1895. When the 3 per cent assessment was levied in January, 1894, Ayers and Lynch, coproprietors, had threatened that abandonment of the fight against the *Times* would lead to a demand for lower wages on the *Herald*. When they relinquished control of the paper in the fall of 1894, a faction within the union seized the opportunity to proselytize for termination of the assessment and boycott. Defeated by one vote in December, 1894, the motion again came up in January, 1895, together with a proposal to open unfair offices to union members, provided the union scale was paid. Notwithstanding a new appropriation of $250 from the ITU and a gift of $50 from District Organizer Parker, the union voted by a small margin to drop the assessment and the boycott, though keeping the *Times* and other unfair offices closed to union printers.[55] Thus the Typographical Union closed an arduous period of its history with a decision tantamount to defeat. The long drain on its resources, the rise of the Merchants' Association, and a realistic interpretation of the *Times'* strength forced the union to acknowledge itself unequal to its adversary.

Yet at the same time the printers' controversy, as the touchstone of unionism's capacity to survive, had helped create a new unity in Los Angeles labor. Moreover, through the printers' persistence, recognition came from the outside. The California Federation of Typographical Unions and the International Union were becoming more and more aware that the printers' struggle in Los Angeles went beyond a single-craft difficulty or a localized dispute. McGlynn's mission was the first open acknowledgment by the San Francisco central labor council that a stronger labor movement in southern California was desirable, by Pacific Coast as well as local criteria. Even the aloof railroad unions were temporarily beguiled into a joint enterprise against the *Times*. Eventually, when all efforts had failed to resolve the impasse, the American Federation of Labor itself was to be drawn into the conflict. The far-reaching significance of the fight against the *Times* cannot be overestimated, as a growing industrial center gradually developed an open-shop philosophy whose impact was to be felt on all organized labor.

X. STRENGTH THROUGH UNITY

AFTER THE APATHY of the late 'eighties, the Los Angeles labor movement came dramatically to life in the 1890's. Into the first four years of the new decade were crowded the printers' strike; development of a new and stronger central labor body; extension of unionism to crafts and workers never before organized; the rise of the People's Party; the march on Washington with Coxey's Army; and participation in the Pullman strike. The new Council of Labor, arising directly from the controversy between the Typographical Union and the *Times* in the fall of 1890, was the guiding spirit which welded disorganized and impoverished fragments of unionism into a federated craft movement. The unity symbolized by this achievement was not accomplished without hard work, discouragements, and mistakes, but throughout the period Los Angeles labor demonstrated a vitality and determination it had never before possessed.

The printers' strike was a gravely needed boost for the local labor movement. In 1890 most of the unions, reduced to impotence by two years of depression and unemployment, existed in name only. As the *Workman,* official organ of the Los Angeles movement, later remarked, "All branches of labor in Los Angeles were in a state of chaos unequalled anywhere else throughout the Pacific Coast."[1] The printers, who alone had kept their union active, expanded their tradition of courage by launching the greatest strike yet known in Los Angeles in this unpropitious setting. Their intrepidity soon brought rewards, for within a month a movement was on foot to reorganize the old Trades Council and, moreover, to enhance its authority through affiliation with a regional organization.

Since the coast federation formed in 1886 had never attained real leadership, central labor councils in California were attaching themselves to the San Francisco central body during this period. On September 7, 1890, the Los Angeles Typographical Union advanced $5 "for procuring a charter from the San Francisco Federated Trades in order to hasten the work of forming a sub-federation in Los Angeles."[2] By the end of the month the new organization, first called the Council of Federated Trades, and later the Council of Labor, was meeting regularly, and on October 3 it formally joined the San Francisco Federated Trades Council. Permanent organization was completed on October 8 by nine member unions. Six of these were the unions of printers, tailors, cigar makers, carpenters, iron molders, and bakers. P. H. Hurley, head of the Typographical Union, was the Council's first president.[3]

The Council began its career with a fresh outlook which sharply distinguished it from its fumbling predecessor of the 1880's. From the first it continuously and insistently emphasized the organization of new unions and the affiliation of independent ones. It carried this policy to the extreme limit of sacrificing the printers' immediate crisis to the necessity of fashioning and consolidating a labor movement strong enough to bring succor to any union in distress. To implement its design, the Council held several organizational mass meetings in the fall of 1890, which brought an immediate response: the painters reorganized as Local No. 206 of the Brotherhood of Painters and Decorators and affiliated with the Council; a new barbers' union joined both its national organization and the local central body; the musicians of Los Angeles and Pasadena jointly organized for the first time as an affiliate of the Council of Labor.[4]

By 1891 the central body had established an organizing committee which zealously spread the gospel of unionism among groups of workers. Public meetings under the Council's auspices were intended to convert other citizens to an unprejudiced view of the labor movement. At one such meeting in August, Michael M. McGlynn, who had been sent from San Francisco to help the printers in their fight against the *Times,* exhorted workers to "revolutionize things in this city."[5] Although progress was less rapid than the San Francisco leader hoped, the Los Angeles Council achieved noteworthy results. Plumbers and American bakers reorganized, and stage mechanics and machinists formed their first unions. All of these, except the stage mechanics, sent delegates to the Council, which by the end of the year included twelve unions. Remaining outside were the railroad brotherhoods, the bricklayers' union, and the revived Pressmen's Union No. 29, whose close association with the printers lessened the need for separate representation. Moreover, all of the Council's members, except the rather weak machinists' union, were affiliated with their respective national bodies. Only one setback marred the Council's organizational record during 1891; the brewery workers ignored a plea to form a union.[6]

A desire to become associated with the now flourishing Los Angeles labor movement infected the San Pedro sailors, whose parent organization, the Coast Seamen's Union, had greatly increased its power and wealth by consolidating with the Steamshipmen's Union in July, 1891, to form the Sailors' Union of the Pacific. In November, 1891, the San Pedro branch asked San Francisco headquarters for permission to join the Los Angeles Council of Labor, but was refused because of the expense of traveling so far—about twenty-five miles—to attend meetings.[7]

Unionism continued to advance during 1892, reaching even into the white-collar class. Organization of a new Clerks' Association followed a successful effort by clothing and shoe store employees to have their establishments close at six instead of eight o'clock every evening except Saturday. (The 6:30 closing won in 1883 had been lost in the intervening years.) Since most merchants were coöperative, the union grew rapidly and enjoyed unusually pleasant labor-management relations. The old stonecutters' union was revived, and the machinists and theatrical stage employees reorganized their unions of the preceding year. The Pasadena painters, organized with the help of Los Angeles painters, received a charter in February as Local No. 92 of the national union. Los Angeles paper hangers reorganized, and boilermakers organized for the first time, during 1892. Early in the year a Hackmen's and Expressmen's Association was formed to work for repeal of a new city ordinance imposing restrictions on hack stands. Having won modification of the regulations in April, the union disappeared. In June the Los Angeles horseshoers organized a branch of the national union in order to increase their rates, and the Pasadena blacksmiths formed a union with the same intent. In September the Los Angeles Stenographers' Association was organized for social and educational purposes.[8]

In contrast to the preceding year, very little gain accrued to the Council of Labor through all this activity. Many of the new organizations were ephemeral, and just two of them made common cause with the older unions. The Clerks' Association and the stonecutters' union affiliated with the central body, but only the former proved a valuable addition. The Council seemed to lose its grip on the labor movement during 1892, partly because of less satisfactory business conditions. The integration which had been a marked feature since 1890 was lacking. A nucleus of seven or eight of the older unions kept the Council going, and the rest failed either to attend meetings or to shoulder any responsibility for joint enterprises. The bricklayers and pressmen remained inactive, and the barbers' and cooks' and waiters' unions disappeared entirely. Attempts to reorganize them toward the end of the year were fruitless, and the Council failed to act on requests from Chicago and Sacramento to organize the woodworkers and harness makers.[9]

The Council, nonetheless, was still seeking new members, and during 1892 it made a determined effort to bring San Pedro labor within its orbit. At the beginning of the year, the only labor organizations in the harbor city were the unions of sailors and longshoremen and a Knights of Labor assembly. In April a San Pedro agency of the Marine Cooks' and Stewards' Association of the Pacific Coast was established with the aid of delegates from San Francisco and from the local Sailors' Union, but it was not yet ready for affiliation with Los Angeles labor. Toward the end of 1892, the Los Angeles Council asked sailors' headquarters in San Francisco to authorize the San Pedro union to join the local central body. This time permission was granted, and the sailors sent their first delegates in December. At about the same time the Long-shoremen's and Lumbermen's Union accepted an invitation to affiliate with the Los Angeles Council.[10]

In 1893 began a period of steady progress which continued for several years. Early in the year the clerks affiliated with the Retail Clerks' National Protective Association as Local No. 83, and the machinists with the International Association of Machinists as Lodge No. 219. A little later the members of the old cooks' and waiters' union formed two new organizations, Cooks' and Pastry Cooks' Union No. 5 and Local No. 48, Waiters' International Union. In July the Council organized the electrical workers for the first time and reorganized the bricklayers. Meanwhile, the Pasadena unions of carpenters and painters had joined the Los Angeles Council. With these additions, the central body claimed twenty-three affiliates with a total membership of three thousand.[11] Only twenty of them are identifiable: the Los Angeles unions of printers, bakers, carpenters, painters, tailors, clerks, molders, cigar makers, stonecutters, plumbers, machinists, paper hangers, cooks, waiters, bricklayers, and electrical workers; the Pasadena unions of painters and carpenters; and the San Pedro unions of longshoremen and sailors. With four of its members outside the city, the central body now changed its name to the Los Angeles County Council of Labor.[12]

The Council was not always successful, however, in its plans to organize new unions, nor did all the local groups join the central body. During 1893 there were unions of butchers, boilermakers, sign painters, letter carriers, hackmen and expressmen, stenographers, and theatrical mechanics, some belonging to their own national bodies but none definitely known to be affiliated with the Los Angeles Council. The central body failed in attempts to organize, or reorganize, barbers, millmen, musicians, and street railway employees. In August, 1893, the last remaining Knights of Labor Assembly, No. 2405, asked to join the Council, but the request was ignored. This assembly now played a very minor role in local labor affairs, and its wish to align with federated craft unionism recognized a national as well as a local trend.[13]

During 1893 the Council of Labor, through a rather remarkable proposal, showed a spirit considerably ahead of the times. In the spring it urged the local school teachers to organize, and promised them the support of trade-unions in a current disagreement with the Board of Education, which was insisting that all teachers be qualified to give instruction in music. When the Board rescinded its decision, however, the teachers felt no need to form a union. The Council's suggestion antedated by four years the first known union of teachers in the country, and by nine years the first affiliation of a teachers' organization with the labor movement.[14]

The Council continued to grow during 1894. New members were a revived barbers' union, including both employers and employees; the pressmen, reorganized as an affiliate of the International Printing Pressmen's Union, now distinct from the ITU; Hotel and Restaurant Employees' Alliance No. 54, composed of cooks and waiters (Cooks' and Pastry Cooks' Union No. 5 was continued, but Waiters' Union No. 48 relinquished its charter); a newsboys' union; a new local of the National Alliance of Theatrical Stage Employees; and the recently formed American Railway Union, prominent in the Pullman strike.[15] Remaining outside the central body were a reorganized boilermakers' union, now affiliated with the Brotherhood of Boilermakers and Iron Shipbuilders as Local No. 92, and a new lathers' union. The musicians also reorganized during 1894 as the Los Angeles Musical Association, chartered as Local No. 19 of the National League of Musicians, but did not affiliate with the Council of Labor until 1895.[16]

The Council could justly be proud of its record in the years 1890–1894. Formed as a direct result of the printers' strike in 1890, it had with verve and enthusiasm taken hold of and recreated an all but dead labor movement. A new vigor and a new sense of direction characterized organized labor during these busy and for the most part prosperous years. After the slow-up of 1892, the years 1893 and 1894 found the Council again pushing forward and making solid membership gains. The progress of this biennium was especially noteworthy because it coincided in part with the business depression after the Panic of 1893. Los Angeles began to feel the effects in 1894, but real hardship was delayed until later in the decade. Isolated and less highly industrialized than San Francisco, the southern city temporarily avoided the slump which had an immediately deteriorating effect on the northern unions. The Los Angeles labor movement, therefore, was for a few years ahead of its San Francisco counterpart in both number and size of unions.[17]

Although during the early 1890's the Council of Labor was aiming primarily at the organization and affiliation of new unions, it felt other obligations. Its own organization had scarcely been completed when, in the fall of 1890, it appointed a committee to visit and pledge legis-

lative candidates to work for adoption of the Australian ballot. This
work, continued into the following year, was part of the campaign initiated by the San Francisco Federated Trades, which received much of
the credit for enactment of a state ballot reform law in 1891. Along
with this, the Los Angeles Council agitated other legislative questions,
such as repeal of the poll tax and defeat of current bills legalizing employment of armed "Pinkertons"[18] and outlawing boycotts.[19]

The Council also approached community problems more positively
than had its predecessors of the 1880's. Official recognition of the central
body as representative of the working people of Los Angeles came for
the first time in 1891, in two instances. The citizens' committee planning the community celebration of July 4th invited the Council to take
part in the parade. Although the invitation came too late for necessary
arrangements, union delegates took their places on the stage with other
dignitaries at the ceremonies after the parade. During the same year
the Council was asked, along with other civic organizations, to submit
a list of nominees from whom the City Council selected a nonpartisan
Board of Freeholders to prepare a new city charter.[20] Early in 1894, on
its own initiative and with the help of Knights of Labor Assembly No.
2405, the Council sought amendment of the charter. The two labor
groups asked for the initiative and referendum, reduction of official
salaries, enforcement of the eight-hour day and employment only of
citizens on public works, a minimum daily wage of $2 for laborers and
the prevailing wage for mechanics, and appointment of a Superintendent of Labor Statistics for the city. The charter committee acted only
on salary reductions.[21]

More successfully, the Council of Labor decided in 1892 to support
an official proposal that the city build and operate a water works for
one section of Los Angeles, the beginning of a plan whereby the community would eventually control the whole water supply system. On
October 24 labor proclaimed its approval at a meeting attended by
seven hundred unionists, and soon afterward both the local Democratic
and Republican platforms came out in support of the proposition.
After the measure had passed, an organization known as the Friends of
the Water Bonds publicly thanked the Council of Labor for getting the
bonds through and turning "a seeming defeat into a victory."[22] Such
generous praise was clear acknowledgment of labor's growing power.

The most outstanding enterprise of the Council was the establishment, early in 1893, of a free employment office, maintained jointly by
the city and county. The idea was not a new one to the city. As far back
as 1884, Isaac Kinley had proposed that the unions set up an employ-

ment agency and prevail upon the municipal authorities to maintain it. During the spring of 1885 the Trades Council had appointed a committee for this purpose, and the *Times* had approved a project which would alleviate the unemployment of that recession period.[23] Nothing was done, however, until 1889, when Barney Fehnemann's Free Labor Exchange had flourished briefly in another period of hard times. The attempt to have the city take over Fehnemann's venture had failed. When the Council was finally successful, in 1893, the only other municipally operated free labor exchanges then functioning in the United States were several established in Ohio in 1890, and their value was cited as an argument for a similar setup in Los Angeles.[24]

The Council of Labor had long held this project in mind. In November, 1891, it had planned to establish its own free labor bureau, but made little headway. By September, 1892, the Council had shifted to the idea of a municipally operated agency, and it began to urge upon the City Council passage of an appropriate ordinance. Labor's agitation extended to the political arena, as Democrats and Republicans were given to understand that in the fall elections workers would be more inclined to vote for advocates of a free employment office. Both parties hastily endorsed the proposal. Labor also had the unqualified support of Mayor Thomas Hazard, whose solicitude for the needy balanced in part the opposition of private employment agencies and the *Times*. The newspaper had gone a long way since 1885, when it upheld the Trades Council's plan to establish a free labor agency; now it fought the scheme because the negotiations made it clear that the unions would be in control. Nevertheless, in January, 1893, the City Council unanimously adopted an ordinance setting up the Free Labor Bureau and appointing W. A. White of the stonecutters' union as manager. The County Board of Supervisors subsequently committed itself to an even share of the financial backing. The Bureau, opened to the public on January 24, made slow progress at the beginning; during the first week it found jobs for only eight of some three hundred applicants. It gradually improved, and within six months had placed 1,381 out of 2,581 applicants and had saved the unemployed over $4,000 in fees. By the end of two years the Bureau had found employment for 5,068 of almost ten thousand applicants.[25]

During 1893 the Council of Labor, through its renewal of anti-Chinese agitation, put Los Angeles workers in the forefront of the national drive for enforcement of the Geary Act of 1892. This law continued for ten years all federal legislation regulating Chinese immigration, and placed upon the Chinese the burden of proving their right to be in the country. The most pertinent clauses were those penalizing unlawful residence by imprisonment and subsequent deportation, and requiring Chinese laborers in the United States to apply within one year for certificates of residence. The Six Companies of San Francisco, functioning as contractors, importers, and despotic rulers of Chinese in the United States,[26] hoped to have the law set aside by the Supreme Court. Acting on their advice, most of the Chinese did not register. When the Geary Act was declared constitutional on May 15, 1893, thousands of Chinese who had been misled by the Six Companies were liable to deportation. Since adequate funds for such a mass undertaking had not been appropriated, labor groups throughout the country bestirred themselves to prevent the law from becoming a dead letter.[27]

In California, leadership of anti-Chinese agitation had traditionally come from San Francisco labor, but the northern movement, now torn by internal dissension and starting its long decline of the 1890's, was unable to serve.[28] The Los Angeles Council stepped into the vacancy with a decision to test the Geary Act, selecting Chinese cooks as the first victims because they competed directly with white labor. When private detectives employed by the Council discovered that only two Chinese cooks had registered in compliance with the law, the Council filed affidavits against sixteen of the offenders. Since local government officials would not move without consulting authorities in Washington, the Council, desiring quick results, relied on a different provision of the Act for its next step. It brought about the arrest of a Chinese cook for illegal entry and, when this case was dismissed on a technicality, lodged charges against a Chinese cigar maker, Wong Dip Ken, for illegal residence. Wong's trial was the first in the United States under the Geary Act. Although defended by counsel retained by the Six Companies, Wong was sentenced on June 16 to two days' imprisonment, to be followed by deportation. Before the sentence could be carried out, the case was appealed to the United States District Court, which in July, 1893, sanctioned the deportation but declared the imprisonment unconstitutional. Through its zeal, the Los Angeles Council of Labor won the first enforcement of the Geary Act in the United States when Wong Dip Ken was deported on August 10.[29]

Meanwhile the Council of Labor, encouraged by Wong's conviction, continued its agitation with the aid of the cooks' and cigar makers' unions. It sponsored an anti-Chinese mass meeting on June 17, the day after Wong was sentenced, and urged the AFL to call similar meetings in other parts of the country. The local gathering adopted resolutions demanding full enforcement of the Geary Act and sent them to government officials in Washington and to all California congressmen. The anti-Chinese fever infected a wide area during the summer of 1893, as communities like Fresno, Tulare, and Compton forcefully expelled resident Chinese, and citizens of Redlands, more lawfully, swore to fourteen warrants for arrest of Orientals. But prosecution did not keep apace, as some thirty warrants in Los Angeles were suppressed on the advice of the United States District Attorney, who hoped that the Chinese would leave voluntarily.[30]

Because federal officials refused to make arrests under the registration clause of the Geary Act, the Council of Labor successfully appealed to Judge Erskine M. Ross, of the United States District Court, to authorize such warrants. The Cahuenga Farmers' Association then swore out complaints against six Chinese in the Cahuenga Valley. Five of them were ordered deported, and as government funds were not available, both the Association and the Council of Labor offered to pay the fares themselves. During September there were more arrests and more orders for deportation, but all the cases were appealed. Both pro- and anti-Chinese sentiment found expression in the now thoroughly aroused community. When a public meeting on September 15 planned to petition Congress for extension of the registration period, union members in attendance voted down the proposal. The Chinese themselves asked Congress for permission to register after the date set by the Act and boycotted Los Angeles by refusing to sell vegetables or launder clothes. The Cahuenga farmers, impatient at delay, persuaded the Chinese remaining in their district to leave, and similar expulsions occurred at Norwalk, Burbank, Vernon, and Pasadena, all suburban to Los Angeles.[31]

Appeals to extend the time for registration continued during the fall of 1893, owing to the shortness of funds for deportation and to a fairly widespread popular belief that the uninformed Chinese should not be held responsible for an error in judgment by the Six Companies. Coincidentally, a new Chinese minister to the United States informed the Attorney General that continued prosecution would lessen his country's responsibility for the safety of American citizens in China. Guided by these representations, Congress amended the Geary Act in November, 1893, to extend the registration period to April 3, 1894. The Chinese in custody in Los Angeles were freed, and the excitement quickly subsided.[32]

In ways less showy than establishment of the Free Labor Bureau and satisfactory testing of the Geary Act, the Los Angeles Council of Labor provided services of direct benefit to its member unions. In contrast to the 1880's, when the painters' assembly had made available a meeting place for the unions, the Council, in 1891, engaged and maintained a hall for the use of organized labor.[33] In 1894 it added a free labor library and reading room, and, for the first time in Los Angeles, put on a promotional campaign to stimulate demand for union labels among both unionists and the general public.[34]

From the time of its organization, the Council of Labor realized that a regular news outlet would be of inestimable aid in the development of a strong craft union movement. It therefore offered to sponsor publication of the *Union Printer*, strike organ of the Typographical Union, as the *Workman*. The printers agreed to the change of title, and in November, 1890, the paper became the official journal of the Council, though continuing to be published, distributed, and financed by the printers. Changing from a semiweekly to a weekly in November, 1891, the *Workman* appeared regularly until April, 1892. Then a compromise agreement with Otis, temporarily suspending the printers' strike, required discontinuance of the *Workman*.[35]

Shortly thereafter, the *Express* inaugurated a weekly labor column, and Joseph Phillis of the Typographical Union founded the *Industrial Age*. This paper was popularly regarded as the official organ of the Council of Labor, though the central body accepted no financial responsibility. In July, 1892, the Council publicly repudiated the *Industrial Age* because of its political stand, and the paper did not long survive. In November, 1892, two members of the Typographical Union, Cyren E. Fisk and Sam J. Chappel, began publishing the *Labor Review*, which was endorsed by the Council of Labor. When Chappel retired in March, 1893, the *Labor Review* merged with the *California Farmer*, organ of the Farmers' Alliance, to form the *Farmer and Labor Review*. Fisk edited the labor section of the new weekly, an influential and progressive paper. The *Farmer and Labor Review* was published continuously until March, 1895, but in August, 1894, the Council of Labor withdrew official sanction from the joint enterprise following a disagreement on policy. Soon thereafter the central body endorsed the Typographical Union's new semimonthly organ, the *California Federationist*.[36]

The Council's aid to individual unions included assistance in disputes with employers and in drives for shorter hours or higher wages or both, to be discussed below. Toward the end of 1891, the central body established formal rules for the levying of boycotts requested by member unions.[37] In several instances the Council was asked to intervene in jurisdictional disputes. In June, 1891, the Musicians' Protective

Association submitted the problem of a rival organization formed by some disaffected members. Although reorganizing in November, the musicians' union was so weakened by the split that it lapsed altogether before the end of the year. In the fall of 1891 disgruntled members of the Los Angeles local of the national bricklayers' union withdrew to form an independent organization. The older union, though not affiliated with the Council of Labor, sought the central body's aid. The San Francisco Federated Trades, asked for a decision, advised preference to the international branch, and shortly thereafter the independent disappeared. Despite its deference to the Council of Labor, the bricklayers' union did not affiliate. Still a third craft faced a jurisdictional dispute, but in September, 1892, the Council of Labor effected amalgamation of the older German-speaking bakers' union with a reorganized American bakers' local. The joint union became Local No. 37 under a new international charter. Early in 1894 the Council restored amicable relations between the sailors' and longshoremen's unions in San Pedro, at loggerheads over water-front jurisdiction.[38]

In the light of the Council's very solid accomplishments between 1890 and 1894, criticism of its failure to deal with all relevant problems would be captious. Yet several fairly important aspects of workers' welfare escaped its attention. For example, the Council gave little heed to the problems of female labor, though several unions, notably the Typographical, accorded women full membership. It was left to an outside organization to help working women. In 1891 the Women's Industrial Exchange replaced the Flower Festival Society, which had been serving women workers in several capacities ever since 1885, and carried on its female labor bureau.[39] Two years later the Council similarly ignored the employment problems of Negroes. In the summer of 1893, the cooks' and waiters' union had split to form two separate unions, and the new waiters' local helped colored waiters to organize a union of their own. The Negro group did not join and received no encouragement from the Council of Labor. In September an Afro-American Protective Association was created to assist unemployed Negroes to find work—especially as replacements for the Chinese who were then leaving—and to obtain lands for Negroes.[40]

The Council was not alert, during these years, to the benefits which might flow from a well-organized celebration of Labor Day. In 1885 the AFL had adopted the first Monday in September as an annual holiday for labor, but for a few years unions were able to gain only local recognition in some of the larger cities. San Francisco labor had begun to observe Labor Day in 1887, and finally in 1891 the governor of California proclaimed the day as a state holiday. Los Angeles labor held no parade in 1891, but did stage an evening meeting so that the public could hear addresses on labor questions.[41] In 1892 the Los Angeles Labor Day mass meeting was the largest labor celebration thus far held in the city, but again there was no parade. A year later the unions contented themselves with a picnic at the beach, including the inevitable speechmaking.[42] By 1894, Labor Day was a national legal holiday for the first time, and Los Angeles labor held its first parade on September 3. The Council was able to muster only seven unions, however, because now California had set aside the first Monday in October as the state holiday (since Admission Day was observed on September 9, too close to the national Labor Day), and the resulting confusion prevented an enthusiastic celebration in Los Angeles.[43]

Regardless of these omissions, the Council of Labor headed a thoroughly progressive labor movement. Immediately plunging into the task of organizing, reorganizing, and directing workers, the Council transmitted its own urgency and spirit to its members. Unions which had been languishing in despondency for several years suddenly awoke, in the fall of 1890, to a new and refreshing hope. Among the first to revive was Local No. 81, Journeymen Tailors' Union of America. In October it gained general acceptance of a higher wage scale. A strike against two recalcitrant employers dragged on for several months and was never resolved. A rumor toward the end of 1890 that employing tailors were combining to resist demands put a damper on the union's aggressiveness, and in the spring of 1892, when employers began to black-list union members and finally formed the Merchant Tailors' Association for "mutual protection," the union lost its original driving power.[44] Immediately after organizing in the fall of 1890, the musicians' union demanded and won wage increases for its members.[45] The older cigar makers' union did its part in reviving a dormant labor movement by reinstituting its anti-Chinese campaign in the fall of 1890. Successfully replacing Chinese cigar makers in Redondo with the aid of the Coast Seamen's Union at San Pedro, the union planned to extend this tactic to other outlying towns. In 1891, noting that many Chinese-made cigars were being bought in Los Angeles, the cigar makers appealed to all local unions to assist them in their fight, and by the end of the year claimed that only one nonunion shop was operating in the city. In 1893 the cigar makers were more active in labor affairs than previously and sent H. E. Martens, president of the Council of Labor, to the union's national convention.[46]

The Los Angeles unions again began to extend their influence beyond the borders of the city, as they had done on a smaller scale in the 1880's. During 1891 many of them contributed financial aid to the San Francisco molders, then engaged in a long and bitter strike against a wage reduction. A more pertinent feature of the expansion for the future security of Los Angeles labor was the effort of certain unions to speed organization in the southern California area. Carpenters' Union No. 56, though never regaining its preboom vitality, was able to revive the carpenters' union in Pasadena. Early in 1892 the Pasadena painters organized with the aid of Los Angeles Painters' and Decorators' Union No. 206. Both the musicians and cigar makers assisted in forming San Diego unions of their respective crafts. In 1892, San Diego bakers, not numerous enough to organize separately, voted to join the Los Angeles bakers' union. In an even wider area, a member of Tailors' Union No. 81 was Pacific Coast organizer for the Journeymen Tailors' Union of America, and in 1891 persuaded the San Francisco tailors to affiliate with the national union.[47]

As in previous periods of prosperity in Los Angeles, the building trades made the most outstanding and most inclusive gains. To them, as to other groups, length of the working day was a prime concern. Since the AFL's eight-hour campaign in May, 1890, had had neither extensive nor permanent results, another national drive for the shorter day was launched in 1891. Following their San Francisco brothers, Los Angeles painters demanded the eight-hour day and a minimum daily wage of $2.50, effective October 1, 1891. The only shop refusing to accede was brought into line in August of the following year. On April 1, 1893, Pasadena Painters' Union No. 92 inaugurated the eight-hour day.[48] Los Angeles Plumbers' Local No. 78 put an eight-hour schedule into effect on August 1, 1892, without difficulty. The plumbers' relations with employers, organized as the Master Plumbers' Association, were unusually close; the eight-hour agreement in 1892 was ratified by a joint banquet of journeymen and masters, reputed to be the first such celebration in Los Angeles and among the first in the United States.[49]

Carpenters' Union No. 56, previously in the vanguard of building-trades agitation, noticeably lagged behind other crafts in winning shorter hours. Early in September, 1892, it organized an Eight-Hour League which announced a reduction of carpenters' working hours from nine to eight for October 24, with no cut in wages. A new employers' association, the Builders' Exchange, offered no resistance, but in October both the Eight-Hour League and its sponsor expired. Weakened by the collapse of the boom and by internal disunity, Carpenters'

Union No. 56 surrendered its charter and was replaced by Local No.
332, organized by disaffected members suspended from "Old 56." The
new union immediately affiliated with the Council of Labor, but it was
not strong enough to establish a shorter working day until 1893. Then,
with a membership of over three hundred, it set June 1 as the inaugural
date. The agitation included a labor parade and demonstration on May
13, attended by more than a thousand members of thirteen unions.
But in August the Council of Labor reported that the carpenters were
still struggling for shorter hours. Their battle was a long one, for not
until 1896 could Arthur Vinette say, "The eight-hour day has been
practically won."[50]

The temporary eclipse of the carpenters' union as leader of the
building trades brought the painters into prominence. Their union
grew rapidly, provided an ample benefit program, and maintained a
free employment agency. In January, 1893, the painters demanded a
wage increase from $2.50 to $3 a day, and won easily when a new master
painters' association adopted the revised schedule on April 17. This
success was cited as the accomplishment of "radical and progressive"
unionism.[51] In November, 1893, the painters, together with the carpenters and the paper hangers, formed a Los Angeles Building Trades
Council, but it was a premature step. When other unions failed to join,
the Council adjourned in July, 1894, subject to call by any member.[52]

The ease with which the painters won their 1893 wage increase was
attributable to their control of the local industry. Before this time,
Los Angeles building trades had not been acutely conscious of the closed
shop as a union objective; only the printers among local crafts had
militantly sought the exclusion of nonunionists. But in the country at
large many unions were trying, in the later 'eighties and early 'nineties,
to achieve this measure of security, and in 1890 the AFL adopted a
resolution that it was "inconsistent" for union men to work with nonunion men. Although discussion of the issue was infrequent, some of
the building trades began to campaign for the closed shop; the painters' international became so thoroughly convinced of its value that
locals were practically obliged to demand it. In Los Angeles, the
painters' union was one of several building trades to gain the closed
shop in this period, winning over the last nonunion employer in 1892;
the molders had claimed complete control of their market at the end
of 1891.[53]

The plumbers likewise enjoyed a closed-shop arrangement. Journeymen and masters carried their coöperation to a then uncommon extreme, temporarily setting up what was, in effect, monopoly control

of the industry. The journeymen had, early in 1893, persuaded the City Council to appoint a union member as plumbing inspector. In July, seeking still greater power, the union, in collaboration with master plumbers, gained passage of an ordinance which established an examining board, composed of both masters and journeymen, to regulate the licensing of all plumbers. Meanwhile, the union had signed a contract with the Master Plumbers' Association, stipulating that union members work only for members of the Association and that the latter employ only union men. Criticism of the high prices resulting from the ordinance was directed against both groups and caused the City Council to repeal the measure before the end of the year.[54]

Although the combination had been balked in its attempt to dictate prohibitive prices for both labor and materials, coöperation between master and journeymen plumbers nevertheless had real substance. Fulfilling the union's contract to work only for Association members, seven plumbers struck in May, 1894, against the W. C. Furrey Company, ousted from the Master Plumbers' Association for an infraction of rules. The walkout forced the rebel back into line, and the strikers returned to work as soon as the employers' disagreement was straightened out.[55] No other union, in the entire early period of Los Angeles labor history, ever achieved such complete unity with employers.

One other building-trades union petitioned for protective legislation during this period. In August, 1894, the electrical workers, organized a year earlier, asked the City Council to adopt various measures for the safety of their trade, and a suitable ordinance embodying their demands was passed in November.[56]

Except in the printers' continuing struggle and the Pullman strike, both described elsewhere, union goals outside the building trades centered mainly on shorter working hours. Retail clerks had begun agitating for a six instead of an eight o'clock closing as early as January, 1891, but had met with no success until a year later. Then, with leading merchants granting early closing, the employees had organized the Clerks' Association. The union, however, had failed to win over the Main Street stores, some of which stayed open until midnight; its caution in exerting pressure was partly dictated by working-class patronage of these establishments. But in July, 1893, the retail clerks decided that uniformity was preferable to partiality and within a few days had convinced all but four of the Main Street stores to close at the earlier hour. The stubborn few were subjected to an intensive campaign, made colorful by nightly parades with banners and a drum corps, and to prounion propaganda by merchants who had already curtailed their hours. A compromise seven o'clock closing was soon arranged, but the Main Street establishments kept the agreement for only two weeks.[57]

Two other groups were concerned over closing hours. In 1891 the barbers' union tried to abolish Sunday work, but the City Council decreed that a Sunday closing ordinance for barber shops would be unconstitutional. Nevertheless, the barbers claimed to have negotiated shorter daily hours and the Sunday holiday by the end of the year.[58] In 1893 the butchers organized as Branch No. 4 of the Journeymen Butchers' Protective and Benevolent Association; their officers were installed by a state organizer coming from San Francisco. As the name implies, the union existed for beneficial purposes and did not interfere in employer-employee issues. The Los Angeles local remained outside the Council of Labor and followed the rules of its parent body until 1894, when it "petitioned" employers to close at six o'clock every day except Saturday. Retail proprietors were agreeable, but opposition by wholesalers defeated the move.[59]

The bakers were also able to improve their working conditions during this period. Until the amalgamation in September, 1892, there were two separate unions, one German and one American. Before that time it was the older German-speaking union which agitated for benefits to the craft. By striking in December, 1891, it forced the Vienna Bakery to discharge nonunion employees and in January, 1892, claimed that all bakers employed in Los Angeles were union members.[60] Late in 1891 bakers throughout the United States had begun a drive for the ten-hour day and elimination of nightwork, to be effected May 1, 1892. Los Angeles bakers were then working twelve to fifteen hours a day, and eighteen on Fridays. Although the German union at once appointed a committee to carry out the national program, both bakers' locals were too involved in their plans for consolidation to make any progress. Early in 1893, with the help of the Council of Labor, the joint bakers' union induced employers to shorten hours to ten, abolish nightwork, observe the union wage scale, and pay 30 cents an hour for overtime. Two weeks later, four of the employers, complaining of heavy losses in the hotel and restaurant trade, returned to the old system. On May 21 all union bakers in the city, fifty in number, struck to retain the concessions, though only fourteen were involved in the dispute. In June the union yielded on nightwork, but gained acceptance of its schedules of wages, hours, and overtime, and two months later all but one of the bakeries were employing union labor. In August, 1894, after two days of negotiation, the one outsider was brought into the union camp.[61]

The waiters were less successful in a strike over wages and hours in 1893. The union scale was $10 to $10.50 for a seven-day week, with an eleven-hour day and twenty minutes off for each meal. On August 3, eleven union waiters employed in Melstead and Maxwell's restaurant, catering mainly to union members, struck because these conditions were not being maintained. In trying to mediate the dispute, the Council of Labor rejected as unsatisfactory a compromise offered by the proprietors. When the restaurant began to employ nonunion help, the Council imposed a boycott. Of five union waiters arrested for picketing, four were dismissed by the court and the fifth was punished by a nominal fine of $1. Attempts to unionize Melstead and Maxwell's continued, while the strikers found employment elsewhere.[62]

Although affiliated with the Council of Labor in 1892, the Sailors' Union of San Pedro was not really an integral part of the Los Angeles labor movement. Its problems differed from those of other unions in the area, and its orientation toward San Francisco headquarters hindered a close association with Los Angeles labor. Throughout this period the sailors concentrated on the triple aim of maintaining their wage scale, establishing their own shipping office, and preventing nonunion crews from sailing. An attempt early in 1890 to force a union crew on an unwilling captain was highly dramatic. On the night of February 26, union members boarded the *Nettie Sundborg,* due to sail the next day with nonunion men. When two of the ship's crew disappeared, seven unionists suspected of implication were arrested. The discovery of an unidentified corpse brought the prisoners face to face with a murder charge, but within a few days officers of the law found and released the abducted seamen, and the charge was changed to kidnaping. In the end the men were tried for false imprisonment, since the place of concealment was Catalina Island, legally a part of Los Angeles County. Strong prounion sentiment in San Pedro led the authorities to hold the trial in Los Angeles. Only one of the defendants was found guilty, and he was punished by a small fine.[63]

Through incidents like this, California seamen waged a continuous campaign against the Shipowners' Association, which had been revived in 1891. Progress made by the spring of 1893 held out the hope of eventual victory, but at this crucial moment the aggressive Manufacturers' and Employers' Association of San Francisco joined the shipowners' fight against the union. Events on the water front at San Pedro reflected the buttressed strength of the employers. The union found it increasingly difficult to hold the line in wages and to ship its members. Friction between nonunion and union sailors grew to serious proportions and resulted in occasional arrests. When the Shipowners' Association reëstablished a shipping office in San Pedro in April, 1893, and protected it with uniformed guards bearing a close resemblance to "Pinkertons," both the union and the community angrily denounced such methods. Arrests of union men on charges of conspiracy or enticing sailors to desert became more frequent, and tension heightened with the appointment of the shipowners' agent, J. W. Davis, as a deputy sheriff. The Los Angeles *Times* helped sharpen the conflict by charging the Sailors' Union with lawlessness and recommending penitentiary terms for its leaders.[64]

Tempers on the San Pedro water front reached the exploding point in May, 1893, when a group of armed sailors boarded the *Halcyon* with intent to remove the nonunion crew. Both sides fired shots, and a union man was killed. Since union men had allegedly opened fire first, one of them was arrested, but confused and admittedly circumstantial evidence brought an acquittal. The affair had a sobering effect, and San Pedro became quieter. With the lessening of tension, the union was occasionally able to ship its members in more peaceable fashion.[65] In September, 1893, the sailors won the moral support of the Los Angeles Council of Labor, which voted "to boycott J. W. Davis of San Pedro and all who do business with him on account of his attempt to ship nonunion crews and his professed antagonism to organized labor."[66] Davis, as editor of the antiunion San Pedro *Sun*, bore somewhat the same relation to labor in the smaller city as Otis did to labor in Los Angeles. The improvement on the local water front was temporary, however, and toward the end of 1893 there were rumors that the Sailors' Union was disbanding. A vigorous denial could not hide obvious deterioration; persistent opposition by the owners, up and down the coast, together with the intervention of the San Francisco Manufacturers' and Employers' Association, had reduced the union to an impotency from which it was not to recover until the turn of the century.[67]

During the years 1890–1894, the Los Angeles Council of Labor had recorded solid achievements in organization, affiliation, and improvement of its community status. Intracommunity guidance of the labor movement extended even to its outpost in San Pedro, where the welfare of the sailors' and longshoremen's unions came to be the concern of the Los Angeles central body. But of greater significance during this crucial half decade was the Council's realization that an effective labor movement, no matter how unified and how much a part of the community, could not prosper if contained within a limited geographical area. Connections with labor outside Los Angeles—in San Francisco, on the Pacific Coast, in the whole United States—were of mounting urgency in the early 1890's. With the decisions that had to be made, and the concomitant policies that had to be established in such external relationships, went new aspects of a long-standing problem which had more than once perplexed Los Angeles labor. Which course would bring greater benefit to labor: to pay close heed to immediate craft union goals, or to strive politically for ultimate revision of the economic structure of society? The Council was to find its answer in 1894, after four years of irresolution, when it affiliated with the American Federation of Labor, an organization dedicated under Gompers' masterful leadership to business unionism, the attainment of here-and-now gains, and the conduct of industrial relations on a day-to-day basis of wages, hours, and working conditions.

XI. THE POLITICAL DILEMMA OF
THE EARLY 1890's

THE PRESSURES tending to push Los Angeles labor into political parti-sanship cannot be separated from the quest for satisfactory regional and national alliances. The possible choices ranged widely from member-ship in the apolitical AFL to amalgamation with the People's Party. Between these two extremes lay a Pacific Coast federation, organized in defiance of the AFL, and wavering on a semipolitical course between out-and-out adherence to Populism and straightforward reliance on craft union principles. So involved were the alternatives that the local movement had to proceed warily, balancing advantage against disad-vantage, making friends where possible, and always following a path charted by need and by the hope of reward. In contrast to the con-scious and largely successful drive for internal unity, the Council of Labor's conduct in external relationships was characterized by con-fusion and disunity, by false starts and sudden changes, by a cumulative frustration not relieved until 1894, when Los Angeles labor chose the AFL as its lodestar.

Formation of the San Francisco Manufacturers' and Employers' Asso-ciation in 1891 had repercussions not only in the fortunes of the water-front unions but also in the development of a stronger regional bond among Pacific Coast labor organizations. The patent weakness of the existing federation, in operation since 1886, had opened the way to its replacement by the San Francisco Federated Trades as the practicing regional council. Other circumstances in the northern city, besides the militancy of the new employers' organization, made 1891 a propitious year for establishment of a bona fide regional body. Alfred Fuhrman, president of the city's central labor council, had broken with the na-tional union of brewery workers to form an independent coast union. Because the San Francisco Federated Trades supported the brewery workers' rebellion, the American Federation of Labor suspended it and thus deepened an existing cleavage between eastern and western labor. In September, 1891, under Fuhrman's ardent leadership, a number of city federations organized the Pacific Coast Council of Trades and Labor Federations to exercise jurisdiction in issues of more than local import, to the exclusion of the AFL. The new body, electing Fuhrman as president, planned to extend and strengthen labor organizations on the west coast, improve social conditions, advance workers' material welfare, and enforce legislation specifying the eight-hour day and regu-lating contract, convict, and Chinese labor.[1]

Because the Pacific Coast Council was so definitely a separatist movement, it posed a problem in loyalties for Los Angeles labor. In the fall
of 1890, the Council had affiliated with the San Francisco Federated
Trades, and in January, 1891, with the old Pacific Coast federation. Did
it now want to join a body organized in defiance of the American Federation of Labor? The issue was the more pointed because Samuel
Gompers, president of the AFL, had spoken in Los Angeles in March,
1891, at the invitation of the Council of Labor. He generously ap-
plauded the Council's insistence on more and yet more organization
and warmed the hearts of his audience by recognizing Harrison Gray
Otis as the focal point of resistance to organized labor. "The time will
soon come," he said, "when our provoked workingmen and women will
show this hero of battles with his pen that it is to his advantage to pay
fair wages and give reasonable treatment to union printers."[2] But a
single visit, no matter how harmonious, could not dispel the feeling
of isolation from the national labor movement. Los Angeles was after
all a part of California, despite north-south friction, and the Council
sent Alex Rose, of the Typographical Union, as delegate to the September, 1891, convention which organized the western federation. When
the Coast Council matched Gompers' comprehension of the key difficulty in Los Angeles by promising both financial and moral aid in the
fight against the *Times,* the Council of Labor decided to affiliate. In
November it adopted the constitution and received a charter.[3]

Before the question of regional or national orientation again became
pertinent during 1893–1894, Los Angeles labor was subjected to temp-
tation by several political groups and politically-minded individuals.
Vacillation with regard to political activity had long characterized
American unions, but it was especially pronounced in Los Angeles,
where the labor movement had been conceived in political turmoil.
Distraction into bypaths of reform had been a recurrent feature, partly
because of the continuity of Workingmen's Party traditions through
a series of third parties, and partly because of the disabilities of the
craft union movement itself. Moreover, during the early 1890's, internal
forces tended to push organized labor toward a closer affinity with
straightforward political movements. The most articulate exponents of
partisan political alignment were Jonathan Bailey and Arthur Vinette,
officers of Carpenters' Union No. 56, and Michael McGlynn, the San
Francisco printer sent down to help the local Typographical Union.
Another craft unionist active as a socialist was P. R. Bellman, a tailor
who was secretary of the Council of Labor early in 1891.[4] The unions
most susceptible to diversion into politics were those of the painters,

carpenters, and tailors, but several others made occasional excursions into the political field.

The two most challenging claimants for local labor's attention during this period were the Socialist Labor Party and the People's Party. The former, organized in Los Angeles late in 1890 by the more radical Nationalists, during the next year sponsored an address by Bailey on the eight-hour question, brought a national party lecturer to Los Angeles, and induced Bellman to laud the party's merits at a meeting of the Council of Labor in August. On this occasion Bellman shared the platform with a representative of the Farmers' Alliance, one of the components of the People's Party, just then emerging in distinct form.[5] From this time on, the Socialist Labor Party sank into obscurity behind the People's Party, whose campaign to enlist the local working class in a political movement was far more intensive. Since Populism originated in farmers' organizations, it could rely on the trend of farmer-labor coöperation begun in the 1870's to enhance any attraction it might otherwise have for union members. Moreover, as a vehicle for all those imbued with reformist ideals, the People's Party was a worthy successor to the Knights of Labor, and could hope to draw in those remnants of now dormant uplift organizations which had found sanctuary in the noble order. Because it possessed such a broad appeal, the People's Party made considerable headway in the Los Angeles area before its final repudiation by organized labor and its own eventual loss of identity through fusion with the Democratic Party.

Like the Union Labor Party of 1888, which was dominated by the agrarian South and West, the People's Party evolved from a coalition of farmer and labor groups, foremost among which were two National Farmers' Alliances, one flourishing in the upper Mississippi Valley and the other in the southern states. The Knights of Labor, though entering into the negotiations for creating a third party, decided in the end that their order must not be completely submerged in a movement of paramount concern to farmers. Individual Knights could find entree through local branches of the new national Citizens' Alliance, one of the party's urban constituents. The People's Party effected preliminary organization at Cincinnati in May, 1891, though its firm establishment dated from the nominating convention at Omaha on July 4, 1892, when General James B. Weaver of Iowa was named as presidential candidate.[6]

The platform adopted at the Omaha convention was a codification of previous statements of principle, and emphasized the grievances of farmers, such as low crop prices, the rapacity of railroads, high interest rates on mortgages, and inequitable taxation. It favored federal crop loans, an adequate and flexible currency issued only by the government, postal savings banks, graduated income tax, government economy, prohibition of land speculation and alien ownership of land, popular election of United States senators, and public ownership of railroads and communication systems. To attract the labor vote, the convention called for the initiative and referendum, the Australian or secret ballot, shorter working hours, enforcement of the eight-hour law on government work, restricted immigration, abolition of the Pinkerton detective system, and discontinuance of government subsidies to private corporations.[7]

California Populists got busy soon after the national party came into being. Preliminary to formal political structure, Farmers' Alliances began to organize Citizens' Alliances as an avenue of participation for trade unionists and other urban dwellers. In Los Angeles the drive for conversion to Populism, aided by Bailey and McGlynn, caught on quickly. Within two weeks the Central Citizens' Alliance in the city was the largest body of its kind on the Pacific Coast.[8] The desire to bring labor into close association with Populist groups was patent in the call of the State Farmers' Alliance for the convention which, meeting in Los Angeles on October 22, 1891, organized the People's Party of California. Trade-unions and Knights of Labor were invited along with Farmers' and Citizens' Alliances, Patrons of Husbandry, the Nationalist Party, and "all other reform organizations . . . in sympathy. . . ."[9] Among the six hundred delegates in attendance was a handful from Los Angeles labor groups: three from the Council of Labor, including McGlynn; seven from the carpenters' union; three from the painters' union; and ten from Knights of Labor assemblies, including Master Workman E. M. Hamilton and Bailey, and a representative from Pasadena. Vinette was present as one of the seven delegates from the Los Angeles Nationalist Club. The platform ratified by the convention was essentially the same as the Cincinnati platform of May, 1891, later to be adopted by the Omaha convention in 1892.[10]

The People's Party grew rapidly in the Los Angeles area, though the extent to which laboring people embraced Populism is debatable. Recognizing a natural affinity, the Los Angeles Knights of Labor formally affiliated with the Citizens' Alliance toward the end of 1891, but craft unions were reluctant to profess an equal degree of conformity. The painters and tailors did try to enlarge the area of coöperation by holding open meetings addressed by Knights of Labor, Nationalists, and members of the Citizens' Alliance, all involved with the People's Party, as well as socialists and single taxers. Such catholicity, however, was not common among the unions; of all the craftsmen, only the painters were really assiduous in steering labor toward politics. In March, 1892, they had helped to organize and subsequently held joint public meetings with the Third Ward Citizens' Alliance. The union was obviously proud of a distinctive characteristic: "The painters are radical and independent in political matters, . . . the first trades Union in the city who believed the Unions should discuss political questions and remedy their wrongs at the ballot box."[11] Although the painters' union tried to convert other labor organizations to its ideology, it was at the same time one of the most alert in tallying economic gains.

Nevertheless, as the year 1892 advanced, Los Angeles labor contracted rather than expanded its participation in political ventures, especially those which might commit it to a specific policy. No union, not even the painters', sent delegates to the convention which in April organized the People's Party of Los Angeles County. The Knights of Labor were represented, and Vinette was on hand as a Nationalist, not a tradeunionist. B. W. Batchelor of the Farmers' Alliance was selected as chairman of the county central committee, E. M. Hamilton as vicechairman, and Vinette as secretary. Alfred Moore, founder of the Workingmen's Party in Los Angeles, was a member of the committee. Again in May, when the San Francisco Building Trades Council sponsored a state labor convention to promote favorable legislation and create a third party if necessary, no Los Angeles union took part. Yet the visiting speaker at the 1892 Labor Day mass meeting was Mrs. Anna L. Diggs, national lecturer for both the Populists and the Knights of Labor, whose avowed intention was to bring workingmen closer to politics. This was, however, a noncommittal gesture implying no outright acceptance of Populism.[12]

The elections in the fall of 1892 were further evidence that Los Angeles labor was by no means convinced that the People's Party was its best potential champion. The Populists' county nominating convention in August drew up a ticket naming a preponderance of farmers with only a sprinkling of labor personages. But the platform was obviously designed for working-class perusal and reflection. After endorsing national principles, it set forth these tenets: antirailroad measures, public work at $2 for an eight-hour day, city and county ownership and operation of public utilities, woman suffrage, an improved mechanics' lien law, weekly payment of wages by all corporations, direct legislation, abolition of the poll tax, proportional representation in legislative bodies, government appropriations for harbors and county improvements, and reduction in the number of county judges. After the convention concluded its business, James B. Weaver, Populist candidate for President of the United States, addressed a crowd estimated at four thousand people.[13]

The city nominating convention of the People's Party, meeting on October 3, 1892, adopted a much briefer platform calling for city ownership of public utilities, initiative and referendum in city government, establishment of a free labor bureau, prohibition of the contract system in city work, and abolition of the chain gang. It is notable that the Council of Labor had just then begun its agitation for a municipal free employment agency. Although some union members went to the convention, the Populist city ticket named nobody of prominence in the labor movement. The People's Party was apparently more willing to garner labor votes than to entrust its fortunes in office, should it be elected, to labor representatives. It did depart from strict party control by endorsing a few Democratic candidates.[14]

Labor was not too impressed by Populist promises. Although the unions of carpenters and painters, together with the San Pedro unions of sailors and longshoremen, sent delegates to several People's Party rallies preceding the election, the major portion of labor's political activity in 1892 was channeled in other directions. Conservative avoidance of third-party tendencies was patent in the endorsement of Democratic or Republican candidates who pledged enforcement of the eighthour law, establishment of a free labor bureau, and support of Chinese exclusion. Both parties, not to be outdone by the Populists, wooed labor through the inclusion of planks specifying these and other benefits, but union leaders felt that the Democrats were more sympathetic. Frank Colver of the Typographical Union was Democratic candidate for county auditor, and Homer C. Katz of the Clerks' Association was a delegate to the city Democratic convention. Sam J. Chappel, a printer, was president of an Independent Political Club whose purpose was to get out the vote. Since Katz was also an officer, the club probably tended toward the Democratic side. Labor's opposition to the Republican Party was concentrated on the candidate for mayor.[15]

The election results are difficult to interpret, with three tickets in the field and with both labor and the Populists endorsing some Democratic candidates. The Republican Party won a majority of county and city offices, except for the mayoralty, and Colver was defeated. No straight Populist candidate was elected in either the county or the city, though some Democratic-Populist choices were successful. Among them were Marion Cannon, elected to Congress in the normally Republican Sixth District by a plurality of 6,500 votes, and H. C. Dillon, elected district attorney. In the legislative contests the Populists received approximately one-third the votes of the winning candidates, and a slightly higher percentage in the county elections. This was conceded to be a "respectable vote" for the local People's Party. Although organized labor could not similarly measure efficiency at the polls by a numerical count, it could compliment itself on a demonstrated ability to gain general support for several of its causes. In January, 1893, the new City Council voted unanimously for the free labor bureau and in February insisted that contractors on public works observe the eight-hour law.[16]

In the 1892 elections in the country at large, the People's Party fared well for a new political venture. Weaver received one million votes as against Grover Cleveland's five and one-half million and Benjamin Harrison's five million. The Populists elected four state governors, fourteen members of Congress, and over three hundred legislators in nineteen states. This impressive showing for a third party of prolabor inclinations caused some liberalizing of government labor policies, and alarmed the two old parties into including labor planks in their platforms. To expedite the forging of a closer bond with labor, People's Party representatives from twenty states organized, in December, 1892, a subsidiary Industrial Legion as a more specific drawing card for craft unionists than the Citizens' Alliance had been. The Panic of 1893, followed by depression, unemployment, and decline in crop prices, exacerbated class antagonism and strengthened Populist agitation for free silver coinage and governmental solution of labor problems. Under the impetus of hard times, labor itself tended toward wider acceptance of Populist principles, particularly restriction of immigration, freedom from the competition of convict labor, and public ownership of utilities.[17]

In the political evolution of Los Angeles labor, however, 1893 was a year of indecision with conflicting pressures and a greater than usual reluctance to formulate and carry out an incisive policy. The People's Party, having reached sizable dimensions, clamored loudly for labor's support. Local branches of the Industrial Legion appeared early in 1893 and, during the summer, sponsored a mammoth conference at Long Beach with a program of discussion on political and legislative reforms, free silver, the future of labor organization, and direct legislation. Even these trenchant questions failed to bring the wholehearted support which the Populists wanted, for only the Knights of Labor and the unions of carpenters, longshoremen, and retail clerks sent delegates. Within the craft union movement there were two extreme points of view, both frankly put forward by front-line unions. The Typographical

Union tersely ordered its Council of Labor delegates to "keep out of politics." The painters, on the other hand, believing strikes "outmoded," urged identification with the People's Party in preference to independent endorsement of old-party candidates with friendly leanings. Such divergence, though precluding unity in political action, did not interfere with unanimity on certain Populist fundamentals. For example, a poll of the Council's unions in 1893 on the initiative and referendum, which found a place in all People's Party platforms, revealed twelve in favor and only one opposed. The attitude of Los Angeles labor to the third party, falling short of full partnership, was a composite of partial doctrinal approval and astute appreciation of the potential usefulness of Populism to the craft union movement. When, in October, 1893, the Council of Labor was setting up the joint committee to cope with the renewed *Times* controversy, it dispatched four official representatives to the county convention of the Farmers' Alliance. More than half of the sixty-six organizations forming the committee were branches of the Alliance and the Industrial Legion.[18]

The Council of Labor's political ambivalence during 1893 was disclosed by a simultaneous tentative approach to the American Federation of Labor. In the spring the central body proposed to organize a Southern California Federation of Labor directly under the AFL, a plan defeated only because labor bodies in neighboring communities offered no encouragement. This strong suggestion of distrust in the Pacific Coast Council, which from the outset had argued for regional separation from the national movement, was followed by the visit of an AFL organizer to Los Angeles in June, while the coast federation was in session. Although the local Council was not represented at the regional gathering, it had just sent off an offer to entertain the 1894 convention in Los Angeles. This invitation in itself was a sign of tolerance toward Populism, for the Pacific Coast Council had gone further than the local central body in ratifying the articles of the People's Party. Yet the appeal of the AFL, then putting on an organizing drive, was sufficiently cogent to induce an abrupt reversal; in July, 1893, the Los Angeles Council withdrew from the coast federation on the plea of "excessive taxation."[19]

The ambiguity continued into the early months of 1894. The Los Angeles Council, asked to reconsider its withdrawal from the Pacific Coast Council, sent delegates to the third and final convention of the regional body, meeting in Sacramento in January, 1894. On this occasion, by concluding with the Farmers' Alliance an agreement for mutual assistance and by sanctioning a few more Populist principles, the coast

federation drew closer to the People's Party. It was not, however, willing to go to the point where the labor organization would be indistin-
guishable from the political party. Accordingly, the Coast Council summoned a Labor Congress to meet in San Francisco in February, and
assigned to it the possibly inflammatory political issues. The Farmers'
Alliance was to have equal representation with labor. The Congress,
as an organization distinct from the unions and from the People's Party,
would permit craftsmen wary of too deep partisan involvement to express freely their aspirations for political reform.[20]

The Los Angeles unions sent Jonathan Bailey (also representing the
Knights of Labor), W. A. Cole, and Frank Colver as delegates to the
Labor Congress. The degree of regard for Populist coöperation could be
measured by the selection of B. W. Batchelor of the Los Angeles
Farmers' Alliance as president of the convention. Socialist representatives were seated only after hesitation and over the protest of the southern California delegation, for the planners of the Congress held that
entanglement with fullfledged political parties was undesirable. For
this reason they had invited the Farmers' Alliance instead of the People's
Party. The recommendations adopted by the gathering included initiative and referendum; proportional representation; compulsory education; the legal eight-hour day; sanitary inspection of places of work;
employers' liability for on-the-job injuries to workers; abolition of contract systems; municipal ownership of public utilities; nationalization
of mines, railroads, telephone, and telegraph; direct issuance of money
by the government; abolition of national banks; graduated income tax;
government work for the unemployed; repeal of tramp and conspiracy
laws; universal suffrage; and a national labor holiday.[21] Clearly the
People's Party had left its mark upon the labor movement.

Yet organized labor on the Pacific Coast, by using a device such as
the Labor Congress to seal off politics in a separate compartment, had
definitely vetoed consolidation with the People's Party. Immediately
after the Congress, two San Francisco union printers, one of whom was
Michael McGlynn, began to publish the *New Union* and in an early
issue urged the continued severance of political and economic goals.
They gave added pertinence to this teaching by pointing to the downfall of the Knights of Labor through an excess of political agitation.
At about the same time the Los Angeles Council of Labor, beginning a
major reorganization, avowed a similar belief by rejecting that portion
of a proposed new constitution which enunciated "certain party principles." Union members, though endorsing the platform of the San
Francisco Labor Congress, strongly objected to the Council's constitu-

tional sanction of specific political policies. While the discussion over the proper form of a governing instrument was delaying Council re-organization, labor's columnist in the *Express,* in April, 1894, adopted the *New Union*'s line of reasoning and exhorted workers to divorce politics from unionism through the medium of political clubs outside craft organizations.[22]

Resolution of the complex political problem facing Los Angeles labor began with the Council's vote, on June 6, 1894, to open negotiations for affiliation with the American Federation of Labor. On July 11 the Typographical Union paid the $5 charter fee, and on September 19 the Council of Labor delegates took the oath of the national federation. A month later Cyren E. Fisk, of the printers' union, received his credentials as AFL organizer for southern California. The Los Angeles Council, unable to send a delegate to the 1894 national convention, arranged for representation by Andrew Furuseth of San Francisco. In November, a group of eight unions demonstrated the sincerity of labor's stand against political partisanship by repudiating a circular, wrongly attributed to them, which endorsed the Democratic nominee for mayor. The carpenters went further, inviting all four of the mayoralty candidates to present their views at a union meeting.[23]

After months of oscillating, the Los Angeles labor movement had taken an important step toward resolution of its political dilemma. Formal association with the American Federation of Labor, although not settling the perplexing problem for all of the future, did establish an explicit policy for the time being, at least. The affiliation also marked the beginning of the end of isolation for local labor. Greater responsiveness to national trends and closer adherence to Gompers' precepts were to follow. Practical benefits were not immediately forthcoming, it is true, but the wisdom of the move became apparent a few years later, when the most crucial threat to Los Angeles labor was recognized by the AFL through moral, financial, and direct organizational aid.

During the period when the Council of Labor was debating its re-organization and, later, negotiating with the AFL, the People's Party drew but scant attention from organized labor. A few unionists, among them S. E. Rude of the painters' union and Cyren Fisk, went to the party's state convention in May, 1894. Among those helping to name the Populist ticket for Los Angeles County in July were Fisk, Bailey, and Fred C. Wheeler, a carpenter who, after 1900, was a key figure in both the local trade-union and socialist movements. Such enthusiasts were simply expressing an individual preference, for the Council of Labor had already turned its back on the People's Party. In August,

1894, the central body openly affirmed its previous tacit decision by refusing representation at a Populist ratification meeting as "tantamount to an endorsement of the People's Party and its nominees." Shortly thereafter the break between the third party and organized labor in Los Angeles became irremediable. The *Farmer and Labor Review,* through all these vicissitudes still the dual organ of the Farmers' Alliance and the Council of Labor, was seeking revenge on the unions for their growing coolness toward the Populist movement. Sniping attacks revealed a sense of injury, even of outrage, because labor had chosen a divergent route. On August 15 the Council, nettled by the unprovoked barrage of criticism, withdrew official sanction from the *Farmer and Labor Review* and in September endorsed the Typographical Union's new semimonthly organ, entitled the *California Federationist* after the *American Federationist* of the AFL. Organized labor could hardly have made clearer its predilection for federated craft unionism and current distaste for partisan politics.[24]

The People's Party, shunned by organized labor, became more and more preoccupied with internal stresses. The 1894 campaign generated open conflict on the question of fusion with the Democratic Party, an issue which had begun to cause trouble early in the previous year. In January, 1893, Los Angeles Populists denounced the recently elected Democratic-Populist Congressman Marion Cannon as a traitor to the People's Party. Two months later a local branch of the Industrial Legion spoke out against the endorsement of other-party nominees on the grounds that fusion candidates in various states, patently without Populist convictions, used the third party only to insure election. Such protests induced the California Populist convention in May, 1894, to write a nonfusion plank into the state party platform. When the People's Party of Los Angeles County convened to nominate a ticket in July, the state provision against fusion did not prevent bitter quarrels over the question of alliance with the Democratic Party. Further dissension arose from a squabble over the chairmanship of the county central committee; Populists with socialist leanings wanted to place one of their number in the key post. The socialists lost out, and the fusion issue was compromised with the naming of some Populists and the endorsing of some Democrats.[25] In the 1894 elections the People's Party, both nationally and locally, received a heavier vote than in 1892, despite internal friction over fusion and, in Los Angeles, a decline in official labor support. The recognized strength of the third party, coupled with the ill effects of the Panic of 1893 and President Cleveland's sanction of the unpopular injunction in the Pullman strike of 1894, frightened the Democrats into a more insistent advocacy of Populist principles. They had agitated for fusion before the elections, but after the Populists' signal demonstration at the polls the Democrats wanted more than ever to have the parties coalesce. The Democratic Party, like the People's Party, was split on the issue of fusion, but the pro-Populist faction took over the 1896 convention and nominated William Jennings Bryan on a platform demanding free silver coinage and other Populist measures. Most of the Populists, though it meant the end of their party, supported the Bryan ticket. The People's Party in Los Angeles County likewise consummated an alliance with the Democrats, thus sacrificing its independent identity.[26]

The contributions of the People's Party cannot be measured solely in terms of its vote-getting ability or its impact on the Democratic Party. Nor can its few years of life as a functioning instrument gauge its influence on the subsequent history of the United States. Populist philosophy can be reduced to two basic interwoven propositions: that the government must represent and be guided by all the people instead of merely the rich and influential; and that the people must use their power through government to bring under reasonable control those who exploit the poor and downtrodden. Many of the tenets of the People's Party have since become law and are today accepted as commonplaces, such as woman suffrage and the direct election of United States senators. Others, more subtly, have permeated political thinking and directed it into channels leading to remedial legislation akin to that demanded by the Populists. As John D. Hicks, the outstanding authority on the People's Party, has said, "Thanks to this triumph of Populist principles, one may almost say that, in so far as political devices can insure it, the people now rule."[27]

XII. ON TO WASHINGTON

THE BELIEFS of the People's Party enjoyed a pervasive currency in many quarters during the early and middle 1890's. Coxey's Army, an organization of unemployed whose march to Washington in 1894 originated in the depression following the Panic of 1893, had features in common with Populism. The social inequities leading to farmer-worker coöperation in the People's Party were the mainspring of the army, as unemployed mining and industrial workers banded together for a protest at the nation's capital against their economic distress. The inflationary schemes that began with the Greenback Labor Party, and moved through the Farmers' Alliance to the People's Party, found a place in the Coxey program; the Populists, though demanding far broader reforms, saw in the industrial army an agency for partial realization of their objectives. Some of them joined the march and stimulated Populist thinking among the Coxeyites, while others gave welcome help along the way.[1]

Jacob S. Coxey, an Ohio farmer and retired businessman, led the army which has perpetuated his name. He had amassed a fortune estimated at $200,000 by 1894, but earlier experience as a laborer plus a humanitarian bent had long inclined him toward social reform. Following admission to the Greenback Party in 1876, he had retained through his later prosperous years ambitions for the economic betterment of society. In 1892 he drafted for presentation to Congress a bill which encompassed his cardinal precepts: (a) that the government should hire the unemployed to build good roads and (b) it should pay them with fiat money. This would solve in part the problem of unemployment, would provide needed highways, and would expand the amount of money in circulation. When Congress failed to act, and the Panic of 1893 vastly increased unemployment, Coxey decided to organize an industrial army as an invincible living protest at the very seat of government against hardships so universal that they could not be blamed on individual inadequacies.[2]

The essence of Coxey's idea for assembling and marching the unemployed to Washington came from Carl Browne, once of Los Angeles. Browne described how bands of unemployed in California wandered from place to place in search of work or relief, and Coxey adapted the technique to his own purposes on a much wider scale. In an unusually colorful career, even for a Californian of the early days, Browne had been printer, editor, painter, cartoonist, rancher, politician, and labor agitator. Coxey, who saw the potential usefulness of these varied qualifications, prevailed upon Browne to become his lieutenant in the industrial movement. Browne's belief that he and Coxey, as a joint reincarnation of Christ, could not fail to have their way with Congress, introduced religious overtones which, for a time, threatened to obscure the economic bases for the enterprise, but in the end proved to have slight influence within the army.[3]

Coxey's Army, sometimes called the Commonweal or the Commonweal of Christ, was organized at Massillon, Ohio, in November, 1893. Numbering a little over a hundred, it began the trek to Washington on March 23, 1894, in military formation with Coxey as commanding general and Browne as marshal. Although, even with additions along the way, the Massillon contingent seldom totaled more than three hundred, other groups, marching simultaneously from all parts of the country under local leadership, gave substance to Coxey's hope of heading an army of one hundred thousand at the nation's capital. Most of the marchers were unskilled and unorganized workers earnestly seeking help in their predicament, but they were sometimes joined by vagrants on the lookout for free provisions. The hardships on the journey, including bad roads, bad food, and bad weather, quickly discouraged these hangers-on, and they gradually dropped out. Because unemployment affected all levels of the working class, some holders of union cards fell in with Coxey's Army on the march to Washington. Although organized labor did not play an integral part in the Coxey movement, Gompers and the AFL approved its aims and methods, and an occasional union group, such as the Central Labor Union and the Building Trades Council of Chicago, gave real help.[4]

The depression was severe in southern California, with unemployment plaguing craft unionists as well as the unorganized and unskilled. In the summer of 1893, five hundred of the unemployed petitioned the City Council for a public works program. When no response was forthcoming, and when new bands of jobless crowded into the city during the fall and winter, the press joined the clamor for city and county relief measures. In January, 1894, new pressure was brought to bear on the city authorities by a Council of Labor committee, including the manager of the Free Labor Bureau, who could speak convincingly of his agency's inability to meet the crisis. At last the City Council was stirred to action, and appropriated $10,000 for a public works program for a six-week trial period. The amount, even with subsequent additions, was insufficient to take care of all those pleading for work, and the undertaking bogged down altogether when the County Board of Supervisors refused to share the burden. Although the Council of Labor continued to agitate for public aid, no relief commensurate with the emergency was provided.[5]

The inadequacy of local measures led to organization of the Los Angeles unemployed by General Lewis C. Fry, whose army was the first and one of the two largest on the Pacific Coast. In all, three regiments totaling about one thousand men left Los Angeles for the long hike to Washington. Fry, through strict discipline and military procedures, made his group one of the most thoroughly organized and well-behaved contingents in the whole Coxey movement. He conceived the idea of forming a local industrial army—quite independently of Coxey, he claimed—in February, 1894, just as the city work for the unemployed was coming to an end. Fry was not simply a quasi-military leader of petitioners for jobs; he had done some serious thinking on the root evils responsible for the current troubles. He evolved a long-range remedial program of government procedures, including employment of the idle on western irrigation projects and reclamation and cultivation of desert areas, nationalization of railroads and industry, and issuance of scrip for financial transactions. For immediate presentation at Washington, he had his army adopt, on March 5, a simple three-point plan: federal work for the unemployed, no immigration for ten years, and no alien ownership of land.[6]

A concrete schedule of this kind, plus official disregard of still another plea for public relief, stimulated rapid growth of Fry's army. Over eight hundred men had enlisted by the middle of March. For the most part citizens were inclined to a sympathetic view of these despairing workers who, after a difficult traverse of mountain and desert, could look forward at best to a dubious welcome at Washington. Yet even so doughty a reformer as Isaac Kinley went against the trend, criticizing the army as a "certain mode of destruction" for the labor movement.[7] To prepare for departure, Fry procured donations of blankets and food from generous well-wishers, wrote to the Secretary of War demanding subsistence along the way, asked the Santa Fe Railroad for free transportation, and appealed to the Merchants' Association for provisions to last five days. Although the railroad and the merchants both responded negatively, and no answer came from Washington, Fry decided, nonetheless, to get his army moving.[8]

On March 16, eight days before Coxey's start, Fry left Los Angeles on foot with six hundred men, entrusting some two hundred left behind to Arthur Vinette, who had taken under his capacious wing the jobless and destitute. Fry's men traveled largely by train after leaving San Bernardino, and were well treated at first, but on March 21, Fry was arrested at El Paso for vagrancy. When the charge was dismissed, the citizens of the inhospitable town corrected the initial affront by hiring a special train to further the army on its way East. By the time Fry reached Little Rock on April 1, he had under his command sixteen companies of fifty each. Most of the group were workingmen or farm hands, with only a negligible number of tramps.[9]

At St. Louis on April 3, Fry divided his army into two sections, selecting Colonel Thomas Galvin as leader of the second. Galvin reached Washington on May 30 with two hundred men. He was one of the most efficient of the Commonweal commanders, and was the only one to stick with his men through all the subsequent tribulations in Washington. Toward the end of April, Fry's army arrived at Indianapolis on a purloined freight train. There, real trouble was encountered as the citizens refused the marchers food, the railroads denied them transportation, and the press was hostile. To raise funds, Fry's men began to sell copies of the recently published *Story of the Commonweal,* written by a Coxeyite named Henry Vincent. On May 7, the army finally left Indianapolis on foot and arrived a month later at Parkersburg, West Virginia, where it split into three companies to hasten progress. Fry, with two hundred followers, arrived in Washington on June 28, after an arduous journey lasting three months and ten days.[10]

Meanwhile, Vinette had been busy securing help for the men left in Los Angeles. Free board and lodging, medical attendance, meal tickets, and some private and public jobs were provided at his urging. The City Council was responsible for a portion of the aid, and in addition appealed for private subscriptions. Although Vinette pleaded that most of the men would rather find jobs at home than set off for Washington, he felt their chances were too slim and proceeded to organize a second regiment. During the preparations, a committee of the unemployed headed by Vinette demanded on March 26 that the City Council make jobs for them or else give them specific assistance toward their coming journey. This ultimatum was endorsed by the Populists, the Knights of Labor, and the unions of electrical workers, painters, and cooks.[11]

When the Council made no response, 160 of the men voted to leave. Vinette's circular asking Los Angeles citizens for food, blankets, and other supplies brought in additional contributions, but his negotiations for rail transportation were as fruitless as Fry's had been. On April 2, Vinette and his army left on foot. They made good progress at first, reaching San Bernardino on the 7th. Enlistments along the way had brought the group up to two hundred men, whose exemplary conduct had earned the respect and help of people on the route. But luck changed at San Bernardino. When requests for rail transportation across the desert were denied, Vinette asked the citizens to subscribe money for the necessary fares. Instead of doing so, the populace hastily organized a Committee of Public Safety which forced the marchers to leave the city. On April 14, Vinette and his men established Camp Determination at Colton, a town reputedly friendly to the Industrial Army.[12]

Confidence in the helpfulness of Colton residents was misplaced, for there Vinette's group encountered its most serious trouble. Attempted seizure of a freight train for the trans-desert trip resulted in the arrest of eight leaders, including Vinette. Charges of evading payment of railroad fares and inciting to riot were lodged against them on April 17. The first count was dismissed on insufficient evidence, but the defendants were tried on the riot charge in Superior Court in Los Angeles on May 10. When the case was dismissed on a technicality, Populist spectators, who had crowded the courtroom to lend friendly support, vociferously cheered the outcome and made Vinette and his colleagues momentary heroes in a righteous cause. During the period between the arrests and the trial, the rank and file at Camp Determination had begun to drift away, despite financial aid from Farmers' Alliances and other Populist groups. Nevertheless, the main portion of Vinette's regiment, still numbering over 160, set out again on April 23. But the desert took its toll and spelled the finish of the army. Early in May, thirty-five men left Palm Springs for Indio and were never heard from again.[13]

After his trial Vinette immediately began arrangements for a third Los Angeles contingent. By May 16 he had enrolled eighty men, some of whom had wandered back to the city from his earlier venture. When the Southern Pacific refused to transport the group free of charge, a few of Vinette's men, accused of trying to steal a train, were arrested and later acquitted. On his second attempt to get to Washington, Vinette made better progress; by the end of June his advance guard was in Kansas City, with the rest of the group scattered over Kansas and Colorado. The smallness of the group made it particularly vulnerable to police interference, and its lateness meant that hospitality en route was all but exhausted. Beset by these unusual difficulties, the third Los Angeles regiment, reduced to a bare handful of eleven men, did not reach Washington until July 25, some weeks after the main Coxey movement had collapsed.[14]

It is likely that Vinette, absorbed in the problems of his march and determined to reach his long-sought goal, was ignorant of Coxey's fate. His disappointment upon arrival must therefore have been the more bitter. Coxey and Browne had reached Washington on May 1, all set for a public demonstration to gain sympathy for their demands upon Congress. In defiance of a previous warning, Coxey paraded his men through the Capitol grounds. For this offense he and Browne were arrested and punished by a twenty-day imprisonment and in addition were fined $5 each for walking on the grass, a ludicrous contretemps for leaders of such lofty purpose. Although Coxey and Browne were released on bail, they could not obtain hearings before Congressional committees to present the relief program. The army gradually disintegrated, and by the middle of June it had almost completely dispersed without accomplishing anything.[15]

Other causes besides the Washington fiasco helped precipitate the decline of Coxeyism. Prosecutions for train-stealing became more frequent as early sympathy for the marchers gave way to growing irritation with their depredations. In June, 1894, the Pullman strike tied up the railroads, making progress to Washington almost impossible and diverting public attention to an apparently more serious outbreak of industrial unrest. The novelty of the adventure gradually wore off, and discouragement mounted with lessening friendliness and increasing transport difficulties. Although remnants of armies continued to straggle into Washington and set up encampments, the public had lost interest. With the food shortage becoming urgent, the Commissioners of the District of Columbia appropriated funds to send the men home in August. Those who remained in the vicinity of Washington suffered arrest and forcible eviction by the authorities of Maryland and Virginia. Estimates of the army's size vary widely, but it is a reasonable assumption that about ten thousand men from all sections of the country took part in the ill-starred march to Washington.[16]

Although Coxey's Army failed of its purpose, there had arisen during Vinette's trials and travels a faint stirring of public responsibility for the unemployed in Los Angeles. In the latter part of April, 1894, prominent citizens presided over mass meetings which outlined a plan to have unemployed county residents construct a boulevard between Los Angeles and Pasadena at wages of $1 a day. Despite a great deal of talk and agitation, the proposal was simply allowed to die. In June the City Council appropriated $100 a week for distribution among the poor, a minimal sum which could have done no more than touch the fringes of current hardship. The depression was more lasting than the Council's charity, and when new pleas for aid were presented in December, 1894, the authorities merely referred them to the incoming Council.[17]

As before, official inertia forced the unemployed to find a remedy of their own. With the help of several Populist leaders, they organized the

New Era Labor Exchange in December. During its few months of life in the winter of 1894–1895, this organization, claiming about three hundred members, established a coöperative hand laundry and a vegetable garden, and offered to contract for orange picking. All proceeds were to be divided among the members. The New Era Labor Exchange unsuccessfully applied to the City Council for assistance and, though commended as infinitely preferable to the march on Washington, was unable to survive after February, 1895.[18]

The industrial army movement was fomented in Los Angeles during the period when the craft unions were preoccupied with questions of national or regional, political or nonpolitical affiliations. Their failure to make a pronounced contribution to the "On to Washington" project stemmed in part from their current distrust of the People's Party, which, in numerous ways, injected itself into the Coxey movement. Before Coxeyism had altogether died out, another great national upheaval, also with local manifestations, signalized continuance of the industrial unrest whose provenance lay in the Panic of 1893. The Pullman strike in the summer of 1894 gave the Populists another opportunity to solicit labor support. The appeal of Populism, however, was less direct than it had been in the Coxey movement and, in Los Angeles, considerably less convincing. The local branch of the American Railway Union, which conducted the Pullman strike, chose alliance with the Council of Labor rather than with the People's Party.

XIII. THE PULLMAN STRIKE

IN 1894, the American Railway Union became a national cynosure through its conduct of the Pullman strike—the outstanding railroad controversy of the decade. Originating in employees' grievances against the Pullman Palace Car Company in Pullman, near Chicago, the strike in some communities involved the railroad brotherhoods, the Knights of Labor, and the American Federation of Labor, but all these were overshadowed by the militant ARU under the leadership of Eugene V. Debs.

The Pullman strike was important to local labor history for two reasons: it was the first labor dispute of national proportions to impinge seriously on Los Angeles, and it led to the integration of the local American Railway Union with the Los Angeles Council of Labor, a clear departure from a long-established trend. From the beginning, railroad workers had refrained from making common cause with other craftsmen, except on rare occasions. The joint committee for the *Times* boycott at the end of 1893 marked the first real collaboration between Los Angeles craft unions and railroad brotherhoods. Although neither permanent nor rewarding, the alliance signalized the need for unity against the *Times'* growing power. The demonstration that the gap could be bridged between the two types of organization prepared, in some degree, for the far closer tie between the local labor movement and the American Railway Union.

The history of railroad unionism in Los Angeles began with the organization of Lodge No. 97 of the Brotherhood of Locomotive Firemen and Division No. 5 of the Brotherhood of Locomotive Engineers in 1882. By 1886, Division No. 111 of the Order of Railway Conductors and Lodge No. 74 of the Brotherhood of Railroad Brakemen had been added, and in 1887, Los Angeles Lodge No. 43 of the Switchmen's Mutual Aid Association was organized. By 1891 a new lodge of firemen, No. 90, had been formed. From the beginning these railroad organizations differed from local craft unions in two important particulars: without exception they were formed as affiliates of national bodies, and they were primarily benevolent and charitable societies. Since the national brotherhoods, desiring no alliance with militant craft unionism, held aloof from the American Federation of Labor, their local branches felt no compulsion to work with Los Angeles craft unions. Furthermore, as benefit organizations, the railroad unions enjoyed the confidence of the Los Angeles press and public to a degree never vouchsafed to unions which regarded strikes and boycotts as justifiable weapons. A prevailing antistrike sentiment, and marked disinterest in the closed shop among railroad workers during this period, deepened the gulf separating them from other unionists.[1]

Nevertheless, the brotherhoods sometimes found that the strike had persuasive power, and did resort to its use. Between 1887 and 1893 the local branches of engineers, switchmen, and brakemen engaged in a series of disputes with both the Southern Pacific and Santa Fe systems. None of these strikes was prolonged or important; most of them were designed to raise or maintain wages, to shorten hours, to prevent discharges, and to establish seniority rights. Several of the disputes were compromised, and about half of the rest marked victories for labor.[2]

Occasional departure from an avowed antistrike policy by the brotherhoods was not the only sign that railroaders saw merit in the walkout. Individuals, too, nursed a desire for more forthright unionism. Long-standing disaffection among members of the national Order of Railway Conductors over an antistrike provision in the constitution culminated in the formation of a rival union toward the end of 1888.

The national Brotherhood of Railway Conductors was organized in Los Angeles in November, 1888, by Santa Fe employees whose immediate impetus was fear that the company would extend a new retrenchment policy to conductors. The constitution sanctioned the use of strikes and named Los Angeles as national headquarters for the first year. Los Angeles Division No. 1 was formed on December 9, and soon claimed that its quick popularity had reduced the local Order of Railway Conductors to negligible strength. Similarly, the Order yielded to the Brotherhood in other parts of the West, as the new movement spread rapidly in ever-widening circles. Within a year the Brotherhood comprised thirty-two divisions with two thousand members throughout the United States; twenty-eight of them, from nineteen states, sent delegates to the first annual convention in Los Angeles in September, 1889.[3]

The convention was a gala affair. The city's hearty welcome and the establishment of friendly relations with the local Brotherhoods of Firemen, Engineers, and Brakemen promised cordial acceptance of the new organization of conductors. Proceeding on the assumption of an assured future, the Brotherhood appointed its national officers as salaried organizers, adopted an insurance plan, and fixed Los Angeles as permanent national headquarters. But these preparations were wasted, for as soon as the Order of Railway Conductors became aware of its rival's popularity, it renounced the antistrike policy. With the main contention between the two organizations disposed of, the Brotherhood disbanded in 1891 and its members flocked back to the Order.[4]

Another group of railroad workers took warning from the conductors' experience. In 1891, the Order of Railroad Telegraphers rescinded its antistrike policy. Immediately the Southern Pacific refused further recognition of the union and announced that it would discharge any members in its employ. The company's request for affidavits of non-membership, present and/or future, precipitated a system-wide strike on December 15, 1891. Coincidentally the Order won its first victory by striking against the Santa Fe for a wage increase. Thus encouraged, the telegraphers forced the Southern Pacific to recognize the union and reinstate the strikers. A Los Angeles branch of the Order of Telegraphers was established during the crisis.[5]

In April, 1893, a wage dispute between the employees and officials of the Terminal Railroad, an independent local company with lines connecting Los Angeles and San Pedro, illustrated the close national supervision characteristic of the railroad unions. The road, unable to pay union wage scales, worked its men twelve hours a day with no overtime pay. Instead of striking, the employees induced national officers of the Order of Railway Conductors and of the Brotherhoods of Engineers and Firemen to come to Los Angeles to settle the controversy. Their conferences with company representatives elicited a promise to raise wages as soon as financially possible, and with this the workers had to be content.[6]

Although the brotherhoods had little in common with the Los Angeles labor movement, signs of a friendly interest began to appear in 1890. In October of that year, the Brotherhood of Railroad Trainmen (formerly the Brotherhood of Brakemen) held its seventh annual convention in Los Angeles. Local craftsmen, with the fight against the *Times* then uppermost in their minds, were gratified when the trainmen's convention endorsed the printers' strike. A year later a more practical step followed this initial overture. A delegation from the various local railroad organizations threatened to boycott a clothing store unless it discontinued patronage of the *Times,* and the store immediately cut down the size of its advertisement.[7] From such gestures, coöperation with the joint committee for the *Times* boycott in the fall of 1893 developed naturally. Still another railroad union, though not participating in the joint committee, supported a different enterprise of the local labor movement. In September, 1893, the recently organized Los Angeles Lodge No. 85 of the Brotherhood of Railway Carmen joined the anti-Chinese crusade then at its height by boycotting firms and individuals employing Chinese help of any kind.[8] These expressions of amity helped create a harmony soon to be of valuable assistance to the new American Railway Union.

In creating the American Railway Union, Debs, formerly an officer of the Brotherhood of Locomotive Firemen and editor of its magazine, protested the exclusiveness of all the railroad unions. In a prospectus issued in the spring of 1893, he stated that the organization would be open to all railroad employees, whether skilled or unskilled and whether members or nonmembers of the brotherhoods. Eligibility was so liberally interpreted that all workers, including even miners or long-shoremen, would be able to join if they were on railroad payrolls. To make admission even easier and more attractive, especially for the un-skilled, the ARU would charge lower fees and dues than the brother-hoods and would eventually provide similar benefits. These ideas were embodied in the constitution adopted when the American Railway Union was formally organized in Chicago on June 20, 1893, with Debs as president and George W. Howard, formerly of the Order of Railway Conductors, as vice-president. Although preferring the old brotherhood policy of avoiding strikes and boycotts, the union permitted branches engaged in disputes to sanction local walkouts if all efforts at mediation had failed. National headquarters could not call a strike without the approval of local unions whose interests were involved.[9]

The American Railway Union was instantly popular. Although the brotherhoods had misgivings, some of their members joined the new organization. But the great majority of converts came from the ranks of hitherto unorganized workers, whose grievances had received scant attention and who saw in Debs' union a promise of fair treatment for even the most inarticulate. Another stimulus to the development of the ARU was a change in the policy of the General Managers' Association, formed in 1886 by railroads with termini in Chicago and holding con-tracts with the Pullman Company. The Association originally proposed to establish uniform rates, but after the Panic of 1893 it began a system-atic reduction of wages. Because the brotherhoods offered only feeble opposition, workers recognized in the ARU a valuable counterpoise to the employers' organization, an instrument which could obtain for "the much oppressed some of the rights to which they were justly entitled." Growing with the rapidity of wildfire, the ARU boasted a membership of one hundred thousand at the end of its first year.[10]

The vitality of the national was reflected in Los Angeles Local No. 80. Formed by 138 charter members on November 28, 1893, it enjoyed astounding growth. Within a week the membership had jumped to 250 and, by the time of the strike in 1894, to one thousand. Although Debs' visit to Los Angeles in the spring of 1894 accounted for some of the popularity, an equally potent stimulus was the tardiness of the Southern Pacific in meeting its payrolls after the Panic of 1893. Employees, provoked beyond endurance and running heavily into debt, looked to the ARU as a likely means of compelling the railroad to discharge its obligations. The Southern Pacific, however, exhibiting no fear of the new organization, simply dismissed those employees known to be members. Lemuel Biddle, a union leader who had incautiously expressed unpopular political opinions, fell a victim to this policy. Black-listing, a weapon used frequently against the ARU, necessitated hidden operations and membership lists. As one ARU man expressed it, "No man knows or can tell whether his co-worker is a member or not. This system is used to avoid the hirelings of the company so they cannot possibly expose any member. . . ." Such persecution did not intimidate the valiant members of Local No. 80. By secretly distributing circulars over a wide area, they helped organize all the Southern Pacific chapters of the ARU and claimed for themselves the honor of belonging to the "banner local."[11]

During the spring of 1894, employees of the Pullman Company were beginning to find the almost feudal paternalism of George Pullman, founder and owner, an intolerable burden. Never very happy over conditions in the company-owned town, they became increasingly restive when business reverses after the Panic of 1893 caused management to cut wages without reducing rents and other living costs. Delay in a promised investigation of alleged shop abuses—black-listing, arbitrary dismissals, and favoritism—intensified dissatisfaction. In March and April of 1894, the workers began to organize branches of the American Railway Union, to which they were eligible because the Pullman Company owned and operated a few miles of railroad. Within a short time they had formed nineteen unions with a total of four thousand members.[12]

Association with a large and flourishing national union encouraged the Pullman employees to believe that their sufferings were at last to be alleviated, and they pressed for quick action. The American Railway Union, however, lacking financial reserves for a major crisis and constitutionally advocating peaceful settlements whenever possible, counseled against any precipitancy. But the workers were too impatient to await the slow processes of mediation, and on May 11, 1894, struck for restoration of predepression wages, reduction of rents, and correction of shop abuses. With the step irrevocably taken, the ARU gamely backed its Pullman members. Balked in an attempt to settle the dispute by the company's refusal to meet with union representatives, the ARU voted a boycott on Pullman cars, effective June 26, and assessed its entire membership ten cents a week to restore the rapidly diminishing relief funds.[13]

Although the railroad brotherhoods did not sanction the boycott, some of their members who did not belong to the ARU, as well as other workers, used the opportunity to strike because of grievances of their own. In an almost completely spontaneous walkout, an estimated eighteen thousand men paralyzed service on many railroads by June 28. The Pullman strike had begun. At its greatest extent it involved twenty-seven states and territories and tied up all transcontinental lines except the Great Northern. Some of the roads, including both the Southern Pacific and the Santa Fe, were struck on Debs' order because they discharged workers for refusing to handle Pullman cars. Thus the strike was resolved into a contest between the American Railway Union and the General Managers' Association.[14]

The ARU, however, was fighting the Pullman Company, not the railroads, and it had authorized walkouts only because the boycott was not being observed. To stress the union's point, strikers asserted their readiness to handle trains which did not carry Pullman cars. But the General Managers' Association, with its teeth into a good scrap which might easily spell the ruin of the ARU, interpreted the strike as an attack on the United States government through interference with the mails. Knowing that members of the ARU would not handle Pullmans, the roads were determined to run only fully equipped trains. Moreover, they deliberately curtailed rail service to aggravate the inconvenience caused by the strike.[15] Foisting the blame for interruption of transportation and of mail service on the strikers, the General Managers' Association gained the support of both the federal authorities and the general public. The people, though sympathetic to the Pullman employees, did not like the intervention of the ARU and the consequent disruption of facilities on lines not even remotely connected with Pullman Company policies.[16]

Los Angeles became involved when Debs called strikes against the Santa Fe and the Southern Pacific. By the end of June, only four days after the boycott went into effect, three thousand men were out of work in the city; some engineers and firemen quit as members of the ARU, though their local brotherhoods were awaiting national decisions before taking a definite stand. Traffic was stalled except for local service, jeopardizing the tourist trade and the marketing of perishable crops. Nevertheless, hatred of the Southern Pacific monopoly went deep enough in California to make public reaction to the strike markedly different from that in other parts of the country; the employees were upheld even by farmers and others suffering financial loss. The press, with such exceptions as the Los Angeles *Times,* also stood by the men.[17]

The Southern Pacific and the Santa Fe followed the course marked out by the General Managers' Association. Acting on appeals from both roads, the United States District Attorney in Los Angeles, George Denis, obtained permission from Attorney General Richard Olney (of known antilabor proclivities[18]) to prosecute the strikers for interference with interstate commerce and passage of the mails. On June 29, Judge Erskine M. Ross, of the United States District Court in Los Angeles, summoned a federal grand jury to determine whether anyone was guilty of conspiracy against the government through such obstructions. The strikers, to counter the allegation that they were acting against the public interest, affirmed their willingness to handle mail cars and, provided the discharged men were reinstated, to move everything but Pullmans. In their opinion the only conspiracy afoot was the collusion between the railroads and the Pullman Company to stop all traffic rather than operate without Pullman cars. Denis retorted that interference with a train carrying mail was a criminal offense, regardless of what other cars were being hauled.[19]

Attacking from another angle, the Southern California Railway prevailed upon Judge Ross to issue, on June 30, an interlocutory writ of injunction directing its employees either to return to work or formally resign their jobs. Use of the unpopular injunction not only strengthened the strikers' determination to stay out, but also rallied support behind them. Although the major brotherhoods were as yet uncommitted, the local Order of Railroad Telegraphers struck against the Santa Fe in defiance of instructions from national headquarters. Early in July, the Los Angeles unions of printers, pressmen, retail clerks, plumbers, bakers, and carpenters endorsed the ARU's fight and contributed monetary aid. The Brotherhood of Locomotive Engineers gave $50. The Council of Labor held a special meeting to assure the strikers of its wholehearted support. Favorable sentiments were also expressed at mass meetings on June 30 and July 2 by members of craft unions and the People's Party. When the Southern Pacific announced that all employees not reporting for work by 10 A.M. on July 4 would automatically be discharged, large numbers of switchmen, firemen, and carmen resigned their jobs before the deadline. By this time all traffic, including local service, was at a standstill.[20]

Meanwhile, District Attorney Denis had telegraphed Olney that illness kept United States Marshal Covarrubias from executing the processes of the courts and preventing obstruction of the mails. To take care of the emergency, six companies of federal troops were dispatched from San Francisco and arrived on July 4. Los Angeles was the first community in California and one of the first four in the country to suffer the intervention of armed forces. To other localities, however, troops were sent to enforce a sweeping government injunction issued in Chicago on July 2, and Denis was careful to stress that only the marshal's incapacitation necessitated troops in Los Angeles, where everything had been peaceful.[21]

Throughout the strike Los Angeles remained remarkably free of violence, though other California communities, notably Sacramento, were not so fortunate. Northern California, lacking the advantage of competing transcontinental lines, was more thoroughly in the grip of the Southern Pacific, and public feeling consequently ran higher. Curiously, one disturbance in Los Angeles arose from the refusal of newsboys to handle the *Times* because of its outspoken criticism of the strikers. Five of the boys were arrested on July 5 on a charge of disturbing the peace after they assaulted a carrier faithful to the *Times* and tore up his papers. The court fined several of the defendants $10, but suspended sentence on promise of good behavior. That same day union printers on the *Herald* entertained the young boycotters at dinner, and on the 7th, the Typographical Union helped them organize Los Angeles Newsboys' Union No. 1, which affiliated with the Council of Labor on July 11. The recently established News and Working Boys' Home turned out some of the residents who belonged to the union.[22]

Only one act of violence was directly attributed to a Los Angeles ARU member. On July 12 a Southern Pacific engineer named Henry Patterson was arrested on a charge of assault against Jesse Martin, another engineer, with intent to murder. Patterson, apprehended in the vicinity of the crime, insisted he had not fired the shot which wounded Martin. His trial in Superior Court in the fall of 1894 was lengthy and confused, but the inability of two juries to agree indicates that the evidence against Patterson was not conclusive.[23]

About the time that federal troops arrived in Los Angeles, the grand jury brought indictments against six local ARU leaders: Philip Stanwood, president; W. H. Clune, secretary; A. T. Johnson, Isaac Ross, C. T. Buchanan, and Richard Gallagher. They were arrested on July 4, under the Sherman Antitrust Act, for conspiring to obstruct United States mails and interstate commerce. The strikers' dismay at federal intervention and arrest of their leaders deepened with the realization that railroad traffic was beginning to move despite the boycott. On July 5 the Santa Fe sent out a San Diego train manned by company officials and a nonunion fireman, and the Southern Pacific trains for Santa Barbara and Santa Ana, both operated by regular brotherhood crews, left unmolested. Once the break was made, increasing numbers of brotherhood members reported for work, and each day witnessed more train departures and arrivals. Within a few days local traffic was almost restored, and on July 7 the Santa Fe sent out the first overland train with a guard of troops. Nevertheless, the ARU, in constant communication with national headquarters in Chicago, stood firm. Despite financial hardship only a few of its members went back to work. By soliciting subscriptions from friendly businessmen and opening a free kitchen, the union was able to care for the most needy. It showed a still unbroken spirit by refusing to endorse a Merchants' Association memorial to President Grover Cleveland proposing arbitration at the national level.[24]

Although the strikers courageously kept up their fight, defeat was almost upon them. By July 12 the strike was virtually over in Los Angeles. Local traffic had reached prestrike proportions, freight was beginning to move, and overland trains with Pullman cars were operating on an almost complete schedule. Firemen and switchmen were still holding out with the ARU, but engineers, conductors, and other employees were seeking reinstatement in increasing numbers. The news that Debs and other national officers had been arrested on July 10 accelerated the back-to-work movement. After July 15 military escorts for trains were discontinued, though the troops did not leave the city for another month.[25]

By July 13 the Chicago strike was at an end, but Debs stubbornly resisted acknowledgment of failure. On July 15 he publicly stated: "We will win our fight in the West because we are better organized there. . . . Men there are loyal, fraternal and true. When they believe they are right, they go out and stay out until the fight is over."[26] Debs was counting heavily on the widespread dislike of the Southern Pacific, which disposed even troops and newspapers to be more friendly to the strikers in California than elsewhere. But his hopes for continuing resistance were doomed. By July 18 the cause of the American Railway Union was lost everywhere. In Los Angeles, service had been completely restored. Most of the railroads reëmployed the strikers, barring only their leaders; the Santa Fe took back fewer men than the Southern Pacific. Despite forebodings, the damage caused by the strike in southern California was not excessive.[27]

The ARU's complete defeat in the Pullman strike eventually led to its disintegration, but some branches survived for a few years. The

Los Angeles local kept going, largely to defend the six leaders who had been arrested for conspiracy. Two of them, Buchanan and Gallagher, were sentenced late in September, 1894, to eighteen months in the county jail and fined $1,000 each. The other four were not tried until November. The prosecution felt that its case was clear-cut, maintaining that the defendants had ordered union members not to handle trains including Pullmans, regardless of whether those trains carried mail. Nevertheless, it took the jury twenty-four hours to reach a verdict of guilty. The sentence, delayed until December 6 so that the defendants could prepare an appeal, was eighteen months in the county jail and a nominal fine of $1 each. Judge Ross denied a new trial and said that he had imposed a lighter punishment than the warranted $1,000 fine and two years' penitentiary imprisonment because the offenses were committed in the heat of a strike. Stanwood, Clune, and Ross were permitted to appeal directly to the United States Supreme Court, but Johnson, too ill to endure further litigation, decided to serve his term, and a few months later was pardoned.[28]

The case of the Los Angeles union leaders was a conspicuous feature of the Pullman strike, the more so because Debs, the outstanding figure in the ARU, was tried only for contempt after conspiracy charges against him were dropped. The Los Angeles local undertook the task of raising a defense fund for its members' Supreme Court appeal. It first broadcast a plea for donations throughout the state of California and then, to solidify local sentiment, decided to affiliate with the Los Angeles Council of Labor. In February, 1894, shortly after the ARU was organized in Los Angeles, it had asked to join the Council, contingent upon its right to independent political action and adoption of proportional representation by the central body. At that time the Council had made too little progress in its own reorganization to give an out-of-hand answer to any individual union, and the application lapsed. Now, however, the ARU was in no position to dictate terms, for it needed all the help it could get. By March, 1895, its delegates were seated in the Council, a good vantage point for raising money. Los Angeles unions were generous in their assistance to the ARU; especially noteworthy contributions came from the printers, plumbers, cooks, and musicians. The San Francisco Typographical Union was also a prominent donor. In the spring of 1895, Local No. 80 brought Debs to California for a speaking tour—a powerful aid in the drive for funds.[29]

All this work was in the end to no avail, for the Supreme Court denied the appeal of Stanwood, Ross, and Clune in the fall of 1895. The prosecution successfully contended that a union which prevented

men from working and thereby interfered with the mails was subject
to the conspiracy statute, though the offense itself was only a misdemeanor. When the decision was handed down, the General Assembly
of the Knights of Labor, itself a contributor to the defense fund, passed
rather extreme resolutions condemning the Supreme Court and the
judiciary of California and Illinois and recommending popular election
of federal judges. The Los Angeles Council of Labor showed its disapproval of judicial proceedings in the Pullman strike by endorsing
these resolutions at a mass meeting celebrating Debs' release from jail in
November, 1895. The central body also manifested a parental concern
for the local ARU. In December, 1895, it collected money for the convicted men, and in February, 1896, appointed a committee to look after
their interests during their prison terms, just then beginning. Several
months later the Los Angeles ARU, then shrunk to only 150 members,
began a final effort in behalf of the prisoners, securing their release
through a presidential pardon in November, 1896.[30]

The reliance of the Los Angeles ARU on federated craft unionism
was determined in part by local circumstances. In other places, particularly Chicago, the Knights of Labor had assumed a protective
interest in the railroad union, but in Los Angeles the order had become
almost a nonentity. The few remaining members had been all but
absorbed by the People's Party, which hoped also to draw in the ARU
and the craft unions. Neither the Knights nor the Populists, however,
offered the ARU anything more constructive than a proposal that government ownership of the railroads would be surety against future
disputes like the Pullman strike. This was cold comfort to the strikers,
whose immediately pressing needs obscured any potential benefits that
might accrue from a doubtful and distant change in railroad management. Since the American Railway Union thus had no feasible alternative to alliance with a tangibly helpful labor movement, it became an
integral part of the Council of Labor.[31]

The Pullman strike, which contributed to the demise of the ARU
and the Knights of Labor and to the growth of the AFL, may also have
strengthened local labor's determination to concentrate more closely on
strict craft unionism.[32] Although the Council of Labor had voted to
enter negotiations with the AFL on June 6, it did not send for a
charter until July 11, when the strike was all but lost. A dramatic
failure of industrial unionism at a critical moment may have brought
to Los Angeles labor, as nothing else could, a conviction that Gompers'
federation was the most useful form of labor organization.

XIV. PROGRESS AND DECLINE

By the end of 1894, after four years of constructive if at times confused effort, Los Angeles labor had taken long strides away from the isolation and uncertainties of the 1880's. It had at once broadened its horizons and accepted a specific form of organization through affiliation with the American Federation of Labor. These accomplishments were supplemented by establishment of a closer bond with San Francisco labor. The barriers separating unions in the two cities had begun to break down, as labor in the north gradually awoke to the far-flung threat of the *Times'* animosity. No less meritorious were the achievements at home through which the Los Angeles Council of Labor had integrated and centralized the union movement arising from the printers' strike of 1890.

The new feeling of unity engendered hope and confidence in the future, as Los Angeles labor resolutely looked forward to further progress. Despite the Panic of 1893, with its bank failures and consequent hard times, the local economic outlook was not unpromising. In the nation at large, and in San Francisco as well, the severity of the depression was felt earlier than in Los Angeles. The southern city was prepared for initial resistance because of the evenness of its growth in the early 'nineties, the relative independence of its commercial life, a good wheat crop in 1893, and improvement in export trade during the Sino-Japanese War of 1894–1895. Thus the worst impact of the depression was delayed in Los Angeles until 1897, enabling the local labor movement to show greater resilience than the considerably more experienced San Francisco unions during the middle 'nineties.[1]

Another encouraging aspect for the southern city was the rapidly increasing production of a cheap fuel. The petroleum industry was already becoming a vital element in the area's economy, and State Labor Commissioner Edward L. Fitzgerald, conducting a general survey of Los Angeles in 1895, foresaw its tremendous potential for the future. Local businessmen, too, were impressed by the industrial possibilities stemming from the discovery of oil. Stimulated in part by the recently formed National Association of Manufacturers, they organized their own Manufacturers' Association in the fall of 1895 and in January, 1896, sent a delegate to the national convention. In June of that year the local group and the Merchants' Association consolidated as the Merchants' and Manufacturers' Association. Since this body, so openly antiunion after 1900, confined itself for the present to promoting local products, any presentiment of its future antagonism could come only from Otis' alleged influence in the Merchants' Association several years earlier.[2]

Such foreboding played little part in labor's thinking during these years, nor were union leaders unduly alarmed by the evidences of hard times. In the summer of 1895, the Council of Labor, revealing only slight sensitivity to depression through a softening of aggressive policies, delineated its primary objectives as economic education of workers, extension of unionism, and substitution of arbitration for open labor conflicts.[3] When Cyren E. Fisk assumed the Council presidency in July, he rejoiced in labor's well-being:

> I feel that a new era is dawning for the Council. New unions are being organized and the old ones are exceptionally active, becoming stronger with each passing hour. The most complete harmony exists, and there is only one feeling discernible, that of the welfare and growth of the organization. Much of the old prejudice against labor unions no longer exists, and public opinion ... has given organization of workingmen its unqualified approval.[4]

Ten months later, in May, 1896, Frank Colver reënforced Fisk's estimate of community approbation of organized labor. Colver wrote that the principles of trade-unionism were currently as much respected in Los Angeles as elsewhere, since labor had painstakingly dissipated a popular misconception that it had radical tendencies.[5]

There was much truth in these assessments of labor's current status. The satisfying internal accord of which Fisk spoke was aptly illustrated by abundant gifts to the American Railway Union and the ARU's reciprocal sharing of responsibility for labor's general welfare. In February, 1895, the ARU's Pacific Coast organizer, D. J. Carr, succeeded W. A. White as manager of the Free Labor Bureau. Moreover, labor's relations with employers and the public were unusually good. Strikes were few and relatively unimportant. The Council of Labor was highly complimented for an "excellent showing" in the community's July 4th parade in 1895, and members of a few unions took part in the summer entertainment of the Turnverein, a German society. The Council was ready to help plan the 1896 Fiesta de Los Angeles when the *Times'* sharp denunciation of labor's inclusion caused the Merchants' Association to withdraw its invitation. The outcome of labor's efforts to remove misunderstandings with the church was happier; Council of Labor delegates addressed a meeting of the Ministerial Union in December, 1895, and two days later several clergymen returned the compliment.[6]

In 1896, the Council made elaborate preparations for a public display of strength on Labor Day in order to enhance its community prestige and attract "moral support to the cause of unionism." Not only the

Council's member unions, but nonaffiliated and out-of-town labor organizations as well were urged to send large delegations for the parade,
and United States Senator Stephen M. White was secured as guest
speaker at the afternoon exercises. The Council's advertising campaign
included the display of posters in streetcars and other public places,
and publication of an *Official Trades and Labor Souvenir Directory of
Los Angeles and Vicinity*. The *Directory* briefly summarized the his-
tories of the more important local unions, and named all labor organizations then functioning in the city. Listed for the Labor Day parade
were thirty-three Council affiliates, seven railroad organizations, the
Industrial Legion, the Knights of Labor, the Socialist Labor Party, and
several new socialist groups, all of Los Angeles, and ten unions from
nearby cities. Moreover, the City Council, invited to witness the festivi-
ties, departed from customary official diffidence toward labor's holiday
doings by donating $250 to the cause. Only twenty-one unions actually
marched in the parade, but the demonstration was impressive enough
to attract large crowds and elicit favorable comment.[7]

Superficially, Los Angeles labor appeared flourishing, particularly
in contrast to the already declining San Francisco Federated Trades.
Such events as the Labor Day celebration evidenced a warmhearted
cordiality in union relations with the public, and estimates of organized
labor's numerical strength were reassuring. In May, 1896, Frank Colver
claimed a membership of 5,400 for the twenty-three unions affiliated
with the Council of Labor, and a few months later, on Labor Day, the
Times placed the number at six thousand.[8] Yet dark clouds loomed on
labor's horizon. Outstanding among the background factors impeding
union progress was the menacing role of the Los Angeles *Times*. The
vigilance of Harrison Gray Otis in indoctrinating the public with antiunion sentiment was to be intensified in the years ahead until his open-
shop philosophy became a vital part of community thinking. In
addition, the agricultural economy, though gradually yielding to nascent industrialism, still delimited the boundaries of unionism. The
impermanence of the labor movement, arising in part from the violent
cyclical fluctuations of the past, was aggravated by the character and
rate of population growth. Neither Fisk nor Colver accurately appraised these hindrances, though the latter glimpsed one of them when
he said that half the population was unsympathetic to trade-union
aims because it was "placed beyond want."[9]

Likewise, the two labor leaders neglected to take into account the
more immediate obstacle of economic distress which, though not disastrous for Los Angeles unions until later in the decade, was slowly

undermining the foundations of the labor movement. Unemployment, noticeable as early as 1893, led in 1894 to participation in the Coxey march to Washington and did not lessen in succeeding years. In 1895, Labor Commissioner Fitzgerald found at least three thousand men out of work in Los Angeles, and wages at a substandard level. Various crafts complained of dull or only fair trade conditions throughout the year, and in May, the Council of Labor warned wage earners in other communities to discount Chamber of Commerce publicity designed to attract new settlers.[10] The disruptive force of economic hardship lay just beneath the surface during the middle 'nineties, an ever-present if not always acknowledged danger.

To the discerning eye, however, signs of the coming collapse were visible in the random nature of labor's activities and in the lack of an integrated program. The Council of Labor, for example, failed to promote campaigns of any magnitude, though it did hold the labor movement together in a semblance of continuing unity and development. Its readiness to forward the enterprises of individual unions was checked by a constitutional prohibition of interference, except upon request, and it could not therefore determine or activate union policies. The Council's declining usefulness was apparent in its indecisive handling of a new problem posed by the importation of Mexican workers, especially by the Southern Pacific Railroad, in violation of the alien contract labor law. Although investigating the extent of Mexican immigration and competition, the Council indefinitely postponed action.[11] This indifference was in sharp contrast to the Council's vigorous campaign to implement the anti-Chinese Geary Act in 1893, only several years earlier.

Signs of coexistent strength and weakness in the Los Angeles labor movement marked the period from 1895 to 1897 as one of paradox, with progress and decline going hand in hand. Organization and reorganization of unions proceeded at a pace comparable in steadiness if not in rapidity to the expansion of the early 'nineties, while a few old and well-established unions faded into obscurity. Despite unemployment, some crafts were able to extend unionization. Wage and hour gains were won by several groups of workers in a period of growing depression. The Council of Labor, either through diffidence or incapacity, no longer stressed its earlier functions of organizing workers and helping them make economic advances, yet it established labor-community relations on a sound basis. Depending on the observer's viewpoint and choice of determining factors, the Los Angeles labor movement in the middle 'nineties could be regarded with equal justification either as a continuing and unimpaired instrument of progress, or as a disintegrating body of unions yielding slowly to the implacable forces of depression. In the end progress was to be altogether nullified by decline, but during these few years at mid-decade the will to survive partially overcame existing handicaps.

The devious course of the pivotal Typographical Union, now aggressive, now enfeebled, illustrated the contradictions of the confused years before collapse became an irrefutable fact. In January, 1895, the printers relinquished the fight against the *Times,* but retained strictures against unfair printing offices. Further compromise followed several months later when members were permitted to work in open-shop job offices which paid union wages. During the spring and summer, with unemployment aggravated by the introduction of typesetting machinery, the union appropriated more than $500 to send printers elsewhere; nearly thirty members left during one week in May. Preoccupation with depression problems and other trade interests crowded out labor disputes until December, 1895, when the *Journal,* a nonunion paper of court news, announced its proposed conversion into a regular morning newspaper. Although the union reduced its composition scale to 40 cents per thousand ems, the proprietor refused to negotiate an agreement. A local assessment and a gift of $200 from the ITU made possible an intensive campaign against the *Journal,* whose proprietor soon grasped the difficulty of establishing "another non-union daily" in Los Angeles. Rather than deal with the union he abandoned his project, and the printers, feeling that a court paper would not compete with union newspapers, dropped the dispute.[12]

The printers had always been preëminent in the provision and maintenance of adequate news outlets for organized labor. They completely unionized the *Record,* a penny sheet known as "the poor man's advocate,"[13] shortly after its establishment in 1895. This paper was consistently prounion and became an outstanding champion of organized labor. Meanwhile, Frank Colver, a member of the Typographical Union, continued his labor column in the *Express,* and favorable news reports of union activities appeared sporadically in the *Herald.* Despite the friendliness of these commercial papers, labor again felt the need of its own organ, since the *California Federationist* established by the Typographical Union in 1894 had lapsed. The Council of Labor was considering publication of such a paper on a daily basis when, in February, 1896, Colver decided to issue a weekly. The *Labor World* appeared in March and, in a now familiar pattern, became the official organ but not the financial responsibility of the central body.[14]

The printers' resistance to conversion of the *Journal* and the reappearance of a regular news outlet for organized labor were signs of a slight upswing in 1896 before the end-of-the-century collapse. The Typographical Union led the way by renewing hostilities against the *Times* and reinvigorating the union label campaign. Since the newspaper had neglected no opportunity "to injure the Typographical Union and labor in general, resorting to many nefarious schemes to carry out its ends,"[15] and had, moreover, sent Fraternity strikebreakers to other cities, the printers deemed the contest one of more than local import. Accordingly, as a preliminary measure, they sounded out the ITU on the possibility of a national assessment sufficient to yield $1,000 a week, offering a new 1 per cent local levy as a pledge of good faith. Although the International promised no full-scale financial backing, the Los Angeles branch voted unanimously on May 31, 1896, to reopen the *Times* boycott.[16]

The printers immediately inaugurated a drive that was both intensive and widespread. Field workers were sent into southern California and Arizona to turn subscribers from the *Times* to friendly newspapers, especially the *Herald* and the *Express,* both of which had offered to help the union. Unemployed members were paid to conduct a similar boycott in Los Angeles. To gain the sympathy and aid of printing craftsmen outside the city, Joseph Phillis attended the annual convention of the State Typographical Union (formerly the California Federation of Typographical Unions) and D. W. Moore, local president, went to the 1896 ITU convention. The national union sent two donations of $200 each to assist the cause. The Los Angeles union tightened internal discipline, ordering its Council of Labor delegation to attend meetings more faithfully and even expelling five members for working in nonunion offices. It urged the printers to turn out in force for the Labor Day parade: "Other unions are looking to the Typographical Union keenly at this time, and failure to attain the position they expect of us will be disastrous."[17] Concessions were granted to union offices. A bonus of $200 enabled a new firm, R. Y. McBride and Company, to contract for the city directory, and reduction of the book and job scale helped friendly proprietors to meet nonunion competition.[18]

By the fall of 1896, the Typographical Union was able to discern progress against its adversary, citing as evidence a decline in the *Times'* sworn circulation figures. The printers also argued that Otis' fulminations against them and his frequent distribution of antiunion circulars to *Times* subscribers and advertisers were defensive tactics. When Otis summarized his account of union misdeeds since 1890 in a pamphlet entitled *A Plain Statement of Bed-Rock Facts and Unanswerable Reasons Sustaining the Attitude of the Times and Its Owners toward Labor during the Past Six Years,* the printers regarded it as proof that the *Times* was losing ground. Furthermore, the union won a considerable victory in September, when the County Board of Supervisors awarded the *Great Register* contract to a union firm in preference to the *Times.*[19]

Later in 1896, the Typographical Union took the first step in enlisting the support of the American Federation of Labor. Otis had been representing himself as President McKinley's political deputy in California, and the Los Angeles printers were discomfited by the implications of such a liaison. Their delegation in the Council of Labor, headed by Cyren E. Fisk, persuaded the central body to write to McKinley explaining the resentment of west coast unions against Otis and asking for a denial of the political tie. In an equivocal response, the President acknowledged Otis as his friend and asked California labor not to be too hard on him. Gompers, also notified of the rumored alliance between Otis and McKinley, had the AFL place the *Times* on its black list for the first time.[20] It was the start of a full program of national assistance in the fight against Otis and his newspaper.

The climax of the local anti-*Times* campaign came in the municipal elections of 1896. Early in the year the Council of Labor, at the instance of the Typographical Union, had summoned a trade-union conference to discuss a legislative program for organized labor, clearly specifying that it would not sanction the formation of a labor party nor accredit delegates from any existing political party. On March 22, representatives of fifteen unions, the Knights of Labor, the Farmers' Alliance, and a new establishment called the Labor Exchange,[21] organized the Labor Congress as a body quite distinct from the Council of Labor. In writing its platform of proposed legislative reforms, the Congress carefully shaped a policy consonant with the political principles of the American Federation of Labor, which since 1892 had been endorsing certain Populist planks without giving formal recognition to the People's Party. The Los Angeles Congress accordingly favored the initiative, referendum, and recall; proportional representation; free coinage of silver at sixteen to one; direct issue of paper currency; government ownership of transportation and communication systems; and establishment of postal savings banks. For workers' direct benefit, the Congress specified the labeling of all goods made by Oriental or convict labor, sanitary inspection of factories, broader powers for the State Labor Commissioner, and a deputy commissioner in each city of over thirty thousand.[22]

In April, before the Labor Congress was a month old, it had an opportunity to show once again the concern of organized labor in community problems. The United States Congress was soon to decide between Santa Monica and San Pedro as the site of a free harbor for Los Angeles, to be developed with the aid of federal funds. Community interest on this very vital question was particularly fervent because the Southern Pacific Railroad was exerting all of its powerful influence on behalf of the Santa Monica location. Both the Labor Congress and the Council of Labor, and all but one of the Los Angeles unions, went along with the majority in favoring San Pedro in opposition to "a great monopoly which has held Southern California by the neck since its infancy."[23] After lengthy deliberations, the United States Congress voted for San Pedro.[24]

Although originally planning to run a union ticket, the Labor Congress eventually decided to support regular party candidates. The tenor of its thinking was indicated by the distribution of its favors; of the first ten nominees endorsed, seven were Populist, two Republican, and one Democratic. Subsequent alterations in the political scene soon forced a change in procedure. By September the Democrats and Populists had fused and nominated a joint ticket; Debs and the American Railway Union had declared for Bryan and free silver; and many prominent trade-union leaders had shown similar leanings, though Gompers succeeded in keeping the AFL nonpartisan. In October, 1896, the Labor Congress, then numbering thirty unions, endorsed Bryan and the fusion ticket, and Colver added the weight of his newspaper, changing its name to *Labor World and Silver Champion.* Union members joined lustily in the campaign for both national and local fusion slates and, their leaders claimed, voted solidly for the Bryan ticket. Bryan did in fact receive a plurality in the city, thanks partly to labor's voice and partly to Colver's persuasive journalism. Nevertheless, Los Angeles labor was at no time so exercised about the issue of free silver as was labor elsewhere.[25]

It was not until the municipal elections that the printers' second major effort of 1896, promotion of the union label, became fused with the anti-*Times* fight. A cardinal point in the Typographical Union's program was official adoption of the label by city and county, so that printing contracts would of necessity go to union firms. Because of the failure of a direct attempt to achieve this goal in 1895, the union proposed the Labor Congress in 1896 with the prime objective of uniting organized labor behind its own label program. When the platform of the Congress made no specific recommendations on this issue, the printers shifted to a different tack. They canvassed all local printing offices, urging them to adopt the union label. They explained to other crafts the meaning and value of the mark of union manufacture. They persuaded white-labor restaurants and laundries to have their printing done by union men in return for the Typographical Union's support of the anti-Oriental program. Through newspaper advertisements they appealed to political candidates to have their election campaign printing bear the union label.[26]

For all this effort, however, the Typographical Union was not suitably rewarded. A few printing firms agreed to adopt the label, and two city councilmen promised to further a petition that official printing go to union firms. The union was especially disturbed by its failure to arouse the labor movement to the importance of the label. It chided all craftsmen for their unresponsiveness, but reproved its own members particularly for their "downright perniciousness" in disregarding the labels of other organizations, since they needed the good will of all unions. The printers were further distressed by the loss of a court case when they prosecuted a firm for affixing the label on printed matter set up by nonunion compositors. A demurrer to the complaint was sustained on the ground that the label was not a legal trade-mark, since the existing law provided no protection against employers so misrepresenting themselves.[27]

As the municipal election drew near, the Typographical Union was determined to get an official decree in favor of the label. To this end it induced the three parties—Republican, Democratic, and Populist—to demand the union label on public printing. With such unanimity prior to the election, the printers had little trouble in persuading the City Council, in October, 1896, to adopt a resolution that "city printing shall hereafter bear the label of the International Typographical Union or its local branch."[28]

This concession to organized labor began a mighty battle fought at City Hall, in newspaper columns, and eventually at the polls, where it obscured almost all other local election issues. Otis, abetted by other nonunion employers and by the Printers' Protective Fraternity, ridiculed the label as a "totem," castigated the councilmen who had voted for it, tried to have the ruling rescinded, and opposed such candidates as were willing to continue the official policy. His chief argument was that nonunion compositors should not be barred from job opportunities because of a preferential edict. *The "Other" Printer,* a campaign paper launched on November 5 by the Fraternity, carried on the *Times'* abuse of "totemism." When the Typographical Union retaliated with the *Union "Totem,"* edited by Joseph Phillis, the campaign reached an extreme of bitterness out of all proportion to the principle at stake. Essentially, however, the label contest was part of the long warfare against the *Times,* and this provided a rationalization for the money and effort expended. The printers levied a local 5 per cent assessment to raise funds, and even brought in the new ITU district organizer, H. H. Watts, who promised to do everything in his power to get national aid.[29]

By December 7, when the municipal elections were held, the Labor Congress and its endorsements of Democratic-Populist candidates had virtually been forgotten. The Typographical Union's campaign, directed toward the election of councilmen who would continue the city's official sanction of the label, had pushed other issues into the background. Moreover, Bryan's defeat in the presidential contest had lessened local advocacy of fusion candidates. The two new tickets of the League for Better City Government, which endorsed the best men for office regardless of party, and of the Socialist Labor Party further confused an evaluation of labor's voting power. The fusion party gained the mayoralty and three other city offices, three of the nine councilmanic seats, and two of the nine places on the Board of Education. All but five of the League's endorsees, some of whom were identical with fusion candidates, were elected. The Socialist Labor Party polled an insignificant vote.[30]

However the labor vote was distributed among the various contenders, the Typographical Union in the end lost the cause which had become paramount to its members. In January, 1897, the new City Council annulled the label resolution as un-American class legislation which limited free competition. Although the ITU belatedly sent $500, the Los Angeles printers lost their spirit after the election. The *Union* *"Totem"* lapsed, and the boycott of the *Times* was not resumed. The election campaign of 1896 had been an eleventh-hour show of vitality, and now the union was indeed in bad straits. Its treasury was depleted, with half of the 142 members owing back dues. Further hardship loomed for some of the printers when a wage concession was granted the *Herald* early in 1897. So discouraging were the prospects that the union's board of directors resigned in a body. Although the printers reinstated them with a vote of confidence, morale was at a very low point. In June, 1897, and again in November, the union extended the *Herald*'s wage reduction and in August cut the book and job scale. At the end of the summer only thirty situations were available for union printers in the whole city.[31]

Nevertheless, the Typographical Union gave careful attention during

1897 to several problems relevant to the *Times*. In March and April the union sent telegrams to Washington to protest the nomination of Otis as Assistant Secretary of War. Labor's ultimate victory in preventing the appointment was a tribute to the political shrewdness of ITU President William B. Prescott, who correctly assessed President McKinley's aversion to loud declamations against Otis. Holding that the Los Angeles union's fight against the *Times* had been characterized by "too much noise and not enough quiet work," Prescott kept his campaign under cover, despite advice to the contrary from Gompers. He negotiated secretly with influential people in Washington, chiefly Senator Marcus Hanna of Ohio, and thus killed the plan to get Otis into the government.[32] Otis himself was not perturbed by his defeat, for he wrote as follows to his friend ex-Governor H. H. Markham:

> You have read about the war office episode. . . . The result was inevitable under the circumstances, and as soon as I found out what the obstacle was, I waived the matter at once. . . . So far as the opposition of the vicious "walking delegates" is concerned, I would not change the attitude I have deliberately and successfully held for years past for the sake of securing any office on earth![33]

In fact, the incident was less useful to the Typographical Union as a victory over Otis than as a means of focusing the attention of both high labor circles and top political figures on Los Angeles. It would never again be so hard for the local union to command the assistance of the ITU and the AFL.

The printers forced recognition from still another national group shortly after the Otis episode. The biennial convention of the Order of Railway Conductors was scheduled to meet in Los Angeles in May, 1897. To defray the expenses of the session, a special "Conductors' Number" of the *Times* had been issued on March 15, the profits going to the local branch of the brotherhood. The Typographical Union, though disconcerted by the railroaders' patronage of an antilabor newspaper, had held its displeasure in abeyance because a formal agreement bound the conductors, and was somewhat mollified when the contract for publishing the convention proceedings went to a union firm. But the open friendship between the conductors and the *Times* while the session was in progress newly affronted the printers, who this time did not refrain from entering protests. To make amends, the conductors endorsed the union label in full convention.[34]

The paradox of progress in a period of decline was pushed a bit further by the printers in 1897, in continuation of their label drive. During the 1896 campaign the pressmen, reorganized in September as Local No. 78 of the International Printing Pressmen's Union, had proposed the formation of a printing trades council, but, despite the Typographical Union's enthusiastic approval, the plan did not then reach fulfillment. After Bookbinders' Union No. 63 was organized in December, 1896, and Press Feeders' and Helpers' Union No. 37 in January, 1897, the project seemed more feasible. In July, 1897, the printers, pressmen, bookbinders, and press feeders organized the first Los Angeles Allied Printing Trades Council, which in November registered its label in accordance with state law. This was the Council's only accomplishment during this period, for efforts to secure wide adoption of the label foundered in the hopelessly depressed latter years of the decade.[35]

Like the printing trades, the building trades illustrated the contradictory trends of the middle 'nineties. Early in 1895 unemployment necessitated the withdrawal of Painters' and Decorators' Union No. 206 from the Council of Labor. In July, the carpenters complained that "owing to the selfish action of those workmen who would not abide by the union scale, wages have been dragged down by cutthroat competition until many carpenters are working for $2 a day and less."[36] Nevertheless, both crafts recovered from the slump and enjoyed relative prosperity for several years. The painters' union rejoined the Council later in 1895, found employment for all of its members, doubled its enrollment by the end of the year, and continued to flourish during 1896. The retrogression which ended in dissolution of the union did not begin until 1897. Carpenters' Union No. 332 also grew rapidly until, with a membership of six hundred in the fall of 1896, it was the largest local labor organization. Unlike the painters' union, it retained its charter through the decade, though sharply curtailing its activities in the later years.[37]

Apart from the temporary lapse of the carpenters' and painters' unions, the building trades were remarkably healthy during 1895–1896. In two years they formed nine new organizations, some of which stepped immediately to the forefront as aggressive units of the labor movement. The Tin, Sheet Iron, and Cornice Workers' Local Union No. 108 was the first to organize, in January, 1895; in April it joined the Council of Labor. The Los Angeles Shinglers' Association, locally reputed to be the first organization of the craft in the world, was formed in August of the same year and sent delegates to the Council in October. The bricklayers reorganized in October and the plasterers in December, but only the latter affiliated with the central body. By the end of 1895 a new paper hangers' union claimed almost complete organization of the craft in Los Angeles. The lathers had bravely started to reëstablish a union in October, 1895, when only three of them were employed, but postponed organization until March, 1896. Their venture, however, was not successful, and early in 1897 an attempted reorganization failed. In August, two groups never before unionized in Los Angeles, the electricians or inside wiremen and the brickmakers, organized. The former split off from Electrical Workers' Union No. 61, in existence since 1893, and the latter was formed in protest against Chinese competition. Within a short time the brickmakers' union, claiming two hundred members, joined the Council of Labor and persuaded employers to discharge their Chinese help. In the fall of 1896 a Housesmiths' and Gas Fixture Hangers' Union was in existence, though not active.[38]

A logical development from this spate of organization was the formation of a central council for construction workers. In November, 1895, the Council of Labor had appointed a committee to promote coöperation among the building trades. In February, 1896, the plumbers called for a more concrete alliance, and in March ten unions organized a Building Trades Council. The new body voted to replace strikes by negotiation, adopted a working-card system to ensure the exclusive employment of union men on construction jobs, and appointed a grievance committee to settle disputes between member unions. By September, 1896, the Building Trades Council embraced all the allied unions in the city, and in December sent its first delegate to the Council of Labor.[39]

One of the outstanding figures in organizing the Building Trades Council was John R. Walker, a shingler by trade. Born in Illinois in 1859, Walker had had an unusually varied career as carpenter, brickmaker, sailor, prospector, and contractor, and he had first joined a union in 1875. Arriving in Los Angeles in 1895, he immediately organized the Shinglers' Association, and later served as its vice-president and delegate to both the Council of Labor and the Building Trades Council. In 1896, the Council of Labor elected him as vice-president and the Building Trades Council as treasurer and member of the grievance committee. It was through Walker's efforts that the City Council was induced to donate $250 to the 1896 Labor Day celebration, the first such occurrence in local labor history. Walker was also one of the most active members of the Labor Congress. He was a socialist who was just as aggressive and positive in promulgating his political doctrines as in furthering the cause of unionism. When the printers reopened their campaign against the *Times* in 1896, he was one of the union agitators who helped make "commercial life a burden for those . . . business men of this community who were toadying to or bulldozed by Otis, and so the weak and vacillating business men were between two fires."[40]

An outstanding achievement of the building trades in the middle 'nineties was their establishment or maintenance of wage scales and of the eight-hour day. In March, 1895, twenty-one members of the Master Plumbers' Association announced a reduction of wages from $4 to $3 for an eight-hour day. Negotiations proved fruitless, despite the hitherto close alliance between journeymen and employers, and on April 1, twenty-five union plumbers refusing to work for $3 were locked out by six of the concerns. The union persuaded the other fifteen firms not to cut wages and eventually reëstablished its scale throughout the industry. In the summer of 1895 two new unions, the Tin, Sheet Iron, and Cornice Workers' Local and the Shinglers' Association, were able to set up uniform wage systems for their members. The former won the eight-hour day at the same time.[41]

In the spring of 1896 the reorganized plasterers' union established a daily wage of $4, and during the summer the painters were granted a minimum daily wage of $2.50. Both worked the eight-hour day. The carpenters' union had more trouble. Although still suffering from imperfect control of the craft, it decided to fix $3 as the minimum wage for the eight-hour day on August 31, 1896. Forty of the leading contractors controlling 90 per cent of the industry agreed to the scale, but the union, with the assurance that national strike benefits would be available and that the local Building Trades Council would assist, struck against several employers who refused. Within two weeks all contractors had met the terms: they unionized their shops, reinstated the strikers, and paid the union scale. Early in 1897 the brickmakers established a uniform wage scale. The bricklayers' union, though winning uniform wages of $4 for the eight-hour day by the end of 1896, was unable to maintain this high level. In the fall of 1897 it had to strike to gain an increase from $2.50 to $3.[42]

The vitality evidenced by the building trades, in organization and in wage and hour gains, brought additional recognition and rewards to some of the unions. In 1895 the carpenters' union, by publicizing eight-hour violations in the construction of new school buildings, forced the City Council to insist that contractors observe the law.[43] The carpenters' enthusiasm in organizing the craft outside of Los Angeles brought a donation of $200 from the national brotherhood in August, 1896, and the appointment of a member of Local No. 332 as district organizer.[44] By the fall of 1896 two crafts, the tin and sheet-iron workers and the electricians, claimed that all Los Angeles contractors in their respective industries were employing only union men.[45]

However encouraging the advances of the building trades, few of the unions could withstand the deepening depression in the middle 'nineties. A mere handful, Carpenters' Union No. 332, Plumbers' Union No. 78, Electrical Workers' Union No. 61, and Pasadena Painters' Union No. 92, retained their charters through the dark years at the end of the decade. Even they hardly remained alive in a period when retention of past gains was of secondary importance to finding jobs, any jobs that would provide the bare essentials of existence.

The activities of unions outside the printing and building trades fell into no distinguishable pattern during the years 1895–1897, partly because these unions lacked a centralizing trade interest. Here again were the characteristic contradictions of the period, as some unions continued to fight for the welfare of their members and to make some progress, while others dropped completely the aggressiveness of the early 1890's. One of the former was Cooks' and Pastry Cooks' Union No. 5, which in October, 1895, struck against the New York Kitchen when it employed a nonunion man and cut wages to $9 a week. Through a boycott upheld by other organized workers, the cooks curtailed the restaurant's business by 40 per cent but were unable to reunionize the establishment. In 1896, the cooks' union, with the help of the Council of Labor and owners of white-labor restaurants, sharply reduced the patronage of Chinese and Japanese eating houses.[46]

Bakers' Union No. 37 helped its members in a number of ways. In September, 1895, it established a sick and death benefit system. In January, 1896, after their request for mediation had been refused, the bakers struck against House's bakery for selecting a nonunion man as foreman. The Council of Labor endorsed the walkout, and within two weeks the dispute was amicably settled. The union also saw to it that sanitary regulations were enforced in bakeries, and in July, 1896, reduced the workweek from sixty-two to sixty hours. By 1897, however, the bakers' union had yielded to hard times, though it did hold on to its charter through the rest of the decade.[47]

Cigar Makers' Union No. 225, as a veteran of the Los Angeles labor movement, commanded the respect of other craftsmen and consistently upheld the principles of unionism. Although its membership never exceeded seventy-five during the years 1891–1896, and had dropped to nine by 1898, the union paid unemployment, sick, and death benefits, enjoyed the eight-hour day and a uniform wage scale, and drove Chinese cigar makers out of the local market, except for Chinatown. One of the union's rare conflicts with employers came in February, 1895, when it struck against a firm employing several nonunion cigar makers and succeeded in reinstating its members. In March, 1897, the cigar makers brought their national vice-president to Los Angeles to speak at a labor mass meeting, and persuaded the Council of Labor to protest certain disadvantageous changes in the tobacco tariff. Although Senator Stephen M. White and several congressmen from California presented the cigar makers' objections, the bill was passed by Congress.[48]

During 1895–1896, Los Angeles Local No. 83, Retail Clerks' National Protective Association, conducted a partially successful campaign for shorter working hours. A constitutional prohibition of strikes and boycotts made this union unusually dependent on the good will of the community. Starting in August, 1895, the clerks accordingly obtained the signatures of more than five thousand citizens on a petition for the six o'clock closing every day except Saturday. The important stores in the central business section quickly yielded, and the new system was instituted on October 1. With considerable pride, Los Angeles complimented itself as the first Pacific Coast community to take this progressive step. In the spring of 1896 the clerks turned to their next objective of Sunday closing. Since legislative action was required, the petition this time went to the City Council. Signed by citizens and endorsed by other unions, it asked for an ordinance prohibiting business on Sundays except in drugstores, livery stables, hotels, and restaurants. The City Council, however, voted five to four against the proposed measure in August, 1896, on the grounds that it was religious legislation and in conflict with state law, and that it would hamper businesses trying to weather the depression. Despite this setback, the clerks' union remained an active affiliate of the Council of Labor and maintained itself through the last years of the century.[49]

The Los Angeles barbers reorganized in February, 1896, with the Sunday holiday as their main objective. The new United Barbers' Association, like its short-lived predecessor of 1894, included both employers and employees and within several months had grown to some two hundred members. Divergent interests soon breached the alliance between management and labor, and in August some of the employees formed a journeymen barbers' union which affiliated with the national as Local No. 30; others chose to remain with the employers in the Barbers' Association. The journeymen's union immediately joined the Council of Labor and made strenuous efforts to organize the city's barber shops preparatory to a drive for Sunday closing. But the defeat of the retail clerks' ordinance for a Sunday holiday halted the barbers' campaign, and their union collapsed before the end of 1896, surrendering its charter in December.[50]

Two groups sharing some common interests, the musicians and the stagehands, were self-contained organizations acting independently of other unions, though both were affiliated with the Council of Labor. Local No. 33 of the Alliance of Theatrical Stage Employees, joining the

Council immediately after its organization in December, 1894, tried during 1895 to unionize the theaters. In June it won over the Burbank Theatre and took in some additional new members. Thereafter it was of minor importance, though it survived the decade.[51] The Los Angeles Musical Association, Local No. 19 of the National League of Musicians, had been organized in the fall of 1894 but did not join the Council of Labor until June, 1895. In July it established a uniform wage scale and by the spring of 1896 claimed that it had unionized all local bands and theater orchestras. In March, 1897, the musicians' union received a charter as Local No. 47 of the American Federation of Musicians, though also retaining its membership in the National League of Musicians. It survived, as Local No. 47, to become an important part of the post-1900 local labor movement.[52]

While some unions were using to advantage the interim before the full impact of the depression was felt, others with equally long and aggressive backgrounds succumbed quickly. Tailors' Union No. 81, for example, though keeping its charter through the turn of the century, was completely lifeless throughout the period. Hotel and Restaurant Employees' Alliance No. 54 was similarly inactive, and had disappeared altogether by 1897. The machinists' union, hard hit by the Pullman strike, was unable to revive. The iron molders, too few in number to maintain their own organization, joined the San Francisco Molders' Union in August, 1896. The stonecutters' union steadily declined in membership during the years 1891–1896; the boilermakers' union simply disappeared. The San Pedro sailors, reflecting the weakness of the coast union after its defeat by the Shipowners' Association at the end of 1893, had withdrawn from the Los Angeles Council of Labor by 1895. Efforts to ship union men, win new members, and raise wages were halfhearted and only occasionally successful. Early in 1896 the *Coast Seamen's Journal* issued a pamphlet entitled "Red Record" in order to expose the abuses suffered by sailors on board ship. The nation-wide publicity accorded the document resulted in a slight improvement in shipping conditions on the coast. In 1898 wages advanced slightly because of the need for vessels in the new Alaska trade.[53]

On the periphery of the labor movement were a few unions which had little to do with other organized workers. The Journeymen Butchers' Association, established primarily for benevolent purposes, restricted its coöperation to financial contributions to needy organizations, particularly the American Railway Union. In 1897, Los Angeles butchers arranged a coast convention which organized the Pacific Coast Butchers' Association, with Albert Winters of Los Angeles as its first president. Los Angeles Branch No. 2, National Association of Stationary Engineers, formed in September, 1895, and the Los Angeles Express and Hackmen's Association, organized in February, 1896, also held aloof from other unions. The hackmen put up a fight against restrictions on hitching, but it was not until August, 1898, that they were freed of irksome regulations. A union of laundry workers, organized in the fall of 1896, fell a victim to a price-raising and wage-cutting combination of proprietors in March, 1897.[54]

Although the Council of Labor ignored repeated requests from several international unions to organize Los Angeles branches, it did make one serious attempt in 1897 to form a local brewery workers' union. In September, following representations from a San Diego brewery which hoped to encroach on Maier and Zobelein's monopoly of the Los Angeles beer trade, the Council of Labor and the Building Trades Council appointed a joint committee to approach Maier and Zobelein; in October the brewery workers' union in San Francisco sent an organizer to confer with the employees. Although the company raised no objection, the men themselves refused to organize on the grounds that their working conditions were as good as, if not better than, those demanded by the union, and that as union members they would have to relinquish their privilege of holding stock in the firm. With the approval of local unions, the Council of Labor immediately imposed a boycott on Maier and Zobelein beer, but in 1898 the brewery workers were still rejecting unionization.[55]

This attempt to form a union among previously unorganized workers drew the first overt expression of hostility from the Merchants' and Manufacturers' Association. When the Council of Labor announced the Maier and Zobelein boycott, the M and M pledged moral support to both the company and its employees, the start of an antiunion career which enabled Los Angeles employers to maintain the open shop for long years ahead. As it happened, Felix J. Zeehandelaar, who was later to acquire a national reputation as an opponent of unionism, became secretary of the M and M in August, 1897, just before the Council of Labor tried to organize the brewery workers.[56]

The Maier and Zobelein incident temporarily hurt the career of one of the oldest and most esteemed members of the Typographical Union, Frank Colver, editor of the *Labor World*. Although Michael McGlynn, now a permanent resident of Los Angeles, had become part owner of the *Labor World* in March, 1897, Colver alone was blamed when the paper opposed the brewery boycott. Reluctant at first to censure a trusted colleague, the Typographical Union finally yielded to mounting pressure from the *Coast Seamen's Journal*, the San Francisco *Voice of Labor*, and the ITU. In February, 1898, it publicly repudiated the

Labor World. Colver left the city, but upon his return in 1899 the printers showed unbroken confidence in him by unanimously electing him as delegate to the Council of Labor.[57]

The inadequacies of Los Angeles labor in the middle 'nineties were painfully apparent, for the progress in some areas could not hide the general trend downward. As hard times intensified and unemployment increased in 1897, disintegration spread from the edges to the heart of the labor movement. In February the carpenters confessed they had reached the lowest point of a twenty-year period. In April only seven of the seventy members of the plumbers' union were employed. Wages in both crafts fell to $2.50 a day. In June, the Building Trades Council advised all its member unions to establish sick and unemployment benefit funds to aid those in distress.[58]

All workers, organized and unorganized, suffered as the depression became ever worse. Estimated unemployment figures for early 1897 varied from two thousand to five thousand, with wages at the lowest level ever known. Farm hands at the bottom of the scale received $15 a month without room or board. Hardship was so acute that the City Council, the Chamber of Commerce, and the Merchants' and Manufacturers' Association jointly tackled the problem of relief measures. In March they inaugurated a large-scale public works program with funds provided by private donation. The president of the Council of Labor represented organized labor on the executive committee in charge of the project, but the unions' own troubles precluded heavy financial contributions. The musicians' union did better than most with a gift of $68. As civic responsibility was aroused, however, the fund grew rapidly and reached a total of over $25,000. Workers hired under the plan were paid only $1 a day in order to spread the benefits as widely as possible. By April 17, 1897, they had completed construction of a new boulevard into Elysian Park, which was opened to the public in a formal ceremony. In the final accounting 765 men had received about $17,000 in total wages. By the time the project was finished, unemployment was beginning to ease; the Free Labor Bureau reports of persons placed in jobs showed an increase from 171 in April to 578 in September.[59]

Although business had improved somewhat by the fall of 1897, the Council of Labor was unable, if indeed it tried, to halt the slump of unionism. As a central body it became less and less efficient, confining itself to gestures like protesting the annexation of Hawaii as a threat of increased Chinese immigration, organizing a volunteer company of union men to fight in the Spanish-American War, and opposing Otis' appointment to high military command. In February, 1898, the Council did select an organizing committee "to bolster up weak unions," but these representatives could not transmit strength that was not there. Only seven unions, with less than four hundred members, remained in the central body. In June, 1898, the Council merged with the Building Trades and Printing Trades Councils to form the United Labor Council, but the reorganization failed to reanimate the local labor movement. The Printing Trades Council retained its own identity, chiefly because the printers refused to let it be submerged, and lasted through the decade. The Building Trades Council, with less vitality, died out in 1899, though it had earlier affiliated with the National Building Trades Council of America, formed at St. Louis in 1897. This body, favoring a system of arbitration, appealed to the Los Angeles building trades which had stipulated, when organizing their own council in 1896, that negotiation with employers be substituted for strikes. The National Building Trades Council, however, drew Gompers' condemnation because of its rivalry with the AFL and it disappeared early in the twentieth century.[60]

Part of the decline of the Los Angeles United Labor Council was its loss of control over the Free Labor Bureau. The first move to end labor's supervision had come in 1895, when the Merchants' Association advised the allocation of public funds to the Associated Charities instead of the labor bureau, but the change was not made. In 1897, the County Board of Supervisors had named S. M. Perry, an ex-employer, as manager. With this appointment, and the defeat of a bill creating local bureaus under the State Labor Commissioner, organized labor saw its control slipping away. In July, 1898, Perry was replaced by Isaac S. Smith, who was popular with workingmen, but his successor, Colonel W. E. Morford, was described as a "superannuated politician."[61]

The central body overlooked several new organizations which it could have brought into the labor movement. In 1893, the Council of Labor had proposed the unionization of teachers, but a Teachers' Alliance formed for mutual benefit and better employment conditions in February, 1898, was disregarded. In June, when the Alliance persuaded the Board of Education to base salaries on seniority, the ever alert *Times* dubbed it a "Debs alliance." At the end of 1899, the Teachers' Alliance, having enrolled about three hundred of the five hundred public school teachers in the city, planned to affiliate with the projected National Federation of Teachers.[62] In 1899 a new local branch of the Barbers' Association of the Pacific Coast, which was sponsoring a bill requiring state licensing of barbers, attracted no more notice from the Council of Labor than had the Teachers' Alliance. The bill failed to pass, and the local union soon disappeared.[63]

In these difficult years, even the resilient Typographical Union sank into apathy. In May, 1898, it failed to join the Council of Labor in protesting a high military post for Otis in the Spanish-American War. It continued to extend the *Herald's* wage reduction, and did not proceed against printing firms employing nonunion labor. Individual members became so disinterested that they could scarcely be induced to hold office. Cyren E. Fisk, elected ITU district organizer in October, 1898, persuaded the union to reverse an earlier decision to withdraw from the State Typographical Union, but poor business conditions, plus the secretary's misappropriation of funds, entailed other economies. The death in 1899 of three prominent members, including McGlynn, was an added blow. Moreover, the printers could foresee no abatement of Otis' opposition to unionism. The *Times,* still as strong as ever, had been triumphant in the long battle which started in 1890. Weakened by depression, the Typographical Union was far from ready to revive the boycott against its old enemy.[64]

The end of a century is in itself a symbolical turning point, suggesting a change of scene or of pace in historical development. In the history of Los Angeles labor, the close of the nineteenth century was a particularly appropriate time for a backward look at progress and accomplishments, for there was a distinct shift from one phase to another. The first twenty-five years of Los Angeles labor history, from the birth of the Typographical Union in 1875 to the decline of unionism at the end of the century, revealed a fair degree of conformity to the broad lines of the national movement. Labor unions throughout the country suffered from the depression after the Panic of 1873, just as the local Typographical Union had to struggle for survival. The insecurity and indecision of the 1880's, seen best in the conflict between the Knights of Labor and craft unionism, were heightened in Los Angeles, where labor clung to the heritage of its political beginnings. Labor's dilemma in finding its most advantageous medium of expression was evident in the abortive Union Labor and United Labor parties of the late 'eighties, both of which flourished briefly in Los Angeles. The "Great Upheaval" of 1886 locally took the form of an anti-Chinese crusade instead of the eight-hour agitation of organized labor elsewhere, but the great increase in union membership during the local real estate boom paralleled a similar expansion in the nation. The deterioration afterward was comparable to the national lull just before 1890.

Although the great eight-hour drive of 1890 under the auspices of the American Federation of Labor excited only feeble response in Los Angeles, the aggressive spirit after the printers' strike reflected the enthusiasm which animated the national organization. The *Times'* developing antagonism after 1890 brought home to Los Angeles labor its need for unity, and the goal of building a strong and effective labor movement as counterpoise to Otis had as great efficacy as the carpenters' eight-hour drive throughout the country. Yet, even with a firmer substructure, the local Council of Labor was unable to make permanent headway in the epochal contest with the *Times*, the crux of labor's troubles in Los Angeles. The local movement was not thereby necessarily marked as incompetent, for national labor was equally inept in meeting the corporate opposition which arose from the post-Civil War economic revolution. The steel strike of 1892 was as much an object lesson to workingmen the country over as was the printers' strike to local labor.

The parallel between Los Angeles and national labor continued into the 1890's, though in this case there was a noticeable lag in local response to cyclical developments. The ill effects of the Panic of 1893 were felt later in Los Angeles than elsewhere, and thus the local labor movement, with confidence born of its resurgence after the printers' strike of 1890, continued to make progress in some areas of endeavor during the middle 'nineties. This gave local substance to Gompers' claim that labor's greater ability to weather business disturbances was a tribute to the steady growth of craft unionism.[65] As the decade wore on, however, labor's advance became more opportunistic and more haphazard. Disintegration was slower than it had been in the aftermath of the real estate boom ten years earlier, but nonetheless certain, as concrete accomplishments dwindled to a thin stream which finally disappeared altogether. Few unions had the inner strength to survive more than nominally the prolonged depression of the 'nineties. National labor, which had also declined in the hard times, responded more quickly than local labor to the return of industrial prosperity in 1898.[66] Los Angeles unions were quiescent until the end of 1899, and real renascence of the local labor movement was delayed until after the turn of the century.

Thus Los Angeles labor closed the first quarter century of its history in weakness and despair. The record it had written disclosed no substantial achievements of lasting value, no remarkable ability to overcome obstacles. Numerous causes contributed to this long-range impotence: an agricultural economy and tardy industrialization; recurrent depressions; physical and psychological isolation during the critical first years; insufficient recognition and help from the AFL, national unions, and San Francisco labor; rapid population growth and a high proportion of transients, health seekers, tourists, and retired persons; absence of outstanding local leadership; instability of central labor bodies; and the constant opposition of Otis and the *Times*. Moreover, the infant labor organizations of Los Angeles were more susceptible than firmly established unions in older industrial centers to the doubts and confusion attending the search for the best means of improving the worker's standard of living. Frequent diversion into political or reform movements might dissipate an all too limited strength which could be more advantageously applied to the development of craft unionism; on the other hand, alliances with other segments of the population in such extra-union agitations might promote wider community understanding and acceptance of labor's goals. The remoteness of Los Angeles labor from the national movement and the background of its leaders intensified its semipolitical, reformist quality. Almost without exception, those who molded local trade-unionism—Vinette, Bailey, Biddle, and Walker among others—proselytized for movements like the Greenback Labor Party, the Union Labor Party, Nationalism, Populism, and Socialism. Although the irresolution was partially resolved when Los Angeles labor joined the American Federation of Labor in 1894, the imminence of depression prevented immediate assessment of the potential benefits of such a decision. Thus an unusual combination of circumstances delayed the building of a solid core of unionism and made way for the extraordinary power of the open shop in Los Angeles.

Nevertheless, Los Angeles labor was ready to enter upon a new and very different phase when it recovered from the long depression of the 1890's. Simultaneously, the American Federation of Labor at last discerned the precarious situation of its Los Angeles affiliate. Although the imminent national assistance could not immediately banish the ill effects of a long period of trial and error nor instantly overcome the disadvantages inherent in the Los Angeles area, it could and did infuse new life and vigor into the surviving unions. The resulting expansion was comparable to the tremendous increase in AFL membership in the dawn of the twentieth century. Local workers had a great asset in being part of a growing community, with its vast building program requiring a steady supply of labor. New vistas of progress were opened by the continuing development of the petroleum industry and of water power, providing the necessary cheap fuel for manufacturing enterprises. Indeed, Los Angeles was accorded a singular triumph of recognition from San Francisco during the 1890's:

There is growing up in the southern part of the state a community which threatens to leave us far behind in the race of progress. If the growth of the country south of the Tehachapi continues at its present rate, the 20th century will not be far advanced when Los Angeles, and not San Francisco, will be the commercial capital of California.[67]

XV. REAWAKENING OF THE LABOR MOVEMENT

ORGANIZED LABOR in Los Angeles enjoyed a prodigious expansion in the early years of the twentieth century. Old unions and new unions, some of them extending to occupations never before organized, flourished alike in a period keynoted by prosperity. A great organizing drive ushered in a new and promising era for Los Angeles labor, different in scope and method from anything that had gone before. Now for the first time the American Federation of Labor evinced real concern for its southern California outpost, and international unions, too, sent assistance to the labor community of the fast-growing city. Local labor shared in organizing and in turn benefited from the first enduring regional body, the California State Federation of Labor. All these forces working together with local leaders soon brought startling changes: the isolation of the pre-1900 period disappeared as Los Angeles labor began to feel at one with national and regional labor; businesslike methods and planned programs replaced the hit-or-miss opportunism of an earlier day; the labor movement became a social institution, more than ever an essential element in a thriving community.

These phenomena made Los Angeles labor an integral part of the national labor movement, sharing in both its fortunes and vicissitudes. By emerging intact from the long depression of the 'nineties, the American Federation of Labor had illustrated its stability and capacity to survive, as well as its superiority over other possible forms of labor organization in the achievement of workers' objectives. When returning prosperity brightened the American industrial scene in 1898, the AFL justified Gompers' prediction that it would be ready to take immediate advantage of a business revival. During the years 1898–1904 the membership of American trade-unions climbed steadily upward from half a million to over two million; the size of the Federation itself increased from approximately a quarter of a million in 1898 to one and two-thirds million in 1904. Thus the AFL grew relative to total union membership as well as in absolute terms, and at the end of this period of expansion included 80 per cent of union members in the country as compared to 55 per cent in 1898. Along with the growth in membership went a net increase in the number of charters issued by the AFL and international unions, though here the high point was reached in 1903 instead of in 1904. Following the great spurt between 1898 and 1904, Federation and total union membership remained almost static until after 1910.[1]

The trend toward organization of labor, and in particular toward federated craft unionism, took place in a changing America. Reasons far more fundamental than the business revival after 1898 impelled workers to join their fellows in collective action. The disappearance of the last frontier and of free land as a "natural" regulator of wages meant dwindling opportunities for the individual worker to achieve proprietary status. Greater consciousness of working-class affinity tended to wean wage earners away from the nineteenth century middle-class antimonopoly and reform parties, invariably ending in dissension and disintegration; from cheap money and related doctrines, outmoded by the depression's end; and from producers' coöperatives, which oftener than not were transformed into capitalist enterprises benefiting the few at the top. The working class also learned that attempts at revolutionary change in the institution of private property aroused public antipathy, and that a labor movement dedicated to slow modification of the existing framework would be more certain of middle-class support against unrestrained employer abuses. The American Federation of Labor was the logical resort of workers disillusioned by the various experiments of the nineteenth century.[2]

The capitalist system had itself undergone a transformation. The population shift from farm to city not only weakened the ties between workers and the earlier agrarian movements, but also made urban dwellers more dependent on wages and brought them closer to others in the same trades or occupations. Along with urbanization went the expansion of competitive areas into national or international markets. The increasing number of persons engaged in industrial pursuits and the extension of market areas forced workers to organize for the maintenance of their standards. At the same time the scale of industry enlarged to keep pace with the changing market structure. By both vertical and horizontal combination the big corporation became the dominant economic unit. The increasing concentration of production in powerful corporations, most of them antiunion and completely impersonal, lowered the status of the individual in both bargaining and personal relationships. Unions were meaningful social organizations and economic bargaining agencies which gave back to the individual a measure of the dignity he had lost.[3]

Two other factors, immigration and mechanization, affected both the development of large-scale industry and the tendency of workers to form labor unions. The peak of immigration into the United States was reached in the first decade of the twentieth century. Its character was changing, however; now the majority came from southern and eastern instead of northern and western Europe. The newer immigrants, with less skill and less familiarity with unionism, represented a competitive menace to organized labor, and at the same time provided employers with a large pool of cheap labor. Technological advance, proceeding at a feverish pace as industrial inventions multiplied, reduced the proportion of skilled craftsmen needed in the factories. As the wider use of machinery simplified tasks and made possible the greater employment of immigrant labor, skilled workers found protection in the extension of unionism and in the elaboration of union on-the-job rules.[4]

What was the character of the labor movement that arose in this industrial, capitalistic, corporation-minded America? Whence came the hundreds of thousands of new members who raised the American Federation of Labor to its practical domination of organized workers? To prevent the destruction of union standards through the large-scale organization of industry, the AFL at first sought to extend its geographical jurisdiction, particularly by penetrating the remoter regions of the South and West where unionism had hitherto made scant progress. A satisfying response in nonurban areas revealed that the organizing drive of the early twentieth century was not confined to large industrial centers or to sections with a long history of unionism. The spread of unionism into outlying regions, however, faltered after 1904 in the face of a determined employer counteroffensive.[5]

There was less effort by the AFL to extend organization into new occupations. Although not lacking in concern for unskilled workers and not excluding some previously unorganized trades from membership, the Federation concentrated on the unionization of skilled craftsmen and of the upper strata of the semiskilled. With the exception of miners and garment and textile workers, the great majority of employees in the mass production industries remained outside union ranks. Labor's fear of competition from the unskilled and often illiterate immigrants prevented acknowledgment of common problems in common resistance to employer pressure, and unions for the most part were concentrated, as before, in a few categories of employment, trades which retained elements of craftsmanship.[6]

Although not changing radically in occupational make-up during this period, the American labor movement did enjoy a favorable turn in its relations with employers. The years 1898–1904 were in general marked by industrial harmony, in spite of occasional strikes, and by a desire on both sides to replace the strife of the 1890's with more peaceable solutions. The National Civic Federation, led by outstanding figures representing labor, management, and the public, was in the forefront of the drive for industrial peace. For a time labor-capital coöperation seemed to thrive, as trade agreements became increasingly prevalent. Such agreements, reached by a process of collective bargaining between organized workers and organized or individual employers, constituted in effect recognition of unions and of their new strength. Although not necessarily stipulating the closed shop, they specified some of the basic conditions of employment and to that extent gave wage earners control over their jobs. But the rapport of the early years did not long continue. Unions, taking an example from employers, became more businesslike in the conduct of their affairs. Shrewd, experienced negotiators followed an aggressive policy, and their demands encroached more and more on the freedom of management. When employers who had expected unions to be more amenable entered upon an intensive open-shop drive, and when contractual relationships in several important industries broke down, the "honeymoon period of capital and labor" came to an end. Although unionism retained its hold upon some key industries and trades, it suffered a perceptible slowing down after 1904, owing chiefly to the employers' counteroffensive.[7]

Like the rest of the United States, California enjoyed a return of prosperity just before the turn of the century. The state was in an enviable location to take commercial advantage of late nineteenth-century developments, such as the Alaska gold rush, the annexation of Hawaii, and the acquisition of the Philippines. California's basic industries of agriculture, manufacturing, shipping, lumbering, and mining were growing, and continuing discoveries of new oil fields predicted further industrial expansion. Steady population growth, meteoric rises in the volume of trade and profits, decline in business failures, extension of railroad mileage, and rapid increases in bank clearings all combined with industrial advance to create an optimistic and highly prosperous era for California. San Francisco, with its centrally placed and well-developed port, enjoyed an immediate upturn in business conditions.[8]

The labor movement of California kept pace with the mounting prosperity, showing a zeal for organization probably never matched by the workers of any other state.[9] Between 1900 and 1902 the number of unions increased by 75 per cent, and union membership by about 125 per cent. San Francisco, with approximately one-fourth of the state's unions and two-thirds of the total California union membership, greatly surpassed other communities in the strength of organized labor. Unlike the AFL, the San Francisco Labor Council campaigned for and accomplished the organization of practically all trades, from the skilled crafts to the previously neglected unskilled occupations, with the result that by 1901 San Francisco was virtually a closed-shop city. Until checked by an employers' counteroffensive—for even San Francisco was not immune to the universal open-shop movement—many unions made unprecedented gains in improvement of working conditions, often without a struggle.[10]

One facet of the expansion of California unionism during these years was a growing tendency to consolidate in central bodies, similar to the national trend toward affiliation with the AFL. In 1900 less than half the unions in the state were represented in central councils, but by 1902 practically all of them had established such local connections. As a logical climax, the tightening of affiliate relationships led to formation of both the California State Federation of Labor and the State Building Trades Council in 1901.[11]

On January 7–9, 1901, delegates from sixty-one unions and five central bodies in the state of California, meeting at the invitation of the San Francisco Labor Council, formed the California State Federation of Labor. Two Los Angeles groups, the Council of Labor and the plumbers' union, were represented. The new organization, operating under an American Federation of Labor charter, restricted its membership to unions and central bodies affiliated with the AFL. Its purposes were to complete the organization of labor in California, improve interunion relations, educate workers, promote the union label, make the eight-hour day universal, prevent black-listing, further authorized boycotts, secure safe and sanitary working conditions and "just and equitable" wage schedules, prevent the passage of unfavorable legislation, win new labor laws, and enforce existing ones. The problem of enforcing labor legislation recurred frequently, for penalties were never onerous enough to deter violations, and the state labor commissioner's facilities were inadequate.[12]

As the San Francisco Labor Council had been instrumental in creating the State Federation of Labor, so the San Francisco Building Trades Council, under the leadership of P. H. McCarthy, began the movement which culminated in organization of the State Building Trades Council in December, 1901. McCarthy, serving as president of the new council from its inception until 1922, became an influential figure in the California labor movement. The struggle for power which had marred the relationship between the San Francisco Labor Council and the San Francisco Building Trades Council ever since 1896 was transferred in part to the two corresponding state organizations. The State Building Trades Council refused to allow its local councils to join the State Federation of Labor until 1910, when McCarthy lifted the ban.[13]

Even without the support of McCarthy's building trades, the State Federation achieved a creditable record in the legislative field. Here, as elsewhere, its mentor was the San Francisco labor movement, which in 1899 had successfully lobbied for favorable labor laws. One measure passed then, a replica of the AFL bill currently before Congress, provided for more stringent observance of the eight-hour day on public works; another safeguarded workingmen by penalizing contractors who defrauded them of their wages. In 1901, the San Francisco Labor Council obtained State Federation sponsorship for a series of bills which it had drafted. Three of these became law: a bill raising the minimum age for child labor from ten to twelve and reducing maximum hours from ten to nine; a bill requiring the licensing of barbers; and a bill providing an adequate blower system in metal polishing factories. The eight-hour law for public works was strengthened by an amendment requiring that contracts specifically stipulate the eight-hour day. Of several measures which did not pass, the most important was an anti-injunction bill. The Legislature rejected it on the plea that judicial restraint of unions had not been widely used in California. Although there had been occasional resort to the injunction in San Francisco, labor's proposal stemmed rather from fears for the future and from AFL efforts to gain a similar federal statute.[14]

Although San Francisco's political, economic, and cultural supremacy in California seemed likely to continue in the flourishing, cheerful atmosphere of the early twentieth century, Los Angeles, too, was making rapid progress. Civic and business leaders, eagerly reaching out for a share of the state's prosperity, were aggressive and forward-looking in their development of the area's potentialities, as Los Angeles "began the new century with a stout heart and confident air."[15] Except for the depression after the Panic of 1907, the decade from 1900 to 1910 was one of almost continuous good times. The city's population, which had doubled between 1890 and 1900, increased more than threefold in the next decade, rising from about 102,500 in 1900 to some 319,000 in 1910. Rainfall was adequate for most of the decade, and sufficient food and water supplies for the growing population were promised in the development of Imperial Valley and the assurance of the Owens River aqueduct. The value of building permits jumped from just over $2,000,000 in 1899 to approximately $21,000,000 in 1910. The future for trade and commerce looked bright, with the beginning of a deepwater harbor at San Pedro, the opening of the Los Angeles, San Pedro, and Salt Lake Railroad, and the start of Henry E. Huntington's interurban network of Pacific Electric lines. Clearinghouse balances, less than $500,000 a day in 1901, rose to nearly $3,000,000 in 1911. Bank deposits more than doubled during the decade, membership in the Chamber of Commerce tripled, and the tourist trade never faltered. The volume of real estate transactions, except for a brief decline in 1904 and a deeper drop in 1907, supplied additional evidence that this was a boom period.[16] It was small wonder that at mid-decade the president of the Merchants' and Manufacturers' Association could say, "We can look forward to the future with the utmost confidence and greatest expectations."[17]

One of the most glowing prospects for the community lay in a steady advance in manufacturing, made possible by increasing production of a cheap fuel. The entrance of the Standard Oil Company into the southern California petroleum fields in 1900 began the flow of eastern capital which raised the oil industry to new heights of achievement. As early as 1901 it was evident that development of this young industry was the most crucial single factor in the city's new prosperity. Manufacturing made great strides in the decade from 1900 to 1910, as value of products increased from some $21,000,000 to about $68,500,000, or by more than 200 per cent. Comparable figures for the state as a whole were somewhat less than $303,000,000 in 1900, and approximately $529,750,000 in 1910. The percentage increase for Los Angeles was thus considerably higher than for California. Along with the greater value of products in Los Angeles went similar gains in number of wage earners, total wages paid, and amount of capitalization. The southern city was rapidly forging ahead to ever greater importance in the state's economy.[18]

The expansion of Los Angeles, in size, in building operations, in commercial activity, in manufacturing, provided abundant work and good wages for the laboring classes. As the city slowly emerged from the crippling depression of the 'nineties, organized labor felt its spirit lifting in the brightening dawn of prosperity. The process of reactivating and rebuilding long dormant unions was, however, very gradual, for a customary lag retarded recovery in Los Angeles. In San Francisco, as elsewhere in the country, business revival and the corresponding reawakening of labor began in 1898, but it was not until very near the end of the century that Los Angeles felt the stimulating impact of returning good times. The labor movement showed only the faintest signs of new life in 1899, and its real growth dated from the fall of 1900. Its development during the years 1900–1904—rapid expansion in both size and number of local unions, inclusion of previously unorganized trades and occupations, and geographical extension of unionism to other parts of southern California—was a microcosm of the national picture. For the first few years of this period, local labor, too, rejoiced in good relationships with management, winning numerous wage and hour concessions and signing trade agreements with various employers. It was not long, however, before union victories transformed latent employer antagonism into the furious counterassault which made Los Angeles par excellence the seat of the open shop. The antiunion drive did not reach full fruition until after 1904, but warning signs of its coming first appeared locally, as in the United States, shortly after the turn of the century.

Los Angeles labor had a sturdy foundation of surviving unions on which to raise a new structure, though some of them had outlasted the depression in name only. The following list shows the organizations which stayed alive to become the nucleus of the greater labor movement of the twentieth century in the Los Angeles area:

Central bodies	*Organization date*[19]
Council of Labor	1890
Allied Printing Trades Council	1897
Unions	
Typographical Union No. 174	1875
San Pedro Sailors' Union	1885
Cigar Makers' Union No. 225	1886
Tailors' Union No. 81	1890
Plumbers' Union No. 78	1891
Carpenters' Union No. 332	1892
Pasadena Painters' Union No. 92	1892[20]
Bakers' Union No. 37	1892
Retail Clerks' Protective Association No. 83	1892
Electrical Workers' Union No. 61	1893
Theatrical Stage Employees' Union No. 33	1896
Printing Pressmen's Union No. 78	1896
Bookbinders' Union No. 63	1896
Press Feeders' Union No. 37	1897
Musicians' Protective Association No. 47	1897
Journeymen Butchers' Association No. 4	1897
Railroad unions	
Brotherhood of Locomotive Firemen No. 97	1882
Brotherhood of Locomotive Engineers No. 5	1882
Order of Railway Conductors No. 111	1886
Brotherhood of Railroad Trainmen No. 74	1886
Switchmen's Mutual Aid Association No. 43	1887
Brotherhood of Locomotive Firemen No. 90	1891

With the exception of the railroad unions and the butchers' association, all of these organizations were integral parts of the local labor movement.

With the waning of the depression in 1899, the Los Angeles labor movement began to reassert itself. During the summer representatives of the Council of Labor appeared before the City Council to urge local observance of the recently passed state law stipulating the eight-hour day on public works. Labor's persistence in focusing public attention on violations by contractors forced the authorities into investigations which culminated in a stricter conformity with the law. In November the Council of Labor promised to help the Los Angeles Traction Company conductors and motormen, whose long dissatisfaction with company policies crystallized with the allegedly unwarranted discharge of four employees. The Council's hope of bringing these previously unorganized workers within its orbit was not, however, immediately realized. Clearer evidence that the Council was shifting from defensive to offensive tactics was its suggestion in November, 1899, that the Typographical Union reactivate its fight against the *Times*. The printers' inability to heed the proposal accentuated a reversal from earlier days, when oftener than not the Typographical Union had pointed the way for the Council of Labor.[21]

The Council became more aggressive in 1900, directing its first attack at the contract system on public works. In January it protested to the City Council that laborers employed in construction of the Third Street tunnel were in danger because of improper roof timbering. The complaint was given dramatic force when, less than a week later, the tunnel caved in, killing three men. Ironically, one of the victims was a city inspector who had just approved the contractor's work. After investigating the disaster, the city engineer agreed that the immediate cause was insufficient bracing of the roof but reënforced labor's contention that the real culprit was the "vicious system of public work." For the next two months the Council of Labor, the carpenters' union, and socialists deluged the City Council with petitions for stricter supervision of contractors and greater precautions in tunnel work. After a full-scale inquiry the City Council replied that it was doing everything in its legal power to safeguard the lives of workingmen. Although the Council of Labor failed to banish private contractors from public work, it utilized the recent tragedy to drive home its point that the contract system was an evil. For a time the city authorities were more than usually scrupulous in watching contractors engaged in public work.[22]

By renewing their customary activities in 1899–1900, the Council's member unions showed that they, too, were no longer willing to remain submerged. The plumbers, who had voluntarily reduced their wages to $2.50 a day in April, 1898, and had persuaded employers to raise them to $3 in October of the same year, tried in August, 1899, to establish a $3.50 level. A few of the smaller concerns paid the higher wage, but two leading firms refused the increase. The union struck against them and called upon the Master Plumbers' Association to deprive the two shops of membership. The former harmony between master and journeymen plumbers was interrupted when the Association failed to exert pressure against the recalcitrants.[23] In the fall of 1899 both the musicians' and the stage employees' unions bestirred themselves to enlarge employment opportunities for their members, and the Allied Printing Trades Council prevailed upon the Los Angeles Printers' Association to sanction the use of the allied label on all labor printing. In November the tailors' union, which had barely managed to retain its charter, was revived, and the cigar makers struck against one employer over a minor issue.[24] Not all of these efforts were successful, nor was any of them separately significant, but together they indicated that an inert labor movement was slowly coming to life.

Another sign of labor's response to the turn of the business cycle was the organization of several new unions before the end of 1899. In August the brewery workers employed by Maier and Zobelein formed a union which immediately affiliated with the Council of Labor. In September the plasterers, dissatisfied with wages of $2.50 to $3 a day, reorganized as Local No. 2 and persuaded employers to raise their daily pay to $3.50. A new branch of the Brotherhood of Carpenters and Joiners, Local No. 426, was organized in November, a sign of immediate improvement in the construction industry. In the same month the Milkers' Protective Association, the first Los Angeles union of milkers, appeared. Early in 1900 both the lathers and bricklayers reorganized, and in May, Machinists' Union No. 311 was chartered by the International Association of Machinists.[25]

With these new organizations the Los Angeles labor movement, at the end of May, 1900, was composed of twenty-nine identifiable unions. The California Bureau of Labor Statistics, in compiling data for the entire state, counted only twenty-six unions, including the railroad brotherhoods, or about 12 per cent of the 217 labor organizations of California. The discrepancy arose because the Bureau, lacking complete information, did not list the local unions of retail clerks, butchers, and switchmen. The Bureau estimated the membership of Los Angeles unions as approximately 2,100 out of a total state membership of 37,500.[26] Compared to the 2,700 members estimated in 1888, and the five to six thousand in 1896, the shrunken size of the Los Angeles labor movement in 1900 revealed the severity of the depression which had sapped its strength.

Yet this weakened labor movement was about to embark on a most rewarding phase of its career, during which it strove for full organization, union recognition, improved working conditions, and, finally, community acceptance of unionism as a social institution. Choosing the first of these objectives as prerequisite to the others, the Council of Labor in 1900 launched a campaign to increase the size of the local union movement. During the spring the Council began to coördinate the existing unions by urging better attendance at meetings and by holding a great labor rally. By the summer it was ready to put a paid organizer in the field, selecting for the job its vice-president, John Ince, a cabinetmaker who had come to Los Angeles from Seattle. After Ince had been at work for a few months, the Council appointed a committee of unpaid volunteers to assist in the organization of unions both in Los Angeles and in other southern California communities, such as San Bernardino, Riverside, and Long Beach. The committee included James Gray, president of the Council, Lemuel Biddle, and Fred C. Wheeler.[27]

Wheeler was one of the outstanding leaders of the Los Angeles labor movement in the early twentieth century. Born in Minnesota in 1867, he joined a carpenters' union in St. Augustine, Florida, at the age of twenty. After leaving Florida he came to California, stayed briefly in San Diego and San Francisco, and arrived in Pasadena in 1892, where he was almost immediately elected president of the carpenters' union. Quickly recognized as a man of unusual ability, Wheeler was chosen in 1894 to preside over an eight-hour convention held in San Francisco. In 1898 he was elected president of the Los Angeles Council of Labor and was sent as the Council's first delegate to the AFL convention. In 1900 Wheeler again headed the Council and represented it at the national convention. In ensuing years he took a major part in the organizing activities of the Council, the California State Federation of Labor, and the American Federation of Labor in the Los Angeles area.[28]

In the fall of 1900 Wheeler, by inducing the Council of Labor to intervene in another abuse of the contract system, was partly responsible for the first organization of Los Angeles teamsters. In October, as vociferous chairman of a Council committee, he aired the wrongdoings of A. P. Cross, street sprinkling contractor, who paid his teamsters wages below the legal $2 minimum and exceeded the legal maximum of eight hours per day. Although the City Council relet the contract to

Cross for the next two and a half years, it stipulated enforcement of state laws regulating wages and hours on public works. Teamsters in general suffered from unsatisfactory working conditions: a twelve-hour day, overtime work on special occasions without compensation, and low wages. Many of the men slept in the livery stables to save room rent. In November, 1900, John Ince organized the teamsters' union with thirteen charter members. The union affiliated with the International Team Drivers' Union, later the International Brotherhood of Teamsters, in December.[29]

The local organizing campaign was given a boost in the fall of 1900 by the American Federation of Labor, the first national body to send assistance to the reviving Los Angeles labor movement. In 1899, at the request of San Francisco delegates, the AFL convention had voted the necessary funds for a Pacific Coast representative, and in November, 1900, general organizer Jefferson D. Pierce arrived in Los Angeles. Closely collaborating with Ince and the Council of Labor, Pierce started the upward spiral of organization which did not falter appreciably until 1904. He formed new unions, increased the size of old ones, and taught local leaders the techniques of organization. When Pierce moved on to San Francisco in January, 1901, Los Angeles labor had profited much from his experience.[30]

In addition to employing both paid and volunteer organizers, the Council of Labor contributed to the growth of the labor movement in other ways. In January, 1901, it sponsored the establishment of an official weekly newspaper for organized labor. L. W. Rogers, formerly a member of the American Railway Union and a close associate of Eugene Debs, became editor of the *Union Labor News,* and John Ince, business manager. They financed the venture by selling stock and subscriptions to unions and union members. When the first issue came off the press on January 25, the veteran *Coast Seamen's Journal* praised it as a reliable and worthy labor organ. Another valuable accomplishment early in 1901 was creation of a union labor bureau. The Council of Labor, seeking a substitute for the old Free Labor Bureau, now completely out of union hands, and for corrupt private employment agencies, had first proposed a union agency in 1900. The project died in the face of strenuous opposition from the printers, who felt that the financing presented an insuperable obstacle. But in March, 1901, the printers endorsed the Council's plan, not because their craft would be directly aided but because they needed the good will of other unions. Financed by per capita union assessments, the bureau began operations in May, 1901, in the Council's new and commodious quarters on South Spring Street.[31]

Through these various channels, the Council of Labor was responsible for initiating a unionizing drive of significant proportions and remarkable results. The Council's leadership stimulated individual unions to place either paid or volunteer business agents in the field, and its coöperation eased the task of outside organizers sent by national and state labor bodies to supplement the work of local representatives. Although the Los Angeles Council had had little to do with the AFL's dispatch of Pierce to the Pacific Coast, it did send a delegate to the 1900 AFL convention which voted to strengthen its organizing campaign in the South and West, areas where local labor particularly needed guidance. The decision to appoint organizers for four specific regions, one embracing the Pacific Coast states, resulted in the selection of John Ince as an AFL district organizer early in 1901. Although Ince's duties frequently took him outside the city, he kept a watchful eye on progress in Los Angeles and retained his office of vice-president of the Council until July, 1901. Then, resigning both as Council official and AFL organizer, he separated himself completely from the labor movement.[32]

Ince's resignation interrupted the organizing work of the AFL in California, though both the State Federation of Labor and the Los Angeles Council of Labor requested a replacement. From the middle of 1901 until the beginning of 1903 Los Angeles received scant consideration from the national federation. Lemuel Biddle served as AFL district organizer for a brief term in the spring of 1902, and W. E. Goodman, a general organizer, spent part of the summer and fall in the city. Goodman's report stressed the need for continued outside help in Los Angeles, where only a few unions could afford full-time business agents, and where sharp antiunion propaganda by the *Times* accentuated the organizing difficulties.[33]

Swayed by Goodman's representations, the 1902 AFL convention made amends for its previous neglect by adopting a resolution introduced by Fred Wheeler:

Whereas, For years past Southern California has received but little attention from the American Federation of Labor in the way of organizers; and

Whereas, The great amount of organizing has been done at our expense; and

Whereas, The great influx of men from the East, mostly non-union, has put us to a great expense in gathering them into the fold, and further that it is the unanimous wish of organized labor in California that we be given a general organizer; therefore be it

Resolved, By this convention that the incoming President of the American Federation of Labor be instructed to appoint an organizer who shall spend at least six months in Southern California to assist in building up the unorganized workers.[34]

Upon the recommendation of the Los Angeles Council of Labor, Gompers named Wheeler as the district organizer for southern California. During 1903 both Wheeler and Biddle, serving respectively the AFL and the local Council, organized many unions in the Los Angeles area.[35]

In 1903 Francis Drake, prominent member of the Typographical Union and president of the Council of Labor, represented Los Angeles at the AFL convention; Wheeler was again on hand as delegate from the carpenters' national union. Both men asked for a full-time special organizer for the Los Angeles area, citing as evidence of need the importation of nonunion workers by employers' organizations and of Mexican labor by the railroads, and the inadequacy of state and local organizing agencies to cope with increasingly militant opposition. Representatives of labor in San Francisco and other west coast areas strongly seconded these appeals. The AFL not only appointed James Gray as organizer for California, but in addition kept Wheeler on its list of paid representatives. When Gray resigned in July, 1904, so that he could devote all his energy to the Los Angeles campaign, Gompers appointed William S. Smith, business agent of the local teamsters' union, to the state post. But despite the work of these various organizers, the second half of 1904 reflected the decline afflicting labor throughout the country.[36]

The California State Federation of Labor and representatives from national and international unions also helped to speed the Los Angeles organizing drive during the years 1900 to 1904. In January, 1903, the State Federation elected Fred Wheeler to a newly created post of state organizer. Serving both the AFL and the State Federation during 1903, Wheeler organized twenty-two unions, assisted in the formation of thirteen others, and induced some existing unions to join the State Federation; he claimed to have brought six thousand new men into unions and over nine thousand into the State Federation. Reëlected state organizer in January, 1904, Wheeler continued to organize and affiliate unions until 1905, when an Oakland delegate narrowly defeated him for the job. Biddle, the unpaid volunteer, and Wheeler, the official organizer, were the two individuals most responsible for the upsurge of unionism in Los Angeles between 1900 and 1904. More sporadic but none the less valuable were the efforts of various national union officials who visited Los Angeles for limited periods in the interest of their particular crafts. Each year saw an increasing influx of these dignitaries, who attended Council of Labor meetings, spoke to their own and allied organizations, and swelled the number of unions and of union members.[37]

The combined endeavors of local, AFL, State Federation, and national union organizers enormously strengthened the Los Angeles labor movement. Tables 3 and 4 give the total number of new unions organized during the years 1900–1904, the first by locality and the second by industry. Until 1904, the labor movements of San Pedro and Pasadena belonged to the Los Angeles County Council of Labor. Table 4 shows which occupations enjoyed the greatest expansion; as expected, the

TABLE 3

FIRST ORGANIZATION* OF LOCAL UNIONS, ALL INDUSTRIES, LOS ANGELES, PASADENA, AND SAN PEDRO, JUNE 1, 1900–DECEMBER 31, 1904

Year	City			Total
	Los Angeles	Pasadena	San Pedro	
1900................	17	0	0	17
1901................	26	4	2	32
1902................	26	2	2	30
1903................	20	5	3	28
1904................	9	0	6	15
Total..............	98	11	13	122

* In cases where exact organization dates are unknown, they are roughly determined from other data.
SOURCE: Table 5.

building trades were easily in the lead. Although table 5, listing individual unions by year of organization, was compiled from all available sources, it may occasionally be in error. Assumptions based on collateral evidence had to be made for unions whose exact organization dates could not be determined. Most of the unions listed survived the period, though some died out and others had to reorganize several times. Such reorganizations are not included in table 5. It should also be noted that these tables refer only to *new* organizations. Those unions which retained their charters through the depression years provided a foundation for the larger labor movement of the new century.

Contemporary estimates of the membership of the whole body of organized labor and of the number of affiliates in the Council of Labor, though not always reliable, indicate continuous growth between 1900 and 1904. As of May 31, 1900, the California Bureau of Labor Statistics claimed twenty-six unions with a total membership of 2,100 for Los Angeles. By the early summer of 1901, the Council of Labor included approximately forty-five unions with a membership of between four and five thousand. In August, more than fifty affiliates comprised the Council, and their total membership approached seven thousand. Toward the end of 1902 there were more than sixty unions, including the railroad brotherhoods, in Los Angeles proper. A year later the labor movement of the area, now ten thousand strong, was organized into eighty-two unions, sixty-four of which belonged to the Council of Labor. In 1904 this membership remained relatively stable. Although the or-

TABLE 4

FIRST ORGANIZATION* OF LOCAL UNIONS, BY INDUSTRY GROUP, LOS ANGELES, PASADENA, AND SAN PEDRO, JUNE 1, 1900–DECEMBER 31, 1904

Industry	Year					Total
	1900	1901	1902	1903	1904	
Building and construction...............	6	10	7	8	3	34
Services, except public...................	1	7	5	9	3	25
Manufacturing..........................	4	6	6	4	3	23
Transportation and storage..............	1	5	4	4	3	17
Metal trades...........................	4	1	6	3	2	16
Printing trades.........................	0	2	2	0	0	4
Public services.........................	1	1	0	0	1	3
Total.............................	17	32	30	28	15	122

* In cases where exact organization dates are unknown, they are roughly determined from other data.
SOURCE: Table 5.

ganizing momentum then began to lag, the years from 1900 to 1904 had brought forth a surge of unionism in Los Angeles, as elsewhere in the country, unlike anything that had gone before.[38]

The centralizing tendency noted in both nation and state was likewise apparent in Los Angeles. Only two central bodies emerged intact from the depression years, the Council of Labor and the Allied Printing Trades Council. In March, 1901, a new Building Trades Council was organized with James Gray, president of the Council of Labor, as business agent. Within a year it claimed jurisdiction over nearly four thousand union members.[39]

The tightening of central authority proceeded in 1902 with the organization of a District Council of Carpenters, a Brewery Workers' Section, and the San Pedro Labor Council. The District Council of Carpenters, starting with two local unions, gradually expanded in size and influence until, in 1904, it employed two full-time business agents

TABLE 5

First Organization* of Local Unions, Los Angeles, Pasadena, and San Pedro, June 1, 1900–December 31, 1904

Year	Total	Local unions first organized

BUILDING AND CONSTRUCTION:

Year	Total	Local unions first organized
1900	6	Bricklayers[1] †Brickmakers[2] Electrical Workers—inside wiremen[3] †Hod Carriers[2] Painters[4] Tile Layers[5]
1901	10	Amalgamated Sheet Metal Workers[6] †Amalgamated Society of Carpenters[7] Carpenters (Pasadena)[8] Cement Workers[9] Composition Roofers[10] †Federal Labor (Pasadena)[9] †Lathers[9] †Plasterers (Pasadena)[7] †Plumbers (Pasadena)[7] †Shinglers[9]
1902	7	†Building Laborers and Hod Carriers (Negro)[11] Carpenters (San Pedro)[12] †Electrical Workers' Helpers[11] Federal Labor[13] †Granite Cutters[14] Sheet Metal Workers (Pasadena)[15] Painters—sign writers[15]
1903	8	†Carpenters[16] Electrical Workers—telephone and switchboard men[17] Electrical Workers (Pasadena)[18] Federal Labor (Mexican)[19] Housemovers and Riggers[20] Shinglers (Pasadena)[21] Sheet Metal Workers, 2d local[18] Structural Iron Workers[18]
1904	3	†Gas and Electric Fixture Workers[22] Painters (San Pedro)[23] Pile Drivers (San Pedro)[24]

TABLE 5—*Continued*

Year	Total	Local unions first organized
SERVICES, EXCEPT PUBLIC:		
1900	1	†Railroad Telegraphers[25]
1901	7	Barbers[26] Bartenders' Alliance[10] Bootblacks[27] Hotel and Restaurant Employees[28] Laundry Workers[29] Messenger Boys[6] Waitresses[30]
1902	5	†Boot and Shoe Repairers[16] †Cooks' Alliance[14] †Newsboys[31] Railroad Clerks[32] Waiters and Waitresses[14]
1903	9	Amalgamated Meat Cutters—retail[33] †Cooks, 2d local[34] Drug Clerks[18] †Fishermen (San Pedro)[35] †Kitchen Helpers[36] †Laundry Workers (San Pedro)[37] Meat Cutters (Pasadena)[17] Retail Clerks (San Pedro)[38] Telephone Operators[39]
1904	3	Barbers (San Pedro)[40] Bill Posters and Billers[41] Shoe Clerks[42]
MANUFACTURING:		
1900	4	Amalgamated Woodworkers[5] Broom Makers[5] Carriage Makers and Horseshoers[43] Garment Workers[44]
1901	6	†Beer Bottlers[9] Glass Workers[45] Leather Workers on Horse Goods[46] Shoemakers[47] Stationary Engineers[6] Woodworkers (San Pedro)[48]

TABLE 5—*Continued*

Year	Total	Local unions first organized

MANUFACTURING (*continued*):

Year	Total	Local unions first organized
1902	6	Bicycle Workers[32] Candymakers[32] Coopers[13] Traveling Goods and Leather Novelty Workers[49] Upholsterers[15] Woodworkers (Pasadena)[15]
1903	4	Butcher Workmen—slaughterers and packers[50] Garment Workers, 2d local[51] Paper Box Makers[17] Stationary Firemen[52]
1904	3	†Flour and Cereal Mill Employees[53] Glass Bottle Blowers[54] †Steam Engineers (San Pedro)[55]

TRANSPORTATION AND STORAGE:

Year	Total	Local unions first organized
1900	1	Teamsters[56]
1901	5	Beer Drivers and Stablemen[57] Federal Labor—longshoremen (San Pedro)[46] Laundry Wagon Drivers[58] †Team Owners[7] United Railway Employees[59]
1902	4	Frieght Handlers[32] †Lumbermen[60] †Railway Carmen[61] Teamsters and Team Drivers (San Pedro)[15]
1903	4	Stablemen[62] Street Railway Employees[63] Teamsters (Pasadena)[18] Winehouse Employees[18]
1904	3	Building Material Team Drivers[64] Longshoremen, 2d union (San Pedro)[65] Lumber Handlers and Tallymen (San Pedro)[66]

TABLE 5—*Continued*

Year	Total	Local unions first organized
METAL TRADES:		
1900	4	Blacksmiths[67] Blacksmiths' Helpers[44] Brass Workers[5] Horseshoers[5]
1901	1	†Pipe and Tank Makers[14]
1902	6	Boilermakers[32] Boilermakers' Helpers[32] Core Makers[15] Cornice Makers[68] Iron Molders[14] Patternmakers[69]
1903	3	Allied Metal Mechanics[70] Blacksmiths (Pasadena)[18] Machinists' Helpers[51]
1904	2	Car Pipemen[71] †Machinists, 2d local[72]
PRINTING TRADES:		
1900	0	....
1901	2	†Lithographers[14] Stereotypers[73]
1902	2	Mailers[74] Photoengravers[74]
1903	0	....
1904	0	....

TABLE 5—*Concluded*

Year	Total	Local unions first organized

PUBLIC SERVICES:

Year	Total	Local unions first organized
1900	I	†Letter Carriers[75]
1901	I	†Postoffice Clerks[76]
1902	0	. . . .
1903	0	. . . .
1904	I	Sanitary Inspectors[77]

* In cases where exact organization dates are unknown, they are roughly determined from other data.
† This sign indicates those unions for which organization dates are so determined.
SOURCE: Footnotes 1–77 in Appendix A.

and represented the carpenters throughout Los Angeles County. The Brewery Workers' Section comprised the unions of brewery workers, bottlers, and brewery wagon drivers. In San Pedro, described by the *Times* as the only "union town" in southern California, the labor movement formed its own central body in 1902 but retained its affiliation with Los Angeles labor until 1904. Late in 1902 an attempt to organize a Los Angeles Metal Trades Council failed, and the number of department councils remained stationary until 1904, when a major reorganization of the Council of Labor systematized interunion and interdepartment relationships.[40]

Backed by a labor movement steadily advancing in size and unification, the Council of Labor during these years took up the job of creating good public relations in the community. One of its methods of winning public recognition was celebration of Labor Day, not only to stimulate union members but to exhibit a rejuvenated labor movement. With floats illustrating different crafts at work and banners proclaiming union principles, Labor Day parades in 1901–1903 made the streets gay with color and vouched for the growth of a new and challenging unionism. Thousands of workers parading the streets gave tangible evidence that Los Angeles labor was on the march. In 1904, when the organizing drive began to slacken, the unions substituted a picnic and rally for the customary public display.[41]

Before 1900, organized labor had more than once sought to make an impression on the life of the community, but its contributions were

limited by its lack of standing. But the greatly increased labor movement of the new century was a force which could no longer be denied
recognition. As spokesman for the unions, the Council of Labor frequently joined in municipal affairs, sometimes by invitation, sometimes
on its own initiative. In 1900 it persuaded the Merchants' and Manufacturers' Association to request that the public library contract for
binding books be awarded to a Los Angeles instead of a San Francisco
firm, in the interest of home industry. Later the same year the Council
decided to investigate local dairies, charged with selling adulterated
milk and flouting sanitary regulations. In 1901, again attacking the
contract system, labor representatives tried to prevent the street sweeping contract from going to a firm evading the state laws for public
works. In 1902 the Council of Labor asked the Board of Education to
bar a textbook slanted against unions. Although such efforts sometimes
failed, they illustrated labor's consciousness of community problems.
In May, 1903, when Los Angeles celebrated the visit of President Theodore Roosevelt with a fiesta, the Council helped plan the event and
entered a float in the procession. Later the same year Francis Drake,
president of the Council of Labor, expounded the principles of unionism and the struggles of the working class to the fashionable and aristocratic Ebell Club.[42]

A governmental change which labor had long advocated was municipal ownership of public utilities. In 1868, the city had voted to complete
purchase of the water system within thirty years, but when the period
expired the water company was reluctant to give up a profitable enterprise. In 1901, after several years of litigation, the City Council finally
ordered an election on a $2 million bond issue for purchase of the plant.
The *Union Labor News* urged all citizens to vote for the bonds, arguing
that it was better to pay an exorbitant price at the time than to be bled
by the company for years and then still have to buy. The *Times* gave
labor high praise for its forthright stand, and agreed with its conten-
tions. The bond issue carried by a majority of five to one in August,
1901, and the city bought the water system for $2 million. Organized
labor had again helped to effect a major transformation in municipal
affairs.[43]

In 1901 Los Angeles labor, though not the prime mover, assisted in
an enterprise extending beyond the city's bounds and bringing at least
a portion of the public into close association with union representatives.
The agitation for continuance of the Geary Act, due to expire in May,
1902, pointed to broad public acceptance of one of labor's earliest
causes, restriction of Chinese immigration. The new movement origi-

nated with the American Federation of Labor, following pressure by western delegates, one of whom represented the California State Federation of Labor. The resulting campaign was of national scope, as labor organizations all over the country followed the lead of the AFL. In California, the mayor of San Francisco summoned an exclusion convention for November, 1901. All cities and counties in the state, all trade and labor organizations, and all civic societies were requested to send delegates; United States senators and congressmen from California, state officials, and governors of other western states were invited to attend. The city and county of Los Angeles, as well as the Council of Labor and a number of unions, sent representatives. The convention, totaling some three thousand delegates from all sections of the state and from groups as disparate as employers' associations and trade-unions, petitioned Congress to continue existing treaties with China and to extend the Geary Act. It also appointed a committee to consider the question of excluding Japanese and other Asiatics from the United States. On April 29, 1902, Congress renewed for an indefinite period all laws prohibiting and regulating Chinese immigration."

Through such events and alliances organized labor was slowly gaining a new community status in Los Angeles. Although its efforts were not always crowned by success, the Council of Labor ably demonstrated that as the representative of workers it had a claim to operate in areas other than collective bargaining. The period from 1900 to 1904 not only saw a great expansion of unionism but also brought union members a sense of dignity as part of a maturing social institution that looked beyond the workshop and the factory for new realms of influence. Another gateway to power was political activity, and in this field organized labor tried the new direction of alliance with the socialists.

XVI. LABOR AND SOCIALISM

ALTHOUGH the early twentieth century collaboration of trade-unionists and socialists was part of labor's search for wider control in a period of expansion, its roots lay in the depression years at the close of the nineteenth century. Then, with economic rewards thinning out, Los Angeles labor looked once again to politics and reform. The orientation differed, however, for now socialism was superseding Populism. The few labor leaders, like Cyren E. Fisk and Jonathan Bailey, who for a time clung to the dying People's Party made the transition to formal socialism easily enough, since "Populists, virtually left without a party after 1900, found a ready welcome with the Socialist Party, at a minimum cost in change of ideology."[1] Trade-unionists of Los Angeles thus helped to lay the foundation for a hardy socialist movement which flourished in the first decade of the twentieth century, and for a socialist-labor political alliance which came to full fruition in the election campaigns of 1902.

The history of socialist parties in Los Angeles paralleled national developments. Three groups contended chiefly for labor support: the Socialist Labor Party, with its subsidiary Trades and Labor Alliance; the Social Democracy, forerunner of the Socialist Party of America; and Christian Socialism. Until the later 1890's, it was the Socialist Labor Party that offered a political outlet to unionists with socialist leanings. Lemuel Biddle and other radical Nationalists had organized a local branch in 1890, just as the Los Angeles labor movement was being stirred to life by the printers' strike against the *Times*. For the next few years the work of rebuilding old unions, fashioning new ones, and consolidating them in a central body absorbed labor's energies; such groups and individuals who desired a fuller expression of the reform spirit than allowed by formal union structure found satisfaction in the People's Party. Controversy over alliance with the Populists continued until 1894, when the Council of Labor officially repudiated the People's Party and affiliated with the American Federation of Labor. For the next several years Los Angeles labor adhered to the AFL policy of accepting and using Populist principles, without fully endorsing the People's Party.

Settlement of the Populist issue did not, however, dispose of all uncertainties on the political front, either nationally or locally. During 1894, the AFL itself was torn by dissension, as socialist members tried to subvert the traditional policy of electing labor's friends and defeating its enemies, regardless of party, and of concentrating on economic rather than political action. At the December convention, hoping to turn the Federation from indirect to direct political participation, the insurgents proposed formation of a labor party based on "collective ownership by the people of all means of production and distribution." Although Gompers defeated the move, the socialist wing was strong enough to oust him from the presidency of the AFL. The schism within the Federation lasted only a year, for the AFL reëlected Gompers as president in December, 1895, and under his guidance emphatically reaffirmed the stand against socialism. In 1896 Los Angeles unions, falling into line, decisively downed a socialist scheme to gain control of the Labor Congress, and further vexed the Socialist Labor Party by adhering to Populist principles, particularly the free coinage of silver.[2]

Certain of the Council of Labor's affiliates, however, were not averse to concert with socialists. In March, 1895, a number of unions sent delegates to a Socialist Labor Party mass meeting, presided over by a member of the American Railway Union. S. E. Fulton of the International Educational Labor Association, organized in August as a forum for socialist ideas, addressed the carpenters' union in October. The Association, though regarded as a "union" for unorganized workers, attracted many members of craft unions, the Knights of Labor, and the American Railway Union. Arthur Vinette, for example, was prominent in its activities. Both the Educational Labor Association and the Socialist Labor Party were invited to participate in the 1895 Labor Day parade, a noncommittal gesture of friendship. Since the Association was not a political party, it was admitted in 1896 to full membership in the Labor Congress after subscribing to the platform of that body.[3] Thus it can be seen that, although organized labor had formally renounced political partisanship, some unions and individuals were still eagerly reaching out for Utopian solutions. When Job Harriman came to Los Angeles in 1895, the local Socialist Labor Party found in him a new source of strength to vitalize the faithful adherence of Lemuel Biddle and other like-minded unionists.

Job Harriman was born in Clinton County, Indiana, in 1861, and lived on a farm until he was eighteen years old. After attending Butler University at Irvington, Indiana, he entered the ministry, but a change in his views soon dictated a shift to the legal profession, and in 1885 he was admitted to the Indiana bar. Because of ill health, Harriman came to Los Angeles in 1895. Although fighting a constant battle with tuberculosis until his death thirty years later, he made few concessions to illness in his devotion to the class struggle.[4]

About 1890, Harriman turned from the Democratic Party to the

Nationalist movement. Later, breaking with the moderates as Biddle had done, he entered the Socialist Labor Party and, upon arrival in Los Angeles, became its southern California organizer. With extraordinary qualities of leadership he made the party a dynamic reform movement during the years 1895–1900. Harriman's agitation up and down the Pacific Coast soon brought him acclaim in national party circles as "a brilliant speaker and untiring worker." But the financial rewards for an itinerant socialist were too meager, and in 1898 Harriman was admitted to the California bar. In the critical years ahead, his courtroom eloquence frequently served unionists on trial.[5]

Harriman firmly believed that socialists should stretch their coöperation with organized labor to political unification. In 1896, however, when the Los Angeles Socialist Labor Party first ventured into politics, circumstances were not favorable to his idea. That was the year of fusion between Democrats and Populists, and of labor's experiment with the Labor Congress, which leaned heavily in the direction of Bryanism and free silver. The socialists, sharply criticizing the People's Party both for losing its identity in a "capitalist" party and for advocating free silver, broke doctrinally with most of organized labor. Only a few unionists appeared on the Socialist Labor Party's county and municipal tickets in 1896, and the vote for all socialist candidates was light. Nevertheless, the Socialist Labor Party in Los Angeles continued to propagandize workingmen. Pointing to the economic system as the chief cause of poverty, its speakers urged workers to transform the competitive system into a vast coöperative enterprise, either by electing their own men to office or by voting the Socialist Labor Party.[6]

Some unionists were converted to Harriman's way of thinking. When, early in 1898, the Merchants' and Manufacturers' Association invited every local union to participate in a home products exhibit, A. Krause of the bookbinders' union caustically rejected the notion that workingmen should join with employers in any undertaking. O. Hesse, secretary of the union, denied official authorization for refusal of the invitation and warned against socialist intrigues within the labor movement:

It is such people as Krause who are constantly giving the enemies of organized labor a club with which to hammer us. We have to stand for the fulminations of the weak-brained cranks who seek to promulgate their impracticable doctrines under the cloak of trades unions. . . . We know that his views are not the opinions of one one-hundredth part of the members of the trades unions of this city. . . .

This attempt of the Socialist Labor Party to turn our labor unions into Socialist organizations has got to be set down upon. We are organized for good, and above all for practical purposes, and we cannot afford to be diverted from the high aims and objects of true trade unionism to go after the dreamy and impracticable.[7]

Hesse, in voicing the traditional AFL rejection of utopian concepts, was at the same time undoubtedly expressing the majority view of organized labor in Los Angeles.

Notwithstanding labor's wariness about socialist intentions, the Council of Labor entered into an unpremeditated and unacknowledged collaboration with the Socialist Labor Party in 1898. Both groups were invited to work with the major political parties, the Merchants' and Manufacturers' Association, the Board of Trade, the Chamber of Commerce, the Teachers' Alliance, and the Christian Socialists in making joint nominations for a Board of Freeholders to write a new city charter. Disparate aims soon revealed the impossibility of agreement on one list of names. Accordingly the conservatives, alleging a coalition of Democrats, Populists, socialists, and labor, withdrew to formulate a slate of their own. Of the fifteen freeholders elected from the competing tickets, seven had been named by the conservatives, four by the "radicals," and four by both sides. Although conservatives held the balance of power, socialists and trade-unionists managed to write the initiative and referendum into the proposed charter. Just before the election, however, labor criticized the instrument for not stipulating a minimum daily wage of $2 on public work and for not outlawing the contract system. The charter was defeated by a decisive majority in December, 1898, despite the support of mercantile organizations, the League for Better City Government, and the *Times*.[8] A few months later, in May, 1899, the City Council voted that all public works contracts must specify payment of the $2 minimum wage in accordance with a state law of 1897.[9]

Heartened by organized labor's coöperation in this first community recognition, the Socialist Labor Party enthusiastically entered the political campaigns of 1898. In May the state convention nominated a full slate, including Job Harriman for governor and Lemuel Biddle for clerk of the supreme court; Los Angeles socialists later named city and county tickets. A feature of the gubernatorial contest was a series of debates between Harriman and James G. Maguire, the Democratic-Populist candidate, on subjects such as "Which Party Best Deserves the Support of the Workingmen?" In the state elections Harriman polled 5,143 out of a total of 287,055 votes cast; the Republican Henry T. Gage won with 148,354 votes. In Los Angeles, the votes for socialist candidates varied between 500 and 750, less than a tenth of those going to the winners. Nevertheless, Harriman saw in the progress made since 1896 a reason for encouragement.[10]

The future of the Socialist Labor Party was, however, by no means assured, either in Los Angeles or elsewhere. The 1898 election occasioned the local emergence of the Trades and Labor Alliance, set up by Daniel DeLeon of the national party in December, 1895, immediately after the AFL rejected socialism and reëlected Gompers as president. DeLeon's object was to draw craft unionists away from the Federation and into the Socialist Labor Party. But his scheme contained the seeds of party disruption, for organization of the Trades and Labor Alliance not only failed to win socialist-minded unionists but also alienated moderates within the party. Remembering the destructive force of the struggle between the AFL and the Knights of Labor, they were apprehensive of a new form of dualism. Moreover, DeLeon's domineering insistence on radical doctrines essentially alien to American ideologies disturbed those of his colleagues who preferred the parliamentary to the revolutionary approach. The underlying conflict between opportunistic socialism and syndicalism became open rebellion in July, 1899, when the disaffected members of the Socialist Labor Party, led by Morris Hillquit and Max Hayes, revolted against DeLeon's leadership. Job Harriman, who had become California state organizer for the party, threw his weight to the Hillquit-Hayes group. In February, 1900, the anti-DeLeon faction nominated Harriman for President and Hayes for Vice-President of the United States.[11]

The 1899 breach was the beginning of the end of the old Socialist Labor Party. The revolt against DeLeon was as much personal as doctrinal, for Hillquit and Hayes and their followers objected to DeLeon's methods of trying to capture labor unions and his attacks on labor leaders like Gompers. Meanwhile, another brand of socialism, first called the Social Democracy, was coming to the front. In June, 1897, Eugene V. Debs wound up the affairs of the American Railway Union and merged it with the Social Democracy, then being formed in Chicago by representatives of labor unions, Socialist Labor Party clubs, colonization societies, religious organizations, and the like. Debs became the leading spirit of the new party, which called for public ownership of all industry, public work for the unemployed, postal savings banks, direct legislation, and proportional representation. Because of its respect for the political neutrality of trade-unions, Debs' party appealed more strongly to workingmen than had the Socialist Labor Party and, moreover, offered a refuge to the anti-DeLeon faction. After the split in the Socialist Labor Party, Hillquit, Hayes, and Harriman attended the Social Democracy convention in March, 1900, to work for unification of the two groups. The convention agreed upon a combination ticket headed by Debs for President and Harriman for Vice-President.

The merger was completed in July, 1901, when the new Socialist Party of America began a long, uphill fight to repair the damage wrought on socialist-union relations by the DeLeon party.[12]

In July, 1897, one month after the Social Democracy had been organized in Chicago, E. J. Mack formed a Los Angeles branch. Mack, formerly active in the American Railway Union, was currently working on Frank Colver's *Labor World and Silver Champion.* The cordial relations between the Los Angeles labor movement and the ARU, as well as deep regard for Debs, contributed to the local popularity of the Social Democracy. Membership grew rapidly, and several prominent unionists, W. C. B. Randolph of the carpenters and A. M. Green of the retail clerks, were interested from the start. In August, 1897, a few days after his election as president of the Council of Labor, Green became chairman of the executive board of the new socialist party. Job Harriman did not find his connection with the Socialist Labor Party a bar to affiliation with the Social Democracy; at the outset he was chosen secretary of the latter's executive board. For several years the Social Democracy and the Socialist Labor Party existed side by side in Los Angeles without open conflict, with Harriman contributing time and energy to both. In November, 1899, at the instance of and with the financial backing of H. Gaylord Wilshire, a wealthy socialist, Debs visited Los Angeles. The Council of Labor urged affiliated unions to attend Debs' lectures as important to the cause of organized labor; the Typographical Union alone purchased one hundred tickets for its members. Large and enthusiastic labor audiences turned out for two meetings, and the Council of Labor expressed gratitude to Wilshire for making Debs' visit possible.[13]

Another doctrine appealing to labor was Christian Socialism, formulated and spread by W. D. P. Bliss, a Congregational clergyman from Boston. Bliss came to Los Angeles early in 1898 and organized a Union Reform League to purify the city government and gain converts to his beliefs. Emphasis on the initiative and referendum gained the adherence of Dr. John R. Haynes, who became chairman of the Committee of One Hundred chosen to guide the work of the League. Among the labor representatives on the committee were Sam Chappel of the Typographical Union, A. M. Green, and W. C. B. Randolph. Bliss spoke publicly on socialist reforms under the auspices both of Green's union of retail clerks and of the Socialist Labor Party. The Christian Socialists were among the groups selecting nominees for the Board of Freeholders in 1898, and the Union Reform League advocated adoption of the charter.[14]

Late in 1900 Bliss' followers organized both a Christian Socialist Club of Los Angeles, with Dr. Haynes as president, and a Christian Social Union. The latter was really a kind of socialist church whose object was "to promote in the community a clearer recognition and a more hearty practice of that perfect equity which is to secure to all people the full and equal possession of their common inheritance."[15] The Christian Socialists' insistence on arbitration rather than strikes and boycotts, and their belief in private enterprise except for public utilities, transportation, and communication, endeared them neither to other socialists nor to labor unionists. The movement soon became relatively unimportant.[16]

Los Angeles Social Democrats lagged behind their national comrades in amalgamating with the anti-DeLeon faction of the Socialist Labor Party. The Debs-Harriman ticket had been nominated in March, 1900, but it was not until August, when campaigns for the fall elections were starting, that the first joint meetings were held locally. Harriman, as vice-presidential candidate for the coalition, was scorned as a traitor by the deserted Socialist Labor Party; Biddle, too, left the party he had helped organize in 1890 to join the Social Democracy.[17] With the beginning of the coalition's 1900 campaign in Los Angeles, Fred C. Wheeler, already prominent in the trade-union movement, took his place beside Harriman and Biddle in the socialist cause.

Wheeler, like Harriman, found his way into socialism when disillusionment made his earlier political affiliation unpalatable. For some years after first joining a union, he had been an earnest and hard-working Republican. His union activities, including prosecution of violators of labor laws, soon convinced him that the two major political parties were indifferent if not antagonistic to organized labor. Accordingly, Wheeler broke away from the Republican Party and allied himself with the socialists. His first experience with the Social Democrats in 1900 marked the beginning of a long political career, which culminated in his election as a socialist to the Los Angeles City Council in 1912. During that campaign the editor of the *Graphic,* a local weekly journal of moderate political slant, praised him in these words: "The Socialist Wheeler is justly regarded as an excellent citizen in spite of his radical political views."[18]

On August 25, 1900, Wheeler presided over the county convention of the Social Democrats. The party pledged support to the national Debs-Harriman ticket, endorsed the state platform, and demanded legal adoption of the eight-hour day and substitution of coöperative government for the competitive system. Wheeler was nominated for state senator and Arthur Vinette for assemblyman. H. Gaylord Wilshire, named to the county central committee, took an active part in the campaign. When the socialists drew up their municipal ticket in October, 1900, they placed Wheeler at the top as candidate for mayor, and nominated Vinette for tax collector and Biddle for city councilman. The city platform specified abolition of the contract system in public work, equal pay for equal work for men and women, minimum wages of $2 for the eight-hour day, union manufacture of all materials used in public work, municipal ownership of utilities, free public baths, public parks in densely populated areas, free universal democratic education, free food and clothing for school children when necessary, free school books and supplies, repeal of vagrancy and gag laws, and use of the union label on city printing. Although the Social Democrats made an insignificant showing at the polls, they won more votes than the Socialist Labor Party.[19]

In August, 1901, the Socialist Party of the United States, which had just been created, sent an organizer to Los Angeles to plead for the unification of all socialists who believed that the competitive system must be destroyed. Responding immediately, the local Social Democrats and bolters from the Socialist Labor Party abandoned their separate organizations and formed a branch of the Socialist Party of the United States. Shortly thereafter Job Harriman went to New York to work at the new party's national headquarters. Even without his aid, the Los Angeles local soon proved a formidable rival to the old Socialist Labor Party. By November, 1901, it had nearly two hundred members, and by the end of the year claimed that the "Socialist Labor Party is completely knocked out."[20]

The Los Angeles branch was host to the convention which organized the Socialist Party of California early in January, 1902. More than one hundred delegates from various parts of the state adopted a constitution and bylaws, voted against alliance with other political parties, and decided to appoint two organizers, one for northern and the other for southern California. Women took an active role in the Socialist Party, both in regular party functions and in their own auxiliary organization. The Women's Socialist League was formed in Los Angeles in December, 1901, and in April, 1902, changed its name to the Women's Socialist Union to conform to national rules. In September, 1902, the Women's Socialist Union of California held its first state convention in San Francisco.[21]

The outstanding organizer for the Socialist Party of California was the Reverend J. Stitt Wilson, who in 1911 was elected socialist mayor of Berkeley. Wilson made frequent speaking tours throughout the state, using his oratorical talents and his sincere convictions to win many converts. By June, 1902, there were fifty locals of the Socialist Party in the state. Many communities in southern California formed branches of the party; in October, 1902, Los Angeles County had ten locals, including those in San Pedro, Pasadena, and Santa Monica.[22]

The center of the socialist movement in southern California was the city of Los Angeles, where a nucleus of eager members worked unceasingly for the party's advancement. On November 2, 1901, a few months after organization, the local established its own weekly newspaper, the Los Angeles *Socialist*. Publication continued with fair regularity for the next eight years, though under the title *Common Sense* after 1904. The socialists of Los Angeles consistently strove for harmonious relations with organized labor by supporting strikes and boycotts and by upholding the broad principles of unionism. As a vehicle through which the desire for close coöperation could be made known, the *Socialist* forthrightly proclaimed in the first issue that it had "but one thought, one aim and one end—the freedom of the working class from industrial slavery. Its studies shall be the condition of labor, its religion, faith in the working class."[23]

The first editor of the Los Angeles *Socialist* was John Murray, a member of the aristocratic New York family for which Murray Hill was named. Born in 1865, Murray came to the Los Angeles area in his early youth because of frail health; like Harriman, he suffered from tuberculosis. During the 1890's he became interested in reform through reading Tolstoi, and spent the rest of his life trying to make the world a better place in which to live. Despite frequent and protracted bouts of the illness which led him to take his own life in 1919, Murray gave "passionate and romantic devotion" to the cause of humanity and left as "an imperishable monument a record of good deeds." Unassuming modesty, tolerance, and unselfishness made him one of the best-loved participants in the Los Angeles working-class struggle.[24] Forced to leave the *Socialist* for a much needed rest after a year's service, he received warm praise from the local party: "Comrade John Murray has performed with unremitting zeal the editorial duties of the Los Angeles Socialist since its inception, being the prime mover in the establishment of the paper . . . whose time and talents have been the means of placing it in the enviable position it occupies in the Socialist Press of America."[25]

Murray was a peripatetic socialist whose forte was journalism. This profession and his later absorption in the fight of Mexican revolutionaries against the corrupt Diaz regime meant that he was only intermittently in Los Angeles. Nevertheless, as a member of the trade-union wing of the Socialist Party, he was an important link between local organized labor and socialism. Early in 1902 he helped to organize Federal Labor Union No. 9614 for unskilled workers and, with a number of other socialists, joined the union. Murray and the others gave the new union a definite socialist tinge; its constitution declared for ultimate abolition of the competitive wage system and substitution of collective ownership by the people of all means of production, distribution, transportation, and communication. When the Federal Labor Union sent Murray as its delegate to the Council of Labor, James Gray, member of the carpenters' union and president of the Council, objected to accepting him on the ground that he would spread socialist propaganda. With Fred Wheeler's vigorous support, Murray won his seat in the central body. The favorable vote indicated the penetrative force of socialist doctrines in the Los Angeles labor movement. According to Murray, the liaison was close: "The Socialist Party and the trades union movement are swiftly but surely merging into one another.... Here in Los Angeles ... the trades unionists and Socialists are throwing off the mutual fear and suspicion bred by the old Socialist Labor Party, in its mistaken understanding of the class struggle."[26]

To educate the working classes to its way of thinking, the Socialist Party employed methods other than journalism, individual missionary work, or influence through unions. The Los Angeles local held numerous public meetings, some of which were designed primarily for unionists. At an International May Day gathering on May 1, 1902, Murray served as chairman and Biddle as main speaker on the topic, "May Day and the Trades Unions." Later in the year all local unions were invited to a series of lectures by J. Stitt Wilson. The local party, more formally, conducted classes in socialism under the auspices of a Training School Institute.[27]

The most picturesque propaganda device, however, was the open-air meeting on street corners or in city parks. Such meetings had the double advantage of attracting large audiences and of saving rental costs. Toward the end of 1901 the socialists selected First and Los Angeles Streets as the scene for a regular Tuesday evening assemblage. A city ordinance of the previous March required that groups holding street or park meetings obtain police permits. At the time H. Gaylord Wilshire, publisher of the socialist journal *The Challenge*, protested that the legislation would stifle freedom of speech among the working classes, but the frequency with which the socialists gathered on street corners during the late months of 1901 supposes their ability to obtain the required permits. Early in 1902 the open-air meetings abruptly ceased, not to be resumed until June. After a series of well-attended gatherings during the summer, the socialists again interrupted the program, but soon determined to test the constitutionality of the ordinance. In November, 1902, J. B. Osborne, a blind socialist orator from Denver, was arrested for speaking in Sixth Street Park (now Pershing Square) after repeated warnings that he was violating the city laws. Job Harriman, who had returned to Los Angeles in August and rejoined the local branch of the party, defended Osborne but lost the case. The constitutionality of the ordinance was upheld. The socialists waited another year before again challenging the validity of the law against outdoor meetings in public places.[28]

The effectiveness of socialist propaganda cannot be adequately assessed through membership data. The size of the Los Angeles branch of the Socialist Party, known as Local Los Angeles, remained static during its early years, by its own admission. The branch had claimed two hundred members before the end of 1901; early in 1903 it reported the identical number to state headquarters.[29] A valid estimate of socialist strength depended, not on the number of dues-paying adherents, but on the volume of socialist votes; many who for one reason or another rejected party affiliation agreed with party doctrines.

The state and county elections of 1902 revealed, for example, that the number of socialist voters was increasing and that it was larger than the tabulated party membership. On June 30, 1902, the Socialist Party of California filed a petition containing some fifteen thousand signatures, more than were needed, to get on the state ballot. A number of Los Angeles unionists were nominated for state or county offices, among them Fred Wheeler for secretary of state, S. H. Laverty of the Typographical Union for state printer, Lemuel Biddle for county clerk, and John Murray for county public administrator. In the elections, Wheeler won about eleven thousand of the approximately 310,000 votes cast; the winning Republican contender for secretary of state had close to 161,500 votes. Laverty's record was similar to Wheeler's. The socialist vote in Los Angeles County, for both state and county offices, varied between twelve and fifteen hundred; Biddle, for example, polled 1,294 votes as against the 18,587 going to his successful Republican opponent. The Los Angeles *Socialist,* however, claimed that official election figures did not show the party's full voting strength, since about two thousand socialist ballots were invalidated because incorrectly marked. It further demonstrated that the socialist vote, even when based on the official reports, had increased by approximately 100 per cent since the 1900 elections.[30]

Thus far Harriman's hope of a close socialist-labor collaboration had not been realized in any election. The Los Angeles municipal contest of 1902, however, afforded an opportunity for precisely the kind of alliance which Harriman envisioned. Beginning at the turn of the century, the local labor movement had enjoyed unprecedented expansion in both number and membership of unions and had made considerable progress in improvement of working conditions and in regularizing industrial relations through reliance on working agreements. The new decade had not advanced very far, however, before a counter open-shop tendency began to narrow the field of union victories; by 1902 labor leaders were noticing more and more interference from militant employers. To the unionists, the solution seemed to lie in gaining representation in the city government, an objective wholeheartedly approved by Harriman and other prominent socialists.

The Union Labor Party of 1902 in Los Angeles had its roots not only in internal quandaries and socialist encouragement, but also in a San Francisco example. Early in the decade the northern city became the scene of violent labor-capital conflict, as the militant Employers' Association, formed in April, 1901, sought to crush organized labor. When the city government abetted the employers by using the police force to quell disorders and make wholesale arrests of strikers and pickets, the unions decided to supplement economic weapons with political methods. In the fall of 1901 they created a Union Labor Party which won a sweeping victory in the November elections. Heading the new administration as mayor was ex-Republican Eugene E. Schmitz, a union musician, but the real power lay in the hands of Abraham Ruef, another former Republican. The Ruef-Schmitz regime, the first in a series of labor administrations which controlled San Francisco for eight of the next ten years, achieved notoriety in the latter part of the decade through the graft prosecutions directed against it. Even in 1901 it was not unreservedly approved by the labor side as an example to be followed. As if with foreknowledge of the Union Labor Party's later corruptibility, the Los Angeles *Socialist* derided the 1901 victory as a betrayal of organized labor. In December, when a California epidemic of union labor parties seemed likely, the *Coast Seamen's Journal* cautioned that labor politicos in other communities might wisely reflect on the peculiar circumstances which alone had made the San Francisco outcome possible.[31]

Despite these warnings, the Los Angeles Council of Labor decided in May, 1902, to adopt political action as a means of strengthening the campaign to win union demands. It started out impartially by appointing one Democrat, one Republican, one Socialist, one Prohibitionist, and one Independent to a committee on procedures. The Los Angeles *Socialist,* instead of repeating its reservations on the San Francisco experiment, rejoiced over the local plan because it would "destroy forever 'no politics in the union.' " Labor found, however, that it was not easy to evolve a policy satisfactory to all groups. From the beginning bitter factionalism disturbed the consideration of how best to serve working-class aims. Conservatives, headed by James Gray, favored endorsement of friendly Democratic and Republican nominees in accordance with the traditional AFL program. On the other hand, unionists with socialist sympathies preferred a complete break with capitalist parties, promulgation of a union labor ticket, and coöperation with the Socialist Party.[32]

When the first labor conference met on July 19, 1902, to choose between these two courses, the committee submitted both a majority and a minority report. The majority report restated the platform of the AFL, which included such tenets as direct legislation, compulsory education, employers' liability for injuries, abolition of the contract system on public work, municipal ownership of utilities, and nationalization of railroads and communication systems, and added a resolution that labor would endorse friendly political candidates regardless of party. The minority report emphasized the struggle between labor and capital as an argument for political safeguards against the oppression of wage earners, stated that labor could not expect favorable laws from legislators who upheld the existing wage system, and proposed that labor support only parties recognizing these truths and nominating candidates from the ranks of trade-unionists. Although not naming the Socialist Party, the minority report clearly had no other in mind. After a long day of debate revealed that the socialist group was in the ascendancy, the conservatives adjourned the conference to July 28 to avoid an immediate showdown.[33]

In the interim before the next meeting took place, extraneous events encouraged both sides in the dispute. The Los Angeles branch of the Socialist Party announced its intention to nominate for municipal office only those members who belonged also to labor unions, obviously a bid for continuance of the trend at the first conference. Sharply counter to this was a warning from Gompers that the Council of Labor would lose its AFL charter if it entered partisan politics or joined in the Socialist campaign. Gompers' threat was enough for James Gray and his followers, who bolted the July 28 conference when it adopted the minority report. The conservatives who remained, however, successfully argued that Gompers, who was due to arrive in Los Angeles within the next several days, would certainly not approve the course chosen. They induced the conference to submit to a referendum vote of all unions in the Council of Labor a compromise proposition that a union convention be held on September 20 "to organize a Union Labor party, advocating the political demands of the American Federation of Labor, present and future, and such state or municipal demands as will benefit the working class, primarily, and finally all classes."[34]

Gompers and his party, including several members of the AFL's Executive Council, arrived in Los Angeles on July 31. The next evening Gompers held a large and enthusiastic audience spellbound for two hours, as he denounced Otis and the *Times,* justified strikes and boycotts, and exhorted local labor to continue its good organizing work. He carefully avoided the subject of politics during his formal appearance, but must have clarified the Federation's official position in private conferences with local labor leaders.[35] The Los Angeles *Socialist,* in urging union members to go in for socialist politics, found it necessary to refute Gompers:

> Samuel Gompers has been "in our midst" this week. Mr. Gompers has been telling you to take the "no politics" route. The Socialist does not wish to impugn any man's motive. The Socialist is willing to concede that Mr. Gompers is an able man. But even great men are fallible and are you, men of the unions, children, that you cannot think for yourselves?[36]

During August and September a labor delegation from San Francisco visited Los Angeles in the hope of arousing sentiment for a state labor party. The Council of Labor responded by naming representatives to a state convention held in San Francisco on September 6. Four of the five local delegates were socialists, including Fred Wheeler and John Murray, who tried to have the convention pledge no endorsement of Republicans or Democrats. They did not succeed, nor did the gathering make any headway toward forming a state party, partly because Mayor Schmitz of San Francisco counseled against it and refused to head a ticket as gubernatorial candidate.[37]

The failure to organize a California labor party disappointed those Los Angeles socialists who had envisioned "a great movement . . . backed by the power of organized labor, for the first time separating itself from the capitalist class, and battling to place the political power in the hands of wage-workers."[38] Yet even among socialists the sentiment for political alliance with organized labor was not unanimous. Many party members were puzzled. They saw as arguments for fusion the Union Labor Party victory in San Francisco and the apparent tendency of trade-unionists to renounce capitalist politics, but at the same time they doubted a thoroughgoing conversion to socialism among labor's rank and file. The enthusiasm and articulateness of outstanding unionists who were also fervent socialists—men like Biddle, Murray, and Wheeler—and of top-rank socialists like Harriman cloaked a suspicion prevalent at lower party levels that fusion would be a perilous course bringing ruin in its wake. The *Socialist,* controlled by the proalliance group, felt that not only unionists but also socialists needed to be awakened to the realization that they were together fighting the battle for wage earners, and that the most powerful weapon was joint political action.[39]

In the end it was a Republican deed, rather than socialist indoctrination, which opened the eyes of union members. The Republican county convention on August 20, seeking to placate organized labor, adopted resolutions pledging the use of the Allied Printing Trades Council label on all party printing, and promised to nominate a union man for the office of sheriff. When the Republicans drew up a ticket completely barren of labor representatives, unionists regarded the duplicity as a compelling reason for naming a slate of their own. On September 20 the union convention voted to place a labor ticket in the field.[40]

In deference to Gompers' warning, the Los Angeles Union Labor Party was completely separate from the Council of Labor. Because of this, it was free to promise support to the socialist state and county tickets in return for full socialist backing of labor's municipal ticket. The decision of Los Angeles socialists not to enter their own ticket in the city elections flouted national party policy and brought a storm of criticism from party members throughout the country. Job Harriman ably defended the fusion by arguing that a socialist party, to be powerful and effective, must have its roots in the working-class movement, must encourage political activity by organized labor, and must save itself from becoming an impotent expression of middle-class aims by recognizing its identity with the workers.[41] The Los Angeles *Socialist* also pleaded valiantly for coöperation with labor:

> The platform of the Union Labor Party in Los Angeles embodies all that the Socialist platform contains. Comrades, what more do you want? Do you still insist that we should stand aloof from the trade unions until such time as their vision is so broadened as to enable them to grasp, theoretically, the Socialist movement as a whole? ... The political must supplement the economic organization. The economic organization must be the base upon which the Socialist party rests.[42]

On October 4, the Union Labor Party nominated a full municipal ticket, composed entirely of union members and headed by George

McGahan, president of the retail clerks' union, as candidate for mayor. Many of the nominees were also members of the Socialist Party. Furthermore, socialists were named to key committees: John Murray was a member of the platform committee, and Lemuel Biddle, E. J. Mack, J. R. Walker, and Murray were all on the executive committee. The party platform, after declaring for the principles of the American Federation of Labor and of the international working-class movement, demanded direct legislation, abolition of the contract system on public work, the eight-hour day on public work, the union label on public printing, civil service reform, equal pay for men and women, weekly payment of wages for municipal employees, city ownership of municipal franchises, better public school facilities, free school books, establishment of night schools and public playgrounds, ample compensation for teachers, and an adequate sewage system.[43]

Several weeks later, McGahan and his associates on the Union Labor Party ticket outlined their reasons for seeking control of the city government. The City Council, whether Republican or Democratic, had regularly turned a deaf ear to the petitions of humble citizens, and had managed city affairs with complete disregard for the people's wishes. Contracts had been awarded to employers who paid substandard wages and violated state laws. Municipal employees, such as school janitors and library girls, had been grossly underpaid. The spoils system had degraded public employment. To correct these and other evils, wage earners wanted to elect their own administration, for they could not expect justice from a Council "owned and controlled by employers of labor who roll up dividends fleeced from the scant earnings of men, women, and children."[44]

Both unionists and socialists regarded the campaign as a genuine class struggle in which any association with the capitalist parties would be a taint on their honor. When the Democratic Party endorsed two labor candidates, the Union Labor Party promptly dispelled the notion that it was in collusion with the Democrats. One of the two candidates refused the Democratic nomination; the other was removed from the labor ticket. The socialists were equally determined to keep free of undesirable alliances. When E. M. Hamilton, independent candidate for the City Council, applied for membership in the Socialist Party, he was rejected because he was running in competition with the Union Labor Party nominee. The Los Angeles *Socialist* was at pains to demonstrate that a vote for either Republicans or Democrats was a vote for all the forces seeking to crush organized labor.[45]

The Union Labor Party commenced its active campaign for the Mc-

Gahan ticket about two weeks before the election. At street meetings
and in circulars distributed to union members the party leaders urged
labor to vote in full strength. According to the *Socialist*, the electioneering was effective: unions, earlier unconvinced of the validity of political
action, swerved to support of the Union Labor Party; Republicans and
Democrats began to fear the outcome on December 1; betting odds
slowly shifted in favor of the McGahan ticket. An agent for Mayor M.
P. Snyder, Democratic candidate for reëlection, even tried to buy off
McGahan a few days before the election.[46]

To give its campaign an impressive windup, the Union Labor Party
brought in Mayor Schmitz of San Francisco for the final week. Local
labor staged a gala demonstration for Schmitz, including a royal reception, a parade of some sixty unions, and a big rally at Hazard's Pavilion.
After the fanfare, Schmitz settled down to stump for the McGahan
ticket, hurrying from union to union, street corner to street corner, rally
to rally. As election day drew near, the Union Labor Party became more
and more confident of winning.[47]

The new party was doomed to disappointment in its hopes for victory. In the mayoralty contest, McGahan polled over three thousand
votes, Snyder, the winning Democrat, over nine thousand, and Pomeroy
Powers, Republican, over six thousand. Labor candidates for other city
offices averaged between twenty-five hundred and three thousand votes.
There was greater variability in the ward elections for the City Council
and the Board of Education; in the Sixth Ward, for example, with
heavy working-class concentration, the ULP candidates received half as
many votes as the winners. Although the Democrats won the mayoralty
and one other city office, the Republicans, with a majority of officials,
city councilmen, and members of the Board of Education, really controlled the ingoing administration. McGahan conceded his defeat in a
dignified way, merely pointing out that his party lacked the money and
organization necessary to carry the elections. Supporters of the Union
Labor Party found an additional cause of defeat in labor's distrust of
Powers. Many unionists, believing that the Republican candidate was
Otis' tool, voted for Snyder rather than McGahan.[48]

Although Los Angeles was the only city in the country where the
socialists actively campaigned for a union labor ticket, the party sought,
in the early years of the twentieth century, to wean the American Federation of Labor away from the nonpartisanship so clearly defined in the
mid-'nineties. Socialist influence in the national body reached high tide
in the conventions of 1902 and 1903. In 1902 numerous resolutions
introduced by socialist delegates proposed overthrow of the wage system

and substitution therefor of a coöperative industrial commonwealth. Fred Wheeler, representing the United Brotherhood of Carpenters and Joiners of America, authored one of these declarations against private ownership of the means of production and distribution.[49] His response to an unfavorable committee report on all such resolutions revealed the intensity of conviction which animated the proponents of socialism:

> I want to say that you can not serve God and Mammon, you can not serve capital and labor at the same time. They tell us to stay out of politics, and some of the men who tell us to stay out of politics have been representatives of the American Federation of Labor at Washington, trying to secure favorable legislation. Their entire course has been one entire, gigantic failure.... I want to say that if we wish to change conditions we must change the cause and we can not do that if we confine our work to trade unions pure and simple.[50]

Delegate Max Hayes proposed a compromise amendment to the report of the resolutions committee stipulating only that the AFL *advise* workers to organize politically as well as economically in order to secure the full equivalent of their toil; socialist strength in the 1902 convention was apparent in the amendment's narrow defeat by a vote of 4,897 to 4,171, with 387 delegates abstaining. The socialists tried again in 1903 to win the coveted AFL approbation, but Gompers' forceful opposition brought overwhelming defeat. For the next decade the socialists were quiescent in the councils of the AFL.[51]

The failure of the Los Angeles Union Labor Party at the polls, following within two weeks of the 1902 AFL convention, demonstrated to both local labor and socialists that even in combination they were too weak to win an election. The enthusiasm of unionists for further political alliance dwindled to the point of nonexistence; socialist advocates of fusion became disillusioned, though for a time the local branch persisted in defending its tactics. As at the start of the campaign, spokesmen answered rebukes by maintaining that it behooved socialists to throw their weight to the anticapitalist side of a sharply drawn class line. But continuing condemnation by the party at large eventually forced Local Los Angeles to admit its betrayal: while socialists dutifully voted the union ticket, union men had voted the capitalist tickets. In January, 1903, the local comrades officially declared that the encouragement of union labor parties was a "menace" to the Socialist Party and urged the national executive committee, soon to meet in St. Louis, to prohibit any such alliance as had disgraced Local Los Angeles. The national committee, in February, reaffirmed its stand of 1901 by adopting resolutions condemning the fusion of the Socialist Party with any reform, radical, or labor party.[52]

The confession of error by Local Los Angeles abated an acrimonious controversy within the ranks of the Socialist Party, though Harriman's tenacious clinging to a contradictory policy repeatedly brought him into disrepute with his colleagues. The abrupt reversal of the local socialists also effectively prevented their political collaboration with organized labor in the critical first decade of the twentieth century. This did not mean total denial of interdependence at every level, for socialists and unionists often joined in common enterprises. Enforcement of labor legislation, fights for free speech, and the battle for woman suffrage were to bring these erstwhile political partners into close association. Segments of the labor movement occasionally supported a socialist for municipal office, and the socialists frequently gave financial and moral assistance to strikers. But the latent distrust generated in 1902 persisted as an undertone throughout the period, and it was not until 1911 that the wounds were completely healed. Then, both internal socialist dissension and strain between socialists and unionists disappeared in common support of Job Harriman's candidacy for the mayoralty of Los Angeles. As will be seen, only very unusual circumstances made the socialist-labor entente of 1911 possible.

XVII. THE RISING TIDE OF CONFLICT

An ESSENTIAL FEATURE of labor's program in the early years of the twentieth century was the drive for better working conditions. Along with the advance in organization, the search for community esteem, and political collaboration with the socialists went demands for higher wages, shorter hours, and union recognition.

1. THE QUEST FOR UNION RECOGNITION

Some of the labor disputes arising from such demands during the years 1900–1902 showed unmistakable signs of keen employer resistance, though a unified drive against unions did not take shape until 1903. The antiunion tendencies which the Merchants' and Manufacturers' Association later integrated into a smoothly functioning system cropped up in the early years with sufficient frequency and effect to make labor's campaign for economic gains less rewarding than its drive for full organization and for improved community standing.

The experience of the street railway employees illustrates one of the ways in which management balked labor. In 1901 the motormen and conductors of the Los Angeles Railway Company, owned by Henry E. Huntington, asked to have their hourly wages raised from 20 to 22½ cents. These men, who were not organized, accepted the company's substitute of a sliding scale ranging from 20 cents for beginners to 22 cents for men with five years' experience. The Traction Railway Company followed Huntington's lead. Then John Ince, of the Council of Labor, began organizing a local branch of the Amalgamated Association of Street Railway Employees, but both companies immediately dismissed those men having the temerity to join the union. A second organizing attempt in 1902 was similarly frustrated by discharges and a voluntary wage increase.[1]

Not all Los Angeles employers were so forthrightly antiunion during the years 1900–1902. Many of them, as yet unafraid that workers would encroach too far on managerial prerogatives, granted labor's demands with little or no opposition. Against a background of business prosperity, the harmony characterizing industrial relations in the country at large was echoed locally, as working agreements with benefits to labor became more prevalent. A tendency to coöperate with organized labor thus existed side by side with antiunionism, but the extent of peaceful negotiation is difficult to ascertain. The quieter aspects of employer-employee relationships were never so newsworthy as strikes and lockouts.

[237]

Contrasted with the complex contracts of today, working agreements of the early twentieth century were simple instruments, usually specifying only wages and hours but occasionally providing for a rudimentary form of arbitration and, rarely, the closed shop. Fairly systematic procedures had been developed by 1901. Most unions drew up contracts for six months or a year, roughly correlating their demands with the cost of living in Los Angeles and with labor's progress elsewhere. After submission to the Council of Labor for approval, the schedules went to the appropriate employers for signature. Unions unable to gain management's consent went back to the central body which, if mediation failed, could then authorize strikes or boycotts. The Council of Labor's control over the working agreements of all its affiliates was part of the current trend toward centralization of power. American Federation of Labor and international union organizers, seated in the Council during their sojourns in Los Angeles, were on hand to give advice and succor to less experienced local officials.[2]

The quest for union recognition was variously manifested. Some unions obtained written agreements, others accepted verbal promises. The teamsters, organized late in 1900, signed an agreement with the city's four large trucking companies in May, 1901, specifying a wage increase, overtime pay, and shorter hours; six months later they renewed the contract. During 1901 the brewery workers and beer wagon drivers persuaded the local breweries to accept terms established by the Pacific Coast Brewery Workers' Union, including the eight-hour day, pay raises, and overtime pay. In 1902 the bottlers followed suit. The bakers' union, controlling 95 per cent of all bakeries in Los Angeles, negotiated an agreement in 1901 reducing the workweek to six days, and the following year expanded the terms to include wage increases for all workers. In 1902 glaziers concluded a compromise agreement denying higher wages but granting the eight-hour day. On the other hand, numerous groups of workers achieved higher wages or shorter hours with less formality, some by merely announcing new schedules, others by obtaining the consent of employers beforehand.[3]

Other differences distinguished union from union. Some crafts were able to establish fairly comprehensive control in their particular fields, but others had to be satisfied with piecemeal conquest. The teamsters and brewery occupations, for example, signed contracts embracing all the principal employers in their industries, but tailors, printers, retail clerks, and the like, working in many small establishments, could convert only one or two shops at a time. The building trades hoped to achieve uniformity with a working-card system, but the process was difficult because many different occupations and employers were in-volved. Within the building trades, some crafts gained more union security than others. By 1901 the plasterers, for example, had virtually a closed-shop agreement with the Master Plasterers' Association, very like the system binding master and journeymen plumbers during the 1890's.[4]

With an unusual degree of harmony, master and journeymen barbers of Los Angeles solved their problems together. A state law passed early in 1901 made a three-year apprenticeship, followed by examination and certification, mandatory for all barbers. In April the journeymen bar-bers of Los Angeles organized a union and secured the appointment of a member as the southern California representative on the state certify-ing board. In May, using the journeymen's hall, barber shop proprietors formed the Master Barbers' Protective Association. The union and the Association then jointly decided to close at 7 instead of 8 P.M., and to raise the price of shaves from 10 to 15 cents and of haircuts from 20 to 25 cents. In October two proprietors, losing trade because of the higher rates, reverted to the old prices. Their union employees, whose earn-ings were proportionately decreased, walked out and levied a boycott. Adamant even against pressure from the Master Barbers' Association, the two shops continued to operate with nonunion help. Their compe-tition finally forced journeymen and master barbers into a compromise agreement in December, 1901, keeping haircuts at 25 cents but putting shaves back to 10 cents, maintaining the 7 o'clock closing, and guaran-teeing employees a minimum weekly wage.[5]

Occasional reliance on arbitration also testified to equable relations between employers and employees in some quarters. An episode in December, 1902, approximated a modern arbitration case. For some months the Typographical Union, which had working agreements with all daily newspapers except the *Times,* had been beseeching the *Herald* to raise proofreaders' wages from $3 to $3.50 a day, basing its request on the prevailing scale in Pacific Coast cities and on the fact that the nonunion *Times* paid the higher rate. When the *Herald* refused the in-crease on the plea of unusually trying competition with the *Times,* the union proposed that Charles D. Willard, secretary of the Board of Trade, serve as arbitrator. Both sides presented arguments at a formal hearing. Willard's decision on December 18, 1902, compromised the wages at $3.25. By an almost unanimous vote the printers accepted the award, and the raise went into effect.[6]

Not all disagreements between labor and management were so ami-cably adjudicated. A number of strikes and/or boycotts during 1900–

1902 frequently concerned some aspect of union security in addition to time-honored wage and hour questions. It was in this struggle for improved working conditions that open-shop tendencies emerged, scattered at first but gradually, with gathered momentum, preparing the way for the great employer offensive later in the decade.

The preponderance of labor disputes in these early years originated with the building trades. The first to make systematic demands were two unions of the International Brotherhood of Electrical Workers. Inside wiremen, or electricians, organized Local No. 116 in September, 1900, and immediately won the eight-hour day and a substantial pay increase. A few days later, the older linemen's union, Local No. 61, inspired by this quick victory, presented comprehensive demands to three electrical companies and the Sunset Telephone and Telegraph Company: reduction of hours from ten to eight; an across-the-board wage increase of 50 cents a day; time and a half for overtime, Sundays, and holidays; the closed shop; and a year's contract. Early in October, 1900, when the companies refused, the men struck. When the walkout spread to other communities in southern California, and threatened to extend even to San Francisco, the companies, unable to find enough competent nonunion workers to keep their lines in repair, offered to compromise. The men, beginning to feel the financial pinch despite the aid of other unionists, agreed to a nine-hour day and a 25-cent wage increase and went back to work in December, 1900.[7]

In February, 1901, without striking, the inside wiremen of Local No. 116 signed a year's contract with the Electrical Exchange, comprising 90 per cent of local dealers in electrical supplies. The agreement specified wages of $3 for the eight-hour day and arbitration of disputes. Each side was to appoint two arbitrators and the four, if unable to settle the issues in dispute, were to select a fifth. The system broke down, however, in August, 1901, when the union's demand for inclusion of travel time to out-of-town jobs in the regular working day was submitted to arbitration. The four arbitrators failed to reach a decision and the union, fearing a biased fifth member, halted the proceedings and annulled the contract.[8]

In July, 1902, the electricians sought a new agreement with employers, now organized as the Electrical Contractors' Association. Their principal demands were enforcement of the eight-hour day; establishment of minimum wages; time and a half for overtime and double time for Sundays and holidays; seven holidays a year; apprenticeship regulations; transportation from job to job and living expenses on jobs outside the city; inclusion of travel time in the eight-hour day; and the closed shop. Inability to compromise resulted in a strike of all electricians in the city on July 17, but within a week the union was forced to yield to a united employer front.[9] Although losing their contest, the electricians demonstrated that some Los Angeles workers were beginning to grapple with questions which are of the utmost importance at the bargaining tables of today.

For construction workers in general, the Building Trades Council tried to achieve union security through the working-card system. In April, 1901, shortly after organizing, the Council forbade members of affiliated unions to work on any job with men who carried no cards. The edict led to a series of short strikes with varying results. Contractors not pressed for time could afford to halt operations until complete nonunion crews could be found, but others, either from necessity or conviction, observed the working-card regulation.[10]

In August, 1901, James Gray, business agent of the Building Trades Council, planned a general strike of construction workers to speed the unionization of building jobs. He could count on the support of all building craftsmen except the bricklayers, who were affiliated with neither the local Council nor their own national union. Under the threat of a general building-trades strike, however, they sought the protection of international affiliation and in August received a charter as Local No. 2. A snag then arose because the Bricklayers' International Union was not a member of the AFL, and the Los Angeles branch therefore persisted in shunning local alliances. Accordingly the building-trades demonstration, planned originally to force the working-card system on employers, turned into a device to exert pressure on the bricklayers. Starting on September 2, 1901, with a walkout of one hundred carpenters, the strike soon involved about five hundred building craftsmen. The futility of the quarrel was quickly manifest, and on the 7th, the Building Trades Council and the bricklayers' union agreed to respect each other's working cards. The Council immediately called off the strike and the men went back to their jobs. With some justification, the *Times* claimed an ultimate victory for the open shop, inasmuch as the Building Trades Council thereafter pushed the working-card system with less vigor. Member unions, however, continued the battle for security in a series of minor walkouts, usually unsuccessful. The most important dispute occurred a year later, in September, 1902, when all the lathers struck for union recognition. Employers, however, banded together to refuse acceptance of the union as bargaining agent.[11]

Although the building trades made slight progress in their closed-shop program, many of them won wage increases without dispute. Even the *Times,* always reluctant to record union victories, admitted that contractors readily granted such demands in order to avoid labor troubles and keep abreast of the current building rush. In July, 1901, when most unions presented new wage scales to employers, only hod carriers and cement workers had to strike to gain acceptance of the higher rates.[12]

During 1902 a number of building trades won further wage advances. In the spring the District Council of Carpenters, representing fifteen hundred members in Los Angeles, pushed the minimum wage for carpenters from $3 to $3.50 a day with very little trouble, and on June 1, Pasadena carpenters likewise instituted the new scale. Dissension within the Building Trades Council, centering about James Gray's leadership, temporarily halted the drive for higher wages and weakened the central body. The *Times* gleefully seized upon this internal conflict to discredit Gray and his associates as a radical element corrupting otherwise docile workingmen. But in September, 1902, with peace restored to the Building Trades Council and Gray again at the helm, wage demands were renewed. Hod carriers, in a two-day strike, persuaded all but three contractors to raise their scale to $4 a day. This motivated more highly skilled workers to press for wage increases, and painters and paper hangers won a year's guarantee for a raise from $3 to $3.50 for the eight-hour day. Other craftsmen temporarily received higher wages on time contracts. But as builders reacted to increased labor costs by refusing new contracts and appealed to the Building Trades Council for relief, workers relaxed their demands.[13]

A protracted and bitterly contended woodworkers' strike, beginning in November, 1901, affected the construction industry. Los Angeles Local No. 144 of the Amalgamated Woodworkers, organized late in 1900, voted to strike on October 7, 1901, unless planing mills cut the working day from nine to eight hours without decreasing daily wages. On October 1, the Millmen's Association, comprising a majority of mill owners, rejected the demand. But when nonunion workers also requested the eight-hour day, employers, faced with a really crippling walkout, began to retract. As the mill owners yielded one by one, the union postponed the strike. By the end of October, ten of the twelve planing mills in Los Angeles had agreed to the shorter working day with no wage reductions. Hughes Brothers and Carpenter & Biles had also accepted the eight-hour stipulation for their regular departments, but refused it for the sash and door sections where competition from ten-hour manufacturers in other communities was particularly keen. The union, abetted by the ten acquiescent proprietors, rejected the proposal because it would constantly threaten the eight-hour day.[14]

A strike and boycott against the two mills began on November 1, 1901, when fifty-four employees at Hughes Brothers and twenty-three at Carpenter & Biles walked off the job. The Council of Labor endorsed the strike and promised help; building-trades unions ordered their members not to work for contractors buying materials from the struck mills, some of them even fining members for disobeying; and the woodworkers began to picket the plants. The boycott proceeded peacefully until A. H. Ryan, one of the pickets, extended his operations to include the Original Mug Saloon, whose proprietor, a stockholder in the Hughes mill, had boasted that he would spend $25,000 to break the strike. Ryan marched up and down in front of the saloon, carrying a banner reading, "The Proprietor of the Original Mug Saloon Is Not Fair to Organized Labor. Boys, Keep Away." On November 28, Ryan was arrested for disturbing the peace after he got into a fist fight with a prospective customer. When bailed out by President James Gray, of the Council of Labor, Ryan went back to his picketing and was again taken into custody for flaunting his banner in front of the saloon. Jury disagreement brought Ryan dismissal on the first charge, and lack of a statute against picketing, acquittal on the second. But the matter did not end there. On December 28, 1901, the City Council passed an ordinance imposing a penalty of fifty days' imprisonment or $50 fine for carrying banners or signs on the streets of Los Angeles.[15]

Although the new law effectively blocked one avenue of union propaganda, the woodworkers continued both strike and boycott after their proposals for arbitration or compromise were ignored. Finally, in September, 1902, Hughes Brothers, evidently feeling the boycott and alarmed by rapidly maturing plans for a coöperative union planing mill, agreed to meet a union committee. Within several weeks, however, the Fire Commission refused to grant a permit for the union establishment, and with the death of that project the prospective rapprochement between Hughes and the union failed to materialize.[16]

The union attack on the two mills eventually ended in defeat. The striking woodworkers found employment elsewhere, picketing gradually ceased, and the strike, though never officially called off, died of inanition. By February, 1903, both Hughes Brothers and Carpenter & Biles were operating all departments on a nine-hour schedule with nonunion employees. The firmness of Hughes Brothers in the controversy with the millmen was a strong boost to the open-shop cause in Los Angeles. All the other planing mill owners, seeing the Hughes victory, gradually reverted to the nine-hour day, and the Millmen's Association instituted the policy, later widely used by other employers' organizations, of conducting its own labor bureau. Such an agency easily became an antiunion technique as the conflict between organized labor and management deepened. The woodworkers' union, having lost every vestige of control, disappeared in 1903. In its stead the District Council of Carpenters organized Local No. 1279 of the Brotherhood of Carpenters and Joiners, which early in 1904 claimed 90 per cent of local planing mill employees.[17]

Workers outside the construction industry had much the same experience as building craftsmen in finding wage concessions easier to win than union security. During 1900 the tailors' union, for example, launched a campaign to eliminate sweatshops, institute the closed shop, and establish uniform pay rates. After several strikes, all employers agreed to the union wage scale, but more than half of them continued to employ nonunion as well as union tailors. Early in 1901, San Pedro longshoremen and lumbermen organized Federal Labor Union No. 8921, destined eventually to surpass the smaller sailors' union and become the leader of the water-front labor movement. In March the longshoremen easily won a strike for a wage increase from $2 to $2.25 for the nine-hour day, but their efforts to prevent employment of non-union workers, though occasionally successful, fell far short of establishing the closed shop. The defeat of a great water-front strike in San Francisco, lasting from July to October, 1901, aggravated the difficulties of San Pedro longshoremen in their quest for control of shipping and unloading.[18]

Another contest as important as the woodworkers' strike occurred in 1901, when the Los Angeles labor movement solidly backed the laundry workers' effort to gain union recognition and a satisfactory wage and hour schedule. Again this dispute illustrated employers' inclination to meet demands other than those affecting union security. John Ince organized Local No. 52 of the Shirt Waist and Laundry Workers' International Union in April, 1901. Despite a preponderance of women, untrained in union methods, the new Council of Labor affiliate soon pushed its membership above the three hundred mark and made plans to improve working conditions. Laundry employees frequently labored twelve or fourteen hours a day without overtime pay, with wages sometimes as low as $4 to $7 a week. In May, 1901, the union drew up an agreement specifying the ten-hour day; time and a half for overtime, Sundays, and holidays; equalization of wages for men and women; establishment of a wage scale; no reductions for employees already earning more than union rates; apprenticeship regulations; arbitration of disputes; union recognition; and the closed shop. With the approval of the Council of Labor, the laundry workers presented the schedule to the Steam Laundry Proprietors' Association, setting June 25 as the deadline for reply.[19]

An uneasy period followed, while the union awaited the reaction of employers. On June 22 the proprietor of Cleaver's Laundry ordered his workers either to quit or renounce union membership. Seven girls walked out and the Council of Labor, dubbing this a lockout, declared a boycott on Cleaver's. The union, meanwhile, had extended the period of grace, but voted to strike on Monday, July 1, should other proprietors follow Cleaver's lead. Most of the laundries professed their willingness to regularize working hours and grant overtime pay, but only one, the American Laundry, agreed to recognize the union. On Saturday, June 29, J. Bonfilio, owner of the Excelsior Laundry and president of the Laundry Proprietors' Association, told his employees that no union members need report for work on Monday. When other proprietors, given one more opportunity to sign the agreement, adopted Bonfilio's policy, the union issued the strike order.[20]

On July 1, 335 of the five hundred employees of seven laundries left their jobs. The Laundry Proprietors' Association publicly stated that it would never recognize the union, but the American Laundry and several smaller establishments stood by the workers. Most of the unions in Los Angeles, and the new Federal Labor Union of San Pedro, helped with cash donations, and a huge benefit on July 6 brought in additional revenue for a strike fund. The laundry workers' union prohibited violence on the picket lines and offered to negotiate with employers. The only break came on July 10, when J. H. Kiefer, proprietor of the Troy Laundry, promised to sign if he could hire nonunion help when no union help was available, such new employees to join the union within two weeks. This unique proposal for a union shop, as distinct from a closed shop, was acceptable to the laundry workers, but Kiefer retracted under pressure from Bonfilio, the most aggressively antiunion proprietor. Several times later Kiefer was on the verge of yielding, but Bonfilio kept him loyal to the employers' association.[21]

The strike dragged on through the rest of 1901 without reaching settlement. The *Times* supported the Laundry Proprietors' Association throughout, claiming that the employees enjoyed excellent working conditions and that owners, although willing to establish the ten-hour day and pay for overtime, could not submit to the tyranny of union dictation. A few strikers gave up union membership and went back to work in Association laundries, but most of them found jobs in the friendly establishments or in other lines of work. About one hundred of them eventually were employed by the New Method Laundry Company, launched in September, 1901, as a union coöperative enterprise. In November, 1901, the drivers employed by the New Method and American Laundries, the only two sizable union establishments, organized to help fight the Laundry Proprietors' Association. Some members of the Association resorted to price-cutting to compete with the union laundries, but they all steadfastly refused to recognize the union. Greatly impaired in strength, the laundry workers had to begin anew the struggle for better working conditions.[22]

After the setbacks of 1901, Los Angeles unions had little heart for serious or prolonged labor disputes. As noted above, the building trades halted their 1902 drive for wage increases upon contractors' representations of the ill effects on the economy; other unions made but few demands. In September, 1902, the molders' union called out the employees of twelve firms, including the leading Baker Iron Works and Llewellyn Iron Works, in an effort to establish the nine-hour day, a uniform wage rate of 35 cents an hour, and time and a half for overtime. Employers, though not yet organized, stood together in resisting the demands at three conferences with the strikers. The dispute was quickly over, with the union making most of the concessions. The final agreement specified 37½ cents an hour for the most competent men, a sliding scale from 24 to 32 cents for the less skilled, and time and a half for overtime after ten hours. In November, 1902, the Los Angeles local of the Upholsterers' International Union struck against three firms for union recognition, the eight-hour day, and an increase from $2.50 to $3 in daily wages. The upholsterers lost the strike, though not relinquishing the struggle until mid-1903.[23]

Although the Merchants' and Manufacturers' Association had not yet turned to an aggressive open-shop policy, employer opposition was obviously tempering the progress of Los Angeles labor's quest for union recognition. In this period it was the *Times* that rallied employers and the public behind the slogan of industrial freedom. In the decade or more since the printers' strike of 1890, Harrison Gray Otis had ramified his initial modest objective of breaking the local Typographical Union into a far-flung design to cripple or destroy unionism wherever it lifted its head. At the same time his newspaper was gaining strength and influence. The city's population had increased by 103 per cent between 1890 and 1900, but the *Times'* daily circulation had jumped 329 per cent.[24] Otis used his newspaper with telling effect to justify employers in labor disputes, to upbraid and ridicule businessmen too friendly to unions, to harass organized labor at every turn, to elevate the nonunion workingman to a pinnacle of nobility, and to commend various nonunion organizations of workers, such as the Printers' Protective Fraternity. Antiunion devices, like the lockout, the black list, and the discharge of union members, received the *Times'* approval and encouragement in its avowed desire to save the richly endowed city of Los Angeles from the closed-shop fate of San Francisco.

2. New Offensive Against the *Times*

Those who watched over the destinies of Los Angeles labor realized that victories at the bargaining table might well be meaningless without a concomitant effort to subdue Otis and the *Times*. The renascence of local unionism had barely begun when the Council of Labor, in November, 1899, suggested reimposition of the boycott which had lapsed during the depression years. The Typographical Union, however, with resources strained and membership reduced by the hard times, rejected the proposal as premature. The printers found another argument for caution in the words of ITU President S. B. Donnelly, who had recently visited Los Angeles. Donnelly had counseled against a new anti-*Times* campaign until such time as the local labor movement had the backing of a strong competing newspaper.[25]

With direct moves against the *Times* temporarily in abeyance, the Typographical Union sought to strengthen itself by gaining wider use of the printing trades label and bringing more work to prounion offices. The impetus came from San Francisco, where the printing trades organized Union Label League No. 1 in October, 1899, and inaugurated a state-wide label campaign. In February, 1900, the Los Angeles Council of Labor opposed the award of the city printing contract to the nonunion *Daily Journal,* the lowest bidder, because as a paper of court news it was not widely circulated. Disregarding the *Journal*'s rebuttal that the circulation argument camouflaged labor's scheme to get official endorsement for the label, the City Council voted six to three for the *Express,* the second lowest bidder. The *Times,* though not competing, criticized the authorities for abandoning the customary assignment of the contract on the basis of cost alone. For the first time the City Council had emphasized circulation more than price.[26]

During the summer and fall of 1900, when political campaigns opened an additional avenue for label agitation, the Typographical Union launched its own drive. Cyren E. Fisk, serving for a month as paid business agent, unionized a number of printing offices, brought to union firms a portion of the contract for the *Great Register* of county voters, almost secured the county printing contract for a union newspaper, and, most important of all, induced the Democratic and Republican local conventions to approve the label for all public printing. The *Times* castigated both parties for the "consummate folly" of making such a vote-catching surrender to organized labor.[27]

More galling to the Typographical Union was a *Times* outburst in September, 1900, when the United Typothetae of America, an association of employing printers, announced the start of an all-out war, including court procedures, against the union label. The *Times,* wholeheartedly approving, denounced the "totem" in outspoken terms:

> It is a form of blackmail, levied by organized ruffianism upon invertebrate employers, weak-kneed politicians and other poltroons who [do] not assert ... their manhood or stand up for their inalienable rights.... Its use by municipalities ... is an unwarranted imposition upon the great majority of the people.... Political committees ... openly violate duty and trample upon common expediency when they slavishly kowtow to the impudent demands that all public and party printing shall bear that badge of servitude, the trades-union totem.[28]

This was too much for the printers. Two days later they decided to give the *Times* "the best run for its money since it posed as a dictator, the most vindictive foe union labor has had to deal with on the Pacific Coast during the past thirteen years."[29]

Nevertheless, the printers cautiously decided to wait until the Council of Labor's organizing drive, then just beginning, had borne results. Meanwhile, they prepared in a small way for the future struggle by sending out anti-*Times* circulars and by acquainting new unions and new union members with the history of their fight against the newspaper. One of the printers' problems was the recurring threat that Otis might receive a cabinet post for his services to the Republican Party. When Otis left for the East in November, 1900, ostensibly for an Associated Press meeting, the union, fearing that he was really seeking appointment as Assistant Secretary of War, immediately wired Gompers and the secretary of the ITU to exert counterpressure on President McKinley. In December the AFL convention entered a formal protest, and local unions and labor federations sent their congressmen letters objecting to the Otis appointment. Such representations helped persuade McKinley to keep the Los Angeles editor out of his administration.[30]

The Typographical Union was less successful in opposing an exhibition of the close personal tie between Otis and McKinley. Elaborate plans for the President's visit to Los Angeles in May, 1901, included a reception and overnight stay at Otis' home. The printers issued a press release stating that Otis was not a proper host for so distinguished a guest and that the city itself should provide the entertainment during a visit of public nature. The Council of Labor endorsed the printers' declaration, but President McKinley accepted Otis' hospitality.[31]

Other disturbing events occurred early in 1901. In January the publishers of the five daily Los Angeles newspapers established a local branch of the United Typothetae. In February the union failed to divert to friendly offices the contract for printing the city directory, verbally promised to the Times-Mirror Company as the only establishment with adequate facilities. The printers sustained another tactical defeat when the 1901 city printing contract went to the nonunion *Journal,* despite their arguments that the *Journal* was not a paper of general circulation. During the spring of 1901 the *Times* instituted a school for linotype operators; its students did local work at less than union rates, and its graduates were potential strikebreakers both at home and in other cities. Moreover, Otis did not even reply when the union, at the request of national headquarters, asked him to discuss an arbitration agreement recently concluded between the ITU and the American Newspaper Publishers' Association.[32]

The Los Angeles printers now believed that the time was at hand for action against the *Times.* By the spring of 1901 the general organizing drive, in operation for some six months, had practically doubled the labor movement, and each succeeding month saw more unions added to the roster. To assess the numerical strength of this potential force and its willingness to join in a *Times* fight, the Typographical Union appointed Frank J. Gregory as special representative. The response was overwhelmingly satisfying, as the Council of Labor, the Printing Trades Council, the Building Trades Council, the District Council of Carpenters, and forty-five unions promised to help the printers. Gregory foresaw that, with the backing of some six or seven thousand union members, as well as of individuals outside the labor movement, the printers had "within their reach the power of crushing the insidious influence of the Times against organized labor.... The present time is more than propitious for launching the fight."[33]

In answer to Gregory's report, the Typographical Union voted on June 30, 1901, to inaugurate a new offensive against the *Times.* A boycott committee under Gregory's chairmanship and including Lemuel Biddle, secretary of the Council of Labor, was empowered to act in the name of the central body; it had barely begun to function when Gregory, exposed by the *Times* as an ex-convict with an unsavory past, left the city. Stepping into his place was Thomas D. Fennessy, an up-and-coming printer destined for a powerful career in the local labor movement. When Fennessy proved unable to rally the badly disorganized committee, the union began negotiating with the ITU for a man of ability and some national reputation to vitalize the local campaign.[34] National President James Lynch strongly favored assisting the Los Angeles local, for a victory there would undoubtedly benefit the ITU: "If we can unionize the Times it will mean a great boom for our organization."[35] Following favorable action by the August, 1901, convention, Lynch chose Arthur A. Hay, president of the Syracuse Typographical Union, for the post of business agent in Los Angeles with orders to concentrate on the *Times.*[36]

Hay's arrival in Los Angeles on October 31, 1901, marked the beginning of his long association with the local labor movement and of a decade of more or less continuous warfare against the *Times* and its advertisers. Assisted by a new Council of Labor committee, including both Fennessy and Biddle, Hay immediately aroused the whole local labor movement to the urgency of the cause. Members of various unions distributed to restaurants, barber shops, and other centers cards defining labor's attitude toward the *Times.* Some unions appointed their own anti-*Times* committees. The Typographical Union paid for five thousand lapel buttons proclaiming "I don't read the Los Angeles Times," and fined its own members $5 for refusing to wear them. The device was so popular that a second five thousand had to be ordered. Members of Hay's committee visited many towns in southern California to solidify anti-*Times* sentiment outside of Los Angeles. At the end of his first month, Hay predicted that "by untiring and unceasing work, by determined and aggressive attacks, regardless of the number of times we are repulsed, we will be absolutely certain to win ... one of the greatest victories ever won by a local Typographical Union."[37]

Far more difficult than unifying the labor movement against the *Times* was the task of winning over businessmen. A renewed canvass revealed that *Times* advertisers were unwilling either to withdraw patronage or to exert pressure on Otis for greater lenience toward organized labor. Stiffened in their resistance by an emphatic edict from the Merchants' and Manufacturers' Association to stay out of the fracas, many businessmen refused even to see Hay. After a series of such rebuffs Hay resolved to concentrate the attack on A. Hamburger and Sons, proprietors of the People's Store. Hamburger was one of the paper's largest advertisers and had, moreover, helped Otis to form a select Employers' Association comprising those businessmen most bitterly antagonistic to organized labor. His establishment was especially vulnerable to union attack because of its heavy working-class trade. Late in November, 1901, the Council of Labor formally declared a boycott on the People's Store, ordering union members to withhold their custom until Hamburger withdrew his advertising from the *Times*. From then on the fight against the *Times* meshed with the fight on Hamburger's to form one great battle by organized labor.[38]

Union members and their friends took up the new aspect of the fight with zest. A committee of delegates from all local unions was organized to channel activities and avoid unnecessary duplication. The Women's Union Label League, formed in September, 1901, by the wives and female relatives of union men, cut down the store's volume of trade by day-to-day appeals to housewives and other prospective purchasers. The holiday season was a particularly fitting time for a boycott on a department store. On the Saturday evening before Christmas, members of the Label League flocked to Hamburger's with no intention of buying and kept clerks so busy exhibiting merchandise that bona fide customers lost patience and went elsewhere. Hay's committee provided another diversion for holiday shoppers. On three evenings just before Christmas, motion pictures giving labor's story and incidentally caricaturing Otis were thrown on a screen placed at a busy street corner. Boys selling the *Union Labor News* at principal intersections shouted, "All about the trouble between Hamburger's and organized labor!" By the end of 1901, Hay claimed that the store's trade had dropped off 25 per cent and that Hamburger, though refusing to budge, admitted embarrassment from labor's inroads.[39]

Hamburger suffered attack from yet another source when Local Los Angeles of the Socialist Party crusaded for enforcement of the state child labor law, passed early in 1901. Beginning in the fall of 1901, the *Socialist* held up for scrutiny all employers who worked their "little wage-slaves" more than the legal nine hours a day. Hamburger's was one of numerous violators of the law. Although the socialists reported the store to the Humane Officer in November, 1901, no action was taken until March, 1902, when John Murray's complaint caused the arrest of William N. Bailie, the store's manager, on a charge of working children sixty hours a week. The judge at first imposed a nominal fine of $2 because the defendant pleaded guilty and admitted ignorance of the law, but raised it when he discovered that the minimum penalty was $50. This experience, revealing the ignorance and indifference of both employers and court officials, illustrated the constant difficulty of enforcing labor laws. After Bailie's conviction, Hamburger's was more careful to observe the statute, and the *Socialist* claimed that other would-be transgressors were deterred.[40]

After the antics of the Christmas season, the boycott committee settled down to serious business. Under the Council of Labor's auspices, a labor parade and mass meeting on January 25, 1902, forcefully displayed labor's united strength. Thousands of union members joined the procession, carrying banners with such inscriptions as "We Will Bear Each Other's Burdens," "The Printers' Fight Is Our Fight," and "The Common People Do Amount to Something." Speakers at the rally were L. W. Rogers, editor of the *Union Labor News,* and J. Stitt Wilson, state organizer for the Socialist Party. The socialists maintained a keen interest in labor's progress, as befitted a party desirous of clarifying the political vision of workingmen. The *Socialist* claimed that Otis, fearing possible violence during the parade, had armed his employees with guns and ammunition. Added the editor, "The working people of Los Angeles will destroy the Times . . . but it will be by killing—not Otis—but the circulation."[41]

The January, 1902, demonstration inaugurated a mammoth publicity campaign by which the Hay committee determined to reach every man, woman, and child in Los Angeles and vicinity. Beginning in February, the Typographical Union distributed twenty thousand circulars a month outlining the causes and progress of the dispute. Thousands of copies of the *Union Labor News* were sent out. Quantities of little boycott stickers, pasted on walls and buildings, were constant reminders not to patronize the *Times* or the People's Store. To help cut the *Times'* circulation, the printers fostered a newsboys' union and urged newsstands, both at home and in other communities, to push the *Herald.* Aided by the Union Label League, they also started a campaign to enlist women's clubs against the *Times.* The national convention of the Federation of Women's Clubs, meeting in Los Angeles in May, 1902, made a wide audience available, but the *Times* boasted that the women were deaf to the union's solicitations. The printers began a drive to wean out-of-town advertisers, particularly manufacturers of medical products, away from the *Times,* and made satisfying headway with the assistance of typographical unions elsewhere. Because of its concentration on these manifold duties and its fear of antagonizing friendly newspapers at a critical time, the local union voted against raising its wage scale in the spring of 1902.[42]

As in previous years, the Typographical Union tried to influence the award of the 1902 city printing contract. Only the *Express* and the *Journal* submitted bids, with the *Journal's* estimate the lower. In March, Hay and Fennessy, accompanied by an attorney, asked the City Council to favor the *Express* because the *Journal* had a limited circulation and allegedly had not fulfilled the terms of its 1901 contract.

The Council, accepting labor's recommendation, gave the contract to the *Express,* but subsequently voted for the *Journal* when accusations of collusion in the bidding led to cancellation of the first award and reopening of the bids. Failure to secure the contract for a union newspaper for the second straight year was one of the reasons behind the formation of the Union Labor Party in 1902.[43]

These undertakings all cost money. Early in 1902, faced by a serious financial predicament, the Los Angeles printers appealed to the ITU for help. An interim grant of $1,000, paid in four monthly installments from April through July, 1902, warded off insolvency until the ITU convention in August could make more substantial provision. During the same period local typographical unions in other cities, particularly in California, gave financial support to the fight against the *Times.*[44]

Such aid was comforting and helpful, but it did not suffice to down the *Times.* Hamburger, suffering serious hardship from the boycott, offered in May, 1902, to cut down his advertising in the *Times,* but Otis had no intention of yielding. On the contrary, he boasted that with the help of the Printers' Protective Fraternity the *Times* was enjoying more than usual prosperity. The Los Angeles branch of the PPF, thriving under Otis' guardianship, now headed the national organization. In March, 1902, it changed the official journal, *The Fraternity,* published in Los Angeles, from a monthly to a weekly and used it to praise the *Times* and attack the Typographical Union. Otis memorialized the beginning of his close tie with the Fraternity by calling one of his presses, used during the 1890 strike, the "Old Guard" and decorating it with the figure of a Roman soldier clad in full armor and the motto, "Stand Fast, Stand Firm, Stand Sure, Stand True." Such symbolism was, however, less alarming to organized labor than Otis' control of the Employers' Association, which in the spring of 1902 began to advertise widely in the East for nonunion workers in various trades. Aided by Secretary Felix Zeehandelaar, of the Merchants' and Manufacturers' Association, the Employers' Association also induced many businessmen to stop advertising in the *Union Labor News.*[45]

Although the M and M still preserved its neutrality, Otis' manipulation of the Employers' Association greatly broadened the lines of labor-management conflict in Los Angeles. The printers' fight became in truth the concern of all organized labor and of its spokesman, the Council of Labor. From the beginning the central body had assumed a high degree of responsibility for the *Times*-Hamburger boycott, but the alliance became even stronger in the spring of 1902. Fennessy, chosen first vice-president of the Council in January, was elected president of the Typographical Union in March. He thus provided the official link that bound the two organizations together in a common enterprise. Indeed, Fennessy reported to the printers in May, 1902, that most of the Council's program was devoted to their affairs. When the Employers' Association began to import nonunion workers and to campaign against the *Union Labor News,* the Council of Labor warned every union in the United States of the damage which could be wrought on organized labor by an open-shop victory in Los Angeles. The response in gifts to the local Typographical Union, spearheading the fight against Otis and, indirectly, the Employers' Association, was gratifying.[46]

Continuance of the Los Angeles offensive, however, depended on an integrated program of support from authoritative national organizations. During 1902 both the AFL and the ITU assisted the local movement. The Federation, which in 1899 had temporarily abolished its unfair list as a step toward labor-management peace, reinstated the Los Angeles *Times* on the renewed list of 1902. At the instance of Arthur Hay, Los Angeles delegate to the August, 1902, convention, the ITU agreed by a five-to-one ratio in a referendum vote to contribute $500 a month for the ensuing year. The ITU membership at large thus expressed confidence in Hay's conduct of the *Times* fight; President James Lynch and other high officials, visiting Los Angeles in October, 1902, likewise evinced satisfaction. At the request of the local union, the ITU's district organizer in San Francisco toured southern California early in 1903 to stimulate more intensive prosecution of the campaign outside the city.[47]

The Typographical Union's siege against the *Times* set in motion a chain of events profoundly significant to the Los Angeles labor movement. The *Times,* vaunting its prosperity under the boycott, proved by circulation and advertising statistics that it was out in front in local journalistic competition and bragged under Lynch's nose that Los Angeles employers were firmly on its side. The People's Store made an about-face from its tentative overtures to the union earlier in the year. Beginning in November, 1902, Hamburger inserted paid advertisements in the *Times* on an almost daily basis, violently attacking the union boycott, claiming good business, and describing his employees' working conditions as excellent. He boasted, for example, that children worked not more than fifty-four hours a week, and that some of them earned a weekly wage of as much as $3. According to labor leaders, Hamburger was secretly responsible for publication of the *Union Press,* a competitor to the *Union Labor News* deliberately given a misleading title to confuse organized labor. The *Union Press,* issued during the fall and winter of 1902–1903, attracted much of the advertising withdrawn from the *Union Labor News* at the request of the Employers' Association.[48]

Most important of all the moves against organized labor in this critical period was a gradual shift in the policy of the Merchants' and Manufacturers' Association. Formed during the 1890's to promote commercial and industrial enterprises, the M and M had consistently refused to interfere in the dispute between the *Times* and organized labor. It had gone so far as to declare itself entirely neutral at a meeting in November, 1901, following Hay's arrival in Los Angeles. Nevertheless, the M and M became less tolerant during 1902, as it gravely considered the maleficent results of prolonged boycotting. Then early in November, under the mistaken impression that the M and M had secretly declared war against organized labor, the Council of Labor denounced the employers' organization and called upon all unions to rally to the support of labor's cherished principles. Although later admitting that the Council's action was hasty and unwarranted, the *Union Labor News* did not cease its derogation of merchants advertising in the *Times*. The M and M thereupon modified its neutrality, submitting that organized labor had goaded it into the new policy.[49] At the annual meeting on January 19, 1903, President Niles Pease declared:

> We regret that these conditions exist today, but we believe that it is the duty of merchants to stand together in a controversy of this character, and to declare that an assault upon one is an assault upon all. The boycott is un-American, unjust, unwarranted and illegal, and we are still more forcibly reminded of this fact when the firm or firms so boycotted are in no manner a party to the controversy existing between the labor organizations and a newspaper. We have acted in this matter in a spirit unbiased, unprejudiced, and totally fair to all concerned.[50]

This warning that employers would unite for common defense was the first step in the transformation of the Merchants' and Manufacturers' Association. From its primary dedication to industrial progress, the Association gradually turned to alliance with the *Times* in an unrelenting assault on unionism. Otis, of course, consistently maintained that he was opposed not to organized labor but to its lawless methods. Yet in reality he approved only of organizations like the Printers' Protective Fraternity, which renounced strikes and boycotts and bargained individually rather than collectively. Trade-unions argued that such an emasculated role would deprive them of their most powerful weapons in gaining their objectives. With the entry of the M and M into the contest, organized labor in Los Angeles found itself lined up against not only the *Times* and a few loyal followers but an ever-increasing body of hostile employers. Thus the bitter open-shop conflict in Los

Angeles had its roots in the printers' "Big Strike" of 1890, and broke out early in the twentieth century when the reopening of the *Times* fight and the boycott on Hamburger's united employers against labor.

3. BEGINNING OF THE OPEN-SHOP FIGHT

Abandonment of neutrality by the Merchants' and Manufacturers' Association, together with intensification of the *Times'* vigilant anti-unionism, tightened the resistance to labor's demands all along the line. Even before 1903, groups such as the Laundry Proprietors' Association, the Millmen's Association, and Otis' little Employers' Association had demonstrated the power of organized management. In 1902 a Master Bakers' Association and a Restaurant Keepers' Association joined the ranks of employers' organizations. In 1903 wallpaper dealers and deco-rators, electrical contractors, master sheet-metal workers, master cornice makers, and master carriage makers organized; two of the most militant antiunion groups, a reorganized Master Builders' Association and the Founders' and Employers' Association, came into being the same year. Employers' organizations, operating in conjunction with the M and M, began a more systematic and more open application of antiunion tech-niques: open-shop declarations, lockouts, black lists, discharges of union members, agencies for the importation and employment of nonunion workers, financial help to struck firms, economic pressure on employers friendly to labor,[51] legislative lobbying, and the like. In October, 1903, the Merchants' and Manufacturers' Association adopted a resolution condemning boycotts and promising moral and financial support to any member suffering from union attack. This declaration was a turning point in Los Angeles industrial relations, for it at once assured em-ployers of authoritative backing and forewarned unions of the uni-versality of the sentiment against them.[52]

Los Angeles was not the only community to launch a counteroffensive against labor unions. Employers in various cities throughout the coun-try began to organize as early as 1900 or 1901—Dayton, Chicago, and San Francisco were outstanding examples—to repress the rampant labor movement of the new century and the hitherto unsuspected power of a new business unionism. Open-shop policies of proven success spread gradually from such centers to other areas, until employers' associations at the national level took up the hue and cry against organized labor. One of the most belligerent was the National Erectors' Association, dominated by the United States Steel Corporation. Formed in 1903, it waged bitter warfare against the International Association of Bridge and Structural Iron Workers, which eventually resorted to terrorism and dynamiting in its hopeless fight against corporate power. Although the open-shop movement was widespread, it still lacked the cohesion of national leadership. The deficiency was supplied in 1903, when the National Association of Manufacturers, organized in 1895 to promote industrial and commercial enterprises, answered the urgent plea of its president, David M. Parry, by declaring against the recognition of unions. This was the first indication of the NAM's future open-shop policy.[53]

With the championship of the NAM, the drive to stop unionism gained new momentum and force. The most determined of labor's foes called a conference of employers and representatives of the public, already organized as Citizens' Alliances in various communities, to coördinate antiunion activities. The convention, meeting in October, 1903, organized the Citizens' Industrial Association of America, selecting Parry as head. The new body immediately launched a vigorous antiunion campaign, fostering the local organization of employers and the public, encouraging the use of nonunion goods and the employment of nonunion men, boycotting union label goods, patronizing firms at odds with organized labor, dispensing information on "law-breakers and undesirable workmen," and publicizing the virtues of the open shop. It declared against the closed shop, boycotts, sympathetic strikes, limitation of output, restrictions on the use of machinery, and apprenticeship regulations.[54] The Citizens' Industrial Association materially aided employers in checking the progress of unionism, and helped put the American Federation of Labor on the defensive against the open shop. Gompers sounded the warning when he spoke to the AFL convention in November, 1903:

> The opponents of organized labor have started an agitation for what they euphoniously designate as the "open shop"; and several employers, otherwise fair, having been persuaded that the proposition on the surface appears to be ethical, have advocated it.... This so-called open shop is the disintegrating factor that leads to the non-union shop; in other words, the shop which is closed to the union man.[55]

It should be pointed out that employers' associations were not undivided in their opposition to unionism. Some of the older and more responsible groups, like the American Newspaper Publishers' Association, preferred to deal with the unions rather than fight them. Guided by the concept that industry is business, not war, they resembled the well-established and experienced unions in their approach to industrial relations. But in both camps—management and labor—there were hastily organized associations which went quickly into battle and disturbed whatever harmony their soberer counterparts had been able to create. Strikes were met with lockouts, boycotts with boycotts, and pickets with detectives or labor spies.[56]

Los Angeles was ripe for the incursion of the Citizens' Alliance. Early in 1904 Herbert George of Denver, who credited himself with originating the idea of organizing the public, began to form Citizens' Alliances in California. Starting in San Francisco, where the new organization soon numbered thousands of members, George moved on to Los Angeles. By the end of January the Los Angeles Citizens' Alliance was functioning with Felix J. Zeehandelaar of the M and M as secretary and Otis as chairman of the executive board. Membership was open to firms, corporations, individual employers, and all citizens who did not belong to labor unions. The Alliance, careful to stress its antagonism to union methods rather than to organized labor as such, set up elaborate rules for the support of members subject to strike or boycott. Struck firms, for example, received compensation of $1 a day for each employee who had walked out. By April, 1904, with a membership of about six thousand, the Los Angeles Citizens' Alliance was reputedly the strongest in the country, proportionate to population. Working closely with the M and M, it included all the prominent employers and businessmen of the city. Henry E. Huntington donated $1,000 to the cause, and offered an additional annual contribution of $250 if needed. The Alliance thrived for a few years, during which its intervention affected the course of numerous labor disputes. Eventually, when the open shop became paramount in Los Angeles and there was no further need for a separate organization, the Citizens' Alliance was absorbed by the Merchants' and Manufacturers' Association, whose subsidiary it had always been.[57]

Thus during 1903 and 1904 the tentative antiunionism of previous years hardened into an almost inflexible opposition to organized labor. Employers and other citizens, banded together under the leadership of the M and M, were determined to make Los Angeles a model open-shop town. Entering more and more into the labor-capital controversy was Henry Huntington, whose great wealth and power added immeasurable strength to the antiunion side. The integration of antiunion forces in 1903–1904 not only blocked labor's progress at the time, but laid the groundwork for the more intense conflict in the middle years of the decade, when Otis' dream of an industrially free city was to be realized in the ascendance of the open shop.

For all the opponents of organized labor—Huntington, the M and M, employers' associations, the Citizens' Alliance—the *Times* was a willing mouthpiece. Moreover, Otis' editorials on the labor question enunciated in the plainest possible language exactly what employers ought to do:

Employers of labor should be ready to meet and vanquish those who make unreasonable and arrogant demands upon them. To be forewarned is to be forearmed.

Employers of labor in Los Angeles, having been thus forewarned, should prepare
for possible disturbances by quietly arranging with skilled workingmen in various
parts of the country, whom they may, if necessary, summon at a moment's notice by
telegraph, to take the place of their present employees, in case the latter should be
persuaded to walk out and leave their work. The latter might then be notified to go
about their business, and never to darken the doors of the establishment again. At
the same time a watch should be kept over the weak and faithless, and all inter-
lopers. Those who are found to be acting the part of the traitor and fomenting disturbance, should be weeded out, and replaced by men who believe in respecting and
protecting the interests of their employer, as well as their own.[58]

This is but one example of the doctrine preached by Otis month after
month and year after year. Couched in different words, the message was
always the same. Otis' contemporaries were well aware of his contribution to the open-shop cause. On July 4, 1903, some three hundred of the
city's industrial and business leaders presented him with a memorial
reading in part:

Your fellow-citizens . . . desire hereby to assure you of their hearty and cordial support in your battle for individual liberty. Under your leadership the Los Angeles
Times has fought and won a great victory for equal rights.

That the City of Los Angeles and environment are free from the tyranny of mis-
guided agitators is chiefly due to the fearless advocacy of the rights of all men and
the relentless condemnation of demagogues by the Times.[59]

Despite the *Times* and the growing open-shop sentiment, a few Los
Angeles workers were able to maintain a collective bargaining relationship with employers in 1903–1904, and to make additional gains.
Brewery employees enjoyed a high degree of control because of the
efficacy of a boycott on beer, the favorite beverage of the working classes.
All local breweries employed only union brewery workers, bottlers, and
drivers, and in 1903, following a brief boycott, signed a closed-shop
agreement with Local No. 72, International Union of Steam Engineers.
When their contracts expired in July, 1904, the brewery trades negotiated two-year agreements with all local firms, specifying wage increases,
overtime pay, and arbitration of disputes. A few months later a new
Los Angeles establishment and an Anaheim brewery accepted the same
terms.[60]

Several other unions concluded working agreements, though few
could match the brewery workers' power over employers. In January,
1903, Garment Workers' Union No. 125 signed a one-year contract with
two important firms after a two-day strike involving two hundred employees. The agreement settled a minor wage and hour dispute, pro-

vided for arbitration, and forbade strikes, boycotts, and lockouts. In
1903 the laundry workers, recovering from their defeat of 1901, signed
a contract with four of the largest laundries in the city, stipulating
higher wages, better working conditions, and the closed shop for laundry workers, drivers, and steam engineers. Early in 1904 two more important firms were added to the union list. This was a signal for proprietors to reorganize, and in March, 1904, they reduced drivers' wages.
The laundry workers' union, with over five hundred members, was
strong enough to maintain its scale; in June it signed one-year agreements with five laundries. The sixth union laundry had gone out of
business in May. The union of steam engineers, having signed up the
laundries and the breweries, tackled the flour mills in January, 1904.
All the mills in the city signed a favorable one-year agreement including
the flour and cereal mill employees as well as the engineers. At the same
time Alex Morrison, president of the engineers' union, was elected
president of the Council of Labor. By March, 1904, probably under
stimulus from the engineers, the flour and cereal mill employees had
organized their own union. The teamsters' union renewed its contract
with the trucking companies for another year in May, 1904.[61]

The nature of retail trade required department store clerks to approach the closed-shop objective in a different way. Late in 1902 Local
No. 83, Retail Clerks' International Protective Association, after re-
cuperating from the depression, launched a drive to place the union
card in mercantile establishments. Store proprietors, though limiting
Saturday hours and closing on holidays, were in the main unwilling to
recognize the union. The San Pedro clerks were more successful. Organized in August, 1903, by Z. W. Craig, business agent of the longshoremen's union, and backed by the strong San Pedro labor movement, they
signed agreements with twenty-eight out of thirty-two local stores in
1904.[62]

Arthur Letts, owner of the Broadway Department Store in Los Angeles, set an example for others in his benevolent method of frustrating
the union. In 1898 he had given his clerks a half-holiday during July
and August, and in 1902 he established overtime pay for employees
working above nine hours a day. A year later the Broadway instituted a
week's vacation with pay for workers of a year's standing. In January,
1904, Letts proposed to the Merchants' and Manufacturers' Association
that stores close at six instead of ten o'clock on Saturdays. Although
other proprietors were loath to sacrifice a lucrative shopping time, Letts
persisted and by the summer of 1906 had enlisted leading merchants in
support of the plan. In 1904, Letts made the union's entry into his estab-

lishment more difficult by organizing his clerks into a Mutual Benefit Association, which dispensed sick and death benefits for many years thereafter.[63]

The Building Trades Council, which had failed in 1901 to gain universal acceptance of the working-card system, tried again in 1903 to unionize the construction industry, partly through the efforts of individual unions and partly through a general strike of all building craftsmen. The outcome, no more satisfactory in 1903 than in 1901, illustrated the growing tendency for employers to unite formally in opposition to union demands and, after winning their victories, to shift to open-shop policies. Leading off in February, 1903, was Local No. 108 of the Amalgamated Sheet Metal Workers' Union, which struck against five shops in an effort to maintain the control it had exercised for several years past and to push wages up another notch. Members of the recently organized Master Sheet Metal Workers' Association locked out unionists who had not struck, substituted their own regulations for the previously recognized union shop rules, employed nonunion men, and broke the strike within six weeks. A similar dispute beginning in April, 1903, just as the sheet-metal workers gave up their fight, ended disastrously for Local No. 116, International Brotherhood of Electrical Workers. The electricians wanted a wage increase and apprenticeship regulations, but the Master Electrical Contractors' Association successfully defied the union.[64]

From February to June, 1903, while the strikes of sheet-metal workers and electrical workers were in progress, small groups of other building craftsmen walked off construction jobs that were not manned completely by union men. Invariably, contractors replaced these strikers with nonunion men. Early in April, the Building Trades Council, trying to systematize the sporadic closed-shop endeavors, ordered all members of affiliated unions to strike if they were working with nonunionists. Although some seven hundred men walked out, the disturbance ended in a few days. Bricklayers, not affiliated with the Council, remained on the job, and other craftsmen soon began to drift back to work, partly because the Council had called the strike without the sanction of member unions. Thereafter, with almost a defeatist policy, the Building Trades Council discontinued the fight for the closed shop in the construction industry. Several minor strikes by carpenters and glass workers in the latter part of 1903 merely emphasized the Council's weakness and the inability of building trades to unionize big contracts. Although some smaller contractors did agree to employ only union members, the most important building jobs in the city were either nonunion or open shop.[65]

Affiliated with the Building Trades Council was Local No. 61, International Brotherhood of Electrical Workers, but its members, electric linemen, had little to do with building contracts and consequently kept out of the disputes affecting other craftsmen. The linemen, however, were simultaneously involved in a strike of their own which reached major proportions and eventually spread throughout the Pacific Coast states. On May 1, 1903, the union presented a list of detailed demands to the Sunset Telephone and Telegraph Company, the Home Telephone Company, and two electrical companies. The most important specifications were pay increases for all grades of workers, the eight-hour day, time and a half for overtime and double time for Sundays and holidays, apprenticeship regulations, and the closed shop. When these demands were rejected on May 5, approximately five hundred Los Angeles linemen and helpers struck against telephone and electrical companies and traction lines. Telephone companies, with 80 per cent of their men out, were the hardest hit. Within a few days the strike spread over southern California, as Sunset Company employees at Riverside, Santa Barbara, San Diego, and various smaller communities walked out. Even then the companies refused to deal with the linemen's union, and began to employ nonunion workers. Huntington quickly freed himself of the dispute by bringing in expert linemen from the East.[66]

Early in June, with the strike stalemated, Local No. 61 asked linemen's unions up and down the Pacific Coast to assist in the fight against the Sunset Telephone Company. Several weeks later President J. J. Sabine of the Pacific States Telephone and Telegraph Company, with which the Sunset Company was affiliated, met in San Francisco with representatives of coast unions, but categorically rejected all demands. On June 23 between fifteen hundred and two thousand linemen in California, Oregon, Washington, and Arizona walked off their jobs. The strike and ensuing boycott, which in some communities extended to removal of telephones from the homes of union members and sympathizers, failed to bring the companies to terms. Nonunion workers replaced the strikers, and Sabine persisted in refusals to negotiate or arbitrate the dispute, saying that he would take the men back only on the old terms and only as individuals.[67]

The deadlock was broken in the fall of 1903, when the annual IBEW convention sent $5,000 to the Pacific Coast strikers, with promises of further aid if necessary. On October 3, Sabine reached agreement with a committee of linemen. The terms, later extended to all struck firms except Huntington's, were not made public, but the boycotts were lifted and the strikers reinstated. The lack of precise information precludes definitive judgment as to which side won the victory, but it seems likely that the terms of settlement embodied at least a compromise. Negotiations between Sabine and linemen's unions toward the end of 1904 revealed that some form of contract had been signed in January, 1904.[68]

In centralization and degree of organization the metal trades of Los Angeles lagged behind the building trades. Without a central body, the individual unions lacked the support of allied craftsmen in their efforts to better conditions in foundries and iron works. In the early part of 1903 boilermakers, iron molders, and pipe and tank makers lost a series of small strikes over wages, apprenticeship regulations, or employment of nonunion men. A more serious pipe and tank makers' strike, extending from mid-June to late August, 1903, and involving practically all of the union's 200 members, was directed against five companies which had refused to reduce the working day from nine to eight hours with no cut in daily wages. After losing this contest, the pipe and tank makers' union was disrupted and soon disappeared.[69]

The two most important metal trades strikes of 1903 were called by the unions of iron workers and iron molders. Shortly after organizing, the iron workers' union gave employers ninety days' notice that as of April 21, 1903, wages would be $3 for the eight-hour day instead of the prevailing $2–$2.25 for the nine-hour day. An unstated but obvious objective was unionization of the two leading concerns, the Baker Iron Works and the Llewellyn Iron Works, which employed most of the union's members but operated as open shops. On April 22, with no response from employers, the union called out its men at Baker and Llewellyn. The two firms, though temporarily embarrassed, eventually imported enough nonunion workers to replace the strikers and defeat the union. Baker and Llewellyn remained open-shop concerns, paying wages of their own choosing; the iron workers' union, which had entered the controversy before it was sufficiently well organized, did not recover from this initial setback for some years.[70]

Of greater significance to the future of the Los Angeles metal trades was a strike of iron molders. On July 30, 1903, Local No. 374, International Molders' Union of North America, presented to all foundries and iron works demands for wages of $3.50 for a nine-hour day, time and a half for overtime, double time for Sundays and holidays, limitation of apprentices, and union recognition. The walkout, beginning on August 3 when employers rejected these terms, involved more than one hundred men and affected all the foundries in the city. When the international union endorsed the strike and began sending strike benefits of $7 a week per worker, the situation was admittedly serious. Even the

Times acknowledged that a majority of the skilled workers had walked out. But the proprietors, instead of dealing with the union, organized the Founders' and Employers' Association with Fred L. Baker of the Baker Iron Works as president, and announced that they would thereafter run nonunion establishments. In January, 1904, when President Joseph Valentine of the International Molders' Union visited Los Angeles and requested consideration of the union's demands, the Founders' and Employers' Association responded by requiring of all job applicants an affidavit of nonmembership in any labor union. By February, 1904, with two-thirds of its members gone to find work in other cities, the local molders' union had all but disintegrated. At the end of that year the Founders' and Employers' Association, including in its membership of twenty-five all of the city's leading foundries, reported that seventeen of those foundries employed nonunion men exclusively.[71]

These metal trades disputes, seriously weakening the unions of pipe and tank makers, iron workers, and molders, and leading to the formation of one of the most aggressive of local employers' organizations, clearly illustrated the trend of industrial relations in Los Angeles.

The existence of a department council did not in itself guarantee victory in labor disputes. Printing pressmen, affiliated with printers, press feeders, and bookbinders in the Allied Printing Trades Council, discovered during a strike in 1903 that sympathetic action by allied trades did not follow as a matter of course. Los Angeles Local No. 78 of the International Printing Pressmen's Union maintained fairly tight control of its trade in Los Angeles, for its members were employed by numerous printing offices that had renounced the Typographical Union, including the Times-Mirror Company. When the local union struck in April, 1903, against nine job offices which refused a wage increase, some members, including those employed by the *Times,* remained on the job pending authorization by the international union. A similar uncertainty about the legality of the strike deterred the Typographical Union from ordering its members out of offices which had not granted the pressmen's demand.[72]

Although some of the smaller concerns yielded, employers who were determined to resist the union formed the Employing Printers' Association several days after the strike began. The Times-Mirror Company, though unaffected by the dispute, was a member. The Association, after conferring with a Printing Trades Council delegation, refused to grant pay increases and began to import strikebreakers from other cities. In June, when the pressmen's international finally endorsed the walkout, the Typographical Union called its members out of offices labeled unfair by the pressmen. The assistance came too late. The pressmen's union, though making satisfactory settlements with a few firms, lost its contest with the Employing Printers' Association. The *Times,* regarding the strike as an oblique attack on itself, rejoiced that yet another effort to down the champion of industrial freedom had failed.[73]

The efforts of another craft to improve working conditions in 1903 led to further organization of employers. In April, Los Angeles Local No. 65, Carriage and Wagon Workers' Union, followed the example of its national body in asking for the eight-hour day, wage increases, and overtime pay. In a pattern becoming ever more familiar, employers refused, locked out union members, and organized the Master Carriage Makers' Association.[74] Typical of this period was the ensuing open-shop declaration:

> We, the undersigned carriage and wagon builders doing business in the city of Los Angeles, Cal., do hereby resolve and agree that we will not in any way recognize any union....
>
> We positively will not recognize or treat with any union or walking delegate, or other representative of any union as to hours of labor, or wages paid, or as to whom we shall employ or discharge. We expressly agree to run our shops as open, independent, and non-union shops.... We shall hire whom we choose, discharge men at our own discretion, and pay such wages as shall be agreed on between ourselves and ... employees ... acting individually. We shall employ union and non-union workmen indiscriminately...
>
> We recognize in unionism as sought to be applied in our shops, nothing but a distinct usurpation of the rights and privileges of the employers by the employees, all of which we declare to be un-American in spirit and not founded upon common sense and business principles.[75]

Despite some confusion in terminology, the intent of this challenge was clear. The carriage workers raised funds for a coöperative establishment, actually in operation for a few months in the summer of 1903 but soon ending in failure. The union survived into the early part of 1904, only to drop out of sight before the end of the year.[76]

The sequence of union formation and self-assertion, of employers' organization and resistance, was repeated in various Los Angeles industries. Employees in the wholesale and retail meat trade were organized into two unions, both affiliated with the national union of Amalgamated Meat Cutters and Butcher Workmen. Local No. 265 comprised the butcher workmen employed in the four local slaughterhouses, Maier, Sentous, Cudahy, and Hauser; the meat cutters of Local No. 266 worked in retail butcher shops. A minor strike in June, 1903, arising from disregard of union shop rules in the Maier plant, involved both unions and forced the four packinghouses to close. Although of brief duration, the tie-up brought the Wholesale Packers' Association and the Retail Butchers' Board of Trade, both organized in 1903, into a collaboration which affected the course of a longer and more serious dispute later in the year.[77]

The second strike began in October, 1903, when nearly two hundred butcher workmen walked out of the Cudahy, Maier, and Hauser slaughterhouses in a dispute over hours. Although some employees were apparently working only nine hours, others were on the job ten hours a day; the union asked to have the nine-hour day regularized with double pay for overtime and holidays. When the firms refused to arbitrate, the Council of Labor imposed a boycott but refrained from calling sympathetic strikes of other workers. Although butchers' unions on the west coast sent money to the strikers, the Los Angeles union made little headway against the two employers' associations until January, 1904, when the Council of Labor lifted the boycott in accordance with a settlement which apparently specified general enforcement of the nine-hour day. The strikers went back to work without prejudice, though the companies reserved the right to rehire on the basis of competency. The parties agreed to adjust future disputes, if possible, before the strike or boycott stage was reached, an amicable arrangement which lasted through the rest of the decade.[78]

An uncommon aspect of the dispute was the resentment of the Sentous Packing Company against the Council of Labor for listing it as fair to organized labor. In December, 1903, declaring that it had not recognized the union, the company requested an injunction restraining the Council of Labor and the butchers' unions from designating it as "fair" on the grounds that the "unwilling affiliation" was ruining its business and disgracing it among local businessmen. Although a temporary restraining order was granted, the court denied a permanent injunction in March, 1904.[79]

In most of the disputes occurring in 1903, the organization of employers was an important factor, but, as Henry Huntington capably demonstrated, a single employer with sufficient power could easily crush unions. The Council of Labor had made two unsuccessful attempts, in 1901 and 1902, to organize streetcar conductors and motormen. Finally, early in 1903, with the help of two outside organizers, Los Angeles Local No. 203 of the Amalgamated Association of Street Railway Employees of America was formed and soon claimed about two hundred members. As in previous years, the traction lines, chief of which was Huntington's Los Angeles Railway Company, discharged those employees known to have joined the union. When the organizers, together with a score of the dismissed men, tried to start a strike in March, 1903, Huntington averted the trouble by calling on the police to disperse the workers, and then ordered that any employees merely talking to the organizers should be fired. In April, determined to test its strength, the union asked the Los Angeles Railway Company for recognition, reasonable wages and hours, and reinstatement of discharged members. Rejection of the demands led to issuance of the strike order; the Council of Labor not only sanctioned the walkout but sent committees to strategic points to urge the men to quit work. Again Huntington prevailed upon the authorities to help. The presence of a policeman on every streetcar on April 30 was sufficiently intimidating to limit the walkout to insignificant proportions. Several days later Huntington tried to insure his employees' loyalty with a wage increase, and set detectives to watch the men to prevent resurgence of the broken union.[80] According to the *Times,* Huntington "was put to great trouble and expense in counteracting the machinations of the organizers who were polluting the minds of his contented employees."[81]

With equal facility Huntington simultaneously downed another union. On April 23, 1903, Lemuel Biddle, of the Council of Labor, organized Mexican laborers, many of whom worked in construction gangs on the street railways, into a federal union numbering some eight hundred members. The next day Biddle and a union committee induced Huntington's superintendent on the Main Street lines to increase wages from the prevailing 15–17½ cents an hour to 20 cents for day work, 30 cents for night or overtime work, and 40 cents for Sunday work. When the superintendent retracted upon orders from Huntington, seven hundred workers struck. The company immediately replaced them, paying its new employees 22½ cents an hour, and had policemen sent to strike headquarters to prevent possible lawlessness. By April 28, approximately fourteen hundred Mexican laborers had gone out. Despite financial help from local unions and the Socialist Party, the strikers were doomed to defeat. Huntington hired Japanese and Negro workers as fast as the Mexicans quit. The Mexican Federal Union, reorganized in February, 1904, with but fifty members, struck again in March when Huntington cut laborers' wages from $1.75 to $1 a day. Living quarters provided to compensate for the loss in pay consisted of two rows of floorless shacks, lacking all conveniences. The company denied the existence of a strike, saying simply that some of its men had quit their jobs with the change in working conditions.[82]

With the organization of the Citizens' Alliance early in 1904 assuring employers of a high degree of community support, labor unions found it even more difficult to make headway. In March, 1904, the paper hangers, members of Painters', Paperhangers' and Decorators' Union No. 267, asked the Wall Paper Dealers' Association, organized in 1903, for higher wages, piecework instead of time rates, and apprenticeship regulations. A strike of sixty paper hangers and painters began on April 11, when the Association rejected the demands. Despite the support of the Building Trades Council and strike benefits from the national painters' union, the local union was forced to capitulate. Within a month its members either returned to work on Association terms or found employment elsewhere. Meanwhile, the union had begun to call out painters receiving less than the union rate of $3.50 a day, but the effort availed the workers nothing. In June, 1904, the *Times* said the painters' and paper hangers' union was ready for the "scrap heap," since its ill-advised strikes had pushed previously friendly employers into open-shop or nonunion policies. Early in 1905 members of the Wall Paper Dealers' Association ordered their employees either to quit work or to surrender their union cards, thus terminating union connections altogether.[83]

During May and June, 1904, the District Council of Carpenters tried to bring the wages of all its members up to the established union rate of $3.50 a day and to achieve the closed shop. The campaign got off to a bad start with an unsuccessful strike against F. O. Engstrom, an important building contractor who replaced the strikers with nonunion carpenters. Subsequent walkouts of a few carpenters here and there lacked spirit and merely lost the strikers their jobs. At about the same time strikes over apprenticeship regulations brought defeat to the Los Angeles gas and electric fixture hangers and to Pasadena Plumbers' Union No. 280; both contests added to the number of open-shop concerns. Early in 1904 the bookbinders' union called its men out of shops which rejected demands for a wage increase, union recognition, and apprenticeship rules. About half the concerns settled with the union, but the rest, aided by the Citizens' Alliance, defeated the bookbinders and continued to operate on an open-shop basis.[84]

Culinary workers scarcely made a dent in the open shop, which prevailed in practically all of the city's hotels and restaurants. The waiters had unionized two cafes in 1903, but one of them, declaring for the open shop in 1904, broke its connection with the union. A strike and boycott against the Rival Restaurant early in 1904 was typical of numerous small disputes of the period. In February, the proprietor decided to sever his relations with the unions; he removed the union card from his window, employed nonunion cooks, and joined the Citizens' Alliance. The Council of Labor called a strike, and when negotiations failed to move the proprietor, levied a boycott on the Rival. The Citizens' Alliance immediately came to the aid of the restaurant. Its appeal to the police resulted in dispersal of pickets, and its agitation in the community, including distribution of several hundred free meal tickets, increased the restaurant's patronage fourfold. The boycott soon ended, with the proprietor clearly the victor.[85]

Barbers and tailors, like the culinary crafts, faced the problem of gaining union recognition in many small establishments. In 1904 the barbers suffered an interruption of three years of amicable relations with employers when one proprietor hired nonunion men and refused to display the union card. With the first break successfully made, other employers were emboldened to throw off union control, and by the end of 1904 a considerable number of them had declared for the open shop. In March, 1904, George Taylor locked out his twenty-eight union tailors when they protested the employment of two nonunion men, and thereafter ran an open-shop establishment. Although his action did not immediately precipitate a general antiunion move among employing tailors, it was a sign of future trouble for the craft.[86]

A clear pattern emerges from the story of Los Angeles labor disputes in 1903–1904. The heaviest concentration of strikes occurred in the first six months of 1903. In the latter half of 1903 and the first half of 1904, labor disturbances were fewer in number and, for the most part, of less significance. Obviously, as resistance to organized labor increased with the formation of more and more employers' associations and of the Citizens' Alliance, the unions slowed down and finally discontinued their drive for better working conditions. Defeat after defeat for union after union, with almost no compensatory victories, demonstrated in unmistakable terms the hold which the open-shop ideal had gained over the community of Los Angeles.

Otis, always on hand to enlighten the public on the progress of management's fight for industrial freedom, regarded 1903 as a decisive year. In April the *Times* said:

The labor situation in Los Angeles presents the gratifying indication that the agitator and jawsmith is an inconsequential and a constantly lessening factor, and that the great body of laboring men, union and non-union, have too much horse-sense to be used as fools and catspaws by these delectable lilies of the field, "who toil not, neither do they spin," except as they spin false tales into the ears of soft-headed and willing dupes.[87]

A *Times* editorial in December, 1903, marked the increasingly generous flow of capital into Los Angeles as a direct result of the establishment of the open shop.[88] But the unions were not yet ready to concede a final triumph to the opposition. Continuation of the *Times*-Hamburger fight during 1903, together with extensive preparations for rebuilding the weakened labor movement, revealed a determination to battle against the new open-shop trend.

XVIII. LABOR'S COUNTEROFFENSIVE

HOWEVER firmly the *Times* might reiterate its contention that the open shop had come to stay, organized labor in Los Angeles was not yet vanquished. Rather, the cumulative power of organized management spurred the labor movement to a reassessment of its own resources and to a realization that countermeasures were essential if it were to survive. Of these, the most consequential were establishment of a prounion commercial newspaper, thorough reorganization of the Council of Labor, and provision for building a Labor Temple to serve not only as central union headquarters but as a symbol of unity.

1. THE LOS ANGELES *Examiner*

Labor's longstanding feud with Otis was responsible for the introduction of a friendly newspaper. During 1903, the Typographical Union continued its fight against the *Times* and the corollary boycott of the People's Store. Both proprietors were as inimical as ever to organized labor. Early in the year Hamburger pointed to a voluntary reduction of working hours in his store as evidence that the employees were well off without the interference of unions. In a series of advertisements appearing in the *Times* during most of 1903, the People's Store proclaimed the futility of the boycott, described its employees' superior working conditions, and exposed what it called the grafting tactics of Arthur Hay and Thomas Fennessy. If Hamburger hoped thus to discredit the Typographical Union leadership, he was doomed to disappointment. The Council of Labor's answer was the distribution of thousands of boycott letters, some of them written in Spanish for the Mexican population. In addition, the Women's Union Label League sponsored a prize essay contest on "Why the Public Should Not Patronize A. Hamburger & Sons." Labor failed, however, to change the policy of the People's Store.[1]

More important than the Hamburger boycott was labor's direct attack on the *Times,* extending over a much wider area and attracting the support of many labor organizations. Locally, the partnership between the Typographical Union and the Council of Labor was once again cemented when another printer, Francis Drake, became president of the central body in July, 1903. Financial contributions from the ITU and sister typographical unions continued, and by mid-1903 had brought in approximately two-thirds of the more than $10,000 spent thus far in the *Times* contest. In August the ITU convention appropriated additional funds to ensure continuance of the fight. Anti-*Times* committees sprang up in other communities to reduce the paper's advertising and subscription lists; labor newspapers like the *Coast Seamen's Journal* regularly appealed to union members everywhere to help down the *Times*. During 1903 the spirit which had so long sustained the Los Angeles printers began to permeate the national labor movement, a development which in a few years was to bring the American Federation of Labor squarely into the battle with the *Times*.[2]

One of the results of this widespread publicity was the termination of advertising contracts with the *Times* by numerous out-of-town firms; in July, 1903, the ITU noted that 137 advertisements had been withdrawn. To counteract such claims, Otis stressed the *Times'* growing circulation, its leadership as an advertising medium at home, and the endorsement of his labor policies by the press and business interests of the nation. As conclusive proof that the printers' boycott had failed, Otis described the new plant occupied by the *Times* early in 1904 as superior to any other newspaper establishment on the west coast.[3]

An incident in the spring of 1903 illustrated a different facet of the *Times*-union contest. For President Theodore Roosevelt's visit to Los Angeles in May, a Citizens' Committee made elaborate plans including the annual fiesta. In the hope of preventing any recognition of organized labor, Otis alleged that the unions were plotting a general strike for the President's visit in order to focus attention on their objectives. There was no general strike, and the Citizens' Committee flouted the *Times* by inviting the Council of Labor to participate in the parade and to seat its representatives on the reviewing stand. Thomas Fennessy, formerly of the Rough Riders, had personal command of Roosevelt's bodyguard; labor delegates sat near the President as he watched the parade; and the Council's float won first prize. Hearing beforehand that Otis planned to ask Roosevelt for a cabinet post, the Council had garnered close to twelve thousand signatures on a petition opposing such an appointment. Like President McKinley, Roosevelt did not name Otis to his cabinet.[4]

Notwithstanding continued support by the ITU and other labor bodies, and an occasional soul-satisfying event like President Roosevelt's visit, the Los Angeles Typographical Union wanted a strong prolabor newspaper as a counterpoise to the *Times*. For successful implementation of any boycott, an alternative must be at hand; the printers had to have a substitute advertising outlet available for firms willing to cancel *Times* contracts. Although the *Record* had unwaveringly championed organized labor ever since its establishment in 1895, it lacked the prestige needed to balance the *Times*, already a nationally known newspaper. As early as October, 1899, President S. B. Donnelly of the ITU had declared that aggression against the *Times* was "impracticable in the absence of a sure-enough competitor for that sheet."[5] Early in 1902, Donnelly's successor, James Lynch, began a long and persevering campaign to bring a rival newspaper to Los Angeles. It is impossible to determine exactly when the printers turned to William Randolph Hearst, but in November, 1902, the newspaper magnate was rumored to be in Los Angeles secretly negotiating for purchase of the *Herald*. A few days later Arthur Hay, who had just returned from the ITU convention, told the local printers that Hearst would shortly establish an entirely new paper in Los Angeles. Such certainty accompanied the report that in January, 1903, the Council of Labor began to circulate subscription blanks for the promised Hearst publication. The following month the *Times* conceded that the rumors about Hearst had real substance.[6]

For some time there was no sign that Hearst intended to make good his promise. Then, in August, 1903, the ITU adopted the following resolution:

Resolved, That the International Typographical Union, in convention assembled, requests W. R. Hearst to acquire a morning newspaper in Los Angeles.[7]

In October Hearst, following a conference with Hay, sent Dent H. Robert, managing editor of the San Francisco *Examiner,* to investigate the Los Angeles situation. On October 19, 1903, after Robert returned a favorable recommendation, the local printing-trades unions entered into a formal agreement with Hearst to be in effect from the day of the Los Angeles *Examiner's* first issue until December 31, 1908. The contract specified complete unionization of the composing room and mechanical departments of the paper; adoption of union wage scales subject to revision by mutual agreement on December 31, 1904; and use of electrotype or stereotype plates produced exclusively by union labor.[8]

A few weeks of excited anticipation followed these preliminary arrangements. Although the *Times* spoke disparagingly of the "advent of yellow journalism,"[9] organized labor expected the Hearst organ to be an unprecedented boon to unionism in Los Angeles. The first issue of the *Examiner* appeared on December 12, 1903. Over ten thousand members of southern California unions showed their appreciation to Hearst by marching in the greatest labor parade held thus far in Los Angeles.[10] The paper itself, crowding its first issue with labor news, declared:

The *Examiner* will support with its whole power the proposition that labor is justified in demanding a fair share of the wealth it produces and its proportion of the country's prosperity; consequently, the *Examiner* will be the friend of the trades unions, and give them its energetic backing when their cause is just.

Local conditions call for the performance of a special function by the *Los Angeles Examiner*. It shall be its endeavor to bring about better relations between Capital and Labor.[11]

For the time being, the *Examiner* amply fulfilled the hopes its coming had inspired. Generous in printing labor news, fair in reporting industrial disputes, it won the gratitude of those who had pinned their faith on adequate competition for the *Times*. Between the two newspapers themselves a furious verbal battle raged during 1904 and 1905, each claiming superiority over the other in circulation and advertising patronage. A curious incident in 1904 gave rise to much speculation in journalistic and labor circles. The *Herald* changed hands in June, following apparently above-board negotiations, but soon rumors began to circulate that Otis had secretly bought a controlling interest in the new management as part of his anti-*Examiner* campaign. The *Herald* continued to employ union printers and remained a Democratic paper, lending credence to the theory that Otis wanted to keep the public ignorant of his ownership. Whatever the truth of such assumptions, the *Examiner* could not in the long run disturb the assured position of the *Times,* backed as it was by the Merchants' and Manufacturers' Association and the powerful interests of Los Angeles. By 1906 the Hearst paper, launched partly to gain labor support for its owner's political aspirations, had begun to recede from its original prolabor position, and the unions suffered gradual disillusionment in the champion from which they had expected so much. In 1907 the *Herald* again changed hands, Otis reputedly relinquishing his interest.[12]

2. Reorganization of the Central Body

San Francisco unionists assessed the cause of labor's troubles in Los Angeles as the lack both of efficient central organization and of adequate newspaper publicity.[13] During 1902 and 1903, while negotiations with Hearst were promising to overcome one of these deficiencies, the Council of Labor addressed itself to the problems of internal organization. There were three reasons why a more tightly disciplined and centralized labor movement was essential. First, the city administration seemed hostile to organized labor. Second, the open-shop tide was gaining momentum. Third, rapid union growth had tended to break down the Council of Labor's control over the labor movement.

Union leaders believed that the municipal government was subservient to organized management because it failed to intervene in the latter's manipulation of the labor market. As early as mid-1902, the Employers' Association controlled by Otis and Hamburger had established an Independent Labor Bureau which, by wide advertising in the East, brought many job-seeking workers to Los Angeles. The *Times* aided the campaign with frequent articles promising employment at high wages to mechanics in all lines. Organized labor saw these maneuvers not only as a union-smashing and wage-depressing scheme but as the cause of dangerously high unemployment and of an epidemic of robberies and burglaries in the winter of 1902–1903. But when the Council of Labor petitioned the City Council in February, 1903, to notify all sizable cities in the United States that no more workers were needed in Los Angeles, its appeal went unheeded. Labor accordingly accused the authorities of kowtowing to Otis and the Employers' Association, of fighting the unions instead of administering the law.[14]

Another official attitude increased labor's distrust. In August, 1903, the City Council passed an ordinance requiring police permits for street meetings within prescribed city limits. Although directed primarily at socialists, the measure was interpreted in labor circles as a scheme to hamper the anti-*Times* campaign, for unionists were convinced that Otis, together with Henry Huntington, controlled the City Council as well as the police department. A Free Speech League, organized by the socialists to protect constitutional liberties and work for repeal of the new law, elected prominent unionists as officers, including President Francis Drake of the Council of Labor. When street-speaking permits were denied socialists but freely granted to religious groups like the Salvation Army, the League announced as a further objective the ouster of Chief of Police Charles Elton. Newspapers other than the *Times,* reminding their readers that crime was still flourishing because of police laxity, joined in the crusade. But endorsement of Elton by the *Times* and the Merchants' and Manufacturers' Association deterred any inquiry into his conduct, and he remained in office. Early in 1904 the socialists were forced to drop the fight against the ordinance because of financial difficulties.[15]

Los Angeles labor felt the power of organized management not only in the procedures of the city administration, but more directly in actual industrial conflicts. Thus far the unions had been unable to curb openshop tendencies, as the *Times* pointed out early in 1903:

The labor unionists are having great trouble in getting their fingers upon the throat of Los Angeles, or entangled in the strands of her flowing locks. So long as the example of San Francisco—poor bedeviled and union-ridden San Francisco—is before this city, we are likely to see the people hereabouts conducting their own business without advice or direction from the jawsmiths and mischief-breeders who assume to represent "labor."[16]

By the middle of the year, Los Angeles unions were in a rather desperate situation. Over a thousand workers were engaged in strikes; union funds were running low; the Employers' Association was rapidly converting businessmen to open-shop policies; nonunion workingmen were steadily coming to the city; and strikebreakers were being deputized as special policemen. In order to tighten union lines and develop cognizance of each other's problems among union members, the Council of Labor established several new policies in June, 1903. It began monthly distribution to every union member of a "Friendly List" of merchants and businessmen who did not advertise in the *Times* and whose labor policy was acceptable. It created, for the first time in its history, a central strike fund to assist unions in financial straits. To bring union members into closer contact, the Council started to hold semimonthly open meetings and urged its member unions to do the same. Union men and women voluntarily organized an informal One-Hour League, whose members pledged themselves to spend at least one hour a week at meetings where they could become better acquainted, discuss methods of avoiding strikes and boycotts, and promote arbitration of labor disputes. These initial steps prepared the way for reorganization of the labor movement.[17]

The third reason why such reorganization was necessary was the changing character of the Los Angeles labor movement. Unions had multiplied so rapidly in the years since 1900 that the central body had become unwieldy and its control of member unions ineffectual. The Council's nominal supervision of industrial disputes, including authorization of strikes and boycotts, had never been fully implemented, and broke down altogether with the affiliation of new and inexperienced unions. President P. H. McCarthy of the State Building Trades Council advised Los Angeles unionists in October, 1903, that in order to have a more efficient labor movement they must create a highly disciplined and centralized body. On December 9, 1903, the Council of Labor adopted a new constitution embodying McCarthy's suggestions and submitted it to member unions for ratification.[18]

Early in 1904, however, the Council expanded the plan for simple constitutional revision into a thoroughgoing reorganization of the whole labor movement. The chief reason for the change was the organization in January of the Citizens' Alliance, a fresh and enthusiastic adversary whose support of management made full mobilization of labor's strength more than ever imperative. The new plan was far more comprehensive than the old, including not only a new constitution and bylaws but complete reorganization of the Council of Labor. Gompers and the AFL executive council endorsed the plan, and an overwhelming majority of local unions approved it. After the arrival of a new AFL charter, dated May 19, 1904, the Council of Labor formally dissolved itself and reorganized as the Los Angeles Central Labor Council, still functioning today as an affiliate of the American Federation of Labor. At this time San Pedro unions decided to withdraw from the Los Angeles labor movement. Although this limitation of the Central Labor Council's jurisdiction permitted greater concentration on exclusively local problems, it had the disadvantage of removing a source of strength, for the San Pedro labor movement was one of the most effective in the state of California. The Los Angeles Central Labor Council simultaneously lost the Pasadena unions, which in August, 1904, formed their own central body.[19]

The new constitution restricted the Central Labor Council's membership to unions affiliated either with their own internationals or directly with the American Federation of Labor. It provided for a series of department councils, which had to affiliate with the central body, and required individual unions to send delegates to the appropriate subordinate council as well as to the Central Labor Council. Representation was proportionate to membership. Precise regulations governing the relationship of unions, department councils, and the central body were designed to preserve the autonomy of each union, but at the same time to create a hierarchy with the real power vested in the Central Labor Council. Each affiliated union had to submit to its department council all changes in trade rules and wage schedules, and all proposals for strikes and boycotts. The latter had to be referred to the Central Labor Council with recommendations. The executive and arbitration committees of the central body were to exhaust every possible means of effecting a settlement before instituting strikes or boycotts, and then a vote of three-fourths of all delegates accredited to the Central Labor Council by organizations in good standing was required. The genuine desire to avoid industrial disturbances was implicit in a further regulation that the central body must make one final attempt to settle the dispute after the interested parties had been notified of a strike or boycott vote. Department councils were given complete jurisdiction over the conduct of strikes and boycotts in their respective fields, subject to the international rules of the union affected. Considerable authority, short of the right to declare strikes or boycotts, was granted to the department councils, which under the new constitution became an important link between individual unions and the Central Labor Council.[20]

The Central Labor Council spent several months setting up its new machinery. As many as seven or eight subordinate councils had been mentioned as possibilities, but only the Electric and Power Council and the Miscellaneous Trades Council were organized to supplement the existing Building Trades Council and Allied Printing Trades Council. The Miscellaneous Trades Council was a catchall for unions which did not fall into the other three categories. By August, 1904, some eighty unions had joined the central body, and in October, AFL district organizer William S. Smith, of the local teamsters' union, was elected to represent the new Los Angeles Central Labor Council for the first time at an annual AFL convention.[21]

During the reorganization, negotiations were also under way for transfer of the *Union Labor News* from private to coöperative union ownership, a change that would give the Central Labor Council absolute control of labor's official organ and enhance its position as the fountainhead of power. In February, 1904, L. W. Rogers retired from the editorship he had held since the paper's establishment three years before. In April, after an accountant had pronounced the business in excellent financial shape, nine unions incorporated the Union Labor News Publishing Company as a joint-stock venture. Most of the stock was bought by unions, though some union members were privileged to buy a few shares. The board of directors, representing all unions in the Central Labor Council, chose H. J. L. Atwood of the laundry workers' union as editor and manager. Atwood had had previous newspaper experience, and had recently been advertising solicitor for the *Union Labor News*. Under his management the official organ flourished. Subscription lists went up, and substantial dividends declared within a few months promised a sound future for the Union Labor News Publishing Company.[22]

3. The End of the Hamburger Boycott

Establishment of the *Examiner*, reorganization of the central body, and union acquisition of the *Union Labor News* were encouraging achievements which in part balanced the numerous industrial defeats suffered by the labor movement during 1903–1904. Labor's preoccupation with these issues, however, had a deleterious effect on one of the most serious aspects of the Los Angeles industrial conflict, the fight with the *Times*. Labor was not alone in assigning unusual significance to the policy of the newspaper. Harry Chandler, representing his father-in-law Otis at the February, 1904, convention of the Citizens' Industrial Association of America, reminded his audience of the *Times'* accomplishments:

> There is one city in the United States where a strike has never been able to succeed: that city is Los Angeles.... The reason ... is because it has ... the Los Angeles Times.... The Times, for some fifteen years, has been working to bring about a wholesome public sentiment, and it has been successful in its efforts.[23]

Recognizing the force of this argument, the International Typographical Union continued to pour money into Los Angeles for the *Times* fight; in two fiscal years ending May 31, 1904, it had sent almost $25,000.[24] Despite the ITU's contributions, the Los Angeles union, temporarily deserted by other local organizations, was compelled to relax its resistance against both the *Times* and the People's Store during 1904.

Another reason for the printers' declining aggressiveness was discord within their union in the early months of 1904. The first sign of restiveness over the conduct of the anti-*Times* campaign appeared in January, when an inquisitive member wondered why the rank and file received no information on disposition of ITU funds. He was told that Arthur Hay was accountable only to the national union, but the undercurrent of dissatisfaction remained. It broke out again when the board of directors, without first gaining unanimous consent of the union, sent to all locals in the ITU a circular advocating the reëlection of President James Lynch. Shortly thereafter seventy-two local members, whose ringleader was C. F. McDonald, similarly broadcast "A Protest" censuring the board for its electioneering and criticizing Lynch and his local cohorts, Arthur Hay, Thomas Fennessy, and Francis Drake, for their methods of conducting the *Times* fight. Before the dissension could be quelled, each side had sent out a further statement, the pro-Lynch faction arguing that the campaign against Otis had borne satisfactory results, and the protestants rebutting the argument with proof that the *Times* was flourishing. McDonald and five of his supporters were tried on a charge of contempt of the union, but were acquitted because the two-thirds vote necessary to convict was not forthcoming. In May, 1904, the union evinced a desire to heal its wounds and present an unbroken façade by electing as president Ben C. Robinson, who had not been prominently identified with either faction.[25]

During the period when the labor movement was absorbed in reorganization and the Typographical Union in internal quarrels, Otis and the *Times* made considerable headway. In January, 1904, when the union asked the Employing Printers' Association to institute the eight-hour day in book and job offices, the employers refused on the ground that printing trade conditions were not good enough to warrant a decrease in working hours. While the union began to build up a strike fund, Otis organized an Employing Printing Trades Alliance to replace the less militant Employing Printers' Association. The new body, pledged to defend the right to work without interference by cajolery, coercion, intimidation, or force, started with only six members, but by June it embraced fourteen firms representing 80 per cent of the capital invested in Los Angeles printing establishments. Although the Typographical Union ordered its members out of offices "which have entered into a combination with Otis to fight the various printing unions when-ever any one of such endeavors to better its conditions,"[26] it felt no disposition to resume the eight-hour negotiations. The campaign for the shorter working day in book and job printing houses was postponed until November, 1904.[27]

Contrary to its habit, the Typographical Union also stayed away from a controversy over the award of the city printing contract in the spring of 1904. The contestants were the *Express,* which had won the 1903 contract, the *Times,* the *Herald,* and the *Journal.* Reversing his stand of several years earlier, Otis now argued that the *Times,* though the highest bidder, merited the award because it had the largest local circulation. On May 23, 1904, the City Council voted six to two in favor of the *Times.* When Mayor M. P. Snyder refused to sign the contract, the Council delegated the duty to the city clerk. Aroused finally, the Typographical Union made last-minute protestations, but to no avail. With the *Times* exulting in a "victory for good government" achieved by a Council that had "risen above the menaces of the union labor agitators,"[28] and the Employing Printing Trades Alliance publicly thanking the administration, union printers and other community groups saw disturbing signs of municipal corruption.[29] From this dis-satisfaction arose a movement to eliminate graft from the city govern-ment, dealing at first with the immediate objective of removing city councilmen allegedly subservient to Otis, but later assuming much larger proportions.

Although the printers were to join in the fight against corruption, particularly as it served their own interests, they decided in mid-1904 to abate one aspect of their contest with the *Times,* the boycott on the People's Store. Several factors entered into this decision. The printers had just seen convincing evidence that the *Times'* economic and polit-ical power had not been diminished through their efforts, direct or indirect. When the city clerk signed the printing contract with the

Times in June, 1904, the Central Labor Council had just been organized with industrial peace as one of its basic premises. The *Examiner* also avowed a policy looking toward the termination of conflicts between unions and employers. The Typographical Union itself had found an alternate and more promising avenue for attacking the *Times* in a plan to recall offending city councilmen. Moreover, the Merchants' and Manufacturers' Association had recently predicated its entry into the management-labor conflict on its dislike of the secondary boycott. Under these circumstances the boycott on the People's Store, almost forgotten in the press of other affairs, seemed an unnecessary survival from a totally different era. Accordingly on August 17, 1904, at the request of the Typographical Union, the Central Labor Council voted unanimously to lift the boycott, citing as reasons the "desire of the conservative newspapers of Los Angeles to bring about an era of harmony between the business interests and organized labor" and its own readiness "to cooperate in any movement that will tend to set aside the strife and the bitterness engendered by . . . the Los Angeles Times."[30]

Commentators pointed out that more practical considerations than a yearning for industrial peace led to termination of the boycott. The *Times* argued that the real causes were the *Examiner*'s need for People's Store advertising[31] and the fact that the boycott had already been defeated: "The Times declares today that the laurels for the superb victory over the dangerous and desperate gang should go to the Hamburgers."[32] The more temperate *Graphic* agreed that the unions had removed the "absurd boycott" just in time to save face and avoid an admission of defeat, but advised Otis to curb his rage against organized labor and to "burn his black list and abolish HIS boycott."[33]

The lifting of the Hamburger boycott symbolized the industrial harmony which prevailed throughout the latter part of 1904. The ban on the People's Store had been unpopular in the community and had contributed to the friction within the Typographical Union. Peace was restored to the union, at least outwardly, and the printers approved the ITU's appointment of Fennessy as state organizer for California in August, 1904. Both factions rejoiced that the end of the boycott did not mean the end of the fight against the *Times;* the 1904 ITU convention again appropriated necessary funds for its continuance. President Lynch helped to end internal dissension by visiting the Los Angeles union in December, 1904, and expressing satisfaction over the conduct of its affairs. A more potent influence in the restoration of harmony was a national drive for the eight-hour day in all printing establishments, scheduled by the ITU for January 1, 1906. Preparations for raising a strike fund were begun early in 1905, and the Los Angeles union, which had postponed its own eight-hour campaign until November, 1904, fell in with the ITU plan. Local No. 174 found the eight-hour crusade, requiring an enormous amount of preparatory work, a healthy substitute for internal quarrels, just as the recall movement arising from the City Council's award of the printing contract to the *Times* united the printers in a cause which appealed to all factions.[34]

4. THE DAVENPORT RECALL

The Typographical Union was able to threaten punitive action against city councilmen who had voted for the *Times* because the Los Angeles electorate had, in 1902, written the initiative, referendum, and recall into the city charter. It was fitting that a trade-union was in the forefront of a movement to make practical application of a charter provision which organized labor had itself helped to promote.

Workingmen had long been aware that their well-being was especially sensitive to the form and processes of city government. In the very infancy of the local labor movement during the 1880's, several farsighted individuals had stressed the importance of workers' participating in framing amendments to the city charter. It was not until 1898, however, that organized labor had played a significant role. Then, it will be remembered, the Council of Labor and several socialist groups had joined with mercantile organizations and political parties in making nominations for a Board of Freeholders to write a new charter. Unionists and socialists together had exerted enough influence to have the proposed instrument provide for the initiative and referendum, but the charter had failed of adoption.

Another opportunity came in 1900, when the mayor invited the Council of Labor to share with other organizations in nominating candidates for a new Board of Freeholders. W. A. Spalding, former editor of the *Herald* and one of labor's two candidates (though not a union man), was elected and subsequently became president of the Board; three more of the fifteen freeholders, J. B. Millard of the Teachers' Alliance, H. Gaylord Wilshire representing the socialists, and Dr. John R. Haynes, candidate at large, had been endorsed by workingmen. For charter amendments the Council of Labor proposed various items of direct benefit to workingmen, such as enforcement of the eight-hour day and elimination of the contract system on public works, as well as direct legislation. The Board of Freeholders wrote most of labor's suggestions into the proposed charter, but because city funds were depleted no charter election was held in 1900.[35]

Inclusion of the initiative, referendum, and recall in the 1900 charter amendment proposals had been due chiefly to Dr. Haynes, long a proponent of direct legislation. Organized labor had given him consistent encouragement and aid, but in 1902 the Los Angeles City Council overlooked both Haynes and labor representatives in appointing another charter revision committee. The Council of Labor, however, petitioned the committee for direct legislation, and Haynes, as the moving spirit of a Direct Legislation League, induced the committee to draw up amendments specifying the initiative, referendum, and recall. With the help of the Union Labor Party, the only political party to espouse direct legislation, Haynes won a signal triumph in the 1902 charter election. By a substantial majority, Los Angeles voters made their city the first in the country to provide the recourse of direct legislation. In January, 1903, the California Legislature approved the amendments to the Los Angeles city charter.[36]

The weapon of the recall was thus ready for use in 1904, when six members of the City Council voted to give the city printing contract to the *Times* at a cost variously estimated to be from $10,000 to $20,000 higher than other bids. Four of the six, hopeful of political advancement, had allegedly subverted the public interest in order to win the backing of the *Times,* the organ of the city's dominant political machine. The cry of "Recall!" went up almost immediately after the Council made the award, some indignant citizens even threatening to remove all six of the offenders. Shortly, however, the Sixth Ward councilman, J. P. Davenport, was chosen for test action, chiefly because many of his constituents were union members. The Typographical Union, as direct sufferer from the Council's choice of the *Times,* was in the vanguard of those moving against Davenport.[37]

Neither organized labor nor Davenport's vote on the printing contract was alone responsible for the recall agitation. Residents of the Sixth Ward believed they had ample evidence that their councilman was corrupt, for many of his official acts had favored corporations. Davenport was accused, for instance, of supporting a street railway which had abolished a transfer privilege enjoyed by the people for four years; of helping a cigar manufacturer to promote his product; of allying himself with the liquor and saloon interests; and of accepting financial remuneration for permitting construction of slaughterhouses in residential districts.[38] The *Graphic* even claimed that Davenport "had bought a seat in the council that he might increase his profits in peddling cigars to saloon keepers."[39]

Unionists talking up the recall speedily found allies among disgruntled Sixth Ward citizens and public-spirited individuals and organizations offended by Davenport's lack of integrity in public office. Prominent among the latter was R. H. Norton, retired businessman and president of the Good Government League. Norton gave untiring and efficient service to the recall campaign because it attacked not only an individual example of corruption but, more important, the practice of using official power to serve private interests. Dr. Haynes, who had a strong desire to see his pet legislation used in a worthy cause, was another civic-minded protagonist in the anti-Davenport agitation. The National Municipal League, though at first skeptical about the validity of the recall, later reversed its stand and employed legal counsel when the constitutionality of the measure was under attack. The League's Los Angeles affiliate was not publicly involved in the Davenport recall, but gave more than casual help to active proponents.[40]

In the Sixth Ward, the signatures of 716 persons, 25 per cent of those qualified to vote, were required to legalize a recall petition. Members of the Typographical Union started the canvass, and on June 13, 1904, submitted to the city clerk a petition containing 951 names and charging that Davenport had perverted public funds by his vote on the printing contract. After checking the names against the *Great Register* of voters, the clerk reported to the City Council that the number of genuine signatures was insufficient to warrant a recall election. On June 27, an amended petition, bearing 952 names, reached the city clerk. When he found it adequate, the City Council set the recall election for August 11.[41]

Davenport, however, determined to contest the Council's action because of obvious imperfections in the petition. Addresses were not always correct, some voters had signed more than once, others had signed more than one name, and different sheets of signatures had been pasted together to form one very long petition. On July 12 Davenport applied to the Superior Court for an injunction restraining the City Council from holding the recall election. His attorneys argued that the recall provision violated the constitutions of the United States and of California, did not apply to city councilmen, and denied public officials equal protection before the law; also that the petition was insufficient, improperly verified, and void of adequate reasons for removing Davenport from office. The local judge, disqualifying himself from hearing the case because he was a taxpayer and a public official against whom the recall could be used, brought in Judge Frank J. Oster of San Bernardino. On July 16 Judge Oster issued a permanent injunction against the recall election on the grounds that the petition was defective because its several parts had been pasted together.[42]

Not to be defeated by a technicality, the recall forces immediately started a second petition at a big public meeting in the Sixth Ward. The new document listed a number of complaints against Davenport, including the issues of the printing contract, the slaughterhouses, and subservience to corporations. This time the canvassers prepared a petition capable of withstanding the closest scrutiny, and on August 1 filed it with the city clerk. Of more than nine hundred names, some eight hundred were found to be correct, and the City Council ordered the Davenport recall election to be held on September 16, 1904.[43]

Late in August Davenport's second appeal for a restraining order was heard before Judge Oster in Superior Court. His attorneys claimed that the city clerk's certification to the City Council was invalid because the names on the petition had been checked against affidavits of registration instead of the *Great Register;* that the statements in the petition were false and therefore did not constitute an adequate basis for an election; that the recall provision was unconstitutional; that it did not apply to an official elected before the legislation was adopted; that the plaintiff had property rights in his office which could not be taken from him without due process of law; and that the recall would violate the contract made between the public and the official at the time of his election.[44]

Judge Oster's decision was a weighty matter, since there was no precedent for judicial action on direct legislation, and future court cases would undoubtedly hinge on the result of Davenport's request for an injunction. The judge, fully aware of his unique responsibilities, decided that the recall provision as remedial legislation merited a liberal construction, and on August 29, 1904, denied the application for an injunction. He held that the charge of unconstitutionality was meaningless without reference to specific sections violated; that the people, not the City Council or the courts, had the right to decide on the truth or falsity of the statements in the recall petition; that a public office is not property but a mere agency which may be terminated at any time by the people; and that an incumbent holds office by no contract or grant. Those primarily concerned over the fate of direct legislation were jubilant, for Oster's decision tacitly if not directly upheld the constitutionality of the recall.[45]

On August 27, two days before the court decision, residents of the Sixth Ward filed a petition with the city clerk naming Dr. Arthur D. Houghton as the candidate to oppose Davenport in the recall election. Houghton ran as a nonpartisan with the support of the unions, the Good Government League, the Direct Legislation League, and newspapers other than the *Times.* The *Times,* the local Republican Party, the street railway companies, the liquor interests, and the gas company lined up behind Davenport. The campaign, of necessity a brief one, was exciting and high-pitched, with three or four meetings held every evening. Property owners and businessmen of the Sixth Ward organized a Davenport Fair Play Club to propagandize the councilman's qualifications for public office. But Davenport's strongest and most vocal ally was the *Times,* which attacked Houghton with scurrilous abuse, ridiculed the recall, defended the incumbent's record in office, and confidently predicted his reëlection up to the time the voters went to the polls. If Otis had indeed placed himself under obligation to Davenport and the others who gave the printing contract to the *Times,* he faithfully discharged his debt during the recall campaign.[46]

The recall election on September 16, 1904, made not only local but national political history. For the first time in the United States a public official was recalled from office by vote of the people. Houghton defeated Davenport by 1,837 to 1,083 votes, carrying all but one of the sixteen precincts in the Sixth Ward, including Davenport's own precinct. The *Times* rationalized Houghton's victory by pointing out that only slightly more than half of the electorate had voted, and that businessmen and property owners had stayed away from the polls; possibly it was the *Times'* preëlection confidence which had kept these known Davenport supporters at home. Houghton's backers readily gave credit for the victory to the labor unions, which had planned and carried out a systematic campaign. They rejoiced, too, in the triumph of free institutions and popular government, for the recall became through its practical application an established principle.[47]

After the election, Davenport went once more to court. Contending that he had been illegally removed from office, he petitioned the Supreme Court of California for a writ of mandamus directing the city of Los Angeles to pay him his salary through the end of 1904, when his term legally expired. The arguments used were identical with those in the earlier litigation. In April, 1905, the Supreme Court ruled that Davenport's removal was illegal because the city clerk had not used the *Great Register* to determine the validity of the signatures on the recall petition, and ordered that Davenport be paid his salary for the last four months of 1904. The court evaded the issue of constitutionality.[48]

The success of the movement to recall Davenport greatly enhanced the popularity of direct legislation. Within several years a number of communities in California had written the initiative, referendum, and recall into their charters, and cities in other states were beginning to take note of these democratic processes. In Los Angeles, proponents of better government found that the mere threat of recall was sufficient to deter councilmen from voting for unpopular measures. After the Davenport affair, two of the other city legislators who had awarded the printing contract to the *Times* were defeated when they sought renomination. Most pleasing to the unionists who had worked indefatigably in the recall campaign, however, was the failure of the *Times* to win later city printing contracts. In 1905 the Council, with little discussion, simply awarded the contract to the lowest bidder, and through the rest of the decade the *Times* was unable to influence the Council in its behalf.[49]

5. THE LABOR TEMPLE

Organized labor was free to devote time and energy to the Davenport recall campaign because it occurred in a period of industrial peace, extending from mid-1904 to early 1905. These six or seven months, completely without strikes and boycotts, were welcomed by both management and labor. The Merchants' and Manufacturers' Association, rejoicing in the current harmony, promised to help stabilize it. The only jarring note was the *Times'* continued belaboring of union leaders and union tactics. Late in 1904 Otis pledged himself to keep up the fight to make Los Angeles industrially the freest city in the United States, while the *Graphic* charged that the *Times,* suffering loss of prestige from the Davenport incident, sought to foment labor unrest as a means of regaining its ascendancy.[50] On the labor side, unions reported that never before in the city's history had so many of their members been employed. Looking toward a horizon where past strife and bitterness would have no place, they had reorganized and reinforced their central body in order to terminate a phase when labor's strength had been sapped and its unity threatened by unauthorized and unwise walkouts. The *Examiner,* taking much of the credit for the harmonious trend, pointed to the lifting of the Hamburger boycott, the absence of industrial disturbances, and the greater authority of the Central Labor Council as healthy signs of labor's new constructive policy. A necessary feature of the program for revitalizing and unifying the labor movement was the building of a labor temple to demonstrate to the community that unions were an integral part of the social order.[51]

The idea of a union headquarters was not new in 1904. In November, 1902, the Council of Labor, forced to move from one hall to another because of steadily mounting rents and a rapidly increasing labor movement, had appointed a committee to devise ways and means of building a labor temple. In the spring of 1903 the Union Labor Temple Association was incorporated with a capital stock of $75,000 in shares of $1 each. Serious industrial disturbances, however, halted the program almost immediately, and the Association returned to donors the funds which had been raised.[52]

In 1904 the Central Labor Council revived and reorganized the Union Labor Temple Association, appointed a Labor Temple Committee representing all unions, and made a fresh appeal for donations. To the nucleus of $1,000 realized from the 1904 Labor Day picnic were added outside contributions (all the daily newspapers except the *Times* gave $100 each) to bring the total to approximately $2,000. In October the Labor Temple Committee purchased one of the two lots forming the Maple Street site where the Temple now stands. Local unions and union members immediately began to buy stock, and by the end of 1904 almost fifteen thousand shares had been sold, enough to permit acquisition of the second lot. The total price of the property was about $19,500.[53]

During 1905, despite the resurgence of industrial disputes, great progress was made on the Temple project. Unions in other sections of the country, appealed to by circular letters, began to invest in the Los Angeles Labor Temple, and local organizations manifested continuing enthusiasm through stock purchases and other contributions. An announced increase in the price of each share to $1.25 effective January 1, 1906, stimulated a great buying rush which raised the total of shares sold to more than 38,000 by the end of 1905. This permitted liquidation of the remaining indebtedness on the two lots and erection of a temporary building on Maple Street, called the Union Labor Bureau, to serve as union headquarters until the Temple should be in readiness.[54]

An increase in the number and intensity of strikes during 1906 slowed down the fund-raising activities and the sale of Temple stock; for example, only one thousand shares were bought in the first five months of the year. Nevertheless, the work of excavating was begun during the summer, and the cornerstone of the building was laid on Labor Day. In 1907, however, financial difficulties increased. Toward the end of the year, in order to reinvigorate the program, the unions organized the Labor Temple Rustlers, a volunteer group which conducted door-to-door canvasses of union members and used revivalist methods at mass meetings to promote the sale of stock. Lemuel Biddle was a leading spirit, cheering his listeners with a song entitled "We Are Building the Temple," written by a member of the Typographical Union. In November, 1907, the printers added to their past record of leadership the further distinction of holding the first union meeting in the Labor Temple, though the building was not yet completed.[55]

From 1907 on, the Labor Temple Association was hard pressed financially. The depression following the Panic of 1907, accompanied by unemployment and low wages, made contributions and stock purchases even more difficult for unions and their members. But the labor movement stuck grimly to its plans for completing the structure. A special appeal to unions to raise the equivalent of $5 per member at the end

of 1908 bore results, and early in 1909 Los Angeles representatives prevailed upon the State Building Trades Council to endorse the Temple
project. Following this action some fifteen thousand shares were sold
in San Francisco. During 1909, weekly dances, a union label bazaar, a
Labor Day picnic, and a Labor Day edition of the official labor paper
were utilized to swell the Temple fund. Despite these unusual efforts,
the Labor Temple Association found it necessary in 1909 to borrow
money in order to complete the building by 1910.[56]

The Labor Temple was finished early in 1910 and dedicated on
February 22 in the presence of thousands of union members. Mayor
P. H. McCarthy of San Francisco was the main speaker, and public
officials from other communities were among the hundreds of out-of-
town visitors. The seven-story building, costing about $180,000, ade-
quately supplied with fire escapes, and as tall as or taller than any other
building in the business district (the Times-Mirror Company could
boast only of a three-story structure), was a source of pride to Los
Angeles unionists. The Labor Temple, containing business offices and
meeting halls for the Central Labor Council and its unions, one large
auditorium and two smaller ones, and some recreational facilities, was
not only a home for the labor movement but a convincing sign that it
could overcome seemingly insuperable obstacles in the achievement of
a cherished objective. It symbolized the feeling of unity whose steady
growth since 1900 had characterized the Los Angeles labor movement.[57]

After the dedication of the building, the Labor Temple Association
faced the problem of paying off the mortgage. Interest payments were
occasionally in default, and in 1914 foreclosure of the mortgage was
actually threatened. The disaster was averted through special levies on
union members, and when business improved during World War I the
Association was able to pay the back interest and renew the mortgage.
Following issuance of one thousand $100 mortgage redemption notes
in 1919, the Association paid off the mortgage by Labor Day of 1920.[58]

These difficulties had been very far in the future in 1904, when the
Central Labor Council took advantage of industrial peace to make a
real start in the campaign for the Labor Temple. During the two years
1903 and 1904 Los Angeles unions had made a creditable record of
achievement. Not only did they plan for a commodious and imposing
central headquarters, but they brought the *Examiner* to Los Angeles,
reorganized the central body, terminated the Hamburger boycott, and
helped to recall a city councilman suspected of being in the pay of the
Times. At the end of 1904 the outlook for the future of Los Angeles
unionism was brighter than it had been since 1900, when the defeated
movement of the 1890's arose to begin a new era.

XIX. ASCENDANCE OF THE OPEN SHOP

AT MID-DECADE, Los Angeles labor—strengthened by its brief respite from industrial strife and by a pervasive optimism springing from the accomplishments of 1903 and 1904—looked forward to the future with serene confidence. Guided by a reorganized central body, the unions began anew the endless struggle for better working conditions with little prescience of the great tribulations in store for them.

1. YEARS OF TRIAL: 1905–1909

Yet the last half of the decade was to provide the supreme test of labor's ability to survive. As depression and unemployment followed major industrial defeats, Los Angeles labor turned upon itself to engage in internecine warfare that left it, at the end of the decade, in a seriously weakened condition.

The pattern was set in the first three years of the period. Intense and bitterly fought industrial conflicts in 1905–1907 quickly dispelled any hope that employers would be more tractable or would abandon their open-shop principles. Employers' organizations had lost none of the verve which characterized their operations in the earlier years of the decade. Through black lists, advertisements for "independent" workingmen, replacement of union by nonunion employees, lockouts, open-shop declarations, importation of strikebreakers, use of Mexican and Negro labor, nonunion employment bureaus, and cancellation of union contracts, the more militant employers shook off the last vestiges of union control. During this period the Merchants' and Manufacturers' Association consummated its partnership with Otis and other antiunion employers, making possible complete financial and moral aid to struck firms, and economic warfare against employers prone to deal with unions. The Citizens' Alliance was a willing and helpful ally until the hegemony of the open shop at the close of the period made its continuance unnecessary.[1]

Although employers' associations were widespread and, thanks to the M and M, adequately armed with both offensive and defensive weapons, they could not dominate every industry nor keep in line every individual employer. Several important strikes were won outright by labor, or at least compromised, because local unions received help from their internationals or worked in concert for a common objective; or because the disputes, like those with railroads, involved larger organizations where union pressure could be applied over a wide area. Some unions, such as those of bartenders, waiters, retail clerks, printers, and barbers, found a program of gradual unionization, shop by shop, best suited to their purposes.[2] Others, notably those in the brewing industry, signed closed-shop contracts with all employers. Yet, despite occasional gains or victories, Los Angeles labor could scarcely challenge the ascendance of the open shop at the end of the 1905–1907 period. Part 2 of this chapter will be devoted to a detailed analysis of this critical phase in labor's development.

One of the most marked characteristics of the entire period 1905–1909 was the local reflection of national trends and a closer connection between local and national labor. Never was the link more clearly seen

TABLE 6

First Organization* of Local Unions, All Industries, Los Angeles, 1905–1909

Year	Number of locals
1905	7
1906	16
1907	6
1908	2
1909	5
Total	36

* In cases where exact organization dates are unknown, they are roughly determined from other data. See Appendix B for details.
Source: Appendix B.

than at the end of 1907, when the American Federation of Labor assessed its entire membership to help Los Angeles unionism maintain its precarious foothold amid ubiquitous open-shop conditions. When the national effort proved futile against M and M opposition and business depression after the Panic of 1907, Los Angeles unions yielded at last to frustration and discouragement. The years 1908 and 1909, to be described in part 3 of this chapter, were marred by crippling internal fights and resultant decline of the labor movement. Offensive actions against employers lapsed as the poison of dissension spread through the ranks of unionism. At no time in its previous history had the Los Angeles labor movement been so near destruction.

Nevertheless, there were a few encouraging signs during the years 1905–1909. For most of the period labor kept its morale at a high level and, when industrial defeats seemed overwhelming, characteristically applied its energies in other areas where compensatory rewards might be forthcoming. This is not to say that union leaders consciously categorized their activities; to them, all endeavors were facets of the one great undertaking of advancing the labor movement. During 1905–

1909 Los Angeles labor showed its inherent vitality in organizing, in accepting community responsibilities, and in seeking progress through legislative enactment and political activity.

With the assistance of AFL and national union organizers, Los Angeles labor continued its policy of expansion through repeated membership drives and excursions into previously unorganized trades. Tables 6 and 7 show new organizations for 1905–1909 by year and by industry. Although the total of thirty-six is far below the ninety-eight new unions formed in Los Angeles during the five years 1900–1904 (see table 3), the record is creditable for a period clouded by industrial defeats, de-

TABLE 7

FIRST ORGANIZATION* OF LOCAL UNIONS, BY INDUSTRY GROUP,
LOS ANGELES, 1905–1909

Industry	Number of locals
Building and construction..	17
Services...	8
Manufacturing...	6
Transportation and storage......................................	3
Metal trades..	1
Printing trades...	1
Total...	36

* In cases where exact organization dates are unknown, they are roughly determined from other data. See Appendix B for details.
SOURCE: Appendix B.

pression, and disharmony. The organizational drive was not confined merely to the formation of new unions. In 1906 and again in 1907 the Central Labor Council was reorganized, both times in response to an acutely felt need, and additional department councils were formed. Moreover, in 1907 the labor movement created an extra-union organization, minutely detailed and ramified, to fight the Citizens' Alliance. (See part 2 below.) These endeavors illustrated sensitivity to the forces operating in the whole complexity of labor-industry and labor-community relationships.

The picture seems less reassuring when the total size of the labor movement is considered. The data, based entirely on estimates by sources friendly to labor, are not reliable; even so, they indicate a static if not a declining labor movement. In September, 1906, there were seventy-two unions in Los Angeles, but by January, 1907, the number had dropped to sixty-three. At the beginning of 1909 the Central Labor Council had forty-eight affiliates, and by the end of the year, fifty-eight. In addition, there were fifteen locals eligible to join the central body but remaining outside. At the close of the decade, therefore, the Los Angeles labor movement comprised seventy-three unions. These data for 1909, compiled by the secretary of the Central Labor Council, are the most authentic for any year during this period.[3] For total union membership the figures are less reliable than those for the number of unions. Estimated at twelve to fourteen thousand in the fall of 1906, membership increased to fifteen thousand a year later, with only two-thirds of that number belonging to unions affiliated with the Central Labor Council. One suspects that fifteen thousand seemed a good round number for continued use, for early in 1909 the Council was still claiming this figure of doubtful accuracy. Early in 1910 sixty-two unions in the Central Labor Council had a combined membership of only six thousand. It is highly unlikely that the fifteen unaffiliated unions had one and a half times that membership or, alternatively, that the labor movement declined numerically to such a serious extent while the city's population was growing. If one accepts the six thousand suggested in January, 1910, as being near the mark, the total membership of the central body was then no larger than it was in 1896.[4]

Organized labor's well-developed sense of community responsibility was manifested in various ways. In 1905, 1907, and 1909 the Central Labor Council supported the issuance of bonds for construction of additional schools. Los Angeles labor felt so strongly the importance of voting in school bond elections that it pushed legislation aimed at extending voting hours so that working people could more easily get to the polls. A state law of 1907, proposed by representatives of the Los Angeles Central Labor Council through the State Federation of Labor, extended voting time by one hour, but complaints in 1909 indicated that labor's objective had still to be reached. Another union aspiration was the supplying of free school books by the state, but bills introduced in the 1907 and 1909 sessions of the Legislature at the instance of Los Angeles labor failed to pass because of sectarian opposition.[5] The unions were equally assertive on the benefits that would accrue to the community as well as to organized labor through the construction of good roads, and in 1908 they helped ensure the passage of bonds in Los Angeles County for this purpose.[6] Still another indication of labor's interest in community welfare was its assistance in raising funds for the 1907 fiesta, an annual celebration sponsored by the Merchants' and Manufacturers' Association. Although some unionists were reluctant to contribute to the M and M, which they felt would regard the overture with indifference and give labor scant credit, the majority prevailed. As an unselfish gesture of civic pride, the Central Labor Council gave the proceeds from a vaudeville show in April, 1907, to the fiesta committee.[7]

The event which afforded labor the best opportunity for exercising its sense of public duty occurred outside of Los Angeles, when the earthquake and fire of April 18, 1906, virtually destroyed San Francisco. Later the same day, as soon as the news reached Los Angeles, the executive board of the Central Labor Council, meeting in special session, sent three representatives north to ascertain the extent of the need and to proffer the aid of Los Angeles unions. That same evening the regular session of the central body called upon all labor organizations to be prepared to help the citizens of San Francisco with money and provisions. Within a few days an Organized Labor Relief Committee with seven departments had been set up in Los Angeles. Under its leadership the first local public mass meeting for collecting funds was held on April 20; additional representatives were dispatched to San Francisco and Oakland to report on developments and distribute money and supplies; thousands of dollars and carloads of provisions and mechanics' tools were contributed by local unions; and refugees were fed and housed in Los Angeles until jobs could be found for them. Los Angeles labor was as prompt and as active in providing relief for earthquake sufferers as any other local agency; although some of its gifts were earmarked for specific unions in San Francisco, its generous outpouring of donations was by no means confined to union members or even to working people. The Organized Labor Relief Committee functioned until May 1, when the need became less desperate, and until then the local unions devoted a large portion of their time and energy to the collection and transfer of money, food, and other supplies to victims of the catastrophe.[8]

During the years 1905–1909 Los Angeles unionists took greater interest than ever before in coöperating with other labor organizations to secure the introduction and passage of favorable state laws, and to oppose measures regarded as dangerous to unions. Such efforts evidenced a mature realization of the many-sided functions of organized labor. In 1905 Los Angeles labor helped to pressure members of the State Legislature into defeating a bill prohibiting black-listing, boycotting, and picketing. Employers' black lists, it reasoned, could hardly be effectively outlawed, but union boycotts could.[9] In 1907 amendments proposed by the Los Angeles Central Labor Council through the State Federation of Labor were added to the employers' liability act. The new measure gave statutory sanction to earlier Supreme Court rulings which clearly defined employers' responsibilities and obligations.[10] Less success, however, attended labor's endorsements in 1905, 1907, and 1909 of bills to raise the minimum daily wage for laborers on public works from $2 to $3.[11]

Another aspect of public works programs in which Los Angeles labor was particularly interested was enforcement of the 1903 law providing the eight-hour day for employees of the state or of any of its political subdivisions. Beginning in July, 1905, the Central Labor Council and the Building Trades Council so publicized violations of the law that within a month the City Council ordered that all future contracts must include the eight-hour clause and the penalties for violation, and instructed the city attorney to proceed against contractors currently disobeying the law. These decisions impressed upon city officials their responsibility for enforcement.[12] The unions made no further complaints about nonobservance of the eight-hour law until 1909, when the Building Trades Council and the District Council of Carpenters sought official action against Carl Leonardt, the contractor building a county hospital and a new Hall of Records. Leonardt admitted infractions of the law but escaped punishment under emergency clauses in the contracts.[13]

For Los Angeles labor the most engrossing issue in the field of remedial legislation was child labor. Local unionists were untiring in their insistence that existing laws be enforced and in their suggestions for amendments, for Los Angeles employers were notably lax in observing child labor regulations. A law of 1901, raising the age limit from ten to twelve and cutting the working day from ten to nine hours, was not thoroughly enforced because the State Labor Commissioner had an inadequate staff. Efforts to raise the age limit to fourteen and add schooling requirements were defeated by the fruit canning and packing industries of the state in 1903. In 1905 the Settlement Association of San Francisco, working with labor organizations, managed by thorough campaigning and by several concessions to the canning interests to push through a new law. It provided that no child under eighteen could work more than nine hours a day; that no child under sixteen could work between 10 P.M. and 6 A.M. or could work at all unless he could read and write English and was attending night school; and that a child under fourteen could work only during school vacations by permission of the juvenile courts.[14]

The State Bureau of Labor Statistics, under State Labor Commissioner W. V. Stafford and his deputy, J. M. Eshleman, made strenuous efforts to arouse public opinion in favor of the 1905 law so that its enforcement would be easier. Eshleman, aided by the Los Angeles Central Labor Council and its attorney, Job Harriman, searched out and prosecuted violators in the southern part of the state. Later the Consumers' League and the Humane Society joined in the enforcement campaign. After numerous arrests and convictions during 1905–1906, and after the California Supreme Court upheld the law's constitutionality, employers in Los Angeles became more careful to observe the regulations.[15]

There was, however, widespread sentiment that the 1905 law was not sufficiently stringent. In 1907 and again in 1909, organized labor's efforts to achieve the eight-hour day for children under eighteen were defeated by the Legislature, but in both years the 1905 law was otherwise amended to give school attendance officers greater authority and to give the State Labor Commissioner and his deputies the power to arrest violators. In April, 1909, Bruce Hatch, a mining engineer, was appointed Deputy Commissioner for southern California with headquarters in Los Angeles. The Central Labor Council, though disappointed that a union man had not been named, was pleased to have a permanent state official whose duties specifically included enforcement of labor laws, particularly the one governing child labor.[16]

Los Angeles labor's more direct political activity often overshadowed its lobbying activities for favorable legislation during these years. Accepting the policy of "Reward your friends, defeat your enemies," established by the AFL in 1906, the Central Labor Council endorsed candidates of either party who promised to favor organized labor. On one occasion the unions went a step further, forming their own party for the municipal elections of 1906 in accord with an AFL corollary sanctioning labor tickets when both major parties were inattentive or hostile to union demands.[17] From 1907 to 1909, organized labor utilized another opportunity to help fashion the governing instrument of Los Angeles, when the Central Labor Council participated with other civic groups in framing amendments to the city charter. In this enterprise, however, labor's role was subordinate to that of progressive groups seeking to free both city and state from the control of the Southern Pacific machine. In its political evolution throughout this period, local labor reflected the attitude of national labor toward the Socialist Party and the Industrial Workers of the World, as well as the relationship of labor in other states to the progressive movement. Both national and local labor benefited in some degree from legislative reforms instigated by progressives, particularly in the fields of child and female labor, workmen's compensation, and factory regulations.[18] The political story of the years 1905–1909, inextricably interwoven with events on the industrial front, will be told in parts 2 and 3 of this chapter.

2. A PRECARIOUS FOOTHOLD

The years 1905–1907 presented the most critical problems that Los Angeles labor had yet had to face, problems requiring solutions not only of immediate urgency but of future significance. During these three years tendencies noticeable as early as 1890 culminated in virtual establishment of the open shop and of the *Times'* brand of "industrial freedom." A series of defeats in major strikes, made possible by the gradual coalescence of the business community under the domination of the Merchants' and Manufacturers' Association, gave the period its pronounced characteristic. Yet, as in the earlier years of the decade, the unions fought hard against the mounting opposition, with strike after strike evidencing a strong determination to break the fastening hold of the open shop. And labor was not always the loser in these encounters with employers. An occasional compromise, or even a victory, illustrated paradoxical trends and gave unions the heartening conviction that their cause was not altogether lost. Moreover, in areas beyond industrial battle lines, labor's continuous reëvaluation of its position gave rise to such measures as structural revisions of the central body, organization of an extra-union group to counteract the Citizens' Alliance, and yet another political attempt to gain control of the municipal government. These efforts demonstrated that the vitality of Los Angeles labor had not been completely vitiated by discouragement and apathy.

The optimism of the last half of 1904 led to a renewal of labor's offensive for better working conditions early in 1905. The first moves, however, bore dismaying rather than propitious results. Four minor strikes in the building trades, following demands for the discharge of nonunion men or the enforcement of union rules, unsuccessfully challenged the open shop. After one of the walkouts, conducted by the structural iron workers, the local foundries set up their own employment agency and required all job applicants to sign an antiunion pledge.[19] Such disputes, although not individually significant, accentuated an existing tendency for employers to predicate their endorsement of "industrial freedom" on "unreasonable" union demands.

Once broken, industrial harmony yielded to prolonged and accelerating conflict on a wide front. One of the important strikes of 1905 had its roots in the millmen's disastrous eight-hour strike of 1901, which had demolished Local No. 144 of the Amalgamated Woodworkers. It was not until 1905 that Carpenters' Union No. 1279, replacing the defunct woodworkers' local, felt able to demand that all planing mills in the city adopt the eight-hour day and the closed shop. Twenty-two out of thirty-three establishments refused, and the strike began on August 8. It closely paralleled the 1901 dispute in respect to both protagonists and procedures. The new carpenters' local of woodworkers, supported by the District Council of Carpenters, the Building Trades Council, and the Central Labor Council, was opposed by the Mill Owners' Association, representing a majority of the industry. The employers hired nonunion workers and advertised in the East for more recruits, while the building-trades unions instituted a boycott on planing mill products, paid strike benefits, and sanctioned walkouts against contractors using boycotted materials. Despite these demonstrations of strength, the woodworkers lost the contest within a few months. They won some independent firms and contractors to the union side but could make no headway with the powerful Mill Owners' Association. The Building Trades Council became so deeply involved in the unsuccessful dispute that it suffered serious loss of prestige and equally harmful discontent among its membership, from which it did not recover for several years.[20]

Like the millmen, the laundry workers in 1905 partially duplicated their experiences of 1901, when they had struck for the closed shop. Although defeated in that dispute, the union had managed by 1904 to obtain written contracts with most of the laundries. One of these was the New Method Laundry, launched in 1902 as a union coöperative enterprise. Despite a gradual change from union to private management, New Method maintained contractual relations until June, 1905, when the laundry workers demanded the nine-hour day. New Method then joined two other large laundries in rejecting the demand, though one of these, along with several small establishments, signed the nine-hour agreement after some two hundred laundry workers struck. Despite strike benefits from the Central Labor Council and the laundry workers' international, the local was unable to institute the shorter working day in all laundries. Early in 1906 the laundry workers established the Puritas Laundry as a second coöperative venture, but, obstructed by the Merchants' and Manufacturers' Association and the Laundry Proprietors' Association, it soon passed from union control. Six years after the strike the laundry workers' union had written contracts with only three Los Angeles establishments.[21]

Two unions lost strikes for higher wages in 1905. The sheet-metal workers, despite aid from their international, were unsuccessful in a strike against twelve out of fifteen firms for a wage increase and the Saturday half-holiday with pay when the Master Sheet Metal Workers'

Association brought nonunion men to the city. The proprietors of four broom factories, aided by the Citizens' Alliance, broke a broom makers' strike for higher wages by threatening to import nonunion reënforcements from the East.[22]

During 1905 organized labor found the boycott a more effective weapon than the strike. The Central Labor Council boycotted the Maier & Zobelein brewery, strictly union in all its regular departments, for contracting some construction work to the nonunion Llewellyn Iron Works. The company capitulated after eight days, agreeing to use only union men in all phases of its business. A telling part of labor's campaign against Maier & Zobelein was its threat to support a current crusade for prohibition. Organized labor enjoyed complete control of the beer industry when the Mathie Brewing Company and the Rainier Brewing Company later signed similar agreements, the latter after an extended Pacific Coast boycott originating in Seattle. Boycotts were also used successfully against a few small concerns, including the Chutes Park Cafe and the Angelus Theatre, which had employed nonunion workers. Cohn, Goldwater and Company, makers of Boss Overalls, yielded after several months to a boycott imposed when the firm hired an open-shop contractor to construct an addition to its plant.[23] These instances illustrate the power of organized labor in negotiations with concerns catering particularly to the working classes.

In December, 1905, the *Times* predicted that labor would consolidate these various expressions of industrial unrest into a general strike for the closed shop, beginning on January 1, 1906. In their quick and angry denials, including an unheeded request that the City Council restrain Otis from such incitement of industrial strife, labor leaders pointed out that only the Typographical Union was planning a demand which might lead to a work stoppage. During most of 1905 the printers had, in fact, been openly preparing for institution of the closed shop and the eight-hour day with no wage reductions in book and job offices, as part of a nationwide ITU program. Their peaceable campaign, spreading over all of southern California, consisted of preliminary negotiations with employers and fund-raising for a possible strike. By the end of 1905 it became apparent that on the Pacific Coast only the Los Angeles printers were going to have trouble. Under Otis' leadership, fifty-five firms controlling 95 per cent of the trade formed a new Employing Printers' Association to oppose the union's demand. The union had gained the support of the pressmen and press feeders, and as 1906 opened both sides were poised for the coming conflict.[24]

On January 2, 1906, almost two hundred printers, pressmen, and press feeders walked out of plants refusing the eight-hour day. They were supported by strike benefits from the ITU and by generous contributions from Pacific Coast labor organizations, in addition to their own accumulated funds. The Employing Printers' Association, with the aid of the Merchants' and Manufacturers' Association and the Citizens' Alliance, imported nonunion workers, continued to operate its plants, and refused union overtures for a settlement. Most employers remained loyal to the Association, though several defections heartened the strikers. Union claims in June, 1906, that incoming strikebreakers were joining the union and that proprietors were having trouble finding competent help were in part substantiated by a decision of the Employing Printers' Association to inaugurate a working day of eight and a half hours on October 1. This concession failed to bring any compromise in the printers' determination to hold out for their eight-hour and closed-shop objectives.[25]

The union was, however, unable to reach its goal. An ITU decision to discontinue the Los Angeles strike benefits, needed more urgently in other cities where the probability of success was higher, terminated local resistance in October, 1906, when twenty-four strikers were still unemployed. The union asserted that firms lost through the strike were balanced by those gained, but it could not gloss over the truth that it had not even approached general establishment of the eight-hour day in Los Angeles. Many of its members had been forced to leave town; others had been expelled for accepting jobs in nine-hour offices. The printers ascribed their defeat to the interference of the Citizens' Alliance and the Merchants' and Manufacturers' Association, as well as to the willingness of some unionists to work in open shops. Throughout the rest of the country, on the contrary, the ITU program met with marked success; the eight-hour day was virtually assured in most communities by the latter part of 1907.[26]

On a national, state, and local basis the Citizens' Alliance provided ample evidence during 1905 that labor could expect no letup in antiunion activities. In January the California Federation of Citizens' Alliances unanimously affirmed an open-shop stand. C. W. Post of Battle Creek, Michigan, replacing David Parry as president of the Citizens' Industrial Association of America in May, emphasized that the molding of public opinion for the open shop was the organization's prime objective. When the *Times* predicted in December that Los Angeles unions would strike in concert for the closed shop, Secretary Felix Zeehandelaar alerted all members of the Citizens' Alliance for the impending crisis.[27] Mayor Eugene Schmitz of San Francisco, speaking to the Los Angeles

Central Labor Council in November, 1905, said: "Every man who believes in fair play and work here in Los Angeles and elsewhere, must in the interest of peace and justice oppose the Citizens' Alliance, which means discontent, poverty, and oppression."[28] The Alliance's intervention in both the broom makers' and printers' strikes convinced labor leaders that Schmitz had voiced an alarming truth.

The activities of the Citizens' Alliance in the printers' eight-hour campaign, particularly the influencing of employers by threats of withdrawing patronage, thoroughly aroused organized labor. At a great mass meeting on January 27, 1906, the unions of Los Angeles gave their answer to the Alliance. After addresses by Schmitz and local labor leaders, the assemblage organized the Anti-Citizens' Alliance with nearly four thousand members and pledged it to a dual policy: no patronage of merchants favoring the Citizens' Alliance, and no votes for political candidates refusing to abjure the Alliance. The Anti-Citizens' Alliance set up ward and precinct organizations, distributed lists of "unfair" merchants, and more than doubled its initial membership by May. Had the original intent been preserved, the ACA might have become a promising instrument of opposition to open-shop forces. From the beginning, however, socialists and others within the labor movement had strongly favored political action, and Schmitz, though hedging on the issue, had intimated that he would support such a movement. Within six months the Anti-Citizens' Alliance was virtually forgotten, though its organization was to prove a useful foundation for another of labor's political efforts in the municipal elections of December, 1906.[29]

The patent growth of open-shop sentiment in Los Angeles gave impetus to another method for strengthening the labor movement. From the beginning of 1905 the Central Labor Council gave serious thought to its form: would the present structure guarantee continuance of harmony and of centralized control? Answering the question in the affirmative, the central body in June, 1905, reiterated its constitutional requirement that individual unions must affiliate with a department council on penalty of forfeiting their representation in the Central Labor Council. The existence of only three subordinate bodies, the Building Trades Council, the Allied Printing Trades Council, and the Miscellaneous Trades Council, limited the choice, and dissatisfaction with the latter heightened a growing resentment among several unions. But union defeats during 1905 and indications that open-shop forces were consolidating proved a strong argument for further tightening central authority. In December, 1905, Lemuel Biddle proposed that individual unions be represented only in department councils whose

delegates in turn would form the Central Labor Council. He acknowledged that such a change, to be acceptable, must be accomplished by
the organization of additional subordinate councils.[30]

Biddle's unanimous election as president of the Central Labor Council on January 31, 1906, prognosticated adoption of his plan. For a few
months, however, the projected reorganization was delayed; it was not
until the Anti-Citizens' Alliance diminished in importance that the
Central Labor Council turned to the development of Biddle's idea.
Even then it was not altogether easy to banish current doubts over
depriving unions of direct representation. But Biddle, aided by the
presidents of the three department councils, crushed the incipient opposition by pointing to the benefits which would accrue from centralization of authority and from elimination of excessive detail in the
central body. By a ratio of seven to one in a referendum vote of all the
unions, the Central Labor Council ratified amendments to the constitution providing for adoption of the new plan on August 1, 1906. The
change gave department councils considerably more control over their
affiliates than they had previously enjoyed, and vested the supreme
authority over union affairs in the Central Labor Council.[31]

The department system, abolishing direct representation, was not
an unqualified success. Organization of new subordinate councils, left
to voluntary action of the unions concerned, was slow and incomplete.
The three old councils continued, an Electrical Trades Council was
formed in September, 1906, and a Metal Trades Council in January,
1907. Projected organization of brewery, provision, and transportation
councils did not materialize. Dissatisfied unionists voiced the suspicion
that the reorganization had been engineered by a power-hungry ring
of labor leaders, who ignored the fact that only a small percentage of
the total union membership had voted in the referendum.[32]

It is highly probable that these murmurs of discontent would have
been recognized as a danger signal had not industrial conflict broken
out afresh in mid-1906. Organized labor, heading into the series of great
strikes at whose end the ascendance of the open shop was almost unchallenged, had no time to answer the small voice of dissatisfaction
occasionally rising from the ranks. Two serious disputes, both beginning in June, 1906, while the printers' eight-hour strike was still un-
settled, demonstrated that neither the Los Angeles labor movement
nor its far more flourishing counterpart in San Pedro could withstand
a strong employer offensive.

The first of these was a strike by Bakers' Union No. 37 of Los Angeles, arising from a previous dispute between the Flour and Cereal Mill

Employees, Local No. 80, and the Globe Flour Mills. In March, 1905, the firm had locked out those employees who refused to forswear their union. The Globe company, with four branches in California, was a powerful concern whose refusal to recognize the flour and cereal mill workers could have a deleterious effect on unionism throughout the state. In April, 1906, after the Los Angeles Central Labor Council had failed to resolve the local dispute, the California State Federation of Labor boycotted Globe products. The International Union of Flour and Cereal Mill Employees backed its local branch, pointing out that the Globe company worked its men thirteen hours a day at a $2 wage, 50 cents below the union scale, and refused to negotiate with the union. The Globe Mills remained impervious to all pressure, however, and continued to employ nonunion men.[33]

Unable to make any headway, the flour and cereal mill workers finally appealed to the bakers' union, which in June, 1906, agreed not to work for bakeries using Globe flour. Despite the protest of the Master Bakers' Association, the bakers' union called a strike in all shops under its jurisdiction. More than twenty bakeries and about a hundred union members were involved. Although aided by its own international and by local labor organizations, the union was no match for the Master Bakers' Association, supported by the M and M, the Citizens' Alliance, the United Cereal and Flour Millers' Association of California, and even the National Master Bakers' Association, which launched a fresh attack on the Bakery and Confectionery Workers' International Union looking toward inauguration of the open shop throughout the United States. The strike was lost by September, 1906, though the boycott on Globe products was continued until October, 1907. Untimeliness and insufficient support by the membership of the two unions were put forward as reasons for the defeat, but the forces arrayed against labor were so strong that any effort to stem the open-shop tide would certainly have been ineffectual. The bakers' union, reduced to a membership of forty-five after the strike, required the services of an international organizer before it could begin, in 1907, to recover from the defeat. The flour and cereal mill employees' union survived into 1907, but then dropped from sight.[34]

A crushing defeat sustained in 1906 by the longshoremen of San Pedro strengthened the open shop and was a psychological blow to unionists in the whole area. Although younger than the sailors' union, the longshoremen's union had become, through force of numbers and the aggressive personality of its business agent, Z. W. Craig, the dominant union in the harbor city. The walkout of San Pedro Local No. 3

of the Pacific Coast Federation of Longshoremen stemmed from a conflict between the Sailors' Union of the Pacific and shipowners in San Francisco. The sailors struck on June 1, 1906, when their demand for a $5 monthly wage increase was denied. Although longshoremen of San Francisco and other ports decided to unload ships whether manned by union or nonunion crews, the San Pedro workers stood firmly against such a concession, and, late in August, demanded a wage increase. There was no water-front violence, though several lumber companies, fearing assaults on nonunion workers, obtained a temporary injunction against picketing. Andrew Furuseth of San Francisco visited San Pedro twice in September, but failed to settle the dispute.[35]

The sailors' strike in San Francisco ended on October 31, when the shipowners granted the $5 raise and signed an agreement with the union, but the San Pedro dispute dragged on until December. Employers then announced a new wage scale, with rates somewhat lower than the union schedule and graduated on the basis of ability and efficiency. The union, with many of its men displaced by strikebreakers, had to accept the employers' terms, including the open shop. The defeat impaired the strength of the longshoremen's union and thus of the whole San Pedro labor movement. For some years thereafter unionists in the harbor city, lacking their previous vitality, were unable to continue the drive for better working conditions.[36]

In the fall of 1906 an effort was made to resuscitate the Los Angeles molders' union, practically wiped out by a strike for higher wages and the nine-hour day in 1903. The Founders' and Employers' Association, organized immediately after that strike, had maintained the open shop ever since. When the business agent of the San Francisco molders' union came to Los Angeles to reorganize his craft in October, 1906, the Association promptly reaffirmed its ruling that no worker following union dictates could retain his job. A successful strike for union recognition against one member of the Association scarcely disturbed the employers' supremacy.[37]

Other metal trades gained some of their objectives during 1906 and 1907. In July, 1906, Los Angeles boilermakers won an across-the-board wage increase in one company following a brief strike. In September the boilermakers successfully struck against the Southern Pacific shops in Los Angeles in support of a helpers' demand for higher wages. Shortly thereafter the Southern Pacific granted a wage increase to all machinists employed on its Pacific Coast lines. After a two months' strike in the summer of 1907, the Pacific Division of the Southern Pacific compromised a dispute with boilermakers arising from the helpers' dislike of a foreman in the Los Angeles shops. These disputes were not individually or even collectively significant, except insofar as they demonstrated that labor had a better chance of success when it was opposing an adversary with widespread organization, like the railroads.[38]

Coöperation among allied crafts occasionally proved helpful to labor during a dispute. This had not been true for the printing trades in 1906, largely because of unified opposition and the character of the industry, but it did apply in some degree to the building trades later the same year. Contractors and builders, anxious to capitalize on current prosperity, had generally been willing to grant wage and hour demands, though balking at the closed shop. For these reasons the Los Angeles building trades met partial success in the fall of 1906 in a concerted drive for various improvements.

The carpenters, the dominant craft in the building industry, greatly increased their bargaining power in April, 1906, by consolidating three locals into one huge union, No. 158. With approximately twenty-five hundred members, the new union was the largest branch of the United Brotherhood of Carpenters and Joiners. Shortly after Local No. 158 affiliated with the Building Trades Council, it voted to demand an increase in wages from $3.50 to $4 a day, the Saturday half-holiday, and the closed shop, effective September 1, 1906. When the Master Builders' Association, the Builders' Exchange, and the Mill Owners' Association resisted all of the demands, practically all union carpenters in the city struck. Aided by the Citizens' Alliance, the employers refused to meet with union representatives, set up their own employment bureau, and carried on as best they could with nonunion workers. The union, with funds sent by the international, transported about five hundred strikers to San Francisco, where the 1906 earthquake and fire had created a demand for building craftsmen.[39]

A conflict of this kind could not reach a decisive end because of the great number of employers involved. Slowly contractors began to yield. Some of them granted all demands except the closed shop. Many more gave the Saturday half-holiday without pay to those workers who wanted it. Eventually, the carpenters achieved fairly general success. By 1907 most of them were working a five-and-a-half-day week at $4 a day, but they did not win the closed shop.[40]

Other building trades presented similar demands at the same time. The plumbers, asking for a raise from $4.50 to $5.50 in daily wages, the Saturday half-holiday, and the closed shop, compromised after a three-day strike. They won the Saturday half-holiday, though without pay, and a wage increase to $5 a day, but the open-shop forces were strengthened when the plumbers agreed to work with nonunion men. In fact, issues not related to union recognition were frequently settled with comparative ease: during 1906 the bricklayers, plasterers, and building laborers gained the Saturday half-holiday, and the bricklayers, steam fitters, and cement workers achieved wage advances.[41]

During 1906 organized labor was also preparing for another political venture. There were several contributory factors. According to a charter amendment effective January 1, 1906, all public construction work in Los Angeles was to be in charge of an appointed Board of Public Works instead of a City Council committee. In November, 1905, led by the Building Trades Council, organized labor appealed to the city authorities for representation on the new body. After several months of argument, the City Council and the mayor ignored unionists in making the appointments, convincing labor that only the election of its own administration could guarantee it a voice in the city government.[42]

Meanwhile, the organization of the Anti-Citizens' Alliance, and increasing interest in the concept of municipal ownership of public utilities, brought labor closer to direct political action. Heading a municipal ownership ticket in New York City in the fall of 1905, William Randolph Hearst received an encouragingly large vote. In October, the Los Angeles Central Labor Council recorded its agreement with organized labor elsewhere in favoring government ownership of utilities. In November, the *Times* outlined a possible political development in Los Angeles. Pointing to Schmitz' reëlection as mayor of San Francisco on the Union Labor Party ticket and to the large vote for Hearst in New York, the *Times* vented the dire prophecy that municipal ownership advocates would combine with organized labor to gain control of the Los Angeles city government and elect Schmitz as governor of California. Contrary to the *Times'* expectations, Schmitz, during his visit to Los Angeles in November, 1905, addressed himself to the evils of the Citizens' Alliance; his exhortation, plus the overt action of the Alliance in several strikes, temporarily diverted labor from politics to organization of the Anti-Citizens' Alliance.[43]

While the *Union Labor News* vigorously denied rumors of a labor political party in Los Angeles,[44] the idea had taken hold. In December, 1905, Machinists' Union No. 311, whose leading spirit was Lemuel Biddle, urged coöperation of all unions in forming a political party to enter the 1906 municipal elections. On the national level, the AFL in 1906 urged central bodies and local unions to oppose the election of legislators who had shown indifference or hostility to such labor demands as an adequate eight-hour law, relief from competition of convict

labor and immigrants, exemption from provisions of antitrust legislation, and relief from injunctions. More important, the orders from the
top sanctioned the nomination of straight labor candidates when both
parties ignored labor's demands. In Los Angeles, as plans for the
Anti-Citizens' Alliance progressed, various individuals expressed sentiments in accord with the latter portion of the AFL policy. James Roche
and Job Harriman, socialists, and union leaders like Biddle and Arthur
Vinette, urged labor to use the ballot box as the most potent weapon
against the Citizens' Alliance. Mayor Schmitz, speaking at the January,
1906, meeting which organized the Anti-Citizens' Alliance, advised Los
Angeles labor to be prepared for political action should it be necessary,
and specifically tied the decline of the San Francisco Citizens' Alliance
to the success of the Union Labor Party there. On the same occasion
Stanley B. Wilson, president of the Typographical Union, attributed
the strength of the local Citizens' Alliance to labor's avoidance of politics. Francis Drake, another printer, called the Anti-Citizens' Alliance
a "party," and the Typographical Union later refused financial aid to
the ACA on the grounds that it could hardly avoid having a political
tinge.[45]

It was soon obvious, indeed, that the Anti-Citizens' Alliance was
semipolitical in nature. Its guiding committee and officers included
such political action proponents as Stanley Wilson, Arthur Hay, James
Roche, Francis Drake, John Murray, and Lemuel Biddle, who was
elected president of the Central Labor Council in January, 1906. The
ACA, moreover, was intentionally structured like a political party, with
well-developed ward and precinct organizations. During the spring of
1906 it began to sound unions on their attitudes to political action.
Within a few months the Anti-Citizens' Alliance practically faded out
of the picture, just as a new labor party was commanding attention.
Early in 1906, when the Board of Public Works was appointed with no
labor representatives, the Central Labor Council expressed determination to choose public officials more sympathetic to unionism at the next
city election, and on February 21 union delegates and other interested
individuals organized the Public Ownership Party on the premise that
private ownership of public utilities was the cause of all political corruption.[46] The new party, which took over the solid political structure
of the Anti-Citizens' Alliance, expected, stated Hay, "to defeat the Otis
control of the Citizens' Alliance."[47] In July, the Central Labor Council
endorsed the movement, and the *Union Labor News* began its advocacy
of the Public Ownership Party.[48]

Late in September the party published its platform and ticket. In

addition to municipal ownership, the platform stressed direct legislation, free school books, increased educational facilities, and the eight-
hour day at fair wages on public works. Heading the Public Ownership
slate as the mayoralty candidate was Stanley Wilson, a gifted speaker
with a warm and friendly personality. His flair for the romantic and
dramatic imparted a flavor quite new in labor politics, and as his whirl-
wind campaign progressed through scores of speeches the opposition
found cause for serious apprehension. Charging that Wilson was merely
a front man for a Central Labor Council ring, including Arthur Hay,
Thomas Fennessy, and Lemuel Biddle, which would control the administration, the *Times* called upon all good citizens to spare Los
Angeles from the closed-shop fate of San Francisco. The assistance
given the local labor campaign by P. H. McCarthy, secretary of the
State Building Trades Council and a powerful figure in the northern
labor movement, provided Otis with further opportunity to denounce
the forces behind Wilson.[49]

By November the Public Ownership Party admittedly had an excellent chance of success. A split in the old parties promised division of
the antilabor vote among Republican, Democratic, and Non-Partisan
candidates. Moreover, the Public Ownership Party, apparently well
supplied with funds, carried out its campaign with a finesse and attention to detail that gained wide respect. It was small wonder that
opponents like the *Times* awaited the election on December 4 with
nervous worry. The results, however, proved their fears unnecessary.
The Democrat Arthur Harper was elected mayor by more than ten
thousand votes; both the Non-Partisan candidate, with over eight thousand votes, and the Republican, with about seven thousand, ran ahead
of Wilson, with just under four thousand. No Public Ownership candidate was elected to any office.[50]

Several developments of great future significance flowed from the
Los Angeles municipal campaign of 1906. The Non-Partisan movement,
beginning at that time as a protest against the local Southern Pacific
machine, was a forerunner of the Lincoln-Roosevelt League and the
progressive movement which ultimately elected Hiram Johnson governor of California and inaugurated a series of reforms, most of which
labor vigorously supported. Although losing the mayoralty, the Non-
Partisans were encouraged by their success in other contests to pursue
the program of cleansing the Republican Party of political corruption.[51]

The results of the election were disheartening for labor, whose political aspirations suffered a clear-cut reverse under what seemed the most
propitious of circumstances. Even its rationalization did not sound

very convincing: Public Ownership funds had been scanty in contrast to those of other parties; many unionists had gone to San Francisco, where the earthquake and fire created an unusual demand for labor; the Democratic platform had adopted some of the Public Ownership planks. The *Union Labor News,* more prophetically than it realized, warned Mayor-elect Harper to expect recall if he did not implement campaign promises. Moreover, the election created a certain coolness between the *Examiner* and organized labor. When the newspaper's manager, fearing serious loss of advertising patronage, disregarded Hearst's order to endorse the Public Ownership Party, the Building Trades Council condemned and boycotted the *Examiner.* The early cordiality between the paper and organized labor was never fully re-established.[52]

Also important to labor's future course was the attitude of the Socialist Party in the 1906 election. Officially, the Socialists derided the Public Ownership Party as a design to win municipal power for the clique which had assured its control of the labor movement through the reorganization of the Central Labor Council. The Socialist Party ran its own ticket in the municipal election to give workers with a true revolutionary spirit an opportunity to cast their votes for public control of *all* the means of production, not merely a few street railways and gas companies. Several unions, in fact, deserted the Public Ownership Party in favor of the Socialist Party; on the other hand, many Socialists admittedly supported Wilson's candidacy. Yet the Socialists and organized labor had not even begun to repair the schism following the Union Labor Party campaign of 1902, and they still had a far distance to travel before a real coalition in 1911 was possible.[53]

The Socialists found further evidence of a political ring in the Central Labor Council in an incident involving the Industrial Workers of the World. The IWW, organized at Chicago on June 27, 1905, was the ideological descendant of such groups as the Knights of Labor, the International Workingmen's Association, and the Trades and Labor Alliance of the Socialist Labor Party. It was a militantly radical organization dedicated to the industrial and political unification of workers of all classes, and as such, bitterly opposed the craft unionism of the AFL. Two Los Angeles locals of the IWW were in existence by the end of 1905, the first having been formed on July 12, only several weeks after national organization. Their program consisted of street meetings, until discontinued by the Police Commission in October, 1906, and of direct efforts to bring the unions into their camp. Labor organizations, however, with the approval of the Central Labor Council, denied the IWW access to their meetings.[54]

The episode which deepened the rift between Socialists and unions occurred in August, 1906, when organized labor throughout the country held meetings to protest the treatment of William D. Haywood, Charles H. Moyer, and George Pettibone, accused of complicity in the murder of Governor Frank Steunenberg of Idaho in December, 1905. Haywood and Moyer were officers of the Western Federation of Miners, affiliated with the IWW. At the Los Angeles protest meeting, held under Central Labor Council auspices, IWW speakers were refused the floor. To the Socialists, this patent demonstration of injustice stemmed from fear that labor's rank and file might be influenced in the direction of revolutionary sentiment and away from the unionists' Public Ownership ticket. Shortly thereafter, the Los Angeles County convention of the Socialist Party adopted resolutions commending the attitude of the IWW toward the socialist movement, thus laying the groundwork for future coöperation between the two groups in the defense of free speech.[55]

At the end of 1906 Los Angeles labor had little cause for self-congratulation. Major industrial disputes had not ended advantageously for unions; Los Angeles was becoming the home of hundreds of nonunion workers; the Citizens' Alliance and the Merchants' and Manufacturers' Association were more and more determined to help employers; the promising Anti-Citizens' Alliance had been transmuted into a political party, which had lost at the polls; the Socialist Party was openly criticizing organized labor, particularly its leaders; dissatisfaction over the concentration of power in the hands of the small group constituting the Central Labor Council was occasionally rising to the surface. In full cognizance of these alarming symptoms, the Central Labor Council asked all its unions to send five delegates each to a meeting on January 19, 1907, to discuss the welfare of organized labor. The two most important issues raised were structural revision of the central body to return the right of direct representation to individual unions, and improvement of labor's official organ, the *Union Labor News*. Decided divergence of views on the former question led to plans for a referendum vote of all unions, but in February the Central Labor Council tabled the proposal, thus postponing indefinitely its own reorganization.[56]

Discussions on the labor press were more immediately fruitful. At the start of 1907, H. J. L. Atwood of the laundry workers' union was president of the Union Labor News Publishing Company and editor and manager of the paper. After Atwood's withdrawal in January and his replacement as editor by the socialist John Murray, the new management agreed to sell enough shares to place 51 per cent of the stock in the hands of unions instead of individuals. Union ownership had actually been intended in 1904, when the Central Labor Council replaced the old Council of Labor, but had not fully materialized. The first issue of the Los Angeles *Citizen,* published as the successor to the *Union Labor News* by the unions of southern California, appeared on March 1, 1907. The weekly organ, with its change in name, was a paper of more general interest and popularity than its predecessor. The *Citizen,* enthusiastically greeted by the labor movement as an exponent not only of good unionism but also of good citizenship, has remained the official organ of the Los Angeles Central Labor Council.[57]

In the early months of 1907, while the labor movement was considering sweeping changes in structure and press, two of the city's smaller unions struck for higher wages. Upholsterers' Local No. 74 had won a wage raise from $3 to $3.50 a day in December, 1906, from all but two firms, the Pacific Purchasing Company and Stockwell & Haley. A strike beginning in January, 1907, brought the former to terms in February, but Stockwell & Haley yielded only after a six-month boycott.[58] A more extended dispute resulted from the request of Cigar Makers' Union No. 225, in March, 1907, for an increase of $1 per thousand cigars in their current average rates of $1 to $3 per thousand. The walkout of all employees on March 18 forced the four cigar factories to shut down pending employment of nonunion workers. By June two of the companies had yielded to the union; over a year later, in October, 1908, the third one settled on terms acceptable to the workers. The fourth firm, the Baer Cigar Manufacturing Company, with significant financial help from the M and M, consistently refused to negotiate with the union. The Central Labor Council kept Baer products on its unfair list, and in 1911 induced the California State Federation of Labor to proclaim a state-wide boycott. Finally, in 1912, the Baer Cigar Company was persuaded to unionize its factory.[59]

More than overbalancing the partial victories, particularly in the area of wages, won by some unions during these years was a crippling defeat sustained by the teamsters' union in 1907. As a blow against one of the most powerful local unions, it psychologically staggered the whole labor movement and added immeasurable strength to the open-shop drive. The teamsters' union, with approximately five hundred members in good standing in 1907, had enjoyed harmonious relations with employers ever since its organization in 1901. Contracts were signed annually and respected by both sides. The agreements with the six major trucking companies in the city, due to expire on April 30, 1907, provided for the union shop, a graduated wage scale from $2 to $3 a day, and a twelve-hour day with pay for overtime. The union wanted renewal of the old contracts with the exception of a 50-cent increase in daily wages. During negotiations in the spring of 1907, employers informed L. W. Butler, the union's business agent, that in order to raise wages they must first increase drayage rates. Butler thereupon persuaded two outside companies to join the Draymen's Association, which was then able on April 1 to raise its rates throughout the city. The union therefore had no reason to expect any trouble in signing agreements with members of the Draymen's Association.[60]

Meanwhile, however, the mercantile interests of Los Angeles had decided, in view of the experience of other cities, that union domination of the carrying trade was dangerous and must be halted. The Merchants' and Manufacturers' Association and the Jobbers' Association, backed by the shipping interests, persuaded the Draymen's Association not to renew its contracts with the teamsters' union. The trucking companies, assured of adequate financial support, posted notices at their barns on April 30 that they would no longer recognize the union but would advance wages by 25 cents a day. Butler was told in conference with the various employers' associations entering into the dispute that the wage difference was not impossible of adjustment but that the open shop was the real issue.[61]

The strike, beginning on May 1, 1907, involved almost all union teamsters. Butler and other union leaders restrained the strikers from acts of violence, and except for one or two incidents the walkout was peaceful. The M and M, which had raised one of the largest funds ever collected to fight a strike, hired deputy sheriffs to assist those provided by the police for the protection of strikebreakers. The union, confronting a united and wealthy opposition, had inadequate resources for a prolonged conflict. The suddenness of the attack had prevented previous amassing of a strike fund, and the union's recent withdrawal from its international deprived the Los Angeles teamsters of strike benefits. The best that Butler could do in conferences with employers was to extract promises of the 25-cent raise and of no discrimination against union members in employment policies. On this understanding, the union called off the strike on May 10.[62]

The strike, assessed thirty years later as one of the most important in Los Angeles history, all but wiped out the teamsters' union, for, according to Butler, the companies broke their pledge of no discrimination. With its membership down to thirty-five after the strike, the union slowly began to rebuild, but several years later had only sixty members. Its power was broken for many years to come, and the open shop had within the short space of ten days won a victory which clinched its hold over the city of Los Angeles.[63]

The defeat of the teamsters, combined with several other motivating forces in the summer of 1907, renewed the agitation for reorganization of the Central Labor Council. In June the Typographical Union adopted resolutions requesting the ITU, at its August convention, to act favorably on an appeal to the AFL for an assessment of its entire membership on behalf of the Los Angeles labor movement. Although focused on the *Times* fight, the printers' plan was rooted in their conviction that the gradual disruption of union after union by persistent and systematic opposition would ultimately crush organized labor in Los Angeles. This in turn would disastrously affect the national labor movement, for weapons used successfully in one community would be turned against unions elsewhere. Reorganization of the Central Labor Council would, it was argued, both influence the AFL to adopt the plan and increase the chances of its success. More direct pressure for reconstruction of the central body came from the Miscellaneous Trades Council, which in June demanded a referendum vote on the plan which had been shelved in February. The Central Labor Council at once submitted the proposals to its member unions; early in August, by a ratio of thirty to one, the unions voted in favor of direct representation in the central body by three delegates each.[64]

In September the new and enlarged Central Labor Council began to prepare for the influx of national organizers it was certain would follow the expected AFL assessment. As many unions took advantage of their restored right of direct representation, the Central Labor Council once again become a truly democratic expression of organized labor. In October the Council purchased the plant of the Union Labor News Publishing Company; as a result the *Citizen,* now edited by Stanley Wilson, was more closely associated with the authoritative labor body. By the end of 1907 the Los Angeles labor movement, hopeful of having achieved unity, stood ready to advance with the help of national labor.[65]

The request for national aid followed its anticipated course without interruption or contradiction. The resolution adopted by the local printers' union on June 30, 1907, emphasized the distressing trend of industrial relations in Los Angeles despite the expenditure of almost $50,000 by the International Typographical Union, and the correlation of the Los Angeles struggle with the fortunes of national labor. The printers asked for ITU sanction of their proposal that the AFL levy a national assessment of 1 cent per capita per month for one year, yielding about $15,000 a month; that the funds thus raised be expended in Los Angeles by an AFL representative directly responsible to Gompers; and that the AFL urge national and international unions to adopt similar resolutions. Arthur Hay, ITU representative in Los Angeles, argued so convincingly at the August convention that the national printers' union speedily endorsed the plan. Although the action of both local and national printers was predicated on the towering influence of the *Times,* it was apparent that favorable response by the AFL would broaden the limits of the local conflict and result in a general effort to make Los Angeles unionism a more effective force against all its opponents.[66]

The reaction of those opponents to the prospective AFL assessment was more violent than labor had anticipated. With a ringing challenge, "Come on, Hay! Come on, Sam Gompers and your Federation of Labor!" the *Times* denied the implication that its antilabor campaign had been financed by the National Association of Manufacturers and asserted that the ITU resolutions were "vain, idle, skyscraping, malicious, truculent, and without any adequate excuse."[67] More significant than the *Times'* loud denunciations of labor's new plan was the decision of the Merchants' and Manufacturers' Association to collect a "peace fund" for the preservation of industrial freedom in Los Angeles. On September 19, 1907, it issued a bulletin placing its goal at $100,000, requesting subscriptions from members and others interested in preventing the advent of the closed shop, and announcing the formation of a special committee of prominent merchants to dispense the money thus raised. In reply to this unprecedented massing of antiunion forces, the Central Labor Council sought to break the solid front of opposition, but it was patently unable to encroach on the M and M's domination of business interests. In order to ensure continued community support of its program, the M and M sponsored an address on the open shop by James A. Emery, secretary of the Citizens' Industrial Association of America, on November 1.[68]

Creation of the M and M's huge "war fund," as Los Angeles unionists called it, redoubled labor's efforts to persuade the AFL convention, meeting in November, to make the assessment a reality. For the first time in several years the Central Labor Council, though forced to borrow money for the purpose, sent a delegate to the national convention. Furthermore, it instructed its member unions to circularize sister locals throughout the country in behalf of the Los Angeles plan. The central body also prepared for distribution at the AFL convention a pamphlet entitled *Los Angeles—A Model Open Shop City,* which stressed the gravity of the local situation by relating the story of such defeats as the teamsters' strike. Hay, who had remained in the East after the ITU convention, persuaded prominent labor officials to endorse the assessment plan. These various efforts created widespread favorable sentiment and in November, 1907, the AFL, for the first time in its history, singled out one community for a thoroughgoing campaign in behalf of unionism. The national body, however, sharply curtailed the original plan by substituting one special levy of 1 cent per capita for the requested monthly assessment, thus reducing an anticipated $180,000 to some $15,000. In addition, it was specified that the fund was to be used not only in Los Angeles but in other places where similar conditions prevailed. The AFL also advised national unions to send one or more organizers to Los Angeles in accordance with demonstrated need.[69]

Coincident with preparation for the new era in Los Angeles unionism, three strikes, all related in one way or another to national labor, were begun. Los Angeles Local No. 48, Commercial Telegraphers' Union, initiated the first of these work stoppages. Early in 1907, Western Union and Postal Telegraph both had granted a 10 per cent wage increase throughout the country, following a revival of organization among their employees. There remained, however, a residuum of dissatisfaction because other grievances were not settled, the wage increase was not universally effected, and the companies were inimical to the union. The undercurrent of resentment among union telegraphers made possible a widespread and almost completely spontaneous walkout in August, 1907, following the discharge of a Western Union operator in Los Angeles. More than one hundred local telegraphers struck on August 7, and within a few days operators in Chicago, New York, and other large cities left their jobs. On August 13, the national union, unable to check the spreading fire, sanctioned the strike.[70]

The telegraphers in Los Angeles, encouraged by the general walkout, asked for a 15 per cent wage increase, an eight-hour day, and company-supplied typewriters. The Central Labor Council endorsed the strike and held a benefit to raise funds. The national union, taken unawares by the membership's precipitate action, had no treasury from which to pay strike benefits. In October, President Samuel Small of the national union recommended to all locals on strike that they return to work inasmuch as there were no funds, negotiations had proved abortive, and the companies intended to fight to a finish. Repudiation of his advice by locals all over the country led to Small's suspension and continuance of the strike under the direction of the national executive board. But from that time on, the union lacked effective leadership, and early in November the strike ended as the men went back to work as individuals on the companies' terms. It was a damaging defeat, caused by insufficient funds, a large supply of nonunion workers, lack of public sympathy for the strikers, poor leadership, and tactical blunders in conduct of the dispute.[71]

In July, 1907, as part of a national drive for a new wage scale, the Los Angeles branch of the Granite Cutters' and Polishers' Union presented demands to the Granite Manufacturers' and Dealers' Association of Southern California, organized about three months before. The union wanted to amend its contracts, due to expire on August 1, by increasing cutters' wages from $4.50 to $5.50 and polishers' wages from $3.50 to $4 a day, and by specifying weekly payment of wages in cash. Identical requests had been made throughout the state; in San Francisco the union compromised cutters' wages at $5 a day. The Los Angeles employers' association, accepting proffered help from the M and M, categorically refused consideration of the union's requests and declared for the open shop. The strike, involving some ninety men and about twelve firms, began on August 2. Only one firm had to close, the others operating with nonunion workers brought in from the outside. In March, 1908, however, the union signed up the more important firms in the city, compromising wages at $5 a day. The granite cutters' success was due in part to the strength of the national union, which paid strike benefits, and to the corresponding deficiency of skilled nonunion men. It was not until March, 1911, however, that the Los Angeles granite cutters were able to win over the remaining firms. At that time the union announced final settlement of the strike which had begun in 1907.[72]

The third Los Angeles dispute affected by national factors was a lockout of union tailors in September, 1907, climaxing several years of conflict between employers and the union. In March, 1904, the firm of George Taylor had locked out its union tailors and thereafter had run an open shop. A year later another employer followed suit.[73] These incidents, plus the growth of open-shop sentiment in the community, influenced about thirty leading employers to organize the Merchant Tailors' Protective Association and issue a "Magna Charta" in October, 1906. The document announced adherence to open-shop principles and complete independence from union domination. The union responded by a piecemeal campaign to wean tailoring shops away from the employers' organization, which enjoyed the hearty support of the Citizens' Alliance and the Merchants' and Manufacturers' Association. By the end of October, 1906, three firms had signed contracts with the union, one after a walkout lasting about a week. The agreements did not specify the closed shop, but guaranteed the union wage scale. In November the union struck against two more employers, one of them George Taylor. By this time the M and M, worried about the earlier defections from the Merchant Tailors' Protective Association, was ready with ample funds to finance the struggle. Nonunion tailors were imported from various parts of the United States, and the union was unable to supplement its promising victories of October.[74]

In 1907 the merchant tailors, who had been less purposive in their open-shop drive than the M and M wanted them to be, shifted to a more aggressive policy. Two of the firms yielding to the union in October, 1906, joined the Merchant Tailors' Protective Association in June, 1907. The two companies struck and boycotted in November, 1906, continued to resist union overtures. Finally, in September, 1907, the Merchant Tailors' Protective Association affiliated with the Citizens' Alliance and voted to lock out all employees who would not give up their union cards. With practically all firms in the city coöperating with the Association, more than one hundred union tailors lost their jobs. Some left town to find work, while others deserted the union. The M and M, employing detectives and special policemen to guard strike-breakers and prevent picketing, poured thousands of dollars into the fight to destroy the tailors' union.[75]

Nevertheless, the dispute ended in ultimate victory for the union. Before the end of 1907 three employers had signed with the union, one of them George Taylor, who was forthwith expelled from the Merchant Tailors' Association and branded a traitor by the *Times*. In April, 1908, another shop agreed to abide by union regulations, and in October all firms sponsoring the lockout of 1907 signed with the union. Almost certain defeat was turned into victory for a variety of reasons, chief among which was the $40,000 sent to Los Angeles by the Journeymen Tailors' Union of America. Furthermore, AFL representatives gave systematic help and encouragement to the local tailors' union, which was able to convert many imported nonunionists to its way of thinking. Employers, never too militant in their open-shop fight, found that union tailors did the most satisfactory work, and accordingly yielded to the union's vigorous campaign.[76]

In the main, however, the close of the period 1905–1907 found Los Angeles labor with little reason for rejoicing, for unionism had suffered a series of major blows which firmly entrenched the open shop. Gains were made, it is true, but for the most part they benefited workers in respect to hours and wages only. Toward the closed-shop objective Los Angeles unions made no progress. In the spring of 1907 the *Times* declared: "This city is unique in having driven to bay the snarling pack of union labor wolves that have infested many other cities of the land and have snapped their red-reeking jaws over the fallen form of industrial freedom."[77] As the *Times'* language was becoming more intemperate with the increasing implementation of its preachings, so its advice to employers was becoming bolder. In May, 1907, it went a step beyond the open-shop doctrine by saying, "The labor unions must be broken up."[78] The less partisan *Graphic,* at the close of the year, described Los Angeles as "the most complete free labor city in the country."[79] The *Times* thus had the great satisfaction of seeing the principles for which it had fought so hard ever since 1890 at last triumphant in Los Angeles.

A noteworthy aspect of this period was the increasing closeness between Los Angeles unions and national labor. The strikes of printers, commercial telegraphers, granite cutters, and tailors amply illustrated this. The most convincing recognition of the interdependence of labor organizations the country over was the AFL assessment at the end of 1907. National trends were felt locally also through the organization of the IWW in Los Angeles immediately after the parent body came into being, and by the disaffection between the Socialist Party and craft unions.[80] The mass offensive of employers in the country at large during the years 1903–1908, following organization of the Citizens' Industrial Association of America, was directed toward establishment of the open shop just as much as was the drive in Los Angeles. While unionism suffered a sharper reversal in Los Angeles than in many other communities, the concerted effort of employers' organizations checked the growth of national labor by strengthening the open shop.[81]

Although in retrospect the period 1905–1907 clearly reveals the ascendance of the open shop in Los Angeles, it was not without its paradoxes. Not all strikes were lost, not all boycotts unsuccessful. Victories were interspersed with defeats in a ratio sufficient to keep alive a hope that persistence might eventually yield rewards. The gains made without conflict added strength to such a conviction and prevented labor organizations from descent to the full darkness of despair. Their continuing power of revival became obvious in the two reorganizations of the central body, the Anti-Citizens' Alliance, and the Public Ownership Party. As the period ended, hope that current trends might be reversed was enormously enhanced by the flow of national funds and organizers into Los Angeles. Local labor had achieved its long-desired objective of convincing national labor that the future strength of unionism depended in part on the course of events in Los Angeles.

3. DARK DAYS FOR LABOR

During 1908–1909 the courage which had illumined previous critical periods all but fled from the hearts and minds of Los Angeles unionists. Although entering the closing years of the decade with hope renewed by the intervention of national labor and by a relatively unimpaired community status, the local labor movement soon encountered seemingly insuperable difficulties. The resultant internal disharmony ushered Los Angeles unionism into the darkest days it had yet known. Torn by dissension of sweeping proportions during most of the year 1909, the labor movement lost the loyalty of many members and much community esteem. By the end of the decade disaster and destruction appeared to be almost inevitable.

The background for decline lay in the Panic of 1907. Despite a shortness of money in the spring of the year, following a period of rampant speculation, the real financial stringency in the fall was successfully met through the declaration of bank holidays and the issuance of scrip. Los Angeles financial institutions, founded on solid business principles, never completely lost their stability during the period of uncertainty throughout the country. The essential soundness of the banks could not, however, prevent a business depression of fairly severe proportions in the first half of 1908. The climatic reputation of Los Angeles and continued advertisements for nonunion workers by mercantile organizations attracted many of the jobless from the East and raised local unemployment to an uncomfortably high level. Estimated figures in January and February, 1908, varied from 10,000 to 20,000.[82]

Various agencies instituted remedial measures to alleviate the widespread distress. Early in 1908, at the behest of organized labor and charitable bodies, the city and county authorities appropriated money for a public works program designed to relieve the most destitute of the sufferers. The charities themselves combined their resources to establish an employment bureau and free soup kitchens. The Southern Pacific and Santa Fe railroads voluntarily repatriated hundreds of Mexicans imported earlier for construction work. Labor unions not only cared for their own unemployed, but attacked one of the underlying causes by publishing in the East the truth about local conditions. By the summer of 1908 these activities, combined with general improvement throughout the country, had ameliorated the situation, and during the winter of 1908–1909 the degree of unemployment was adjudged normal for that season of the year.[83]

The depression inflicted considerable hardship on unions. In January, 1908, three of them were suspended from the Central Labor Council for nonpayment of dues. During the spring and summer, wage reductions were suffered by various groups of workers, including retail clerks, plumbers, steam fitters, carpenters, laundry workers, and longshoremen. In April, 1908, financial difficulties temporarily halted construction work on the Labor Temple. The year 1908 also witnessed a decline in the number of new unions organized; only two were formed, contrasted with six in 1907 and sixteen in 1906. (See table 6.) Estimates of total union membership are too inconclusive to determine a trend, though the *Citizen* claimed ten thousand members for affiliated unions in November, 1907, and twelve thousand in October, 1908.[84]

Circumstances were hardly propitious for demands for better working conditions or union recognition, since the oversupply of labor tended to further the ends of open-shop proponents while defeating the aims of unions. The AFL campaign to unionize Los Angeles thus began inauspiciously, though both national and local labor did their utmost to provide the necessary machinery. Arthur Hay, appointed as special representative in charge of an AFL branch in Los Angeles, began his work on December 1, 1907, and before the end of the year the Central Labor Council and four department councils had each named five delegates to an advisory board to assist him in judicious use of assessment funds. In January, 1908, the AFL sent a general organizer, W. E. Terry, to Los Angeles and kept him there most of the year; a month later Treasurer John B. Lennon of the AFL visited southern California to arouse local unionists. Gompers requested both Hay and Lennon to report to him personally on the Los Angeles situation. During 1908, at the instigation of the AFL, many national and international unions sent representatives who functioned as accredited delegates to the Central Labor Council during their sojourns. In addition to the advisory board responsible to Hay, the central body had its own organizing committee in the field.[85]

This galaxy of organizers faced not only depression conditions but the unrelaxed opposition of the Merchants' and Manufacturers' Association. Maintaining a solid front internally, the M and M went beyond its own membership to solicit help in the defense of industrial freedom. In March, 1908, it asked all property owners to contribute to its peace fund at the rate of $2 per front foot. According to Hay's report to the AFL early in the year, both the M and M and the Citizens' Alliance aggravated the already heavy local unemployment by advertising in eastern papers that workingmen would find good jobs at high wages in Los Angeles. This accusation was borne out in part by a director of the Chamber of Commerce, who, preferring to remain anonymous, advised mercantile organizations to cease their representations of southern California as a place of golden opportunity. Another facet of the M and M's contest with organized labor was pressure on banks and wholesalers to refuse credit and supplies to employers making concessions to unions. In appraising these evidences of opposition, Hay charged that the National Association of Manufacturers had chosen Los Angeles, geographically isolated and already far advanced toward realization of the open shop, for the first intensive campaign to crush unionism. Whether the antiunion drive was sponsored entirely by local agencies or partly by national groups, it was powerful enough to check labor's plan for unionization; even the combined might of the AFL and international unions could not prevail against the open shop in Los Angeles.[86]

The AFL branch office accomplished very little during its first year of operation. Plans for the campaign, drawn up in March, 1908, were centered on the device of holding open meetings to arouse and strengthen existing unions and gain new converts to the cause of organized labor. In order to generate a unity that would cut across the usual craft lines, the city was divided into thirty-four districts. At periodic district open meetings, members of different unions became acquainted with each other and with such nonunionists as could be persuaded to attend; speakers educated and stimulated their audiences with expositions of the aims and accomplishments of unionism; organizers called on outsiders to join unions and on merchants to handle only union label goods. In addition to these district conclaves, an occasional mass meeting brought the whole body of organized labor together, and many unions held their own open meetings addressed by able speakers.[87]

This largely inspirational program was continued through 1908 without alteration or expansion. It cost, mainly in salaries and personal expenses for Hay and Terry, approximately half of the more than $15,000 raised by the assessment. Hay claimed at the end of the year that the Los Angeles labor movement showed considerable improvement, particularly in the strength of unions. The AFL agreed that the results warranted continuance of the campaign, and at its 1908 convention renewed Hay's commission for another year. Nevertheless, the degree of improvement is open to some question. Certainly the labor movement had not reached a point where it could again take the offensive, and such data as are available do not indicate an overwhelming upsurge of unionism. And not all local unionists shared in the AFL's commendation of Hay. A rebellious spirit had first manifested itself among Los Angeles printers in 1904, when Hay was ITU representative, had become gradually stronger in intervening years, and finally broke forth with furious intensity in 1909. An animosity directed chiefly against Hay sharply divided the labor movement, and on these shoals of dissension the AFL campaign foundered, helpless to safeguard Los Angeles labor from external enemies or internal disruption.[88]

During 1907 and 1908, before completely sacrificing progress to internal quarrels, the Los Angeles labor movement displayed a continuing sense of community and social responsibility which threw into sharp relief its conviction that economic unionism was not in itself an all-embracing goal. The defense of Mexican liberals fighting the despotic regime of President Porfirio Diaz brought local labor squarely into a battle for justice and freedom for an oppressed people. Los Angeles, as the center of Mexican population in the United States, became the seat of the Mexican Liberal Party and its organ, *La Revolucion*. When three of the party's leaders, Antonio Villareal, Librado Rivera, and Ricardo Magon, were arrested and lodged in the Los Angeles city jail in August, 1907, allegedly at the request of Diaz, President Samuel Gompers of the AFL came to their aid. His repeated intercessions with the United States government helped prevent extradition of the three revolutionaries to Mexico, and his appeals to the labor movement launched a defense movement of national proportions. Labor's constant protests against the persecution of political refugees could not, however, save the defendants from punishment in United States courts. In May, 1909, they were convicted of violating neutrality laws by conspiring to send a revolutionary force into Mexico from the Territory of Arizona. After eighteen months' imprisonment, they were released in the fall of 1910, the year in which the Diaz regime was overthrown. Thereafter labor organizations and progressive political parties could work openly in Mexico.[89]

In Los Angeles, both organized labor and the Socialist Party rose valiantly to the defense of the Mexican revolutionaries. The labor movement not only gave of its slim financial resources and gravely needed time and energy, but provided one of the leaders of the national movement in the person of John Murray. Los Angeles socialists also raised money for defense of the Mexicans on trial, and organized a branch of the party for resident Mexicans, just as the Central Labor Council formed a Mexican federal union and secured an AFL charter for it. These common endeavors brought socialists and unionists into closer harmony than they had enjoyed for some years. Murray, who was a socialist as well as a labor leader, resigned as editor of the *Citizen* in October, 1907, devoting the rest of his life to the Mexican cause. In 1918 he assisted Gompers in organizing the Pan-American Federation of Labor.[90] After Murray's death a year later, a friend paid this fitting tribute to his life work: "The peons in the wastes of Mexico will mourn for John Murray. . . . The driven and the oppressed have lost a friend who understood as few have understood."[91]

During 1908, Los Angeles labor, without forming a party of its own, was unusually active on the political scene. Its opportunistic course first led it into collaboration with the Lincoln-Roosevelt League. Started by Edward A. Dickson of the Los Angeles *Express* and Chester H. Rowell of the Fresno *Republican* after the success of reform movements in both San Francisco and Los Angeles in 1906, the League perfected its organization in August, 1907. Its main objectives were emancipation of the California Republican Party from domination by the Southern Pacific Railroad; selection of delegates to the 1908 Republican national convention pledged to the nomination of Theodore Roosevelt; election of a free, honest, and capable legislature; direct primaries; and popular election of United States senators. Prominent Los Angeles members of the League, in addition to Dickson, were Dr. John R. Haynes and Meyer Lissner, both imbued with the spirit of reform. The first test of the Lincoln-Roosevelt League came in the Republican state convention in May, 1908. By that time Roosevelt had withdrawn and urged the nomination of William Howard Taft, a change to which the League subscribed. Although the League was in the minority in the convention, with the help of Thomas Fennessy and other labor representatives it elected one of its four candidates for delegate-at-large, defeating the regular Republican nominee, Harrison Gray Otis, by the narrow margin of one vote. This, with the election of several district delegates, brought the League acclaim as a promising instrument for future reform.[92]

Labor's maneuvering with the Lincoln-Roosevelt League for the defeat of Otis at the Republican state convention was soon revealed as a measure of expediency rather than a policy based on conviction. Although the Typographical Union had known as early as March, 1908, that the League's printed matter did not carry the Allied Printing Trades label, it was not until the summer that the Central Labor Council investigated. Upon discovery that the League contracted its printing indiscriminately to union and nonunion shops, the Council notified union members "to take heed and act accordingly at the primaries on August 11."[93] When only two League candidates were nominated in the primaries, labor credited itself with the defeat. In the 1908 presidential contest, the Central Labor Council followed the lead of the AFL in suggesting that the Democratic Party was friendlier to labor than the Republican Party. Fearing that Taft's election would ensure Otis the appointment as Secretary of War, California unionists campaigned vigorously through the medium of Anti-Otis Clubs. Their apprehension proved groundless, for President Taft did not name Otis to his cabinet.[94]

The civic responsibilities of organized labor were recognized once again in the summer of 1907, when the City Council asked the Central Labor Council, along with the Chamber of Commerce, the Merchants' and Manufacturers' Association, the Municipal League, the Voters' League, the Clearinghouse Association, and the Bar Association, to name representatives to an advisory committee which was to consider revision of the city charter. Representing labor were John Murray and Thomas Fennessy; among the other delegates were Dr. Haynes of the Voters' League, Meyer Lissner of the Municipal League, and John D. Works of the Chamber of Commerce, key figures in pushing certain reforms designed to break the hold of the Southern Pacific machine over both the local Republican and Democratic parties.[95]

In June, 1908, with a new charter drafted, the committee and its component organizations urged the City Council to call a special election for a Board of Freeholders, the only body legally empowered to frame the document for submission to the people. Viewing the Council's refusal to call the election as yet another evidence of machine control, nonpartisans and reformers, united in a Good Government League, determined to bring the most vital parts of the new charter before the electorate in the form of amendments. Using the initiative, they forced the City Council to call a special election for February, 1909. Two important amendments were submitted; they provided for election of city councilmen at large instead of by wards, and for the direct primary, with candidates listed in alphabetical order without party designation. Organized labor objected to the former on the ground that recall of a corrupt councilman would be virtually impossible if the whole city electorate were involved, but it favored the direct primary. The Good Government forces had done their work well, and both amendments passed by comfortable pluralities. Reformers regarded this victory as a preliminary to cleansing the city government of machine politics.[96]

Even before the election on charter amendments was held, the Good Government League had decided that the next step in the reform campaign should be the recall of Mayor Arthur Harper. Although Harper was a Democrat, he was allegedly tied to the Southern Pacific machine, and was reputedly sanctioning the protection of vice. Early in 1909, through the agency of its managing editor, Frank E. Wolfe, the *Herald* uncovered and published details of corruption and graft in Harper's administration that involved the mayor himself. The recall election, set for March 26, 1909, was the first attempt in the United States to remove a mayor from office. Harper announced his candidacy for reëlection, and the Good Government League nominated George Alexander, an elderly man heretofore unknown in municipal affairs.[97]

The Socialist Party of Los Angeles, believing that Alexander represented organizations hostile to the working classes, nominated Fred C. Wheeler, a prominent labor leader, for the mayoralty. The selection of a well-known union man reënforced a growing community of spirit between socialists and organized labor. Socialist speakers had occasionally addressed union meetings, and common defense of the Mexican revolutionaries had brought the two groups closer together. During 1908 the socialists had put on a remarkable fight in defense of free speech. Refused the same permission generously granted to religious groups, they deliberately violated a city ordinance forbidding street meetings without police permits. Socialist speakers, as well as those representing the IWW, so crowded the jail and clogged court calendars that the City Council repealed the objectionable ordinance in July. Although new restrictions limited the area where street meetings were permitted, they were applied fairly to all groups.[98]

The free speech fight at once gained the commendation of organized labor and weakened the bond between the Socialist Party and the IWW, since the latter had not participated as an organization. It was easier for the Central Labor Council, which had refused the IWW access to the Labor Temple in March, 1908, to approve a socialist movement at odds with the radical fringe. Another important development after the free speech fight was the readmission of Job Harriman to the Socialist Party; this termination of his disaffection prepared the way for the labor-socialist coalition of 1911. In addition to their desire for union support, the socialists had an excellent internal reason for entering a candidate in the recall election. Factionalism and financial hardship had gravely weakened the party by the end of 1908, and the campaign for Wheeler promised to reunite socialists behind a platform demanding the eight-hour day for all workers, union wages, and abolition of the contract system on public works; public work and free lodgings for the unemployed; an efficient municipal labor bureau; and collective ownership of public utilities.[99]

Shortly before the election in March, 1909, Mayor Harper resigned his office and withdrew as candidate for reëlection. Nevertheless, the Good Government League, backed by the opinion of the city attorney, insisted that the recall election must be held. At the last minute the machine made a desperate effort to prevent the election by applying for an injunction, but the court refused to grant the restraining order. Although Wheeler received votes from many unexpected sources, including friends of Harper and disgruntled machine supporters, he lost to Alexander, who was elected by a plurality of only seventeen hundred votes in a total of twenty-six thousand. Jubilant over this victory and the subsequent complete rout of the Southern Pacific machine in the regular municipal elections at the end of 1909, reformers were encouraged to continue their campaign to break the railroad's power throughout the state. After his election, Alexander promised fairness and justice to all groups: capitalists, merchants, manufacturers, workers, and property owners.[100]

The position of organized labor in the recall election was not clearly defined. The Central Labor Council rejected proposals for open discussion of the issues either in the *Citizen* or at public mass meetings because there was no likelihood of unanimity. Excluded from the councils of the Good Government organization, labor would not endorse Alexander, though some unionists approved the recall and hoped for better treatment from a reform administration. Others favored Harper (prior to his withdrawal) or Wheeler, though few were yet ready to commit labor to open support of the Socialist Party. Some of labor's doubts were resolved when Alexander, on the day he was sworn into office, named Ben C. Robinson of the Typographical Union to the Fire Commission. The Central Labor Council unanimously congratulated the mayor for this first appointment of a union man to any important municipal commission.[101]

The disunity preventing endorsement of either candidate in the recall election was but one expression of the factionalism which brought Los Angeles labor to the brink of disaster during 1909. The failure of the AFL assessment provided a focus for criticism and a whipping boy for the malcontents in the person of Arthur Hay. The opposition to Hay first split the Typographical Union into warring groups struggling for power and then, spreading through a wider area, involved the Central Labor Council and the Building Trades Council. The cleavage was so sharp that Stanley Wilson, though presumably neutral as editor of labor's official organ, found that he had to take sides. A prominent labor leader, Secretary L. W. Butler of the Central Labor Council, directly attributed the misfortunes of Los Angeles unionism to this lack of unity when he said, in 1909, that internal dissension had done more to disrupt unions than the enemies of organized labor or the Panic of 1907.[102]

The violent quarrels over Hay's alleged misconduct in the AFL campaign did not suddenly break out in 1909, but climaxed the conflict which began in the Typographical Union in 1904. Linking Thomas Fennessy and Francis Drake, prominent union officials, with the unpopular Hay, a dissident faction charged that the triumvirate spent huge sums of money with no visible result except creation of a powerful ring. Although the trouble quieted down during 1905, when the printers concentrated on preparations for their eight-hour campaign, it came to the surface again during the 1906 strike. In April Stanley Wilson, then president of the union, resigned from the strike committee in protest over Chairman Fennessy's methods. Wilson was persuaded to withdraw his resignation, but the incident revealed latent antagonism between the two men. Fennessy's power was increased by the election of members of his group to key union offices in May, 1906, when Wilson ended his term as president. Peace was again temporarily restored as the union unanimously backed Wilson's candidacy for mayor on the Public Ownership ticket in 1906. After the defeat at the polls, Francis Drake left Los Angeles, but Hay and Fennessy continued in undisturbed leadership of the Typographical Union.[103]

Distrust of Hay again became manifest when Los Angeles delegates to the 1907 ITU convention raised the question of his fitness for the position he held. Nevertheless, despite revelations of extensive local factionalism, the convention reappointed Hay as special ITU representative in Los Angeles. Several months later Hay's elevation to the post of AFL representative in charge of the assessment fund shifted the printers' animosity against him to Fennessy, whom the ITU named to take over Hay's old job. In March, 1908, the dissident faction requested the ITU to delegate the *Times* fight to the union's regularly elected officers. Although the union later rescinded the resolution, factional lines were clearly drawn at the annual election in May, 1908. A close race resulted in the election of W. E. McLernon, replacing Drake as the third leading member of the Hay-Fennessy clique, as president. But when his opponent, C. F. Howe, pledged support to the new officers, a cessation of fighting within the union seemed likely. Shortly thereafter, Fennessy's voluntary resignation as ITU representative and his replacement by the less unpopular McLernon increased the feeling that harmony could be restored.[104]

Meanwhile, the anti-Hay feeling outside the Typographical Union had been growing stronger, particularly among the building trades. Over the objection of the Building Trades Council, the Central Labor Council elected Hay as delegate to the 1908 AFL convention in preference to W. E. Terry, special AFL building trades organizer. The Building Trades Council thereupon withdrew from the Central Labor Council, removing one-fifth of the central body's total membership. The cleavage deepened in December, 1908, when the AFL Executive Council, overwhelmed with requests for organizers, sent Terry to San Francisco. Another very popular organizer, E. Rosendahl of the Brotherhood of Carpenters and Joiners, was ordered to Texas early in 1909. Stanley Wilson accused Hay of having engineered these transfers because Terry and Rosendahl, as incorruptible officials, presented too sharp a contrast to Hay's own alleged grafting tactics. Another source of conflict between the two bodies was the Central Labor Council's refusal to list as unfair the clothing firm of Hunter & Company, which had employed nonunion building mechanics for construction work. The department council also clashed with the central body over the parade of the Benevolent and Protective Order of Elks in the summer of 1909. At first all labor organizations had welcomed the opportunity to participate, but upon discovery that the Elks had used nonunion labor in their preparations for the parade, the Central Labor Council asked the building trades to respect its final decision not to march. The Building Trades Council replied firmly that its unions would keep their promises to the Elks.[105]

These unpleasant episodes heightened the distrust between the two councils. Another attack on Hay by Secretary R. A. Woodbury of Carpenters' Union No. 158 in June, 1909, in a letter to the AFL, revived the original provocation of disagreement over Hay and spurred national bodies to remedial measures. After a series of communications between the AFL and its Building Trades Department and their respective local branches, peace was restored to the Los Angeles councils. The building trades were mollified by the dispatch of AFL Organizer Oscar W. Frederickson to Los Angeles to fill the vacancy left by Terry's removal, and by the return of the carpenters' organizer, Rosendahl. In October, 1909, the Building Trades Council reaffiliated with the Central Labor Council.[106]

Settlement of one thorny aspect, however, did not end all dissension in the Los Angeles labor movement, for the dislike of Hay and Fennessy was as potent as ever. While top-level negotiations to reunite the Building Trades and Central Labor Councils were under way during the summer of 1909, trouble broke out afresh within the Typographical

Union. At the annual elections in May the anti-Hay-Fennessy faction gained control of the union, with C. F. Howe winning the presidency. The printers' first action was to request President James Lynch of the ITU to replace W. E. McLernon as district organizer with a representative respected and liked by the local union. Taking this move against McLernon as a signal, Stanley Wilson published in the *Citizen* during July a series of editorials attacking the powerful ring which had so long dominated the local Typographical Union. Wilson's most stinging rebukes were directed against Fennessy, who after resigning as ITU representative had obtained an AFL organizer's commission which gave him a seat in the Central Labor Council. Fennessy thus had a vantage point from which to continue his machinations for control of the local labor movement. Wilson was severely reprimanded by the Central Labor Council for using the *Citizen* to express personal animosities, but he continued to criticize those leaders he believed incapable of furthering the cause of unionism.[107]

In July, 1909, the Typographical Union, led by the anti-Hay-Fennessy faction, appealed to the AFL to abolish the office of special representative and, to bolster the request, prepared elaborate arguments on Hay's and Fennessy's alleged extravagance and mismanagement in dispensing the more than $100,000 sent to Los Angeles by the ITU since 1902. The Central Labor Council, disregarding the request of the local Typographical Union for endorsement of the appeal, reaffirmed its confidence in Hay. The ITU convention in August, 1909, made an exhaustive survey of the Los Angeles situation, calling on Hay, Fennessy, and McLernon, as well as on representatives of the opposition, to testify. Although recognizing the disaffection within the local union, the ITU by an overwhelming vote expressed satisfaction with past accomplishments and present activities. The convention, however, made one concession in stipulating that McLernon would be removed as organizer on June 1, 1910, if he had not by that time produced desired results or gained the confidence of the Los Angeles printers.[108]

Although lacking the support of both the ITU and the Central Labor Council, the local printers' union was determined not to stop short of completely discrediting the Hay-Fennessy ring. Backed by the *Citizen* and the Building Trades Council, which also requested Hay's removal, the printers asked the ITU to impeach President Lynch, requested Gompers to terminate Fennessy's commission as AFL organizer, and began to issue a monthly journal called *Publicity* to inform the ITU membership of the true conditions in Los Angeles. Lynch's visit to Los Angeles in October, 1909, caused the union to backtrack on its impeachment request, but had no other visible effect on the bitter factionalism. In November, a local delegate of the Brotherhood of Carpenters and Joiners petitioned the AFL convention to abolish the branch office in Los Angeles. Since assessment funds were all but exhausted, the AFL Executive Council did not renew Hay's commission as special representative, but did keep him on as organizer for California, a post in which he created far less friction in local labor circles. This was tantamount to discontinuance of the branch office.[109]

But Fennessy was still potentially troublesome, even though Gompers had revoked his AFL commission in October, 1909. The following month Fennessy became foreman of the *Examiner*'s composing room and immediately discharged several printers belonging to the opposing faction. The violent and recriminatory fight thus provoked climaxed the prolonged dissension and threatened to destroy the union. By its very extremes, however, the quarrel seemed to dismay even its protagonists, and returned them to a saner course during the winter of 1909–1910. The union discontinued publication of *Publicity,* endorsed Lynch for the presidency of the ITU, elected members of both factions to local offices falling vacant, worked with McLernon in organizing nonunion shops, and finally, in May, 1910, selected Ralph Criswell as president. Under Criswell's fair and just administration the union completed the restoration of harmony: it accepted an ITU decision absolving Fennessy of improper conduct as foreman of the *Examiner,* commended McLernon for his work as ITU organizer, and even gave Hay wholehearted praise for his past faithful services in July, 1910, when he resigned as AFL organizer and left the area. By October 1, 1910, when the bombing of the Los Angeles *Times* shocked the whole country, the local Typographical Union was once more ready to face its external problems with unity.[110]

Because of the failure of the AFL assessment and the ensuing internal dissension, the Los Angeles labor movement was financially and psychologically ill-equipped for resumption or continuance of its normal functions. Straitened circumstances prevented the Central Labor Council from sending delegates to the 1909 AFL and California State Federation of Labor conventions, and necessitated the borrowing of money to continue work on the Labor Temple. During the fall AFL organizer Oscar Frederickson reported that labor conditions in Los Angeles were below standard. Yet there were scattered signs of encouragement during the dark days of 1909. The depression following the Panic of 1907 had lifted, and many union men were at work. In the fall of 1909 a new union of ladies' tailors struck against two shops because they discriminated against union members. One of the firms yielded to the union, but the other was granted a court injunction against picketing. Some unions, notably those of garment workers, brewery trades, and steam engineers, which had maintained contractual relations with some employers throughout the decade, won wage increases upon renewal of their agreements in 1909. In July, Plumbers' Union No. 78 demanded a wage increase promised its members a year earlier when, because of hard times, they had accepted a cut from $5 to $4 a day. When employers refused to honor the previous agreement, all union plumbers struck. Within two weeks they arrived at a satisfactory arrangement specifying continuance of the $4 scale until November 1, 1909, when an advance of 50 cents a day would be granted, and restoration of the $5 scale on June 1, 1910.[111]

Much more than a few achievements by individual unions, however, was required to resuscitate a labor movement which had been on the defensive ever since 1905. During the long years of trial, hardship, and dissension, even such moves as reorganization of the central body had arisen from the need to strengthen labor's safeguards against the rapidly encroaching open shop. The AFL assessment, in the midst of hard times and unemployment, had failed to launch the hoped-for offensive against employers, and had finally boomeranged against unions by creating a deep schism within the labor movement. To repair the damage wrought by internecine quarrels, to rehabilitate unions as a prerequisite to simple survival, and to change from defensive to offensive were the great problems facing Los Angeles labor at the turn of the decade. Realizing that real revival must come from within, responsible labor leaders and groups in Los Angeles drew upon their own resources of fortitude and will power to keep alive the spirit of unity and organization which alone could save unionism. Beginning the process of reconstruction by slow degrees on the very threshold of disaster, they prepared the way for the imposing effort of San Francisco labor to unionize Los Angeles in 1910 and 1911. The agitation resulting from these several lines of development ushered in one of the most turbulent periods in the whole of local labor history.

XX. UPHEAVAL ON THE LABOR FRONT

Among all her [Los Angeles'] splendid material assets, none is so valuable ... as her possession of that priceless boon, industrial freedom. Her hold
upon that great asset has already proven of inestimable value, and is destined
to yield vastly greater and more substantial returns in the future. We have
not yet, it may be, entirely thrown off industrial thralldom—but we are
steadily approaching that magnificent goal for which brave and free men
everywhere should contend, until the entire country is free in this respect.[1]

IN THESE WORDS, written in January, 1910, Harrison Gray Otis expressed
his conviction that Los Angeles was the citadel of the open shop and the
cradle of industrial liberty in America. Few individuals were better
qualified than the editor of the *Times* to comment on this evolution,
for Otis had for almost thirty years been the apostle of antiunionism in
Los Angeles. Nevertheless, through all his violent denunciations of
labor and his flagrant journalistic distortions of industrial disputes,
Otis was enough of a realist to avoid the error of underestimating the
renascent strength of the labor movement whose development he had
observed from its infancy. A nagging doubt as to complete suppression
of the spirit of unionism thus tempered his paean of open-shop supremacy.

Otis' conscientious admission that organized labor was not yet ready
to bow before the unqualified domination of the Merchants' and Manufacturers' Association was well founded. Even before the disruptive
internal warfare of 1908 and 1909 had run its full course, Los Angeles
labor began within its own ranks a revival which, attracting enthusiastic
support from the outside, led it into a supreme contest with organized
capital in 1910 and 1911. The two major sources of the flow of revitalizing energy were the Central Labor Council and the Building Trades
Council, both of which launched independent constructive campaigns
several months prior to the building trades' reaffiliation with the central
body in October, 1909.

Beginning in the summer of 1909, the Central Labor Council seized
upon minor disputes in the moving picture theaters as a cause which
would simultaneously harmonize warring factions within the labor
movement, dispel community doubts about the unity of organized
labor, build up smaller unions, and establish union control in a new
and developing industry. Between May and September, following negotiations and short boycotts, the Central Labor Council settled disagreements over wages and contracts between three theaters and the unions
of stage employees, musicians, electricians, and motion picture operators.[2]

These disputes were preliminary to a prolonged and sharply contested fight with the Regal Theatre, a fight which more clearly demonstrated labor's intent to present a united front in behalf of less important unions. The trouble began in the summer of 1909 when the Regal's manager refused to discharge nonunion employees. At the behest of the Amusement Department Council, created by the unions of stage employees, musicians, motion picture operators, bill posters, and the Allied Printing Trades Council specifically for this dispute, the Central Labor Council placed the Regal Theatre on its unfair list in August. Because the Regal's patronage came mainly from the working classes, labor regarded this case as a critical test of its power. In October, 1909, after being advised by its attorney that boycotting must be confined to mild and peaceable publications and oral statements, the Central Labor Council authorized an active campaign against the Regal within the prescribed legal limits.[3]

During the winter of 1909–1910 the Amusement Department Council, aided by a Central Labor Council committee and donations from many local unions, kept up a lively and zestful boycott. Crowds of unionists blocked the sidewalk in front of the theater; special editions of the *Citizen,* distributed without charge, advised the public not to patronize the Regal; pickets were constantly on duty; boycotting signs were posted throughout the city; and unionists operated a free moving picture theater near the Regal. With scrupulous care pickets avoided violations of the law and were thus able to continue their activities unmolested. By February, 1910, however, the campaign had slowed down, since the Regal Theatre, backed by the Merchants' and Manufacturers' Association and the *Times,* was obviously determined not to yield. The boycott, though continued for several years, gradually became submerged in the great industrial upheavals which signified the full awakening of Los Angeles labor.[4] The dispute with the Regal Theatre had, however, been psychologically useful. By solidifying the labor movement in a common endeavor, it did much to heal the wounds of dissension. As Stanley Wilson commented, "It is a long time since Los Angeles saw such evidence of real life in the unions."[5]

The contribution of the Building Trades Council to the revival of Los Angeles unionism was functionally different from that of the Central Labor Council, chiefly because the building trades needed to concentrate first on their own rehabilitation. The Building Trades Council had had a checkered career in the years just previous to 1909. After several withdrawals from and reaffiliations with the State Building Trades Council, it had again dropped out in the spring of 1908 because of financial vicissitudes following the Panic of 1907. Reorganizing as the Los Angeles County Building Trades Council, it rejoined the state council toward the end of 1908 on an impetus from the new Building Trades Department of the AFL. This move, however, coincided with the separation from the Central Labor Council, and the prolonged dissension within the Los Angeles labor movement delayed for some months the reconstruction of the Building Trades Council. A number of unions had disaffiliated, membership lists were low, finances were still a problem, and spirit was lacking.[6]

The revival began in August, 1909, when the AFL sent organizer Oscar Frederickson to Los Angeles to concentrate on the building trades. Although Frederickson remained only two months, his contagious enthusiasm and organizing talents provided the necessary stimulus. The campaign he initiated was carried on by local leaders after his departure; many unions came back into the Building Trades Council, membership rolls increased, and, by the spring of 1910, the building trades had been lifted out of the doldrums. These determined local efforts aroused the interest of national building-trades unions, many of which sent representatives to Los Angeles to speed local rehabilitation. Before the end of 1909, organizers from the unions of carpenters, lathers, painters, and structural iron workers (affiliated with the building trades) had come to the city, and early in 1910 representatives of the sheet-metal workers and plumbers joined them. The carpenters' organizer was A. J. Mooney of San Francisco, who chose to remain in Los Angeles. He was elected business agent of the District Council of Carpenters in January, 1910, and secretary of the Building Trades Council in October of the same year.[7]

The organizing fever among the building trades, together with the Central Labor Council's boycott of the Regal Theatre, aroused widespread activity in behalf of the Los Angeles labor movement. National unions outside the building trades began to send organizers to the city; during the winter of 1909–1910 representatives of the bakers, teamsters, longshoremen, blacksmiths, iron molders, and machinists spent varying lengths of time in the Los Angeles area. The October, 1909, convention of the California State Federation of Labor, at which only one Los Angeles union was represented, voted to hold its 1910 session in the southern city, possibly to reassure local labor of renewed concern over its problems and to give an open-shop community an illustration of the orderly processes of a responsible labor body. Although an expected west coast tour by Gompers and the AFL Executive Council in the spring of 1910, with special emphasis on Los Angeles, did not materialize, the AFL sent Stuart Reid, a general organizer, to Los Angeles in June with orders to stay until the city was unionized. The coöperative nature of the effort to rebuild the local labor movement was well illustrated at an open meeting of the bartenders' union, when the roster of speakers included Arthur Hay of the AFL, W. A. Engle, president of the Central Labor Council, E. Rosendahl, organizer for the carpenters' union, and Stanley Wilson of the *Citizen*. With union after union enjoying the same flattering attention, it is not surprising that the response was quick and enthusiastic.[8]

In view of subsequent developments, the most significant feature of this almost spontaneous campaign to unionize Los Angeles was the participation of San Francisco labor organizations and leaders. J. B. Bowen, organizer for the International Union of Wood, Wire, and Metal Lathers, and first vice-president of the State Building Trades Council, made two trips to Los Angeles in the fall of 1909. In December, speaking to the Central Labor Council, he pledged the full assistance of the state council in the organizing of Los Angeles. Many of the national union representatives flocking to Los Angeles came directly from San Francisco. More than one hundred unionists from the Bay area attended the dedication of the Los Angeles Labor Temple on February 22, 1910. Among the speakers were P. H. McCarthy, Mayor of San Francisco and president of the State Building Trades Council; O. A. Tveitmoe, secretary of the State Building Trades Council; and Andrew Gallagher, secretary of the San Francisco Labor Council. At both the Temple ceremonies and a meeting of the local Building Trades Council a few days later, these powerful figures promised that the labor movements of California and San Francisco would aid Los Angeles unions to the fullest possible extent. That this was much more than idle talk was evident in May, when the State Building Trades Council sent organizer Anton Johannsen to Los Angeles for a thorough canvass of the local union situation as a preliminary to the launching of a more formal campaign to organize the city.[9]

The insistence of San Francisco labor that the long-delayed unionization of Los Angeles must be realized in 1910 was predicated largely on the situation of the metal trades in the northern city. The contracts between the San Francisco Metal Trades Council and the California Metal Trades Association, due to expire on June 1, 1910, specified the eight-hour day. Northern employers, however, who had long suffered from the competition of manufacturers in Los Angeles and other coastal cities where labor costs were lower and the working day longer, declared against renewal of these contracts unless San Francisco unions equalized wages and working conditions up and down the coast. Los Angeles was selected as the locale for commencement of the eight-hour campaign, and the San Francisco contracts were extended until August 1, 1910, to allow adequate time for the test. The ultimatum was a powerful incentive for a supreme effort to organize Los Angeles. This campaign was linked to the contemporaneous building-trades drive through the bridge and structural iron workers, who belonged to the Building Trades Council but would be affected by metal trades maneuvers. The national union of iron workers had sent its secretary, John J. McNamara, to Los Angeles in August, 1909, and in March, 1910, notified the local Building Trades Council that it would defray its share of the expense of any general organizing campaign.[10]

The agitation among the metal trades was to lead to the greatest local industrial upheaval of 1910, but before it reached maturity several other disturbances broke out on the labor front. Among union representatives coming to Los Angeles late in 1909 was E. J. Baker, president of the International Union of Leather Workers on Horse Goods. His purpose was to inject life into Local No. 72, a weak union with about forty members, in preparation for a national campaign to reduce working hours from ten to eight and increase wages by 15 per cent. The leather workers planned to strike on March 21, 1910, if their demands were refused. The two leading firms in Los Angeles were the Los Angeles Saddlery and Finding Company and Brydon Brothers Harness and Saddlery Company. The former, with 110 employees, was the larger and more militant of the two; it had been operating an open shop for the past decade. When, as a result of Baker's visit, its employees began to join the union, Los Angeles Saddlery forestalled the anticipated eight-hour strike; on February 19, 1910, it locked out those workers known to be union members. On March 19, just two days before the strike deadline, Brydon Brothers followed suit. Some nonunion workers at both plants walked out in support of the eight-hour demand, but the firms continued in operation by employing students from the Indian Industrial School.[11]

On March 21, when leather workers struck in many sections of the United States, local union members working at firms other than Los Angeles Saddlery and Brydon Brothers walked off their jobs. The strikers were supported by contributions from their national organization, various local unions, and the Central Labor Council. As the number of unemployed gradually increased through the conversion of more nonunion employees, several unions, notably those of bartenders and printers, guaranteed weekly strike benefits to the leather workers for limited periods. Nevertheless, the national union, opposed by the National Saddlery Manufacturers' Association, was compelled to compromise the disputed issues in June, 1910. It permitted its members to go back to work in those firms which agreed to a 10 per cent wage increase and a nine-hour day. Three shops in Los Angeles granted these terms and took back their union employees, but Los Angeles Saddlery and Brydon Brothers refused any concessions. Local No. 72, with continued assistance from other Los Angeles unions, settled down to a protracted fight against the two unfair firms.[12]

A small but not insignificant part of the campaign to unionize Los Angeles during 1910–1911 was the effort to organize unskilled workers, migratory labor, and minority groups. The impetus came from the California State Federation of Labor, which in 1909 called for the unionization of unskilled and migratory labor to offset the appeal of the IWW and prevent the use of such workers as strikebreakers. The first evidence of activity along these lines in Los Angeles was an informal organization of Mexican laborers employed by street railways, but their demand for an increase from $1 to $1.50 in daily wages in March, 1910, was not met. Early in 1911, the Central Labor Council, aided by organizer Juan Ramirez of the State Federation, formed United Laborers' Union No. 13097 for Mexicans, and Laborers' Protective Union No. 13149 for Russians, Slovenes, and other East Europeans. During 1911 both of these unions affiliated with the Central Labor Council and the State Federation. Ramirez also organized migratory and unskilled workers in Long Beach, San Pedro, and other southern California communities.[13]

Another aspect of organizing the unskilled was the formation in 1910 of unions of machinists' helpers, blacksmiths' helpers, molders' apprentices, and marble workers' helpers. In April, 1910, the last of these struck for higher wages, and the marble workers' union ordered a sympathetic walkout. The helpers, however, were not affiliated with the Building Trades Council, and when their strike threatened to have an adverse effect on other building crafts, the Council urged the marble workers to terminate the walkout and try to negotiate with employers for the helpers' increase.[14]

During 1911 Los Angeles labor made a special effort to reach colored workers, following a declaration of the 1910 AFL convention favoring the organization of Negroes. The Central Labor Council readily enlisted the help of the Afro-American League, which had strongly resented the treatment accorded Negroes by employers who hired them as strikebreakers during the teamsters' strike of 1907. In 1911 union representatives and the Afro-American League formed the Mutual Organization League, whose purposes were to bring Negroes into unions and to promote better understanding among all wage earners regardless of race, color, or creed. The Mutual Organization League was admitted to the Central Labor Council and had its headquarters at the Labor Temple. It was active through most of 1911.[15]

Labor's attitude to Orientals was in sharp contrast to its concern for the welfare of other minority groups. With Chinese immigration checked by federal legislation, organized labor turned to the problem of the Japanese, who came to the United States in increasing numbers after 1900. In 1905 San Francisco labor leaders organized the Asiatic Exclusion League to agitate against Japanese immigration. Some employers, particularly restaurant and laundry proprietors who suffered from Japanese competition, shared labor's sentiments for exclusion. With pressure from various sources mounting, the United States entered into the "Gentlemen's Agreement" with Japan in 1907. Under its terms skilled and unskilled Japanese laborers, except for those who had formerly been residents of the United States or were relatives of residents, were not granted passports by the Japanese government. Although the agreement temporarily decreased Japanese immigration, its operation did not completely satisfy west coast exclusionists, and organized labor felt the need to continue its agitation. The Los Angeles Central Labor Council took little part until early in 1910, when it sponsored the organization of a local branch of the Asiatic Exclusion League. Although meeting regularly, the League made no important contribution to the cause of Japanese exclusion.[16]

Amid all the bustle on the labor front during the winter of 1909–1910 the Merchants' and Manufacturers' Association had taken no overt antiunion steps, possibly because the activity had not as yet eventuated in a major strike. The two firms opposing the leather workers' union apparently needed no local assistance. But in May, 1910, when the various unions working in Los Angeles breweries began to renegotiate their contracts, the M and M jerked to attention. Here indeed was a splendid opportunity to win a telling victory, for brewery owners had never before been able to hold out for long against a boycott by organized labor. If they could be induced to break contractual relations with their employees, the unions would lose their best foothold in the city.[17]

The unions holding contracts with the breweries were the brewery workers, bottlers, and beer drivers, all affiliated with the International Brewery Workers' Union; the steam engineers, stationary firemen, coopers, and machinists. Through a series of minor boycotts over the years, these unions had won closed-shop agreements with the following breweries and brewery agencies: Maier & Zobelein, Los Angeles Brewing Company, and Mathie Brewing Company in Los Angeles; the Union Brewery of Anaheim; and the Los Angeles agencies of Anheuser-Busch, Rainier, and Wieland. These firms comprised the entire brewing industry in the area. With the exception of Anheuser-Busch, all were members of the Southern California Brewers' Association, affiliated with the California State Brewers' Association.[18]

The contracts between the seven unions and the companies were due to expire on May 15, 1910. The new agreements, presented to employers on April 30, differed from the old chiefly in respect to the wages of bottlers and drivers, the lowest paid brewery employees on the west coast. The drivers demanded an increase of $3 a week, the bottlers $2 a week. Anheuser-Busch signed the new contracts at once, but when it became apparent that the other employers were disinclined to grant the wage increases without discussions, each union named three delegates to a contract committee to meet with a representative of the Southern California Brewers' Association.[19]

Conversations between the chairman of the contract committee and the secretary of the Brewers' Association on May 10 and 11 resulted in the division of the committee into two sections; one represented the engineers, firemen, and machinists, the other the brewery workers, bottlers, drivers, and coopers. A conference between the former and the representative of the employers on the morning of May 12 brought agreement on the contracts in the mechanical departments. But, on the afternoon of the same day, the Brewers' Association refused to increase the wages of bottlers and drivers and rejected the brewery workers' appeal that they be allowed to talk directly to the brewery owners. On May 14 the full contract committee met with the secretary of the Association, and agreed on minor points in the contracts, but could win no concessions on the wage issue. At this point in the negotiations the secretary requested that the unions take no drastic action until a representative of the International Brewery Workers' Union could be brought to Los Angeles.[20]

Members of all unions remained at work until May 19, four days beyond expiration of the contracts. On that day Joseph Proebstle of the international union arrived in Los Angeles and, with the contract committee, immediately conferred with the secretary of the Brewers' Association. He was told that no wage increases would be granted and that union representatives would not be allowed to discuss the contracts with the brewery owners. All seven unions immediately called out their members working at Maier & Zobelein, the Los Angeles Brewing Company, the Mathie Brewing Company, and the Union Brewery of Anaheim. In consideration for their employers, they temporarily kept skeleton crews at work to safeguard plant operations until the companies could find other workers. The Rainier and Wieland agencies, not included in the strike order, locked out their employees. The brewery owners, in a last-minute effort to settle the dispute, summoned the unions' contract committee to a conference on the afternoon of May 19. When the unions countered the owners' proposal for arbitration with a suggestion that the whole question be submitted to the State Brewers' Association, the conference broke up. This first major brewery strike in Los Angeles involved a total of 315 employees of four breweries and two agencies.[21]

No time was wasted by either side in establishing the lines of the dispute. On May 20, Secretary Felix Zeehandelaar pledged the active support of the Merchants' and Manufacturers' Association to the Southern California Brewers' Association. Brewery owners, also assured of assistance from their state and national organizations and from local associations of hotel and restaurant proprietors, posted a notice that former employees willing to work under open-shop conditions might return to their jobs. Also on the 20th, the Central Labor Council laid a boycott on all beer made in Los Angeles until the companies and agencies would come to terms with the unions. Picketing was begun immediately, but was conducted so peacefully that only rarely were there complaints of violence. The strikers received benefits from their national unions. As the boycott continued, the *Times* claimed that the breweries were slowly winning the fight through desertions of union members and employment of nonunion workers, while the *Citizen* insisted that sales of local beer were drastically reduced. There was to be no break in the deadlock, however, until almost a year had passed.[22]

The strike of the brewery workers, employed in the only Los Angeles industry which had been completely unionized, must have forewarned the metal trades to expect trouble when their current organizing campaign reached the point for action. For years the local metal-trades unions had been kept in subjection by the Founders' and Employers' Association and the Merchants' and Manufacturers' Association. Wages were low, the working day was ten hours, and, with union membership a sufficient cause for discharge of employees, labor organizations were helpless to improve conditions. Workers could get jobs through an employment agency conducted by Secretary William B. Hoswell of the Founders' and Employers' Association, but only by renouncing and abstaining from union membership. With the aid of the strongly anti-union National Erectors' Association, the Founders' and Employers' Association hired detectives to ferret out employees who showed pro-union leanings. Foundries, machine shops, and other plants employing metal trades workers were able by such means to maintain absolute control of their industries.[23]

Partly to improve the lot of these workers, partly to safeguard their own closed-shop benefits, the San Francisco metal trades had been trying for several months to meet the terms of their employers' ultimatum through an intensive unionizing campaign in Los Angeles. Picked organizers, representing ten metal-trades unions in the northern city, had been ordered to go to Los Angeles and stay until they accomplished the desired objective. Among them were John Nolan, member of the executive board of the International Molders' Union; William Hannon, sixth vice-president of the International Association of Machinists; Godfrey Dawson, organizer for the Pattern Makers' League of North America; William Murphy, vice-president of the International Union of Boilermakers, Iron Shipbuilders, and Helpers; W. Flannigan, vice-president of the International Brotherhood of Blacksmiths; J. E. Timmons, organizer for the Bridge and Structural Iron Workers; and George Gunrey, organizer for the International Molders' Union.[24]

After a thorough preparation, during which many employees had joined the unions, these representatives believed that the local metal trades were ready to make their demands. On May 18, 1910, Gunrey, Dawson, and E. H. Misner, organizer for the machinists and an official of the Los Angeles Metal Trades Council, wrote to employers proposing that they enter into a working agreement with the unions of machinists, molders, patternmakers, boilermakers, brass workers, and sheet-metal workers. The contract, to be effective until May 1, 1911, would establish a minimum wage of $4 for the eight-hour day, time and a half for overtime, and double time for holidays. The unions suggested a joint conference with employers to discuss details, and requested a reply by no later than June 1. The Founders' and Employers' Association, meeting within a few days, told the metal-trades unions that their letter had been thrown into the waste basket.[25]

Several days before the deadline of June 1, Wilson & Willard Manufacturing Company and Western Gas Engine Company locked out their union employees. On the 1st, the walkout ordered by the metal-trades unions began, and by the 10th, some fifteen hundred workers had left their jobs. In addition to the six crafts mentioned above, the strike involved blacksmiths and structural iron workers. The most important

of the twenty-five firms affected were Baker Iron Works, Llewellyn
Iron Works, Western Pipe and Steel Company, Union Tool Company,
Fulton Engine Works, Lacy Manufacturing Company, Keystone Iron
Works, Los Angeles Manufacturing Company, and Pacific Ornamental
Iron Works, all in Los Angeles, and the Craig shipbuilding plant at
Long Beach. Many of the strikers in all these plants were nonunion
workers who subsequently joined the metal-trades unions.[26]

The metal trades strike, as the greatest industrial disturbance Los
Angeles had thus far experienced, stimulated unusual defense measures
by employers. Members of the Founders' and Employers' Association
agreed to stand by previous open-shop declarations and induced outside firms to join the group for mutual protection and aid. The Merchants' and Manufacturers' Association promised unstinting aid to
metal trades employers, urging them to shun any compromise with
labor unions and asking landlords to make rental concessions to proprietors of small shops crippled by the walkout. Toward the end of
June the M and M began collecting funds for the protection of local
industries from union domination; not only manufacturers, but bankers, retailers, and professional men responded generously.[27] Job Harriman, speaking to the 1910 AFL convention, claimed that Henry
Huntington alone contributed $100,000 of the $350,000 raised by the
M and M to defeat the eight-hour strike of the Los Angeles metal
trades.[28]

The financing of the Los Angeles strike was undertaken by labor
organizations of the state and of the Bay area under the leadership of
San Francisco unions. Early in June, 1910, the State Federation of
Labor, the State Building Trades Council, the San Francisco Labor
Council, the San Francisco Building Trades Council, the Alameda
County Central Labor Council, and the Alameda County Building
Trades Council organized a General Campaign Strike Committee, composed of five delegates from each of the six bodies. The committee was
to supervise the collection and disbursement of funds for the Los Angeles strikers, to continue the campaign for unionizing Los Angeles, and
to assist in directing the strike. Each of the participating groups levied
a weekly assessment of 25 cents per capita on its entire membership.
The committee selected O. A. Tveitmoe as chairman and Andrew Gallagher as secretary-treasurer. George Gunrey, with the title of assistant
secretary-treasurer, was the committee's representative in Los Angeles.
Gunrey was a capable official who laid down strict rules for the management of the strike. The authenticity of all applicants for strike benefits
of $7 a week was first determined, and those deemed eligible were re-

quired to register for picket duty. Gunrey's complex tasks, including the distribution of some $8,000 or $9,000 a week during the early months of the strike, required precisely the businesslike attention to detail which he exhibited.[29]

The General Campaign Strike Committee, holding weekly meetings in San Francisco, got into operation very quickly. Within a few weeks it had sent $22,000 to Los Angeles. Its officers, Tveitmoe and Gallagher, visited Los Angeles early in July to assure the strikers that San Francisco labor would give them complete moral and financial support. The organizers who had helped prepare the ground for the metal trades offensive remained in Los Angeles to assist in the campaign and continue the work of organizing. On his return to San Francisco Tveitmoe reported that there was an excellent spirit among the rank and file, and that Los Angeles labor showed unfaltering enthusiasm and determination. Strikers were regularly picketing the struck shops, and many nonunion workers were being brought into the unions.[30] As Tveitmoe said, "Not even the most sanguine organizer would have dared to dream a year ago that such a state of affairs could come to pass in Los Angeles."[31]

Employers, too, were impressed by the earnestness of organized labor's campaign to unionize Los Angeles. Deeming their position unusually critical, they used the M and M fund to find nonunion workers; to tide the smaller firms over the first difficult period; and to employ detectives to spy on the activities of strike leaders, assist the regular police force in preserving the peace, and prevent disturbances on the picket lines. Employers found the city authorities coöperative. On June 17, Mayor George Alexander issued a proclamation to the citizens of Los Angeles that the police would take action against pickets who unlawfully obstructed the streets, and a week later the chief of police enforced the dictum by ordering the immediate arrest of violators of the ordinance which forbade pickets to annoy or molest passers-by or to loiter in the streets. These measures did not completely satisfy the metal trades employers. By the end of June, ten of the struck firms had obtained injunctions restraining members of the Metal Trades Council and its affiliated unions from assembling in the vicinity of the shops, from picketing, from intimidating or using force or violence against present or prospective employees, and from following such employees to or from their homes. Among the companies obtaining the injunctions were Baker Iron Works, Llewellyn Iron Works, and other prominent firms.[32]

Although the pickets, kept in firm check by Gunrey and other strike officials, displayed no tendency to resort to violence or step beyond legal limitations on boycotting, the employers sought still more protection from the city authorities. Late in June two prominent lawyers, Earl Rogers for the Merchants' and Manufacturers' Association and Wheaton A. Gray for the Founders' and Employers' Association, prepared an antipicketing ordinance which the city attorney brought before the City Council on July 1. When C. F. Grow, local business agent for the machinists and a prominent strike official, and W. A. Engle, president of the Central Labor Council, protested that the proposed legislation was more drastic than any court injunction, the City Council and its legislative committee asked both sides in the dispute to present their points of view. Attorneys Rogers and Gray, iron manufacturers Fred L. Baker and John Llewellyn, and L. W. Jutton of the Chamber of Commerce spoke in favor of the ordinance, arguing that picketing was dangerous and anarchistic and that labor unions should not be allowed to carry their warfare into the streets. Speaking for labor, lawyers Job Harriman and Fred Spring and union delegates from the metal trades and the brewery workers (who were still on strike) defended their position in the name of liberty and freedom of speech. On July 16, 1910, the City Council unanimously passed the ordinance without discussion, and one hour later Mayor Alexander signed it. The new legislation became effective on July 18 under an emergency clause claiming need for "immediate preservation of the public peace, health and safety."[33]

The antipicketing ordinance was sufficiently restrictive to satisfy the most militantly antiunion employer. It forbade picketing, loitering, and displaying of signs or banners in the vicinity of any business establishment for the purpose of coercing or intimidating any present or prospective employee or customer; it prohibited loud or unusual noises or verbal proclamations in the streets of Los Angeles; and it provided as penalty for violation a fine of not more than $100, or imprisonment of not more than fifty days, or both. On July 29 the Long Beach City Council unanimously passed a similar ordinance, after hearing Earl Rogers and Job Harriman argue its merits and demerits.[34]

Labor's reaction to the Los Angeles antipicketing ordinance, which it denounced as "class legislation," was particularly violent. A supposedly progressive City Council, elected by the Good Government League, had passed the law without a dissenting voice; this patent subservience to employers by a self-styled reform administration only intensified the bitterness.[35] Job Harriman, addressing the 1910 AFL convention, said: "These were Good Government Fathers, with old

Father Alexander at the head. He dresses to look like Uncle Sam, combs his hair and trims his whiskers to look like the popular whiskers of Uncle Sam."[36] Ben Robinson of the Typographical Union, whom Mayor Alexander had appointed to the Fire Commission upon his election in March, 1909, resigned his post in protest against the ordinance.[37] Andrew Gallagher reported that unionists at first regarded the ordinance as a death blow, but, quickly rallying, evidenced their loyalty to constitutional principles by continuing to picket even when they knew it meant going to jail.[38]

The first violators of the ordinance, E. P. Kraemer and Carl Schnitzer of the brewery workers, were arrested on July 19. Attorney Fred Spring, representing the defendants, demanded jury trials which were held early in August. Both men were convicted and sentenced to a $50 fine or fifty days in jail. By the time of the Kraemer and Schnitzer trials, a total of fifty-seven pickets had been arrested; among them were two important strike leaders, C. F. Grow of the machinists and V. J. O'Leary of the boilermakers. According to the *Times,* the unions deliberately planned wholesale arrests so as to arouse public sympathy for their cause. After the first two convictions, arrests proceeded at a rapid rate. With each defendant demanding a jury trial, the court calendars were filled up until early in 1911. By September, 1910, of nine antipicketing cases tried, four had brought convictions and five had been set for retrial because of jury disagreements.[39] The *Times* expressed high approval of the police and judiciary; describing an attempt of unionists to visit their colleagues in jail, the newspaper remarked that the police went after them "stick in hand" and soon "had the ruffians on the run."[40] The courts had proven a bulwark of industrial peace, said the *Times:* "May the citizens of Los Angeles county never place upon the bench in the Superior Courts any judge less worthy of honor and confidence than those who during this last summer have so effectively guarded the interests of the people."[41]

The antipicketing ordinance not only aroused the strikers to defiance of the law, but stimulated more intensive efforts by outside labor organizations. The General Campaign Strike Committee sent four attorneys from San Francisco to help defend arrested pickets, added the leather workers (still on strike) to the benefit lists, organized pickets in squads of ten under captains, insisted that strikers do picket duty on pain of losing their benefits, sent Tveitmoe and other labor leaders to Los Angeles to encourage the strikers, appealed to national unions for contributions to the strike fund, established a Labor Temple Grocery Store stocked with provisions sent from San Francisco for sale to strikers at cost, and urged local unions not involved in industrial disturbances to assess their memberships for the strike fund. The San Francisco Labor Council ordered member unions delinquent in the assessment to pay up or withdraw, and sent an appeal for funds for Los Angeles to labor organizations all over the country. The Executive Council of the California State Federation of Labor ordered a special organizer to the southern part of the state, and international unions continued to send in their representatives. During August, 1910, organizers from the cement workers, coopers, steam engineers, and brewery workers spent some time in Los Angeles. The local labor movement responded enthusiastically to the intensified campaign in its behalf. Unions unconnected with the strikes increased their organizing activities; the District Council of Carpenters, for example, had six business agents in the field in September. At the end of September the *Citizen* claimed that never had there been such militance and vitality in Los Angeles unions.[42]

The renewed spirt of opposition led to three small strikes in the summer and early fall of 1910. In July the laundry workers struck when the Sanitary Laundry broke its agreement with the union and declared for the open shop. A month later the electricians employed by the Los Angeles Pacific Railway Company walked out when refused a wage increase. In September the Building Trades Council authorized a strike against the New Method Laundry, which had employed non-union workers to construct a new building. All these efforts were unsuccessful.[43]

By the end of September, 1910, the General Campaign Strike Committee had expended, in strike benefits, lawyers' fees, bail and fines for pickets, and organizing and operational costs, slightly more than $80,000. The bulk of this came from the assessment levied by the committee's member bodies, but unions outside of California had contributed about $2,500, and Los Angeles organizations accounted for $1,500 of the total. The wide variance between the sum spent in four months in 1910 and the total realized from the AFL assessment of 1907 (which amounted to only some $15,000 instead of the requested $180,000) was reflected in actual results. Between January and September, 1910, the Central Labor Council had grown from sixty-two unions with six thousand members to eighty-five unions with approximately ninety-five hundred members. Seventeen unions not affiliated with the central body, with a total of twenty-five hundred members, brought the combined strength of organized labor in Los Angeles to about twelve thousand. Both the General Campaign Strike Committee and local bodies felt that such strides more than justified the effort to organize Los Angeles.[44]

The events on the industrial scene stimulated concurrent political developments of great future significance to organized labor and the Socialist Party in Los Angeles. The rapprochement between these two groups, beginning in 1907 with the common defense of the Mexican revolutionaries and growing slowly stronger, became in 1911 a genuine coalition much like that of 1902, when the Socialist Party had endorsed the union labor ticket in the municipal elections.

Since its organization of the Public Ownership Party in 1906, Los Angeles labor had done relatively little in the political field. The AFL assessment and the ensuing decline of the labor movement precluded anything more than a superficial interest in politics. In the fall of 1909, however, just as the union revival was starting, the Central Labor Council sponsored the organization of a Union Labor Political Club, composed of delegates from all interested unions. Since labor was always chary of the Good Government League, the Political Club endorsed the regular Republican ticket in the 1909 municipal elections.[45]

The metal trades strike on June 1, 1910, the injunctions issued against picketing, and the willingness of the police to protect employers and their strikebreakers, reawakened labor's interest in politics. On June 26, a mass meeting of more than one thousand unionists reorganized the 1909 Union Labor Political Club. The revived movement, endorsed by San Francisco labor leaders and by Stuart Reid, AFL organizer, was modeled after the San Francisco Union Labor Party. Local leaders included prominent socialists and union men; among them were Job Harriman, Fred Spring, W. A. Engle, Fred Wheeler, L. W. Butler, Charles Feider of the barbers' union, W. A. Vanna of the laundry workers' union, and Frank Sesma of the bartenders' union.[46]

Passage of the antipicketing ordinance on July 16 completed labor's repudiation of the Good Government administration and stimulated further development of labor's political movement. On July 31, 1910, the Union Labor Political Club adopted a platform specifically attacking the M and M, the Good Government League, and the Democratic and Republican parties as a combination of capitalistic bodies bent on the destruction of unionism. The platform called for municipal ownership of public utilities, public works for the unemployed, municipal housing, enforcement of child labor laws, compulsory education and free school books, extension and perfection of direct legislation measures, a workmen's compensation law, statutory recognition of the right to strike and boycott, legal prohibition of the injunction in labor disputes, popular election of judges and United States senators, and nationalization of communication systems and railroads. The Union Labor Political Club did not enter a ticket of its own in the 1910 elections. Instead, it endorsed the state and county tickets of the Socialist Party, and split its favors for municipal officers among Socialists, Republicans, and Democrats, on the basis of individual merit.[47]

Meanwhile, the Socialist Party, with a sprinkling of union men among its membership, had clearly shown its sympathy for labor in the current industrial upheavals. Shortly after the metal trades walkout, Los Angeles socialists pledged moral and financial support to the strikers and boycotted all products made by "scab" labor. On July 1, 1910, the Socialist Party moved its headquarters into the Labor Temple, a patent sign that the bond between the two groups was strengthening. After enactment of the antipicketing ordinance, not only the local but the state Socialist Party condemned the Lincoln-Roosevelt League and the Good Government League, as well as the M and M. The county and state tickets of the Socialist Party included union members like Fred Wheeler and C. F. Grow. It was obvious that the socialists were actively propagandizing for the votes of union labor, and that unionists were beginning to recognize the value of socialist support in their industrial troubles. The *Citizen,* for example, urged its subscribers to read the truth about labor disputes in the *People's Paper,* which had replaced *Common Sense* as the local socialist organ. In the three months after its move into the Labor Temple, the Los Angeles Socialist Party claimed a membership increase of almost one thousand as a direct result of the industrial struggle going on in the city.[48]

By the end of September, 1910, Los Angeles labor felt that it had made real advances. Within the past year it had banished internal dissension and had supplied from its own spiritual strength the original impetus for an organizing drive that far transcended any previous effort to unionize Los Angeles. The Central Labor Council had increased its membership by more than 50 per cent. National unions and California labor organizations were more than adequately compensating for their earlier neglect of Los Angeles problems. Through all the vicissitudes of police interference, court injunctions, and the antipicketing ordinance, organized labor steadfastly refused to countenance defeatism. Instead, it seemed to flourish in adversity. There were few desertions from the ranks of strikers, whether they were leather, brewery, or metal workers. Moreover, the unions had formed a political organization which attracted widespread support, and they were progressing toward a firm alliance with the Socialist Party. In all its aspects the Los Angeles labor movement showed boundless energy and great faith in the future.

Then, at an early morning hour of October 1, 1910, the *Times* building was destroyed by an explosion and resultant fire. Twenty employees lost their lives in the conflagration. The *Times* labeled the disaster the "crime of the century," and Otis at once laid the blame at the door of organized labor, charging that the unions had at last resorted to the use of dynamite in retaliation for his work in the cause of industrial freedom. Local labor as quickly denied any knowledge of or responsibility for the catastrophe, and refuted the statement that organized labor in the country at large employed or even condoned violence in its struggle with employers. The immediate offer of the Los Angeles Typographical Union, which ever since 1890 had borne the brunt of the *Times* fight, to supply Otis with printers so that he could continue publication without a break, exemplifies the attitude of local labor. Because the *Times* bombing—and a grand jury declared that it was in fact a bombing—presents one of the most dramatic and involved stories in the history of American unionism, the detailed account will be reserved for chapter xxi of this volume. It will be sufficient for the purposes of this chapter to mention only those developments in the *Times* case which currently affected the course of the labor movement.

The brewery workers immediately felt the impact of the *Times* disaster. In July, 1910, the strikers and the companies had called an armistice pending a settlement attempt by the State Brewers' Association. The Rainier agency soon compromised the issue in dispute, and the men returned to work in August, but negotiations with other agencies and companies lasted longer. Finally, on September 30, L. W. Butler and C. F. Grow of the local strike committee signed contracts with the brewery owners. Grow, suspected of implication in the *Times* bombing, was jailed on October 1; on the same day the brewery proprietors cancelled their contracts with the unions, and several months passed before they were again willing to negotiate.[49]

Another event indicated the effect on the community of Otis' instantaneous charge that organized labor was responsible for the destruction of his building. The California State Federation of Labor convened in Los Angeles on October 3. The scheduled parade to protest the anti-picketing ordinance was postponed; Mayor Alexander, who had joined the Central Labor Council in inviting the convention to meet in Los Angeles and had agreed to welcome the delegates, did not appear; nor did anybody else represent the city government or mercantile organizations. The State Federation was ignored while a bankers' convention meeting concurrently was given an effusive welcome. To organized labor the rebuff was an alarming indication that its guilt was taken for granted even before an investigation had been started.[50]

Ten days after the *Times* explosion, the metal-trades unions tried to bring their strike to an end. Some of the smaller foundries and machine shops, hard hit by the walkout, had earlier signed eight-hour agreements with the unions. These minor victories, however, had no bearing on the main course of the strike, and on October 10 a delegation, headed by C. M. Feider, and including C. F. Grow (who had been released from jail), asked Mayor Alexander to notify metal trades employers that the affected unions desired a conference with a view to terminating the conflict. Three days later the Founders' and Employers' Association rejected the suggestion on the ground that the union representatives, who had condoned boycotting and picketing, were not responsible leaders; that the metal trades employers had never had and did not now want to have business relations with unions; and that their non-union employees were adequate in number and skill to maintain production. Nevertheless, in December, 1910, the Llewellyn Iron Works had to ask, and was granted, an additional six months for fulfilling its contract to build a new Hall of Records. When it became obvious that settlement in Los Angeles was as remote as ever, San Francisco metal trades, after several time extensions for their unionization program outside of the city, began negotiating and finally signed an agreement with their employers in January, 1911. It stipulated that the unions would ask no wage increase for three years, that the eight-hour day would be enforced until November 9, 1911, and that thereafter working hours would be determined by the average working day of the metal trades throughout California, Oregon, and Washington.[51]

Even before the Los Angeles metal trades had made their unsuccessful plea for collective bargaining, the California State Federation of Labor, a few days after the *Times* disaster, declared that the general campaign to unionize Los Angeles must continue until the city's working men and women won the right to organize and better their working conditions. This fighting resolve set the tone for the next few months. President James Lynch of the ITU, pointing to the longstanding campaign of his own union to help local labor, urged other national organizations to continue the battle to organize the city. In October the national conventions of carpenters and plasterers each voted $2,000 for the unionization of Los Angeles; a little later the national painters' union sent $400. The national unions of molders, brass workers, sheet-metal workers, plumbers, restaurant employees and bartenders, bakers, and cement workers sent new representatives to Los Angeles. The General Campaign Strike Committee and its affiliated bodies intensified their agitation, ordering San Francisco labor leaders south to hearten the strikers, and continuing the payment of benefits to metal trades and leather workers. Local labor, as in previous crises during the revolutionary year of 1910, rallied to the standard. On November 4, 1910, more than ten thousand Los Angeles union members marched through the streets in a silent and sober demonstration of their earnest and orderly attempt to win for themselves the benefits of organization.[52]

Thus far the participation of the American Federation of Labor in the unionization campaign had been minimal. Organizer Stuart Reid had not been an outstanding strike leader, nor had he been constantly in Los Angeles. He had not, for example, sent to headquarters the customary regular reports on the local situation. The standoffish policy of the AFL may have stemmed partly from the failure of both the California State Federation of Labor and the Los Angeles Central Labor Council to elect delegates to the 1909 national convention. But in November, 1910, California and local labor made a concerted effort to persuade the AFL to assume its just share of the burden. Telegrams from the State Building Trades Council and the Los Angeles Allied Printing Trades Council pleaded with the convention for assistance. Job Harriman, speaking for Los Angeles labor, made a long and impassioned appeal on the convention floor for aid for the embattled unionists of southern California. Strike leaders, including Tveitmoe, Gallagher, Butler, and Grow, reviewed the Los Angeles industrial disputes, the antipicketing ordinance, and the role of the Merchants' and Manufacturers' Association. Convinced of the urgency of the cause, the AFL convention asked all national and international unions, all state federations, all central bodies, and all local unions in the United States to contribute to the support of strikers on the west coast, particularly in Los Angeles. In December, 1910, Gompers implemented the convention's action by sending to the organized workers of America a circular letter which stressed the sinister plot of the M and M, as a subsidiary of the National Association of Manufacturers, to exterminate unionism in Los Angeles and on the Pacific Coast. With the AFL's entry, the coöperation of organized labor in behalf of Los Angeles unionism became nationwide.[53]

There was no letup in activity on the local battle front. The brewery owners' repudiation of their agreements on October 1 and the foundry owners' refusal to sit at the bargaining table with union representatives meant that the two major strikes continued. The leather workers, still at odds with Los Angeles Saddlery and Brydon Brothers, were receiving strike benefits from the General Campaign Strike Committee. After the lapse of a few days following the shock of the *Times* explosion, strike leaders ordered a renewal of picketing. Trials of arrested pickets proceeded very slowly because of the difficulty of finding unprejudiced jurymen. Moreover, many cases were dismissed for insufficient evidence; arrests had been made so long before that witnesses could not always be found or, if available, could no longer identify the defendants. In November, 1910, when 280 pickets still awaited trial, the deputy city prosecuting attorney announced that because of these difficulties pending cases would be fully investigated before they were brought into court. This policy, plus additional dismissals in court, had by the end of 1910 reduced the number of pickets awaiting trial to fifty.[54]

Some of the violators of the antipicketing ordinance during this period were messenger boys, who had recently formed a union and in November, 1910, had struck against Western Union and its subsidiary, the American District Telegraph, when the companies objected to the boys' organizing activities. Two of the four messengers brought to trial for picketing were convicted; the other two were released, one because of insufficient evidence and the other because of jury disagreement. The Central Labor Council endorsed the strike, boycotted the companies, and raised funds to support the boys. The striking messengers set up a coöperative service of their own at the Labor Temple, and eventually forced one Western Union branch out of business. But the strike was long and unsuccessful; in August, 1912, the Central Labor Council lifted the boycott because it no longer served any useful purpose.[55]

Industrial unrest in the Los Angeles area heightened as two more strikes broke out late in 1910. The first of these involved some of the workers on the aqueduct then being constructed to bring the Owens River water to Los Angeles. The men's resentment against D. J. Desmond, in charge of the mess halls along the aqueduct route, had first been aroused in the fall of 1909. At that time the Board of Public Works had responded to an appeal from Desmond by ordering a weekly $5 meal deduction from wages whether or not the men ate in the mess halls. According to organized labor, Desmond's financial insecurity had been caused by the workers' refusal to eat the ill-prepared and inadequate food he served. When Desmond raised the prices in November, 1910, and the Board of Public Works refused to authorize a corresponding increase in wages, the men struck. Supported by unions in Los Angeles and by the General Campaign Strike Committee, the aqueduct workers remained on strike until the end of 1911, when a satisfactory arrangement was made. In August, 1912, the Central Labor Council reported that industrial troubles at the aqueduct were over.[56]

In December, 1910, union photoengravers working for the Thorpe Engraving Company of Los Angeles struck because the company was making the plates for the *Times'* mid-winter edition. The strikers found jobs elsewhere while Thorpe, with the aid of nonunion workers, fulfilled its contract with the *Times* and thereafter ran an open shop.[57]

At the end of 1910 it was apparent that industrial strife in Los Angeles was going to continue. The strikes of long standing were not even close to settlement, and several new ones had broken out. The AFL, national unions, and San Francisco labor were all determined to see the struggle through to a satisfactory end. On the other hand, employers were equally opposed to compromise. So certain of this was Mayor Alexander that when a strikers' committee from the metal trades, on December 28, 1910, asked him a second time to intercede with employers, he bluntly replied that the Founders' and Employers' Association was doing everything in its power to prevent a settlement. Because he saw no hope for peace, and because he was favorably impressed by the reasonable attitude of the metal-trades unions in their conversations with him, the mayor proposed that organized labor ask the 1911 State Legislature for an act specifying compulsory arbitration of industrial disputes. The *Record,* which had been the only Los Angeles paper remaining friendly to labor throughout the strikes and the *Times* disaster, commented approvingly, arguing that many employers would be glad to arbitrate but were prevented by the M and M from doing so. However, in 1911, labor opposed a compulsory arbitration bill because it was limited to public services only. The bill, satisfactory to neither side, failed to pass.[58]

Labor believed that Mayor Alexander's shift to greater friendliness toward unions was symptomatic of a more favorable community sentiment. In October, 1910, within a few weeks of the *Times* explosion, the Central Labor Council had been invited to participate with the Chamber of Commerce, the M and M, and other mercantile groups in the dedication of a new federal building. Job Harriman, in his address to the 1910 AFL convention, assured the delegates that public opinion, outraged by the excesses of the *Times'* denunciations of organized labor, was slowly becoming less hostile to unions. He cited as examples the cheering crowds which witnessed the labor parade on November 4, and the outspokenness of occasional jurors who believed the antipicketing ordinance an affront to free men. During 1910 and 1911 organized labor was much interested in the proposed establishment of a municipal newspaper, a movement growing out of citizens' resentment over the distortion or withholding of news by all Los Angeles newspapers. A not unimportant factor in this movement was the *Times'* ceaseless labor-baiting. The Central Labor Council was represented on a charter revision committee functioning during 1910, and in December endorsed an amendment enabling the City Council to publish a weekly newspaper which would give equal space to all political parties polling 3 per cent of the vote, print only accurate, unbiased facts, and avoid the publication of libelous or defamatory material. Although this unique journalistic experiment did not materialize until the spring of 1912, the idea germinated in a period when the *Times* was subjecting organized labor to extraordinary verbal punishment.[59]

Organized labor, unwilling to rely too strongly on fickle community sentiment, found its strongest allies in the Socialist Party. Following the *Times* bombing there was a noticeable trend toward closer coöperation between the two groups. Several unions endorsed the complete socialist ticket, and visiting socialists, like Emil Seidel, candidate for vice-president of the United States, spoke to large audiences at the Labor Temple. After the fall elections of 1910, in which the Socialist Party polled over eleven thousand votes in Los Angeles County, the Union Labor Political Club decided to form a permanent organization and enter its own ticket in the next municipal election. Observers, however, believed that all the signs pointed instead to a labor-socialist coalition. Max Hayes, for example, in an editorial in the *International Socialist Review,* claimed that the drift of Los Angeles workers toward socialism precluded the development of a real labor party. J. Stitt Wilson, defeated socialist candidate for governor of California in 1910, saw in the Los Angeles labor parade and political rally of November 4 a clear indication of strong sympathy between organized labor and socialists. By the end of 1910 the Los Angeles branch of the Socialist Party numbered over two thousand members, a German branch had just been formed, and a Children's Socialist Lyceum had been organized. The Women's Socialist Union decided to collaborate more frequently with the Women's Union Label League. A flourishing socialist movement, supported in part if not wholly by organized labor, was in the making in Los Angeles.[60]

As the year 1911 opened, the vitality of Los Angeles unionism seemed unimpaired. The labor movement had shared to some extent in community enterprises; it had begun the search for political solutions; it had twice appealed to the city administration for help in ending industrial strife; and it had supported its striking members to the fullest extent of its capacity. By the end of 1910 the General Campaign Strike Committee had spent close to $160,000 in Los Angeles, continuing the collection and disbursement of funds with uninterrupted regularity. The results were gratifying. Up to January, 1911, only twenty-four strikers had deserted the unions. During the six months ending in February, 1911, twelve new unions had been organized, and twenty-five hundred new members had joined the labor movement. Both the metal trades and the building trades had doubled their membership lists since the start of the unionizing campaign. With many unions reporting notable membership gains in the early months of 1911, the upward trend seemed to be a continuing one. According to Tveitmoe, a militant labor movement with tremendous staying power had been created in Los Angeles.[61]

Picketing, which had subsided temporarily because large sums were tied up in bail, was resumed in March, 1911. On April 7, in an unusually large haul for one day, the police arrested thirty-five pickets loitering in the vicinity of the Baker Iron Works. The city authorities, hoping to end these intermittent disturbances once and for all, set bail at $300 per man instead of the usual $50; charged the pickets with conspiracy to violate the ordinance, a more serious offense than picketing itself; and refused the defendants' request for individual trials. The conspiracy charge led to several unsuccessful efforts to stay court proceedings. The Supreme Court of California denied a petition for a writ of prohibition, and the local court overruled defense attorney Job Harriman's demurrer. Both documents stressed the defendants' claim that they were not guilty of conspiracy to commit a crime.[62]

With seven defendants dismissed because of lack of witnesses for identification, the remaining twenty-eight were brought to trial at the end of April, 1911. When the jury was unable to agree on a verdict, the trial was reset for May 20. But both sides were growing tired of the excessive litigation resulting from the antipicketing ordinance. Following Harriman's pledge that pickets would stay out of industrial districts for the duration of current labor disturbances, the prosecution dismissed the twenty-eight defendants. This agreement ended picketing for the time being, but the ordinance remained on the statute books for many years. The total of three hundred arrests in 1910–1911 brought five convictions, four acquittals, four jury disagreements, and 247 dismissals; forty cases were pending when prosecution ceased. The thirty-five arrested on the conspiracy charge have not been included in the above summary.[63]

Part of the renewal of the campaign in early 1911 was the eruption of fresh labor disputes. In February the Bishop Cracker & Candy Company locked out some thirty employees because they had recently formed a cracker bakers' local of the Bakery and Confectionery Workers' International Union. The Central Labor Council, after trying unsuccessfully to have the dispute submitted to arbitration, boycotted the company. Representatives visited more than one thousand local grocery stores, inducing many of them not to handle Bishop products. The central body also circularized merchants in nearby states to advertise the boycott over a wide area. Both the Central Labor Council and the General Campaign Strike Committee provided financial assistance to the locked-out employees, and the State Federation of Labor placed the company on its unfair list. Although by January, 1912, all of the workers had found other jobs, the Central Labor Council continued to boycott the Bishop firm because it was operating as an open shop.[64] Shortly after the cracker bakers' lockout, labor won two shorter disputes. After a one-day strike in March, 1911, the cigar makers established a new and higher wage schedule in all firms except the nonunion Baer Cigar Manufacturing Company. In May the relatively new and flourishing union of ladies' tailors, after a strike lasting three weeks, won recognition in all departments of the firm of Krystal & Company.[65]

Of far greater consequence to organized labor was settlement of the brewery workers' strike in April, 1911, following negotiations begun at the request of Edward Maier of Maier & Zobelein. Representatives of Maier & Zobelein, the Los Angeles Brewing Company, and the Mathie Brewing Company met with C. F. Grow of the local strike committee, E. P. Kraemer of the local brewery workers' union, and Emil Muri of the state organization of brewery workers. They agreed to sign the old contracts substantially without change, except for a compromise on the disputed wages for drivers and bottlers. The drivers were granted an increase of $2 a week, the bottlers of $1 a week, instead of the $3 and $2, respectively, demanded by these workers at the time of the strike. Before the end of April all local breweries and agencies had signed the agreement, and in August the Union Brewery of Anaheim accepted the terms. The strike was over, and the brewery unions, though forced to compromise the wage issue, had demonstrated once again their ability to write closed-shop contracts with all their employers.[66]

Although not closely related to the Los Angeles organizing campaign, certain political developments of 1910–1911 were of profound importance to labor's progress in the state of California. The first of these came in November, 1910, when progressive Republicans under the standard of the Lincoln-Roosevelt League won their fight to destroy the Southern Pacific machine by electing Hiram Johnson Governor of California and giving him substantial majorities in both houses of the Legislature. The progressives were no more anxious than employers' associations to increase the power and prestige of labor; however, their dedication to the welfare of the people compelled them to implement, in the 1911 Legislature, their program of reform measures which in many cases either directly or indirectly benefited organized labor. As a result, the California State Federation of Labor acclaimed this legislative session as the most significant one in the history of the state.[67]

Organized labor had not endorsed the Lincoln-Roosevelt progressive movement, but it could take some credit for the beneficial results of Johnson's reform program. The State Federation of Labor, at its 1910 convention, had mapped out a series of legislative proposals for presentation to the 1911 session. Moreover, labor lobbyists were on hand in Sacramento to use their influence in favor of desirable bills and against those they believed inimical to the interests of working people. The State Federation, the San Francisco Labor Council, and the Joint Legislative Board of the Railroad Brotherhoods maintained a lobby throughout the entire session, and the Building Trades Councils of California and San Francisco kept representatives there for the last two months. Various outside groups such as the American Association for Labor Legislation, the Consumers' League, and the California Conference of Social Agencies assisted the legislative program of organized labor. Of forty-nine bills advocated by union groups, thirty-nine became law through the action of the 1911 Legislature; Governor Johnson vetoed some of the labor legislation because he believed the bills unnecessary, bad, or not clear in purpose or wording.[68]

The most important prolabor laws passed by the 1911 Legislature and signed by the Governor provided for workmen's compensation in cases of injury and for the eight-hour day for women. The former was a compromise preserving the doctrine of "contributory negligence" and providing for voluntary instead of compulsory compensation. The proposal to limit the working day for women originated with W. A. Vanna, delegate of the Los Angeles laundry workers' union to the 1910 State Federation of Labor convention. The new law stipulated the eight-hour day and the forty-eight hour week for all women except those employed in the processing of perishable fruits and vegetables. Other labor measures made misuse of the union label illegal, regularized payment of wages, amplified restrictions on child labor, provided for full train crews, gave the governor power to appoint and remove the State Labor Commissioner, established safety regulations for electrical workers, improved the mechanics' lien law, provided for temporary floors in buildings under construction, ordered that cases of occupational disease must be reported to the Board of Health, voided temporary injunctions if not brought to trial within a certain period, and limited prison labor to the manufacture of articles for public use.[69]

Two measures not directly contributing to the immediate welfare of organized labor, but embodying longstanding union objectives, were passed by the 1911 Legislature. They provided for submission to the electorate of constitutional amendments for woman suffrage and direct legislation. When, later in 1911, the voters adopted these amendments, the State Federation of Labor claimed that woman suffrage would not have passed without labor support, and that its own history was the history of the struggle for the initiative, referendum, and recall. Ever since its organization in 1901 the State Federation had advocated direct legislation. Other 1911 laws of indirect benefit to organized labor provided for inspection of weights and measures and for state regulation of public utilities and railroads; appropriated funds for investigating the prevalence of tuberculosis; and specified standards of ventilation, sanitation, and lighting in tenement houses.[70]

Organized labor failed to secure legislation on some of its proposals. A bill limiting the use of injunctions in labor disputes, prohibiting yellow-dog contracts, and legalizing boycotts and peaceful picketing was allowed to die in the Assembly. This measure, which would have invalidated the Los Angeles antipicketing ordinance, aroused a violent controversy, with many of the progressives opposed to it. The Los Angeles *Times* denounced it as a threat to industrial freedom in southern California, and only one prominent newspaper in the state endorsed labor's view. Among the other bills failing to pass were those appropriating funds for a tuberculosis sanitarium, closing barber shops on Sundays, regulating the use of guards and detectives, establishing free state labor bureaus in San Francisco and Los Angeles, prohibiting blacklisting, providing for the licensing of barbers, and providing for state inspection of mines and scaffolding.[71]

Passage of the eight-hour law for women workers was a source of pride to Los Angeles labor. Not only had the local laundry workers proposed the measure, but the Los Angeles Central Labor Council and Building Trades Council had sent telegrams urging southern California legislators to vote for the bill. To celebrate achievement of an objective for which they had worked hard, Los Angeles unionists staged a huge demonstration, including a parade and mass meeting, on April 15. The main speakers were Job Harriman, Stanley Wilson, C. F. Grow, and O. A. Tveitmoe. The enthusiastic celebration denoted the confidence and good spirits of Los Angeles unionists during the period when their welfare was the concern of many state and national labor organizations.[72]

The rejoicing of organized labor was dimmed, however, by an event which occurred during the same month as settlement of the brewery strike and celebration of the eight-hour law for women. In April, 1911, following months of investigation by private detective agencies and officers of the law, Secretary John J. McNamara of the International Association of Bridge and Structural Iron Workers and his brother James B. McNamara were arrested on suspicion of complicity in the *Times* bombing. For the time being, the arrests did no more than restrict the boundaries of a proposed building trades drive for higher wages, but in the months to come they had a telling effect in dampening the ardor of the unionizing campaign and in diverting contributions from the General Campaign Strike Committee to a McNamara defense fund raised by the American Federation of Labor and a number of national unions.

In December, 1910, the Los Angeles District Council of Carpenters had planned to demand a wage increase from $3.50 to $4 a day in May, 1911. With assurances of support from the Brotherhood of Carpenters and Joiners and the California State Building Trades Council, the plan was gradually expanded until, in the spring of 1911, it was expected to be a general movement for higher wages among the Los Angeles building trades. Apprehension following the arrest of the McNamaras, however, weakened the determination of crafts other than the carpenters to make any demands upon employers.[73]

The carpenters, who had notified the Master Builders' Association of their wage designs several months prior to May 1, went ahead with their plans. During March and April, organizers worked intensively to build up union strength, and negotiations with employers ended in many individual promises to raise carpenters' wages. The Master Builders' Association, however, refused to consider the demand for a $4 scale; it set up a nonunion employment agency and prepared for a showdown. Several of its members even anticipated the strike deadline of May 1 by discharging all their union carpenters. On May 1, 1911, some eight hundred carpenters left their jobs. The strikers received benefits from the national union, and help from local labor organizations. Gradually, as more and more employers were induced to grant the pay increase, the strike rolls dwindled; by mid-July only one hundred and fifty carpenters were out of work, compared to "normal" unemployment of about one hundred. Since the beginning of the strike, eleven locals in the area had gained a total of five hundred new members. At this point, the District Council of Carpenters quietly ordered the men back to work on the tacit understanding that all contractors would assent to the wage raise. Termination of the strike before the increase actually went into effect was a face-saving concession to large contractors who were unwilling to appear the losers in a contest with their union employees. In August the *Times,* while claiming a defeat for labor, reported that builders were "voluntarily" paying their workers from 50 cents to $1 more than the old union scale of $3.50 a day. In September both the lathers and plasterers won daily wage increases of $1 and 50 cents, respectively, without striking.[74]

Like the carpenters, the union bakers of Los Angeles enlarged and solidified their organization through a concurrent drive for shorter hours. Some members were working as long as fifteen hours a day, and the union threatened to strike on May 1, 1911, if employers refused to institute the nine-hour day. Instead of striking, however, the union, encouraged by early successes with some employers, continued to negotiate, and by June had signed up all companies except the two large firms of Meeks-Barnes and Walker. The Central Labor Council sanctioned a boycott against these two bakeries, and in July, 1912, they were still listed as unfair. Meanwhile, in February, 1912, the union had renewed its contracts with other companies, with a new clause stipulating time and a half for overtime.[75]

While the bakers and several of the building trades were able to make some progress in the summer of 1911, the general unionizing campaign in Los Angeles began to show the first signs of faltering. These indications were by no means obvious, for on the surface there was the same determination to shape the local labor movement into an effective weapon against employer opposition. In June, 1911, Gallagher reported no material change in the Los Angeles strike situation, and the General Campaign Strike Committee kept its machinery in full operation, even though benefit rolls were dwindling as the strikers gradually found jobs. During the year from June, 1910, to June, 1911, the committee had expended almost $260,000, most of it in Los Angeles; an additional $85,000 contributed by national unions brought the total to an imposing $345,000. But in August the committee was forced to issue a fresh appeal for funds in order to "hold out" in Los Angeles, and twice during the summer the Central Labor Council strongly urged local unions to contribute to the campaign being waged for their benefit. Such insistent pleas were necessary because unions all over the country were being asked at the same time to give to the McNamara defense fund.[76]

In June, 1911, the *Times* claimed that hundreds of workers had left local unions since the arrest of the McNamaras, and that unionism was on the decline in Los Angeles. Although this statement was not completely accurate, it contained an element of truth. During the year beginning in June, 1910, close to seven thousand new members had joined Los Angeles unions, an average weekly increase of about 115. Thereafter there was a perceptible decline in the rate of growth, except for a brief period in the fall of 1911, when initiation of the great strike of railroad shop workers for recognition of the Harriman System Federation caused a temporary spurt in accretions to union membership lists. Between June, 1910, and June, 1911, twenty-five new unions had been organized in Los Angeles, but in this respect, too, the campaign began to slow down. By October, 1911, the Central Labor Council, with ninety-one affiliated organizations, represented a total of approximately fifteen thousand union members. In comparison with the strides made in the organizing campaign during 1910 and the early months of 1911, the progress following the McNamara arrests was less noteworthy.[77]

Another sign that the Los Angeles campaign was tapering off was deterioration in the caliber of the work of national and international union organizers, which obviously lacked the intensity and urgency formerly characterizing such activity. Between June and November, 1911, the unions of bartenders, coopers, garment workers, painters, carpenters, pressmen, laundry workers, and boot and shoe workers sent representatives to Los Angeles. The results of their efforts varied from union to union. New members of the coopers' union, for example, were locked out by the Western Cooperage Company when their union affiliation was discovered, while the garment workers' organizer succeeded in signing contracts with a number of local firms.[78]

Despite this general slackening of the organizing campaign in the months following the arrest of the McNamaras, the spirit of local unionists remained confident. In July the Central Labor Council issued a revised unfair list of all members of the Merchants' and Manufacturers' Association so that union workers could give their patronage to firms friendly to organized labor. The Labor Day parade of 1911, a large but orderly demonstration, received favorable press comments. Gompers' visit to Los Angeles in September, though devoted primarily to consultation with the McNamaras and their defense lawyers, served once again to remind local labor that its interests were not being neglected in high quarters. Both Gompers and organizer Juan Ramirez of the State Federation of Labor reported that Los Angeles unionists were undaunted by the many obstacles, both old and new, that confronted them. There was no evidence that the metal trades were yet ready to yield in the long strike which had already lasted more than a year, or that the leather workers would terminate the boycott of Los Angeles Saddlery and Brydon Brothers.[79]

The sustained aggressiveness of Los Angeles unionism was manifested during the latter part of 1911 by unions not involved in the serious industrial disturbances contingent on the organizing campaign. Mailers' Union No. 9, affiliated with the International Typographical Union, had by 1911 signed contracts with all the union newspapers in the city. During the same year the union of trunk and case workers, following a quiet but persistent campaign, signed up all local firms employing its members. By the end of 1911 the horseshoers' union claimed to have organized 95 per cent of workers in the trade. In October, 1911, the musicians' union, one of the strongest in Los Angeles, established a new pay scale providing for a 16 per cent increase in all but seven theaters in the area. (One of these was the Regal, which had been on the Central Labor Council's unfair list since the fall of 1909.) In 1912, after a boycott, three of the theaters signed an agreement with the musicians' union, but the other four refused to yield. After a strike lasting three weeks in October, 1911, the tailors' union signed contracts with all important firms in the city specifying the union wage scale, reduction of hours from nine to eight, and recognition of the union. The fact that most of the nonunion tailors joined the union during the strike helped to make this sweeping victory possible. Another affiliate of the Journeymen Tailors' Union, Ladies' Tailors' Local No. 52, struck in November, 1911, for the same benefits, but after six weeks called off the strike. The defeat was attributed to the union's poor financial condition and its failure to obtain the sanction of either its own international or the Los Angeles Central Labor Council.[80]

During the latter months of 1911 the spirits of Los Angeles unionists were buoyed by political developments, outstanding among which was the cementing of the alliance between local organized labor and the Socialist Party. The rapprochement, which had begun in 1907 and 1908, was hastened and vastly strengthened by vigorous socialist support of union labor in the industrial upheavals of 1910 and 1911. This support, both moral and financial, had been so vital in the organizing campaign that the General Campaign Strike Committee made a special acknowledgment of gratitude to the Socialist Party and to Job Harriman, its leading Los Angeles member, for the frequent use of his legal talent in behalf of unionists charged with offenses against the law. In January, 1911, Stanley Wilson, editor of the *Citizen,* joined the Socialist Party. The following month E. H. Misner, prominent strike leader, succeeded Fred Wheeler as president of the Central Labor Council; both were socialists. So close were such ties between socialists and unionists that political collaboration in 1911 seemed the only logical development.[81]

Both the Socialist Party and the Union Labor Political Club were independently gaining strength in the early months of 1911. In January the Socialist Party of California, which during the past year had increased its membership from fifteen hundred to sixty-four hundred, claimed to have more adherents than any other state branch of the party. The Socialists of Pasadena were numerous enough to enter a complete ticket in the city election in March. New party locals were being formed in other southern California communities; and in Los Angeles a Young People's Socialist League, a Christian Socialist Fellowship, a Socialist Proletarian Club, and a Negro branch of the party were organized. In March, the Los Angeles Socialist Party claimed a dues-paying membership of one thousand, and a "voting membership" of eight thousand. In June, 1911, the *California Social Democrat* was incorporated to replace the *People's Paper* as the socialist organ. The Union Labor Political Club, meanwhile, had successfully been urging unions to affiliate with it; by April it claimed a voting strength of eighteen thousand. The club took to itself the credit for ending antipathy to socialism among unionists, and for bringing working people to the realization that furtherance of their aims depended upon political expression.[82]

In April, 1911, a joint committee of the Socialist Party and the Union Labor Political Club drew up a tentative list of nominees for the forthcoming municipal elections. As finally endorsed by both groups, the ticket named Job Harriman as candidate for mayor and three other socialists for the offices of city attorney, city auditor, and city assessor. Nominees for the City Council included unionists Fred Wheeler, C. F. Grow, Frank Wolfe, A. J. Mooney, and Alexander Kane; G. W. Whitley, a Negro businessman guiding the work of the Afro-American League; and several socialists not members of unions. Nominees for the Board of Education, including three women, were socialists rather than union members. On July 4 Job Harriman formally accepted the mayoralty nomination of the socialists and unionists who had joined forces under the banner of the Socialist Party. In their platform, adopted on August 6, the socialists promised to abolish graft in construction of the aqueduct from the Owens River, extend the municipally owned water system, establish a single municipally owned telephone system, work for the municipal ownership of all public utilities, extend the city's park and playground system, construct a municipal railway between Los Angeles and San Pedro, improve the school system, provide a building for the public library, erect publicly owned hospitals, abolish the chain gang, establish a municipal free employment bureau, abolish the contract system on public work, improve the harbor facilities at San Pedro, shift the tax burden from small home owners to speculators in land, investigate the housing situation, and improve the garbage disposal system. In an early campaign speech, Harriman promised that the first action of his administration would be repeal of the antipicketing ordinance.[83]

Both partners in the joint enterprise rallied to the cause. The National Executive Committee of the Socialist Party urged all its local branches to unite with labor organizations in a fund-raising campaign for the socialist ticket in Los Angeles. The local branch of the party formed a Socialist Campaign Committee to bring in speakers like J. Stitt Wilson, socialist mayor of Berkeley; to solicit contributions; and to arrange for electioneering meetings in halls, on street corners, and at factory and shop doors. All candidates participated in an exhausting round of speech-making, some of them appearing as frequently as thirty-five times a week. The socialists published and distributed one hundred thousand copies every week of a campaign leaflet entitled "The Coming Victory," and in addition circulated other items of socialist literature. Organized labor was just as enthusiastic. Not only the Union Labor Political Club, but the Central Labor Council, the Building Trades Council, the Metal Trades Council, and many individual unions endorsed the socialist ticket. Metal trades strikers worked in the political campaign. The Central Labor Council asked all of its affiliates to donate to a campaign fund, the *Citizen* advocated voting for the Socialist Party, the Union Labor Political Club arranged joint meetings with the socialists, and numerous unions formed Harriman clubs. A registration office was established at the Labor Temple as part of an intensive campaign to register all potential Harriman voters. President Samuel Gompers of the AFL visited Los Angeles in September, 1911, and urged unionists to vote for Harriman; his advocacy caused members of organized labor to believe that the barrier separating the AFL and the Socialist Party would be broken down. Certainly all local indications pointed to a realization among unionists that the Socialist Party was the political expression of the working-class movement.[84]

The first contest was the primary election on October 31, 1911. The only full ticket competing with the socialists, entered by the Good Government League, was headed by Mayor George Alexander, candidate for reëlection. A Republican, W. C. Mushet, was also running for mayor. Among daily newspapers only the *Record* supported the Socialist Party; the *Times* advised its readers to vote against Harriman, but did not come out strongly for either Alexander or Mushet; the rest of the papers backed Alexander's candidacy. While the *Citizen* claimed that employers were ordering their employees to vote for Alexander if they wanted to keep their jobs, there was no fervent anti-Socialist campaign before the primaries. There was little apprehension concerning potential Socialist strength, for the Good Government forces expected their man to receive a majority on October 31 and thus be elected without a runoff. Unionists and Socialists, however, were confident of a good showing; in addition to their own votes, they were counting on six thousand Negro votes which G. W. Whitley of the Afro-American League promised to deliver. A final rally on election eve, addressed by Harriman and J. Stitt Wilson, demonstrated that the Socialist-labor forces formed a solid bloc dedicated to the election of the Harriman ticket.[85]

The Socialist Party won a clear victory in the primary, but it lacked the majority necessary for election. Of about 45,500 votes cast for mayor, Harriman received slightly over 20,000, Alexander approximately 16,800, and Mushet about 7,500. The Good Government nominees for city attorney, city auditor, and city assessor ran ahead of their Socialist contenders by 500 to 2,000 votes; however, returns for eight of the nine councilmanic seats favored the Socialists, and Fred Wheeler received 18,410 votes, the highest number obtained by any City Council candidate. Socialists were also ahead in five of the seven contests for membership on the Board of Education.[86]

The unexpected popularity of the Socialist ticket led to an extraordinary and unprecedented amalgamation of anti-Socialist and anti-labor sentiment in Los Angeles in preparation for the final election on December 5. The *Times* proposed immediately after the primaries to do all in its power, which was certainly not inconsequential, to defeat the Socialist menace to the peace and security of the city.[87] The campaign to defeat Harriman and save Los Angeles from a Socialist administration, however, became inextricably involved with developments in the *Times* bombing case. Until this point the investigations and the arrest of the McNamaras had not greatly altered the course of either the campaign to organize Los Angeles or the political entente between unionists and Socialists. But the outcome of the December 5 election hinged directly on proceedings in the McNamara case, and the account must therefore be deferred until the following chapter.

The connection between the unionizing campaign and the beneficial results of a Harriman victory in December was fully recognized by Los Angeles labor. In September the General Campaign Strike Committee had informed the Central Labor Council that local unions would thereafter have to finance the fight alone, since San Francisco and California labor organizations could not carry on the assessment indefinitely. The Central Labor Council thereupon urged continuance of the outside assistance at least until after the elections. Should Harriman ultimately be defeated, local leaders argued, they would willingly assent to termination of the state-wide assessments for Los Angeles strikers. They clearly felt that the catastrophe of a Harriman defeat would negate any further efforts to continue the organizing campaign.[88] The General Campaign Strike Committee, heeding the local appeal, remained in operation until the end of 1911. Indirectly, therefore, the conclusion of the great organizing campaign and of the metal trades strike depended on the outcome of the McNamara case, and discussion of these events also will be delayed until a later chapter.

XXI. THE "CRIME OF THE CENTURY"

1. THE BOMBING OF THE *Times*

ON THE MORNING of October 1, 1910, a slim, four-page issue of the *Times*, printed in antiquated type, gave mute evidence of the catastrophe announced in a bold headline, "Unionist Bombs Wreck The Times." Some hours previously, at 1 A.M., an explosion had occurred in Ink Alley, a passageway separating the stereotyping and press rooms of the *Times* building at First Street and Broadway. The initial blast blew out the first floor wall on one side of the building, and caused tons of ink stored in the alley to explode. Within seconds the entire three-story structure was on fire, and the hundred or more employees at work inside were making frantic efforts to escape. The firemen and equipment hastily summoned to the scene could make no headway against the rapidly spreading flames, and when some hours later the fire had spent itself, only a skeleton of the building remained. Total property damage was assessed at slightly over half a million dollars, though more than half of this loss was recovered through insurance and salvage.[1] Oddly enough, an eagle which the *Times* regarded as a symbol of the newspaper's indomitable spirit was not dislodged from its perch on top of the building. The idea that the indestructible eagle represented the imperishable quality of the *Times*' fight for industrial freedom was expressed in a poem entitled "The Times Holocaust":

> High on the ruins of the battlement
> The Eagle stood, unscathed, above the wreck
> Of dynamite and death. The morning sun
> Threw o'er its grimy wings a sheen of gold
> To symbolize that Liberty shall live,
> While in the arms of God the martyred dead
> Shall rest eternally, and willing hands
> Shall take their places here and rear again
> A thousand temples unto Liberty
> For every one that falls.[2]

The difficulty of identifying the bodies found in the ashes led to an initial estimate that twenty-one persons had lost their lives in the explosion and fire; the number was later corrected to twenty. The *Times* memorialized the victims in the following inscription on a monument dedicated in November, 1911:

This imposing pile, reared by the Los Angeles Times, stands here to perpetuate the names, the virtues and the memories of those Honored Dead who in life toiled in the ranks of the journal which they served so long and so well, and who fell at their posts in the Times Building on the awful morning of October 1, 1910—victims of conspiracy, dynamite and fire: The Crime of the Century.[3]

No summary of the meaning imputed by the *Times* to its "Crime of the Century" could have been more apt than these words from the dedicatory oration of the Reverend Dr. Robert L. Burdette: "Above your dust, oh, sacred dead, we consecrate this monument. We dedicate it to the cause for which you died. To free labor for free men; to the unfettered hand; to the unshackled mind; to the free soul."[4]

Underneath the public display of emotionalism, however, lay an opportunity to extract benefit from the catastrophe: to fasten the deed on unionists would not only enhance the righteousness of the *Times'* battle for industrial freedom but also discredit the cause of organized labor. Harrison Gray Otis, proprietor of the *Times,* was en route home from Mexico at the time of the disaster. Arriving on the afternoon of October 1, he immediately reaffirmed his newspaper's accusation of union responsibility. So serious a charge did not go unchallenged by local unionists. Denying all prior knowledge of and any responsibility for the explosion, they placed the blame on faulty gas fixtures and inadequate escape facilities in the building. For some weeks previous, *Times* employees had complained of gas leakages; because of this Ben Robinson of the Typographical Union, during his membership on the Board of Fire Commissioners, had fruitlessly requested an investigation. Several employees reported that the odor of gas was particularly strong on the night of the explosion. Although some extremists went so far as to charge that Otis had blown up his own plant in order to "frame" organized labor, most local unionists accepted and proclaimed the gas theory. Thus at the very start the conflicting accusations of dynamite and gas were clearly delineated.[5]

The *Times* disaster, whether deliberately contrived or caused accidentally through carelessness, was not wholly unexpected. As far back as the spring of 1908 the editor of the local Socialist organ had written: "Sufficient proof that the powers that be have not commenced to worry over the growth of the labor movement in Los Angeles lies in the fact that they have thus far failed to unearth a dynamite bomb or a plot to assassinate Gen. Otis."[6] For at least a year prior to the explosion, according to local labor leader Charles Feider, Otis himself had been intimating that a unionist resort to violence against him or his property would not surprise him.[7] Immediately after the catastrophe the *Times* remarked that "numerous threats [by laborites] to do this dastardly deed had been received."[8] A less prejudiced local weekly journal commented, "And on the morning when the tragedy was announced nine men out of every ten in Los Angeles said in their thoughts: 'Well, I have long expected something to happen.' "[9]

Even labor leaders who hesitated to place direct responsibility upon Otis found indications that the *Times* proprietor was well prepared for the disaster. Since 1901 he had made no substantial improvements in the old building, evidently a fire trap with a faulty gas system, but instead had drawn up complete plans for a new structure. Furthermore, Otis had built and fully equipped an auxiliary plant for any emergency. Even more curious, according to an investigatory committee of the California State Federation of Labor, was the fact that despite the quickness of the flames the *Times* had lost no valuable records and no executive personnel in the conflagration. With a speculative eye on such coincidences, labor unionists could not help wondering whether Otis had himself had a guilty hand in the destruction of life and property on the morning of October 1.[10] A national Socialist paper gave more forthright expression to this notion. Pointing out that antiunion forces would gain far more than organized labor from an outrage fraudulently attributed to union members, it asked: "Was this a huge conspiracy against union labor in Los Angeles? General Otis admits that he 'expected' the calamity. What led him to expect it and are his own hands clean?"[11]

Although Otis' direct implication in the disaster was usually more obliquely suggested than this, his moral responsibility for goading unionists into violence—if organized labor were indeed guilty—was openly proclaimed by observers both friendly and neutral to labor unions. Eugene Debs accused the *Times* management of instigating if not actually perpetrating the crime.[12] The *Pacific Outlook,* a local weekly journal edited by Charles Willard of the Chamber of Commerce, said: "The Times . . . hates labor unions. . . . When there is industrial trouble, it makes a business of throwing kerosene on the flames, and it hurls taunts and insults that are a very fair moral substitute for dynamite."[13] It did not, however, exonerate organized labor on this account. Describing the bomb as a blow at the privilege of free speech, it added: "The Times incident is worse than many strikes."[14] After a visit to Los Angeles, Frederick Palmer wrote for *Hampton's Magazine:* "You hear talk of the hateful baiting which breeds hate; of a man of power and position using his newspaper weapon with such venom in beating down his enemies that he created the elements which could find no voice except nitroglycerin to answer the dynamite of Otis' language."[15]

These opinions represented the school of thought which, while tacitly assuming labor's guilt, suggested that the *Times* proprietor must accept a share of the responsibility. At the other extreme were journalistic expressions like that of Alfred Holman, editor of the San Francisco

Argonaut, who conceded no extenuating circumstances to lessen the blame on organized labor: "The world will understand . . . that this incident represents the spirit and criminal aggression of labor unionism as we have it on the Pacific Coast."[16] The reaction of newspapers, news agencies, and journals in California and the rest of the country varied between these two points of view. Many, like the Associated Press and the California Press Association, sent messages of sympathy to Otis and, without naming names, demanded that the guilty be brought to justice. A typical example of a reasoned argument inculpating organized labor was the following: ". . . No one can help knowing that it was the labor union men who felt aggrieved that nonunion men were employed, and it is they who stood to gain profit, or at least revenge, by this dynamite explosion. . . . It is the natural suspicion that some member or representative of the unions exploded the dynamite or at least planned the outrage."[17] In Los Angeles, the *Record* was the only paper which faithfully subscribed to the innocence of organized labor. The *Express* felt that, in view of the suspicious atmosphere, it behooved the unions to call off the strikes of brewery workers and metal trades.[18] A few editors, distressed by the contravention of justice in presuming the accused guilty until proven innocent, spoke up with words of caution. The *Citizen* reprinted the following from the Pasadena *News*:

Certain papers are already assuming that the labor union is responsible for this outrage. While there is evidence on which to ground the belief that the editorial policy of the Times toward labor unions prompted the outrage, the News still advises a suspension of final judgment in the interest of a full and fair investigation and the ultimate punishment of the guilty.[19]

There was equally wide variation in the opinions expressed by other individuals and groups. Governor James N. Gillett of California left no doubt whatsoever as to his position: "Whether guilty or not, the labor unionists will have to be blamed for the crime, until shown they are not guilty, as everything points to a desire to wipe out property and lives of those who have been fighting organized labor for years."[20] Hiram Johnson, soon to succeed Gillett, made no identification of the guilty in his statement: "No punishment is great enough for the criminal who planned it or for the loathsome miscreant who carried it into execution."[21] Citizens' groups, clubs, chambers of commerce, and similar bodies in Los Angeles and other communities confined themselves, for the most part, to expressions of sympathy for the *Times* and the families of victims, or of horror at the enormity of the crime. With but one or two exceptions, local clergymen and church groups charitably refrained from prejudgments, merely voicing hopes that the culprits would be apprehended and punished.[22]

Organized labor was unanimous in denying its responsibility for the disaster. Local unions, pointing out that the major strikes then under way were on the verge of success and that violence could only damage their cause, were quick to condemn the crime, insist on a thorough investigation, and offer their coöperation. George Gunrey, speaking for the Los Angeles Metal Trades Council and the General Campaign Strike Committee, referred to labor's consistent preaching against violence as evidence of innocence. The California State Federation of Labor, meeting in Los Angeles on October 3, 1910, called off its scheduled parade out of respect for the dead and in the interest of the public peace, and appointed a committee to make a full investigation of the *Times* explosion.[23] The sincerity of labor's belief in its own innocence was clear in a personal letter, not intended for publication, from Frank Roney, a San Francisco unionist then visiting Los Angeles, to Professor Ira B. Cross of the University of California: "... You have heard no doubt and been appalled at the Times calamity in this town. You have also been made aware of the fact that the catastrophe has been as usual laid at the door of the trades unionists by the Times people and their allies. You are morally certain I am sure that the charge is wholly unfounded."[24]

At the national level, organized labor exhibited the same shock of horror and the same disbelief that union members could have so rashly violated their obligations to society and to their own organizations. As the *Times* noted, "Passionate denials of guilt from all the 'big' union leaders of America are being clicked in over the telegraph."[25] Within a few days of the explosion, President Samuel Gompers elucidated the stand of the American Federation of Labor by affirming his confidence in the innocence of union members; he added that even if a union man should eventually be found guilty, unionism per se could hardly be held accountable for the actions of a man so devoid of human feelings.[26] Speaking at a public meeting in Battle Creek, Michigan, on October 5, 1910, Gompers said: "The greatest enemies of our movement could not administer a blow so hurtful to our cause as would be such a stigma if the men of organized labor were responsible for it."[27]

Neither such disclaimers from the highest authorities in the American labor movement nor the logic of their arguments had power to deter those who were bent on making organized labor the culprit. The Merchants' and Manufacturers' Association, accepting without deviation the *Times'* accusation of union responsibility, immediately appropriated $50,000, part of which was earmarked for hunting down the guilty "unionite fiends" who had bombed the *Times* building. The remainder provided a nucleus for a "defense fund" of $1,000,000, which the M and M confidently expected to raise in the short space of one week. "Now is the time," said Secretary Felix Zeehandelaar, "to concentrate on the defense of Los Angeles from any and all encroachments by labor unionism."[28] The National Association of Manufacturers fell into line with its Los Angeles branch. Urging Otis to continue his splendid fight for industrial freedom, the NAM's board of directors unanimously adopted resolutions placing the responsibility for the disaster squarely on the International Typographical Union because of its long history of opposition to Otis and the *Times*. A New York newspaper, the *Commercial,* particularized the charge by alleging that Los Angeles members of the Typographical Union could fairly be blamed for the destructive explosion, and advocated hanging for the perpetrators of union labor crimes as a means of restoring normal industrial conditions in California.[29]

Voices were raised in defense of both the Typographical Union and local labor. President James Lynch of the ITU reminded the public, through an Associated Press reporter, that his organization had conducted its long, hard fight against the *Times* with the utmost fairness and had, through more than sixty years of continuous existence, established a record that was honorable and free from violence.[30] The editor of the Los Angeles *Graphic,* noting that the respected Springfield *Republican* placed no credence in the charges against the Typographical Union, paid high tribute to the printers: "Few persons hereabouts entertain the slightest suspicion that any member of the Typographical Union was remotely connected with the dastardly deed.... The membership of the Typographical Union is enrolled from men of a high order of intelligence, having a genuine respect for the laws of their country and for the laws of humanity. Their attitude toward the *Times* in this crisis ... has been one of admirable poise."[31] Both the *Graphic* and the *Pacific Outlook* suggested that San Francisco rather than local labor had plotted and carried out the destruction of the *Times* building; Mayor George Alexander and the Los Angeles chief of police also contended that the guilty ones must be sought outside the city.[32]

There was, indeed, little for an impartial observer to criticize in the attitudes of local labor. Immediately after the disaster, President Ralph Criswell of the Los Angeles Typographical Union wrote to Harry Chandler, business manager of the *Times,* offering the services of union printers in preparing the newspaper for publication. Although the

Times made no acknowledgment of the overture other than mentioning Criswell's name in a general list of those offering sympathy and aid, union printers did serve Otis indirectly. The auxiliary plant could not adequately handle the full printing load, and for several weeks after the explosion, sections of the *Times* were set up by the *Herald* and other establishments manned exclusively by union printers. Moreover, the union declared a sixty-day amnesty in its fight against the *Times,* permitted members to work in nonunion shops where union wage and hour schedules were maintained, and instructed its officers to proffer assistance to any workmen deprived of their means of subsistence by the disaster. The local Typographical Union also voted $100 to the widow of an international member who lost his life in the explosion, but at the time withheld this information for fear that her husband's union affiliation would prevent her from receiving payments from relief funds.[33]

Talk of raising money to assist the families of victims began immediately after the disaster. On October 2, the *Times,* while thanking those friends who had already proffered aid, promised that it would take care of the families of those who had perished. Nevertheless, when Mayor Alexander and the City Council set up the machinery for an official relief fund on October 3, Otis said in a signed editorial that his newspaper would serve as one of the collecting agencies, and added: "To this fund we ourselves will contribute according to our reverent inclination and our manifest duty."[34] The final accounting in December, 1910, revealed that more than $75,000 had been accumulated and distributed; several unions had made donations to the fund. Neither Otis nor Chandler nor the *Times,* however, had subscribed to the public relief, though the newspaper's owners had paid out about $15,000 for hospital and other expenses incident to the disaster. The *Times* justified its failure to contribute to the official fund on the ground that its stockholders had suffered a loss of some $300,000 through destruction of the building. The *Pacific Outlook* commented that the newspaper preferred a public subscription to its own payment of the bills because of the sympathy and friendship which would thus be created.[35]

Despite all evidences of union helpfulness and all union denials of guilt, the *Times* was not shaken from its belief that organized labor was responsible for the explosion. Joseph Phillis, a union printer, believed that Otis would have given half his fortune to have proved that the local Typographical Union was implicated.[36] Unable to do this, Otis made general charges that organized labor had instigated the crime. His utmost concession in reference to local labor was embodied in an editorial statement: "The plot may never have been discussed at a general meeting of trade unionists in this city."[37] Other events occurring both before and after the *Times* explosion strengthened Otis' contention of labor's guilt, and at the same time weakened the gas theory.

During the summer and fall of 1910 the industrial situation in Los Angeles was tense. The city was frequently the resort of San Francisco labor leaders, locally regarded as possessing a high potential for violence; major strikes were under way with no sign of a speedy end; arrests under the antipicketing ordinance were common; and there were occasional encounters between strikers and police. Although labor claimed that deliberate police efforts to incite pickets to violence had failed, there was still an anxious feeling in the community that inflamed tempers on both sides could easily enlarge minor disturbances into serious riots or desperate acts of violence.[38]

It was small wonder, in an atmosphere so clouded by suspicion and fear, that the discovery of several sticks of dynamite near the Alexandria Hotel annex caused an emotional eruption of some magnitude. At 10:30 on the evening of September 1, 1910, a hotel employee saw an intoxicated man drop a small package in a gutter near the entrance, and immediately notified the police. Upon finding that the contents were dynamite, the police jumped to the conclusion that unionists had plotted the destruction of the annex since it was being constructed by nonunion labor. Albert Kennedy, who identified himself as a former member of the miners' union and as the owner of the dynamite, was arrested. He was, however, released the following day when he satisfied the police that he planned to use the explosive for legitimate purposes on his ranch and that it had been dropped near the Alexandria as a practical joke by a friend.[39] The incident would doubtless have been forgotten had it not been for subsequent events and for the *Times'* unwillingness to let the matter drop. After the major explosion on October 1, the newspaper reminded its readers that Kennedy's story "was not more logical than the theory that he had carried it [the dynamite] to the building for a purpose and attempted to rid himself of it when he found he had arrived at an inopportune time."[40]

A more serious and prolonged case grew out of the finding of dynamite near the Hall of Records, then in process of construction by the antiunion Llewellyn Iron Works. On the evening of September 8, the police were alerted by a phone call from an unidentified union man. His report of a plot to blow up the Hall of Records caused them to set a guard on the building and to scrutinize all loiterers in the vicinity. At about midnight a policeman spotted H. B. Connors, a striking iron worker, near the building and began to question him. Connors struck the officer and then tried to run away, but was apprehended and charged with drunkenness. At daybreak on September 9 the police found two sticks of dynamite with fuses attached on the route of Connors' flight, and accordingly booked him on suspicion of attempting to blow up the Hall of Records. Two men seen near the building at the time of Connors' apprehension had escaped, but A. B. Maple, another iron worker arrested on the evening of the 9th on a vagrancy charge, was believed to be one of them and was accordingly held as a suspect in the dynamite attempt. George Gunrey, speaking for the local Metal Trades Council, said that the unions had had no part in the attempted outrage and would coöperate with the authorities to preserve order and to find those who were really guilty. After a thorough police investigation failed to connect Connors and Maple with the dynamite found near the Hall of Records, the charges against them were dropped.[41]

The authorities, however, did not relinquish their conviction that Connors had guilty knowledge of a union conspiracy against the *Times* and its allies in the Los Angeles industrial warfare. In May, 1911, in another effort to clear up the Hall of Records case and elicit information about the conspiracy, they arrested Connors and Maple, together with F. Ira Bender, president of Los Angeles Local No. 282 of the International Brotherhood of Blacksmiths. These three were later indicted by a grand jury for complicity in the dynamiting attempt at the Hall of Records. Los Angeles unions, consistent in their belief that the accused were innocent, raised money to employ Job Harriman and several other lawyers as defense counsel. In Connors' trial, beginning early in January, 1912, the prosecution tried to prove the existence of a Labor Temple conspiracy to dynamite both the Hotel Alexandria annex and the Hall of Records, but the jury was unable to agree, standing ten to two for acquittal. In February the cases against Bender and Maple were dismissed for lack of evidence, and Connors' trial was reset for April. But failure to unearth new evidence caused the prosecution to move for dismissal, and Connors was released without standing trial a second time. L. W. Butler, secretary of the Central Labor Council at the time, insisted that there had never been a plot to blow up the Hall of Records, though he did admit that certain hotheads in the local union movement occasionally had to be curbed. Union officials suspected that some of these advocates of violence were *agents provocateurs* planted by the M and M, but they could adduce no proof.[42]

Because of the Alexandria Hotel and the Hall of Records incidents, dynamite was much in people's minds on October 1, 1910, when the

Times explosion occurred. Attributing the disaster to union agitators was perhaps a natural reaction for a community whose indoctrination with open-shop principles had been a calculated policy over the years. When, on the same day, bombs were found at the homes of the two men who had done most to establish industrial freedom in Los Angeles, organized labor was a logical suspect. As the *Times* said, "There could be no further doubt where the finger of guilt should point when the tools of anarchists were found at the home of Gen. Harrison Gray Otis, and at the residence of F. J. Zeehandelaar, secretary of the Merchants and Manufacturers Association."[43]

Shortly before 1 P.M. on October 1, a box containing fifteen sticks of dynamite attached by electric wires to an alarm clock, set to go off at one o'clock, was found beneath a window at Zeehandelaar's home. The bomb failed to explode because the alarm had been wound too tightly and the clock had stopped. At 1:45 P.M. a caretaker at Otis' home, inspecting the grounds after hearing of the Zeehandelaar bomb, discovered a suspicious-looking suitcase directly outside Otis' own apartments. The police, hastily summoned, were examining the suitcase when they heard the ticking of a clock inside. They barely managed to escape injury when the bomb exploded a few seconds later. It had been set to go off shortly after 2 P.M., at a time when Otis was expected to arrive home from Mexico. Michael Eagen, said to have been an anarchist who had advocated the use of violence in labor disputes, was arrested in the vicinity, but was released two days later for lack of evidence.[44] Because of the overwhelming disaster at the *Times* building, neither labor nor its accusers attached great significance to these two bombs, though the *Times* said that they reduced the gas theory to an absurdity[45] and the *Citizen* suggested that "they were placed there by agents of those who are eager to make the *Times* catastrophe appear to have been the work of the labor unions."[46]

The events of October 1 did nothing to abate the tenseness of Los Angeles. Industrial firms took precautionary measures, such as increasing the number of guards on night duty; the County Board of Supervisors suspended until December 1 the law permitting private citizens to transport and store explosives; and the Chamber of Commerce, the M and M, and a mass meeting of citizens petitioned the City Council to enlarge the police force by two hundred men. Their plea pointed out that unusual demands on the police deprived residential districts of adequate protection and severely overworked the present force, many of whose members were on duty from twelve to fifteen hours a day. The City Council made provision for employment of an additional hundred officers and men.[47]

The prosecution of a legal case against three local unionists, Charles F. Stevens and Claude Mars of the iron workers' union and Cyrus F. Grow, business agent of Local No. 311 of the International Association of Machinists, indicated a panicky feeling after the *Times* explosion. Stevens and Mars had been arrested on September 24 on a charge of assault with intent to murder Edward Hoffman, a nonunion worker attacked and beaten by four assailants on September 19. Grow was arrested on September 29 on the same charge, but was released on bail. On the day of the *Times* explosion he was again picked up on the original charge and as a suspect in the bombing; an effort to have him released on a writ of habeas corpus failed, and he was held for questioning until October 8. At the trials in the winter of 1910–1911, Stevens was found guilty of assault with intent to murder and sentenced to two years in San Quentin, while Mars and Grow, convicted of simple assault, went to the county jail for terms of ninety days. Spokesmen for organized labor contended that the three men had been subjected to unusually harsh treatment when maximum sentences were imposed, since Hoffman's injuries were slight, identification of the accused was open to question, and good alibis had been established.[48]

As week after week followed the *Times* disaster without further dynamite alarms, the uneasiness of the community gradually subsided. Then, at 1:55 A.M. on Christmas Day of 1910, an explosion heard as far away as fourteen miles partially wrecked the plant of the Llewellyn Iron Works, causing $25,000 damage and inflicting minor injuries on one of the five night watchmen. Llewellyn and other iron works immediately employed additional guards, who were sworn in as special police officers and armed; the Chamber of Commerce and the M and M proffered financial assistance to the city for investigation of the crime; citizens talked of forming a vigilance committee; and the usual charges of complicity were lodged against organized labor, since Llewellyn was notoriously antiunion in its policies and practices. Unionists again denied their guilt, but this time even the previously tolerant *Record* evinced a suspicious attitude toward organized labor.[49] The *Graphic,* however, described the community as unconvinced that the explosions at the *Times* and at Llewellyn were related.[50] Nevertheless, investigation of the Llewellyn explosion merged into the *Times* investigation which, by this time, was well under way.

The first consideration in investigating the *Times* explosion was determination of its cause. Both the *Times* and the civic authorities were quick to establish the premise that the explosion was deliberate, not accidental. At 3 A.M. on October 1, after only two brief hours had elapsed, the chief of police stated flatly: "That the building was wrecked by dynamite seems certain from all my men can learn."[51] With every issue of the *Times* talking "dynamite" and "union responsibility," the climate of opinion leaned toward the dynamite rather than the gas theory postulated by organized labor. An investigatory committee of experts in the fields of mining, engineering, chemistry, and high explosives was appointed by Mayor Alexander on October 1. On October 8, it reported that detonation of nitroglycerin or a product of nitroglycerin, placed in a passageway on the street floor, had caused the destruction of the *Times* building.[52] This was enough for the newspaper management, which declared that even if the perpetrators, "lashed into a frenzy of bitter hatred by the vicious utterances of designing, unscrupulous union leaders," were never caught, the tragedy would be a blight on organized labor until the end of time.[53] The report of the coroner's jury, submitted much later, established incineration as the cause of death, and agreed with the mayor's committee in imputing the fire to a dynamite explosion.[54]

On October 4, before the mayor's committee had concluded its investigation, the California State Federation of Labor, in annual convention in Los Angeles, appointed its own committee to inquire into the disaster. Although frustrated in efforts to work with the mayor's committee and to gain admission to the scene of the explosion, the labor committee spent three weeks in an exhaustive inquiry, questioning witnesses, inspecting the wrecked building from an adjacent property, and utilizing every possible method of ascertaining the truth. It reported on October 26 that the explosion had been caused by gas; that Otis, though perfectly aware of this, was exploiting the dynamite theory in order to escape the consequences of negligence and to further his antiunion campaign; and that various rewards offered for the apprehension of the guilty were intended to fasten the blame on unions and to tempt unscrupulous detectives to fabricate a case against organized labor.[55]

Sizable rewards were posted immediately after the *Times* explosion. On October 1 the City Council appropriated $25,000 for the mayor's discretionary use in discovering the perpetrators of the crime. Of this amount Mayor Alexander designated $2,500 as a reward for information leading to the arrest and conviction of the guilty. Within the next two days, however, the reward was substantially increased, as the mayor first raised it to $10,000, and then to $10,000 for each person convicted of complicity in the crime. On October 3 the Board of Supervisors offered a reward of $5,000 for each person so convicted, and authorized an unusually large expense account for the use of John D. Fredericks,

District Attorney of Los Angeles County, in tracking down the criminals. At a special session of the State Legislature, called on October 3 for reasons other than the *Times* explosion, the Assembly voted $10,000 from its contingent fund as a reward for the apprehension and conviction of the criminals. The Merchants' and Manufacturers' Association of Los Angeles announced a reward of $15,000, which was gradually increased to $50,000 by personal subscriptions of businessmen. On the labor side, the California State Building Trades Council offered $5,000 and the General Campaign Strike Committee $2,500 for apprehension of the guilty.[56]

These rewards added an extra stimulus to the nationwide hunt for the perpetrators of the crime. Three agencies conducted simultaneous investigations, sometimes pooling their knowledge, sometimes working independently. District Attorney Fredericks delegated the official police inquiry to his chief of detectives, Samuel L. Browne; all information uncovered by regular city police, in Los Angeles and elsewhere, was channeled to Browne. The Merchants' and Manufacturers' Association, intent on defense of the open shop, decided to put a special investigator in the field. For this purpose it chose Earl Rogers, the lawyer who had represented the M and M in formulating the antipicketing ordinance earlier in the year, and provided him with a staff of assistants. Rogers and Detective Browne collaborated closely in their search for the guilty. The third agency concerned in the hunt was the Los Angeles city government, headed by Mayor Alexander, who feared that failure to uncover the criminals would discredit his administration. The mayor appointed as special investigator William J. Burns, head of a famous detective agency, who at the time of the disaster was on his way to Los Angeles for the convention of the American Bankers' Association. Neither the *Times* nor the M and M approved the choice of Burns, who had recently opposed Rogers in the San Francisco graft investigations. Burns, though not happy at the prospect of association with his erstwhile opponent, finally yielded to Alexander's pleading and agreed to take the case on the understanding that his activities and discoveries be kept secret.[57]

Burns' insistence on working under cover gave rise to much confusion and acrimony over his role. The *Times,* openly applauding Rogers, tended to belittle the contribution of Burns. Day-to-day reports of progress toward identification and apprehension of the guilty gave no indication of collaboration between the two special investigators, though it was clearly specified that Rogers enjoyed the full confidence of police officials. These daily accounts, indeed, suggested that the major discoveries in unraveling the case were directly attributable either to the regular police or to the M and M investigator. However, Burns, in his own story of the manhunt, emphasized that he, not Rogers, outlined the course of the investigation. Burns also complained that he was "somewhat hampered with the endeavors of the Los Angeles local investigators, but managed to keep in the background while the newspaper men followed them and were given interviews."[58] It is not surprising that an uninformed public misunderstood the part played by Burns.

Burns quite naturally wanted his agency to be credited with solution of the mystery. As it happened, he was in an extraordinarily good position at the start of the investigation to make accurate predictions of the probable identity of the guilty, and he did in fact acquaint Mayor Alexander with his suspicions. An assignment recently handled by the Burns agency in another section of the country enabled the detective to relate the *Times* bombing to a series of dynamitings of nonunion plants, construction jobs, and materials which had occurred throughout the country during the past five years. This destruction of property, Burns believed, could be traced to the International Association of Bridge and Structural Iron Workers. The presumption gave Burns an initial advantage not shared by police investigators, for, according to the *Times,* it was not until October 9 that they connected the local disaster with the outrages Burns believed attributable to the iron workers' union. This tardy realization suggests that Burns had been careful to reveal no pertinent information to Rogers.[59]

The International Association of Bridge and Structural Iron Workers was, in 1910, a comparatively new union in a relatively young industry. Organized in 1896 by six locals, it had lacked cohesion until a firmer national organization had been effected at the turn of the century. Then the BSIW, whose members earned their livelihood through hard, dangerous, and poorly paid work, adopted an aggressive policy. In 1902, when its membership had risen to ten thousand, the union called a general strike against the American Bridge Company, a subsidiary of the United States Steel Corporation. As a result, the company entered into a union-shop agreement to run from May 1, 1903, to January 1, 1905. This agreement was later accepted by the other members of the National Association of Manufacturers and Erectors of Structural Steel and Iron Work, which had been organized in March, 1903, to deal specifically with labor problems.[60]

Although the contract was not renewed on a national basis in 1905, the union maintained satisfactory relations with many employers. In

July, 1905, however, the American Bridge Company refused to hire union members, and the BSIW called another strike against it. A few months later, in September, the union elected Frank M. Ryan to succeed Frank Buchanan as president, and chose John J. McNamara as secretary-treasurer. This change in leadership had a marked effect on subsequent union activities, for Buchanan had always exhausted the possibilities of negotiation before consenting to strikes, whereas Ryan, with the support of McNamara, favored a more militant policy. Early in 1906, when the union extended the strike against the American Bridge Company to other firms, the employers' organization, changing its name to the National Erectors' Association, took a strong open-shop stand. Under the belligerent leadership of the American Bridge Company, the National Erectors' Association, controlling the major portion of the industry, succeeded in establishing the open shop in all large cities except Chicago and San Francisco.[61]

In retaliation, the union turned to dynamite. During the five years from 1906 to 1911 eighty-seven bombs were exploded in various parts of the United States, causing property damage amounting to millions of dollars but involving no loss of life. The dynamiting program was directed against structures on which nonunion labor was employed or in which materials made by nonunion labor were used. Operations were directed by John J. McNamara from the union's Indianapolis headquarters. Given discretionary use of a monthly appropriation averaging $1,000, earmarked for "organization purposes," McNamara decided where and when to strike, provided the high explosives, and commissioned his underlings to do the jobs. Two of the men most frequently employed by McNamara were his brother, James B. McNamara, and Ortie McManigal, who was a member of the union.[62]

Although the public certainly failed to link this reign of terror to the BSIW, the extent of knowledge within the union and the National Erectors' Association is debatable. Walter Drew, attorney for the employers' organization, was trying to combat the dynamite campaign, but kept his activities secret. Several commentators have suggested that many of the union's members must have been aware of what their officers were doing, and that they kept reëlecting McNamara as secretary precisely because he believed in and was willing to use dynamite.[63]

A more pertinent question was just how much William J. Burns knew about the dynamite conspiracy on October 2, 1910, when he agreed to accept Mayor Alexander's commission to investigate the *Times* explosion. In the summer of 1910 the McClintic-Marshall Construction Company of Pittsburgh, Pennsylvania, had called upon the Chicago office of the Burns agency to investigate the dynamiting of a railroad bridge at Indiana Harbor, Indiana, which the company had built. Although failing to reach a solution, the operative assigned to the case reported to Burns that the construction company was open shop. Seizing upon this as a clue, Burns turned his attention to the International Association of Bridge and Structural Iron Workers. Upon further inquiry, he formulated his first tentative theory that the Indiana Harbor explosion was one of a series engineered by the union. Thereupon he sought permission from McClintic-Marshall to reopen the investigation. This was refused, even though Burns had impressed the company with his initiative and sagacity.[64]

Several months later, on September 4, two explosions occurred simultaneously at Peoria, Illinois. One of these blew up the iron works of Lucas & Sons; the other destroyed a pile of McClintic-Marshall steel girders awaiting shipment in a freight yard. McClintic-Marshall immediately summoned Burns to investigate. The detective discovered that H. S. Hockin, organizer for the BSIW, and John J. McNamara had visited the Lucas company a few days previously to urge institution of the closed shop. Moreover, McClintic-Marshall had been secretly notified that the explosion would take place and had warned Lucas & Sons, but the advice went unheeded. Burns became convinced that his theory about the BSIW was correct. One of the bombs placed under the girders had failed to explode, and Burns was thus able to ascertain the kind of dynamite used and the method of construction employed. Starting with these clues, he discovered that a man giving his name as J. W. McGraw had purchased the dynamite. Armed with a description of McGraw, Burns secured a tracing of his signature at a hotel in Muncie, Indiana, and followed his trail to the scene of the explosions.[65]

Before the end of September, 1910, Burns had a conference with organizer Hockin of the BSIW. Burns had learned from McClintic-Marshall that Hockin, who had been furnishing the company with inside information about the union, wanted to see him. Although nervous and reticent during the interview, Hockin told Burns that he had turned stool pigeon because he believed that McNamara's policy of violence could bring only disaster to organized labor. Hockin also informed Burns that James B. McNamara and Ortie McManigal were the men who actually planted the dynamite, but he apparently did not at that time identify McGraw. Nevertheless, Burns, well supplied with information from Hockin and from the Peoria investigation, was primed for the search for evidence that would expose all the ramifications of the dynamite conspiracy, from the union higher-ups to the men sent out to execute their orders.[66]

Rapid progress was made in the tripartite investigation of the *Times* disaster by Detective Samuel Browne of the district attorney's office, Earl Rogers for the M and M, and William Burns for the mayor of Los Angeles. Except for Burns' private knowledge that the unexploded bombs found at Zeehandelaar's home in Los Angeles and under the girders in Peoria were identical, most of the information turned up was shared by all parties. The clue which served as the starting point of the investigation was the unusually strong 80 per cent dynamite found in the unexploded Zeehandelaar bomb. It was stamped with the name of the Giant Powder Works, a DuPont subsidiary located in Contra Costa County across the bay from San Francisco, and had been made to special order. This made identification of the purchasers simple, and within three weeks the investigators had discovered the salient facts about them. Three men giving their names as J. B. Bryce, J. B. Leonard, and William Morris had purchased five hundred pounds of dynamite, transported it across the bay to a rented house in San Francisco, and removed fifty pounds for the destruction of the *Times* building and the homes of Otis and Zeehandelaar. With complete descriptions supplied by various witnesses, the movements of the three men had been traced up to the time of the explosion; after that the trail had been lost. J. B. Leonard was identified as Matthew A. Schmidt, a former member of the Chicago woodworkers' union who had been living in the San Francisco area for some time and had become acquainted with Olaf Tveitmoe and other northern labor leaders. William Morris, who had also used the alias William Capp, was discovered to be David Kaplan, a Russian who had fled his native country fifteen years previously and had lived in San Francisco for the past seven years. Both Schmidt and Kaplan had the reputation of being anarchists, and had at one time lived in an anarchist settlement known as Home Colony, located about twenty miles from Tacoma, Washington. At this stage little was known about the third man, J. B. Bryce, except that he had come from Chicago to San Francisco several months prior to the *Times* bombing and had soon thereafter got in touch with Schmidt. Bryce and Schmidt, the latter using the alias F. A. Perry, had stayed in a Los Angeles hotel from September 29 to October 2. It was believed that they returned to San Francisco for shelter after the bombing and fled the northern city at their earliest opportunity. Bryce had last been heard of on October 2, Schmidt on October 7, and Kaplan, who had apparently not accompanied the other two to Los Angeles, had left San Francisco on October 9.[67]

Much of the investigation had centered in San Francisco, where the three conspirators had made their preparations for the Los Angeles explosion. This gave rise to the supposition that northern labor leaders, particularly Tveitmoe and Anton Johannsen, were implicated in the plot. A secret visit of Tveitmoe, accompanied by three labor lawyers, to Los Angeles during September, 1910, was another suspicious circumstance. When questioned by the police, however, Tveitmoe denied all knowledge of the Los Angeles plot. He admitted having met both Schmidt and Kaplan through Johannsen, but said he did not know Bryce at all and had never heard of him. Bryce, apparently the most important figure in the conspiracy, was at the same time the most mysterious. He was not a San Franciscan, nobody seemed to know anything about him, and he had vanished without leaving a trace. Burns knew from descriptions in his possession that Bryce was not J. W. McGraw of the Peoria bombings, and that McGraw had apparently had nothing to do with the Los Angeles episode. The formidable task of identifying Bryce and of apprehending the conspirators, all three of whom were at large, was still ahead of the investigators. On October 19, Detective Samuel Browne and Earl Rogers left San Francisco to arrange for the empaneling of a grand jury in Los Angeles, and Burns, commissioning his son Raymond to start the search for Bryce, left for Tacoma to begin the hunt for Schmidt and Kaplan.[68] His secret departure caused the *Times* to make a very inaccurate observation: "Burns . . . can now be considered to have been gently, but firmly eliminated from the case."[69]

A special grand jury of nineteen members, charged with ascertaining the cause of the *Times* disaster and returning indictments against identifiable culprits, commenced its deliberations on October 27, 1910. Although proceedings were secret, it was learned that 174 witnesses, including a considerable number from San Francisco, were subpoenaed. Tveitmoe and Johannsen were among those who testified. Because of his investigations in San Francisco and his preliminary talks with witnesses, Earl Rogers was appointed as special prosecutor before the grand jury. The granting of official status to a representative of an organization opposed to unionism stirred the anger of organized labor into active protest, but the district attorney, though promising to extend the same privilege to Job Harriman, did not give the labor lawyer the opportunity of appearing before the grand jury. On January 5, 1911, after twenty-five days of investigation, the grand jury returned twenty-three indictments in the *Times* case. In the absence of an official statement, newspapers conjectured that there were twenty-one triple indictments against J. B. Bryce, Matthew Schmidt, and David Kaplan for the murder of the victims of the *Times* explosion (the correction to twenty had not yet been made), and two triple indictments against the same persons for placing dynamite at the homes of Otis and Zeehande- laar. Within a few days the district attorney's office distributed fifty thousand posters describing Bryce, Schmidt, and Kaplan to all chiefs of police, sheriffs, and postmasters in the United States. The circular announced a reward of $25,000, including $15,000 from the Board of Supervisors and $10,000 from the mayor, for apprehension of the three men. The grand jury proceeded with other investigations, and at the end of its deliberations in October, 1911, returned three indictments for the attempted bombing of the Hall of Records and two for the Llewellyn explosion.[70]

Toward the end of January Earl Rogers withdrew as investigating attorney for the Merchants' and Manufacturers' Association because, it was rumored, Zeehandelaar objected to his expenditures from the fund subscribed by Los Angeles businessmen. The two men had never been overly friendly, and it is possible that Zeehandelaar compared the results of Rogers' efforts in the *Times* case disadvantageously with those of Burns, who was known to be spreading his operatives over a wide area in an intensive hunt for the three men presumed guilty of the crime.[71]

Burns was indeed very busy during the weeks that the grand jury was in session, though his operations were still held secret. Only Mayor Alexander, to whom a Burns employee made regular reports, was ap- prised of the agency's activities. Burns, with several of his operatives, had left San Francisco on October 19 and proceeded to Tacoma for investigation of the anarchist settlement. He hoped to catch Schmidt and Kaplan and extract from them a confession which would lay bare the activities of all those involved in the dynamite conspiracy, for Burns was certain that prominent labor officials, particularly in the Inter- national Association of Bridge and Structural Iron Workers, were be- hind the destructive campaign against open-shop firms. His conviction was strengthened when he discovered that Bryce had been in Seattle, where one of the bombings had occurred, and had there exhibited dynamite bought in Portland, Indiana, the very place where McGraw had purchased the explosives for the Peoria job. Burns kept operatives constantly on duty trailing high officials of the BSIW in Indianapolis.[72]

The Tacoma investigation proved a disappointment. Several Burns detectives, disguised as engineers and surveyors, thoroughly explored the Home Colony, talking to residents and acquainting themselves with the manner of life. Burns himself, though occasionally visiting the colony, depended on daily reports from his men. He learned many details about Schmidt and Kaplan, both of whom had earlier lived in the community, but efforts to pick up their trail proved fruitless. Burns encountered a further annoyance at this time in the cessation of payments from Mayor Alexander. In faithfully observing the detective's request to reveal nothing about his movements, the mayor had even refused to turn Burns' reports over to the grand jury. The city authorities accordingly ordered Alexander to withhold compensation until the detective produced results. Although the manhunt was very expensive, Burns determined to finance it with his own or borrowed funds because he was certain that he would in the end overtake the wanted criminals. He did not succeed at the time in finding Schmidt and Kaplan, but other lines of investigation began to look promising.[73]

During the unsuccessful Tacoma inquiry, detectives from the Burns agency had been busily at work in Los Angeles, San Francisco, Chicago, and Indianapolis, concentrating on the search for J. B. Bryce and trying to pick up leads that would link the *Times* explosion to the iron workers' union. A real break came when a man answering the description of J. W. McGraw, connected with the Peoria bombings, was seen talking to John J. McNamara. Burns was thus able to spot McGraw and to have him shadowed day and night thereafter. McGraw finally was followed to his home in Chicago and identified as Ortie McManigal, already known by Burns to be one of the outside men in the dynamite conspiracy.[74]

In a few weeks Burns was to realize the full impact of the McManigal identification. On November 5, 1910, under constant surveillance, McManigal left Chicago to meet one Frank Sullivan at Kenosha, Wisconsin. From there the two men went into the Wisconsin woods on a hunting trip, establishing a camp near Conover. Burns operatives immediately set up headquarters at Conover, where they became friendly with local inhabitants, frequented places where gossip flowed freely, and eventually struck up acquaintance with McManigal and Sullivan. Sullivan, who was drinking heavily, was prone to talk when under the influence of liquor, and the Burns men observed that McManigal acted as a watchdog to keep Sullivan from talking too much. Finally, the detectives succeeded in getting two snapshots of Sullivan and samples of his handwriting, and these, with descriptions of the man, enabled Burns to identify him as the mysterious J. B. Bryce involved in the Los Angeles bombing. Burns could then have had McManigal and Bryce arrested, but he held off, hoping they would lead him to the mastermind behind the dynamitings.[75]

On December 3, McManigal left Wisconsin for his Chicago home, and Bryce, lacking companionship, began to show signs of nervousness and fear. A few days later he suddenly left Conover for Chicago, where he talked briefly with McManigal, and then proceeded to Indianapolis. There he stayed over night and presumably contacted union head-quarters by telephone. The next day he went to Cumminsville, a Cincinnati suburb, where he met a third man. At this point three lines of inquiry merged. The man whom Bryce met was John J. McNamara, who had been shadowed from Indianapolis. The place of their meeting was the home of Mrs. Mary T. McNamara and her son James, brother of John and one of his outside men in the dynamite conspiracy. The McNamara home in Cumminsville had been under surveillance for some time by a Burns operative. Burns thus took the final step in identifying Bryce, who was none other than James B. McNamara. Although Burns had ample evidence to connect both McManigal and James McNamara with the dynamite plot, he still had nothing definite against John McNamara. Nor did he have evidence against Frank Ryan, H. S. Hockin, Olaf Tveitmoe, or any other labor leaders whose implication he suspected. He therefore stayed his hand, hoping by continued patient and thorough inquiry to leave no aspect of the conspiracy unsolved. From the time of the brothers' meeting early in December, 1910, Burns had his operatives trail the various suspects night and day.[76]

The McNamaras and McManigal were kept under the most careful watch, for Burns hoped to surprise John McNamara in the act of participating in a dynamite scheme. Burns found out not only all the details about the personal lives of his suspects, but also where the explosives were stored, how the bombs were made and set off, how frequently Ryan and John McNamara held conferences, and much other related information. He did not, however, catch McNamara in the kind of overt act which would have simplified his arrest. Moreover, Burns was still having money troubles, as no payments had come from Los Angeles since November, 1910. He had already invested $14,000, including $10,000 of borrowed money, in order to continue the investigation. Burns believed that to implicate John McNamara, a lawyer and high union official, he would have to extract a confession from one of the suspects. He therefore decided, in April, 1911, after some six months of one of the most exciting and dramatic manhunts in American history, to close the net on McManigal and James McNamara in the hope of obtaining the needed confession from McManigal.[77]

After this decision, Burns merely had to wait until the two men set off on another dynamiting job. He did not have long to wait. McManigal and McNamara met in Toledo on April 11, 1911, spent the night there, and together went to Detroit on the morning of the 12th. From information received, Burns suspected that their objective was destruction of the new $2,000,000 railroad station at Detroit. With police officers from both Detroit and Chicago, Burns' son Raymond arrested McManigal and McNamara under their assumed names ten minutes after they had checked into the Oxford Hotel, carrying heavy suitcases. Their luggage was examined by the police and found to contain six clock batteries like those used in the unexploded bombs in Peoria and Los Angeles, as well as three guns, one equipped with a silencer. The prisoners, on being told they were wanted for a recent bank robbery in Chicago, for which they had alibis, waived extradition and voluntarily accompanied the police to Chicago. On the train, however, McNamara began to suspect that he had been arrested in connection with the *Times* explosion. In desperation he attempted to bribe his captors into letting him and his fellow prisoner escape. He raised his initial offer of $5,000 to $30,000 before acknowledging defeat, and finally remarked that if the detectives would not take the money it would go to Clarence Darrow. This was the first indication that the famous criminal lawyer would be considered as defense counsel if and when such were needed. Upon arrival at their destination, the prisoners were taken to the home of Chicago Police Sergeant William H. Reed for questioning. This maneuver was part of Burns' plan to keep the arrests secret until he could extract a confession from McManigal and take John McNamara into custody.[78]

William Burns took upon himself the task of getting a confession from McManigal at the Reed home in Chicago. Told by McNamara that it was now every man for himself, McManigal was in a receptive mood for a conversation with Burns. On the afternoon of April 13, Burns pointed out to McManigal that he could hardly expect the same support from the union that his fellow prisoner (the brother of a top official) would get; that the detectives knew all about his life and his criminal activities; that under the conspiracy laws McManigal was as guilty of the *Times* explosion as the two McNamaras; and that his rights under the law entitled him to counsel, but that Burns would make no efforts in his behalf if he engaged such a lawyer, though he could not promise him immunity. Leaving the prisoner to ponder these circumstances, Burns withdrew to his Chicago headquarters to await the announcement that McManigal was ready to talk. He delayed until McManigal had called him four times, and then returned to the Reed home. In the presence of Burns, a member of the Chicago police force, and a police stenographer, McManigal dictated and signed his confession. Beginning about midnight of April 13 and continuing until morning, he gave a complete and detailed account of the bombings. His statements, revealing the inner workings of the dynamite conspiracy, implicated John McNamara, Frank Ryan, H. S. Hockin, and other union leaders in a deliberately planned war against the National Erectors' Association.[79]

McManigal's story of the *Times* bombing confirmed the discoveries made by Burns in his investigations, and added other details. In June, 1910, John McNamara instructed his brother to go to the west coast and report to E. A. Clancy, business agent of the iron workers' local in San Francisco and vice-president of the national union. When James McNamara arrived in San Francisco in July, Clancy introduced him to Matthew Schmidt and David Kaplan and gave the three men orders for the Los Angeles job. Olaf Tveitmoe also helped with the preliminaries, according to McManigal. McNamara was the one who actually placed the bombs in Los Angeles, after which he immediately left for San Francisco where he remained in hiding for four days. He was then sheltered by friends and relatives in various places until McManigal took him into the Wisconsin woods for the hunting trip.[80]

Included also in McManigal's confession was an account of the Llewellyn Iron Works bombing. On December 9, 1910, John McNamara, having promised the "coast bunch" a Christmas present, ordered McManigal to blow up the *Times* auxiliary plant, Llewellyn's and Baker's iron works, the Hall of Records, and the Alexandria Hotel annex on Christmas Day. McManigal arrived in Los Angeles on December 15, registered as T. F. McKee at the Rosslyn Hotel, cached his explosives in the Los Angeles River bed, and proceeded to inspect the scene. He found the *Times* auxiliary plant and the Baker works so well guarded and lighted that he was afraid to attempt their destruction, and, curiously, could not locate either the Hall of Records or the Alexandria Hotel. He placed a bomb against an outside wall of the Llewellyn plant, set it to explode early on Christmas morning, and departed for San Francisco. Several days later he contacted Clancy, who had known in advance of McManigal's assignment in Los Angeles, and then left for Chicago. On January 15, 1911, John McNamara summoned him to Indianapolis and reprimanded him because there had been only one explosion in Los Angeles instead of the five which had been ordered.[81]

With McManigal's confession, Burns was ready to proceed against John McNamara. The necessary papers for extradition of the three men to California arrived at Indianapolis on April 21, and were signed by the Governor of Indiana. On the 22nd, Burns, accompanied by representatives of the Indianapolis police and armed with a search warrant and a warrant for McNamara's arrest, walked in on a meeting of the executive board of the iron workers' union. McNamara, charged with murder in connection with the *Times* bombing and with implication in the Llewellyn bombing, was immediately rushed to police court, where he was arraigned before Judge James A. Collins. The judge, denying McNamara's request for counsel, granted the requisition for extradition. The prisoner was then hustled into an automobile and within half an hour of his apprehension was on his way out of Indianapolis in the custody of Burns operatives and a police officer representing the state of California. It was obviously Burns' design to get McNamara out of sight before his friends could muster their resources to fight the extradition. On the afternoon of April 22, James McNamara and McManigal had been turned over to two Los Angeles police officers, who took them to Joliet, Illinois. That night the party boarded a special car on a Santa Fe train bound for Los Angeles. John McNamara was placed on the same train at Dodge City, Kansas, and the three prisoners arrived in Los Angeles on April 26 and were lodged in the county jail.[82]

News of the arrests did not break until after John McNamara was apprehended. Then organized labor the country over raised a great outcry against the methods used to arrest a high union official and convey him out of the state. The entire proceeding, unionists claimed, smacked of kidnaping: the arraignment in a police court, which did not have jurisdiction in extradition cases; the refusal to allow the prisoner to consult a lawyer; the failure to notify the prosecuting attorney of the court proceedings; the use of extradition proceedings against a man who was not a fugitive from justice; the use of an automobile to convey McNamara out of the state. Voices outside the labor movement joined in the protest against what was at best a dubious method of rushing a prisoner into a state where he had not been at the time of his alleged crime. Although Burns and other parties in the case maintained that all proceedings were entirely legal, an ingredient of doubt lent force to labor's claim that the McNamaras had been "framed." Only the enormity of the offense against human life and property stilled the voice of protest.[83]

Burns' work was not finished when McManigal and the McNamaras were safely locked up in jail. McManigal's confession was the basis for the rest of Burns' job: finding the evidence to support McManigal's statements and to ensure conviction of the accused. His agency immediately renewed its search for Schmidt and Kaplan, who had been implicated in the *Times* bombing by the confession. Burns himself participated in the police search of union headquarters in Indianapolis, which revealed a store of dynamite in the basement of the building. Subsequent investigation located three other places where explosives were kept until needed. One was a barn near Indianapolis, rented by John McNamara; the other two were McManigal's flat in Chicago and his father's home near Tiffin, Ohio. The books of the iron workers' union, seized by the police, contained sufficient data to confirm the story of the dynamite plot.[84]

Burns had done a spectacular job in his investigation of the *Times* bombing and other dynamite atrocities. Even those who, deceived by the secretiveness of his operations, had earlier disparaged his role now acclaimed him a great detective. The *Times,* for example, said that the McNamara case was destined to be the crowning event in Burns' career, and the *California Outlook* called Burns the greatest living American detective, and his capture of the McNamaras a triumph of skill and energy and persistence.[85] And yet Burns had considerable difficulty in collecting remuneration from both the city and county of Los Angeles. By July, 1911, Mayor Alexander had paid him some $13,000, leaving a balance due of $7,700. In August the City Council finally authorized full settlement of Burns' account. As late as 1913, Burns aggrievedly complained that Los Angeles County had paid him only $5,000 of the $15,000 reward offered by the Board of Supervisors. He apparently had overlooked the fact that Schmidt and Kaplan were still at large and felt that his work in apprehending McManigal and the two McNamaras was sufficient to give him a claim on the entire amount.[86]

With the arrest of the McNamaras and McManigal, tension over the "crime of the century" noticeably relaxed. Those who believed that the guilty had been caught anticipated the end of the terrorism of dynamite in industrial warfare. They foresaw only conviction in the trials ahead, and rejoiced that organized labor would have learned the futility of violence in employer-employee relationships. Labor itself, confronted with specific charges against its own members, turned to the problem of defending those whom it considered innocent until proven guilty. For this purpose it chose Clarence Darrow, whose reputation as the foremost criminal lawyer in the United States was based partly on his previous defense of unionists charged with crimes. As Burns had been the central figure in the first part of the McNamara story, so Darrow dominated the scene in the critical period before and during the McNamara trial.

2. THE McNAMARA CASE

The months between the arrests and the opening of the trial in October, 1911, were crowded with preparatory activities by both prosecution and defense for a legal contest which promised to be highly dramatic. The prosecution had the easier task. District Attorney John Fredericks and his assistants had ample financial resources as well as important clues disclosed in the confession of Ortie McManigal, the evidence uncovered in the initial investigations, and the confiscated books and records of the iron workers' union. Oscar Lawler, a former assistant attorney general of the United States and an ex-district attorney of Los Angeles County, also helped to prepare the prosecution's case. Not to be discounted was the enthusiastic assistance of William Burns, who would crown his early achievements in the investigation with great personal glory should the McNamara case end in conviction. It was therefore very much to Burns' advantage to be a willing aid to the prosecution.[87]

Although Burns claimed as early as May, 1911, to have sufficient evidence for conviction, his agency continued its patient digging throughout the summer. Through verification of McManigal's statements and fresh discoveries, Burns was able to tighten the net around John McNamara. Since he suspected that the defense was intimidating and threatening the state's witnesses, he placed reliance chiefly on exhibits, inanimate objects which could not lie or be subjected to cross-examination. Burns was also busy checking the activities of San Francisco labor leaders, trying to find Matthew Schmidt and David Kaplan, seeking to uncover evidence pointing to Samuel Gompers' knowledge of the dynamite conspiracy, and preventing his star witness, McManigal, from retracting his confession. According to Burns, the defense used both McManigal's wife, Emma McManigal, and his uncle, George Behm, in an effort to persuade McManigal to repudiate his statement.[88] Labor people could not believe that McManigal would have confessed voluntarily; Matthew Schmidt claims that Burns extracted the confession only by assuring McManigal that James McNamara had already admitted the guilt of the two dynamiters.[89]

Labor's defense of the McNamaras was predicated on the assumption that the brothers were innocent of any crime. In particular, labor leaders could not accept as true any allegations against John McNamara, whom they regarded as a model citizen and a union official of proven integrity and reliability. His statement shortly after his arrest that he had broken no law, either in word or in deed, strengthened his

supporters' belief that Burns had manufactured the evidence against
the accused. Labor also charged that Burns, with his great show of
protecting state witnesses from harm, was trying to make the case so
spectacular and sensational that the press and the public would find
the defendants guilty long before they appeared in court to face trial.
Labor maintained that in any event the McNamaras and McManigal
were entitled to a fair and impartial trial and that under the constitution they were presumed innocent until proven guilty. The defense
plans included McManigal until he made it clear that he desired no
legal aid. He had, within a few days of his arrival in Los Angeles, repeated his confession to District Attorney Fredericks, and thereafter
remained steadfastly on the side of the prosecution.[90]

The International Association of Bridge and Structural Iron Workers
made the first move toward defense of the McNamara brothers. On
April 24, two days after the arrest of John McNamara, Clarence Darrow
was called to Indianapolis for a conference with officials of the iron
workers' union. Darrow had already achieved fame through defending
Charles H. Moyer, William D. Haywood, and George Pettibone in the
Western Federation of Miners case, and James McNamara had revealed
shortly after his arrest that he had been ordered to get in touch with
Darrow if he needed help. Early consultation with the well-known
criminal lawyer thus came as no surprise, and it was taken for granted
from the start that Darrow would head the counsel for the defense. Yet
Darrow hesitated to accept so serious a responsibility. He was in ill
health and weary of fighting the battle of unionism, however worthy,
against the powerful forces of society. Hence he postponed his decision
and recommended the retention of a younger, more vigorous lawyer.
The BSIW, unwilling to employ a lesser talent, formed a Legal Defense
Committee with seven other national unions in Indianapolis and invited Gompers to a conference on May 10 for the purpose of exploring
the whole problem of the McNamara defense.[91]

Meanwhile, pending Darrow's decision, President Frank Ryan of the
BSIW engaged the services of Job Harriman and of ex-Judge E. M.
Hilton of Pomona who had collaborated with Darrow in the defense
of Moyer, Haywood, and Pettibone. He also sent Leo M. Rappaport,
counsel for the BSIW, to Los Angeles to take interim charge of the Mc-
Namara defense. Hilton and Harriman conferred with the McNamaras
several times, but delayed final defense plans until after arraignment
of the prisoners and after Darrow's decision. With Harriman, Rappaport represented the McNamaras on May 5 when they were arraigned
before Judge Walter Bordwell in Superior Court. Assistant District

Attorney W. J. Ford presented nineteen indictments against the brothers, charging them with the murder of nineteen of the twenty victims of the *Times* bombing, and one indictment against John McNamara for the dynamiting of the Llewellyn plant on December 25, 1910. The judge set June 1 as the date for entering pleas. McManigal, to be charged with the Llewellyn dynamiting, was not arraigned with the McNamaras.[92]

The American Federation of Labor was quick to assume responsibility for the McNamara defense. On May 6, before Gompers conferred with the Indianapolis unions, the Executive Council issued "A Call to Labor" for funds to provide adequate legal defense for the accused. The document expressed the AFL's repugnance to crime and its sorrow over the destruction of life and property, but also emphasized that the McNamaras, faced by the formidable combination of wealth, power, and influence arrayed behind the prosecution, would need funds to ensure a fair trial. The Indianapolis conference on May 10–12, 1911, attended by Gompers, urged the AFL to take over the administration and distribution of defense funds. Gompers approved the plan and submitted it to the Executive Council, which delegated the task to AFL Secretary Frank Morrison.[93]

With plans under way to finance the undertaking, Gompers himself asked Darrow to accept the job of defending the McNamaras. Darrow, though suspecting that the prosecution's case was airtight,[94] finally gave his reluctant consent. He could resist neither the pressure of organized labor nor the promptings of his own conscience. Arriving in Los Angeles on May 25, Darrow immediately engaged the services of two prominent local attorneys in addition to Harriman and Hilton. One of these was LeCompte Davis, a leading trial lawyer and a respected and cultured gentleman; the other was Joseph Scott, an attorney of wide acquaintance and high repute. The community standing and legal ability of Scott and Davis increased the respectability of the McNamara defense in the eyes of many Los Angeles citizens. Darrow also employed ex-Judge Cyrus F. McNutt of Indiana, a lawyer of unusual ability who had displayed marked sympathy for the working class. Darrow then proceeded to establish his headquarters and to organize his staff. The headquarters comprised an entire floor in a large office building, and the existing staff was enlarged to include John Harrington, an experienced investigator for the Chicago City Railway, whom Darrow had brought with him, and Bert Franklin, formerly a deputy sheriff and a deputy United States marshal in Los Angeles. These two men he put in charge of a force of investigators who were to inquire into the con-

nection between the *Times* explosion and the bombings attributed to
the BSIW, prepare evidence for the trial, interview witnesses, and ascertain the religious and political affiliations of prospective jurors. Darrow
and his staff of lawyers visited the McNamaras in jail, worked out a
program for the defense, and familiarized themselves with laws appli-
cable to the case, particularly those relating to conspiracy. Because he
and Scott and Davis were unfamiliar with the testimony before the
grand jury which had drawn the indictments, Darrow obtained a continuance of the time for pleading from June 1 to July 6. Then, with
the investigatory and legal aspects of the defense program provided for,
Darrow returned to Chicago for a few weeks.[95]

Meanwhile, organized labor had commenced its fund-raising activities in behalf of the McNamaras. Before the end of April, the Seattle
Central Labor Council and the San Francisco Building Trades Council
had pledged substantial sums. On May 1, Los Angeles unionists held a
mass meeting at which contributions were solicited, and several weeks
later the Central Labor Council appointed a committee to take charge
of local money-raising. At the national level, the American Federation
of Labor in June organized a permanent McNamara Ways and Means
Committee, including Frank Ryan of the BSIW, Samuel Gompers and
Frank Morrison of the AFL, and the presidents and secretaries of the
Building Trades, Metal Trades, and Union Label Trades Departments
of the AFL. The committee appealed to all national and international
unions, city central bodies, and local and federal unions for a 25 cents
per capita contribution for defense of the McNamaras. The response
was generous from all groups except the American Federation of
Musicians, which passed resolutions condemning lawlessness and censuring the McNamaras. The reason behind this exceptional conduct
was inside information obtained by C. L. Bagley, president of Los
Angeles Local No. 47, from the district attorney's office. Bagley, convinced that the brothers were guilty and that their case was hopeless,
persuaded his national union to refrain from assisting the defense. The
Ways and Means Committee adopted several other money-raising devices. It designed stamps and buttons reading "McNamara Brothers
Not Guilty" for sale to union members, and made a motion picture
telling the story of the arrest and "kidnaping" of John McNamara. The
committee also urged a more earnest and general celebration of Labor
Day, and ordered that the proceeds be turned over to the McNamara
defense fund.[96]

On July 6, 1911, the McNamara brothers made their second appearance in court, this time to enter their pleas. They were represented by

Darrow—who had returned to Los Angeles on June 25—Harriman, Davis, Scott, and McNutt, while District Attorney Fredericks and his assistant Ford appeared for the prosecution. Counsel for the defense filed motions challenging the jurisdiction of the Superior Court in Los Angeles County on the ground that the indictments had not been found in accordance with the Penal Code of California and that the defendants had been taken from their homes in other states without due process of law. After several days of argument on these motions, Judge Bordwell disallowed the pleas of the defense and ruled that his court had jurisdiction. On July 12 the McNamaras pleaded not guilty to all the indictments against them. The prosecution wanted the trial to open on October 1; the defense preferred a December date. Judge Bordwell set October 11 for the trial of John and James McNamara on the charge of murdering the victims of the *Times* bombing.[97]

The prosecution and the defense used the three-month interval between the pleading and the opening of the trial to put the final touches on their cases, while organized labor continued to build up a fund sufficient to meet the heavy expenses. Most of the money came from outside Los Angeles, for local unionists, many of whom were out of work because of the metal trades strike, had strained their resources to the utmost to support the year-old effort to unionize the city. Yet they did their best to aid the McNamara cause: many unions made contributions, the *Citizen* sponsored its own defense fund, the Central Labor Council ordered ten thousand McNamara buttons for local sale, and a Labor Day celebration netted $1,000 for the McNamara defense.[98] Moreover, the officers of the Central Labor Council worked tirelessly in behalf of the defendants, disseminating information and serving as a kind of clearinghouse for all the agitation and work that was in progress. This publicity from the storm center of the McNamara case was a valuable asset to the fund-raising program.[99]

The union drive for funds throughout the state of California received an impetus in September when Gompers toured the west coast, speaking in many cities and urging demonstrations of sympathy for the McNamaras. The AFL president stopped twice in Los Angeles where, accompanied by Darrow, he visited the McNamaras in jail and received fresh assurances of their innocence. Armed with a strengthened belief that the brothers were not guilty, Gompers was able to make his pleas for contributions the more convincing. Early in October, the California State Federation of Labor seconded Gompers' appeal with a suggestion that every union man and woman in the state give one day's wages, and Anton Johannsen, speaking to the Los Angeles Central Labor Council, pleaded for more generous donations. As a result of these renewed requests for money, a state-wide McNamara Defense League was organized by representatives of the State Federation, the State Building Trades Council, and various central bodies in the San Francisco area. Shortly thereafter, Los Angeles unions organized their own defense league to solicit larger contributions and systematize the collection of donations. Both state and local leagues continued in operation throughout the trial.[100]

As the moment approached when the McNamaras would go on trial for their lives, Darrow became increasingly apprehensive. A highly sensitive and emotional man, he had been frequently depressed through the long months of preparation by the fear that his clients would receive the death penalty. He seemed to doubt that his learning and resourcefulness were equal to the task of preventing conviction or even of holding the penalty to a minimum, should the evidence prove the defendants guilty. Although Darrow was a great fighter, he knew only too well the bitter partisanship and intensity of feeling which threatened to obscure the vision and becloud the judgment of ordinarily fairminded people. He knew, moreover, that an almost endless series of trials might lie ahead, since District Attorney Fredericks was determined to try the McNamaras on each of the nineteen murder indictments, if necessary, to obtain a conviction. With the prosecution claiming an abundance of evidence, Darrow felt that the situation was nearly hopeless. His fears for his clients, for the cause of organized labor, and for his own fortitude in meeting the challenge so soon to be presented created a heaviness of spirit that was not to be lightened as the trial proceeded.[101]

The McNamara trial was a *cause célèbre*. Some sixty correspondents were in Los Angeles to report developments to all the leading United States newspapers and news services, as well as to papers in the European capitals of London, Paris, and Berlin. Not only Darrow, but all the players in the drama were keyed to a high pitch of excitement. There were to be ten lawyers appearing in the courtroom for prosecution and defense together, and forty more working behind the scenes. Some six hundred detectives had taken part in preparing the case for its final public stage. Not the least of the reasons why unusual interest attended the McNamara trial was the fact that not only the defendants but the whole of organized labor was to be judged at the bar of public opinion. It was much more than a simple case of murder; social, industrial, and political overtones made the McNamara trial an event of unlimited significance in American labor history.[102]

With the prosecution expecting to call over four hundred witnesses, and the defense more than one hundred, the trial promised to be a long, drawn-out affair. In order to expedite proceedings, Judge Bordwell drew the names of one hundred and twenty-five veniremen for the jury on September 29, more than ten days before the formal opening of the trial. A hint of the enormous difficulties to be experienced in selecting a jury came when two-thirds of this first group were excused for reasons of physical disability or business preoccupation. Only forty were asked to report to court on October 11. At this time, as well as later, many prospective jurors, reluctant to serve for the long period which seemed inevitable, sought to evade the duty.[103]

On the morning of October 11, 1911, in Department 9 of the Superior Court of Los Angeles County, Judge Walter Bordwell opened the McNamara trial. At the outset Darrow moved for a change of judge on the ground that Bordwell was prejudiced against the defendants, but after due consideration the court ruled that the judge was not biased. District Attorney Fredericks, having ascertained that the defense desired separate trials for the brothers, chose James McNamara as the first defendant. By agreement of prosecution and defense, the trial began upon the indictment for the murder of Charles J. Haggerty, foreman of machinists, who was killed near the spot where McNamara allegedly had placed the dynamite. With these preliminaries disposed of, the court proceeded to the task of selecting a jury.[104]

It was soon apparent that days, or even weeks, would be consumed in the process of filling the jury box and providing the two alternate jurors Judge Bordwell required. On the first day of the trial the question of pro- or antiunion prejudice in the minds of prospective jurors was brought to the fore. The defense opposed selection of jurors who might be swayed by antiunion predilections, while the prosecution was equally determined to keep out those who strongly favored organized labor. Other reasons for disqualification of jurors were certainty that the defendant was guilty, unwillingness to convict on circumstantial evidence when the defendant's life was at stake, aversion to capital punishment, and belief that dynamite caused the explosion. The examination by both prosecution and defense to determine the attitudes of veniremen on these questions was a long, wearisome process which occupied most of the time that the court was in session. In addition to excuses for cause, twenty peremptory challenges were allocated to the defense and ten to the prosecution.[105]

On October 25, two weeks after the start of the trial, the first venire was exhausted and only six jurors had been seated. It was not until

November 7 that the jury box was temporarily filled for the first time, after some two hundred talesmen had been examined, and then only three of the twelve survived peremptory challenges. By November 17, when more than four hundred veniremen had been summoned, five permanent jurors had been seated in the box, and the defense had used nine of its peremptory challenges, the prosecution five. At the end of November, eight permanent jurors had been chosen, five hundred and fifty-five veniremen had been summoned and more than five hundred examined, the defense had seven peremptory challenges left and the prosecution five.[106]

As jury selection proceeded thus slowly and tediously, it became more and more obvious that, except for some unexpected occurrence, the McNamara trial would last a long time. Early in November, the *Times* estimated that the giving of testimony in court would begin on December 1, but a week or so later Darrow ventured the opinion that the jury would not be complete until December 15. Accepting this date, Assistant District Attorney Ford guessed that a verdict could not be reached before April 1, 1912. The longer the trial, the heavier would be the expense of defending the McNamaras. Accordingly the AFL convention, meeting late in November, 1911, took measures to increase the defense fund. All paid officials of the labor movement were requested to donate one week's wages, and all delegates to the convention other than paid officials, one day's wages. Gompers broadcast a general appeal for more contributions, contradicting a recent statement by William Burns that labor had already raised $1,000,000. The exaggeration, said Gompers, was a deliberate device on the part of Burns to make unionists think that no more money was needed. The convention sent a message to the McNamaras, informing them that the AFL believed in their innocence and pledging continued moral and financial support, and Gompers reiterated his earlier statement that the whole case was a plot to ruin organized labor by bringing false accusations against union members.[107]

The tenseness in the courtroom during November was in part induced by the political situation. On October 31, in the primary election, Socialist Job Harriman had run ahead of the other candidates for the mayoralty of Los Angeles. The final election on December 5 was to be a runoff between Harriman and incumbent George Alexander, the Good Government nominee. Even the opposition admitted that the Socialist ticket, officially supported by local organized labor, stood an excellent chance of capturing the city administration, a prospect which induced a state of alarm bordering on panic. Both sides in the Mc-

Namara case were aware that a relationship existed between the trial and the election, particularly in respect to timing. Any delays that would postpone a verdict, or even the testimony of witnesses, until after the election would work to the advantage of the Harriman forces. Since the district attorney was reputedly a tool of Otis and capitalistic interests, who were bent on defeating the Socialists, the prosecution felt an urgent need to discredit organized labor before the election. These considerations made the preëlection campaign extraordinarily intense and bitter.[108]

The Good Government organization based its campaign for Alexander on the need to save Los Angeles from the rule of socialists and unionists, who would institute the closed shop, repeal the antipicketing ordinance, and subject the city to a government modeled upon the labor administration of San Francisco. It was pointed out, over and over, that Harriman was nothing more than a tool in the hands of the labor clique in the northern city, and that his election would result in business stagnation, unemployment, and hard times. Fear of such dire consequences attracted diversified support for Alexander. All the daily newspapers except the *Record,* regardless of any previous objections to the Good Government party, rallied to the cause. The Merchants' and Manufacturers' Association, the Chamber of Commerce, the Founders' and Employers' Association, the Los Angeles Realty Board, the Women's Progressive League, nonunion workingmen, and old-line Republicans and Democrats united against a common danger. Under the auspices of a nonpartisan Citizens' Committee of One Hundred, organized early in November, these groups and individuals collaborated in the campaign to elect Alexander, providing the necessary funds, registering voters, engaging in precinct work, forming Alexander clubs, and holding almost daily meetings throughout the month of November. Special appeals were made to Negroes and to women who were eligible to vote for the first time through passage of a state woman suffrage amendment on October 10, 1911.[109]

The Socialists were just as active as the Alexander forces. Starting immediately after the primaries, they organized a campaign committee, collected funds, and arranged for frequent meetings and rallies. The national headquarters of the party sent Alexander Irvine to assist in the campaign; Anne Malley, national Socialist organizer, and Winfield Gaylord, Socialist state senator in Wisconsin, came to Los Angeles to speak in Harriman's behalf. Harriman himself undertook a major portion of the campaign speeches, spending so much time working for a Socialist victory that he was forced to slight his duties as one of the Mc-

Namara defense counsel. The Socialist-labor coalition, like the Good Government party, made particular efforts to win the votes of Negroes and of women.[110]

Early in November, betting odds on a Harriman victory were very close to even, but by the end of the month the Alexander forces believed their candidate had gained considerable ground while the Socialists had done no more than hold their own. There were, however, a number of imponderables. Registration for this election was the largest in the city's history, totaling about one hundred and eighty-five thousand. How would the thousands of new registrants vote? Some eighty thousand women would cast their first ballots, a sufficiently large number to be the deciding factor. How would these women vote? The McNamara case was in progress. Would there be pertinent developments before December 5? True, at the end of November four jurors and two alternates still had to be selected, but in such a trial almost anything could happen. These unanswerable questions raised the community to a feverish pitch of excitement in the last, tense days of November, 1911. Rumors, speculations, doubts filled the air, as people wondered whether the city of Los Angeles would elect a Socialist administration in which organized labor would carry great weight.[111]

On Tuesday, November 28, an unexpected development in the McNamara case rocked the community. Detective Samuel Browne of the district attorney's office arrested Bert Franklin, Darrow's chief investigator, on a charge of bribing a prospective juror to hold out for James McNamara's acquittal. Browne, having learned several weeks earlier that Franklin was busily canvassing veniremen, had had him closely watched and was on hand to witness the actual transfer of money. At nine o'clock on the morning of November 28, Franklin handed $500 to George Lockwood and $3,500 to Charles White, who as stakeholder, according to Browne, was to pay the balance to Lockwood when the latter fulfilled his promise to vote for acquittal. The officers impounded the money and released White and Lockwood after questioning. At Franklin's arraignment the next day, the prosecution demanded a trial before the end of the week. However, ex-Governor Henry T. Gage, Franklin's defense counsel, obtained a later date in December on the plea that he would not have time to prepare his case, since November 30 was Thanksgiving Day.[112]

The sensational arrest of Franklin brought fresh speculations. Even intimate friends had not known that Franklin was working for Darrow, and, though Darrow's name was not officially mentioned in connection with the bribery charge, people wondered if Franklin had acted on orders from his chief. The odd circumstance that a former deputy marshal would let himself be caught so easily in such a suspicious transaction suggested that Franklin might have been paid by the prosecution to time his apprehension at a critical moment. Contemplation of Darrow's possible implication and the effect this might have on both the election and the trial served to increase the already high tension in Los Angeles.[113]

Before the community had had time to assess the full import of Franklin's arrest, it received a second shock far more startling than the first. When court convened on Friday, December 1, after a Thanksgiving recess, District Attorney Fredericks requested an adjournment until afternoon on the plea that he had "grave matters" to consider. This unusual procedure, when the court had been engaged in the monotonous process of selecting a jury, caused premonitions of impending courtroom drama. Newspaper correspondents, recalling the bribery allegations and the recent harassed demeanor of the defense counsel, believed a crisis was at hand and turned out in full force for the afternoon session. When court reconvened, the spectators were not disappointed. Their first surprise came with the appearance of John McNamara, who for the first time since the opening of the trial accompanied his brother into the courtroom. It was obvious to all that the defense lawyers were under a great strain, yet few were prepared for the most dramatic moment of the entire case. To a courtroom hushed by expectancy, LeCompte Davis announced in a low voice that the defense desired to change its plea; James McNamara then pleaded guilty to murder, and John McNamara in his turn pleaded guilty to conspiracy in the dynamiting of the Llewellyn Iron Works. Both prisoners were ordered to appear on December 5 for sentencing.[114]

Dumbfounded newspaper reporters hastened to question the principals in the case. District Attorney Fredericks refused anything more than a simple statement that the McNamaras were guilty and had confessed. James McNamara said that he realized he might hang for his crime, but he was willing to pay this penalty to uphold his principles and to save his brother from execution. It was generally understood, however, that James would receive a life sentence and John a shorter term. Darrow, almost incoherent from fatigue, said the confession was the only way out of a hopeless situation, for the prosecution had a complete case; he had seen a chance to save a life and had grasped it. Questioned about the timing, Darrow observed that he had had to take advantage of clemency when it was extended, and added that the defense had been considering the change of plea for several weeks; it had

not been a sudden decision, and certainly had had nothing to do with
the bribery charge against Franklin.[115]

The events leading to the dramatic finish of the McNamara case
began in the middle of November, when writer Lincoln Steffens arrived
in Los Angeles to cover the trial for a syndicate of twenty-one newspapers. He had returned from Europe expressly to solicit the job so
that he might present through the conservative press his view that the
Times bombing had been as much a manifestation of social injustice
as a legal offense. Steffens first sought permission from the McNamaras
to use their case as the basis for a series of articles which would reveal
the fundamental issues in the war between labor and capital, and thus
partially justify the occasional violence and ultimate use of dynamite
by union workers. James McNamara, who appeared to Steffens the
more decisive, convinced his brother of the value of a sympathetic
presentation of their story, and both men consented, subject to Darrow's approval.[116]

Because Darrow represented the defendants and, by implication,
organized labor, he refused to approve the plan. He did, however, urge
Steffens to stand by and watch the progress of the case, which he felt
was going badly. Darrow confessed to Steffens that he was quite apprehensive of the outcome. He knew that the prosecution would not rest
until it got a conviction, and that the penalty would certainly be execution. He was frightened because District Attorney Fredericks was able
to find out very quickly the most secret plans of the defense. He suspected that the prosecution was employing informers, and his suspicion
was shown to be well founded when Detective Browne later admitted
he had kept spies in Darrow's office from the moment the defense had
organized its headquarters until the brothers had confessed their guilt.
Darrow, of course, had had informers at the headquarters of the prosecution, but they merely confirmed his own belief that the defense was
on very shaky ground.[117]

With these gloomy thoughts constantly in mind, Darrow began to
consider the possibility of a settlement out of court. He put the idea
into words during the week end of November 18–19 when he and
Steffens were visiting newspaper publisher E. W. Scripps in San Diego.
Steffens then proposed an experimental application to the McNamara
case of Christian principles, particularly the Golden Rule, as a possible
method of solving Darrow's difficulties as well as the Los Angeles labor
problem. By obtaining the coöperation and backing of a group of
prominent citizens, including employers, Steffens hoped to convince
the prosecution that the McNamaras should go unpunished and that

further pursuit of other suspects should be abandoned. The advantages of such an arrangement, he felt, would accrue to the entire community, since it would mean the peaceful termination of the McNamara case which, if tried, could only intensify class war and hatred, regardless of its outcome. Steffens wanted next to call a conference of leading employers and union officials, who would work in harmony for wiser and saner industrial relations than had previously characterized the city. The end result, he fervently believed, might well be a transformation of Los Angeles from the worst to the best city for labor in the United States. Scripps was enthusiastic about Steffens' plan, and offered any help that he or his newspapers might give. Darrow, expressing the hope that his clients would not have to make a confession of guilt, gave his tentative approval.[118]

When Steffens and Darrow returned to Los Angeles, the former began immediately to put the plan into operation. He first consulted Meyer Lissner of the Lincoln-Roosevelt League and Thomas E. Gibbon, a popular businessman and member of the Harbor Commission. Both were skeptical of success, but promised to lend their assistance to any plan which might eventuate in happier labor relations in Los Angeles. With their help, Steffens next tackled Otis and Harry Chandler of the *Times.* Surprisingly enough, he found them amenable to his suggestion. Darrow, amazed but heartened by the compliance of Otis, wired the AFL to send a representative to Los Angeles for the talks which now seemed likely to bear fruit. Meanwhile, he had discussed the proposal with all his colleagues except Job Harriman, who stood to lose his contest for the mayoralty in the event the settlement required admissions of guilt. With these preliminaries disposed of, Steffens asked LeCompte Davis to submit the plan to the district attorney. Here the first obstacle appeared. Fredericks, though willing to settle out of court, would not entertain a proposal involving no punishment for the Mc-Namaras. The National Erectors' Association, which had supplied some of the funds for investigating the dynamite conspiracy, had heard of the Los Angeles negotiations and was pressing for uncompromising terms. The district attorney therefore demanded that the McNamaras plead guilty, and that James receive a life sentence and John a shorter term in prison, possibly ten years.[119]

Steffens, Darrow, Davis, and McNutt then placed the proposal, modified to meet the district attorney's stipulations, before the two defendants. James McNamara at first opposed any settlement which would force his brother to plead guilty. He himself was prepared to hang, if necessary, to save his brother's life, but he did not want John, as a union official, to make an admission of guilt that would by implication inculpate organized labor. Darrow, however, insisted that no one must die, and that settlement out of court was possible only if both brothers pleaded guilty. He further expounded the enormous difficulties the defense would face in continuing the case in court, and the possibility that both brothers might receive the death penalty. James then agreed to the change of plea, involving a life term for himself and a ten-year term for John, on condition that the prosecution abandon the pursuit of other suspects and that labor and capital in Los Angeles hold a peace conference.[120]

At this point in the negotiations, the defense believed that settlement was practically certain. The McNamaras had accepted Fredericks' terms; Edward C. Nockels, representing the AFL, had arrived and signified his approval; Judge Bordwell, consulted by Steffens, had indicated that he would not interfere with the plan; and Darrow's colleagues were in favor of terminating the case in this fashion. Moreover, Steffens had obtained approval for the labor-capital conference from a representative group of leading citizens, including among others Edwin T. Earl, proprietor of the *Express;* Fred Baker of the Baker Iron Works; Paul Shoup, vice-president of Southern Pacific; James Slauson, president of the Chamber of Commerce; William Mulholland, chief engineer on the Los Angeles aqueduct; Charles Willard of the Chamber of Commerce; Lissner; and Gibbon. The arrest of Bert Franklin on the heels of these arrangements threatened to halt the settlement proceedings. However, when Darrow insisted that any charges implicating him in Franklin's crime should be considered outside the McNamara negotiations, the district attorney stuck to his bargain. During the evening of Thanksgiving Day, November 30, Davis and Fredericks settled on the final terms: pleas of guilty with no confessions, life imprisonment for James McNamara, a ten-year term for John McNamara, abandonment of the pursuit of other suspects, and a local labor-capital conference. The district attorney had yet to see Judge Bordwell, but promised Davis there would be no opposition from that quarter.[121]

The arrangements thus concluded, the McNamaras carried out their part of the agreement by pleading guilty on the afternoon of December 1. James McNamara, however, had reservations about Judge Bordwell. Throughout the negotiations he had been skeptical of the judge's intention to abide by any agreement reached. Immediately after adjournment on December 1, James expressed his doubts to Steffens, predicting that the judge when he pronounced sentence might well impose more severe penalties than those agreed upon. Another worrisome factor was the district attorney's press statement after the pleas that no bargain had been made regarding the length of the prison terms and that the court would make that decision. On Darrow's advice, Steffens visited Judge Bordwell on Saturday, December 2, to prevail upon him to make a statement from the bench which would express understanding of the crime and emphasize the good will of the settlement. The judge promised Steffens to carry out the spirit of the agreement.[122]

In his own story, filed for publication on December 2, Steffens interpreted the court proceedings of the day before as a plea of guilty by both capital and labor. The McNamaras, he reported, had made no confession which involved other persons in their crime, but rather had entered into the agreement so that the labor problem in the most anti-union city in the country would receive fair consideration by both sides. Steffens himself did not emphasize the principles of Christianity upon which he had based his negotiations, but other reporters caught the implicit idea of the Golden Rule and gave it nationwide publicity. Steffens was therefore dismayed when a cry of hate and revenge went up from the churches on Sunday, December 3. According to him, the sermons preached by those supposed to be practicing the teachings of Christ were vindictive and self-righteous attacks on organized labor, on the McNamaras, and on those who had contrived to lighten the punishment of the guilty.[123]

Steffens felt that this reaction from the churches was responsible for the change of heart which Judge Bordwell exhibited when he pronounced sentence on December 5. When court opened, District Attorney Fredericks read a brief confession signed by James McNamara. The statement revealed that McNamara had placed sixteen sticks of 80 per cent dynamite in Ink Alley at 5:45 P.M. on September 30, 1910, set to explode at one o'clock the next morning; that his object was merely to damage the building and scare the *Times* proprietor, not to take human life; and that he would gladly give his own life if by so doing he could restore the victims of the disaster to their families. The district attorney then asked the court to sentence McNamara to life imprisonment instead of death because of his service to the state. Judge Bordwell accordingly sentenced James McNamara to a life term, but instead of the expected ten years he sentenced John McNamara to fifteen. Bordwell also reneged on his promise of a kindly, humane statement from the bench. In pronouncing sentence, he excoriated both prisoners with a torrent of denunciation, allowing no extenuating circumstances for their crime. It was the exact opposite of what Steffens had hoped for, and as the McNamara case reached its end, he felt that all his altruistic efforts to bring industrial peace to Los Angeles and mercy to an embattled labor movement had been in vain.[124]

The final chapter in the story of the "crime of the century" began on December 9, 1911, when James and John McNamara were taken under heavy guard from the Los Angeles jail and put on a train for San Francisco. On the morning of December 10, escorted by twelve armed guards, the brothers entered San Quentin prison. The authorities had conducted the transfer in the utmost secrecy, to avoid any possible attempts to help the McNamaras escape. At San Quentin the prisoners were put to work in the jute mills, where they were lost to a labor movement bewildered by their confession of guilt, and to a world that was to feel for some time the impact of their crime.[125]

XXII. REACTIONS AND AFTERMATH

THE HOSTILITY of the crowds which gathered in the streets of Los Angeles at the time of the McNamara confessions was directed primarily against Clarence Darrow and Lincoln Steffens. With the sudden shattering of their long-held faith, previously loyal partisans of the defense turned against the two they regarded as responsible for the debacle, as well as against the confessed criminals. Angry men threw their McNamara buttons to the ground, spoke harsh words, and made rash threats; others wept tears of defeat over a lost ideal. Deep emotional stress was the activating force among workers and Socialists who had given generously of time and money because of their firm belief in the innocence of the accused and in the probity of Clarence Darrow.[1]

Among the criticisms leveled against Darrow, two were predominant. The first was that he had sacrificed the McNamaras to save himself from possible conviction of bribery. This theory was generally accepted by the press, and was strengthened by the assertions of Judge Walter Bordwell and District Attorney John Fredericks, that the arrest of Bert Franklin had indeed precipitated the confessions. The second criticism was that Darrow had deliberately timed the confessions to occur before the municipal elections on December 5, even in the knowledge that his colleague, Job Harriman, might lose the mayoralty.[2]

Harriman, whose opinion regarding Steffens' plan had never been sought, had known nothing about the confessions until they took place. He then freely acknowledged that the blow had been a staggering one and that, had he been consulted, he would have urged a defense fight through to the end. Although Harriman buttons "fell off like leaves off a tree"[3] after the confessions, the Socialists conquered their apprehensions and continued to campaign vigorously in the few remaining days. Nor did the Alexander forces relax their efforts, for they foresaw an outgrowth of apathy through overconfidence. They need not have feared, however: the complete official election returns gave Alexander 85,492 votes and Harriman 51,423; all other Good Government candidates ran ahead of their Socialist rivals in approximately the same ratio. The consensus at the time was that Harriman's defeat was directly attributable to the McNamara confessions and that Darrow had been partly responsible by authorizing the change of plea before the election. In recounting the story some forty years later, however, Frank Wolfe, Socialist candidate for the City Council in 1911, insisted that the timing bore no relationship to the political situation. Darrow had been faced with the dilemma of choosing between continued prosecution of the

McNamara case or confessions of guilt from both brothers and, fearing the death penalty for his clients, had accepted the latter alternative. Harriman's revelation shortly after the election that Darrow had explained to him the defense's desperate need for a settlement out of court gives Wolfe's conjecture a ring of truth.[4]

The motives behind the confessions—the prosecution's desire to terminate the case before the election and to save trial costs and Darrow's compulsion to save the defendants' lives—seemed to rule out any credit to Steffens for the settlement. In fact, Judge Bordwell told newspapermen that the district attorney had not been swayed in the slightest degree by the ideals or hopes of Steffens. Steffens was widely ridiculed for his missionary fervor and Christian idealism and was pictured as the dupe not only of Fredericks but of Otis and other employers who would never, it was argued, seriously contemplate either release of the McNamaras without punishment or readjustment of labor relations in Los Angeles.[5] It is true that the *Times* sounded conciliatory in its editorial reaction to the confessions:

> It is a fateful hour for labor; it is a fateful hour for the employers of labor; it is the hour for the cultivation of that true spirit of justice, equality and fair play which is the solution of all these problems. To make the most of this fortunate outcome ... will be the effort of The Times and of those who have stood with it in all this twenty years' struggle.[6]

However, the *Times'* simultaneous pledge to work for a compact between labor and management that, under the "benign rule of industrial freedom," would eliminate the "real" causes of industrial conflict was tantamount to a decree that unions and not employers should renounce their principles for the sake of peace between labor and capital.[7]

On the other hand, the spirit of Steffens' approach to the problem was recognized in some quarters. The *California Outlook,* for example, had this to say:

> It is not incredible that out of the great awakening that this dramatic event gives to the public mind all over the country, bringing the subject of unionism and its claims and purposes up for new consideration, that we may all be brought to a better adjustment and understanding. Particularly is this possible in Los Angeles where the dismal tragedy had its culmination.[8]

In the weeks immediately following the confessions, Steffens' hopes for labor-management peace in Los Angeles did indeed seem realistic. On December 2, at the call of President James Slauson of the Chamber of Commerce, a group of prominent citizens met to make preliminary arrangements for the peace conference. Immediately the Los Angeles Typographical Union announced its support of the proposal, and the

Central Labor Council appointed a committee to represent organized labor. It was not until February, 1912, however, that representatives of industry and labor first met as a joint Peace Conference Committee. Although Secretary L. W. Butler of the Central Labor Council believed that this was a sincere effort to improve employer-employee relationships in Los Angeles, the joint committee held no further meetings. With one of its foremost objectives relegated to the scrap heap, Steffens' great experiment seemed a failure.[9]

Those who believed that Darrow had betrayed the McNamaras in return for his own immunity had misjudged him, for it soon became apparent that the district attorney intended to prosecute Darrow as well as Bert Franklin for attempted bribery of the jury. Testimony at Franklin's preliminary hearing on the Lockwood indictment on December 11, 1911, led to issuance of a second complaint charging him with bribing a permanent juror, Robert Bain, and also linked Darrow with the bribery of both Lockwood and Bain. Before coming to trial Franklin pleaded guilty to both charges and promised to testify against Darrow. Franklin's fine of $4,000, his only penalty for a self-confessed crime, was paid with the bribe money which Detective Samuel Browne had taken from George Lockwood and Charles White at the time of Franklin's arrest.[10]

The fact that Franklin was not personally inconvenienced either by going to jail or by paying the fine out of his own pocket led to speculations that he had been in the employ of District Attorney Fredericks, whose reputation would be much enhanced and whose gubernatorial aspirations greatly aided by conviction of the most famous criminal lawyer in the country. On the other hand, it was felt that Darrow could hardly have been ignorant of his agent's activities, and this, plus Franklin's willingness to testify, induced a widespread belief that Darrow was guilty. Organized labor, still vexed over Darrow's presumed betrayal of the McNamaras, was indifferent to his fate. Early in February, 1912, the grand jury brought two indictments against Darrow, charging him with bribing Lockwood and Bain. In order to have the best possible defense, Darrow chose Earl Rogers, whose reputation as a resourceful and expert criminal lawyer outweighed the possible disadvantage of his past service as adviser to and investigator for the Merchants' and Manufacturers' Association. Rogers' acceptance of a case so diametrically opposed to his recent activities in connection with the *Times* bombing was predicated on his belief in Darrow's innocence and a natural desire for personal fame. When Rogers failed in an attempt to have the indictments set aside on technical grounds, Darrow pleaded not guilty.[11]

Darrow's trial on the first charge began in Superior Court before Judge George H. Hutton on May 15, 1912, with District Attorney John Fredericks heading the prosecution. The chief witnesses for the state were Franklin and Lockwood, both of whom testified that Darrow had been nearby when the bribe money was transferred and that he had crossed the street to talk to them. Franklin particularized in great detail the bribery campaign, alleging that in all his operations he had acted under Darrow's orders, and even the brilliant cross-examination of Rogers failed to shake him in this damaging testimony. In response to Franklin's statements, Darrow denied that he had planned or put into operation the attempted bribery of any jurors and claimed that he knew nothing whatsoever about the transactions. His presence at the time of Franklin's arrest was, he testified, completely coincidental, and he had crossed the street because he wanted to talk to Franklin.[12] Rogers, in his argument for Darrow, appealed to common sense:

Will you tell me how any sane, sensible man who knows anything about the law business—and this defendant has been at it for thirty-five years—could make himself go to a detective and say to him: "Just buy all the jurors you want. I put my whole life, my whole reputation, I put everything I have into your hands. I trust you absolutely. I never knew you until two or three months ago, and I don't know very much about you now; but there you are, go to it!"[13]

The essence of Darrow's defense, however, came in his own plea to the jury on August 14–15, a highly emotional speech which Fredericks called one of the greatest ever heard in a courtroom. Darrow pointed to various absurdities implicit in the charge that he was guilty of bribery: as a stranger in Los Angeles, he could not have known the parties involved well enough to trust them; an astute lawyer would hardly have sent an agent to do his bribing and then have turned up on the scene himself; by November 28, when the bribe money had changed hands, negotiations for a settlement out of court in the McNamara case had been in progress for a week and were practically concluded; and he could have had no reason for jeopardizing not only his reputation but also the settlement negotiations by stupidly involving himself in a criminal act. In a moving and eloquent plea, Darrow represented himself as the victim of a conspiracy which sought his downfall because, as a friend of the poor and the oppressed, he had lent his legal talents to the defense of men like the McNamaras. Even had he known they were guilty, he claimed he would have defended them, for their crime grew out of the conditions of society. He agreed with Steffens that inquiry into the fundamental political and sociological causes of such crimes would do far more to end industrial warfare than would penitentiary terms or the death penalty. No, concluded Darrow, he was not on trial for bribing a juror, but for his love of justice for the downtrodden of the world.[14]

Darrow's plea reached the hearts of his jurors, though most of them had been antilabor when the trial started. They returned a verdict of not guilty after only half an hour of deliberation. Judge Hutton, too, had been won over by the magic of Darrow's courtroom eloquence. After the verdict he congratulated the defendant, saying that the whole country would ring with hallelujahs because of Darrow's acquittal. A few days later the judge, the jurors, and Steffens, who had come to Los Angeles to testify for the defense, gave Darrow a dinner to celebrate his victory. The prosecution, cheated of its anticipated conviction, set the wheels in motion on the second charge accusing Darrow of bribing Bain, though its case was in this instance much weaker. The trial was set for October, 1912, but several postponements delayed it until January, 1913. By that time events which had transpired in Indianapolis threatened to affect the Darrow trial.[15]

Inquiries into the alleged dynamite conspiracy had been instituted both at Indianapolis and at Los Angeles by the Attorney General of the United States, acting on the order of President William Howard Taft. The Los Angeles investigation began on December 6, 1911, under the direction of Oscar Lawler. Indictments of illegal transportation of dynamite via interstate carriers were brought against Olaf Tveitmoe, E. A. Clancy, and Anton Johannsen of San Francisco, and J. E. Munsey, secretary of the Salt Lake City iron workers' union. In January, 1912, however, it became apparent that Indianapolis was the focal point of the national campaign against open-shop firms, and the Los Angeles grand jury therefore adjourned sine die. The indictments it had issued were later quashed because the defendants were to be tried at Indianapolis.[16]

The Indianapolis investigation also began in December, 1911, and resulted in similar indictments against some fifty union members. The grand jury based its action largely on the statements of Ortie McManigal, who had been taken to Indianapolis early in January, 1912, to testify against the alleged conspirators. Subsequently, several indictments were dropped, so that only forty of those originally charged had to stand trial. All of these were labor union officials, and most of them were affiliated with the International Association of Bridge and Structural Iron Workers.[17]

The trial began in the United States District Court at Indianapolis on October 1, 1912. The prosecution based its case on McManigal's testimony and on union records and correspondence files. On December 28, the jury acquitted two and convicted thirty-eight of the defendants. The judge sentenced President Frank Ryan of the BSIW to seven years in prison, and Tveitmoe, Clancy, and Munsey each to six years. Other terms varied from six years to a year and a day; five defendants who had pleaded guilty were released under suspended sentences. Tveitmoe never served his term, for on July 3, 1914, a higher court reversed the decision in his case and he was set free.[18]

Two aspects of the Indianapolis proceedings were particularly invidious, in the view of organized labor. The first was the attempt to implicate the American Federation of Labor and its high officials, especially Gompers, in the dynamite conspiracy. Detective William Burns, who took to himself the credit for discovering the plot, had frequently suggested that Gompers was guilty and obviously wanted to see him brought to trial. In fact, Tveitmoe asserted that the prosecuting attorney at Indianapolis had at Burns' insistence promised him immunity if he would testify that Gompers was involved. After examination of AFL books and records, however, the Indianapolis grand jury completely exonerated the Federation and its officials.[19] The second aspect was an apparent bias in the attitude of the judge and the prosecution. Throughout the trial the prosecution referred to the defendants as murderers and dynamiters, though they were charged only with illegal transportation of explosives. The court permitted introduction of evidence of bombings and violence, while ruling out testimony on bad working conditions and on the methods used by employers in their war with labor. Labor felt that, even though some of its members were guilty of breaking the law, the wrongdoings of capital should also be aired. When the judge, in pronouncing sentence, remarked that government by injunction was preferable to government by dynamite, Gompers was moved to public protest. Speaking before a Senate committee, he said: "If ever the time shall come when government by dynamite shall be attempted . . . it will have as its main cause . . . government by injunction—personal government foisted upon our people instead of a government by law."[20] With a truculence born of the sense of injury, Gompers and other labor notables attended an iron workers' convention held after the Indianapolis trials.[21]

These trials were concluded just before Darrow's second bribery trial opened in Los Angeles in January, 1913. Darrow believed that the Indianapolis verdict, accorded a full measure of local publicity, would adversely affect his chances in court. Another discouraging factor was Earl Rogers' illness, which became so critical after the trial opened

that Darrow had to relieve him and assume the difficult task of defending himself. Moreover, Darrow's funds were running low. He had been
absent from his regular Chicago practice for some eighteen months,
and the money received from the AFL for the McNamara defense was
exhausted. Without Rogers' restraining influence, Darrow tried in his
plea to the jury to condone as a social crime the destruction of the
Times building and the murder of its employees. He went so far beyond
his statements in the first trial that now several jurors turned against
him and held out for his conviction. After several days' deliberation,
the jury reported its inability to reach a verdict. It appeared that
Darrow might stand trial a third time, but the district attorney eventually, in December, 1913, had the indictment dismissed on the grounds
of insufficient evidence. Darrow, weary and discouraged by the whole
course of events in Los Angeles, returned home with a debt of $20,000.[22]

Meanwhile, William Burns, with the tenacity of a bulldog, had continued to pursue Matthew Schmidt and David Kaplan, who were suspected of having assisted James McNamara in the purchase and
transport of the dynamite used to destroy the *Times* building. Shortly
after the explosion, Schmidt had gone from San Francisco to New
York, via Seattle and Butte, arriving at his destination on October 23,
1910. From New York he had gone south to look for a job. For a time
he had worked ten hours a day at 25 cents an hour, but for safety's
sake he had not stayed too long in any one place. He had also been very
careful in small details, such as never using the same telephone twice.
To conceal his identity, Schmidt had changed his name and pretended
to be a German immigrant, a disguise that came easily because of a
boyhood spent among the German-speaking people of Wisconsin. He
gloated over escaping detection by Burns on two occasions, once when
they had stayed for several days at the same hotel, and again when
Burns entered a phone booth which Schmidt was just leaving. Schmidt
eventually had returned to New York, where, in February, 1915, the
Burns agency finally tracked him down after a chase lasting more than
four years. He was arrested on February 13, only five days before a
similar fate befell Kaplan who had been trailed to Seattle.[23]

After apprehending Schmidt, Burns detectives tried to extract a confession by telling him that Kaplan had been caught and had given the
police a complete story. Skeptically, Schmidt refused to talk, and never
at any time did he admit that he had played any part in the *Times*
bombing. According to his own account, he was in San Francisco when
the explosion occurred, and first knew about it from the newspapers.
James McNamara, he said, had placed the dynamite in Ink Alley after

John McNamara had sent him to Los Angeles to blow up nonunion building supplies as part of the BSIW program. He suggested, however, that the order to destroy the *Times* building might have come from a source other than the union. In fact, he accused detectives of having engineered some of the bombings attributed to the BSIW: they planted the dynamite, then "discovered" it, and blamed it on organized labor. Schmidt held only contempt for Burns who, he said, pretended to be an unusually clever detective while he constantly received inside information from H. S. Hockin, organizer for the BSIW. Hockin had been on Burns' payroll since July, 1910, Schmidt claimed, so small wonder that Burns, with the help of a high union official's betrayal of his co-workers, was able to apprehend the McNamaras and Ortie McManigal.[24]

The trial of Matthew Schmidt on a charge of murder began in Superior Court in Los Angeles on October 4, 1915, almost exactly five years after the *Times* bombing. Organized labor throughout the country had raised $30,000 for the defense of Schmidt and Kaplan, and Job Harriman was employed as one of Schmidt's lawyers. Jury selection occupied a month, and the actual trial dragged on slowly, for there were frequent clashes between prosecution and defense, and 147 witnesses were called to testify.[25] Schmidt's address to the court made the public aware once more of the social causes of industrial warfare: "The same forces back of the prosecution of my case have opposed at each and every turn every measure for the relief of the toilers."[26] In January, 1916, the jury returned a verdict of guilty with a recommendation that Schmidt be sentenced to life imprisonment. Upon appeal, the conviction was upheld, and Schmidt entered San Quentin prison in 1917. He was a model prisoner, studious and industrious. In 1939, after serving twenty-two years of his life term, he was paroled and subsequently his sentence was commuted to time served.[27]

David Kaplan's trial on a charge of murder began in March, 1916, in Los Angeles. Since the Schmidt-Kaplan defense fund had been exhausted for Schmidt's trial, the San Francisco Labor Council and the State Building Trades Council of California raised money for Kaplan's defense. In May, the jury reported its inability to agree after seventy-six hours of deliberation. Kaplan's second trial, in the fall of 1916, ended in a verdict of voluntary manslaughter and a sentence of ten years' imprisonment in the penitentiary. Again, as in previous trials, counsel for the defense emphasized that bad working conditions in industrial centers were responsible for the *Times* bombing, and that such disasters would end only when society abolished the causative evils. Kaplan entered San Quentin prison in January, 1917, after his motion for a new trial was denied. He was released after serving two-thirds of his term.[28]

In the trials of both Schmidt and Kaplan, the testimony of Ortie McManigal was admitted. In fact, throughout all the litigation incident to the *Times* bombing, except the bribery trials, his testimony was important. McManigal's confession at the time of his arrest was one basis for accumulation of evidence against John McNamara and other labor officials, as well as against James McNamara. McManigal testified before the grand jury which returned indictments against the McNamaras; after the brothers confessed, he was taken to Indianapolis, where his testimony was heard both by the grand jury which indicted the dynamite conspirators and by the court which tried them. During the year or more that McManigal spent in Indianapolis he was under indictment in Los Angeles on a charge of illegally transporting the dynamite used in the Llewellyn bombing. Just before he was brought back to Los Angeles in February, 1913, however, it was rumored that because of his services to the state he would be given his freedom and would go to South or Central America. Shortly after his return he did in fact disappear, so quietly that local labor was unaware of his whereabouts. But during Schmidt's trial in 1915, defense counsel Job Harriman charged that Los Angeles County had given McManigal, a self-confessed criminal, not only his freedom but a bonus of $1,000 with which to start life anew. Presumably McManigal later returned to Los Angeles under an assumed name, for Schmidt claims that he worked in the sheriff's office until his retirement a few years ago.[29]

Organized labor appears to have shown more animus against the McNamara brothers than against McManigal. From top to bottom of the labor hierarchy, opinions expressed after the McNamara confessions carried implicit condemnation of the brothers' deceitfulness in encouraging the belief that they were innocent. Since this belief became the cornerstone of a policy which affected the pocketbooks of workers, the betrayal seemed particularly reprehensible. Labor's chagrin at having been so badly misled and its consequent humiliation in the eyes of the public were manifest in the indignant repudiation of the McNamaras.

Gompers, when informed of the confessions, was astounded almost beyond belief. Speaking for the national labor movement, he condemned the McNamaras' unlawful acts and declared their punishment commensurate with their crime, while stressing once again the AFL's consistent discouragement of violence. He promised that unexpended defense funds would be returned, and that the AFL would immediately cease its activities on behalf of the brothers. John Mitchell, vice-president of the AFL, was similarly shocked by the confessions. He had difficulty in renouncing the belief so tenaciously held that the McNamaras had been entirely innocent and that the *Times* disaster had been an accident. The AFL Executive Council and the McNamara Ways and Means Committee both denounced violence and condemned the McNamaras for their departure from the high ideals of organized labor. In its subsequent accounting of funds in May, 1912, the Ways and Means Committee revealed that of the $236,000 raised for defense purposes all but approximately $10,000 had been spent. On December 1, 1911, by which time $170,000 had been sent to Darrow in Los Angeles, the AFL discontinued its appeals for funds and its transmission of money to Darrow.[30]

Denunciatory pronouncements came from labor groups other than the AFL at both national and local levels. The Indianapolis unions which had launched the defense movement revealed their abhorrence of crime and violence, while President Frank Ryan of the iron workers' union declared he was shocked by John McNamara's lack of integrity. Labor leaders of Chicago and of San Francisco were horrified by the knowledge of the brothers' guilt; the latter promptly disbanded the McNamara Defense League of California and returned the $6,000 balance in the treasury in amounts proportionate to original contributions. In Los Angeles, the Central Labor Council and the Typographical Union condemned lawlessness and disorder and castigated the McNamaras for their deception of union members. These and other opinions from all sections of the country made abundantly clear the bewilderment and shock which temporarily seized the American labor movement. The only variation lay in the recommendations for punishment. Although most groups agreed with Gompers that imprisonment was reasonable, extremists in the labor movement felt that nothing short of hanging was an adequate penalty.[31]

Organized labor was thus unanimous in its vehemence toward the McNamaras. At the same time it justified past loyalty on the grounds of every man's right to a presumption of innocence until proven guilty. Anxious to free the American labor movement of any taint of suspicion, union leaders stressed over and over again that only a firm conviction of the McNamara's innocence had guided their actions. When they had clarified this issue, labor officials pointed an accusing finger at society for permitting the maladjustments which gave rise to the crime of the McNamaras. It was an illuminating commentary on existing conditions, they maintained, that normally law-abiding workers could be driven to such drastic acts by the oppressive and hostile measures of organized employers, while the public looked on in placid unconcern. Although not condoning crime, no matter how strong the provocation, labor leaders stuck to their belief that the McNamara case was a vivid example of the possible ill effects of repression, whether practiced by government, capital, or society. The responsibility, they said, should not only be placed on the shoulders of the guilty individuals, but should burden the hearts and minds of all those who had given tacit assent to industrial conditions which bred dynamiters like the Mc-Namaras.[32]

Although organized labor seemed more condemnatory of the McNamara offense than those outside the labor movement, the most anti-union elements certainly did not spare their calumniation. President John Kirby of the National Association of Manufacturers said:

> The type of unionism represented by the American Federation of Labor and advo-cated by Gompers and Mitchell is as great a menace, if not a greater one, to society than the Ku-Klux-Klan, the Molly McGuires, the Mafia and Black Hand societies.... The institution of which I am speaking has proved itself to be a cold, merciless and murderous organization.[33]

Harrison Gray Otis regarded the confession as the most significant event in the United States since the close of the Civil War, and felt that it gave labor unionists an unparalleled opportunity to purge their organizations of criminal elements. Without the evil leadership of the past, Otis said, unions could quickly renounce their indefensible policies of violence, boycotting, industrial monopoly, and persecution of non-union workingmen, and attain the status of responsible and honorable organizations. Their usefulness in an industrial society would then be unquestioned.[34]

The moderation with which the *Times* proprietor clothed his comment on the McNamara confessions was symptomatic of a changing attitude toward labor unions in the country at large. John R. Commons has pointed out that public tolerance had noticeably advanced since 1886, when the Haymarket riots in Chicago led to a demand for revenge and suppression. By 1912, people wanted an unbiased investigation into the basic causes of industrial unrest with the object of preventing McNamara cases in the future. The shock of the dynamite conspiracy had, then, the healthy effect of bringing home to the nation the urgent need for a look at both sides of the labor-capital controversy.[35]

Although the efforts of Lincoln Steffens to bring industrial peace to Los Angeles met with failure, his concept of management's responsibility for evoking labor violence seemed to gain momentum and was propounded in many areas. Speaking for the Socialist Party, Eugene

Debs called the *Times* bombing labor's answer to government by injunction, to the employers' war of extermination against unions, and
to antipicketing ordinances and other such devices for impeding workers' progress.[36] Louis D. Brandeis, later a Supreme Court justice, placed
blame for industrial unrest at the doorstep of the great trusts and
corporations:

> In the midst of our indignation over the unpardonable crimes of trade union
> leaders disclosed at Los Angeles, should not our statesmen and thinkers seek to
> ascertain the underlying causes of this widespread, deliberate outburst of crimes of
> violence?
>
> What was it that led men like the McNamaras really to believe that the only
> recourse they had for improving the condition of the wage-earner was to use dyna-
> mite against property and life?
>
> Was it not because they... believed that the wage-earner, acting singly or col-
> lectively, is not strong enough to secure substantial justice?
>
> Is there not a causal connection between the development of these huge, indom-
> itable trusts and the horrible crimes now under investigation?... Is it not irony to
> speak of the equality of opportunity in a country cursed with their bigness?[37]

Professor Edwin Seligman of Columbia University attributed the actions of the McNamaras to both "the extreme conservatives in the capitalist class who push their individualism to the point of opposing labor
unions as such ... and, on the other hand, the extremists in the labor
ranks ... who incessantly preach the inevitability of class conflict...."[38]

The most eloquent plea for social justice came from the lips of
Clarence Darrow:

> You may hang every agitator to the highest tree; you may hang every labor leader
> in America and the world; you may drive them into their holes like rats; you may
> destroy the last spark of courage in their breasts; and you may leave the injustice
> and the wrong that exists in the world today and new men will be born to take their
> places.
>
> Do you want to know who is responsible for this struggle? It is the men who have
> reached out their hands and taken possession of all the wealth of the world.... You
> may kill and kill and kill; you may destroy every man who in a blind way has reached
> out with dynamite or anything else to fight against the social system; you may kill
> them, and you may send me and every other lawyer that dares to speak for them
> to the penitentiary for life, and you may leave this injustice in the world and other
> men will come to take our places forever and forever, until the blind world sees and
> the dumb world speaks.[39]

Convinced that neither individual depravity nor union policy was
alone responsible for labor unrest, a group of leading national citizens,
including Henry Morgenthau and Louis Brandeis, presented to President Taft on December 30, 1911, a petition requesting federal investigation of unions, employers' associations, strikes, working conditions,

and other factors in industrial relations. The theory behind this unusual procedure postulated a necessity for choosing between violence and progress in the solution of labor problems: if capital continued its policies of the past without restraint, obvious dissatisfaction among workers would lead to more and more eruptions like the dynamite conspiracy. As a result of the petition, in August, 1912, Congress authorized the appointment of an investigatory commission which was to report in three years.[40]

The chairman of the United States Commission on Industrial Relations was the capable and versatile Frank P. Walsh of Kansas City. His manner of conducting the hearings and of focusing public attention on them brought the cause of trade-unionism favorable publicity throughout the nation. For the first time in history the practices of employers were exposed to the public view by a commission whose impartiality was unquestioned. In this manner, the investigation performed an invaluable service for organized labor, which could no longer be regarded as the sole miscreant in the use of oppression or aggression. The final report of the Commission on Industrial Relations dignified the American trade-union movement as an indispensable national institution for settlement of labor disputes.[41]

A labor movement whose political influence was sufficient to warrant a congressional commission inquiry and whose integrity was evident enough to merit a favorable report from such a commission could not suffer irreparable damage from the McNamara case and the whole dynamite conspiracy. Although the confessions brought forth many dire predictions that unionism would be extinguished as an effective instrument for representing workers, the fact was that the national labor movement quickly recovered from the obloquy of the iron workers' campaign of violence. After the initial public indignation died down and was replaced by a desire for honest appraisal of the causes of industrial unrest, organized labor entered upon one of its most prosperous eras. Federal and state legislative successes, an AFL membership spurt between 1911 and 1913, and marked growth of the iron workers' union after the termination of the Indianapolis trials testified to the labor movement's uninterrupted progress.[42] The dynamite conspiracy, though it had caused extreme anguish, did not in the final analysis interfere with the advancement of the American labor movement, and may even have stimulated it. However, as will be shown, Los Angeles unionism was not so easily able to overcome the consequences of an act of violence committed in its own territory.

XXIII. LOS ANGELES: CITY OF
THE OPEN SHOP

THE EVENTS beginning with the *Times* bombing and culminating in the McNamara confessions and the Socialist defeat were to affect Los Angeles labor for years to come. The immediate and perhaps inevitable result was a trying period of readjustment, of declining membership, of waning vitality. More important than these setbacks, however, was nullification of a possible victory for labor in the great struggle of 1910–1911. The two-year unionizing campaign was designed essentially to break the hold of the open shop, established by the *Times* and its allies in the tempestuous decade of 1900–1910. Marked by an almost revivalistic enthusiasm, and reaching a pitch of ardor unmatched by any previous agitation among the city's workers, the campaign held the promise of a new era for Los Angeles labor. Defeat of the open shop seemed a realizable objective as neither destruction of the *Times* building, attempts on the Otis and Zeehandelaar homes, bombing of the Llewellyn Iron Works, nor even the McNamara arrests brought the organizing drive to a halt. Then suddenly, in December, 1911, the McNamaras pleaded guilty and a few days later Socialist-labor aspirations for control of the city administration were defeated. This climax sounded the death knell of both the unionizing campaign and the hope of raising labor to equality with management in collective bargaining. Thus through the *Times* bombing and related events local labor lost its clearest opportunity to vanquish the open shop. From labor's point of view it was extremely unfortunate that promised victory and expansion were defeated by forces outside the local labor movement—forces consciously identified with violence. The supremacy of the open-shop principle in industrial relations was to give Los Angeles one of its most distinctive characteristics far into the future.

The first retraction of the organizing drive resulted from dissolution of the General Campaign Strike Committee. This did not come without warning, for in the fall of 1911 the Committee had notified the Los Angeles Central Labor Council that its general strike assessment must be terminated because of demands on its members for McNamara defense funds. Local leaders, however, had prevailed upon their northern colleagues to prolong the effort at least until after the municipal election. When the McNamaras changed their pleas, and Harriman was defeated, the Committee voted to call off the assessment on January 1, 1912, but stipulated that subsequent voluntary contributions would be forwarded to the southern city. Los Angeles union leaders, though fully aware that the decision meant the collapse of their campaign, comforted themselves with the somewhat cheerless observation that in the final analysis organization of workers depends primarily upon the efforts of local unions and their business agents.[1]

In its final accounting, the General Campaign Strike Committee revealed that total collections in its year and a half of operation had amounted to nearly $334,000, and that all but about $600 of this sum had been expended. Almost half of the total had been raised by unions affiliated with the San Francisco Labor Council; another $130,000 had come from the State Building Trades Council. Of the latter amount, approximately $14,000 had been given by the building-trades unions of Los Angeles County. The local Carpenters' Union No. 158 had collected some $7,000. The second largest contributor in Los Angeles was the Typographical Union which gave over $4,000. Donations throughout the country had varied from one-dollar contributions sent in by individual union members to the $17,500 raised by the San Francisco machinists' union.[2]

The campaign had indeed been expensive, but the Committee, despite its inability to reach the goal of unionizing Los Angeles and overcoming the open shop, proudly pointed to solid gains: during the period of the assessment, twenty-two new unions had been organized; over ten thousand new members had joined the local labor movement; and the political power of organized labor had grown in rapid strides, as demonstrated by the tremendous though unsuccessful vote for Harriman. The Committee also claimed that Otis had lost prestige through his unwarranted charges against organized labor, and that the circulation of his newspaper was diminishing. Further, while labor had dug deep into its resources for the exceptional effort of 1910–1911, the Merchants' and Manufacturers' Association had at the same time poured so much money into the counteroffensive that it was forced to make special appeals to rebuild its treasury. From the Committee's point of view, therefore, the Los Angeles labor movement had reaped some benefit from the campaign.[3]

The prime concern of the General Campaign Strike Committee had been the Los Angeles metal trades strike which began on June 1, 1910. After the assessment ended, strike leaders in Los Angeles realized the impracticability of trying to continue the dispute. Accordingly, late in February, 1912, organizer George Gunrey of the molders, V. J. O'Leary of the boilermakers, and E. H. Misner of the machinists represented the metal trades in a conference with Secretary William B. Hoswell and another official of the Founders' and Employers' Association. Under a verbal agreement reached by the joint committee, the unions called off the strike and the employers promised to rehire the men, as opportunity permitted, without discrimination against union members. At the same time the Metal Trades Council requested the Central Labor Council to discontinue local strike assessments, since they were no longer needed. Although no formal arrangements as to wages and hours were made as part of the agreement, the five most important crafts participating in the walkout—molders, machinists, boilermakers, blacksmiths, and patternmakers—gained pay increases averaging 5 cents an hour, a nine-hour day for the first four groups, and an eight-hour day for the patternmakers.[4] Despite these incidental improvements, the strike had failed to win its main objectives of the eight-hour day and union wage schedules for all Los Angeles metal trades. The real battle had thus been lost, a defeat which both local and national labor leaders attributed to the bombing of the *Times* and the McNamara confessions.[5]

Although working conditions were slightly better after the strike, and although the promise of no discrimination theoretically improved the status of the unions, the effects of the prolonged dispute of 1910–1912 were in the main deleterious to the metal-trades unions. The unions of boilermakers and machinists' helpers relinquished their charters; other unions met irregularly if at all; most of them suffered declining membership; and the seriously weakened Metal Trades Council was compelled to reorganize in the spring of 1912. All of the unions complained that employers were flouting their promise of no discrimination, so that union members had great difficulty in getting back into the struck plants and, in fact, in finding any kinds of jobs. The future of the Los Angeles metal trades appeared so gloomy that both the Metal Trades Department of the AFL and the California State Federation of Labor made extraordinary efforts in their behalf during 1912 and 1913.[6] As late as 1914, J. W. Buzzell, then secretary and business agent of the Los Angeles Metal Trades Council, testified before the Commission on Industrial Relations that only the patternmakers approached conditions comparable to those before the strike.[7]

Not only the metal trades, but the whole local labor movement suffered from partial atrophy during 1912. Early in the year, Secretary L. W. Butler of the Central Labor Council recommended the needed stimulants of new organizing efforts, assistance to unions formed during the preceding two years, greater emphasis on the union label, and affiliation of all unions with the central body. These general proposals for rehabilitation were particularized in March when, after the failure of Lincoln Steffens' management-labor peace conference, the Central

Labor Council called a union "Get Together Conference." The conference drew up an eight-point program:

1. The first duty of union members shall be to purchase union-made goods and patronize union establishments.
2. Lists of unfair merchants shall be read at all union meetings.
3. Union meetings shall be made more attractive, with a joint lecture bureau furnishing data and speakers.
4. Delegates to department councils and the Central Labor Council must attend meetings.
5. Each union shall have an organizing committee to visit nonunion workers and distribute literature.
6. Moral and financial support shall be given to unions on strike.
7. The labor movement shall be politically active in support of working-class candidates who have received the unanimous approval of all Los Angeles unions; the unions shall consider the advisability of forming local branches of the Socialist Party within the unions.
8. All members of the trade union movement shall support campaigns to protect freedom of speech and freedom of the press.[8]

Although such a prospectus would appear to be a promising start for a labor movement bent on retaining past gains and striking out for new ones, it did not serve to create the necessary enthusiasm. After a poorly attended second meeting later in March, the Get Together Conference disintegrated.[9]

Manifold specific problems of narrower scope than those of the Get Together Conference faced the Central Labor Council in 1912. With the collapse of the great organizing campaign, the central body found that it had to abandon expansionist plans in favor of efforts to hold and consolidate its past membership gains. As the year opened, the Central Labor Council had ninety-three affiliated unions with a total of 11,290 members; twenty-two unions remained outside the central body. In July, 1912, the Council still had ninety-three member unions, since three new affiliations balanced the loss of two by disbandment and one by withdrawal. Total membership, however, had declined to 10,737, and among the fifteen unaffiliated unions were the important organizations of painters and paper hangers. In making this semiannual report, Secretary Butler warned Los Angeles labor of the futility of internal quarrels, and urged continuance of the Council's program to unionize the city. But his report for the half-year ending in January, 1913, although giving no data on total union membership, revealed that the number of central body affiliates had dropped to eighty-eight, and the number of unaffiliated unions had increased to twenty. During the last six months of 1912, therefore, the number of unions in Los Angeles, and possibly also total union membership, had remained static.[10]

Dissolution of the General Campaign Strike Committee on January 1, 1912, had other results less tangible than the membership problems arising from cessation of the organizing campaign. Both the central body and its member unions were financially embarrassed. Some of the latter were unable to pay their pro rata assessments for the still unpaid legal fees for defense of the three Los Angeles unionists accused of the Hall of Records bombing attempt. The Council itself, in November, 1912, announced that it could give no money, but only moral support, to unions on strike. There was, moreover, a decline in the coöperative spirit which had animated Los Angeles unionists during 1910–1911, when their labor movement was the cynosure of working people all over the country. In August, 1912, the Central Labor Council felt compelled to amend its bylaws so that the executive board could fine or censure member unions disobeying the rules of the central body. Later in the year the Council tried to bring in the unaffiliated unions and to devise ways and means of revivifying the labor movement which it headed. Although a number of unions, including some of those in the Metal Trades Council, began to report membership gains toward the end of 1912, the Central Labor Council had yet to hit upon a formula which would restore to Los Angeles unionism the inspired ardor of 1910 and 1911.[11]

Various segments of the labor movement reflected the difficulties of this period of readjustment in 1912. The Building Trades Council was at a particularly low ebb. In May the executive board discontinued its regular meetings and in the fall appealed for the assistance of a national organizer. The Council's largest union, Carpenters' Local No. 158, suffered heavy membership losses and in June instituted lower initiation fees in order to increase enrollment. So many members were in arrears in dues that the union prevailed upon the Central Labor Council to return its per capita assessment for the first half of 1912. With allied crafts faring little better than the carpenters, the Building Trades Council did not begin to recover from its slump until the end of the year, and even then its membership was only slightly larger than it had been a year before.[12] The leather workers' union, exhausted by its long boycott against Brydon Brothers and Los Angeles Saddlery, was in poor financial condition. The teamsters, not yet recovered from their disastrous strike of 1907, complained that other unionists were failing them by not demanding the working card, and asked their international union to send an organizer to southern California. The local union of retail clerks, disappointed in the fruitless activities of a national official who visited Los Angeles, decided to depend on its own resources, and in May reorganized and sent for a new charter. But the clerks, like the teamsters, found their progress hampered by the neglect of other unionists.[13]

There were, however, a few bright spots for labor in its relations with management. During 1912 the printing trades made steady progress toward the closed-shop ideal of organized labor. The printers, mailers, stereotypers, and pressmen had closed-shop contracts with all daily newspapers except the *Times*. Union press feeders and photoengravers were employed along with nonunion men in every shop except the *Times*. The printers, photoengravers, and press feeders negotiated wage increases during 1912, and the bookbinders and mailers made notable membership gains.[14] In January, 1912, the Los Angeles plumbers' union signed closed-shop agreements, overcoming employer opposition primarily because it included in its ranks most of the competent plumbers in the city.[15] The bakers, though unable to establish the closed shop, signed union agreements, effective May 1, 1912, with eighteen local shops.[16]

The brewery unions continued their closed-shop contracts signed at the end of their strike in April, 1911. The Los Angeles bartenders' union, which had benefited to some extent from the strength of the brewery unions, and was a thriving, progressive organization, increased its membership during 1912 to over five hundred. It was easily able to sign new agreements specifying a wage increase, effective May 1, and by June it claimed enforcement of the wage scale in most of the Los Angeles saloons.[17] An interesting commentary on the brewery workers' spirit of independence is their reaction to a workingmen's compensation and old-age pension fund proposed by the International Brewery Workers' Union and the United States Brewers' Association in 1912. Both employers and employees were to contribute. Los Angeles and San Francisco locals voted against the measure because they objected to a plan supported in part by employers. Their action helped to defeat the proposal in a referendum vote of the union's membership at large.[18]

Examples of union progress during 1912, scattered though they were, show that Los Angeles labor refused now, as it had refused in the past, to bow its head in complete submission to the powerful opposition it had faced and would continue to face. Pauline Jacobson wrote in January, 1912: "Despite the terrific obstacles and despite all their losses the unions of Los Angeles have not lost out entirely. They still retain their foothold."[19] Los Angeles unionism had lived through one of the most trying series of events ever to confront a local labor movement and, though it did not emerge unimpaired, it never completely lost the will to survive or the desire to continue the struggle for better working conditions. Yet local labor leaders were objective in their assessment of conditions in the years immediately following the *Times* disaster. Reports of Los Angeles delegates to the State Federation of Labor in 1912 and 1913 realistically admitted that local labor was going through a period of reconstruction and that it could show no marked improvement. The paralysis following the shock of the McNamara confessions held progress to a minimum. The best that labor could do was attempt to consolidate previous membership gains and lay a foundation for future constructive work.[20]

Furthermore, no labor official denied the supremacy of the open shop in Los Angeles. No voice was raised to contradict the *Times'* pronouncement as the year 1912 opened:

The efforts of the misleaders of union labor to make Los Angeles a cringing suppliant at their feet have utterly failed. The confession of the McNamaras and the defeat of Harriman...saved our city from the disgrace and disaster of socialistic rule. The effort to force the closed shop upon the employers of labor has been completely abandoned. Boycotting, picketing, and assaulting, and dynamiting are at an end....Industrial freedom reigns supreme.[21]

Although the *Times'* assumption of the unions' complete rejection of their traditional weapons of boycotting and picketing may have been unwarranted, its premise that labor's closed-shop objective had been defeated found general agreement among commentators. Frederick Palmer, in 1911, criticized antilabor forces such as the M and M for beating down the unions until no protection whatsoever remained for employees.[22] Various observers in later years spoke of the open shop in Los Angeles as something taken for granted, and as the most important factor contributing to the industrial growth of the city.[23] Even labor representatives concurred in the prevalence of the open shop. An official of the International Printing Pressmen's Union said in 1912: "There is probably no city in America where such unfriendly sentiment obtains against organized labor as in this beautiful city of Los Angeles."[24] Later in the same year a local union of engineers opposed labor's endorsement of a state license law for their craft on the ground that enforcement authorities in a union-hating community like Los Angeles would always discriminate against union engineers.[25] In 1916, Olaf Tveitmoe referred to Los Angeles as a "benighted city" in its attitude to labor relations.[26] These samples of opinion indicate general acceptance by both management and labor of the truth that Los Angeles was preëminently the open-shop city of the United States.

There was no escaping the conclusion that Harrison Gray Otis was the leading protagonist in the fight to make Los Angeles a haven for nonunion workingmen. Frederick Palmer, noting that the city "bears his [Otis'] stamp as probably no other city bears the stamp of any one man," spoke of Otis' pride in being "the most aggressive, successful, and unyielding foe of organized labor in America."[27] Early in 1912 a national monthly journal had this to say about the owner of the *Times:*

> With political power regained, with the cause of union labor terribly hit by its own fool-friends, with his paper making a yearly profit of from three to five hundred thousand dollars and carrying more advertising, it is claimed, than any other newspaper in the world, Harrison Gray Otis, at the age of seventy-four, still rides the crest of the wave triumphant, as uncompromising as ever, grim, peppery, militant, probably the most hated man in America today, but glorying in that hatred, as well as in the equally intense loyalty of his own employees and followers.[28]

In 1929 the *Times* published a supplement entitled *The Forty-Year War for a Free City.* The publication described the history of the open shop in Los Angeles, as seen by the management of the newspaper, and placed particular emphasis upon 1910, that revolutionary year in the development of the local labor movement:

> The year 1910 was the most important of all the forty during which the war for the open shop has been in progress in Los Angeles—perhaps, in its results, the most important in the whole history of the struggle for industrial freedom everywhere.... Its real significance lies in the fact that its grim events finally ripped the mask from the sinister agencies of death and destruction that long had masqueraded as the friends and defenders of the American workingman and left them stark and horrible for an incredulous world to shudder at.... The series of revelations marked an industrial turning-point not only in Los Angeles but in the country at large. From that year forward the open shop has been definitely in the ascendant.[29]

In both the title and message of this special supplement, as well as in its daily news columns, the *Times* placed the beginning of the open-shop contest in Los Angeles in 1890, the year of the printers' "big strike." By selecting 1910—the year of the bombing—as the date when the ascendancy of the open shop could no longer be questioned, the *Times* ascribed crucial significance to events in which the newspaper itself played a leading role. As has been seen, time and again, there were many observers who echoed Otis and his newspaper in crediting the *Times* with establishing, for good or for ill, "industrial freedom" in Los Angeles. In the opinion of the National Association of Manufacturers, the Merchants' and Manufacturers' Association, employers' organizations, and other like-minded bodies, Otis was the hero of the battle fought out in the score of years between 1890 and 1910; by the same token, in the eyes of organized labor, he was the villain of the

drama. But certainly there was no disagreement on the net result of
the contest or on the significance of Otis' contribution to that result.

Of all the influences that retarded the development of the Los Angeles labor movement, the *Times* was the most striking, the most dramatic, and the most obvious. It is therefore easy to slip into the error
of exaggerating its importance to the extent of belittling other factors
which certainly did not lack weight in determining the final outcome.
The tardy shift from an agricultural to an industrial economy, the slow
development of manufacturing, the geographical and psychological
isolation of Los Angeles in early decades, the phenomenal population
growth, the character of immigration into the area, the climate, the
relatively easy life—all these were essential parts of the composite
atmosphere in which the labor movement came into being and advanced through its various stages of growth, and each of them worked
in some way to the disadvantage of organized labor. Nevertheless, without discounting or neglecting the largely unseen operation of such
influences, observers could justifiably, without prejudice or partisanship, assess the *Times* as the outstanding single determinant of the
trend of industrial relations in Los Angeles, and the twenty years between 1890 and 1910 as the period when the characteristics of the local
labor movement were set.

Although a labor movement had existed in Los Angeles before 1890,
its activities were too experimental in nature to contribute any specific
or lasting quality to the unionism of a later day. Its only source of continuity was the Typographical Union, organized in 1875 and persistently clinging to life through adversities that might have defeated
groups of lesser spirit. But, whatever its strength and stability, one
union alone could not transform a weak and fumbling infant labor
movement into a powerful and purposeful body of organized labor.
The unions which sprang up and flourished briefly during the prosperous 1880's provided only the first hesitant approach to the solution of
workers' problems. Their trial and error procedures, however, were
adequate enough in a situation as yet uncomplicated by united employer opposition or by the militant enmity of the *Times*. The newspaper, founded in 1881 and joined by Otis in 1882, utilized the pre-1890
period to establish itself on the sound business basis essential to a successful enterprise. Preoccupation with its own commercial and political
problems ruled out any overt antilabor moves by the *Times,* and limited
it to occasional exploratory attempts to ascertain union strength or
community sentiment. Yet the paper's editorial tone revealed a strong
predisposition against the aims and methods of unionism, and a more

experienced labor movement might have taken warning of trouble on the horizon. But the unions of the 1880's, almost without exception, were too superficial to survive the hard times of the latter part of the decade, and were in a badly disorganized state by 1890.

The printers' strike of 1890 set in motion the forces which determined the character of the Los Angeles labor movement for many years to come. The unions found it a stimulus which, added to their unhappy experiences of the previous decade, spurred the creation and expansion of a centralized labor movement. This body of organized labor, in continuous existence ever since 1890, was far more aware of its obligations to workers and to the community than its predecessor of the 1880's. In 1894 it affiliated with the American Federation of Labor, thus establishing a link with the national labor movement that was later to be of inestimable benefit. It progressed sufficiently far in unification and in strength to prevent complete collapse in the long depression of the 1890's. Although greatly weakened by the hard times at the end of the century, the Los Angeles unions retained enough vitality and spirit to respond quickly in 1900 to more advantageous conditions.

The printers' strike not only instigated the organization of a labor movement with staying power, but it brought the latent hostility of the *Times* into the open. At no time after 1890 was there serious or prolonged doubt concerning the attitude of Otis and his convenient vehicle of a newspaper toward the problems of labor relations. During the 1890's, while the labor movement was developing, the *Times* began in earnest to create a community sentiment against organized labor. Although little progress was made in unifying employer opposition to unionism, a solid groundwork was laid in the organization first of the Merchants' Association, then of the Manufacturers' Association, and finally, in 1896, of the Merchants' and Manufacturers' Association through consolidation. The M and M, although not openly antiunion before 1900, provided a necessary nucleus for later implementation of a concerted drive for the open shop. Thus the decade of the 1890's was a period of preparation for the great contest between organized labor and organized management which characterized the first decade of the twentieth century. Heard throughout the period, above all else, was the insistent voice of the *Times,* castigating labor leaders, decrying union methods, singing the praises of industrial freedom, and lauding the independence of workingmen free of the shackles of unionism.

The *Times* became still more insistent after 1900, when it was apparent that the labor movement was steadily advancing in size and strength and that employers were more willing than before to pool their resources in an effort to retard unionism. Encouraged and publicized by the *Times,* employers' associations became more numerous and more militant as the decade advanced, and gave overwhelming evidence of their ability to thwart even the most powerful of unions. But Otis, though noting with satisfaction the progress of such organizations, wanted a more general alliance of employers to confront the whole body of organized labor. Early in the decade he formed a small Employers' Association which performed for several years the antiunion functions later assumed by the Merchants' and Manufacturers' Association. The latter body turned from its early avoidance of labor-management disputes to active intervention as a direct result of the fight between the unions and the *Times.* Labor's secondary boycott against *Times* advertisers, particularly the People's Store, convinced the M and M that it could no longer shut its eyes to union practices which it regarded as harmful to the business community. Once the decision was made, the M and M threw its powerful weight behind the employers' associations in ever-increasing measure, until it became a full partner with the *Times* in the cause of preserving industrial freedom and establishing the open shop.

Against such an array of wealth and influence, organized labor was almost helpless. All the counteroffensives it could devise—strikes, boycotts, the *Examiner,* reorganizations of the central labor body, creation of an authoritative hierarchy, political endeavors—were nullified by the powerful combination of forces in opposition to unionism. Even the American Federation of Labor was unable to impede the victorious march of the open-shop principle in Los Angeles. Industrial freedom became the ideal of the community just as it was the hallmark of the *Times* and the guiding concept of employers. Even before the calamitous events of 1910–1911, the open shop had been firmly established in Los Angeles.

Whether the rise of industrial freedom would have been so certain and the influence of the open shop so predominant if there had been no Los Angeles *Times* and no Harrison Gray Otis is one of the unanswerable questions of history. Yet the conclusion seems almost inescapable that, other factors remaining constant, organized labor would have found the battle easier without the *Times.* The power of the press in influencing public opinion and in fostering a pet theory had been forcibly brought home to Los Angeles labor through bitter experience. The determination of Otis to fashion community thinking into a pattern of his own devising, and to make it reflect the antiunion principles on which his newspaper operated, was in its successful implementation the overshadowing influence which made Los Angeles an open-shop city.

APPENDIXES

APPENDIX A

Sources for organization dates in table 5

NOTE

[1] *Times*, September 4, 1900.
[2] *Times*, September 4, 1901.
[3] *Record*, October 1, 1900.
[4] *Record*, December 6, 1900.
[5] *American Federationist*, January, 1901, p. 26.
[6] *American Federationist*, September, 1901, pp. 386–7.
[7] *Record*, September 2, 1901.
[8] *Souvenir Program 20th Annual Convention, California State Council of Carpenters, 1948* ([Los Angeles, 1948]), p. 15.
[9] *Record*, May 28, 1901.
[10] *American Federationist*, February, 1902, p. 76.
[11] *Union Labor News*, November 7, 1902.
[12] *Souvenir Program 20th Annual Convention, California State Council of Carpenters, 1948* ([Los Angeles, 1948]), p. 19.
[13] *American Federationist*, May, 1902, p. 243.
[14] *Union Labor News*, April 18, 1902.
[15] *American Federationist*, November, 1902, p. 821.
[16] California State Federation of Labor, *Proceedings, 1903*, p. 7.
[17] *American Federationist*, May, 1903, p. 387.
[18] *American Federationist*, April, 1903, p. 282.
[19] *Record*, April 24, 1903.
[20] *American Federationist*, March, 1903, p. 186.
[21] *American Federationist*, September, 1903, p. 950.
[22] *Times*, June 1, 1904.
[23] *Examiner*, September 18, 1904.
[24] *Examiner*, March 8, 1904.
[25] *Record*, November 13, 1900.
[26] *Times*, April 4, 1901.
[27] *Times*, April 3, 1901.
[28] *Record*, May 29, 1901.
[29] *Record*, May 1, 1901.
[30] *Record*, May 31, 1901.
[31] LATU, *Minutes 1898–1902*, p. 326.
[32] *American Federationist*, September, 1902, p. 525.
[33] *Examiner*, March 10, 1904.
[34] *Record*, May 4, 1903.
[35] *Times*, May 14, 1903.
[36] *Union Labor News*, December 18, 1903.
[37] *Union Labor News*, December 25, 1903.
[38] *American Federationist*, October, 1903, p. 1070.
[39] *Times*, May 19, 1903.
[40] *American Federationist*, May, 1904, p. 421.
[41] *American Federationist*, August, 1904, p. 664.
[42] *Examiner*, June 7, 1904.
[43] *Record*, December 7, 1900.
[44] *American Federationist*, February, 1901, p. 61.
[45] *American Federationist*, December, 1901, p. 556.
[46] *American Federationist*, April, 1901, p. 134.
[47] *Record*, April 1, 1901.
[48] *American Federationist*, April, 1901, p. 134.
[49] *Common Sense*, February 1, 1907.

[50] *Record,* April 16, 1903.

[51] *American Federationist,* November, 1903, p. 1176.

[52] *Examiner,* January 13, 1904.

[53] LATU, *Minutes 1902–1905,* p. 174.

[54] *Examiner,* January 29, 1905.

[55] *Examiner,* January 13, 1905.

[56] *Record,* December 12, 1900.

[57] *Times,* May 30, 1901.

[58] *Record,* November 22, 1901.

[59] *Record,* October 29, 1901.

[60] *Union Labor News,* March 28, 1902.

[61] *Tenth Biennial Report, 1901–1902,* California Bureau of Labor Statistics, p. 68.

[62] *Record,* July 8, 1903.

[63] *Times,* February 12, 1903.

[64] *Examiner,* June 17, 1904.

[65] *Examiner,* September 18, 1904.

[66] *Eleventh Biennial Report, 1903–1904,* California Bureau of Labor Statistics, p. 38.

[67] *Record,* November 2, 1900.

[68] *Times,* September 17, 1902.

[69] *Tenth Biennial Report, 1901–1902,* California Bureau of Labor Statistics, p. 73.

[70] *American Federationist,* January, 1904, p. 58.

[71] *Examiner,* May 26, 1904.

[72] *Eleventh Biennial Report, 1903–1904,* California Bureau of Labor Statistics, p. 39.

[73] *American Federationist,* October, 1901, p. 434.

[74] Board of Publishers of the Organized Labor Movement, *Official Year Book and Reference Manual of the Organized Labor Movement of Los Angeles, 1922,* p. 37.

[75] *Times,* August 22, 1900.

[76] *Record,* June 26, 1901.

[77] *Record,* February 1, 1904.

APPENDIX B

Industry	Year of organiza-tion	Source
BUILDING AND CONSTRUCTION		
†Building laborers...............	1905	*Union Labor News*, November 24, 1905
Elevator constructors............	1905	*American Federationist*, February, 1906, p. 101
†Plumbers' helpers...............	1905	*Examiner*, February 1, 1905
Woodcarvers and modelers.......	1905	*Examiner*, October 11, 1905
Brick, tile and terracotta workers..	1906	*Examiner*, July 29, 1906
Hardwood floor layers...........	1906	*Examiner*, September 1, 1906
†Marble setters..................	1906	*Examiner*, August 30, 1906
Paper hangers...................	1906	*Union Labor News*, March 9, 1906
Plaster casters..................	1906	*Examiner*, May 29, 1906
Plumbers—steamfitters..........	1906	*Examiner*, May 16, 1906
Marble setters' helpers...........	1907	*Union Labor News*, January 25, 1907
Painters........................	1907	*Citizen*, December 13, 1907
Stone masons...................	1907	*Citizen*, March 8, 1907
†Art glass workers...............	1909	*Citizen*, June 18, 1909
†Electrical workers..............	1909	*Citizen*, March 26, 1909
Steam engineers—hoisting and portable engineers............	1909	*Citizen*, July 16, 1909
Stonecutters...................	1909	*Citizen*, March 5, 1909
SERVICES, EXCEPT PUBLIC		
†Commercial telegraphers........	1905	*Union Labor News*, January 4, 1907
Elevator operators..............	1906	*Examiner*, November 14, 1906
Fruit and vegetable vendors......	1906	*Examiner*, April 8, 1906
Junk peddlers..................	1906	*Union Labor News*, February 16, 1906
†Railway postal clerks...........	1906	*Examiner*, June 8, 1906
†Cooks........................	1907	*Citizen*, July 5, 1907
Moving picture machine operators	1907	*Citizen*, November 22, 1907
†Waitresses.....................	1908	*Citizen*, February 28, 1909
MANUFACTURING		
Asbestos workers...............	1906	*Union Labor News*, December 14, 1906
†Bakers' helpers.................	1906	*Union Labor News*, June 8, 1906
Boot and shoe workers..........	1906	*Union Labor News*, March 9, 1906
†Cloak makers..................	1907	*Citizen*, May 12, 1907
†Millmen......................	1908	*Citizen*, October 9, 1908
Ladies tailors..................	1909	*Citizen*, October 8, 1909

† This sign indicates each union for which the year of organization is estimated.

Industry	Year of organization	Source
TRANSPORTATION AND STORAGE		
Automobile drivers and helpers....	1905	*Examiner*, November 14, 1905
Ice wagon drivers...............	1906	*Union Labor News*, October 5, 1906
Milk wagon drivers.............	1906	*Union Labor News*, January 11, 1907
METAL TRADES		
Machinists' helpers.............	1906	*Examiner*, December 30, 1906
PRINTING TRADES		
Web pressmen.................	1905	Board of Publishers of the Organized Labor Movement, *Official Year Book and Reference Manual of the Organized Labor Movement of Los Angeles, 1922*, p. 37

NOTES

Chapter I

ANTECEDENTS OF THE LABOR MOVEMENT

[1] *Fourteenth Census of the United States, 1920*, Vol. I, *Population*, p. 82.

[2] James Bryce, *The American Commonwealth* (2d ed., rev.; New York: Commonwealth Publishing Co., 1908), II, 439.

[3] *Loc. cit.*

[4] Nathan Fine, *Labor and Farmer Parties in the United States, 1828–1928* (New York: Rand School of Social Science [c. 1928]), p. 35; Lucile Eaves, *A History of California Labor Legislation* (Berkeley: The University Press [c. 1910]), pp. 6–8; Ira B. Cross, *A History of the Labor Movement in California* (Berkeley: University of California Press, 1935), pp. 28–9; Carl Plehn, "Labor in California," *Yale Review*, IV (Feb., 1896), 420.

[5] [Helen Hunt Jackson], "Outdoor Industries in Southern California," *Century Magazine*, XXVI (Oct., 1883), 803.

[6] Laurance L. Hill, *La Reina—Los Angeles in Three Centuries* (Los Angeles: Security Trust and Savings Bank [c. 1929]), pp. 35–8; Cross, *op. cit.*, p. 249.

[7] Robert Glass Cleland, *The Cattle on a Thousand Hills* (San Marino: The Huntington Library, 1941), pp. 185–6; Robert Glass Cleland and Osgood Hardy, *March of Industry* (Los Angeles: Powell Publishing Co. [c. 1929]), pp. 133–6; John S. Hittell, *The Commerce and Industries of the Pacific Coast of North America* (San Francisco: A. L. Bancroft & Co., 1882), p. 114; *Manufactures, California*, U. S. Bureau of the Census, Bulletin no. 136 (Washington: 1902), pp. 3–4; *Weekly Star*, Dec. 3, 1859. (Unless otherwise specified, newspapers cited were published in Los Angeles.)

[8] [John Albert Wilson], *History of Los Angeles County, California* (Oakland, Calif.: Thompson and West, 1880), pp. 76–7; George A. Tracy, comp., *History of the Typographical Union* ([Indianapolis]: International Typographical Union, 1913), pp. 194–5; Julia Norton McCorkle, "A History of Los Angeles Journalism," *Publications of the Historical Society of Southern California*, X (1915–1916), 25–6. Information about Los Angeles Typographical Union No. 44 was supplied from the records of the International Typographical Union by Mr. Clark B. Hicks, Research Director, in a letter to the author dated April 1, 1948. Mr. Hicks found the membership list in the November, 1859, issue of *The Printer*, official organ of the national union from 1859 to 1866.

[9] John R. Commons and Associates, *History of Labor in the United States* (New York: Macmillan, 1921–1935), I, 104, 109; Cross, *op. cit.*, pp. 15, 21, 24, 28, 303; Tracy, *op. cit.*, p. 187; Harris Newmark, *Sixty Years in Southern California, 1853–1913* (New York: Knickerbocker Press, 1916), p. 256; J. J. Warner, Benjamin Hayes, and J. P. Widney, *An Historical Sketch of Los Angeles County, California, from the Spanish Occupancy, by the Founding of the Mission San Gabriel Archangel, September 8, 1771, to July 4, 1876* (Los Angeles: Louis Lewin & Co., 1876), p. 12; *Semi-Weekly Southern News*, Feb. 8, 1860; Apr. 5, 10, 1861.

[10] Charles Dwight Willard, *History of Los Angeles City* (Los Angeles: Kingsley-Barnes and Neuner Co., 1901), pp. 304–6; Cleland and Hardy, *op. cit.*, pp. 231–2; Warner, Hayes, and Widney, *op. cit.*, pp. 125–6.

[11] Philip S. Foner, *History of the Labor Movement in the United States* (New York: International Publishers [c. 1947]), p. 369; Fine, *op. cit.*, p. 23.

[12] Eaves, *op. cit.*, pp. 16–19, 199–201; Cross, *op. cit.*, pp. 37–48.

[13] Eaves, *op. cit.*, pp. 22, 204–6, 210–11; Cross, *op. cit.*, pp. 50–2; Commons and Associates, *op. cit.*, II, 108; *Semi-Weekly News*, Feb. 25, Mar. 10, 1868.

[14] *Semi-Weekly News*, May 22, 1868.

[15] *Ibid.*, July 14, 1868.

[16] *Daily News*, Apr. 26, 1869.

[17] [Wilson], *op. cit.*, p. 123.

[18] *Daily News,* Mar. 21, 1869.

[19] Eaves, *op. cit.,* pp. 19, 22, 212–13; Cross, *op. cit.,* pp. 51, 54–5.

[20] Warner, Hayes, and Widney, *op. cit.,* pp. 128, 130–1; Cleland and Hardy, *op. cit.,* pp. 82–4; Cross, *op. cit.,* p. 269; Willard, *op. cit.,* pp. 316–19; *Fourteenth Census of the United States, 1920,* Vol. I, *Population,* pp. 82, 95; James J. Ayers, *Gold and Sunshine, Reminiscences of Early California* (Boston: Richard G. Badger [c. 1922]), pp. 267–80; San Francisco *Bulletin,* Oct. 29, Nov. 6, Dec. 12, 1879; June 19, 1880.

[21] Solon J. Buck, *The Granger Movement,* Harvard Historical Series, vol. 19 (Cambridge: Harvard University Press, 1913), p. 60; [Wilson], *op. cit.,* p. 123; *Daily Star,* July 15, 22, 1873.

[22] Anna Rochester, *The Populist Movement in the United States* (New York: International Publishers [c. 1943]), pp. 20–1; Buck, *op. cit.,* p. 52; Fine, *op. cit.,* p. 56.

[23] Ezra Slocum Carr, *The Patrons of Husbandry on the Pacific Coast* (San Francisco: A. L. Bancroft & Co., 1875), pp. 228–66 *passim;* [Wilson], *op. cit.,* p. 123; *Daily Star,* July 17, 29, Aug. 10, Sept. 23, 1873.

[24] William A. Spalding, comp., *History and Reminiscences, Los Angeles City and County, California* (Los Angeles: J. R. Finnell & Sons Publishing Co. [1931]), I, 219; Herald Publishing Co., *The Herald Pamphlet for 1876* (Los Angeles: Herald Publishing Co., 1876), p. 59; Buck, *op. cit.,* p. 264; Carr, *op. cit.,* p. 167; [Wilson], *op. cit.,* p. 126; *Daily Star,* Oct. 3, 1873; Feb. 1, 1878; *Herald,* Dec. 4, 5, 1873; *Times,* July 1, 1883.

[25] Buck, *op. cit.,* pp. 59–60; Bryce, *op. cit.,* II, 441; Rochester, *op. cit.,* p. 22.

[26] Solon J. Buck, *The Agrarian Crusade,* Chronicles of America Series, vol. 45 (New Haven: Yale University Press, 1921), p. 35; *Daily Star,* July 13, 27, Aug. 24, Sept. 2–4, 6, 11, 1873.

[27] *Herald,* Oct. 4, Nov. 14, 1873.

[28] *Ibid.,* Nov. 11, 14, 15, 27, Dec. 2, 1873.

[29] Selig Perlman, *A History of Trade Unionism in the United States* (New York: Macmillan, 1922), p. 62; Eaves, *op. cit.,* pp. 5–6; Mary Coolidge, *Chinese Immigration* (New York: Holt, 1909), pp. 384, 389–90.

[30] Eaves, *op. cit.,* pp. 20, 115, 117, 126–7, 134–8; Commons and Associates, *op. cit.,* II, 148–51.

[31] *Eighth Census of the United States, 1860,* Vol. I, *Population,* pp. 24–5; *Ninth Census of the United States, 1870,* Vol. I, *Population,* pp. 15–16; Eaves, *op. cit.,* p. 140; Willard, *op. cit.,* pp. 279–80; *Express,* June 24, 1873; *Daily Star,* June 27, 1873.

[32] *Express,* Nov. 2, 1876.

[33] *Daily Star,* May 10, 1876.

[34] *Ibid.,* May 18, 1876.

[35] *Ibid.,* June 2, Aug. 24, Sept. 15, 1876; *Express,* Aug. 23, 1876; *Constitution and By-Laws of the Anti-Coolie Club No. One of Los Angeles, California* (Los Angeles: Herald Steam Job Printing House, 1876), *passim.*

[36] Eaves, *op. cit.,* p. 27.

Chapter II

LABOR VENTURES INTO POLITICS

[1] See chapter iii for a discussion of the printers' union organized in 1875.

[2] The sand lots were a vacant plot of ground in front of the San Francisco courthouse, used for years by soapbox orators.

[3] Ira B. Cross, *A History of the Labor Movement in California* (Berkeley: University of California Press, 1935), pp. 88–93; Lucile Eaves, *A History of California Labor Legislation* (Berkeley: The University Press [c. 1910]), pp. 23–5, 150.

[4] Cross, *op. cit.,* pp. 93–6.

⁵ *Ibid.*, pp. 96–112; Eaves, *op. cit.*, pp. 31, 34–5.

⁶ Eaves, *op. cit.*, p. 27; James J. Ayers, *Gold and Sunshine, Reminiscences of Early California* (Boston: Richard G. Badger [c. 1922]), pp. 275–80, 305–6; *San Francisco Bulletin*, Nov. 6, Dec. 12, 1879; June 19, 1880.

⁷ *Herald*, Aug. 2, 1877; *Express*, Aug. 2, 1877.

⁸ This led to a not wholly acceptable argument that the Los Angeles movement would have arisen independently of San Francisco, based on the claim that the party's first political meeting was convened in Los Angeles and that the first ticket was offered in Los Angeles County. Priority of meetings rests on an individual interpretation of San Francisco chronology, but it is true that the party's first political venture came with the Los Angeles elections of September, 1877. See the *Herald* of July 31, 1879, for elaboration of the argument.

⁹ *Express*, Aug. 3, 1877.

¹⁰ *Ibid.*, Aug. 4, 1877.

¹¹ *Herald*, Aug. 7, 10, 28, 1877; *Express*, Aug. 9–11, 14, 25, 28, 1877.

¹² *Express*, Aug. 14, 30, 1877.

¹³ *Herald*, Mar. 8, 9, 1878.

¹⁴ *Ibid.*, Aug. 11, 29, 1877; *Express*, Aug. 11, 14, 25, 1877.

¹⁵ *Express*, Aug. 18, 1877.

¹⁶ *Ibid.*, Apr. 16, 1873; Aug. 28, Sept. 3, 4, 7, 1877; Mar. 6, 1878; *Herald*, Feb. 24, 1878; July 31, 1879. Page was referring to Leland Stanford and the Central Pacific Railroad.

¹⁷ Cross, *op. cit.*, p. 107; *Herald*, Nov. 8, Dec. 18, 20, 1877; *Express*, Dec. 10, 1877.

¹⁸ *Herald*, Dec. 23, 27, 1877.

¹⁹ *Express*, Nov. 2, 1876; Feb. 27, 1882; *Porcupine*, May 5, 1883. *Porcupine*, a weekly, was established on November 11, 1882, by Horace Bell, who was also editor. It was neutral in politics and claimed to uphold the interests of the people.

²⁰ *Express*, Jan. 4, 1878.

²¹ *Daily Star*, Feb. 1, 1878; *Herald*, Feb. 3, 1878; *Express*, Feb. 4, 21, 1878.

²² *Express*, Feb. 4, 1878.

²³ Cross, *op. cit.*, pp. 113–17, 119.

²⁴ *Herald*, Feb. 24, Mar. 3, 14, 1878; *Express*, Feb. 25–27, Mar. 4, 8, 13–15, 1878; *Daily Star*, Mar. 20, Oct. 1, 4, 12, 27, 29, Nov. 13, 16, 1878.

²⁵ *Herald*, Mar. 22, Apr. 10, 11, 13, 1878; *Express*, Mar. 23, Apr. 10, 18, 19, 27, 30, May 6, 7, 1878; *Daily Star*, Apr. 14, 17, 21, 1878; Cross, *op. cit.*, pp. 113–17.

²⁶ *Express*, Feb. 21, Mar. 2, 4, Aug. 1, 1878; *Daily Star*, Mar. 10, 12, 1878. A party leader's suggestion that women establish a female labor bureau to supplant Chinese domestics with white servants was not followed. (*Herald*, Jan. 13, 1878.)

²⁷ J. C. Stedman and R. A. Leonard, *The Workingmen's Party of California* (San Francisco: Bacon & Co., 1878), p. 21; *Daily Star*, Mar. 6, Oct. 11, 12, 31, Nov. 8, 1878; *Express*, Apr. 17, July 17, 22, Aug. 12, 1878; *Herald*, Nov. 27, 1878.

²⁸ *Daily Star*, Apr. 19, 28, May 2, 22, June 18, 24, 1878; *Express*, May 21, 31, 1878; *Herald*, June 18, 1878.

²⁹ *Herald*, Nov. 28, 1877; July 25, Dec. 5, 1878; Apr. 10, 19, May 30, 1879; *Express*, Jan. 15, Aug. 1, Dec. 31, 1878; *Daily Star*, Dec. 4, 1878; *San Francisco Post*, Apr. 5, 1879; Julia Norton McCorkle, "A History of Los Angeles Journalism," *Annual Publications of the Historical Society of Southern California*, X (1915–1916), 32. Kinley had interests outside the welfare of the working class. He was one of the founders of the Historical Society of Southern California, organized in November, 1883, and was president for 1886. In the same year he published in Los Angeles a collection of poems under the title *Labor Rhymes*, a copy of which is in the Huntington Library.

³⁰ *Express*, May 27, July 3, 1878.

³¹ D. G. Waldron and T. J. Vivian, eds., *Biographical Sketches of the Delegates to the Convention to Frame a New Constitution for the State of California, 1878* (San

Francisco: Francis & Valentine, 1878), p. 171 and *passim;* Cross, *op. cit.,* pp. 117–18; Ayers, *op. cit.,* pp. 305–6; *Herald,* Feb. 27, Mar. 19, Apr. 22, 1879.

[32] San Francisco *Post,* July 31, Aug. 8, 1878. Workingmen and farmers together nominated A. M. Rodgers, a Vernon farmer, for supervisor. He received 832 votes, his nearest competitor polling only 188. (*Express,* Aug. 20, 26, Sept. 5, 9, 1878.)

[33] *Daily Star,* Nov. 14, 1878.

[34] *Herald,* June 18, Sept. 12, 1878; *Express,* Sept. 3, 11, 1878; *Daily Star,* Oct. 11, 12, Nov. 1, 27, 1878.

[35] *Herald,* July 31, 1879.

[36] *Daily Star,* Nov. 12, 1878.

[37] *Express,* Nov. 18, 19, 1878; *Herald,* Nov. 26–28, Dec. 2, 1878; *Daily Star,* Nov. 26, Dec. 1, 1878.

[38] *Express,* Nov. 30, 1878; *Daily Star,* Dec. 1, 1878.

[39] *Express,* Dec. 3, 1878.

[40] San Francisco *Post,* Dec. 31, 1878; *Herald,* Jan. 26, July 31, 1879.

[41] *Herald,* Jan. 29, 30, Feb. 4–7, 9, 12, 14, Apr. 11, 15, May 4, July 31, Aug. 8, Sept. 26, 1879; Eaves, *op. cit.,* pp. 145, 153–4, 157.

[42] *Herald,* May 18, July 9, 1879; Dec. 4–6, 1885.

[43] *Ibid.,* July 31, 1879.

[44] *Ibid.,* Jan. 17, Feb. 14, Mar. 30, Apr. 1, 4, 10, 18, May 30, June 6, July 4, Aug. 19, 22, 1879.

[45] *Ibid.,* May 25, June 27, July 1, 2, 1879.

[46] *Ibid.,* July 22, 23, Aug. 10, 21, 28, 31, Sept. 2, 12, 1879. Plans to continue the *Voice of Labor* as a weekly after the election did not materialize. Isaac Kinley had started the *Weekly Commoner,* sympathetic to the Workingmen, in May, 1879, but suspended publication in June because of an attempt on his life. (*Herald,* Apr. 22, May 24, June 1, 6, 1879.) A new Workingmen's organ, *The Outlook,* enjoyed a brief existence in November, 1879. (*Herald,* Nov. 8, 1879.)

[47] *Herald,* Sept. 26, Nov. 5, 15, 16, 19, 26, Dec. 2, 5, 1879; San Francisco *Bulletin,* Oct. 25, 27, 29, 1879. Estimates of the amount embezzled by Hamilton varied between $10,000 and $20,000.

[48] Cross, *op. cit.,* pp. 125–7; *Express,* May 19, 20, 1880.

[49] *Herald,* Dec. 3, 4, 10, 12, 1879; *Express,* May 4, 5, 7, 8, June 7, 1880.

[50] *Express,* June 18, 28, July 6, 16, 17, 1880.

[51] *Ibid.,* Aug. 9, 10, 1880; Solon J. Buck, *The Agrarian Crusade,* Chronicles of America Series, vol. 45 (New Haven: Yale University Press, 1921), pp. 77–90, 93–6.

[52] *Express,* Aug. 10, 11, 23, Oct. 5, 11, 25, 30, 1880.

[53] *Ibid.,* Nov. 5, 19, Dec. 6, 9, 1880.

[54] Cross, *op. cit.,* p. 129; Paul S. Taylor, "Foundations of California Rural Society," *California Historical Society Quarterly,* XXIV (Sept., 1945), 222; *Migratory Labor in California,* State Relief Administration, Division of Special Surveys and Studies ([San Francisco]: 1936), p. 67.

[55] Cross, *op. cit.,* p. 129.

[56] *Ibid.,* p. 120.

Chapter III

GENESIS OF THE LABOR MOVEMENT

[1] Ira B. Cross, *A History of the Labor Movement in California* (Berkeley: University of California Press, 1935), pp. 60–8, 312; George A. Tracy, comp., *History of the Typographical Union* ([Indianapolis]: International Typographical Union, 1913), pp. 245, 247; J. J. Warner, Benjamin Hayes, and J. P. Widney, *An Historical Sketch of Los Angeles County*...(Los Angeles: Louis Lewin & Co., 1876), pp. 127–31; [John Albert Wilson], *History of Los Angeles County*...(Oakland, Calif.: Thompson and

West, 1880), pp. 76–8; William A. Spalding, comp., *History and Reminiscences, Los Angeles City and County* ... (Los Angeles: J. R. Finnell & Sons Publishing Co. [1931]), I, 205. The *Weekly Mirror* was one of the earliest "throw-away" papers in Los Angeles. Its publishers, Jesse Yarnell and T. J. Caystile, were among the group which established the Los Angeles *Times* in 1881. A chart of the real estate cycle in Los Angeles County from 1850 to 1945 appears in the September 13, 1947, issue of the *Monthly Summary, Business Conditions in Southern California,* published by the Security-First National Bank of Los Angeles.

[2] George E. McNeill, *The Labor Movement: The Problem of To-day* (Boston: Bridgman, 1887), p. 355; Tracy, *op. cit.,* p. 113; letter from Clark B. Hicks, Research Director of the International Typographical Union, to the author, April 1, 1948.

[3] "... We see the Trade Union springing, not from any particular institution, but from every opportunity for the meeting together of wage-earners of the same occupation." (Sidney and Beatrice Webb, *The History of Trade Unionism* [rev. ed., extended to 1920; London: Longmans, Green, 1935], pp. 22–3.)

[4] *Express,* Jan. 8, 12, 19, 20, 22, 23, 1874; Oct. 25, 1875; *Herald,* Jan. 9, 13, 14, 1874; *Tribune,* Mar. 24, 1888; Cross, *op. cit.,* p. 269; Los Angeles Typographical Union No. 174 (hereinafter cited as LATU), *Minutes 1875–1885,* pp. 3–5, 6–15; *Minutes 1888–1890,* p. 27; *Golden Jubilee, 1875–1925* (Los Angeles: Typographical Union No. 174, 1925), unpaged. Paynter paid the charter fee out of his own pocket.

[5] *Official Trades and Labor Souvenir Directory of Los Angeles and Vicinity* (Los Angeles: Council of Labor and Building Trades Council, [1896]), p. 37. This source will hereafter be cited as *Official Trades and Labor Directory, Los Angeles, 1896.*

[6] LATU, *Minutes 1875–1885,* pp. 16–29 *passim,* 31, 33.

[7] *Ibid.,* pp. 34–49 *passim; Official Trades and Labor Directory, Los Angeles, 1896,* p. 37.

[8] LATU, *Minutes 1875–1885,* pp. 46–7.

[9] Cross, though mistakenly dating this dispute in 1876, claims that the *Star* was unionized but gives no authority. (Cross, *op. cit.,* p. 269.) In an unpublished master's thesis, Helen Flannery states that the dispute was settled to the union's satisfaction. Her authority was Joseph Phillis, whom she personally interviewed and whose notes and memoranda she used. Phillis became a member of the Los Angeles Typographical Union in 1886, and was for many years prominent in the labor movement. (Helen Flannery, "The Labor Movement in Los Angeles, 1880–1903" [unpublished M.A. thesis, University of California, Berkeley, 1929], p. 4.)

[10] LATU, *Minutes 1875–1885,* p. 53; *Times,* May 9, 1883; [Wilson], *op. cit.,* p. 78. The *Commercial,* established as a Republican paper on March 6, 1879, expired in May, 1883.

[11] LATU, *Minutes 1875–1885,* pp. 56–61.

[12] *Ibid.,* pp. 62–71.

[13] Cross, *op. cit.,* pp. 130–2.

[14] *Ibid.,* pp. 269–70; LATU, *Minutes 1875–1885,* pp. 72–7, 80–3; *Official Trades and Labor Directory, Los Angeles, 1896,* p. 38.

[15] Spalding, *op. cit.,* I, 245–6; III, 79. The remark was made by Charles Edward Locke, bishop of the Methodist Episcopal Church, at the unveiling of the Otis statue in Westlake Park, Los Angeles. It is quoted from Spalding, *op. cit.,* III, 79.

[16] Frederick Palmer, "Otistown of the Open Shop," *Hampton's Magazine,* XXVI (Jan., 1911), 29–44. The quotation is from page 32.

[17] Spalding, *op. cit.,* III, 77; *Mr. Otis and the Los Angeles "Times"* (Los Angeles: Typographical Union No. 174, 1915), p. 2; *Examiner,* July 24, 1906. O. P. Wharton, a resident of Pasadena, had been editor of the Rock Island *Courier* in 1852, when the Otis incident occurred. In the *Examiner's* article revealing Otis' early interest in unionism, Wharton reported that he had chided Otis for his change of front, and that Otis had excused his youthful indiscretion by saying that he was only an apprentice printer at the time.

[18] Tracy, *op. cit.*, p. 903.

[19] *Times*, Aug. 7, 1883.

[20] LATU, *Minutes 1875–1885*, pp. 94, 97, 160; *Herald*, Aug. 15, 1883.

[21] *Official Trades and Labor Directory, Los Angeles, 1896*, p. 38.

[22] *Ibid.*, p. 38; LATU, *Minutes 1875–1885*, pp. 98–100; *Herald*, Aug. 18, 1883; *Free Lance*, Aug. 21, 1883. *Free Lance* first appeared in July, 1883, as a daily Republican paper, circulated gratuitously. It survived for only a few months. See chapter iv for a discussion of the Knights of Labor.

[23] LATU, *Minutes 1875–1885*, pp. 101–2, 106; *Herald*, July 6, 17, Aug. 21, 1883; *Free Lance*, Aug. 18, 21, 1883; *Times*, Aug. 29, 1883.

[24] *Free Lance*, Aug. 21, 1883; *Herald*, Aug. 21, 1883.

[25] *Times*, Aug. 18, 1883.

[26] *Official Trades and Labor Directory, Los Angeles, 1896*, p. 38.

[27] LATU, *Minutes 1875–1885*, p. 104; Norman J. Ware, *The Labor Movement in the United States, 1860–1895* (New York: Appleton, 1929), pp. 236–9.

[28] LATU, *Minutes 1875–1885*, pp. 104–8; Cross, *op. cit.*, p. 270; *Official Trades and Labor Directory, Los Angeles, 1896*, pp. 38–9; Flannery, *op. cit.*, pp. 6–7 and n. 16.

[29] Joseph Phillis, "Capt. F. B. Colver," *Citizen*, Feb. 10, 1911; *Citizen*, June 23, 1911; LATU, *Minutes 1875–1885*, pp. 108–11; San Francisco *Call*, May 4, 1896. The *Citizen* has been the organ of the Los Angeles Central Labor Council since 1907.

[30] Stereotyped plates, often called "boiler plate," consisted of miscellaneous reading matter set up and electrotyped. Their use considerably reduced publication costs, since the equivalent of one thousand ems could be bought at this time for about 15 cents. The Typographical Union objected to plates because they meant employment for fewer printers, and because they might have been set up by nonunion men.

[31] LATU, *Minutes 1875–1885*, pp. 114, 117–18, 153–4, 156, 158, 161; *Cactus*, Oct. 20, 1888.

[32] LATU, *Minutes 1875–1885*, pp. 116, 164–5.

[33] *Ibid.*, pp. 175–6; *Times*, July 7–17 passim, 1885; *Herald*, July 7, 1885.

[34] *Times*, July 10, 12, 15, 18, 30, 1885; Jan. 7, 9, 1886; *Weekly Mirror*, July 18, 1885; LATU, *Minutes 1875–1885*, p. 178. The *Evening Union* became a weekly in January, 1886, and was discontinued shortly thereafter.

[35] *Times*, Aug. 1, 1885.

[36] LATU, *Minutes 1886–1888*, pp. 15–19, 22–4. The 1875–1885 volume of the *Minutes* ends with August 8, 1885. Entries for the rest of 1885 are in the 1886–1888 volume.

[37] There is a statement in *California Labor Notes: Miscellaneous Material, Unions and Protective Associations* that a paper called *Labor Union* was published in Los Angeles in March, 1885. No other reference to it has been found. *California Labor Notes* are the manuscript notes used by Ira B. Cross in the compilation of his *History of the Labor Movement in California*. They are in the Bancroft Library, University of California, Berkeley.

[38] Harris Newmark, *Sixty Years in Southern California, 1853–1913* (New York: Knickerbocker Press, 1916), pp. 553, 555; Spalding, *op. cit.*, I, 264; *Henry H. Markham Papers*, Huntington Library, San Marino, California, letters from Otis to Markham dated Jan. 6, Sept. 29, and Dec. 14, 1885.

[39] Robert Glass Cleland and Osgood Hardy, *March of Industry* (Los Angeles: Powell Publishing Co. [c. 1929]), pp. 72–87, 148; John S. Hittell, *The Commerce and Industries of the Pacific Coast* ... (San Francisco: A. L. Bancroft & Co., 1882), pp. 753–86 passim; San Francisco *Examiner*, Mar. 17, 1881; *Express*, Nov. 3, 1881; *Times*, Apr. 25, May 2, June 7, 1882; Aug. 13, 1885; *Daily Commercial*, May 7, 1882; *Herald*, May 26, June 14, 17, 21, 1883; Aug. 12, 1885; San Pedro *Shipping Gazette*, Dec. 29, 1883.

[40] Cross, *op. cit.*, pp. 130–4, 325–6; Hittell, *op. cit.*, pp. 99, 102; Samuel Gompers, *Seventy Years of Life and Labor* (New York: Dutton [c. 1925]), I, 219–20, 227–8; *First Biennial Report, 1883–1884*, California Bureau of Labor Statistics (Sacramento: 1884), pp. 11–13; *Times*, Apr. 12, July 27, Aug. 30, Sept. 10, 1882; Aug. 10, 1883; *Express*, Oct. 10, 23, Dec. 1, 12, 1882; *Herald*, May 25, July 1, 1883.

[41] *Express*, July 5, 1881; Oct. 6, 13, 14, 1882; *Times*, Aug. 27, 31, Sept. 1, 27, Oct. 3, 1882.

[42] *Times*, Oct. 3, 1882.

[43] *Ibid.*, July 1, Oct. 24, Nov. 3, 1883; *Herald*, Dec. 14, 30, 1883; Jan. 1, 1884. The Los Angeles Horseshoers' Mutual Protective Association adopted a higher scale of prices on September 1, 1882. In October, 1882, the Pioneer Foundry denied a rumor that its molders had struck for higher wages and that it had brought in strikebreakers from San Francisco. Instead, the company had hired additional men because of the pressure of work.

[44] *Herald*, Feb. 14–16, 21, Mar. 1–3, 1883. In 1882, the grocers had changed their closing hour from 9 P.M. to 8 P.M., possibly as a result of employee action. (*Times*, June 25, 1882.)

[45] *Third Biennial Report, 1887–1888*, California Bureau of Labor Statistics (Sacramento: 1888), p. 129; Cross, *op. cit.*, p. 271; *Official Trades and Labor Directory, Los Angeles, 1896*, p. 17; *Herald*, Apr. 22, 1884.

[46] *Official Trades and Labor Directory, Los Angeles, 1896*, p. 17.

[47] Cross, *op. cit.*, p. 341, n. 7; *Cactus*, Aug. 24, 1889; *Union Labor News*, July 27, 1906; Joseph Phillis, "Arthur Vinette," *Citizen*, Jan. 20, 1911. The *Union Labor News* was the organ of the Los Angeles Central Labor Council from 1901 to 1907, when it became the Los Angeles *Citizen*.

[52] Phillis, "Arthur Vinette," *Citizen*, Jan. 20, 1911.

[49] *Common Sense*, Aug. 20, 1904; Phillis, "Arthur Vinette," *Citizen*, Jan. 20, 1911. *Common Sense* was a socialist paper published in Los Angeles from 1904 to 1909.

[50] *Official Trades and Labor Directory, Los Angeles, 1896*, p. 19.

[51] *Herald*, June 19, 1884.

[52] Phillis, "Arthur Vinette," *Citizen*, Jan. 20, 1911.

[53] *Third Biennial Report, 1887–1888*, California Bureau of Labor Statistics, p. 130; McNeill, *op. cit.*, pp. 387–8; *Official Trades and Labor Directory, Los Angeles, 1896*, p. 25; *Reports of the Industrial Commission on Labor Organizations, Labor Disputes, and Arbitration, and on Railroad Labor*, U.S. 57th Cong., 1st sess., H. Doc. 186 (Washington: 1901), XVII, 149; *Herald*, May 21, Oct. 3, 5, 1884; *Times*, Apr. 8, 1885.

[54] Cross, *op. cit.*, pp. 143–5, 147; *Official Trades and Labor Directory, Los Angeles, 1896*, p. 18; *Herald*, Aug. 5, 13, 16, 17, 19, Sept. 6, 1884; *Democrat*, Aug. 23, 1884; *Weekly Slogan*, Oct. 18, 1884; Phillis, "Arthur Vinette," *Citizen*, Jan. 20, 1911; Flannery, *op. cit.*, p. 8.

[55] *Times*, Oct. 25, 1884; McNeill, *op. cit.*, p. 357.

[56] *Times*, Mar. 3, 1885.

[57] *Ibid.*, Mar. 8, 1885.

[58] *Ibid.*, Mar. 7, 12, July 21, 26, Sept. 26, 27, Nov. 28, 1885; Jan. 8, 1886; *Herald*, May 15, June 4, 11, 27, July 4, 24, 1885; *Official Trades and Labor Directory, Los Angeles, 1896*, p. 18; Cross, *op. cit.*, p. 272.

[59] *Times*, Mar. 11, 18, 25, Apr. 1, 8, July 22, 29, 1885.

[60] *Herald*, Mar. 22, 1884; LATU, *Minutes 1875–1885*, p. 162; Cross, *op. cit.*, p. 271. In October, 1884, the Typographical Union set aside $50 for the tailors to use in an impending strike. Cross says the strike took place, but gives no details. Cross also suggests that the hod carriers and cigar makers organized in 1884, but there is no supporting evidence. In April, 1884, the Letter Carriers of Los Angeles held their first annual ball, indicating prior organization. They did not make common cause with other labor organizations in Los Angeles. (*Herald*, Apr. 6, 25, 1884.)

[61] Cross, *op. cit.*, pp. 148–67, 173–5; *Monthly Summary, Business Conditions in Southern California* (published by Security-First National Bank of Los Angeles), Sept. 13, 1947; *First Biennial Report, 1883–1884*, California Bureau of Labor Statistics, p. 9; *Porcupine*, Sept. 15, 1883; *Times*, Jan. 17, Mar. 12, Apr. 15, 1885; *Herald*, Apr. 15, 1885; Phillis, "Arthur Vinette," *Citizen*, Jan. 20, 1911.

[62] *Times*, Oct. 14, 1884.

[63] *Ibid.*, Oct. 30, 1884.

[64] LATU, *Minutes 1875–1885*, p. 163.

[65] See chapter v.

[66] *Times*, Dec. 6, 1884; Jan. 21, Mar. 3, 4, 7, 11, 12, Apr. 15, 1885; *Herald*, Mar. 14, Apr. 15, 18, 19, May 22, 29, June 28, Aug. 7, 1885; Lucile Eaves, *A History of California Labor Legislation* (Berkeley: The University Press [c. 1910]), pp. 229, 231–2. The quotation is from the *Times*, Apr. 15, 1885. In March, 1885, the Los Angeles Women's Club investigated women's working conditions in Los Angeles. Appalled by what it found, the club organized the Flower Festival Society to raise money for a charitable improvement program. The movement received general support from the community and labor organizations.

[67] *California Labor Notes: 1847–1885*. The information relative to this conference was drawn from the personal notes of Frank Roney, one of the leaders, and from a broadside issued by the Pacific Coast Central Labor Union, the new organization.

[68] *Times*, June 27, July 14, 1885; *Herald*, Aug. 13, 1885; LATU, *Minutes 1875–1885*, pp. 171, 173; *California Labor Notes: 1847–1885*, from the San Francisco *Daily Report*, Nov. 5, 1885; Cross, *op. cit.*, p. 271. The local cigar makers' union shortly disbanded, not to reorganize until April, 1886.

[69] LATU, *Minutes 1886–1888*, pp. 26–7, 33; *Herald*, Dec. 4–6, 1885; *Times*, Dec. 6, 8, 1885.

[70] Cross, *op. cit.*, pp. 175–7; Eaves, *op. cit.*, pp. 43–4; John R. Commons and Associates, *History of Labor in the United States* (New York: Macmillan, 1921–1935), IV, 71; Paul S. Taylor, *The Sailors' Union of the Pacific* (New York: Ronald Press, 1923), p. 49; *California Labor Notes: 1847–1885*, from the San Francisco *Daily Report*, Dec. 1, 3, 7, 9, 22, 1885.

[71] *Herald*, Dec. 5, 1885; Mar. 27, Apr. 27, 1886; *Times*, Jan. 8, Mar. 5, June 19, 1886; *Third Biennial Report, 1887–1888*, California Bureau of Labor Statistics, p. 128.

[72] *Herald*, July 22, Sept. 7, 14, 16, 1884; *Times*, Nov. 14, Dec. 16, 19, 1884.

Chapter IV

THE NOBLE ORDER

[1] Philip S. Foner, *History of the Labor Movement in the United States* (New York: International Publishers [c. 1947]), pp. 433–7; Norman J. Ware, *The Labor Movement in the United States, 1860–1895* (New York: Appleton, 1929), pp. xiii–iv.

[2] Foner, *op. cit.*, pp. 437, 479–80, 484, 506; Selig Perlman, *A History of Trade Unionism in the United States* (New York: Macmillan, 1922), pp. 114–15.

[3] Foner, *op. cit.*, pp. 507–8; Ware, *op. cit.*, pp. xi, 117.

[4] Foner, *op. cit.*, pp. 437, 509–12; Ira B. Cross, *A History of the Labor Movement in California* (Berkeley: University of California Press, 1935), pp. 152–3.

[5] Cross, *op. cit.*, pp. 142, 149, 152–4; T. V. Powderly, *Thirty Years of Labor, 1859–1889* (rev. and corr. ed.; Philadelphia: [c. 1890]), p. 161.

[6] *Times*, July 14, 20, 1882; *Daily Commercial*, July 15, Aug. 27, 1882; Knights of Labor, *Proceedings of the General Assembly, 1883* (n.p., n.d.), p. 552; *Proceedings of the General Assembly, 1884* (n.p., n.d.), p. 826; *Proceedings of the General Assembly, 1885* (n.p., n.d.), pp. 210, 215; John R. Commons and Associates, *History of Labor in the United States* (New York: Macmillan, 1921–1935), II, 199, 339–40; Ware, *op. cit.*, p. 70.

[7] *Times*, Feb. 4, 1885; Jan. 10, Feb. 24, Sept. 7, 1886; *Herald*, Jan. 10, June 25, 1886; *Porcupine*, Apr. 3, 1886; *Tribune*, Oct. 29, 1886; Joseph Phillis, "J. D. Bailey," *Citizen*, Jan. 27, 1911; Powderly, *op. cit.*, p. 336; Knights of Labor, *Proceedings of the General Assembly, 1886* (n.p., 1886), p. 327; Cross, *op. cit.*, p. 153.

[8] *Truth*, Oct. 6, 1883; *Herald*, June 18, 19, 1885; July 22, 1886. *Truth* was a San Francisco labor paper.

[9] *Citizen,* Apr. 9, 1909; Joseph Phillis, "J. D. Bailey," *Citizen,* Jan. 27, 1911.

[10] *Workman,* Feb. 11, 1892; Phillis, "Arthur Vinette," *Citizen,* Jan. 20, 1911; Phillis, "J. D. Bailey," *Citizen,* Jan. 27, 1911. *The Workman* was the organ of the Los Angeles Council of Labor from 1890 to 1892.

[11] Ware, *op. cit.,* p. xv.

[12] *Times,* Feb. 4, 1885.

[13] *Ibid.,* July 11, 12, 17, 1885.

[14] *Ibid.,* Aug. 13, 16, 18, 1885.

[15] Cross, *op. cit.,* p. 176. The Los Angeles assembly sending delegates was listed as No. 2157, but it could have been only Painters' Assembly No. 3167.

[16] Knights of Labor, *Proceedings of the General Assembly, 1885,* pp. 4, 127, 160; *Proceedings of the General Assembly, 1886,* pp. 18, 161, 182, 198, 227, 274, 304, 325.

[17] *Herald,* Nov. 1, 1884; *Tribune,* Nov. 22, 1886.

Chapter V

UNION AGAINST THE CHINESE

[1] Lucile Eaves, *A History of California Labor Legislation* (Berkeley: The University Press [c. 1910]), pp. 40–1, 172–3, 177–9; Ira B. Cross, *A History of the Labor Movement in California* (Berkeley: University of California Press, 1935), pp. 135–41; Samuel Gompers, *Seventy Years of Life and Labor* (New York: Dutton [c. 1925]), I, 220, 227–8; John R. Commons and Associates, *History of Labor in the United States* (New York: Macmillan, 1921–1935), II, 267–8.

[2] *Times,* Mar. 3–5, Apr. 9, 22, 25, 30, May 2, 7, 12, Aug. 6, 8, 1882.

[3] *Tenth Census of the United States, 1880,* Vol. I, *Population,* p. 416; *Eleventh Census of the United States, 1890,* Vol. I, *Population,* part 2, pp. 290–1; *Fourteenth Census of the United States, 1920,* Vol. I, *Population,* p. 82.

[4] Elmer Clarence Sandmeyer, *The Anti-Chinese Movement in California* (Urbana, Ill.: University of Illinois Press, 1939), pp. 96–8; Cross, *op. cit.,* pp. 171–6, 272.

[5] *Times,* May 24, 1890.

[6] *Ibid.,* Nov. 19, 1886.

[7] *Herald,* Sept. 20, Oct. 5, 1884. The quotations are from the issue of Oct. 5, 1884.

[8] *Times,* Oct. 16, 19, 25, Nov. 1, 1884; *Democrat,* Oct. 18, 1884; *Herald,* Oct. 19, 1884. The quotation is from the *Times,* Oct. 19, 1884.

[9] *Herald,* Feb. 28, Mar. 3, 14, 15, 21, 28, Apr. 9, 15, 25, 30, May 2, 3, 8, 1885; *Times,* Feb. 28, Mar. 10, 15, 21, 22, 1885. In 1886 Janes changed the title of his paper to *Advocate,* retaining the *Shipping Gazette* as a subordinate part of the publication. His faculty for creating disturbances continued, for on one occasion in 1886 he was thrown out of the City Council for smoking a "nefarious" cigar and interrupting with foolish questions while reporting the proceedings for his newspaper. His subsequent threat to "blow the whole Council to h—l" if he only had the dynamite was presumably not taken seriously. Late in 1886 Janes was reported to have given up politics, and to have opened a fish market which also served as headquarters for his publishing activities. (*Times,* May 11, Nov. 19, 1886.) In 1890 he became involved in an abortive filibuster in Lower California. (Andrew F. Rolle, "Futile Filibustering in Baja California, 1888–1890," *Pacific Historical Review,* XX [May, 1951], 162–4.)

[10] *Times,* June 24, 26, 28, July 2, 14, 15, 22, 1885; *Herald,* July 5, 7, 10, 12, 1885.

[11] *Herald,* Feb. 5, 1886; *Times,* Feb. 5, 1886; LATU, *Minutes 1886–1888,* p. 41. The quotation comes from the last source.

[12] *Herald,* Feb. 12, 16, 28, 1886; *Times,* Feb. 21, 23, 24, 27, 28, 1886. Somewhat later Captain Janes, whose intimate association with the anti-Chinese movement gives his opinion considerable validity, referred to the Knights of Labor as the important group in the movement. (*Advocate,* Apr. 24, 1886.)

[13] *Herald,* Feb. 23, 28, 1886.

[14] *Ibid.*, Mar. 9, 21, May 6, 23, July 3, 1886; *Times,* Mar. 11, 12, 14, Apr. 4, May 8, July 3, 1886.

[15] *Herald,* Mar. 23, 1886; *Times,* Apr. 17, 1886; LATU, *Minutes 1886–1888,* pp. 48, 77 ff.

[16] Cross, *op. cit.,* pp. 179, 181; Selig Perlman, *A History of Trade Unionism in the United States* (New York: Macmillan, 1922), pp. 91–106; *Herald,* Mar. 13, Apr. 13, 21, May 2, 1886; *Times,* May 2, 1886. Los Angeles was not represented at the Sacramento convention, though the Trades Council had asked the County Board of Supervisors to send delegates.

[17] *California Labor Notes: 1886–1890,* from the *Open Letter* (published in San Francisco), May 18, 1886.

[18] *Times,* May 4, 1886; *Herald,* May 6, 8, 25, 1886.

[19] *Times,* May 11, June 4, 1886; *Herald,* May 19–30 *passim,* Aug. 18, 24, 31, 1886; *Porcupine,* June 5, 1886; LATU, *Minutes 1886–1888,* pp. 56, 58, 61–2, 77–8, 84; Sandmeyer, *op. cit.,* p. 98. The City Council's excuse for failing to act on the laundry receipt proposal was that such a requirement might stimulate the Chinese to learn English and thus make them better able to compete with white labor.

[20] Cross, *op. cit.,* p. 332, n. 18; *California Labor Notes: 1886–1890,* from the San Francisco *Daily Report,* May 11, 1886; *Tribune,* Nov. 17, Dec. 1, 10, 24, 1886; *Times,* Dec. 1, 1886.

Chapter VI

LABOR GROWS WITH LOS ANGELES

[1] Glenn S. Dumke, *The Boom of the Eighties in Southern California* (San Marino: The Huntington Library, 1944), pp. 17–26; Charles Dwight Willard, *History of Los Angeles City* (Los Angeles: Kingsley-Barnes and Neuner Co., 1901), pp. 325–8; James M. Guinn, "The Great Real Estate Boom of 1887," *Annual Publications of the Historical Society of Southern California,* I (1890), 15.

[2] Dumke, *op. cit.,* pp. 28–9, 33. As early as 1883 the Los Angeles Board of Trade sent a representative to New Orleans to disseminate information on business opportunities in southern California. (*Herald,* May 20, 1883.)

[3] Dumke, *op. cit.,* pp. 24–5. Normal railroad fares from the Mississippi Valley to southern California were in the neighborhood of $125. At the end of 1885, when the Santa Fe began to offer competition to the Southern Pacific, they dropped to $95. The sharpest cuts came in March, 1887, when the Santa Fe acquired its own roadbed all the way to the coast. Early in the month the rate from Chicago to Los Angeles dropped from $32 to $25, but the real war between the roads was fought on the rate from Kansas City to southern California. On March 6 that rate fell to $1. Fares were soon raised to a more realistic level, but for a year a passenger could travel from the Midwest to Los Angeles for less than $25.

[4] *Ibid.,* pp. 5, 9–11, 16, 43, 55, 278; [Thomas Richardson, ed.], *The Industries of Los Angeles, California* (Los Angeles: Industrial Publishing Co., 1888), p. 23.

[5] [Richardson], *op. cit.,* pp. 11–12; Ira B. Cross, *A History of the Labor Movement in California* (Berkeley: University of California Press, 1935), p. 271; Walter Lindley and J. P. Widney, *California of the South* (New York: Appleton, 1888), pp. 110–11; [Bascom A. Stephens, ed.], *Resources of Los Angeles County, California* (Los Angeles: Sprague & Rodehauer, 1887), pp. 27, 29–31; *Annual Report, 1888,* Los Angeles Board of Trade (Los Angeles: Evening Express Co., 1888), pp. 57–8; *Tribune,* Oct. 4, 1887.

[6] *Herald,* July 22, 1886; *Official Trades and Labor Directory, Los Angeles, 1896,* p. 18. The quotation is from the latter source.

[7] *Times,* June 30, Aug. 8, Sept. 7, 9, 15, 23, 29, 30, Oct. 6, Dec. 15, 1886; Sept. 22, 1887; *Tribune,* Oct. 25, Dec. 15, 29, 1886; May 27, Aug. 21, 27, 29, 1887; Cross, *op. cit.,*

p. 194. In December, 1886, the carpenters' union reported 463 members in good standing, an average monthly benefit payment of $125, and a balance of $1,500 in the bank.

[8] *Tribune*, Mar. 11, Apr. 22, May 27, Oct. 15, 25, 1887; *Times*, Apr. 22, Oct. 14, Nov. 8, 1887; Jan. 31, 1888; *Official Trades and Labor Directory, Los Angeles, 1896*, p. 19; LATU, *Minutes 1886–1888*, p. 134.

[9] *Tribune*, Oct. 29, 1886; Apr. 6, May 27, Sept. 7, 28, Nov. 5, 1887; *Times*, Apr. 9, 12, Sept. 2, 7, 28, 1887; *Architect, Builder, and Mechanic of Southern California*, July 22, 1887; *Official Trades and Labor Directory, Los Angeles, 1896*, p. 25; *Reports of the Industrial Commission on Labor Organizations, Labor Disputes, and Arbitration, and on Railroad Labor*, U.S. 57th Cong., 1st sess., H. Doc. 186 (Washington: 1901), XVII, 149.

[10] *Times*, Sept. 11, 14, Oct. 16, 1886; Oct. 1, 1887; *Tribune*, May 27, Aug. 21, Oct. 1, 1887; *Third Biennial Report, 1887–1888*, California Bureau of Labor Statistics (Sacramento: 1888), p. 130.

[11] *Times*, Aug. 16, 24, 25, 28, 31, 1887; Jan. 16, 1888; *Tribune*, Aug. 18, 28, 1887; *Final Report and Testimony Submitted to Congress by the Commission on Industrial Relations*, U.S. 64th Cong., 1st sess., S. Doc. 415 (Washington: 1916), VI, 5567–8, 5782.

[12] *Times*, Nov. 6, 1886; LATU, *Minutes 1886–1888*, pp. 44, 49, 52, 55, 64–73, 80–4, 131, 136, 143, 161.

[13] *Times*, Apr. 6, 1887; LATU, *Minutes 1886–1888*, pp. 96–110, 125.

[14] *Herald*, Sept. 16, 1886; *Tribune*, Oct. 29, 31, 1886; Jan. 16, 1887; LATU, *Minutes 1886–1888*, pp. 113, 117–18; William A. Spalding, comp., *History and Reminiscences, Los Angeles City and County, California* (Los Angeles: J. R. Finnell & Sons Publishing Co. [1931]), I, 264. The quotation is from the *Tribune*, Jan. 16, 1887.

[15] LATU, *Minutes 1886–1888*, pp. 141–3, 147–9.

[16] *Ibid.*, pp. 168–9.

[17] *Ibid.*, pp. 130, 169, 188–9, 191.

[18] *Ibid.*, pp. 210–11, 213–14; *Times*, Aug. 30, Oct. 22, 1887; *Tribune*, Aug. 30, Oct. 22, 1887; W. L. Mackenzie King, "The International Typographical Union," *Journal of Political Economy*, V (Sept., 1897), 471.

[19] LATU, *Minutes 1886–1888*, pp. 39, 43, 124, 164, 169–70, 174–5, 177–82, 187, 208. See chapter ix for more detailed discussion of the Printers' Protective Fraternity.

[20] LATU, *Minutes 1886–1888*, pp. 77–222 *passim*.

[21] *Times*, Aug. 10, Nov. 23, 24, 1886; Mar. 5, 13, 1887; *Tribune*, Nov. 23, 25, 1886; Nov. 17, 1887.

[22] LATU, *Minutes 1886–1888*, p. 161.

[23] *Tribune*, Jan. 22, May 27, Aug. 19, Sept. 5, Nov. 27, 1887; *Times*, Sept. 5, 6, Nov. 30, 1887; *Coast Seamen's Journal*, Nov. 9, 1887; *Statistical Report of Unions Represented in the Council of Federated Trades and Labor Organizations on the Pacific Coast, November 1, 1887*, California Bureau of Labor Statistics (Sacramento: 1887), p. 15; *Citizen*, June 23, 1911. The *Coast Seamen's Journal* was published in San Francisco. The quotation is from the *Times*, Nov. 30, 1887.

[24] *Tribune*, May 27, June 10, 26, July 4, Sept. 27, 1887; *Times*, Sept. 26, 1887.

[25] *Times*, Sept. 15, 1886; May 20, June 19, July 12–15, 1887; *Tribune*, Mar. 17, Apr. 2, July 13–15, Sept. 21, 25, 1887.

[26] *California Labor Notes: Miscellaneous Material, Unions and Protective Associations*, from *Proceedings of the California State Assembly, Knights of Labor*, September 16, 1886.

[27] *Times*, Nov. 30, 1886; LATU, *Minutes 1886–1888*, p. 134.

[28] *Herald*, Sept. 26, 1886; Cross, *op. cit.*, p. 186. The quotation is from the *Herald*.

[29] *Times*, Oct. 10, 24, Nov. 18, Dec. 2, 7, 1886; *Tribune*, Oct. 11, 30, Nov. 22, Dec. 2, 4, 1886; LATU, *Minutes 1886–1888*, p. 84.

[30] *Times*, Nov. 2, 5, 1887.

[31] This was an English order. The date of its organization in Los Angeles is not known.

[32] *Tribune*, Nov. 5, 1887; LATU, *Minutes 1886–1888*, pp. 214–15.
[33] *Times*, Jan. 23, 1888.
[34] *Ibid.*, Oct. 16, 1887.
[35] *Tribune*, Dec. 23, 1887.

Chapter VII

TROUBLE ON THE WATER FRONT

[1] Knights of Labor, *Proceedings of the General Assembly, 1886*, p. 327; *Proceedings of the General Assembly, 1887*, pp. 1630, 1681, 1755, 1849; *Times*, Oct. 16, 1887. The new Los Angeles assembly was Local No. 44, mentioned only once during 1887.

[2] *Times*, Mar. 27, 1910.

[3] Ira B. Cross, *A History of the Labor Movement in California* (Berkeley: University of California Press, 1935), pp. 169, 330–1.

[4] *Ibid.*, p. 168; Paul S. Taylor, *The Sailors' Union of the Pacific* (New York: Ronald Press, 1923), pp. 46–9; *Times*, May 30, 1885.

[5] Taylor, *op. cit.*, pp. 51–2; Cross, *op. cit.*, p. 183.

[6] Taylor, *op. cit.*, p. 52; Cross, *op. cit.*, pp. 156–9, 183; *Fifth Biennial Report, 1891–1892*, California Bureau of Labor Statistics (Sacramento: 1893), p. 176; *Advocate*, Aug. 21, 1886; *Herald*, Aug. 28, 1886.

[7] Taylor, *op. cit.*, p. 53; *Statistical Report of Unions Represented in the Council of Federated Trades and Labor Organizations on the Pacific Coast, November 1, 1887*, California Bureau of Labor Statistics (Sacramento: 1887), pp. 9–10; *Fifth Biennial Report, 1891–1892*, California Bureau of Labor Statistics, p. 166; *Times*, May 7, 1887.

[8] Cross, *op. cit.*, p. 169; *Statistical Report of Unions Represented in the Council of Federated Trades . . .* , p. 9.

[9] *Statistical Report of Unions Represented in the Council of Federated Trades . . .* , p. 10; *Coast Seamen's Journal*, Nov. 2, 1887; *Times*, Nov. 6, 1887.

[10] *Times*, Nov. 6, 7, 9, 10, 1887; *Coast Seamen's Journal*, Nov. 9, 1887.

[11] *Tribune*, Nov. 10, 11, 1887; *Times*, Nov. 11, 12, 1887; *Coast Seamen's Journal*, Nov. 16, Dec. 7, 1887.

[12] *Coast Seamen's Journal*, Nov. 30, Dec. 7, 1887; *Times*, Dec. 2–4, 6, 1887; *Tribune*, Dec. 2, 3, 5, 1887; Taylor, *op. cit.*, p. 55; *Third Biennial Report, 1887–1888*, California Bureau of Labor Statistics (Sacramento: 1888), pp. 161–2, 165.

[13] *Times*, Dec. 4, 1887; *Tribune*, Dec. 4–6, 1887; Taylor, *op. cit.*, p. 55; *Third Biennial Report, 1887–1888*, California Bureau of Labor Statistics, pp. 162–4.

[14] *Tribune*, Dec. 3–6, 1887; *Times*, Dec. 4–6, 1887; *Coast Seamen's Journal*, Dec. 7, 1887; *Third Biennial Report, 1887–1888*, California Bureau of Labor Statistics, pp. 161, 163. The quotation is from the *Times*, Dec. 6, 1887.

[15] *Times*, Dec. 5, 1887; *Third Biennial Report, 1887–1888*, California Bureau of Labor Statistics, p. 164. Isaac Kinley had apparently withdrawn from office in the Knights of Labor, for he took no part in these negotiations.

[16] *Tribune*, Dec. 4, 5, 1887; *Times*, Dec. 5, 1887.

[17] *Tribune*, Dec. 5, 1887.

[18] *Times*, Dec. 5, 7, 1887; *Tribune*, Dec. 5, 7, 1887; *Coast Seamen's Journal*, Dec. 14, 1887; *Third Biennial Report, 1887–1888*, California Bureau of Labor Statistics, p. 165.

[19] *Tribune*, Dec. 7, 1887; *Times*, Dec. 8, 1887.

[20] *Coast Seamen's Journal*, Dec. 14, 1887.

[21] *Tribune*, Dec. 10, 12, 16, 1887; *Times*, Dec. 14, 1887; *Third Biennial Report, 1887–1888*, California Bureau of Labor Statistics, pp. 162, 165–6; Taylor, *op. cit.*, p. 55.

[22] Although the *Tribune*, on December 12, 1887, claimed that "Mr. Farsweth, the grand master of the Coast Seamen's Union," spoke at a mass meeting in San Pedro on December 11, there is no confirming evidence that Furuseth came to San Pedro during the strike.

Chapter VIII

AFTERMATH OF THE BOOM

[1] Glenn S. Dumke, *The Boom of the Eighties in Southern California* (San Marino: The Huntington Library, 1944), pp. 50–3, 55, 241, 259–60, 262–3, 267–8, 276–7; Charles Dwight Willard, *History of Los Angeles City* (Los Angeles: Kingsley-Barnes and Neuner Co., 1901), pp. 333–4, 337, 339, 345; James M. Guinn, "Great Real Estate Boom of 1887," *Annual Publications of the Historical Society of Southern California,* I (1890), 21; *Charles Dwight Willard Letters,* Huntington Library, San Marino, California, undated letter from Willard to his mother, to which the editor has assigned the date May 28, 1888; *Times,* Mar. 30, Sept. 15, 1890.

[2] *Times,* Nov. 28, 1887; Jan. 12, 16, 18, 23, 25, Feb. 6, Apr. 18, 1888; *Tribune,* Feb. 18, Mar. 28, June 20, 1888; *Porcupine,* June 23, 1888; *Herald,* Oct. 19, 1891; *Third Biennial Report, 1887–1888,* California Bureau of Labor Statistics (Sacramento: 1888), pp. 128–9.

[3] *Times,* Sept. 19, 1886; Dec. 5, 1887; Jan. 16, 18, 23, 25, 30, Feb. 6, Mar. 28, Apr. 11, May 9, 11, 30, 31, June 2, 13, 14, 30, July 3, 5, 1888; *Tribune,* Nov. 22, 30, Dec. 5, 7, 1887; Jan. 21, 25, Mar. 28, 30, May 11, 13, 30, June 3, 5, 13, July 2, Dec. 19, 1888; *Pacific Opinion,* May 12, 1888; *Express,* June 11, 1895; *Third Biennial Report, 1887–1888,* California Bureau of Labor Statistics, p. 128; Knights of Labor, *Proceedings of the General Assembly, 1887,* p. 1410; *Official Trades and Labor Directory, Los Angeles, 1896,* p. 19.

[4] *Times,* Nov. 19, 1887; Jan. 16–18, 20, 23, 30, Feb. 6, 1888; June 24, 1889; LATU, *Minutes 1886–1888,* pp. 77–8, 131; *Constitution and By-Laws of the Journeymen Tailors' Protective Union of Los Angeles, California* (Los Angeles: 1888), p. 1.

[5] LATU, *Minutes 1886–1888,* pp. 187, 227, 238, 241–56 *passim; Minutes 1888–1890,* pp. 3–17, 21, 25–34; *Official Trades and Labor Directory, Los Angeles, 1896,* p. 39; George A. Tracy, comp., *History of the Typographical Union* ([Indianapolis]: International Typographical Union, 1913), pp. 415–17; Marion Dixon, "The History of the Los Angeles Central Labor Council" (unpublished M.A. thesis, University of California, Berkeley, 1929), pp. 187–8; *Labor Gleaner,* Feb. 11, 1888; *Tribune,* Feb. 15, 19, 1888; *Times,* Feb. 20, 1888. The Typographical Union began to publish the *Labor Gleaner* in February, 1888, as a vehicle for news of organized labor in southern California and eventually in the whole state. The paper came out only once and was devoted wholly to the printers' current fight with the job offices. It implied that the Commercial Printing House was employing members of the Printers' Protective Fraternity.

[6] *Third Biennial Report, 1887–1888,* California Bureau of Labor Statistics, p. 113. Doubt as to the time when these data were collected reduces the value of comment on obvious inaccuracies. It is certain, however, that the membership statistics are not reliable. For example, the cooks' and waiters' union is noted elsewhere in the same report as having 170 members, and in a local newspaper as having 400 members. (*Third Biennial Report . . . ,* p. 131; *Times,* Jan. 16, 1888.) The painters' union, wage workers' union, and mixed assembly of the list are identifiable as Painters' Assembly No. 3167 and Mixed Assemblies No. 7647 and No. 2405, Knights of Labor. The separate unions of plasterers' and plumbers' helpers were subsidiaries of the journeymen's organizations. The report omitted some known unions, notably Hod Carriers' Union No. 1 and the Teamsters' Association. Both of these continued into the winter of 1887–1888. (*Commercial Bulletin of Southern California,* Jan. 28, 1888; *Annual Report, 1888,* Los Angeles Board of Trade [Los Angeles: Evening Express Co., 1888], p. 17.)

[7] LATU, *Minutes 1886–1888,* pp. 242, 244; *Minutes 1888–1890,* pp. 20, 33; *Times,* Jan. 23, Feb. 13, May 2, 28, 29, Aug. 10, 11, 1888; *Tribune,* Feb. 10, 13, Mar. 9, May 28, 29, 1888; *Citizen,* July 7, 1911; *Overture,* June 15, 1925, p. 5; Sept. 1, 1926, p. 7.

Overture, official organ of Musicians' Mutual Protective Association, Los Angeles Local No. 47, American Federation of Musicians, was consulted in the office of C. L. Bagley, legal counsel for the union.

[8] Lucile Eaves, *A History of California Labor Legislation* (Berkeley: The University Press [c. 1910]), pp. 7–8.

[9] *Times,* May 29, 1888.

[10] Norman J. Ware, *The Labor Movement in the United States, 1860–1895* (New York: Appleton, 1929), pp. 362–4; John R. Commons and Associates, *History of Labor in the United States* (New York: Macmillan, 1921–1935), II, 461–8.

[11] *Times,* Feb. 28, June 11, 16, 18, 1888; *Tribune,* Apr. 9, June 11, 28, 1888; LATU, *Minutes 1888–1890,* pp. 20, 33.

[12] *Tribune,* June 15–18, 20, 1888; *Times,* June 16–18, 1888; *Porcupine,* June 23, 1888; *Cactus,* Sept. 8, 1888.

[13] *Times,* Oct. 10, 15, 1888; *Cactus,* Oct. 13, 20, 1888; LATU, *Minutes 1888–1890,* p. 56.

[14] LATU, *Minutes 1888–1890,* pp. 56–7.

[15] *Tribune,* July 20, Sept. 6, 14, Nov. 11, 18, 1888; *Cactus,* Sept. 22, 1888; Ira B. Cross, *A History of the Labor Movement in California* (Berkeley: University of California Press, 1935), p. 154; *Official Trades and Labor Directory, Los Angeles, 1896,* p. 25.

[16] *Charles Dwight Willard Letters,* letter to his mother, Jan. 13, 1889.

[17] *Ibid.,* letter to his mother, Sept. 29, 1889.

[18] *Times,* Jan. 23, May 19, 20, 22, 24, 1889; *Tribune,* Jan. 25, 1889; *Herald,* May 19, 20, 22, 24, 1889.

[19] *Herald,* Aug. 3, 1889.

[20] *Times,* Oct. 20, Dec. 7, 9, 11, 1889; Jan. 11, Feb. 26–28, Mar. 1, 4, 1890; *Herald,* Dec. 9, 10, 1889; Feb. 26–28, Mar. 4, June 23, 1890.

[21] *Times,* Jan. 24, Feb. 5, 11, 12, 14, 18, 29, Mar. 4, Apr. 9, 17, 23, May 30, June 3, 4, 1889.

[22] *Ibid.,* Aug. 14, 1888; Cross, *op. cit.,* pp. 106, 117, 127, 217; *California Labor Notes: Biography.*

[23] *Times,* Mar. 9, June 18, 25, 28, Aug. 27, 29, 31, 1889; Los Angeles *Life,* July 20, 1889; *Herald,* Aug. 10, 1889.

[24] LATU, *Minutes 1888–1890,* pp. 39–60 *passim.*

[25] *Ibid.,* pp. 61–99 *passim,* 104–5, 111–50 *passim,* 160–88 *passim; Times,* May 5, 1890; *Cactus,* May 10, 1890; Tracy, *op. cit.,* pp. 413, 425, 429.

[26] *Times,* Feb. 28, Mar. 27, Apr. 9, 17, 26, May 8, 29, June 3, July 5, Aug. 13, 1889; San Francisco *Examiner,* Apr. 7, 1889; *Herald,* Apr. 17, 24, May 29, 1889; Cross, *op. cit.,* pp. 200–1, 274; Eaves, *op. cit.,* pp. 217–19.

[27] *Times,* Apr. 9, 16, 1889; *Herald,* Apr. 17, 1889; *Weekly Nationalist,* June 7, 1890; Cross, *op. cit.,* pp. 198–9.

[28] *Times,* May 18, June 4, 7, 1889; *Herald,* May 31, July 16, 1889.

[29] Alfred Fuhrman was prominent in the San Francisco labor movement until 1893, when he turned to the practice of law. One of his accomplishments was organization of the Brewers' and Maltsters' Union of the Pacific Coast in 1886. He was president of the Federated Trades Council in 1890–1891 and of its successor, the Pacific Coast Council of Trades and Labor Federations, which he founded, from 1891 to 1893. (Cross, *op. cit.,* pp. 190, 333.)

[30] Michael M. McGlynn was a member of the St. Louis Typographical Union in 1881. After participating in the labor movements of Chicago and Colorado, he arrived in San Francisco in 1887, where he was a capable and conservative labor leader. In 1890 he was sent to Los Angeles to assist the printers in their fight against the *Times.* (Cross, *op. cit.,* p. 336.)

[31] *Coast Seamen's Journal,* Apr. 17, May 22, June 5, 12, 1889; *Herald,* May 25, 27, July 2, Aug. 4, 1889; *Times,* June 24, 1889; LATU, *Minutes 1888–1890,* pp. 86, 90, 101–2, 128, 147; Cross, *op. cit.,* p. 274; Helen Flannery, "The Labor Movement in

Los Angeles, 1880–1903" (unpublished M.A. thesis, University of California, Berkeley, 1929), p. 23. H. E. Martens of the cigar makers said that only his union and the printers' union remained when the central labor body dissolved. (Dixon, *op. cit.*, p. 7.)

³² *Herald*, June 22, Aug. 10, Sept. 25, 1889; July 16, 1893; *Times*, Apr. 20, May 18, 25, 26, Oct. 8, Dec. 1, 1889; *California Labor Notes: 1886–1890*, from the San Francisco *Call*, Nov. 24, 1889.

³³ Charlotte Perkins Gilman, *The Living of Charlotte Perkins Gilman* (New York: Appleton-Century, 1935), p. 122; J. O. Hertzler, "Edward Bellamy," *Encyclopedia of the Social Sciences*, II (1930), 504.

³⁴ *Times*, Sept. 9, 1889; Jan. 11, 15, 20, Feb. 8, Apr. 28, May 24, 25, Sept. 16, 1890; Cross, *op. cit.*, pp. 165, 175, 177, 274, 341; F. I. Vassault, "Nationalism in California," *Overland Monthly*, 2d Series, XV (June, 1890), 660–1; Burnette G. Haskell, *Personal Notes: A Collection of Labor Miscellany, 1879–1893*, II, 117 (from a letter written by Arthur Vinette to the San Francisco *Star*, Aug. 31, 1889), 169. Haskell's *Notes*, a number of manuscript volumes, are in the Bancroft Library, University of California, Berkeley.

³⁵ Joseph Phillis, "L. D. Biddle," *Citizen*, Mar. 3, 1911; Philip S. Foner, *History of the Labor Movement in the United States* (New York: International Publishers [c. 1947]), p. 475.

³⁶ Phillis, *op. cit.*; *Citizen*, Sept. 15, 1916.

³⁷ *Citizen*, Sept. 15, 1916.

³⁸ *Ibid.*, Sept. 8, 15, 1916.

³⁹ *Times*, June 10, 1889; Jan. 12, 15, 18, Feb. 2, 7, Apr. 9, 11, 13, May 5, 7, 11, 12, 19, 1890; *Herald*, May 16, 1890; *Express*, Aug. 9, Sept. 4, 1890; Haskell, *Personal Notes...*, III, unpaged, from the *Alta California* (published in San Francisco), Apr. 9, 1890; F. I. Vassault, "Nationalism in California," *Overland Monthly*, 2d Series, XV (June, 1890), 659–61.

⁴⁰ *Times*, Mar. 3, 4, 11–31 *passim*, Apr. 1, 5–8, May 6, 1890.

⁴¹ *Ibid.*, Mar. 14, 18, 22, 30, Apr. 14, 15, 22, May 6, 20, July 27, 1890; *Weekly Nationalist*, May 31, 1890; *Herald*, June 5, 6, 12, 24, 1890.

⁴² *Times*, Apr. 8, May 1, 11, 1890; *Herald*, Apr. 29, May 11, 1890; Cross, *op. cit.*, pp. 200–1, 274.

⁴³ *Times*, Oct. 5, 15, 27, 1890; *Evening Post*, Nov. 11, 1890; Hertzler, *op. cit.*, p. 504.

⁴⁴ Frank B. Colver, "Los Angeles Labor Council," San Francisco *Call*, May 4, 1896.

⁴⁵ *Tribune*, Nov. 12, 1887; Apr. 9, 1888. The anarchist group was said to have a large and prominent membership and to have sent a long petition to Governor Oglesby of Illinois requesting a pardon for the men sentenced to die for their alleged connection with the Haymarket bombing in May, 1886.

⁴⁶ *Fourteenth Census of the United States, 1920*, Vol. I, *Population*, p. 82.

⁴⁷ George Hamlin Fitch, "Races and Labor Problems in California," *Chautauquan*, XXIV (Jan., 1897), 432; Dixon, *op. cit.*, pp. 1–4. Dixon used the personal notes of Joseph Phillis.

Chapter IX

THE "BIG STRIKE"

¹ *The Forty-Year War for a Free City; A History of the Open Shop in Los Angeles* (Los Angeles: Times-Mirror Publishing Co., 1929), p. 3.

² Harrison Gray Otis, *The Los Angeles Times: A Plain Statement of Bed-Rock Facts and Unanswerable Reasons Sustaining the Attitude of the Times and Its Owners toward Labor during the Past Six Years* (Los Angeles: Times-Mirror Publishing Co., 1896), p. 2; Harrison Gray Otis, "A Long, Winning Fight against the 'Closed Shop': An Account of a Seventeen-Years' Conflict between the Los Angeles 'Times'

and the Typographical Union," *World's Work*, XV (Dec., 1907), 9675. The quotation is from the latter source.

³ *Official Trades and Labor Directory, Los Angeles, 1896*, p. 39.

⁴ Pauline Jacobson, "Otis: 'Jehovah of Industrial Freedom,' " San Francisco *Bulletin*, Dec. 9, 1911. This was the first of a series of eight articles by Miss Jacobson, dealing with the labor movement in Los Angeles and appearing in the *Bulletin* between December, 1911, and February, 1912. Most of the articles dealt with the period in which they were written, under such colorful titles as "Industrial Freedom Versus Feudalism," "In the Grip of Greed," and "Industrial Freedom—For Whom?" In the summer of 1912 the Central Labor and Building Trades Councils of Los Angeles brought the articles together and published them as a pamphlet entitled *The Struggles of Organized Labor in Los Angeles*. The edition was prepared for and inscribed to Samuel Gompers, president of the American Federation of Labor. It attracted much attention in labor circles, and the Central Labor Council was called upon to send copies to various labor organizations in all parts of the country.

⁵ *Citizen*, Sept. 15, 1911, in an article reprinted from *Pacific Union Printer*, Sept., 1890.

⁶ See p. 109.

⁷ *The Forty-Year War for a Free City* ..., p. 3; LATU, *Minutes 1888–1890*, pp. 190–5; *Herald*, Aug. 12, 1890; *Times*, Aug. 14, 1890. The *Times* claimed that Otis asked for only a 5-cent reduction at the initial conference. The *Herald* said the proprietors had not stipulated the amount of reduction desired.

⁸ *Citizen*, Sept. 15, 1911, in an article reprinted from *Pacific Union Printer*, Sept., 1890.

⁹ Jacobson, *op. cit.*

¹⁰ LATU, *Minutes 1888–1890*, pp. 196–9, 202, 218; Ira B. Cross, *A History of the Labor Movement in California* (Berkeley: University of California Press, 1935), p. 275; Helen Flannery, "The Labor Movement in Los Angeles, 1880–1903" (unpublished M.A. thesis, University of California, Berkeley, 1929), p. 24; *Times*, Aug. 6–8, 1890; *Tribune*, Aug. 6–8, 1890; *Herald*, Aug. 6, 7, 9, 1890; *Express*, Aug. 6–8, 1890. Officially, the union called the dispute a lockout because Otis dismissed his employees before the strike vote had been taken. To avoid confusion, the term "strike" will be used in this study.

¹¹ LATU, *Minutes 1888–1890*, p. 199; Flannery, *op. cit.*, p. 24, and n. 24. Flannery obtained information from Joseph Phillis, a member of the Typographical Union at the time. The quotations are all from the former source.

¹² LATU, *Minutes 1888–1890*, pp. 200–1, 205, 212.

¹³ *Ibid.*, p. 213; *Express*, Aug. 8, 1890; *Tribune*, Aug. 8, 10, 1890.

¹⁴ *Times*, Aug. 6, 7, 14, 1890.

¹⁵ *Henry H. Markham Papers*, Huntington Library, San Marino, California, from an incomplete letter in Otis' handwriting, dated Aug. 9, 1890, and addressed "Dear Colonel."

¹⁶ *Times*, Aug. 14, Sept. 13, 1890; Otis, "A Long, Winning Fight against the 'Closed Shop'...," p. 9675.

¹⁷ Cross, *op. cit.*, p. 276.

¹⁸ LATU, *Minutes 1888–1890*, pp. 213–23.

¹⁹ LATU, *Minutes 1888–1890*, pp. 205–6, 217; *Weekly Nationalist*, Aug. 9, 1890; *Herald*, Aug. 10, 1890; *Times*, Aug. 11, 13, 1890; Los Angeles *Life*, Aug. 16, 1890.

²⁰ The Printers' Protective Fraternity first appeared in Kansas City in 1878 or 1879, following a lockout of union printers and the temporary dissolution of the Kansas City Typographical Union. (In this study, the terms "union" and "nonunion" will be used to distinguish between members and nonmembers of the International Typographical Union.) There was no serious conflict between the two organizations until 1885, when the Kansas City Fraternity sent nine members to Topeka to replace striking union printers. In March, 1886, the National Printers' Protective Fraternity

was organized with a constitution which banned strikes, lockouts, and boycotts, admitted proprietors and stockholders to membership, and instituted an arbitration system. It maintained headquarters in Kansas City, whence replacements were sent out for union strikers. The Fraternity organized its first California branch in San Diego in the spring of 1887; Los Angeles Local No. 33 was formed in September, 1890. Otis' support of the Fraternity helped prolong its existence. The *Times* branch flourished even when, in the late 1890's, the order was elsewhere declining. Eventually Los Angeles became national headquarters and the Fraternity's main stronghold. The official organ, *The Fraternity*, was first published in Kansas City, then in Nashville, and finally, in 1902, in Los Angeles. It was issued in small editions intended mainly for newspaper proprietors employing union printers, in the hope that they would change over to Fraternity members. (John C. Baker, "Birth and Demise of the P. P. F.," *Typographical Journal*, CXI [July, 1947], 25–7; George E. Barnett, *The Printers*, American Economic Association Publications, Third Series, Vol. X, no. 3 [Cambridge, Mass.: American Economic Association, 1909], pp. 52–3; Clark B. Hicks, "The Printers' Protective Fraternity," *Typographical Journal*, CX [Feb., 1947], 80–2; James A. Coates, "The Printers' Protective Fraternity," *Kansas Weekly*, Aug. 28, 1947, unpaged; *Constitution and By-Laws of the National Printers' Protective Fraternity* [Kansas City, Mo.: Ramsey, Millett & Hudson, 1886], pp. 5, 13; L. M. Schnitzer, *Truth—Strikes* [(Oakland: 1897)], pp. 5–10; *California Labor Notes: 1891–1896*, from *Pacific Union Printer*, Dec., 1891; *Times*, Apr. 28, 1887; *Workman*, Mar. 4, Apr. 8, May 13, 1891.)

[21] LATU, *Minutes 1888–1890*, p. 224; *Official Trades and Labor Directory, Los Angeles, 1896*, pp. 39, 41; *Mr. Otis and the Los Angeles "Times"* (Los Angeles: Typographical Union No. 174, 1915), p. 4; *Final Report and Testimony Submitted to Congress by the Commission on Industrial Relations*, U.S. 64th Cong., 1st sess., S. Doc. 415 (Washington: 1916), VI, 5536–7; *Henry H. Markham Papers*, letter from Alfred Pennington, chairman of the Executive Committee, San Francisco Typographical Union, Aug. 27, 1890; Jacobson, *op. cit.*; *Times*, Aug. 14, 16, 21, 27, 30, 1890; *Herald*, Aug. 29, Sept. 3, 1890; *Evening Post*, Sept. 29, 1890.

[22] LATU, *Minutes 1888–1890*, pp. 224–5, 227, 230; *Minutes 1890–1893*, pp. 1–24 *passim*, 41, 65, 72–3; *Mr. Otis and the Los Angeles "Times,"* p. 4; Cross, *op. cit.*, p. 200; Flannery, *op. cit.*, p. 28, and n. 34.

[23] LATU, *Minutes 1888–1890*, p. 230; *Minutes 1890–1893*, pp. 5, 7, 9–11, 16; *The Forty-Year War for a Free City . . .*, p. 3; *Herald*, Oct. 19, 20, 31, 1890. In September, 1890, the Los Angeles union requested the Columbia Typographical Union of Washington, D.C., to remove Otis' name from its honorary list.

[24] Barnett, *op. cit.*, pp. 268–71. The new central body was called the Council of Labor. For a detailed discussion of the labor movement in general during this period, see chapter x.

[25] LATU, *Minutes 1890–1893*, p. 13; *Times*, Aug. 14, Oct. 10, 12–14 ff., Nov. 2, 12, 20, 1890. The quotation is from the *Times*, Nov. 12, 1890.

[26] LATU, *Minutes 1888–1890*, pp. 217, 228; *Minutes 1890–1893*, pp. 4, 16–18, 26; *Herald*, Nov. 6, 1890; *Workman*, Jan. 10, Feb. 14, 1891.

[27] LATU, *Minutes 1890–1893*, pp. 28–36, 41, 49, 56–8, 61, 64–5, 67; *Workman*, May 16, 1891.

[28] LATU, *Minutes 1890–1893*, pp. 69, 72–87 *passim*; *Workman*, Jan. 10, Apr. 1, 15, 18, May 9, 13, 16, June 6, Aug. 1, 1891; *Times*, Apr. 5, 9, 20, Aug. 6, 1891.

[29] *Herald*, June 14, Aug. 6, Sept. 12, 1891; *Times*, Sept. 2, 13, 1891; *Workman*, Sept. 12, 16, 1891; LATU, *Minutes 1890–1893*, pp. 104, 106, 110.

[30] LATU, *Minutes 1890–1893*, pp. 117–37 *passim*, 141, 156, 163. The quotation appears on the last page cited.

[31] LATU, *Minutes 1890–1893*, pp. 155–87 *passim*; Cross, *op. cit.*, p. 202; *Times*, Jan. 17, 1892; *Workman*, Jan. 21, 1892; *California Labor Notes: 1891–1896*, from *Pacific Union Printer*, Feb., 1892. The *Times* expressed reluctant admiration for the Typo-

graphical Union in February when the printers voted a 10-cents-per-week assessment for the Pittsburgh union, an example of good fellowship since the ITU had done less than expected for its Los Angeles branch. (*Times*, Feb. 21, 1892.)

[32] LATU, *Minutes 1890–1893*, pp. 164, 167; *Workman*, Mar. 10, 17, 24, 1892. The printers paid for the circulars distributed by the Council.

[33] LATU, *Minutes 1890–1893*, pp. 183, 201, 203–7; William A. Spalding, comp., *History and Reminiscences, Los Angeles City and County, California* (Los Angeles: J. R. Finnell & Sons Publishing Co. [1931]), I, 299; *Workman*, Apr. 7, 1892; *Times*, Apr. 7, 1892; *Express*, Apr. 12, 1892.

[34] LATU, *Minutes 1890–1893*, p. 205.

[35] Otis, *The Los Angeles Times: A Plain Statement of Bed-Rock Facts . . .* , pp. 10–11.

[36] LATU, *Minutes 1890–1893*, pp. 210, 212; *Workman*, Apr. 7, 1892.

[37] LATU, *Minutes 1890–1893*, pp. 204–7, 220, 229; *Official Trades and Labor Directory, Los Angeles, 1896*, p. 41; *Times*, Dec. 7, 1902.

[38] *Express*, Jan. 7, 1892; *Official Trades and Labor Directory, Los Angeles, 1896*, p. 41; Pauline Jacobson, "The 'M. and M.' and the Struggle of Labor," San Francisco *Bulletin*, Dec. 16, 1911.

[39] LATU, *Minutes 1890–1893*, pp. 174–6, 203–4. The Los Angeles delegate, elected earlier, resigned when it became apparent that union members would have to be assessed to pay his expenses. (LATU, *Minutes 1890–1893*, pp. 188, 202.)

[40] LATU, *Minutes 1890–1893*, pp. 160–1, 167, 218–19, 235–6, 241, 243, 259–60, 268; *Minutes 1893–1896*, pp. 23–4; *Workman*, Feb. 11, Mar. 10, 1892. The printers believed that nonunion workmen from the *Times* were employed by the *Journal* after the walkout.

[41] LATU, *Minutes 1890–1893*, p. 276; *Minutes 1893–1896*, pp. 2, 22–5, 27.

[42] LATU, *Minutes 1893–1896*, p. 41; *Herald*, Oct. 8, 28, 29, 1893.

[43] *Citizen*, Feb. 3, 1910.

[44] LATU, *Minutes 1893–1896*, pp. 28–37, 39, 41–2.

[45] *Coast Seamen's Journal*, May 17, 1893; *Farmer and Labor Review*, Sept. 2, 1893.

[46] LATU, *Minutes 1893–1896*, pp. 42–3, 45.

[47] *Ibid.*, pp. 41, 44; *Times*, Nov. 24, 1893; Apr. 11, July *passim*, Sept. 17, 1894; H. W. Frank, "The Merchants' and Manufacturers' Association," *Land of Sunshine*, VI (Apr., 1897), 213, 216.

[48] LATU, *Minutes 1893–1896*, pp. 44–57; *Express*, Feb. 17, 20, 27, June 19, 27, 1894; *Times*, Mar. 4, 1895.

[49] LATU, *Minutes 1893–1896*, pp. 54–5, 58–63, 71; *Express*, Mar. 27, 1894.

[50] *California Federationist*, Sept. 15, 1894; LATU, *Minutes 1893–1896*, p. 70. The quotation is from the latter source.

[51] LATU, *Minutes 1893–1896*, pp. 77–80, 86–8, 95, 112; *Times*, July 25, Aug. 22, 1894; *California Federationist*, Sept. 15, 1894; *Express*, Sept. 18, 1894.

[52] LATU, *Minutes 1893–1896*, pp. 88, 95–113 *passim*; *California Federationist*, Sept. 15, 1894; *Express*, Oct. 2, 1894.

[53] LATU, *Minutes 1893–1896*, pp. 90–3, 98–9, 109, 114.

[54] *Ibid.*, pp. 103, 106–7; George A. Tracy, comp., *History of the Typographical Union* ([Indianapolis]: International Typographical Union, 1913), pp. 439, 461, 478–9, 503–10.

[55] LATU, *Minutes 1893–1896*, pp. 107–8, 111, 113–18; *Times*, Sept. 30, Oct. 5, 1894.

Chapter X

STRENGTH THROUGH UNITY

[1] *Workman*, Jan. 7, 1892.

[2] *California Labor Notes: 1886–1890*, from *Pacific Union Printer*, Sept., 1890; Ira B. Cross, *A History of the Labor Movement in California* (Berkeley: University of Cali-

fornia Press, 1935), pp. 204–5; LATU, *Minutes 1888–1890,* pp. 229–30. The quotation is from the last of these sources.

[3] *Herald,* Oct. 10, Nov. 1, 1890; LATU, *Minutes 1890–1893,* p. 4.

[4] *Herald,* Nov. 1, 6, 7, 13, 20, Dec. 18, 31, 1890; *Evening Post,* Nov. 13, 1890; *Workman,* Dec. 13, 1890; Jan. 13, 31, 1891; *Official Trades and Labor Directory, Los Angeles, 1896,* p. 25.

[5] *Herald,* Aug. 11, 1891.

[6] *Workman,* Jan. 13, Apr. 7, June 20, Aug. 15, Nov. 5, 12, 19, Dec. 24, 1891; *Herald,* Jan. 17, Oct. 19, 1891; LATU, *Minutes 1890–1893,* p. 126. A union of tram men was mentioned by the printers in October, 1891.

[7] *Coast Seamen's Journal,* Aug. 5, Nov. 11, 25, 1891; Paul S. Taylor, *The Sailors' Union of the Pacific* (New York: Ronald Press, 1923), pp. 62–5.

[8] *Herald,* Jan. 9, 26, Mar. 17, Apr. 6, 12, 13, May 13, 17, June 6, 24, 25, 28, July 2, Sept. 16, Nov. 5, 1892; *Workman,* Jan. 21, 28, Feb. 18, Mar. 17, 24, Apr. 7, 1892; *Times,* Apr. 1, 19, 20, 26, 29, May 6, Oct. 12, Nov. 6, 1892; *Express,* Apr. 12, June 7, 9, Aug. 2, 24, 30, 31, Nov. 1, 1892; *Labor Review,* Dec. 3, 1892.

[9] *Workman,* Jan.–Apr. *passim,* 1892; *Herald,* Mar. 20, 1892; *Express,* June 7, July 12, Aug. 24, 1892; *Labor Review,* Dec. 3, 1892.

[10] *Coast Seamen's Journal,* Feb. 17, Apr. 27, June 22, Oct. 19, Nov. 16, Dec. 21, 1892; *Express,* Aug. 16, 1892; *Herald,* Oct. 2, 1892.

[11] *Farmer and Labor Review,* July 29, 1893.

[12] *Express,* Feb. 21, 28, 1893; *California Farmer,* Mar. 18, 1893; *Farmer and Labor Review,* Apr.–May *passim,* June 10, 24, July 5, 15, 22, Sept. 2, 1893; *Coast Seamen's Journal,* June 14, 1893; *Herald,* July 9, 16, 23, 25, Aug. 2, Sept. 10, 1893.

[13] *Express,* Jan. 24, Mar. 7, 1893; *Times,* Feb. 17, 1893; *Farmer and Labor Review,* Apr. 15, Aug. 5, 1893; *Herald,* May 4, June 3, July 9, Aug. 6, Sept. 10, Oct. 1, 1893. The Council of Labor had assisted the boilermakers to organize in April. A new theatrical mechanics' union, organized in August, at once joined its own national union.

[14] *Farmer and Labor Review,* Mar. 25, Apr. 15, 1893; Aileen W. Robinson, *A Critical Evaluation of the American Federation of Teachers* (Chicago: American Federation of Teachers [1934]), p. 8.

[15] Later in 1894, some of the cooks revived their own local, while retaining membership in the Hotel and Restaurant Employees' Alliance. (*Official Trades and Labor Directory, Los Angeles, 1896,* p. 22.) See chapter xiii for discussion of the American Railway Union and the Pullman strike and for details concerning the newsboys' union.

[16] *Express,* Feb. 13, Mar. 13, 27, May 8, 15, 23, June 19, July 17, Aug. 21, Nov. 13, Dec. 4, 11, 25, 1894; June 27, 1895; *California Federationist,* Sept. 15, 1894; *Overture,* Sept. 1, 1926, p. 7; *Official Trades and Labor Directory, Los Angeles, 1896,* p. 22.

[17] *Express,* Mar. 7, 1893; *Farmer and Labor Review,* Apr. 15, July 8, Aug. 5, 1893; *Herald,* Oct. 28, 1893; Cross, *op. cit.,* pp. 217–18.

[18] "Pinkertons" were men furnished by the Pinkerton Detective Agency to employers and agents of employers' associations to act as strikebreakers and guards during industrial strife or as labor spies. Pinkerton detectives began to specialize in labor disputes in the 1870's and by 1892 the use of "Pinkertons" was so prevalent that the platform of the newly organized People's Party called for their outlawing. (John R. Commons and Associates, *History of Labor in the United States* [New York: Macmillan, 1921–1935], II, 415–16; Foster Rhea Dulles, *Labor in America* [New York: Crowell (c. 1949)], p. 181.)

[19] *Herald,* Nov. 1, 6, 1890; Feb. 13, 1891; *Workman,* Jan. 31, 1891; Cross, *op. cit.,* p. 204. Neither bill was passed by the legislature. The bill outlawing boycotts was favorably recommended by an assembly committee, but never came to a vote. The bill regulating the use of detectives was killed by a senate committee. (California Legislature, *Journal of the Assembly,* 29th sess. [1891], pp. 80, 214; *Journal of the Senate,* 29th sess. [1891], pp. 178, 366.)

[20] *Workman,* July 8, 1891; William A. Spalding, comp., *History and Reminiscences, Los Angeles City and County, California* (Los Angeles: J. R. Finnell & Sons Publishing Co. [1931]), I, 305.

[21] *Express,* Mar. 13, 27, Apr. 21, 28, May 12, 1894.

[22] *Herald,* Oct. 25, Nov. 3, 9, 1892; *Times,* Oct. 26, Nov. 2, 1892.

[23] *Weekly Slogan,* Oct. 18, 1884; *Herald,* Apr. 15, 1885; *Times,* June 21, 1885.

[24] *Express,* Sept. 17, 1892; *Times,* Jan. 17, 1893; *Free Public Employment Offices in the United States,* by J. E. Connor, U.S. Bureau of Labor, Bull. no. 68 (Washington: 1907), pp. 7–8. Connor is in error in stating that the Ohio experiment was unknown in Los Angeles; references were made to it at the City Council meeting of January 16, 1893.

[25] *Workman,* Nov. 12, 1891; *Times,* Sept. 7, 13, 17, 21, Oct. 26, 28, Nov. 2, 15, 29, 1892; Jan. 10, 11, 17, Feb.–June *passim,* 1893; *Herald,* Sept. 13, 17, 1892; Feb.–June *passim,* 1893; *Express,* Sept. 14, 17, Oct. 27, 1892; Jan. 10, 16, 18, 23, Feb.–June *passim,* 1893; Nov. 29, 1894; *Weekly Citizen,* Feb. 4, 1893. In February, 1895, the Los Angeles Council of Labor drafted for presentation to the California Legislature a bill to provide for a Free State Labor Bureau. Although endorsed by other labor groups in California, the bill did not pass. (*Express,* Feb. 7, 21, 1895; *Coast Seamen's Journal,* Feb. 27, 1895; California Legislature, *Journal of the Assembly,* 31st sess. [1895], p. 1274.)

[26] Cross, *op. cit.,* p. 76.

[27] *Workman,* Feb. 18, Mar. 17, 1892; *Express,* Oct. 20, 1892; *Times,* May 16, 1893; Elmer Clarence Sandmeyer, *The Anti-Chinese Movement in California* (Urbana, Ill.: University of Illinois Press, 1939), pp. 102–5.

[28] Cross, *op. cit.,* pp. 214–18.

[29] *Herald,* May 24–July 3 *passim,* Aug. 1, 11, 1893; *Farmer and Labor Review,* May 27, June 3, 10, 24, 1893; *Times,* June 4–6, 10, 12, 1893; *Coast Seamen's Journal,* June 7, 21, 1893.

[30] *Herald,* May 30, June 16–18, July 16, Aug. 13–29 *passim,* Sept. 4, 1893.

[31] *Ibid.,* Aug. 31–Oct. 1 *passim,* Oct. 29, 1893; *Coast Seamen's Journal,* Sept. 13, 1893.

[32] *Herald,* Sept. 8, 12, 13, 17, 27, Nov. 17, 19, 1893; *Times,* Nov. 4, 17, 1893.

[33] LATU, *Minutes 1890–1893,* pp. 47, 53.

[34] *Express,* Apr. 17, May 4, 22, June 1, 12, 19, 27, Nov. 13, 1894.

[35] *Evening Post,* Nov. 3, 1890; *Workman,* Nov. 5, 1890; Nov. 5, 1891; LATU, *Minutes 1888–1890,* pp. 218, 228; *Minutes 1890–1893,* pp. 16–17, 187.

[36] *Express,* Aug. 14, 21, Sept. 10, 1894; *Citizen,* Feb. 3, 1910. The first issue of *Farmer and Labor Review,* on March 25, 1893, was numbered consecutively with preceding issues of *California Farmer.* The name was changed to *Civic Review* in March, 1895. (*Civic Review,* Mar. 30, 1895.)

[37] *Workman,* Dec. 24, 1891.

[38] *Ibid.,* Apr. 8, June 20, Aug. 29, Nov. 12, 1891; *Herald,* Sept. 30, 1891; *Express,* Nov. 17, 1891; July 6, Aug. 2, 16, 30, Sept. 14, 1892; Feb. 27, Mar. 27, 1894; *Overture,* Sept. 1, 1926, p. 7.

[39] *Times,* July 2, 17, 18, 24, Aug. 23, 1891.

[40] *Herald,* July 23, 30, Aug. 6, 1893; *Evening Telegram,* Sept. 20, 1893.

[41] *Herald,* Sept. 7, 1891; *Workman,* Sept. 8, 1891.

[42] *Express,* Aug. 16, Sept. 6, 1892; *Herald,* Sept. 5, 6, 1892; *Times,* Sept. 6, 1892; Sept. 5, 1893.

[43] *Express,* July 17, 24, Sept. 1, 3, Oct. 1, 2, 1894.

[44] *Evening Post,* Oct. 30, Nov. 15, 1890; *Herald,* Nov. 1, 1890; Mar. 20, 1892; *Times,* Nov. 13, 1890; *Workman,* Feb. 18, 1892.

[45] *Herald,* Nov. 1, 6, 7, 13, 1890; *Evening Post,* Nov. 13, 1890.

[46] *Workman,* Dec. 13, 1890; Nov. 19, Dec. 17, 1891; *Herald,* Dec. 18, 1890; *Farmer and Labor Review,* Aug. 12, 1893.

[47] *Workman,* Mar. 25, May 23, Nov. 12, 19, Dec. 17, 1891; Jan. 21, 1892; *Herald,* May

26, 1891; *Express,* Nov. 10, 1891; *Coast Seamen's Journal,* Mar. 16, 1892; Cross, *op. cit.,* pp. 199–200.

⁴⁸ *Workman,* May 2, 23, Aug. 29, 1891; *Express,* Aug. 16, 1892; *Herald,* Apr. 26, 1893; Cross, *op. cit.,* p. 207; *Official Trades and Labor Directory, Los Angeles, 1896,* p. 25.

⁴⁹ *Express,* June 7, July 19, 27, Aug. 2, 4, 1892.

⁵⁰ *Workman,* Feb. 18, Mar. 17, Apr. 7, 1892; *Express,* Apr. 19, May 10, July 19, Aug. 2, 18, 29, Sept. 5, Oct. 5, Nov. 3, 1892; *Herald,* Aug. 21, Sept. 6, 7, 18, Nov. 3, 6, 13, 1892; Apr. 15, May 12, 15, 1893; *Times,* Aug. 22, Sept. 7, 1892; *Farmer and Labor Review,* Apr. 1, 29, May 20, June 10, 17, 30, Aug. 5, 1893; *Coast Seamen's Journal,* Aug. 23, 1893; *Official Trades and Labor Directory, Los Angeles, 1896,* p. 19. The quotation is from the last of these sources.

⁵¹ *Workman,* July 8, 1891; *Farmer and Labor Review,* Mar. 25, Apr. 8, 15, July 8, 1893; *Express,* Mar. 28, 1893; *Official Trades and Labor Directory, Los Angeles, 1896,* p. 26.

⁵² *Herald,* July 25, 1893; *Official Trades and Labor Directory, Los Angeles, 1896,* p. 13.

⁵³ *Workman,* Nov. 12, 1891; *Express,* Aug. 16, 1892; Frank T. Stockton, *The Closed Shop in American Trade Unions,* Johns Hopkins University Studies in Historical and Political Science, Series 29, no. 3 (Baltimore: Johns Hopkins Press, 1911), pp. 39–42.

⁵⁴ *Times,* Feb. 2, July 14, Oct. 27, 30, 31, Nov. 7, 1893; *California Farmer,* Mar. 18, 1893; *Herald,* Aug. 17, Oct. 7, 28, 1893.

⁵⁵ *Times,* May 27, 28, 1894; *Express,* May 30, 1894.

⁵⁶ *Times,* Aug. 7, 11, Nov. 20, 27, 1894.

⁵⁷ *Herald,* Jan. 17, 1891; July 25, 30, Aug. 6, 13, Sept. 24, 1893; *Farmer and Labor Review,* Aug. 12, 1893.

⁵⁸ *Times,* Feb. 17, 25, 1891; *Workman,* Dec. 24, 1891.

⁵⁹ *Times,* June 13, 15, 1893; *Express,* May 15, 28, June 12, 1894.

⁶⁰ *Herald,* Dec. 31, 1890; *Workman,* Dec. 17, 24, 1891; Jan. 21, 1892; *Express,* Sept. 14, 1892.

⁶¹ *Workman,* Nov. 25, Dec. 3, 1891; *Express,* Aug. 30, 1892; Aug. 21, 1894; *Farmer and Labor Review,* Apr. 1, 15, 29, May 13, 27, 1893; *Times,* Apr. 20, May 22, June 5, 1893; *Herald,* Apr. 26, 27, May 22, 27, June 17, Aug. 6, 1893; *Coast Seamen's Journal,* June 7, 1893; Cross, *op. cit.,* pp. 276–7.

⁶² *Farmer and Labor Review,* July 15, Aug. 5, 12, 26, Sept. 2, 1893; *Herald,* July 16, Aug. 3, 20, 23, Sept. 24, 1893; *Times,* Aug. 27, Sept. 2, 1893; *Coast Seamen's Journal,* Sept. 20, 1893.

⁶³ *Times,* Mar. 1–18 *passim,* Apr. 12, 15, July 21, Aug. 5, 6, Oct. 5–18 *passim,* 1890; *Herald,* Mar. 5–18 *passim,* Apr. 10, Aug. 7, 12, 22, Oct. 8, 10, 15, 18, 1890; *Express,* Aug. 11, 1890; *Evening Post,* Oct. 4–13 *passim,* 1890; *Coast Seamen's Journal,* Oct. 22, 1890.

⁶⁴ San Pedro *Times,* Feb. 18, Mar. 11, 18, 25, Apr. 1, 8, 15, 1893; Los Angeles *Times,* Mar. 21, 29, Apr. 8, May 7–9, 14, 22, 1893; *Herald,* Apr. 4, 5, 1893; *Farmer and Labor Review,* Apr. 8, June 24, 1893; *Coast Seamen's Journal,* Apr. 12, 19, 26, 1893; Cross, *op. cit.,* pp. 212–13.

⁶⁵ *Herald,* May 7, June 22, 24, Sept. 24, 1893; Los Angeles *Times,* May 7–9, 13, 16, 18, June 22, 1893; San Pedro *Times,* July 1, 1893.

⁶⁶ San Pedro *Times,* Sept. 9, 1893.

⁶⁷ *Coast Seamen's Journal,* July 12, 1893; Cross, *op. cit.,* p. 213.

Chapter XI

THE POLITICAL DILEMMA OF THE EARLY 1890's

¹ Ira B. Cross, *A History of the Labor Movement in California* (Berkeley: University of California Press, 1935), pp. 204–6, 210; Lucile Eaves, *A History of California Labor Legislation* (Berkeley: The University Press [c. 1910]), pp. 52–3, 58.

[2] *Workman,* Jan. 31, Mar. 11, 1891; *Herald,* Mar. 12, 14, 1891. The quotation is from the *Herald,* Mar. 14, 1891.

[3] *Workman,* Aug. 22, 29, Sept. 12, Nov. 12, 25, 1891; LATU, *Minutes 1890–1893,* pp. 130–1.

[4] *Workman,* Mar. 28, 1891.

[5] *Herald,* Apr. 17, June 1, Aug. 11, 1891.

[6] Anna Rochester, *The Populist Movement in the United States* (New York: International Publishers [c. 1943]), p. 49; John R. Commons and Associates, *History of Labor in the United States* (New York: Macmillan, 1921–1935), II, 489–92; John D. Hicks, *The Populist Revolt* (Minneapolis: University of Minnesota Press [c. 1931]), pp. 96–127, 205–37. The Citizens' Alliances of the 1890's are not to be confused with those of the early 1900's, which were antiunion.

[7] Commons and Associates, *op. cit.,* II, 493–4; Nathan Fine, *Labor and Farmer Parties in the United States, 1828–1928* (New York: Rand School of Social Science [c. 1928]), p. 77; Rochester, *op. cit.,* pp. 51–2, 61, 65–70; Solon J. Buck, *The Agrarian Crusade,* Chronicles of America Series, vol. 45 (New Haven: Yale University Press, 1921), pp. 107, 109–10; Hicks, *op. cit.,* pp. 439–44.

[8] *Herald,* July 7, 8, 1891; *Alliance Farmer,* July 23, 1891.

[9] *Workman,* Sept. 23, 1891; *Times,* Oct. 18, 19, 1891. The quotation is from the first source cited.

[10] *Alliance Farmer,* Sept. 24, 1891; *Herald,* Oct. 23, 1891; *Times,* Oct. 23, 1891.

[11] *Alliance Farmer,* Dec. 17, 1891; *Workman,* Jan.–Mar. *passim,* 1892; *Herald,* May 15, 1892; *California Farmer,* May 28, June 25, July 16, 1892; *Official Trades and Labor Directory, Los Angeles, 1896,* p. 27. The quotation is from the last of these sources. The Knights of Labor assemblies still in existence were Pasadena Local No. 1051 and Los Angeles Locals No. 2405 and No. 7647.

[12] *Times,* Apr. 8, 1892; *Herald,* Apr. 8, Sept. 5, 1892; *Express,* Apr. 12, May 24, Sept. 6, 1892; *Coast Seamen's Journal,* May 25, 1892; Cross, *op. cit.,* pp. 214–15; LATU, *Minutes 1890–1893,* p. 197.

[13] *Herald,* July 14, 1892; *Times,* Aug. 7, 1892.

[14] *Times,* Oct. 4, 7, 1892.

[15] *Ibid.,* Oct. 26, Nov. 2, 1892; *California Farmer,* Oct. 29, 1892; *Herald,* Oct. 30, Nov. 1, 4, 8, 14, Dec. 4, 1892; *Labor Review,* Dec. 3, 1892.

[16] *Herald,* Nov. 19, 1892; *Times,* Nov. 19, 21, Dec. 3–7, 1892; *Express,* Feb. 2, 4, 6, 14, 20, 23, 28, 1893.

[17] Fine, *op. cit.,* pp. 79–80; Rochester, *op. cit.,* pp. 80–98 *passim; Times,* Dec. 28, 1892.

[18] *Farmer and Labor Review,* Apr. 29, June 24, 30, July 8, 1893; *Herald,* May 5, July 9, Oct. 8, 1893; *Times,* June 28, July 3, 5, 1893; LATU, *Minutes 1890–1893,* p. 269. The quotation is from the last of these sources.

[19] *California Farmer,* Mar. 18, 1893; *Farmer and Labor Review,* Apr. 15, May 6, 20, 1893; *Herald,* June 8–10, 12, July 2, 23, 1893; *Coast Seamen's Journal,* June 14, 1893.

[20] *Farmer and Labor Review,* Aug. 5, 1893; *Coast Seamen's Journal,* Jan. 10, 1894; *Express,* Jan. 31, 1894; *California Labor Notes: 1891–1896,* from *Pacific Union Printer,* Feb., 1894; Cross, *op. cit.,* p. 206.

[21] *Express,* Feb. 6, 13, 20, Mar. 6, 1894.

[22] *Ibid.,* Feb. 13, 27, Mar. 13, 27, Apr. 11, 24, 1894; Cross, *op. cit.,* p. 221. The quotation is from the *Express,* Feb. 13, 1894.

[23] *Express,* June 12, July 17, Aug. 21, Sept. 25, Oct. 10, 30, Nov. 24, 27, 28, 30, Dec. 11, 1894; *California Federationist,* Sept. 15, 1894; *Times,* Nov. 24, 28, 1894; LATU, *Minutes 1893–1896,* p. 77.

[24] *Express,* May 23, 24, Aug. 7, 14, 21, Sept. 10, 1894; *Times,* July 27, 28, 1894; *California Federationist,* Sept. 15, 1894; LATU, *Minutes 1893–1896,* p. 116. The quotation is from the *Express,* Aug. 7, 1894.

[25] *Times,* Jan. 26, 1893; July 27, 28, 1894; *California Farmer,* Mar. 11, 1893; *Herald,* Dec. 3, 1893.

[20] *Times,* Sept.–Oct. *passim,* Nov. 7, 23, Dec. 4, 1894; *Express,* Oct. 5, 1894; *Herald,* Sept. 13, 1896; *Civic Review,* Sept. 19, 1896; Fine, *op. cit.,* pp. 80–6; Hicks, *op. cit.,* pp. 338–79.

[27] Hicks, *op. cit.,* pp. 404–23. The quotation is from page 422.

Chapter XII

ON TO WASHINGTON

[1] Donald L. McMurry, *Coxey's Army: A Study of the Industrial Army Movement of 1894* (Boston: Little, Brown, 1929), pp. 6, 262, 268, 271–2; John D. Hicks, *The Populist Revolt* (Minneapolis: University of Minnesota Press [c. 1931]), p. 322.

[2] McMurry, *op. cit.,* pp. 22–3, 25.

[3] *Ibid.,* pp. 30–3, 37–8; Henry Vincent, *The Story of the Commonweal* (Chicago: W. B. Conkey Co., 1894), p. 16.

[4] McMurry, *op. cit.,* pp. 45–7, 50–2, 58–60, 262; Vincent, *op. cit.,* pp. 16, 56, 95, 175, 212.

[5] *Times,* Aug. 29, Sept. 5, Nov. 3, 5, 1893; Jan. 6, 10, 11, 16, 24, 25, Feb. 2, 20, 1894; *Herald,* Oct. 28, Nov. 2, 5, 1893; *Express,* Jan. 5, 23, Feb. 5, Mar. 10, 12, 1894.

[6] McMurry, *op. cit.,* pp. 20, 127–9; Vincent, *op. cit.,* p. 163; *Express,* Feb. 6, 27, Mar. 1, 3, 10, 12, 13, 1894; *Times,* Feb. 13, 20, 27, 1894.

[7] *Express,* Mar. 13, 1894.

[8] *Ibid.,* Mar. 13–15, 1894; *Times,* Mar. 14, 1894; McMurry, *op. cit.,* p. 131.

[9] *Express,* Mar. 16, 1894; *Times,* Mar. 17, 19, 20, 23, 1894; McMurry, *op. cit.,* pp. 131–5.

[10] *Times,* Apr. 4, 27, 1894; *Express,* May 4, 7, 8, June 6, 1894; McMurry, *op. cit.,* pp. 142–5, 147–8, 246.

[11] *Express,* Mar. 16, 17, 20–22, 24, 26, 28, 1894; *Times,* Mar. 17–20, 22, 1894.

[12] *Express,* Mar. 28, 1894; *Times,* Apr. 3, 4, 7, 10, 13–15, 1894; McMurry, *op. cit.,* p. 197; Vincent, *op. cit.,* p. 199.

[13] Henry Winfred Splitter, "Concerning Vinette's Los Angeles Regiment of Coxey's Army," *Pacific Historical Review,* XXVII (Feb., 1948), 33–5; *Times,* Apr. 15, 17–20, 22, 24, 26, 28, May 1, 4, 10, 11, 1894; *Express,* May 10, 11, 1894.

[14] Splitter, *op. cit.,* p. 36; McMurry, *op. cit.,* p. 198; *Express,* May 16, 18, 21, 23, 1894; *Times,* June 26, 1894.

[15] McMurry, *op. cit.,* pp. 104–26, 244.

[16] *Ibid.,* pp. 241–58.

[17] Splitter, *op. cit.,* p. 35; *Express,* Apr. 26, 30, 1894; *Times,* June 19, Dec. 4–20 *passim,* 1894; Jan. 1, 1895.

[18] *Times,* Dec. 20, 25, 1894; Jan. 12, 1895; *Express,* Dec. 26, 29, 1894; Jan. 11, 15, 23, 31, Feb. 5, 1895.

Chapter XIII

THE PULLMAN STRIKE

[1] *Express,* Dec. 1, 1882; Mar. 13, 1893; *Firemen's Magazine,* VII (Jan., 1883), 47; VII (July, 1883), 320; *Times,* June 3, Nov. 29, 1883; *Herald,* Mar. 9, June 1, 1886; *Fraternal Reporter,* Oct. 21, 1887; Ira B. Cross, *A History of the Labor Movement in California* (Berkeley: University of California Press, 1935), p. 194; John R. Commons and Associates, *History of Labor in the United States* (New York: Macmillan, 1921–1935), II, 310. *Firemen's Magazine* was the official organ of the Brotherhood of Locomotive Firemen, and at this time was edited by Eugene V. Debs.

[2] *Times,* July 30, Oct. 2–4, 1887; Mar. 4, 5, 17, 21, May 24, 26–29, Nov. 2, 3, Dec. 7,

1888; June 1, 1889; Aug. 31, 1893; *Tribune,* Oct. 6, 1887; Mar. 17, 19–21, May 24, 26–29, Nov. 2–4, 21, Dec. 6, 1888; *Herald,* May 29, 1889; Sept. 22, 26, 27, 1890; Apr. 22, 29, May 11, 12, 15, 22, 1892; Oct. 30, 1893; *Farmer and Labor Review,* Apr. 29, 1893; Selig Perlman, *A History of Trade Unionism in the United States* (New York: Macmillan, 1922), pp. 130–1; *The Forty-Year War for a Free City; A History of the Open Shop in Los Angeles* (Los Angeles: Times-Mirror Publishing Co., 1929), p. 4.

³ *Tribune,* Nov. 14, Dec. 10, 11, 15, 1888; Jan. 1, 14, Feb. 4, 1889; *Herald,* May 26, June 26, Sept. 17, 1889; Commons and Associates, *op. cit.,* II, 310; Edwin C. Robbins, *Railway Conductors: A Study in Organized Labor,* Columbia University Studies in History, Economics and Public Law, vol. 61 (New York: Columbia University Press, 1914), pp. 22–3, 108, 111; *Brotherhood Relief and Insurance of Railway Employees,* by Emory R. Johnson, U.S. Dept. of Labor, Bull. no. 17 (Washington: 1898), p. 557; *Constitution and By-Laws of the Grand International Brotherhood of Railway Conductors* (Los Angeles: 1889), *passim.*

⁴ *Herald,* Sept. 16–21, 1889; *Times,* Sept. 17, 18, 21, 1889; Sept. 7, 1890; *Workman,* May 16, 1891; *Brotherhood Relief and Insurance of Railway Employees,* p. 557.

⁵ *Times,* Oct. 16, 1891; *Herald,* Dec. 16, 17, 19–31 *passim,* 1891; Jan. 1, May 10, 1892; *Workman,* Dec. 24, 1891; *California Farmer,* Feb. 6, 1892; Archibald M. McIsaac, *The Order of Railroad Telegraphers* (Princeton: Princeton University Press, 1933), pp. 5–7.

⁶ *Herald,* Apr. 23, 25–27, 1893; *Farmer and Labor Review,* May 6, 1893.

⁷ *Times,* Oct. 20, 21, 1890; *Herald,* Oct. 21, 1890; *Evening Post,* Oct. 31, 1890; *Workman,* Aug. 26, 1891.

⁸ *Herald,* Sept. 9, 1893.

⁹ *Times,* Apr. 16, 1893; Almont Lindsey, *The Pullman Strike* (Chicago: University of Chicago Press [c. 1942]), pp. 110–13. In 1894 the first annual ARU convention voted down a proposal to admit Negroes by 113 to 102. (*Express,* June 27, 1894.)

¹⁰ *Times,* June 13, 1894; Commons and Associates, *op. cit.,* II, 502; *Official Trades and Labor Directory, Los Angeles, 1896,* pp. 43–6. The quotation is from page 45 of the last source cited.

¹¹ *Express,* Mar. 27, May 15, 29, July 3, 1894; *Times,* July 16, 1894; *Seventh Biennial Report, 1895–1896,* California Bureau of Labor Statistics (Sacramento: 1896), p. 142; *Official Trades and Labor Directory, Los Angeles, 1896,* pp. 57–9. The quotation is from page 59 of the last source cited.

¹² Lindsey, *op. cit.,* pp. 95–105, 110; Commons and Associates, *op. cit.,* II, 502; Foster Rhea Dulles, *Labor In America* (New York: Crowell [c. 1949]), p. 172.

¹³ Lindsey, *op. cit.,* pp. 105, 123–5, 128–9, 133; *Times,* June 16, 23, 1894; *Express,* June 22, 25, 1894.

¹⁴ Lindsey, *op. cit.,* pp. 133–5, 239; Commons and Associates, *op. cit.,* II, 502; *Times,* June 27, 1894.

¹⁵ Lindsey, *op. cit.,* p. 142.

¹⁶ *Ibid.,* pp. 139, 144, 239–40, 249.

¹⁷ *Ibid.,* pp. 134, 248–9; Cross, *op. cit.,* pp. 219–20; Thomas R. Bacon, "The Railroad Strike in California," *Yale Review,* III (Nov., 1894), 241–50; "The Situation in California," *Nation,* LIX (July 12, 1894), 23; *Express,* June 26–29, 1894; *Times,* June 27–29, 1894.

¹⁸ Lindsey, *op. cit.,* pp. 148–9.

¹⁹ *Ibid.,* p. 150; *Express,* June 28–30, 1894; *Times,* June 29, 30, July 1, 1894.

²⁰ *Times,* July 1–4, 6, 1894; *Express,* July 2–4, 7, 9, 11, 1894.

²¹ Lindsey, *op. cit.,* pp. 161–5, 250; *Times,* July 3, 5, 7, 8, 1894; *Express,* July 3, 4, 6, 18, 1894.

²² *Times,* Mar. 30, July 6, 7, 13, 1894; *Express,* July 4–6, 9, 12, 17, 1894; LATU, *Minutes 1893–1896,* p. 88; "Southern California and the Strike," *Land of Sunshine,* I (Aug., 1894), 59; *Charles Dwight Willard Letters,* letter to his father, July 9 [1894]. Willard was one of the publishers of *Land of Sunshine,* the first issue of which appeared in June, 1894.

[23] *Express,* July 11, 1894; *Times,* July 13–15, Sept. 30, Dec. 22, 23, 1894.

[24] *Express,* July 4–7, 9–12, 1894; *Times,* July 5–10, 1894.

[25] Lindsey, *op. cit.,* pp. 226–34; *Express,* July 12–14, 1894; *Times,* July 13, 14, 1894.

[26] Lindsey, *op. cit.,* p. 235, from the New York *World,* July 16, 1894.

[27] Lindsey, *op. cit.,* pp. 249–51, 269–70; *Express,* July 4, 17, 18, 20, 1894; *Times,* July 18, 22, 1894; "Southern California and the Strike," p. 59.

[28] Lindsey, *op. cit.,* p. 270; *Times,* Sept. 21, 23, 25, Nov. 17, 18, 21, 22, 27, Dec. 7, 8, 18, 25, 1894; Mar. 24, 1895; *Coast Seamen's Journal,* Dec. 12, 1894.

[29] Lindsey, *op. cit.,* pp. 290–2, 300–3; McAlister Coleman, *Eugene V. Debs* (New York: Greenberg [c. 1930]), pp. 176–7; *Express,* Feb. 13, Mar. 13, Apr. 24, Nov. 28, Dec. 25, 1894; Jan. 23, 30, Feb. 7, 21, 27, Mar. 7, 8, 14, 29, 31, Apr. 1, July 25, 1895; *Times,* Mar. 29, Apr. 1, 1895.

[30] *Express,* Nov. 23, Dec. 12, 26, 27, 30, 1895; Feb. 20, 1896; *Coast Seamen's Journal,* Nov. 6, 27, 1895; Mar. 25, Nov. 18, 1896; *Times,* Nov. 9, 20, 23, 24, 29, Dec. 9, 24, 1895; *Civic Review,* Feb. 29, 1896; *Labor World,* Apr. 2, 1896; Caroline Augusta Lloyd, *Henry Demarest Lloyd, 1847–1903* (New York: Putnam, 1912), I, 144–54.

[31] Lindsey, *op. cit.,* pp. 225, 322; *Express,* June 27, July 4, Aug. 7, 1894; *Times,* July 27, 1894. At this time a Populist leader, Mrs. M. W. Alex, was master workman of the Knights of Labor.

[32] *The Forty-Year War for a Free City* . . . , p. 5.

Chapter XIV

PROGRESS AND DECLINE

[1] Charles Dwight Willard, *History of Los Angeles City* (Los Angeles: Kingsley-Barnes and Neuner Co., 1901), p. 344; Ira B. Cross, *A History of the Labor Movement in California* (Berkeley: University of California Press, 1935), pp. 217–18; Robert Glass Cleland and Osgood Hardy, *March of Industry* (Los Angeles: Powell Publishing Co. [c. 1929]), pp. 238–9; Selig Perlman, *A History of Trade Unionism in the United States* (New York: Macmillan, 1922), p. 163; Lucile Eaves, *A History of California Labor Legislation* (Berkeley: The University Press [c. 1910]), pp. 62–3; *Herald,* Nov. 5, 1893.

[2] *Times,* Dec. 13, 1894; Jan. 25, July 17, 28, 31, Aug. 9, 15, 22, 23, Nov. 5, 1895; Jan. 14, Feb. 5, June 10, 23, 24, July 15, 21, 1896; Cross, *op. cit.,* p. 278; *Constitution and By-Laws of the Merchants and Manufacturers Association of Los Angeles* (Los Angeles: 1896), pp. 5–7.

[3] LATU, *Minutes 1893–1896,* p. 118; *Express,* July 3, 11, 1895.

[4] *Herald,* July 24, 1895.

[5] Frank B. Colver, "Los Angeles Labor Council," San Francisco *Call,* May 4, 1896.

[6] *Express,* Jan. 23, 24, Feb. 21, Mar. 7, 21, Apr. 4, June 4, 8, 21, July 24, 25, Sept. 5, 11, Nov. 7, 21, Dec. 16, 19, 1895; *Times,* Mar. 1, Sept. 6, 7, Dec. 19, 1895; *Herald,* July 24, 1895; LATU, *Minutes 1893–1896,* pp. 128, 135.

[7] *Herald,* Aug. *passim,* Sept. 6, 8, 1896; *Record,* Aug. 25, 1896; *Times,* Sept. 8, 1896; LATU, *Minutes 1896–1898,* pp. 32, 40–1; *Official Trades and Labor Directory, Los Angeles, 1896,* pp. 3–5, 65–7.

[8] Colver, *op. cit.; Times,* Sept. 8, 1896.

[9] Colver, *op. cit.*

[10] *Express,* Feb. 21, Apr. 4, May 1, 9, 16, 23, June 8, Aug. 1, 6, 21, 1895; *Times,* May 28, Aug. 1, 18, 1895; *Herald,* July 15, 1895; *Coast Seamen's Journal,* Aug. 28, 1895; LATU, *Minutes 1893–1896,* pp. 125–6, 128.

[11] *Express,* Nov. 7, Dec. 5, 1895; Jan. 16, Feb. 12, 20, Mar. 5, 19, Apr. 2, Sept. 20, Dec. 4, 1896; *Times,* May 26, 1896; *Civic Review,* June 6, 1896; *Herald,* Aug. 23, Sept. 14, 1896; LATU, *Minutes 1896–1898,* pp. 20, 26–7; *Charles Dwight Willard Letters,* letter to his father, July 13, 1896; *Official Trades and Labor Directory, Los Angeles, 1896,* p. 8.

[12] *Express*, Oct. 10, 1895; LATU, *Minutes 1893–1896*, pp. 115–80 *passim*.

[13] Harris Newmark, *Sixty Years in Southern California, 1853–1913* (New York: Knickerbocker Press, 1916), p. 610.

[14] *Herald*, July 15, 24, 1895; Aug.–Sept. *passim*, 1896; *Express*, Feb. 20, Apr. 2, 1896; *Coast Seamen's Journal*, Mar. 25, 1896; *Record*, May 4, 12, 1896; LATU, *Minutes 1893–1896*, pp. 130, 192.

[15] *Official Trades and Labor Directory, Los Angeles, 1896*, p. 41.

[16] LATU, *Minutes 1893–1896*, pp. 178–81, 184–5, 193–5; *Minutes 1896–1898*, p. 10.

[17] LATU, *Minutes 1896–1898*, pp. 8–47 *passim*; *Herald*, Aug. 16, 1896. The quotation is from page 41 of the former source.

[18] LATU, *Minutes 1896–1898*, pp. 17, 20–2; *Express*, Aug. 8, 9, 1895; *Pacific Union Printer*, Aug., 1895.

[19] LATU, *Minutes 1896–1898*, pp. 40, 53, 63–4; *Herald*, Aug. 16, Sept. 2, 17, 18, 1896; *Times*, Sept. 18, 1896.

[20] LATU, *Minutes 1893–1896*, p. 202; *Minutes 1896–1898*, p. 24; *Proceedings of the American Federation of Labor, 1896*, p. 34; *Labor World*, Apr. 2, 1896; Joseph Phillis, "C. E. Fisk," *Citizen*, Feb. 3, 1910.

[21] The Los Angeles Labor Exchange was organized in January, 1896, as Branch No. 39 of a national order formed in Missouri in 1890 to facilitate the exchange of labor and commodities by a certificate system. The local organization maintained a coöperative store and harness shop, but was not mentioned after May, 1897. ("The Labor Exchange," in *The Encyclopedia of Social Reform*, ed. by W. D. P. Bliss [1897], p. 786; *Civic Review*, Jan. 25, Feb. 15, Mar. 7, 28, Apr. 18, June 6, 1896; *Times*, May 5, 1897.)

[22] *Express*, Mar. 5, 12, 19, 23, 1896; *Civic Review*, Mar. 7, 1896; Colver, *op. cit.*; LATU, *Minutes 1893–1896*, pp. 181, 185–7, 190; *Official Trades and Labor Directory, Los Angeles, 1896*, p. 23; John R. Commons and Associates, *History of Labor in the United States* (New York: Macmillan, 1921–1935), II, 509–14.

[23] *Times*, Apr. 7, 9, 12, 16, May 3–5, 1896; *Express*, Apr. 20, May 1, 1896; *Record*, May 1, 1896; *Herald*, Nov. 30, 1896. The quotation is from a letter of Frank Colver's published in the *Times*, May 3, 1896.

[24] Willard, *op. cit.*, pp. 348–51.

[25] *Herald*, July 6, Aug. 31, Sept. 7, 14–16, 26, 28, Oct. 5, 12, 19, Nov. 1, 2, 9, 23, 1896; Joseph Phillis, "Capt. F. B. Colver," *Citizen*, Feb. 10, 1911; Commons and Associates, *op. cit.*, II, 514.

[26] LATU, *Minutes 1893–1896*, pp. 133, 139, 153, 197–200; *Minutes 1896–1898*, pp. 11–14, 44; Helen Flannery, "The Labor Movement in Los Angeles, 1880–1903" (unpublished M.A. thesis, University of California, Berkeley, 1929), p. 46; Eaves, *op. cit.*, pp. 385–6; E. R. Spedden, *The Trade Union Label*, Johns Hopkins University Studies in Historical and Political Science, Series 28, no. 2 (Baltimore: Johns Hopkins Press, 1910), pp. 9–12, 16–21.

[27] *Herald*, Sept. 15, Nov. 5, 1896; *Times*, Nov. 5, 1896; LATU, *Minutes 1896–1898*, pp. 11–12, 35, 44–5, 53–4.

[28] *Herald*, Sept. 12, 1896; *Times*, Oct. 7, 1896; LATU, *Minutes 1896–1898*, pp. 49–52, 64. The quotation is from page 64 of the last source cited.

[29] *Times*, Oct. 8–11, 18, 20, 27, 29, Nov. 6, 7, 10, 12, 16, 17, 19, 20, 24, Dec. 1, 1896; *Herald*, Oct. 9, 11, Nov. 9, 13, 16, 1896; *Record*, Nov. 17, 23, 1896; *Union "Totem,"* Nov. 19, 1896; LATU, *Minutes 1896–1898*, pp. 65, 83–7.

[30] *Express*, Mar. 5, 1896; *Times*, July 31, Aug. 3, 7, Sept. 3, 20, Oct. 13, 14, 30, Dec. 8, 9, 1896; *Herald*, Oct. 26, Dec. 2, 7, 8, 1896; *Charles Dwight Willard Letters*, letters to his father, July 13, Sept. 12, Nov. 13, 1896, and Jan. 23, 1897.

[31] LATU, *Minutes 1896–1898*, pp. 90–198 *passim*; *Times*, Jan. 5, 6, 18, 19, 1897; *Herald*, Jan. 19, Apr. 5, Aug. 2, 23, 1897.

[32] LATU, *Minutes 1896–1898*, pp. 131, 137; photostatic copies of Prescott's letters and telegrams between the dates March 15 and 29, 1897, in the files of the International Typographical Union at Indianapolis.

[33] *Henry H. Markham Papers,* letter from Otis to Markham, Apr. 13, 1897.

[34] *Times,* Aug. 25, 1896; Feb. 2, Mar. 15, Apr. 21, May 11, 15, 19, 1897; *Herald,* Mar. 22, May 7–13, 20, 24, 1897; LATU, *Minutes 1896–1898,* pp. 113, 141–2; *Twenty-Sixth Session of the Grand Division of the Order of Railway Conductors, May 11th, 1897, Los Angeles, Cal.* (Los Angeles: R. Y. McBride [1897]), *passim.*

[35] *Herald,* Sept. 5, 29, 1896; Apr. 5, 12, 19, May 17, June 21, 28, 1897; *Record,* Dec. 18, 1896; July 23, 1897; *Times,* Mar. 23, Sept. 22, 1898; LATU, *Minutes 1896–1898,* pp. 85, 96, 104, 133–4, 159–214 *passim,* 246–7; *Minutes 1898–1902,* pp. 22, 24–5, 40, 51, 66, 94–5.

[36] *Herald,* July 15, 1895.

[37] *Express,* May 23, July 11, Sept. 12, 1895; Jan. 1, 1896; *Herald,* July 15, 24, 1895; Aug. 2, Sept. 14, Oct. 12, 1896; Apr. 19, June 1, July 12, Aug. 23, 1897; Colver, *op. cit.*

[38] *Express,* Jan. 18, Feb. 7, May 1, 6, Sept. 12, 20, Oct. 10, 15, 18, 31, Nov. 7, Dec. 5, 26, 1895; *Times,* May 7, Aug. 30, 1895; *Herald,* Aug. 7, 16, Dec. 28, 1896; Apr. 19, June 1, 1897; Colver, *op. cit.; Seventh Biennial Report, 1895–1896,* California Bureau of Labor Statistics (Sacramento: 1896), p. 137; *Official Trades and Labor Directory, Los Angeles, 1896,* pp. 70–1, 81, 83.

[39] *Express,* Nov. 7, 1895; Mar. 5, 1896; *Record,* May 25, Dec. 18, 1896; *Herald,* Aug. 16, Sept. 14, 1896; Colver, *op. cit.; Official Trades and Labor Directory, Los Angeles, 1896,* pp. 13, 15.

[40] Joseph Phillis, "J. R. Walker," *Citizen,* Feb. 24, 1911.

[41] *Express,* Mar. 26, Apr. 4, 17, 1895; *Times,* Mar. 28, 29, Apr. 1–4, Aug. 30, 1895; *Herald,* July 15, 1895; Aug. 16, 1896; *Record,* Aug. 19, 1896; *Seventh Biennial Report, 1895–1896,* California Bureau of Labor Statistics, pp. 138–9.

[42] Colver, *op. cit.; Record,* June 2, July 6, Aug. 17, 1896; July 23, Sept. 10, 11, 13, 1897; *Herald,* Aug. 2, 9, 23, 31, Sept. 3, 6, 12, Nov. 30, 1896; Feb. 16, Aug. 2, Sept. 14, 1897; *Times,* Sept. 3, 1896; *Seventh Biennial Report, 1895–1896,* California Bureau of Labor Statistics, pp. 142–3.

[43] *Times,* July 28, 30, Aug. 6, 25, 27, Dec. 10, 12, 1895; *Herald,* Aug. 23, 1895.

[44] *Herald,* Aug. 9, 23, Sept. 14, Nov. 23, 1896.

[45] *Ibid.,* Aug. 16, Sept. 12, 1896.

[46] *Express,* Sept. 19, Oct. 9, 18, 1895; Jan. 20, Feb. 20, Mar. 5, 1896; *Times,* Oct. 9, 1895; *Labor World,* Apr. 2, 1896; LATU, *Minutes 1893–1896,* pp. 150–1, 197; *Seventh Biennial Report, 1895–1896,* California Bureau of Labor Statistics, p. 139.

[47] *Express,* Feb. 25, Sept. 12, 1895; Jan. 1, 16, 23, 24, 1896; *Record,* July 6, 1896; *Herald,* Nov. 9, 23, 1896; Aug. 30, 1897; *Times,* Jan. 17, Feb. 8, 1897; Colver, *op. cit.; Seventh Biennial Report, 1895–1896,* California Bureau of Labor Statistics, p. 142; LATU, *Minutes 1896–1898,* pp. 104, 139.

[48] *Express,* Feb. 21, 1895; *Herald,* Mar. 15, 22, Apr. 5, 1897; *Record,* Feb. 7, 1898; Colver, *op. cit.; Seventh Biennial Report, 1895–1896,* California Bureau of Labor Statistics, p. 139.

[49] *Express,* Aug. 15, 21, 28, Sept. 12, Oct. 3, 1895; Apr. 8, July 1, 1896; *Times,* Oct. 3, 24, 1895; Mar. 24, June 23, 25, July 14, 21, Aug. 6, 19, 25, 1896; *Coast Seamen's Journal,* July 1, 1896; *Herald,* July 8, Aug. 19, 20, 25, 29, Oct. 6, Nov. 9, 16, 23, 1896; Aug. 2, 1897; *Record,* July 14, Dec. 3, 1896; Feb. 7, Mar. 5, Aug. 5, 1898; July 21, 1899; LATU, *Minutes 1893–1896,* pp. 145, 153; *Seventh Biennial Report, 1895–1896,* California Bureau of Labor Statistics, p. 138.

[50] *Express,* Feb. 20, Mar. 19, 26, 1896; *Herald,* Aug. 9, 16, 23, 1896; *Record,* Dec. 3, 1896; Colver, *op. cit.; LATU, Minutes 1896–1898,* pp. 78, 96.

[51] *Express,* Dec. 11, 25, 1894; Jan. 15, 17, Mar. 21, June 8, 1895; *Herald,* Nov. 16, Dec. 14, 1896; *Voice of Labor* (published in San Francisco), Apr. 10, 1897.

[52] *Express,* June 27, 1895; Jan. 1, 1896; *Herald,* Aug. 2, 1896; Apr. 19, Aug. 30, 1897; *Times,* June 27, 30, July 3, 1897; Feb. 19, 1898; *Record,* Jan. 8, 24, 1898; *Overture,* Sept. 1, 1926; Colver, *op. cit.; Constitution and By-Laws of the Los Angeles Musical Association* (Los Angeles: 1895), p. 30; *Fiftieth Anniversary of Musicians Local 47, A. F. of M., 1894–1944* (Los Angeles: 1944), unpaged.

[53] San Pedro *Times,* Jan. 12, 26, Apr. 15, 1895; Aug. 15, 22, Dec. 5, 1896; Jan. 16, May 22, July 31, Aug. 28, Oct. 16, 1897; *Coast Seamen's Journal,* 1895, *passim;* Jan. 22, 1896; *Express,* Jan. 23, Feb. 7, 21, Mar. 20, 28, May 9, July 11, Aug. 18, Sept. 12, Nov. 7, 1895; Jan. 16, Feb. 20, 1896; *Civic Review,* Mar. 30, 1895; Los Angeles *Times,* Apr. 24, 26, 1895; Feb. 19, Mar. 2, Nov. 12, 1898; *Record,* May 9, Aug. 22, 1896; Jan. 8, 24, 1898; *Herald,* Sept. 29, 1896; Feb. 8, Aug. 30, 1897; Colver, *op. cit.; Seventh Biennial Report, 1895–1896,* California Bureau of Labor Statistics, pp. 137, 148; Cross, *op. cit.,* p. 213; Paul S. Taylor, *The Sailors' Union of the Pacific* (New York: Ronald Press, 1923), pp. 73–5, 92.

[54] *Express,* Feb. 20, May 25, Sept. 26, Dec. 24, 1895; *Times,* Apr. 19, June 30, Oct. 7, 1895; Mar. 1–July 9 *passim,* 1896; Oct. 5–20 *passim,* Nov. 2, Dec. 9, 1897; Apr. 5, May 11, 26, June–Aug. *passim,* 1898; *Record,* Aug. 17, 1896; Aug. 10, 12, 1897; *Herald,* Aug. 23, Sept. 16, Oct. 5, 1896; Mar. 8, Apr. 19, May 17, 24, Aug. 16, 1897; Colver, *op. cit.; Official Trades and Labor Directory, Los Angeles, 1896,* p. 73.

[55] *Herald,* July 24, 1895; Nov. 23, 1896; Mar. 1, 29, Sept. 14, 1897; *Express,* Sept. 19, 1895; *Record,* Sept. 20, 1896; Sept. 13, Nov. 24, 1897; *Times,* Oct. 7, 11, 12, Nov. 11, 1897; LATU, *Minutes 1896–1898,* pp. 186, 212, 220.

[56] *Times,* July 28, Oct. 19, 1897; Cross, *op. cit.,* p. 278; *The Forty-Year War for a Free City; A History of the Open Shop in Los Angeles* (Los Angeles: Times-Mirror Publishing Co., 1929), p. 6; *Fiftieth Annual Report of the Merchants and Manufacturers Association, 1896–1946* (Los Angeles: [1946]), pp. 24–5.

[57] *Herald,* Mar. 29, 1897; *Times,* Oct. 11, 1897; Joseph Phillis, "Capt. F. B. Colver," *Citizen,* Feb. 10, 1911; LATU, *Minutes 1893–1896,* p. 207; *Minutes 1896–1898,* pp. 178–220 *passim; Minutes 1898–1902,* p. 99.

[58] *Herald,* Feb. 1, 8, 22, Mar. 8, 22, 29, Apr. 5, 12, 19, May 17, June 1, 14, July 12, Sept. 14, 1897; *Record,* Sept. 13, Nov. 20, 1897; Feb. 19, June 8, 1898; *Charles Dwight Willard Letters,* letters to his father, Jan. 23, May 12, 1897.

[59] *Times,* Jan. 22, 24, 27, 29, Feb. 9, 13, 15, 20, 24, Mar. 2, 3, 5, 9, 14, 18, 21, 26, Apr. 17, July 9, Aug. 3, 1897; *Herald,* Jan. 31, Feb. 2, 12, 13, 16, Mar. 1, 8, 15, Sept. 2, 1897; *Record,* Aug. 7, 1897; *Express,* Oct. 4, 1897.

[60] *Record,* Nov. 2, 18, 20, 1897; Feb. 7, Apr. 21, 25, June 9, 1898; *Citizen,* Oct. 7, 1910; Sept. 1, 1911; Commons and Associates, *op. cit.,* IV, 365–6.

[61] *Times,* Jan. 31, Feb. 5, 12, 29, 1895; May 25, 1897; July 23, 26, 1898; Dec. 31, 1899; California Legislature, *Journal of the Assembly,* 32d sess. (1897), p. 1453; *Journal of the Senate,* 32d sess. (1897), p. 1307.

[62] *Record,* Feb. 12, 24, 1898; *Times,* Mar. 11, June 10, 11, 1898; Nov. 4, 1899; June 23, 1900.

[63] *Times,* Jan. 13, 25, 27, 29, Mar. 7, June 11, 1899.

[64] *Record,* May 12, 1898; *Times,* May 16, 1901; LATU, *Minutes 1896–1898,* pp. 192–4, 247; *Minutes 1898–1902,* pp. 3–114 *passim,* 132; George A. Tracy, comp., *History of the Typographical Union* ([Indianapolis]: International Typographical Union, 1913), pp. 542, 569.

[65] Perlman, *op. cit.,* pp. 135–6.

[66] *Ibid.,* p. 163.

[67] *Herald,* June 28, 1893, from the San Francisco *Argonaut,* n.d.

Chapter XV

REAWAKENING OF THE LABOR MOVEMENT

[1] John R. Commons and Associates, *History of Labor in the United States* (New York: Macmillan, 1921–1935), IV, 13–15; Harry A. Millis and Royal E. Montgomery, *Organized Labor* (New York: McGraw-Hill, 1945), pp. 81–5.

[2] Commons and Associates, *op. cit.,* IV, 3–5; Millis and Montgomery, *op. cit.,* pp. 86–7.

[3] Commons and Associates, *op. cit.*, IV, 11; Millis and Montgomery, *op. cit.*, pp. 87, 89–91; Foster Rhea Dulles, *Labor in America* (New York: Crowell [c. 1949]), p. 205.

[4] Commons and Associates, *op. cit.*, IV, 9–11; Millis and Montgomery, *op. cit.*, pp. 88–9.

[5] Commons and Associates, *op. cit.*, IV, 15–19, 110–16, 129–37; Millis and Montgomery, *op. cit.*, pp. 86, 89; Selig Perlman, *A History of Trade Unionism in the United States* (New York: Macmillan, 1922), pp. 143, 165. Unions in certain industries had long been hampered by militant employers' associations. Stove molders faced the resistance of the Stove Founders' National Defense Association, dating from 1889; the National Founders' Association of 1898 gradually shifted from peaceful negotiations with unions to aggressive attack. There was no unification of antiunion policies, however, until 1903, when the National Association of Manufacturers, organized in 1895 for trade purposes, dedicated itself to the establishment and preservation of the open shop. The Citizens' Industrial Association of America, formed in 1903 under the leadership of the NAM, provided the necessary centralizing agency for all employers' organizations and citizens' groups concerned over the growing size and strength of labor unions. See chapter xvii, part 3, for a fuller discussion of this subject.

[6] Commons and Associates, *op. cit.*, IV, 19; Millis and Montgomery, *op. cit.*, p. 85; Perlman, *op. cit.*, p. 165; Dulles, *op. cit.*, p. 185.

[7] Commons and Associates, *op. cit.*, IV, 10, 110–16; Millis and Montgomery, *op. cit.*, pp. 92–8; Perlman, *op. cit.*, pp. 166–7; Dulles, *op. cit.*, pp. 186–8, 204–5.

[8] Robert Glass Cleland, *California in Our Time* (New York: Knopf, 1947), pp. 5–7; Ira B. Cross, *A History of the Labor Movement in California* (Berkeley: University of California Press, 1935), p. 228.

[9] Cross, *op. cit.*, p. 229.

[10] *Ibid.*, pp. 228–31, 337.

[11] *Ibid.*, p. 234; Espiridion B. Lopez, "The History of the California State Federation of Labor" (unpublished M.A. thesis, University of California, Berkeley, 1932), pp. 2–3.

[12] Cross, *op. cit.*, pp. 234–6; Lopez, *op. cit.*, pp. 4–10; LATU, *Minutes 1898–1902*, pp. 223, 308; *Proceedings of the American Federation of Labor, 1901*, p. 34; *Proceedings of the California State Federation of Labor, 1901*, pp. 4, 13–14, 40; San Francisco *Call*, Dec. 30, 1900.

[13] Cross, *op. cit.*, pp. 222, 235–7, 336–7.

[14] Lucile Eaves, *A History of California Labor Legislation* (Berkeley: The University Press [c. 1910]), pp. 221–2, 298, 394, 415; *Times*, Feb. 11, 14, 18, 23, Mar. 10, 1899; *Coast Seamen's Journal*, Jan. 30, Feb. 6, Apr. 3, 1901.

[15] William A. Spalding, comp., *History and Reminiscences, Los Angeles City and County, California* (Los Angeles: J. R. Finnell & Sons Publishing Co. [1931]), I, 332.

[16] *Monthly Summary, Business Conditions in Southern California* (published by Security-First National Bank of Los Angeles), Sept. 13, 1947; Cleland, *op. cit.*, p. 6; Los Angeles County Chamber of Commerce, *Los Angeles, "The Magic City and County"* (Los Angeles: 1951), pp. 6, 44; Charles Dwight Willard, *History of Los Angeles City* (Los Angeles: Kingsley-Barnes and Neuner Co., 1901), appendix, pp. i–vi; *Times*, Jan. 1, Mar. 13, July 6, Nov. 4, 1899; Apr. 28, 1901; Jan. 1, Apr. 29, 1904; Jan. 18, 1905.

[17] *Times*, Jan. 17, 1905.

[18] *Ibid.*, Aug. 31, Nov. 19, 1900; Jan. 1, Feb. 4, 1901; Feb. 15, 1902; *Twelfth Census of the United States, 1900*, Vol. VIII, *Manufactures*, p. 38; *Thirteenth Census of the United States, 1910, Abstract of the Census with Supplement for California*, pp. 445, 448–9, 675, 684–5.

[19] These organization dates are summarized from preceding chapters. In a few cases where exact information was not obtainable, the date of organization was inferred from other evidence.

[20] In February, 1952, Painters' Union No. 92 of Pasadena celebrated its sixtieth anniversary. It is the oldest painters' union west of the Rocky Mountains. This infor-

mation was communicated to the author by A. C. Miller, financial secretary of the union, in a telephone conversation on February 5, 1952.

²¹ LATU, *Minutes 1898–1902*, pp. 126–7; *Times,* Feb. 11, 14, 18, 23, Mar. 10, May 16, 21, 23, 28, 1899; *Express,* May 15, 22, 25, 29, June 1, 8, 10, 16, 24, 1899; *Record,* Nov. 18, 1899.

²² *Times,* Jan. 16, 22, 23, 25, 27, 30, Feb. 4, Mar. 3, 6, 9, 11, 13, 20, 1900; *Record,* Jan. 25, Mar. 19, 1900.

²³ *Times,* Aug. 16, Sept. 1, 1899.

²⁴ *Record,* Sept. 12, 27, Nov. 23, 1899; *Times,* Oct. 21, 1899; LATU, *Minutes 1898–1902,* p. 119.

²⁵ *Record,* Aug. 24, Nov. 8, 10, 23, 1899; *Citizen,* May 27, 1910; July 28, 1911; LATU, *Minutes 1898–1902,* p. 108; *Ninth Biennial Report, 1899–1900,* California Bureau of Labor Statistics (Sacramento: 1900), pp. 93–4.

²⁶ *Ninth Biennial Report, 1899–1900,* California Bureau of Labor Statistics, pp. 92–7.

²⁷ *Record,* Oct. 22, 1900; Apr. 22, May 28, 1901; *Times,* July 17, 1901; *Examiner,* Sept. 19, 1904; LATU, *Minutes 1898–1902,* pp. 145, 151, 189, 209, 220; Cross, *op. cit.,* p. 279; Helen Flannery, "The Labor Movement in Los Angeles, 1880–1903" (unpublished M.A. thesis, University of California, Berkeley, 1929), p. 58; Robert DeWitt Morgans, "A History of Organized Labor in Long Beach, California" (unpublished M.A. thesis, University of California, Berkeley, 1939), pp. 1–5.

²⁸ *Citizen,* Mar. 19, 1909; Joseph Phillis, "Fred Wheeler," *Citizen,* June 9, 1911; *Western Comrade,* Aug., 1913, p. 166. *Western Comrade* was a socialist journal published in Los Angeles from 1913 to 1918.

²⁹ *Times,* Oct. 2, 6, 16, 1900; *Record,* Oct. 6, Dec. 11, 1900; *Citizen,* Mar. 19, 1909; July 14, 1911; interview with L. W. Butler, July 26, 1951. Butler joined the teamsters' union in 1902, and served for some years as secretary of the Council of Labor.

³⁰ *Proceedings of the American Federation of Labor, 1897,* p. 42; *1898,* pp. 20, 56; *1899,* pp. 58, 70–1, 88; *1900,* p. 67; *American Federationist,* Jan., 1901, p. 26; LATU, *Minutes 1898–1902,* p. 196; *Record,* Nov. 15, 22, 24, 1900; *Coast Seamen's Journal,* Jan. 23, 1901.

³¹ *Coast Seamen's Journal,* Jan. 30, 1901; *Record,* Feb. 28, Mar. 28, May 2, 22, 28, 1901; *Times,* Apr. 25, July 4, 5, 17, 1901; Feb. 15, 1903; LATU, *Minutes 1898–1902,* pp. 153, 158, 160–1, 211, 238–42; Francis Drake, "Board of Publishers of the Organized Labor Movement," *Official Year Book and Reference Manual of the Organized Labor Movement of Los Angeles, 1922,* p. 49.

³² *Proceedings of the American Federation of Labor, 1900,* pp. 10, 57–8, 95; *1901,* p. 52; LATU, *Minutes 1898–1902,* pp. 189, 194, 230–1; *Record,* Mar. 28, May 2, 10, 1901; *Times,* Apr. 30, July 4, 11, 17, Aug. 21, 1901; Los Angeles *Socialist,* Nov. 9, 1901.

³³ *Proceedings of the American Federation of Labor, 1901,* pp. vi, 105–6, 175; *1902,* p. 41; *American Federationist,* Feb., 1902, p. 76; May, 1902, p. 243; Aug., 1902, p. 446; Sept., 1902, pp. 525–6; Nov., 1902, p. 821; LATU, *Minutes 1898–1902,* pp. 330, 339, 349, 357; *Record,* July 11, 1901; *Union Labor News,* Apr. 18, 1902.

³⁴ *Proceedings of the American Federation of Labor, 1902,* p. 74.

³⁵ *Proceedings of the American Federation of Labor, 1903,* p. 56; *American Federationist,* Mar., 1903, pp. 186, 205; Apr., 1903, p. 282; May, 1903, p. 387; June, 1903, p. 481; Nov., 1903, p. 1176; Dec., 1903, p. 1308; *Times,* Dec. 4, 1902; *Herald,* Mar. 22, 1903.

³⁶ *Proceedings of the American Federation of Labor, 1903,* pp. iii, xi, 72–3, 103–4, 172; *1904,* pp. 56–7; *American Federationist,* Apr., 1904, pp. 322–3; June, 1904, p. 514; July–Dec. *passim,* 1904; Aug., 1904, p. 664; *Proceedings of the California State Federation of Labor, 1905,* p. 29; *Record,* Nov. 21, 1903; Aug. 3, Oct. 6, 1904; *Examiner,* Jan. 2, 24, Feb. 14, 21, 25, 28, Apr. 9, 12, July 8, 22, Aug. 30, Sept. 28, Oct. 25, 1904.

³⁷ *Proceedings of the California State Federation of Labor, 1902,* pp. 12, 15–17,

36–9; *1903*, pp. 59, 71–6; *1904*, pp. 64, 84, 86–7; *1905*, pp. 30, 87, 96–7, 99–102; Lopez, *op. cit.*, pp. 6, 16; *Coast Seamen's Journal*, July 30, 1902; Jan. 13, 1904; *Record*, Jan. 3, 6, 1903; *Times*, Jan. 7, 1903; *Union Labor News*, Dec. 18, 1903; *Examiner*, Jan. 8, 1904; *Labor Clarion* (published in San Francisco), July 1, 1904.

[38] *Tenth Biennial Report, 1901–1902*, California Bureau of Labor Statistics (Sacramento: 1902), p. 78; *Eleventh Biennial Report, 1903–1904*, California Bureau of Labor Statistics (Sacramento: 1904), pp. 67–78; LATU, *Minutes 1898–1902*, p. 257; *American Federationist*, Feb., 1901, p. 61; *Record*, May 22, Aug. 8, 1901; May 28, Sept. 7, 1903; Jan. 6, 1904; *Times*, July 17, Aug. 10, 1901; *Union Labor News*, Nov. 7, 1902; Dec. 18, 1903; *Examiner*, Jan. 30, Feb. 19, 1904.

[39] *Record*, Mar. 28, Apr. 4, May 28, 1901; May 2, 1902; *Times*, Aug. 2, 1901; *Citizen*, Sept. 1, 1911.

[40] *Union Labor News*, Apr. 18, Nov. 7, 1902; *Times*, May 23, Sept. 19, 1902; May 28, 1904; *Record*, Apr. 21, 1904; *Examiner*, May 21, July 16, 1904.

[41] *Record*, Sept. 2, 1901; Aug. 25, Sept. 1, 1902; Sept. 7, 1903; Aug. 17, 1904; *Times*, Sept. 3, 1901; Sept. 2, 1902; Sept. 7, 1903; Sept. 5, 6, 1904; Los Angeles *Socialist*, Aug. 30, Sept. 6, 1902; *Coast Seamen's Journal*, Sept. 16, 1903; *Examiner*, Sept. 6, 1904.

[42] LATU, *Minutes 1902–1905*, pp. 56–7; *Times*, Aug. 26, 1900; June 25, July 2, 3, 1901; Apr. 24, May 10, 1902; May 3, 10, 1903; *Record*, Nov. 23, Dec. 13, 1900; June 24, 1901; Apr. 21, 1903; Los Angeles *Socialist*, Mar. 22, Apr. 12, 1902; *Examiner*, Dec. 15, 1903; *Union Labor News*, Dec. 18, 1903.

[43] *Times*, Aug. 28, 29, 1901.

[44] *Proceedings of the American Federation of Labor, 1901*, pp. 21–3, 63–6, 68–70, 96–8, 154; LATU, *Minutes 1898–1902*, pp. 308–9, 334–5; Eaves, *op. cit.*, p. 196; *Proceedings and List of Delegates, California Chinese Exclusion Convention Held at San Francisco, November 21 and 22, 1901* (San Francisco: The Star Press [1901]), pp. 6, 11, 19, 22, 25–92; *Coast Seamen's Journal*, Oct. 23, 1901; *Times*, Nov. 12, 22, 23, 1901.

Chapter XVI

LABOR AND SOCIALISM

[1] John R. Commons and Associates, *History of Labor in the United States* (New York: Macmillan, 1921–1935), IV, 229.

[2] Foster Rhea Dulles, *Labor in America* (New York: Crowell [c. 1949]), p. 181; Frank B. Colver, "Los Angeles Labor Council," San Francisco *Call*, May 4, 1896; Los Angeles *Times*, Aug. 3, 1896.

[3] *Express*, Jan. 11, Feb. 21, Mar. 21, July 30, Aug. 6, 26, Sept. 2, 9, Oct. 4, 14, 20, 28, Nov. 7, 21, 1895; Apr. 20, 1896; *Herald*, Aug. 19, 1895; *Civic Review*, Aug. 1, 1896.

[4] Joseph Clement Bates, ed., *History of Bench and Bar in California* (San Francisco: Bench and Bar Publishing Co., 1912), p. 343; *Citizen*, June 2, Sept. 1, 1911; *Times*, Oct. 28, 1895; "Job Harriman," *Who's Who in America*, X (1918–1919), 1194.

[5] "Job Harriman," p. 1194; Morris Hillquit, *History of Socialism in the United States* (New York: Funk & Wagnalls, 1903), p. 329; Bates, *op. cit.*, p. 343; *Times*, Aug. 4, 1902; *Citizen*, June 2, Sept. 1, 1911; *Southern California Labor Press*, Oct. 30, 1925.

[6] *Times*, Aug. 3, Dec. 8, 1896; Mar. 26, Oct. 3, 1897; Aug. 1, 1898; *Herald*, Oct. 26, 1896.

[7] *Labor World and Silver Champion*, Jan. 22, 1898.

[8] *Times*, Feb. 25, Mar. 11, 18, 20, May 10, June 8, 15–17, July 1, 7, 9, Sept. 28, Nov. 19, 20, 23, Dec. 6, 7, 1898.

[9] *Ibid.*, May 16, 1899.

[10] *Ibid.*, May 20, Aug. 1, 22, 29, Sept. 4, 6, Oct. 3, 5, Nov. 14, 20, Dec. 6, 1898; *California Blue Book, 1899* (Sacramento: [1899]), p. 227.

[11] Harry W. Laidler, *Social-Economic Movements* (New York: Crowell, 1946), pp. 581–2, 585–6; Selig Perlman, *A History of Trade Unionism in the United States* (New York: Macmillan, 1922), pp. 210–12; Commons and Associates, *op. cit.*, IV, 222, 224; Dulles, *op. cit.*, p. 210; Nathan Fine, *Labor and Farmer Parties in the United States, 1828–1928* (New York: Rand School of Social Science [c. 1928]), pp. 163–7; *Times,* Aug. 29, 1898.

[12] Laidler, *op. cit.*, pp. 583–7; Hillquit, *op. cit.*, pp. 331–8; Fine, *op. cit.*, pp. 163–76 *passim,* 179; Commons and Associates, *op. cit.*, IV, 229; Perlman, *op. cit.*, pp. 211–12; *Citizen,* Sept. 1, 1911.

[13] *Ninth Biennial Report, 1899–1900,* California Bureau of Labor Statistics (Sacramento: 1900), p. 109; Perlman, *op. cit.*, p. 212; LATU, *Minutes 1898–1902,* p. 116; *Record,* July 20, Aug. 6, 21, 1897; Aug. 24, Oct. 30, 31, Nov. 1, 2, 6, 10, 1899; *Herald,* Aug. 2, 9, Oct. 31, 1897; *Times,* Oct. 18, 1897; Nov. 6, 10, 1899; Joseph Phillis, "E. J. Mack," *Citizen,* Apr. 7, 1911.

[14] "William Dwight Porter Bliss," in *The Encyclopedia of Social Reform,* ed. by W. D. P. Bliss (1897), p. 179; Arthur M. Schlesinger, *The Rise of the City, 1878–1898,* History of American Life Series, Vol. X (New York: Macmillan, 1933), pp. 341–2; *Times,* Jan. 21, Feb. 3, 7, 10, Mar. 5, Aug. 29, 1898; Mar. 6, 1899; Nov. 27, 1900; *Herald,* Feb. 10, 1898.

[15] *Times,* Sept. 27, Nov. 27, 1900. The quotation is from the issue of November 27, 1900.

[16] *Times,* Jan. 27, 30, 1901.

[17] *Ibid.,* Aug. 13, Sept. 30, 1900; Joseph Phillis, "L. D. Biddle," *Citizen,* Mar. 3, 1911.

[18] *California Blue Book, 1913–1915* (Sacramento: 1915), p. 454; *Citizen,* Mar. 19, 1909; June 9, 1911; *Graphic,* June 15, 1912. The quotation is from the last source cited.

[19] *Times,* Aug. 27, Sept. 30, Oct. 20, Dec. 4, 13, 14, 1900.

[20] *Ibid.,* Dec. 30, 1900; Aug. 5, Sept. 1, 1901; Los Angeles *Socialist,* Nov. 23, Dec. 28, 1901; *Record,* Jan. 1, 1902. The quotation is from the last source cited.

[21] *Record,* Dec. 21, 1901; Jan. 1, Apr. 26, Sept. 13, 1902; *Times,* Jan. 2–5, 1902; Los Angeles *Socialist,* May 17, 1902.

[22] Los Angeles *Socialist,* Nov. 30, Dec. 21, 1901; Feb. 1, 8, June 14, Sept. 27, Oct. 11, 1902.

[23] *Ibid.,* Nov. 2, 1901.

[24] *Citizen,* Oct. 31, Dec. 5, 1919.

[25] Los Angeles *Socialist,* Nov. 22, 1902.

[26] *Ibid.,* Feb. 22, Mar. 1, 8, 15, 1902; *Times,* Mar. 8, 1902; *Union Labor News,* Apr. 18, 1902; *Common Sense,* June 3, 1905. The quotation is from Los Angeles *Socialist,* Feb. 22, 1902.

[27] Los Angeles *Socialist,* Apr. 19, 26, June 28, July 12, 1902.

[28] *Challenge,* Mar. 27, Apr. 3, 1901; Los Angeles *Socialist,* Nov. 2, Dec. 7, 14, 1901; June 14, July 5, 12, 19, Aug. 23, 30, Nov. 22, 1902; *Times,* Aug. 4, Nov. 15, 22, 1902.

[29] Los Angeles *Socialist,* Nov. 23, 1901; Mar. 7, 1903.

[30] *Ibid.,* Nov. 15, 22, 1902; *Times,* Nov. 17–19, 1902; *California Blue Book, 1903* (Sacramento: [1903]), pp. 333, 336.

[31] *Coast Seamen's Journal,* Sept. 11, Oct. 30, Dec. 4, 1901; Mar. 27, 1907; Los Angeles *Socialist,* Nov. 2, 9, 1901; Robert Glass Cleland, *California in Our Time* (New York: Knopf, 1947), pp. 9–11; Walter V. Woehlke, *Union Labor in Peace and War* (San Francisco: Sunset Publishing House [c. 1918]), p. 66; Ira B. Cross, *A History of the Labor Movement in California* (Berkeley: University of California Press, 1935), pp. 229–47; Commons and Associates, *op. cit.*, IV, 72–4; Walton Bean, *Boss Ruef's San Francisco* (Berkeley: University of California Press, 1952), pp. 153–231.

[32] *Times,* Apr. 28, May 15, June 28, 1902; Los Angeles *Socialist,* May 17, 24, 1902; *Record,* July 16, 23, 24, 1902. The quotation is from the Los Angeles *Socialist,* May 17, 1902.

[83] Los Angeles *Socialist,* June 21, July 19, 26, 1902; *Times,* July 24, 1902; *Record,* July 25, 1902.

[84] Los Angeles *Socialist,* July 26, Aug. 2, 1902; *Times,* July 28, 29, 1902; *Record,* July 28, 29, 1902. The quotation is from Los Angeles *Socialist,* Aug. 2, 1902.

[35] *Record,* July 31, Aug. 1, 1902; *Times,* Aug. 1, 1902.

[36] Los Angeles *Socialist,* Aug. 9, 1902.

[37] *Record,* Aug. 26, Sept. 5, 10, 1902; Los Angeles *Socialist,* Sept. 6, 13, 1902.

[38] Los Angeles *Socialist,* Sept. 13, 1902.

[39] *Ibid.,* Aug. 2, 30, 1902; M. W. Wilkins, "The California Situation," *International Socialist Review,* III (Jan., 1903), 416.

[40] Los Angeles *Socialist,* Aug. 23, 1902; *Record,* Sept. 4, 1902; *Times,* Sept. 21, 1902.

[41] *Record,* Aug. 7, Sept. 22, 1902; *Times,* Sept. 21, 1902; Los Angeles *Socialist,* Sept. 27, Oct. 4, 11, 18, 1902.

[42] Los Angeles *Socialist,* Nov. 8, 1902.

[43] *Times,* Oct. 5, 7, 1902; *Record,* Oct. 7, 1902; Los Angeles *Socialist,* Oct. 11, 1902.

[44] *Express,* Oct. 22, 1902.

[45] *Record,* Oct. 27, 28, 1902; *Times,* Oct. 31, 1902; Los Angeles *Socialist,* Nov. 1, 8, 1902; *Union Labor News,* Nov. 7, 1902.

[46] *Record,* Nov. 15, 26, 1902; Los Angeles *Socialist,* Nov. 22, 1902; *Times,* Nov. 27, 1902.

[47] *Times,* Nov. 19, 26–28, 1902; *Record,* Nov. 20, 24, 25, 28, 1902; Los Angeles *Socialist,* Nov. 29, 1902.

[48] *Herald,* Dec. 3, 1902; *Times,* Dec. 6, 1902; *Union Labor News,* Jan. 9, 1903.

[49] Commons and Associates, *op. cit.,* IV, 150–1; *Proceedings of the American Federation of Labor, 1902,* pp. iii, 122, 178–80.

[50] *Proceedings of the American Federation of Labor, 1902,* p. 181.

[51] Commons and Associates, *op. cit.,* IV, 150–1.

[52] Los Angeles *Socialist,* Nov. 29, Dec. 6, 20, 1902; Jan. 3, 10, 31, Feb. 14, Oct. 24, 1903; May 21, 1904; *Common Sense,* Dec. 8, 1906; Wilkins, *op. cit.,* pp. 416–19.

Chapter XVII

THE RISING TIDE OF CONFLICT

[1] *Times,* Mar. 7, 27, Apr. 8, May 23, 30, June 5, July 4, 5, 1901; Apr. 20, June 19, 1902; *Record,* Mar. 7, Apr. 15, May 30, 31, June 24, July 4, 16, 1901; June 11, 1902; Los Angeles *Socialist,* Apr. 26, May 3, 1902.

[2] *Times,* July 3, 1901; *American Federationist,* Aug., 1902, p. 446; Sept., 1902, p. 526.

[3] *Final Report and Testimony Submitted to Congress by the Commission on Industrial Relations,* U.S. 64th Cong., 1st sess., S. Doc. 415 (Washington: 1916), VI, 5665; *Souvenir Program 20th Annual Convention, California State Council of Carpenters, 1948* (n.p. [1948]), p. 15; *American Federationist,* Apr., 1901, p. 134; *Coast Seamen's Journal,* Aug. 1, 1900; *Times,* Sept. 30, 1900; Feb. 14, Apr. 3, 16, May 20, 21, 28, June 1, July 18, Aug. 3, 16, Oct. 30, Dec. 15, 1901; Sept. 6, 19, 1902; *Record,* Oct. 22, 1900; Mar. 23, Apr. 1, 2, May 5, 20, June 3, 1901; July 10, Sept. 18, 1902; Los Angeles *Socialist,* June 7, 1902; *Citizen,* July 21, 1911; Sept. 8, 1916.

[4] LATU, *Minutes 1898–1902,* pp. 329, 350, 395; *Times,* Aug. 8, 1901; *Record,* Aug. 14, 1901; Sept. 18, 1902; *Coast Seamen's Journal,* Oct. 8, 1902; *Union Labor News,* Nov. 7, 1902.

[5] *Times,* Mar. 29, Apr. 4, 11, 16, 23, May 14, 22, 28, July 16, Oct. 2–4, 6, 8, 9, 16, Nov. 12, Dec. 10, 1901; *Record,* Apr. 8, 23, June 3, Oct. 1, 2, 4, 8, 21, Nov. 5, 25, 1901.

[6] LATU, *Minutes 1902–1905,* pp. 16–24.

[7] LATU, *Minutes 1898–1902,* pp. 185–6, 189, 199–200; *Times,* Oct. 2, 4, 6, 9, 10, 14,

20, Dec. 4, 1900; *Record,* Oct. 2–5, Dec. 7, 25, 1900; *Coast Seamen's Journal,* Oct. 10, 1900; San Francisco *Call,* Oct. 26, 1900.

[8] *Times,* Aug. 21, 1901.

[9] *Ibid.,* July 16, 19, 25, 1902; *Record,* July 17, 18, 1902.

[10] *Times,* Aug. 2, Oct. 4, 1901; *Record,* Aug. 9, 14, 1901; Helen Flannery, "The Labor Movement in Los Angeles, 1880–1903" (unpublished M.A. thesis, University of California, Berkeley, 1929), pp. 64–5.

[11] *The Forty-Year War for a Free City; A History of the Open Shop in Los Angeles* (Los Angeles: Times-Mirror Publishing Co., 1929), p. 9; *Times,* Aug. 6–8, 14, 16, Sept. 4–9, 12, 1901; Sept. 13, 1902; *Record,* Aug. 6, 7, 9, 14, Sept. 3–7, 9, 1901; Sept. 6, 8, 11, 1902.

[12] *Twelfth Biennial Report, 1905–1906,* California Bureau of Labor Statistics (Sacramento: 1906), pp. 186–7; Flannery, *op. cit.,* pp. 184–5; *Record,* July 1, 3, 5, Aug. 6, 1901; *Times,* July 2, 4–6, 14, Aug. 6, 7, 1901.

[13] *Souvenir Program 20th Annual Convention, California State Council of Carpenters, 1948,* p. 15; *Union Labor News,* Apr. 18, 1902; *Record,* May 2, 3, 5, 6, Sept. 18, 1902; *Times,* May 2, 3, 6, June 6, 26, 28, Sept. 9, 11, 19, 20, 24, 25, 1902; Los Angeles *Socialist,* May 3, 1902.

[14] *Times,* Sept. 14, 26, Oct. 2, 8, 9, Nov. 2, 4, 5, 1901.

[15] *Ibid.,* Nov. 2, 8, 29, Dec. 3, 6, 11, 14, 15, 24, 1901; *Record,* Nov. 5, 6, 1901; Los Angeles *Socialist,* Nov. 30, Dec. 21, 1901; Jan. 25, 1902.

[16] *Times,* Dec. 27, 1901; Jan. 3, 1902; *Record,* Mar. 19, 24, Sept. 11, 17, 24, 1902; *Union Labor News,* Apr. 18, 1902.

[17] *Twelfth Biennial Report, 1905–1906,* California Bureau of Labor Statistics, pp. 186–7, 190–1, 196–7; *Final Report and Testimony Submitted to Congress by the Commission on Industrial Relations,* VI, 5616–23; *Times,* Jan. 19, 23, Apr. 24, 25, May 7, Aug. 15, Dec. 25, 27, 28, 1902; Feb. 5, 1903; *Record,* Apr. 23, May 2, Dec. 25, 1902; *Union Labor News,* Dec. 25, 1903; *Examiner,* Mar. 6, 1904; *Graphic,* May 13, 1905, p. 15.

[18] LATU, *Minutes 1898–1902,* p. 207; Ira B. Cross, *A History of the Labor Movement in California* (Berkeley: University of California Press, 1935), pp. 242–5; Paul S. Taylor, *The Sailors' Union of the Pacific* (New York: Ronald Press, 1923), pp. 96–8; *American Federationist,* Feb., 1901, p. 61; Apr., 1901, p. 134; *Record,* Mar. 9, 10, Oct. 20, 1900; Aug. 30, Sept. 7, 1901; *Times,* Oct. 20, 1900; May 12, 20, Aug. 5, 19, 28, 30, Sept. 1, 12, Oct. 30, 1901; *Coast Seamen's Journal,* Oct. 24, 31, 1900; Apr. 3, 1901; San Francisco *Call,* Mar. 29, 1901.

[19] *Record,* Apr. 29, 30, May 1, 4, 15, 29, June 5, 11, 22, 1901; *Times,* May 1, 2, 15, July 2, 1901.

[20] *Record,* June 24–26, 28, 29, 1901; *Times,* June 25–27, 1901.

[21] *Times,* July 2–6, 8, 9, 1901; *Record,* July 2–6, 8, 9, 11, 15, 16, 1901.

[22] LATU, *Minutes 1898–1902,* pp. 282, 286, 294; *American Federationist,* Sept., 1901, p. 387; Dec., 1901, p. 556; *Times,* July 5, 8, 11–14, 19, 27, 28, Aug. 1, 4, 1901; Mar. 9, 1902; *Record,* July 5, 10, 11, 13, 19, 20, 25, 31, Aug. 7, 28, Sept. 6, 23, 28, Nov. 22, Dec. 19, 1901; Feb. 8, Mar. 19, 1902; *Coast Seamen's Journal,* Oct. 2, 1901; Los Angeles *Socialist,* Dec. 21, 1901; *Citizen,* Sept. 1, 1911.

[23] *Twelfth Biennial Report, 1905–1906,* California Bureau of Labor Statistics, pp. 188–9; *Times,* Sept. 4, 5, 9, 14, 1902; *Record,* Sept. 8, 11, 13, Nov. 26, 29, 1902; June 6, 1903; *Coast Seamen's Journal,* Sept. 17, 1902; Los Angeles *Socialist,* Nov. 29, 1902.

[24] *Times,* Oct. 9, 1900.

[25] LATU, *Minutes 1898–1902,* pp. 116–19, 126–7.

[26] *Ibid.,* p. 144; Cross, *op. cit.,* pp. 238–9; *Record,* Feb. 10, 1900; *Times,* Feb. 11, 13, 20, 1900.

[27] LATU, *Minutes 1898–1902,* pp. 168–9, 173, 179–83, 190–1, 202; *Record,* Oct. 4, 1900; *Times,* Oct. 9, 13, 14, 27, Dec. 7, 1900.

[28] *Times,* Sept. 28, 1900.

[29] LATU, *Minutes 1898–1902,* p. 181.

[30] *Ibid.*, pp. 186–92, 194, 197–8, 201, 204, 207–8, 213–14, 216, 223, 226; *Proceedings of the American Federation of Labor, 1900*, pp. 50, 75; *Record,* Dec. 3, 1900.

[31] LATU, *Minutes 1898–1902*, pp. 243–5; *Times,* Apr. 2, 30, May 8, 9, 1901; *Record,* Apr. 30, May 2, 1901.

[32] LATU, *Minutes 1898–1902*, pp. 214, 216, 220–2, 224–5, 231–3, 243, 258, 268; *Times,* Dec. 8, 1900; Jan. 4, 6, 18, Mar. 3, 10, 12, 19, 1901; *Record,* Mar. 2, 1901.

[33] LATU, *Minutes 1898–1902*, pp. 254, 257–9; Flannery, *op. cit.,* p. 65. The quotation is from page 259 of the *Minutes.*

[34] LATU, *Minutes 1898–1902*, pp. 258, 261–4, 272, 275–7; Marion Dixon, "The History of the Los Angeles Central Labor Council" (unpublished M.A. thesis, University of California, Berkeley, 1929), p. 57; *Times,* July 10, 21, Aug. 10, 1901.

[35] LATU, *Minutes 1898–1902*, p. 292.

[36] *Ibid.*, pp. 246, 255, 278, 283–4, 288–9, 291–2, 297.

[37] *Ibid.*, pp. 301, 303–5, 307, 314–15; *Times,* Aug. 11, 1903. The quotation is from page 307 of the *Minutes.*

[38] LATU, *Minutes 1898–1902*, pp. 305–7, 314; Los Angeles *Socialist,* Nov. 30, 1901; *Times,* Sept. 11, 1907.

[39] LATU, *Minutes 1898–1902*, pp. 314–17; *Final Report and Testimony Submitted to Congress by the Commission on Industrial Relations,* VI, 5716; *Record,* Sept. 26, Oct. 24, 1901; *Times,* Oct. 2, 1901. The quotation is from page 315 of the *Minutes.*

[40] Los Angeles *Socialist,* Nov. 16, 23, 30, Dec. 7, 1901; Mar. 1, 8, Apr. 26, May 17, 24, 1902.

[41] LATU, *Minutes 1898–1902*, pp. 322–3, 326, 329; Los Angeles *Socialist,* Jan. 18, Feb. 1, 1902; *Times,* Jan. 20, 25, 26, 1902; *Record,* Jan. 24, 1902; *Herald,* Jan. 26, 1902. The quotation is from Los Angeles *Socialist,* Feb. 1, 1902.

[42] LATU, *Minutes 1898–1902*, pp. 335–40, 346–7, 350, 358, 360, 368; Los Angeles *Socialist,* Feb. 22, 1902; *Times,* May 2, 15, 1902.

[43] LATU, *Minutes 1898–1902*, pp. 310, 328–30, 344–5; *Times,* Mar. 8, 11–13, 18, 20, 25, Apr. 1, 8, 15, May 6, 13, 1902; *Union Labor News,* Mar. 28, 1902; *Record,* May 5, 14, 15, 1902.

[44] LATU, *Minutes 1898–1902*, pp. 333, 347, 351, 354, 359, 364, 376, 388, 393, 396; *Minutes 1902–1905*, pp. 4, 8–9, 13, 26.

[45] LATU, *Minutes 1898–1902*, pp. 338, 346, 365–8, 379–82; *Times,* Jan. 5, Mar. 8, July 11, 1902; *The Fraternity,* Mar. 5, 1902; Los Angeles *Socialist,* Mar. 15, July 5, Sept. 6, 1902; *Record,* July 21, 1902.

[46] LATU, *Minutes 1898–1902*, pp. 338, 342, 346, 350, 357, 374, 381–2; *Labor Clarion* (published in San Francisco), May 30, 1902; *Times,* Sept. 20, 29, 1902.

[47] LATU, *Minutes 1898–1902*, pp. 334–5, 368, 374, 381, 393–4, 396; *Minutes 1902–1905*, pp. 4, 7, 9, 10, 12–14, 26; *Proceedings of the American Federation of Labor, 1900*, pp. 73–4; *1902*, p. 59; George A. Tracy, comp., *History of the Typographical Union* ([Indianapolis]: International Typographical Union, 1913), pp. 705–6, 712–13, 731; *Times,* July 10, Oct. 5, 1902; *Record,* Sept. 30, 1902; *Coast Seamen's Journal,* Oct. 15, 1902.

[48] LATU, *Minutes 1902–1905*, p. 25; *Record,* Sept. 11, 1902; *Times,* Sept. 29, Oct. 5, 12, 15, Nov. 18–23, 26, 28, 30, Dec. 1, 2, 4, 7, 9, 13, 14, 1902; Jan. 1, 1903; *Union Labor News,* Nov. 7, 1902.

[49] *Union Labor News,* Nov. 7, 1902; *Times,* Jan. 20, 1903.

[50] *Times,* Jan. 20, 1903.

[51] In an interview on May 27, 1952, Archie J. Mooney, Chief of the Division of Apprenticeship Training, California Department of Industrial Relations, asserted that during the open-shop fight in Los Angeles the banks withdrew credit from companies which granted the union shop, and that unions frequently had to protect friendly employers by keeping their union agreements secret. Mr. Mooney, who was prominent in the local labor movement for a number of years after 1908, confirmed the fact that the real open-shop drive in Los Angeles started about 1902 or 1903.

[52] *Fiftieth Annual Report of the Merchants and Manufacturers Association, 1896–1946* (Los Angeles: [1946]), p. 27; *Times*, Sept. 6, 11, 1902; Feb. 27, Mar. 18, 19, Apr. 15, 1903; Jan. 28, Apr. 14, 1904; *Examiner*, Apr. 13, 1904.

[53] John R. Commons and Associates, *History of Labor in the United States* (New York: Macmillan, 1921–1935), IV, 72, 129–33, 318–20; Cross, *op. cit.*, p. 239; Selig Perlman, *A History of Trade Unionism in the United States* (New York: Macmillan, 1922), pp. 190–6; Foster Rhea Dulles, *Labor in America* (New York: Crowell [c. 1949]), p. 195; F. W. Hilbert, "Employers' Associations in the United States," *in* Jacob H. Hollander and George E. Barnett, eds., *Studies in American Trade Unionism* (London: Hodder and Stroughton, 1906), pp. 183–217; Ray Stannard Baker, "Organized Capital Challenges Organized Labor," *McClure's Magazine*, XXIII (July, 1904), 279–81.

[54] Commons and Associates, *op. cit.*, IV, 133–7; Perlman, *op. cit.*, pp. 195, 208; *Bulletin No. 1*, Citizens' Industrial Association of America (Indianapolis: 1903), p. 18; *A Statement of the Character and Purposes of the Citizens' Industrial Association of America* (Indianapolis: n.d.), p. 7.

[55] *Proceedings of the American Federation of Labor, 1903*, p. 20.

[56] Baker, *op. cit.*, pp. 282–91.

[57] Commons and Associates, *op. cit.*, IV, 134–5; *The Forty-Year War for a Free City . . .*, p. 8; *Times*, Aug. 1, 1903; Jan. 17, 24, 28, 29, Feb. 3, 7, 19, 23, Apr. 13, Nov. 30, 1904; *Express*, Jan. 23, 1904; *Record*, Jan. 25, 29, 1904; *Coast Seamen's Journal*, Feb. 24, Mar. 2, 1904; Los Angeles *Socialist*, July 23, 1904.

[58] *Times*, Mar. 29, 1903.

[59] *Ibid.*, Aug. 2, 1903.

[60] *Record*, June 4, 5, 8, 1903; July 19, 28, 1904; *Times*, June 10, 1903; *Union Labor News*, Dec. 18, 1903; *Examiner*, Feb. 20, July 8, Nov. 1, 3, 1904.

[61] *American Federationist*, Apr., 1903, p. 282; LATU, *Minutes 1902–1905*, p. 174; *Record*, Jan. 20, 1903; *Times*, Jan. 21, 1903; May 7, 15, 1904; Los Angeles *Socialist*, Jan. 24, 1903; *Coast Seamen's Journal*, Aug. 19, 1903; *Examiner*, Dec. 21, 25, 29, 1903; Jan. 20, Feb. 11, 26, Mar. 22, 24, June 8, 1904.

[62] *American Federationist*, Oct., 1903, p. 1070; *Record*, Aug. 26, Sept. 18, 1902; *Times*, Jan. 31, Feb. 17, Aug. 26, 1903; July 6, 27, 1904; *Examiner*, Dec. 24, 1903; Jan. 5, 20, Mar. 27, Apr. 3, May 6, June 7, 30, July 3, 23, 1904; *Union Labor News*, Dec. 25, 1903.

[63] [William H. B. Kilner], *Arthur Letts, 1862–1923* ([Los Angeles: privately printed, 1927]), pp. 201–9; *Final Report and Testimony Submitted to Congress by the Commission on Industrial Relations*, VI, 5703–4.

[64] *Twelfth Biennial Report, 1905–1906*, California Bureau of Labor Statistics, pp. 192–3; *American Federationist*, Sept., 1901, pp. 386–7; *Record*, Feb. 27, 28, Apr. 16, June 6, 1903; *Times*, Feb. 27, 28, Mar. 1, 7, 19, Apr. 2, Dec. 9, 1903.

[65] *Twelfth Biennial Report, 1905–1906*, California Bureau of Labor Statistics, pp. 192–3, 196–7; Flannery, *op. cit.*, p. 89; *Times*, Feb. 26–28, Mar. 1, 27–29, Apr. 7, 9–12, 14, 16, Oct. 13, Nov. 28, Dec. 3, 1903; *Record*, Mar. 28, Apr. 10, 11, 13–16, June 19, 1903.

[66] *Twelfth Biennial Report, 1905–1906*, California Bureau of Labor Statistics, pp. 194–5; *Record*, May 2, 5, 6, 8, 11, 25, June 1, 3, 5, 6, 23, 24, 26, 27, July 1–3, 1903; *Times*, May 6–9, 12, 13, 19, 24, 31, June 3, 5, 15, 17, 18, 28, July 2–4, 18, 19, 1903.

[67] LATU, *Minutes 1902–1905*, pp. 89, 91; *Times*, June 5, 19, 24, July 14, 1903; *Record*, June 19, 23, 25, 29, July 9–11, 13, Aug. 8, 10, 11, 14, 17, 25, 1903; *Coast Seamen's Journal*, July 1, 22, 1903; Los Angeles *Socialist*, July 25, 1903.

[68] *Twelfth Biennial Report, 1905–1906*, California Bureau of Labor Statistics, pp. 194–5; *The Forty-Year War for a Free City . . .*, p. 9; Cross, *op. cit.*, p. 280; LATU, *Minutes 1902–1905*, p. 133; *Record*, Sept. 21, Oct. 3, 5, 16, 1903; *Coast Seamen's Journal*, Oct. 7, 14, 1903; *Examiner*, Nov. 20, 1904.

[69] *Twelfth Biennial Report, 1905–1906*, California Bureau of Labor Statistics, pp. 192–5, 198–9; *Times*, Mar. 24, June 17, July 21, Aug. 18, 23, 1903; *Record*, Apr. 23, June 26, July 1, 25, 1903.

[70] *Record,* Apr. 21, 22, 29, May 1, 2, 12, 30, June 6, 1903; *Times,* Apr. 22, 23, May 2, 13, 28, 1903; *Citizen,* May 29, Dec. 18, 1908.

[71] *Twelfth Biennial Report, 1905–1906,* California Bureau of Labor Statistics, pp. 194–5; *Times,* Aug. 1, 27, 1903; Jan. 19, 1905; *Record,* Aug. 4, 6, 1903; Feb. 4, 1904; *Examiner,* Jan. 6, Feb. 4, 1904.

[72] *Twelfth Biennial Report, 1905–1906,* California Bureau of Labor Statistics, pp. 196–7; LATU, *Minutes 1902–1905,* pp. 50–1; *Record,* Apr. 11, 14, 15, 1903; *Times,* Apr. 14, 15, 1903.

[73] LATU, *Minutes 1902–1905,* pp. 54–6; *Times,* Apr. 14, 15, 17–19, June 5, 1903; *Record,* Apr. 14, 15, 17, 18, 21, 29, June 5, 6, 1903.

[74] *Times,* Apr. 12, 1903; *Record,* Apr. 13–15, May 1, June 6, 1903.

[75] *Times,* Apr. 15, 1903.

[76] LATU, *Minutes 1902–1905,* p. 174; *American Federationist,* Sept., 1903, p. 954; *Record,* Apr. 24, May 1, June 6, 1903; Los Angeles *Socialist,* May 30, 1903.

[77] *Times,* May 31, June 6–9, 1903; *Record,* June 1, 4–6, 9, 1903.

[78] *Times,* Oct. 14, 17, 21–23, 26–27, Nov. 6, 1903; Jan. 10, Apr. 10, 1904; *Record,* Oct. 21–24, 26, 30, Nov. 11, 17, 18, 1903; Jan. 26, 1904; *Coast Seamen's Journal,* Nov. 4, 1903; Los Angeles *Socialist,* Nov. 7, 1903; *Union Labor News,* Dec. 18, 25, 1903; *Examiner,* Dec. 23, 27, 1903; Jan. 10, 27, 1904.

[79] *Record,* Nov. 11, 1903; Mar. 14, 1904; *Times,* Dec. 2, 8, 19, 1903.

[80] *Times,* Feb. 12, 20, Mar. 26, 29, Apr. 12, 29, 30, May 8, Oct. 7, Nov. 11, 1903; *Record,* Apr. 30, May 2, 1903.

[81] *Times,* Oct. 8, 1903.

[82] *Twelfth Biennial Report, 1905–1906,* California Bureau of Labor Statistics, pp. 198–9; *Record,* Apr. 24, 25, 27, 28, May 1, June 6, 1903; Mar. 2, 3, Apr. 6, 7, 1904; *Times,* Apr. 26, 27, 1903; Los Angeles *Socialist,* May 2, 1903; *Examiner,* Feb. 9, 1904.

[83] *Twelfth Biennial Report, 1905–1906,* California Bureau of Labor Statistics, pp. 200–1; *Times,* Mar. 3, Apr. 12, 14, May 14, June 12, 29, 1904; *Record,* Apr. 13, 1904; *Examiner,* Apr. 13, 21, May 6, June 11, 21, 1904; Mar. 11, 1905; *Common Sense,* Aug. 5, 1905.

[84] *Twelfth Biennial Report, 1905–1906,* California Bureau of Labor Statistics, pp. 200–3; *Times,* May 5, 16, 17, 19, 24, 25, 27–29, June 1, 2, 8, 17, 27, July 27, Aug. 2, 1904; *Examiner,* May 21, 24, 27, 29, June 5, 1904; *Record,* June 1, 1904; Los Angeles *Socialist,* July 16, 1904.

[85] *Record,* Sept. 29, 1903; *Union Labor News,* Dec. 25, 1903; *Times,* Feb. 4, 5, 12, 13, 26, Mar. 1, 31, June 28, 1904; *Examiner,* Feb. 5, 6, 12, 14, 1904.

[86] *Twelfth Biennial Report, 1905–1906,* California Bureau of Labor Statistics, pp. 212–13; LATU, *Minutes 1902–1905,* pp. 153, 178, 180; *Examiner,* Jan. 22, 26, 1904; *Record,* Jan. 29, 1904; *Times,* Feb. 3, Mar. 3, 8, 17, Apr. 9, Dec. 7, 1904.

[87] *Times,* Apr. 12, 1903.

[88] *Ibid.,* Dec. 19, 1903.

Chapter XVIII

LABOR'S COUNTEROFFENSIVE

[1] *Times,* Jan. 15, 28, Feb. 3, Mar. 12, 15, 18, 25, 26, Apr. 7, 9, 15, 21, 22, May 7, 12, 17, June 3, July 30, Aug. 11, Sept. 13, 29, 1903; *Record,* May 11, 26, 1903; *Coast Seamen's Journal,* Sept. 2, 1903; Los Angeles *Socialist,* Oct. 17, 1903.

[2] *Times,* Feb. 10, Dec. 31, 1903; *Coast Seamen's Journal,* May 13, June 3, 10, 24, Aug. 19, 26, 1903; *Record,* Oct. 26, 1903; *Labor Clarion* (published in San Francisco), Apr. 1, 1904; *Proceedings of the American Federation of Labor, 1903,* pp. 52, 72, 255; *Proceedings of the California State Federation of Labor, 1904,* pp. 25–6; LATU, *Minutes 1902–1905,* pp. 27, 30, 33, 38, 64, 66, 78, 80, 82, 99, 139–40; Leo Wolman, *The Boycott in American Trade Unions,* Johns Hopkins University Studies in Historical

and Political Science, Series 34, no. 1 (Baltimore: Johns Hopkins Press, 1916), p. 121, n. 65; George A. Tracy, comp., *History of the Typographical Union* ([Indianapolis]: International Typographical Union, 1913), pp. 734, 748–9.

[3] *Coast Seamen's Journal,* Mar. 18, May 13, June 3, 10, 17, July 1, 15, Oct. 14, 1903; Jan. 6, Apr. 13, May 18, 1904; *Times,* Apr. 10, 24, July 11, Sept. 7, Dec. 6, 1903; *Record,* July 17, 1903; LATU, *Minutes 1902–1905,* p. 34; Wolman, *op. cit.,* p. 91, n. 47.

[4] *Coast Seamen's Journal,* Apr. 29, May 6, 20, 27, 1903; *Record,* May 13, 1903; LATU, *Minutes 1902–1905,* p. 59.

[5] LATU, *Minutes 1898–1902,* p. 117.

[6] *Times,* Nov. 27, 1902; Feb. 10, 1903; LATU, *Minutes 1902–1905,* pp. 12, 31, 151; Wolman, *op. cit.,* p. 92; *The Forty-Year War for a Free City; A History of the Open Shop in Los Angeles* (Los Angeles: Times-Mirror Publishing Co., 1929), p. 7; Julia Norton McCorkle, "A History of Los Angeles Journalism," *Annual Publications of the Historical Society of Southern California,* X (1915–1916), 29.

[7] LATU, *Minutes 1902–1905,* p. 121.

[8] *Ibid.,* pp. 121–4.

[9] *Times,* Dec. 9, 1903.

[10] *Coast Seamen's Journal,* Dec. 9, 23, 1903; *Record,* Dec. 12, 1903; *Times,* Dec. 13, 1903; *Examiner,* Dec. 13, 23, 1903; *Union Labor News,* Dec. 18, 1903; LATU, *Minutes 1902–1905,* p. 139.

[11] *Examiner,* Dec. 12, 1903.

[12] *Ibid.,* Dec. 14, 1903; Jan. 3, Mar. 1, 23, 25, 1905; *Record,* Dec. 15, 1903; June 23, 1904; *Union Labor News,* Dec. 18, 1903; *Times,* Dec. 24, 1903; Jan. 17, June 19, 22, 23, Aug. 15–18, 1904; *Labor Clarion,* Apr. 1, 1904; May 24, 1907; *Graphic,* Aug. 13, 1904, pp. 4–5; Nov. 11, 1905, p. 8; Dec. 9, 1905, p. 23; July 27, 1907, p. 11; Oct. 26, 1907, p. 11; LATU, *Minutes 1902–1905,* p. 232; *Mr. Otis and the Los Angeles "Times"* (Los Angeles: Typographical Union No. 174, 1915), pp. 9, 12; *The Forty-Year War for a Free City . . . ,* p. 7; McCorkle, *op. cit.,* p. 29; Frederick Palmer, "Otistown of the Open Shop," *Hampton's Magazine,* XXVI (Jan., 1911), 34–5. Frank E. Wolfe, managing editor of the *Herald* during this period, told the author in an interview on February 15, 1952, that the *Examiner's* prolabor stand lasted for only a few years. L. W. Butler, one of the most prominent men in the Los Angeles labor movement from 1902 to 1915, said in an interview on June 19, 1952, that the *Examiner* gradually altered its policy toward organized labor.

[13] *The Forty-Year War for a Free City . . . ,* p. 7.

[14] Los Angeles *Socialist,* June 28, 1902; Jan. 3, 1903; *Times,* Sept. 3, 17, Oct. 26, 1902; Feb. 26, Mar. 3, 4, 10, 31, June 21, 1903; *Coast Seamen's Journal,* Sept. 23, 1903; *Labor Clarion,* Mar. 4, 1904; *American Federationist,* Mar., 1903, p. 186; *Proceedings of the California State Federation of Labor, 1903,* p. 61.

[15] *Times,* Aug. 25, 27, Sept. 21, Oct. 4–7, 17, Nov. 14, 1903; Apr. 27, 1904; Los Angeles *Socialist,* Sept. 19, 26, Oct. 3, 10, Nov. 17, Dec. 12, 1903; Mar. 19, Apr. 30, May 7, 1904; *Coast Seamen's Journal,* Sept. 30, Oct. 7, Dec. 30, 1903; *Examiner,* Dec. 21, 1903.

[16] *Times,* Mar. 2, 1903.

[17] *Ibid.,* May 20, 24, June 21, July 4, 17, Oct. 15, 1903; *Record,* June 18, 20, July 7, 8, 1903; *Coast Seamen's Journal,* July 8, 1903; Los Angeles *Socialist,* July 18, 1903; *Union Labor News,* Dec. 18, 1903; LATU, *Minutes 1902–1905,* pp. 89–91, 96.

[18] *Times,* Oct. 1, 5, 11, 1903; Los Angeles *Socialist,* Nov. 14, 1903; *Record,* Dec. 7, 10, 1903; LATU, *Minutes 1902–1905,* pp. 132–3.

[19] *Times,* Dec. 22, 24, 1903; Feb. 26, Mar. 10, 22, Apr. 9, June 2, 1904; *Examiner,* Jan. 21, Feb. 19, Mar. 3, 6, 8, 15, 21, 29, Apr. 21, 28, May 5, 13, 26, 27, Aug. 6, 17, Sept. 18, 1904; *Coast Seamen's Journal,* Mar. 2, 1904; *Record,* Mar. 2, 14, 15, 19, 21, Apr. 20, 21, May 12, June 2, 1904; *Labor Clarion,* Mar. 25, 1904; LATU, *Minutes 1902–1905,* pp. 146, 170; *American Federationist,* May, 1904, p. 421; Ira B. Cross, *A History of the Labor Movement in California* (Berkeley: University of California Press, 1935), p. 280.

[20] LATU, *Minutes 1902–1905,* pp. 171–4.

[21] *Examiner,* July 9, 14, 23, 29, 31, Aug. 3, 16, 23, Sept. 1, 15, Oct. 6, 27, 29, Nov. 3, 24, Dec. 9, 15, 21, 1904.

[22] *Ibid.,* Apr. 7, 16, 22, 23, May 14, June 18, July 9, Sept. 10, Nov. 13, 1904; *Coast Seamen's Journal,* June 1, 1904; LATU, *Minutes 1902–1905,* pp. 162, 169, 182–3, 189, 258.

[23] *Proceedings of the Adjourned Session of the First Convention of the Citizens' Industrial Association of America, 1904* (Indianapolis: [1904]), p. 93.

[24] Tracy, *op. cit.,* p. 763.

[25] LATU, *Minutes 1902–1905,* pp. 149–52, 155–60, 163, 178–81, 183, 191–214, 216–18, 222; *Times,* Apr. 26, 1904.

[26] LATU, *Minutes 1902–1905,* pp. 178, 180.

[27] *Ibid.,* pp. 150, 152–3, 168, 183–4, 221; *The Forty-Year War for a Free City . . . ,* pp. 8–9; *Times,* Jan. 14, Apr. 24, May 15, 22, June 8, 19, 1904; *Examiner,* Feb. 3, Mar. 1, 5, 1904; *Labor Clarion,* Apr. 1, 1904.

[28] *Times,* June 7, 1904.

[29] *Ibid.,* May 5, 1903; Apr. 20–23, 26, May 3, 10, 24, 29, June 1, 7, 8, 1904; *Examiner,* Sept. 17, 1904; C. V. Barton, *The Recall* (unpublished manuscript, Haynes Foundation, Los Angeles, 1905), p. 4; *Proceedings of the National Municipal League, 1909,* p. 328.

[30] *Examiner,* Aug. 18, 1904.

[31] *Times,* Aug. 16, 1904.

[32] *Ibid.,* Aug. 19, 1904.

[33] *Graphic,* Aug. 27, 1904, p. 5.

[34] *Times,* July 12, 1904; *Examiner,* July 25, Aug. 9, Sept. 2, Nov. 19, 29, Dec. 3, 1904; *Record,* Aug. 9, 1904; *Graphic,* Aug. 13, 1904, p. 4; LATU, *Minutes 1902–1905,* p. 278; Tracy, *op. cit.,* pp. 785–6, 808.

[35] *Times,* May 25, June 9, 23, July 28, Aug. 8, Sept. 22, 1900; Jan. 5, Feb. 3, 1901; *Record,* Nov. 7, 1900.

[36] Espiridion B. Lopez, "The History of the California State Federation of Labor" (unpublished M.A. thesis, University of California, Berkeley, 1932), p. 6; LATU, *Minutes 1898–1902,* p. 378; J. W. Park, *The Adoption of the Recall in Los Angeles* (unpublished manuscript, Haynes Foundation, Los Angeles, 1909), p. 9; *Times,* Sept. 29, 1900; Feb. 11, Apr. 25, 1902; Los Angeles *Socialist,* Feb. 8, 15, 1902; *Record,* Apr. 4, 1902; *Union Labor News,* July 25, 1902; Jan. 9, 1903; R. H. Norton, *The First Recall Campaign* (unpublished manuscript, Haynes Foundation, Los Angeles, n.d.), p. 1.

[37] *Examiner,* Sept. 17, 1904; *Graphic,* Dec. 31, 1904, p. 4; *Pacific Outlook,* June 11, 1910, p. 3; Norton, *op. cit.,* p. 1; Barton, *op. cit.,* p. 4; John R. Haynes, *The Recall of Councilman Davenport* (unpublished manuscript, Haynes Foundation, Los Angeles, n.d.), pp. 1–3; Eltweed Pomeroy, "Really Masters," *Arena,* XXXIII (Jan., 1905), 51; *Proceedings of the National Municipal League, 1905,* pp. 104–5.

[38] Haynes, *op. cit.,* p. 3; *Proceedings of the National Municipal League, 1905,* pp. 102–3, 105; Pomeroy, *op. cit.,* p. 51; Eltweed Pomeroy, "The First Discharge of a Public Servant," *Independent,* LVIII (Jan. 12, 1905), 69; letter from John R. Haynes to Lincoln Steffens, *Examiner,* Jan. 26, 1907.

[39] *Graphic,* Dec. 10, 1904, p. 3.

[40] *Record,* May 27, 28, June 2, 1904; *Times,* June 1, 1904; *Examiner,* Sept. 17, 1904; Barton, *op. cit.,* p. 4; Haynes, *op. cit.,* pp. 5, 13–14; Norton, *op. cit.,* p. 2; Pomeroy, "The First Discharge of a Public Servant," p. 69; *Proceedings of the National Municipal League, 1905,* pp. 104–5.

[41] Pomeroy, "Really Masters," p. 51; "The First Discharge of a Public Servant," p. 69; Norton, *op. cit.,* pp. 2–3; Barton, *op. cit.,* p. 6; *Times,* May 28, June 14, 18, 21, 28, July 6, 12, 1904.

[42] Barton, *op. cit.,* p. 6; Haynes, *op. cit.,* p. 4; *Times,* June 14, July 6, 8, 11–13, 16, 17, 1904; *Examiner,* Sept. 17, 1904.

[43] Pomeroy, "Really Masters," p. 51; "The First Discharge of a Public Servant," p. 69; Barton, *op. cit.*, p. 6; Haynes, *op. cit.*, p. 4; *Times*, July 18, 21, Aug. 2, 9, 1904.

[44] Pomeroy, "Really Masters," p. 52; *Times*, Aug. 25–27, 1904.

[45] Pomeroy, "Really Masters," pp. 51–2; "The First Discharge of a Public Servant," pp. 69–70; Barton, *op. cit.*, pp. 6–7; Haynes, *op. cit.*, pp. 9–10; Norton, *op. cit.*, p. 3; *Times*, Aug. 30, 1904.

[46] Pomeroy, "Really Masters," p. 52; "The First Discharge of a Public Servant," p. 71; Barton, *op. cit.*, p. 7; Norton, *op. cit.*, pp. 2, 6; *Times*, Aug. 28, 30, Sept. 4, 6, 7, 9–11, 13–15, 1904; *Examiner*, Sept. 17, 1904; *Graphic*, Dec. 10, 1904, pp. 2–3; Dec. 31, 1904, p. 4.

[47] Pomeroy, "Really Masters," p. 52; "The First Discharge of a Public Servant," p. 71; Barton, *op. cit.*, p. 1; Haynes, *op. cit.*, p. 15; *Times*, Sept. 17, 1904; *Examiner*, Sept. 17, 1904; *Graphic*, Sept. 24, 1904, p. 5.

[48] *Times*, Oct. 4, 18, 1904; Apr. 6, 1905; *Herald*, Apr. 6, 1905; *Common Sense*, June 3, 1905.

[49] *Graphic*, Dec. 31, 1904, p. 5; *Times*, May 16, 1905; *Pacific Outlook*, June 11, 1910, p. 3; letter from John R. Haynes to Lincoln Steffens, *Examiner*, Jan. 26, 1907.

[50] *Times*, Dec. 1, 1904; Jan. 10, 17, 1905; *Graphic*, Dec. 31, 1904, p. 6.

[51] *Examiner*, Dec. 11, 22, 1904.

[52] *Times*, Dec. 4, 1902; *Examiner*, Dec. 24, 1903; *Union Labor News*, Dec. 25, 1903; *Citizen*, Feb. 8, 1910; LATU, *Minutes 1902–1905*, pp. 34–5, 48, 57–8, 117, 138.

[53] *Examiner*, May 13, July 8, Sept. 13, 22, 27, Oct. 6, 8, 13, 20, 21, 23, 30, Nov. 1, 3, 20, Dec. 18, 20, 21, 25, 1904; *Record*, Oct. 6, 1904; *Common Sense*, Dec. 10, 17, 1904; *Citizen*, Feb. 8, 1910; LATU, *Minutes 1902–1905*, pp. 245, 249–50, 258, 267.

[54] *Examiner*, Jan. 14, 25, Feb. 3, 8, 17, Mar. 15, 25, 30, Apr. 14, May 7, 9, 17, 30, June 9, July 8, Aug. 23, Oct. 20, 1905; Jan. 1, 1906; *Coast Seamen's Journal*, Feb. 22, 1905; *Union Labor News*, Nov. 17, Dec. 8, 29, 1905.

[55] *Examiner*, Jan. 23, Feb. 23, May 11, July 3, 1906; *Union Labor News*, Feb. 16, 1906; *Times*, Feb. 21, Mar. 5, 1907; *Citizen*, Aug. 16, Nov. 22, 29, 1907; Feb. 8, 1910; Feb. 21, 1936; LATU, *Minutes 1905–1908*, pp. 212, 217.

[56] *Times*, Apr. 6, 1908; *Citizen*, Apr. 10, Dec. 11, 1908; Jan. 22, Feb. 12, Apr. 2, May 7, July 2, Aug. 6, 20, Oct. 8, 1909; Feb. 21, 1936; LATU, *Minutes 1905–1908*, p. 289.

[57] *Examiner*, July 29, 1906; *Citizen*, Jan. 14, 28, Feb. 18, 25, Apr. 8, 1910.

[58] *Citizen*, Feb. 21, 1936.

Chapter XIX

ASCENDANCE OF THE OPEN SHOP

[1] Pauline Jacobson, "The 'M. and M.' and the Struggle of Labor," San Francisco *Bulletin*, Dec. 16, 1911; *Times*, Apr. 25, 1907; *Citizen*, July 5, 1907; LATU, *Minutes 1905–1908*, pp. 184, 191.

[2] *Examiner*, Jan. 12, Mar. 12, May 23, Aug. 2, Sept. 21, 24, Oct. 17, 21, 27, 28, Nov. 11, 15, 23, Dec. 29, 1905; July 1, Sept. 15, 22, Oct. 6, 1906; *Union Labor News*, Nov. 10, 17, 24, Dec. 22, 29, 1905; *Citizen*, May 12, 1907.

[3] *Examiner*, Nov. 5, 1905; Sept. 17, 1906; *Citizen*, Dec. 31, 1909; Feb. 4, 1910; *Proceedings of the California State Federation of Labor, January, 1908*, p. 61.

[4] *Examiner*, Sept. 17, Oct. 25, 1906; *Citizen*, Nov. 8, 1907; Jan. 8, 1909; Feb. 4, Sept. 2, 1910.

[5] *Examiner*, Mar. 23, 1905; *Union Labor News*, Jan. 4, 11, 1907; *Citizen*, Mar. 15, 1907; Dec. 25, 1908; Jan. 15, 1909; *Times*, Dec. 20, 23, 27, 1908; Jan. 5–7, 1909; LATU, *Minutes 1905–1908*, p. 154; *Proceedings of the California State Federation of Labor, 1907*, pp. 4, 16, 20; *January, 1908*, p. 94; *October, 1908*, p. 18; *1909*, p. 82.

[6] *Citizen,* July 17, 24, 1908; *Herald,* July 26, 31, 1908; *Times,* July 31, 1908.

[7] *Citizen,* Apr. 5, 1907; *Examiner,* Apr. 7, 1907; LATU, *Minutes 1905–1908,* pp. 153–4, 161–2.

[8] *Union Labor News,* Apr. 20, 27, May 11, 25, 1906; *Examiner,* Apr. 20–29, May 1–3, 10, 1906; LATU, *Minutes 1905–1908,* pp. 74–5, 91.

[9] *Examiner,* Jan. 18, 19, 1905; *Times,* Jan. 8, 1905.

[10] *Times,* Mar. 3, 1907; *Citizen,* Mar. 15, 1907; *Proceedings of the California State Federation of Labor, 1907,* pp. 4, 19; *January, 1908,* p. 94; Lucile Eaves, *A History of California Labor Legislation* (Berkeley: The University Press [c. 1910]), pp. 382–6.

[11] San Francisco *Chronicle,* Mar. 7, 1905; *Examiner,* Mar. 8, 11, 1905; *Union Labor News,* Feb. 15, 1907; *Times,* Mar. 3, 1907; *Proceedings of the California State Federation of Labor, January, 1908,* p. 95; *1909,* p. 83.

[12] *Examiner,* July 25, 27, 29, Aug. 3–5, 8, 9, 13, 15, 18, 22, 1905; *Common Sense,* Aug. 12, 1905; Eaves, *op. cit.,* pp. 219–23.

[13] *Times,* Aug. 6, Sept. 28, 1909; Feb. 9, 1910; *Citizen,* Aug. 20, 27, Sept. 3, 10, 17, 24, Oct. 8, Dec. 3, 17, 24, 1909; Jan. 14, Feb. 11, 1910.

[14] *Graphic,* Jan. 7, 1905, pp. 7–8; *Examiner,* Feb. 11, 14, 1905; *Coast Seamen's Journal,* Mar. 1, 1905; *Times,* Apr. 7, 1905; Eaves, *op. cit.,* pp. 298–304; W. V. Stafford, "Child Labor in California," *Transactions of the Commonwealth Club of California,* II (Jan., 1906), 106–7.

[15] *Examiner,* Sept. 7, 9, 21, Nov. 17, 1905; Jan. 24, Mar. 10, 16, 18, 22, 30, Apr. 7, June 29, July 26, 27, 29, 31, Sept. 7, Nov. 21, 26, 1906; *Times,* Mar. 10, 23, 24, 30, Sept. 13, 14, 1906; *Union Labor News,* Mar. 16, 23, July 27, Aug. 24, Sept. 14, 1906; Eaves, *op. cit.,* p. 307; Stafford, *op. cit.,* pp. 107–11, 113–14.

[16] *Times,* Apr. 6, 1906; May 4, 1909; *Pacific Outlook,* Dec. 1, 1906, pp. 5–6; Dec. 8, 1906, pp. 11–12; *Union Labor News,* Feb. 1, 1907; *Citizen,* Mar. 15, 29, 1907; Oct. 16, 1908; Apr. 2, 9, 1909; Eaves, *op. cit.,* p. 307; *Proceedings of the California State Federation of Labor, 1907,* pp. 4, 16–17, 19; *January, 1908,* p. 95; *October, 1908,* pp. 19–22; *1909,* p. 82; *Thirteenth Biennial Report, 1907–1908,* California Bureau of Labor Statistics (Sacramento: 1908), p. 188; *Fourteenth Biennial Report, 1909–1910,* California Bureau of Labor Statistics (Sacramento: 1910), p. 28; Earl C. Crockett, "The History of California Labor Legislation, 1910–1930" (unpublished Ph.D. dissertation, University of California, Berkeley, 1931), p. 100.

[17] John R. Commons and Associates, *History of Labor in the United States* (New York: Macmillan, 1921–1935), IV, 152–3; *Legislative Achievements of the American Federation of Labor* (Washington: 1916), p. 4.

[18] Foster Rhea Dulles, *Labor in America* (New York: Crowell [c. 1949]), pp. 184–207; Harold U. Faulkner, *The Quest for Social Justice, 1898–1914,* History of American Life Series, Vol. XI (New York: Macmillan [c. 1931]), pp. 52–80; George E. Mowry, *The California Progressives* (Berkeley: University of California Press, 1951), pp. 135–57, 295–6.

[19] *Times,* Jan. 24, Mar. 23, May 5, 1905; *Examiner,* Apr. 24–26, May 5, 27, 1905; *Twelfth Biennial Report, 1905–1906,* California Bureau of Labor Statistics (Sacramento: 1906), pp. 212–13.

[20] *Examiner,* Jan. 1, 3, 4, 6, 8, 12, Aug. 8, 12, 13, 15–18, 21, 23, 24, 26, 27, 29, 31, Sept. 3, 6, 8, 12, 21, 27, 29, Oct. 1, 17, Nov. 9, 15, Dec. 5, 1905; *Times,* Jan. 6, Aug. 13, 15–17, 24, 29, 1905; *Common Sense,* Aug. 12, 19, 1905; *Union Labor News,* Nov. 10, 17, 24, 1905; *Citizen,* Sept. 1, 1911; *Twelfth Biennial Report, 1905–1906,* California Bureau of Labor Statistics, pp. 206–7.

[21] *Examiner,* June 14, 29, July 1–3, 5–8, 13, 14, 30, Aug. 1, 13, 31, Sept. 16, 23, 24, 1905; June 28, 1906; *Times,* July 1–3, 18, 1905; Feb. 21, 1906; *Common Sense,* Aug. 12, 1905; *Union Labor News,* Dec. 8, 1905; Feb. 23, 1906; *Citizen,* Sept. 1, 1911; *American Federationist,* Sept., 1905, p. 640; Oct., 1905, p. 769; Nov., 1905, p. 854; *The Forty-Year War for a Free City; A History of the Open Shop in Los Angeles* (Los Angeles: Times-Mirror Publishing Co., 1929), p. 10.

[22] *Times,* July 26, 28, 30, Aug. 20, 25, Dec. 8, 23, 1905; *Examiner,* July 27–29, Aug. 24, 30, Dec. 7, 1905; *Common Sense,* Aug. 5, 1905; *Union Labor News,* Nov. 10, Dec. 8, 15, 1905; Feb. 23, 1906; *Twelfth Biennial Report, 1905–1906,* California Bureau of Labor Statistics, pp. 204–5.

[23] *Examiner,* Jan. 29, Feb. 1, 23, 28, Mar. 8–10, Apr. 13, 20, May 28, July 9, 13, 20, 22, 28, Aug. 17, Sept. 20, Oct. 8, Nov. 4, Dec. 23, 1905; Feb. 4, 15, 24, 1906; *Record,* Mar. 2, 9, 1905; *Times,* Mar. 9, May 28, July 17, 23, 24, 1905; *Graphic,* Mar. 11, 1905, p. 5; *Union Labor News,* Dec. 8, 22, 1905; Feb. 16, Dec. 29, 1906; *Proceedings of the California State Federation of Labor, 1906,* pp. 79–80.

[24] *Examiner,* June 20, July 15, 17, Aug. 6, 21, Sept. 20, Nov. 7, 20, Dec. 4, 5, 8, 18, 25, 29, 1905; *Times,* July 19, 31, Nov. 18, Dec. 5, 7, 22, 28, 30, 31, 1905; *Union Labor News,* Nov. 17, 24, Dec. 8, 22, 1905; LATU, *Minutes 1902–1905,* pp. 278, 283, 289, 293–4, 298; *Minutes 1905–1908,* pp. 6, 8–9, 14–16, 20, 26–8, 33, 38, 41–3, 47–9.

[25] *Times,* Jan. 3, 9, 30, Feb. 6, 10, Mar. 29, 1906; *Examiner,* Jan. 3, 8, 19, Feb. 7, 11, 20, 25, 27, Mar. 7, 25, 27, May 1, June 6, 12, Aug. 4, 7, Sept. 27, 1906; *Union Labor News,* Jan. 5, 12, Mar. 2, Sept. 28, 1906; *Common Sense,* Jan. 13, 1906; LATU, *Minutes 1905–1908,* pp. 61, 65, 67, 69, 90, 95, 102, 119–21, 269; Ira B. Cross, *A History of the Labor Movement in California* (Berkeley: University of California Press, 1935), p. 288.

[26] *Times,* Nov. 18, 1905; Nov. 3, 1906; Sept. 11, 1907; *Union Labor News,* Feb. 16, Oct. 12, 1906; Jan. 27, 1907; LATU, *Minutes 1905–1908,* pp. 107–8, 119–21, 269; George A. Tracy, comp., *History of the Typographical Union* ([Indianapolis]: International Typographical Union, 1913), pp. 893, 896–9, 902.

[27] *Examiner,* Jan. 4, Dec. 4, 5, 8, 1905; *Coast Seamen's Journal,* June 7, 1905; *Times,* Dec. 5, 7, 1905; *Union Labor News,* Dec. 8, 15, 1905; Commons and Associates, *op. cit.,* IV, 136–7.

[28] *Union Labor News,* Nov. 17, 1905.

[29] *Examiner,* Jan. 3–5, 7, 14, 19–21, 24, 27–29, 31, Feb. 9, 23, May 6, 9, 1906; *Union Labor News,* Jan. 5, 12, 19, Mar. 9, May 11, 1906; *Common Sense,* Jan. 13, 1906; *Times,* Jan. 14, 27, 28, 1906; LATU, *Minutes 1905–1908,* pp. 57, 64–5, 72.

[30] *Examiner,* Jan. 29, Feb. 1, 8, 11, Mar. 19, June 16, Aug. 19, 23, Sept. 24, Oct. 6, 14, Nov. 7, 9, 22, Dec. 9, 17, 1905; *Union Labor News,* Nov. 24, Dec. 8, 22, 1905.

[31] *Examiner,* Feb. 1, Apr. 18, May 1, 2, 10, 30, June 5, 10, 14, 17, July 19, 1906; *Union Labor News,* June 15, July 27, 1906.

[32] *Examiner,* Dec. 9, 1905; June 27, Sept. 14, Nov. 29, 1906; *Common Sense,* Aug. 18, 1906; *Union Labor News,* Nov. 2, 1906; Jan. 18, 1907.

[33] *Examiner,* Mar. 21, 22, July 9, Aug. 19, 1905; *Union Labor News,* May 11, June 22, 1906; LATU, *Minutes 1905–1908,* p. 2; *Proceedings of the California State Federation of Labor, 1907,* pp. 59–60.

[34] *Examiner,* June 14, 15, 17, 24, July 7, 27, Aug. 11, 1906; *Times,* June 18, 19, 24, 27, 1906; *Union Labor News,* June 22, July 6, 13, 20, Sept. 7, 1906; Jan. 25, 1907; *Citizen,* Aug. 9, Sept. 6, 1907; June 23, 1911; Sept. 1, 1939; *Proceedings of the American Federation of Labor, 1906,* p. 257; *Proceedings of the California State Federation of Labor, January, 1908,* p. 62; *The Forty-Year War for a Free City . . . ,* p. 10.

[35] *Union Labor News,* Jan. 21, 1904; Jan. 26, Apr. 20, 27, Aug. 24, 31, Sept. 7, 21, 1906; *Examiner,* Jan. 25, June 2, 17, 24, Aug. 7, 19, 21, 27, 28, 30, Sept. 30, 1906; *Times,* Aug. 3, 7, 21, Sept. 6, 14, 1906; *Coast Seamen's Journal,* Aug. 29, 1906; *Graphic,* Sept. 1, 1906, pp. 29–30; Paul S. Taylor, *The Sailors' Union of the Pacific* (New York: Ronald Press, 1923), pp. 104–6; Cross, *op. cit.,* p. 247.

[36] *Examiner,* Dec. 16, 1906; *Times,* Dec. 16, 1906; Taylor, *op. cit.,* p. 107; Cross, *op. cit.,* p. 247.

[37] *Times,* Oct. 7, 17, 19, 26, 1906; *Union Labor News,* Oct. 26, 1906.

[38] *Examiner,* July 6, 7, Sept. 13, 14, 1906; *Union Labor News,* Sept. 21, 1906; *Citizen,* June 28, 1907; *Times,* Aug. 9, 10, 12–14, 1907; *Coast Seamen's Journal,* Aug. 21, 1907.

[39] *Union Labor News,* Apr. 7, 13, July 6, Aug. 17, 24, Sept. 14, Oct. 5, 12, 14, 1906;

Times, Aug. 15, 18, 23, Sept. 12, Oct. 2, 7, Dec. 12, 20, 1906; Jan. 3, 1907; *Examiner,* Sept. 20, 1906.

[40] *Union Labor News,* Sept. 28, 1906; Jan. 11, 1907; *Times,* Oct. 7, 1906; *Citizen,* May 3, 1907.

[41] *Times,* Apr. 15, Sept. 5, 6, Oct. 24, 31, Nov. 13, 14, 1906; Jan. 22, 24, 31, 1907; Feb. 23, 1908; *Examiner,* May 15, July 21, Sept. 8, 9, 1906; *Coast Seamen's Journal,* Sept. 12, 1906; *Union Labor News,* Oct. 12, Nov. 16, 1906.

[42] *Examiner,* Nov. 23, 28, Dec. 2, 6, 8, 20, 1905; *Union Labor News,* Nov. 24, Dec. 8, 15, 1905; Jan. 26, 1906; *Times,* Dec. 8, 19, 20, 29, 1905; Feb. 15, 22, 27, 1906.

[43] *Examiner,* Aug. 6, Oct. 12, Nov. 8, 12, 16, 18, 1905; *Times,* Nov. 10, 15, 16, Dec. 7, 1905; *Union Labor News,* Nov. 17, 1905.

[44] *Union Labor News,* Dec. 22, 1905.

[45] *Examiner,* Dec. 19, 1905; Jan. 14, 20, 21, 27, 28, 1906; *Union Labor News,* Feb. 23, 1906; LATU, *Minutes 1905–1908,* pp. 57, 64–5, 72; Commons and Associates, *op. cit.,* IV, 152–3.

[46] *Times,* Dec. 7, 1905; Apr. 12, May 27, 1906; *Examiner,* Jan. 25, Feb. 1, 9, 14, 15, 18, 22, Mar. 1, 7, 1906; *Union Labor News,* Feb. 23, Mar. 2, 9, 23, 1906.

[47] LATU, *Minutes 1905–1908,* p. 125.

[48] *Examiner,* July 19, 1906; *Union Labor News,* Aug. 3, 31, 1906; *Common Sense,* Aug. 18, 1906.

[49] *Union Labor News,* Oct. 5, 1906; *Times,* Nov. 10, 11, 13, 15, 24, 1906; *Pacific Outlook,* Nov. 17, 1906, pp. 8–9.

[50] *Graphic,* Aug. 11, 1906, p. 23; Nov. 10, 1906, p. 14; *Times,* Nov. 24–26, Dec. 5, 15, 1906; LATU, *Minutes 1905–1908,* pp. 125–6.

[51] J. Gregg Layne, "The Lincoln-Roosevelt League," *Historical Society of Southern California Quarterly,* Sept., 1943, pp. 8–9; Mowry, *op. cit.,* pp. 38–43.

[52] *Times,* Nov. 24, Dec. 15, 1906; *Graphic,* Nov. 24, 1906, p. 23; Dec. 28, 1907, p. 3; *Union Labor News,* Dec. 7, 1906; Jan. 4, Feb. 22, 1907; LATU, *Minutes 1905–1908,* p. 134; *The Forty-Year War for a Free City . . . ,* p. 7.

[53] *Common Sense,* Mar. 10, Aug. 18, Sept. 15, Dec. 1, 29, 1906; *Times,* Oct. 19, Nov. 19, 1906; *Union Labor News,* Dec. 7, 1906.

[54] *Common Sense,* July 15, Sept. 23, Oct. 28, 1905; Apr. 21, June 30, July 28, Aug. 18, 1906; *Examiner,* Nov. 4, 1905; Mar. 21, 24, 1906; *Union Labor News,* Nov. 17, 1905; Jan. 26, 1906; *Times,* Mar. 16, Sept. 26, Oct. 3, 1906; Paul F. Brissenden, *The I. W. W.* (New York: Columbia University Press, 1919), pp. 28–9, 31, 40–3, 46, 54, 57, 82, 123–4, 136, 143; Hyman Weintraub, "The I. W. W. in California, 1905–1931" (unpublished M.A. thesis, University of California, Los Angeles, 1947), pp. 18, 20.

[55] *Examiner,* Aug. 2, 3, 6, 1906; *Common Sense,* July 28, Aug. 11, 18, Sept. 1, 1906; Commons and Associates, *op. cit.,* IV, 208–13.

[56] *Union Labor News,* Jan. 11, 25, Feb. 1, 8, 22, 1907; *Times,* Jan. 15, 1907; *Citizen,* June 21, 1907.

[57] *Union Labor News,* Jan. 11, 18, 25, Feb. 1, 22, 1907; *Citizen,* Mar. 1, 1907.

[58] *Examiner,* Dec. 8, 20, 1906; *Union Labor News,* Jan. 4, 18, Feb. 8, 15, 1907; *Citizen,* Mar. 1, June 7, 28, 1907; *American Federationist,* Feb., 1907, p. 107; *Proceedings of the California State Federation of Labor, January, 1908,* p. 61.

[59] *Times,* Mar. 19, Sept. 11, 1907; Aug. 1, 1909; *Citizen,* May 12, June 21, 28, July 5, Aug. 2, 23, 1907; Sept. 25, Oct. 16, 1908; Feb. 4, 1910; Oct. 13, 1911; May 24, 1912; *Proceedings of the California State Federation of Labor, 1911,* p. 29; *1912,* p. 96.

[60] *Times,* May 1, 4, 1907; *Citizen,* May 3, 1907; *Thirteenth Biennial Report, 1907–1908,* California Bureau of Labor Statistics, p. 181; *Final Report and Testimony Submitted to Congress by the Commission on Industrial Relations,* U.S. 64th Cong., 1st sess., S. Doc. 415 (Washington: 1916), VI, 5667–9; interview with L. W. Butler, June 19, 1952.

[61] *Times,* May 4, 1907; *Final Report and Testimony Submitted to Congress by the Commission on Industrial Relations,* VI, 5667–9.

[62] *Times,* May 2, 3, 5, 10, 11, 1907; *Citizen,* May 10, 17, 1907; *Final Report and*

Testimony Submitted to Congress by the Commission on Industrial Relations, VI, 5496–7, 5667–9; Walter V. Woehlke, "Terrorism in America," *Outlook,* 100 (Feb. 17, 1912), 360–1; interview with L. W. Butler, June 19, 1952.

[63] *Citizen,* July 14, 1911; Feb. 21, 1936; *Final Report and Testimony Submitted to Congress by the Commission on Industrial Relations,* VI, 5667–9; Woehlke, *loc. cit.;* interviews with L. W. Butler, July 26, 1951; June 19, 1952.

[64] *Citizen,* June 21, 28, July 5, Aug. 9, 23, 1907; LATU, *Minutes 1905–1908,* pp. 173–5, 187–8; interview with L. W. Butler, June 19, 1952.

[65] *Citizen,* Sept. 6, 27, Oct. 4, 11, Dec. 13, 1907.

[66] *Times,* Aug. 4, 1907; *Citizen,* Aug. 16, 23, 1907; LATU, *Minutes 1905–1908,* pp. 173–5; Tracy, *op. cit.,* pp. 886, 903.

[67] *Times,* Aug. 25, 1907.

[68] *Ibid.,* Sept. 11, Oct. 27, Nov. 1–3, 1907; *Citizen,* Oct. 11, 25, 1907.

[69] *Citizen,* Oct. 11, Nov. 1, 8, Dec. 6, 13, 1907; Feb. 21, 1908; *Graphic,* Nov. 23, 1907, p. 3; *Times,* Dec. 4, 18, 1907; Jan. 21, 1908; *Coast Seamen's Journal,* Jan. 8, 1908; San Francisco *Call,* Jan. 10, 1908; LATU, *Minutes 1905–1908,* p. 210; *Proceedings of the American Federation of Labor, 1907,* pp. 321–3; *Los Angeles—"A Model Open Shop City"* (Los Angeles: Central Labor Council, 1907), *passim.*

[70] *Express,* Feb. 25, 1907; *Citizen,* Mar. 15, June 28, July 26, Aug. 16, 1907; *Herald,* Mar. 17, 1907; *Times,* Aug. 10, 12–14, 1907; "A Senseless Strike," *Outlook,* 86 (Aug. 17, 1907), 794–5; "The Strike of the Telegraphers," *Outlook,* 86 (Aug. 24, 1907), 841; *American Federationist,* Dec., 1907, p. 973.

[71] *Citizen,* Aug. 30, Sept. 6, 20, Nov. 29, Dec. 20, 1907; *Common Sense,* Oct. 19, Nov. 9, 1907; "The End of Two Strikes," *Outlook,* 87 (Nov. 16, 1907), 552; LATU, *Minutes 1905–1908,* pp. 187, 192; Robert F. Hoxie, "The Failure of the Telegraphers' Strike," *Journal of Political Economy,* XV (Nov., 1907), 545–7; Graham Taylor, "The Industrial Viewpoint," *Charities and the Commons,* XVIII (Sept. 7, 1907), 697.

[72] *Times,* Aug. 3, 5, Sept. 14, 27, 1907; *Citizen,* Nov. 8, 1907; Mar. 20, 1908; Mar. 10, 1911; *Proceedings of the California State Federation of Labor, January, 1908,* p. 62; *Proceedings of the American Federation of Labor, 1908,* p. 241; Los Angeles Central Labor Council, *Minutes 1911–1912,* meeting of Mar. 3, 1911.

[73] *Twelfth Biennial Report, 1905–1906,* California Bureau of Labor Statistics, pp. 212–13.

[74] *Times,* Oct. 13, 17, 18, 23, 26, Nov. 4, 1906; Sept. 11, Dec. 6, 1907; *Union Labor News,* Nov. 2, 16, 1906; Jan. 25, 1907; *Citizen,* Oct. 16, 1908.

[75] *Times,* June 13, Sept. 24, Nov. 15, Dec. 6, 1907; *Citizen,* Oct. 4, 11, Nov. 8, 29, 1907; Jan. 24, Feb. 21, Sept. 25, 1908; *Coast Seamen's Journal,* Oct. 16, 1907; *Proceedings of the American Federation of Labor, 1907,* p. 196; *American Federationist,* Sept., 1910, p. 777.

[76] *Citizen,* Oct. 11, Nov. 8, Dec. 13, 1907; Apr. 24, Oct. 16, 23, 1908; *Times,* Dec. 6, 1907; *Record,* Jan. 29, 1908; *Proceedings of the American Federation of Labor, 1908,* p. 241; *American Federationist,* Sept., 1910, p. 777; Charles Jacob Stowell, *Studies in Trade Unionism in the Custom Tailoring Trade* (Bloomington, Ill.: Journeymen Tailors Union of America, 1913), pp. 56, 127.

[77] *Times,* Apr. 2, 1907.

[78] *Ibid.,* May 22, 1907.

[79] *Graphic,* Dec. 28, 1907, p. 3.

[80] Commons and Associates, *op. cit.,* IV, 151, 364–5.

[81] *Ibid.,* IV, 131–7, 489–91.

[82] *Graphic,* Apr. 13, 1907, p. 10; Jan. 25, 1908, p. 8; *Citizen,* Nov. 8, 15, Dec. 6, 1907; Jan. 24, Feb. 14, 28, 1908; *Herald,* Jan. 19, 25, 1908; *Times,* Jan. 21, Feb. 10, 1908; *Record,* Jan. 22, 1908; *Labor Clarion,* Feb. 21, 1908; *Pacific Outlook,* Feb. 22, 1908, p. 7; *American Federationist,* Dec., 1907, p. 987.

[83] *Herald,* Jan. 1, 6, Feb. 7, 9, 11, 1908; *Graphic,* Jan. 4, 1908, p. 6; Jan. 25, 1908, p. 8; Apr. 4, 1908, p. 3; *Times,* Jan. 25, 28, 30, 31, Feb. 10, 11, 1908; Jan. 19, 1909;

Citizen, Mar. 20, Nov. 26, 1908; Apr. 2, 1909; *American Federationist*, May, 1908, p. 394; June, 1908, pp. 476–77; July, 1908, p. 546; Apr., 1909, p. 365; LATU, *Minutes 1905–1908*, pp. 223–24, 226.

⁸⁴ *Citizen*, Nov. 8, 1907; Jan. 10, Mar. 20, Apr. 10, June 13, Aug. 21, Oct. 2, 1908; Dec. 31, 1909; July 21, 1911; *Common Sense*, Jan. 18, 1908; *Times*, Feb. 23, Mar. 6, 18, 1908; *Proceedings of the California State Federation of Labor, January, 1908*, p. 63.

⁸⁵ *Citizen*, Dec. 13, 20, 1907; Jan. 24, Feb. 14, 21, May 29, June 13, July 3, 1908; *Coast Seamen's Journal*, Jan. 22, Nov. 25, 1908; *Times*, Feb. 6, 11, Mar. 8, 1908; *Record*, Feb. 13, 1908; *American Federationist*, Mar., 1908, pp. 217, 226; LATU, *Minutes 1905–1908*, p. 226; Tracy, *op. cit.*, p. 928.

⁸⁶ *Herald*, Jan. 25, 1908; *Times*, Feb. 6, Mar. 8, July 3, 8, 1908; *Labor Clarion*, Feb. 21, 1908; *Citizen*, Feb. 21, Mar. 13, 1908; *Coast Seamen's Journal*, Feb. 26, 1908; interview with A. J. Mooney, May 27, 1952.

⁸⁷ *Graphic*, Jan. 11, 1908, p. 11; *Citizen*, Mar. 27, June 19, 26, 1908; *American Federationist*, May, 1908, p. 394; June, 1908, pp. 476–77.

⁸⁸ *Citizen*, Nov. 6, Dec. 4, 1908; *Coast Seamen's Journal*, Nov. 18, 25, 1908; *Proceedings of the American Federation of Labor, 1908*, pp. x, 43, 241; Tracy, *op. cit.*, p. 928.

⁸⁹ *Citizen*, Aug. 30, Sept. 20, Oct. 4, 25, Nov. 15, 29, 1907; Jan. 3, 17, 1908; May 21, 1909; Sept. 9, 1910; *Herald*, Jan. 29, 1908; *Times*, Nov. 3, 10, 17, Dec. 17, 23, 1908; Jan. 5, Mar. 3, 1909; *Proceedings of the American Federation of Labor, 1908*, pp. 59–60; Samuel Gompers, *Seventy Years of Life and Labor* (new ed.; New York: Dutton [c. 1925]), II, 304–7.

⁹⁰ *Pacific Outlook*, Aug. 10, 1907, p. 7; Aug. 31, 1907, p. 6; Oct. 3, 1907, p. 8; *Times*, Aug. 27, 1907; *Citizen*, Sept. 20, Oct. 4, 25, Nov. 8, 15, 29, Dec. 20, 1907; Jan. 3, 10, 17, Apr. 17, Sept. 11, Oct. 23, 1908; *Common Sense*, Sept. 21, Dec. 7, 1907; Jan. 25, Feb. 15, Apr. 4, 1908; *Herald*, Jan. 4, 1908; Gompers, *op. cit.*, II, 309, 317–18; *Mexican Labor in the United States*, by Victor S. Clark, U.S. Bureau of Labor, Bull. no. 78 (Washington: 1908), pp. 507, 511.

⁹¹ *Citizen*, Dec. 5, 1919.

⁹² *Graphic*, May 23, 1907, p. 7; *Times*, Apr. 26, 30, May 1–3, 6, 7, 14, 1908; *Citizen*, May 8, June 19, 1908; LATU, *Minutes 1905–1908*, pp. 255–7; Mowry, *op. cit.*, pp. 57–79; Layne, *op. cit.*, pp. 5–6, 8–9, 13–17, 19–21.

⁹³ LATU, *Minutes 1905–1908*, pp. 246, 279; *Citizen*, Aug. 14, 1908. The quotation is from the latter source.

⁹⁴ *Times*, Aug. 19, 21, 22, 28, Oct. 6, 14, 21, Nov. 2, 4, 5, 1908; *Herald*, Aug. 23, 1908; *Citizen*, Sept. 25, Oct. 2, 9, 16, 30, Nov. 13, 1908; *Labor Clarion*, Oct. 2, 1908; *California Weekly*, Jan. 29, 1909, p. 145; Mowry, *op. cit.*, pp. 79–80; LATU, *Minutes 1905–1908*, pp. 282, 287–9.

⁹⁵ *Times*, July 31, Sept. 14, 28, Oct. 3, 5, 15, 25, 29, 1907; Jan. 22, 1908; *Citizen*, Aug. 2, Nov. 1, 1907; Jan. 17, 1908; *Express*, Oct. 28, 1907; *Herald*, Jan. 12, 16, 1908.

⁹⁶ *Herald*, Feb. 12, July 12, 1908; *Citizen*, June 26, July 3, 10, 17, 1908; Jan. 25, Feb. 5, 1909; *Times*, June 27, 30, July 14, 15, 18, Sept. 29, Nov. 17, 29, 1908; Feb. 4, 1909; *Pacific Outlook*, July 25, 1908, p. 3; Dec. 11, 1909, p. 2; "The Municipal Reform in Los Angeles," *Outlook*, 91 (Mar. 13, 1909), 570–1; John D. Works, "A City's Struggle for Political and Moral Freedom," *Arena*, XLI (Mar., 1909), 353–5; Mowry, *op. cit.*, p. 44.

⁹⁷ Los Angeles Central Labor Council, *Minutes 1909–1910*, meeting of Jan. 29, 1909; "The Municipal Reform in Los Angeles," pp. 570–1; *Graphic*, Mar. 13, 1909, p. 2; Mar. 20, 1909, p. 1; Mowry, *op. cit.*, pp. 44–5; Franklin Hichborn, *Story of the California Legislature of 1909* (San Francisco: James H. Barry Co., 1909), pp. 194–5; interview with Frank E. Wolfe, Feb. 15, 1952.

⁹⁸ *Common Sense*, Mar. 2, Apr. 6, 13, 20, May 18, June 15, Dec. 7, 1907; Feb.–July *passim*, 1908; *Record*, Jan. 6, 1908; *Herald*, Feb. 5, 6, July 21, 28, 1908; *Times*, Feb. 14, 25, Mar. 4, 14, 15, 25, 1908; *Citizen*, Feb. 21, Mar. 6, July 17, 24, 1908; Feb. 26, 1909; *Pacific Outlook*, July 11, 1908, pp. 4–5; "A Notable Triumph for Free Speech in Los Angeles," *Arena*, XL (Oct., 1908), 350–1.

[99] *Citizen,* Mar. 27, 1908; Feb. 26, 1909; *Common Sense,* Aug. 8, 15, Oct. 17, 31, Nov. 28, 1908; Jan. 23, 1909.

[100] *Graphic,* Mar. 13, 1909, p. 2; Mar. 20, 1909, p. 1; Apr. 3, 1909, p. 2; Aug. 21, 1909, p. 1; *Coast Seamen's Journal,* Mar. 24, Apr. 14, 1909; *Times,* Mar. 27, 1909; *Common Sense,* Mar. 27, Apr. 3, 1909; *Pacific Outlook,* Apr. 3, 1909, pp. 3–4; Dec. 11, 1909, p. 2; "The House-Cleaning in Los Angeles," *Outlook,* 91 (Apr. 3, 1909), 757–8; *Proceedings of the National Municipal League, 1909,* pp. 330–1; Mowry, *op. cit.,* pp. 45–6; Works, *op. cit.,* pp. 355–7; *Charles Dwight Willard Letters,* letter to his father, Nov. [11], 1909; letter to his sister, Nov. 12, 1909.

[101] *Citizen,* Feb. 26, Mar. 5, 12, 19, Apr. 2, 9, 1909; *Times,* Apr. 2, 1909; Mowry, *op. cit.,* p. 45.

[102] *Citizen,* Dec. 31, 1909.

[103] *Times,* May 27, Dec. 10, 1906; LATU, *Minutes 1905–1908,* pp. 81, 85, 125–6.

[104] LATU, *Minutes 1905–1908,* pp. 196, 199–200, 244–5, 248, 254, 259–61, 279; Tracy, *op. cit.,* pp. 902–5, 928–9.

[105] *Citizen,* July 31, Sept. 11, Nov. 6, 13, Dec. 4, 1908; Mar. 5, 12, 19, 26, Apr. 2, 16, 30, May 7, 14, June 18, 25, July 2, 23, Aug. 13, 1909; *Times,* Nov. 1, 1908; July 17, 1909; Los Angeles Central Labor Council, *Minutes 1909–1910,* meetings of Mar. 19, 24, 31, Apr. 2, 7, 14, May 7, June 11, 1909; *American Federationist,* Mar., 1909, p. 268; LATU, *Minutes 1908–1911,* p. 73.

[106] Los Angeles Central Labor Council, *Minutes 1909–1910,* meetings of Mar. 31, June 16, 18, 22, July 23, 1909; *Citizen,* July 23, 30, Aug. 6, 13, 27, Sept. 24, Nov. 5, 12, 19, 26, Dec. 10, 1909; LATU, *Minutes 1908–1911,* p. 50.

[107] *Citizen,* July 2, 9, 16, 1909; Los Angeles Central Labor Council, *Minutes 1909–1910,* meetings of July 9, 21, 1909; LATU, *Minutes 1908–1911,* pp. 35, 46, 62, 64.

[108] *Times,* July 29, 31, 1909; *Citizen,* July 30, Aug. 6, 13, 1909; LATU, *Minutes 1908–1911,* pp. 53–5, 60–4, 69–77, 154; Tracy, *op. cit.,* pp. 951–3.

[109] *Citizen,* May 21, 28, June 4, July 9, 16, Aug. 6, 13, 20, 27, Sept. 24, Oct. 1, 15, 22, Nov. 19, 1909; Jan. 7, Feb. 25, Mar. 18, 1910; LATU, *Minutes 1908–1911,* pp. 68–9, 78–9, 81–3, 86, 88–92, 96–8; *Proceedings of the American Federation of Labor, 1909,* pp. 48, 202–3, 244; *1910,* pp. 65, 82.

[110] *Citizen,* Nov. 12, 1909; *Times,* Nov. 27, 1909; May 8, 22, 29, 1910; Tracy, *op. cit.,* pp. 985–6; LATU, *Minutes 1908–1911,* pp. 92, 105–7, 110–13, 118–19, 122–4, 126, 128–9, 132, 135–8, 141, 143–4, 147–56, 162–4, 173, 176–9, 184–5, 190–2, 201.

[111] *Citizen,* May 21, July 23, Aug. 6, 20, Sept. 3, 24, Oct. 1, 8, 15, Nov. 19, Dec. 17, 31, 1909; Feb. 4, 1910; *Times,* July 21, 23, 29, Aug. 7, Sept. 16, 24, 1909; Los Angeles Central Labor Council, *Minutes 1909–1910,* meetings of June 25, Oct. 20, 1909; *American Federationist,* Oct., 1909, p. 88; *Proceedings of the California State Federation of Labor, 1909,* p. 73.

Chapter XX

UPHEAVAL ON THE LABOR FRONT

[1] Harrison Gray Otis, "Los Angeles—A Sketch," *Sunset,* XXIV (Jan., 1910), 14.

[2] *Citizen,* July 2, 9, 30, Aug. 27, Sept. 3, Oct. 1, 8, 1909; Los Angeles Central Labor Council, *Minutes 1909–1910,* meetings of May 26, June 16, 18, 22, 25, July 7, 21, Aug. 4, 18, Sept. 8, 10, 22, 29, 1909.

[3] *Citizen,* July 2, Aug. 20, Oct. 15, 22, 1909; *Times,* Oct. 26, 1909; Los Angeles Central Labor Council, *Minutes 1909–1910,* meetings of July 21, 30, Aug. 13, Oct. 6, 1909.

[4] *Times,* Oct. 16, 17, 20–22, 26, Dec. 28, 1909; Dec. 20, 1910; *Citizen,* Oct. 22, 29, Nov. 19, Dec. 3, 17, 24, 1909; Jan. 7, 14, Feb. 4, 11, 18, 25, 1910; July 21, Aug. 11, 1911; Los Angeles Central Labor Council, *Minutes 1909–1910,* meetings of Oct. 22,

Dec. 6, 27, 1909; *Minutes 1912–1913*, meetings of July 5, Aug. 23, 1912; LATU, *Minutes 1908–1911*, pp. 115–16, 123.

⁵ *Citizen*, Oct. 22, 1909.

⁶ *Ibid.*, May 8, Oct. 9, Nov. 13, 20, Dec. 11, 18, 1908; Feb. 18, Mar. 4, 1910; Sept. 1, 1911; San Francisco *Call*, July 1, 1909; *Times*, Apr. 10, 1910; John R. Commons and Associates, *History of Labor in the United States* (New York: Macmillan, 1921–1935), IV, 367.

⁷ *Citizen*, July 16, Aug. 6, 13, 27, Oct. 1, 8, 15, Dec. 24, 1909; Jan. 7, 21, Feb. 11, 18, 25, Mar. 4, 11, 18, 25, May 13, 20, 27, July 1, 1910; *Final Report and Testimony Submitted to Congress by the Commission on Industrial Relations*, U.S. 64th Cong., 1st sess., S. Doc. 415 (Washington: 1916), VI, 5643.

⁸ *Citizen*, July 9, Aug. 13, Oct. 8, Nov. 19, 26, Dec. 31, 1909; Feb. 25, Apr. 1, May 13, 1910; *Times*, Mar. 13, 20, 27, 30, Apr. 24, May 15, Aug. 19, 1910; *Labor Clarion* (published in San Francisco), June 17, 1910; Los Angeles Central Labor Council, *Minutes 1909–1910*, meetings of Sept. 24, Nov. 26, Dec. 3, 1909; *Proceedings of the California State Federation of Labor, 1909*, pp. 26–7, 29.

⁹ *Citizen*, July 16, Oct. 8, Dec. 17, 1909; Jan. 28, Feb. 18, 25, Mar. 4, May 27, 1910; *Times*, Feb. 23, July 10, 1910; *Proceedings of the State Building Trades Council of California, 1911*, p. 64; Andrew J. Gallagher, "Something Doing in Los Angeles," *International Socialist Review*, XI (Sept., 1910), 166.

¹⁰ *Citizen*, Aug. 6, 1909; Mar. 11, 18, 1910; *Times*, June 21, 1910; *Pacific Outlook*, July 6, 1910, p. 1; *American Federationist*, Sept., 1910, p. 819; *Proceedings of the State Building Trades Council of California, 1911*, p. 64; Ira B. Cross, *A History of the Labor Movement in California* (Berkeley: University of California Press, 1935), p. 282; Frederick Palmer, "Otistown of the Open Shop," *Hampton's Magazine*, XXVI (Jan., 1911), 38–9; Huntington Manuscript 1152, *The United States vs. Frank Ryan et al.*, United States District Court, Indiana, No. 7, p. 1462.

¹¹ *Citizen*, Dec. 24, 1909; Mar. 18, May 20, June 17, Aug. 5, 1910; *Labor Clarion*, Mar. 4, 1910; *Times*, Mar. 22, May 28, July 16, 1910; Los Angeles Central Labor Council, *Minutes 1909–1910*, meeting of Dec. 17, 1909; *Proceedings of the California State Federation of Labor, 1910*, p. 30.

¹² *Citizen*, Mar. 11, Apr. 15, May 20, June 24, July 22, Aug. 5, 19, Sept. 2, 9, 1910; July 21, 1911; *Times*, Mar. 22, July 16, 1910; San Francisco *Call*, June 10, 1910; LATU, *Minutes 1908–1911*, pp. 169–70, 179.

¹³ *Citizen*, Oct. 15, 1909; Jan. 14, Nov. 11, 1910; Jan. 27, Feb. 3, 24, Apr. 7, May 12, July 21, Aug. 4, 1911; *Times*, Feb. 20, Mar. 2, May 1, 8, 1910; *Proceedings of the American Federation of Labor, 1911*, p. 70; *Proceedings of the California State Federation of Labor, 1911*, pp. 58, 67–8, 99; Austin Lewis, "The Drift in California," *Internationalist Socialist Review*, XII (Nov., 1911), 273.

¹⁴ *Citizen*, Apr. 1, 15, Sept. 2, 1910; *Times*, Apr. 7, 1910.

¹⁵ *Citizen*, Mar. 24, Apr. 21, June 2, 9, 16, 30, July 7, Aug. 4, Oct. 20, 1911; LATU, *Minutes 1908–1911*, p. 236; *History, Encyclopedia Reference Book* (Washington: American Federation of Labor, 1919), pp. 300–1.

¹⁶ San Francisco *Call*, Feb. 20, 1910; *Times*, Feb. 27, 1910; *Labor Clarion*, Mar. 4, 1910; *Citizen*, Mar. 4, 11, 18, Apr. 29, 1910; July 14, 1911; Cross, *op. cit.*, pp. 262–7; LATU, *Minutes 1908–1911*, p. 137.

¹⁷ Pauline Jacobson, "The 'M. and M.' and the Struggle of Labor," San Francisco *Bulletin*, Dec. 16, 1911, and "Industrial Freedom Versus Feudalism," San Francisco *Bulletin*, Jan. 27, 1912; *Proceedings of the California State Federation of Labor, 1910*, p. 53.

¹⁸ *Citizen*, May 20, 27, Aug. 5, 1910; *Union Label Bulletin*, July, 1910, p. 2.

¹⁹ *Citizen*, May 27, 1910; *Union Label Bulletin*, July, 1910, p. 2.

²⁰ *Ibid.*

²¹ *Citizen*, May 20, 27, Aug. 5, 1910; Apr. 21, 1911; *Times*, May 24, 1910; *Union Label Bulletin*, July, 1910, p. 2.

[22] *Times,* May 21, 22, 25–27, June 2, 6, 8, Aug. 16, 1910; *Citizen,* May 27, June 10, July 15, 29, Aug. 5, Sept. 23, 1910; San Francisco *Call,* June 14, 1910.

[23] *Citizen,* Oct. 21, 1910; Pauline Jacobson, "Los Angeles and the Piece System," San Francisco *Bulletin,* Dec. 30, 1911; *Final Report and Testimony Submitted to Congress by the Commission on Industrial Relations,* VI, 5548, 5626, 5629.

[24] *Citizen,* Nov. 19, Dec. 3, 1909; Mar. 11, 18, Aug. 5, 1910; *American Federationist,* Sept., 1910, p. 819; Gallagher, *op. cit.,* p. 167.

[25] *Times,* May 26, 1910; *Citizen,* June 3, 1910; *Proceedings of the American Federation of Labor, 1910,* p. 208.

[26] *Citizen,* June 3, 10, 24, Aug. 5, 1910; Sept. 1, 1911; San Francisco *Call,* June 4, 24, 1910; *Times,* June 10, 1910; *Final Report and Testimony Submitted to Congress by the Commission on Industrial Relations,* VI, 5552, 5796–7.

[27] *Times,* May 27, June 3, 9, 22, 28, Aug. 5, 1910; *Citizen,* June 3, 1910; San Francisco *Call,* Aug. 20, 1910.

[28] *Proceedings of the American Federation of Labor, 1910,* p. 208.

[29] *Times,* June 4, 1910; *Labor Clarion,* June 17, 1910; *Citizen,* June 17, 24, 1910; San Francisco *Call,* June 19, July 10, 14, 1910; *Proceedings of the California State Federation of Labor, 1910,* pp. 53–4; Palmer, *op. cit.,* p. 39; *California Labor's Greatest Victory; Final Report of the General Campaign Strike Committee for the Unionizing of Los Angeles, Embracing Receipts and Expenditures June 1, 1910—April 1, 1912* ([San Francisco: 1912]), p. 8.

[30] *Labor Clarion,* July 8, 15, 1910; San Francisco *Call,* July 10, 1910.

[31] San Francisco *Call,* July 10, 1910.

[32] *Times,* June 3, 7, 9, 18, 21, 24, 26, 28, 29, July 1, 1910; *Record,* Dec. 12, 1910.

[33] *Times,* July 2, 6–8, 12, 15–17, 1910; *Citizen,* July 22, 1910; Aug. 23, 1912; *Proceedings of the American Federation of Labor, 1910,* p. 208; Jacobson, "The 'M. and M.' and the Struggle of Labor," San Francisco *Bulletin,* Dec. 16, 1911. The quotation is from the *Times,* July 16, 1910.

[34] *Times,* July 16, 30, 1910; *Proceedings of the American Federation of Labor, 1910,* p. 209.

[35] *Citizen,* July 22, 1910; *Graphic,* July 23, 1910, p. 1; *Pacific Outlook,* July 23, 1910, p. 1; Palmer, *op. cit.,* p. 41.

[36] *Proceedings of the American Federation of Labor, 1910,* p. 208.

[37] LATU, *Minutes 1908–1911,* p. 178.

[38] *California Labor's Greatest Victory; Final Report of the General Campaign Strike Committee for the Unionizing of Los Angeles . . . ,* p. 5.

[39] *Times,* July 20, 21, Aug. 5, 6, 9–11, 13, 14, 23, 25, 31, Sept. 27, 1910; *Citizen,* Aug. 12, 26, Sept. 17, 1910; Marion Dixon, "The History of the Los Angeles Central Labor Council" (unpublished M.A. thesis, University of California, Berkeley, 1929), p. 67.

[40] *Times,* Sept. 29, 1910.

[41] *Ibid.,* Aug. 30, 1910.

[42] *Citizen,* Aug. 5, 26, Sept. 2, 9, 16, 30, 1910; *Labor Clarion,* Aug. 5, 12, 26, Sept. 23, 1910; *Times,* Aug. 24, 31, 1910; San Francisco *Call,* Aug. 28, Sept. 4, 11, 1910; *Organized Labor* (published in San Francisco), Sept. 17, 1910.

[43] *Citizen,* July 8, Sept. 2, 23, 1910; Feb. 3, 1911; *Times,* Sept. 23, 1910.

[44] *Citizen,* Sept. 2, Oct. 7, 1910; *Labor Clarion,* Oct. 28, 1910; *Proceedings of the California State Federation of Labor, 1910,* pp. 73, 75–80.

[45] *Citizen,* Oct. 8, Dec. 3, 1909; Los Angeles Central Labor Council, *Minutes 1909–1910,* meetings of Oct. 8, Nov. 26, 1909.

[46] *Citizen,* June 10, 24, July 1, Aug. 5, 1910; San Francisco *Call,* June 22, July 2, Aug. 2, 1910; *Times,* June 27, 1910; *Labor Clarion,* Oct. 6, 1910.

[47] *Citizen,* July 22, 29, Aug. 5, 12, 19, 26, Sept. 2, 23, 30, 1910.

[48] *Ibid.,* June 17, July 1, 8, 22, Sept. 23, 1910; *Pacific Outlook,* Sept. 3, 1910, p. 4.

[49] *Labor Clarion,* July 29, Aug. 12, 1910; *Citizen,* Aug. 5, 1910; *Times,* Aug. 16, 1910; interview with L. W. Butler, June 19, 1952.

[50] *Proceedings of the State Building Trades Council of California, 1911*, p. 40.

[51] *Times*, June 8, July 22, Oct. 11, 14, 1910; Jan. 22, 1911; *Citizen*, July 22, Aug. 5, Dec. 2, 1910; San Francisco *Examiner*, Nov. 12, 1910; *Express*, Dec. 30, 1910; *American Federationist*, Sept., 1910, p. 189; "Employers at Last Awake," *The Review*, Oct., 1910, pp. 27–8. *The Review* was published by the National Metal Trades Association and the National Founders Association.

[52] *Citizen*, Oct. 14, 21, 28, Dec. 2, 1910; Jan. 6, 27, Mar. 3, 10, 1911; *Times*, Oct. 21, 1910; *Labor Clarion*, Nov. 11, 1910; San Francisco *Call*, Feb. 28, 1911; Los Angeles Central Labor Council, *Minutes 1911–1912*, meetings of Feb. 10, Mar. 3, 1911; *Proceedings of the California State Federation of Labor, 1910*, pp. 6, 12; *Proceedings of the State Building Trades Council of California, 1911*, pp. 25–6, 40, 111–12, 114.

[53] *Citizen*, Nov. 18, Dec. 9, 1910; Feb. 3, 1911; *Labor Clarion*, Nov. 25, 1910; *Graphic*, Dec. 24, 1910, p. 6; *Record*, Feb. 17, 1911; *Times*, Feb. 19, 1911; *American Federationist*, *passim*; Jan., 1911, p. 65; *Proceedings of the American Federation of Labor, 1909*, p. 14; *1910*, pp. 167, 207–10, 233, 256–7; *Proceedings of the California State Federation of Labor, 1909*, p. 16.

[54] *Labor Clarion*, Oct. 6, 1910; *Times*, Oct. 14, Nov. 15, 1910; *Citizen*, Oct. 28, 1910; *Examiner*, Nov. 23, 1910; *Record*, Dec. 12, 31, 1910.

[55] *Times*, Nov. 14, 1910; Jan. 6, 11, 12, 26, Feb. 1, 1911; *Express*, Nov. 15, 1910; *Citizen*, Nov. 18, 25, Dec. 2, 1910; Feb. 3, 17, Mar. 10, June 9, Dec. 24, 1911; *Record*, Dec. 23, 1910; Los Angeles Central Labor Council, *Minutes 1912*, meetings of Mar. 11, Apr. 1, 1912; *Minutes 1912–1913*, meetings of July 19, 22, Aug. 2, 1912; LATU, *Minutes 1908–1911*, p. 219; *Proceedings of the California State Federation of Labor, 1912*, p. 75.

[56] *Times*, July 1, Sept. 8, 1909; Nov. 16, 1910; *Citizen*, Aug. 20, 27, Sept. 3, Oct. 1, 1909; Nov. 18, Dec. 9, 1910; Feb. 3, 17, Aug. 4, 1911; Los Angeles Central Labor Council, *Minutes 1911–1912*, meetings of Dec. 17, 22, 1911; *Minutes 1912–1913*, meeting of Aug. 16, 1912.

[57] *Times*, Dec. 18, 1910; Jan. 17, 1911; *Citizen*, Dec. 23, 1910; Jan. 20, Feb. 3, 1911; Los Angeles Central Labor Council, *Minutes 1911–1912*, meeting of May 12, 1911.

[58] *Record*, Oct. 14, Dec. 29, 30, 1910; *Graphic*, Dec. 24, 1910, p. 6; *Express*, Dec. 29, 1910; *Citizen*, Dec. 30, 1910; *Proceedings of the California State Federation of Labor, 1911*, p. 86; Franklin Hichborn, *Story of the Session of the California Legislature of 1911* (San Francisco: James H. Barry Co., 1911), p. 261.

[59] *Pacific Outlook*, Jan. 22, 1910, p. 5; *Times*, Feb. 16, 1910; *Citizen*, Feb. 25, Mar. 4, Oct. 21, Dec. 9, 1910; Nov. 3, 1911; *Labor Clarion*, Nov. 11, 1910; *Proceedings of the American Federation of Labor, 1910*, p. 210; Carey McWilliams, "The City That Wanted the Truth," *Pacific Spectator*, III (Spring, 1949), 177–81.

[60] *Citizen*, Sept. 2, Oct. 7, 14, 21, 28, Nov. 4, 11, 18, 25, Dec. 9, 16, 23, 30, 1910; *Herald*, Nov. 4, 1910; *International Socialist Review*, Sept., 1910, p. 186.

[61] *Citizen*, Nov. 11, 1910; Jan. 27, Feb. 3, Mar. 24, 31, May 5, 19, June 9, 1911; Los Angeles Central Labor Council, *Minutes 1911–1912*, meetings of Apr. 21, 28, May 12, 1911; *Proceedings of the State Building Trades Council of California, 1911*, pp. 40, 63.

[62] *Times*, Mar. 4, Apr. 8, 9, 14, 25, 1911; *Citizen*, Apr. 14, 21, 1911.

[63] *Times*, May 6, 9–11, 30, 1911; *Citizen*, Aug. 4, 1911.

[64] *Citizen*, Mar. 17, Apr. 28, May 5, 19, June 2, July 21, Aug. 4, 1911; *Labor Clarion*, Mar. 24, 31, 1911; Los Angeles Central Labor Council, *Minutes 1911–1912*, meetings of Apr. 28, Aug. 18, Dec. 15, 1911; Jan. 19, 1912; *Proceedings of the California State Federation of Labor, 1911*, pp. 29, 59; *1912*, p. 76.

[65] *Citizen*, Mar. 3, 31, Apr. 28, May 5, 19, 1911.

[66] Los Angeles Central Labor Council, *Minutes 1911–1912*, meetings of Apr. 14, Aug. 11, 1911; *Times*, Apr. 16, 1911; *Citizen*, Apr. 28, May 5, 1911; *Final Report and Testimony Submitted to Congress by the Commission on Industrial Relations*, VI, 5557; interview with A. J. Mooney, May 27, 1952.

[67] George E. Mowry, *The California Progressives* (Berkeley: University of California Press, 1951), pp. 133–47.

[68] *Proceedings of the California State Federation of Labor, 1910*, pp. 9–11, 18–19, 32; *1911*, p. 92; Hichborn, *op. cit.*, p. 227; Earl C. Crockett, "The History of California Labor Legislation, 1910–1930" (unpublished Ph.D. dissertation, University of California, Berkeley, 1931), p. 3.

[69] Mowry, *op. cit.*, pp. 144–5; Crockett, *op. cit.*, pp. 35, 37, 116, 121–9, 165, 261; Hichborn, *op. cit.*, pp. 143, 235, 237, 247–50, 325, 327, 333; *Proceedings of the California State Federation of Labor, 1910*, p. 9; *1911*, pp. 80–3, 85, 87; *Citizen*, Mar. 31, 1911.

[70] Mowry, *op. cit.*, pp. 139–42, 149–50; Hichborn, *op. cit.*, pp. 93, 95, 102, 123, 331; *Proceedings of the California State Federation of Labor, 1911*, pp. 82–4; *American Federationist*, Sept., 1912, p. 693.

[71] Mowry, *op. cit.*, pp. 145–7; Crockett, *op. cit.*, pp. 234, 273, 290–2, 294; *Proceedings of the California State Federation of Labor, 1911*, pp. 82, 85–6, 89.

[72] Crockett, *op. cit.*, pp. 6–9, 12–14, 16; Hichborn, *op. cit.*, pp. 247–50; Los Angeles Central Labor Council, *Minutes 1911–1912*, meeting of Feb. 20, 1911; *Citizen*, Mar. 3, 24, Apr. 14, 21, 28, 1911; *Times*, Mar. 15, Apr. 14, 16, 1911.

[73] Cross, *op. cit.*, p. 284; *The Forty-Year War for a Free City; A History of the Open Shop in Los Angeles* (Los Angeles: Times-Mirror Publishing Co., 1929), p. 18; San Francisco *Call*, Jan. 20, 1911; *The Carpenter*, XXXI (Mar., 1911), 50.

[74] San Francisco *Call*, May 2, 1911; *Labor Clarion*, June 9, 16, 23, July 14, 1911; *The Carpenter*, XXXI (Aug., 1911), 20–4; XXXI (Nov., 1911), 23–4; Los Angeles Central Labor Council, *Minutes 1911–1912*, meeting of May 12, 1911; *Proceedings of the California State Federation of Labor, 1911*, p. 59; *Final Report and Testimony Submitted to Congress by the Commission on Industrial Relations*, VI, 5631; *Times*, Apr. 30, May 2–4, June 9, July 2, 10, Aug. 20, Sept. 20, 24, 1911; *Citizen*, May 5, 12, 19, 26, June 2, 9, 16, 30, July 14, 28, Sept. 1, 1911; interview with A. J. Mooney, May 27, 1952.

[75] *Times*, May 1–3, 8, 1911; *Citizen*, May 12, June 9, 16, 23, 30, July 7, 1911; Feb. 2, 1912; Los Angeles Central Labor Council, *Minutes 1912*, meetings of Feb. 3, 26, Mar. 15, July 12, 1912; *Proceedings of the California State Federation of Labor, 1911*, p. 59.

[76] *Citizen*, June 23, 30, July 7, 21, Aug. 4, 11, 25, 1911; *Labor Clarion*, July 7, Aug. 4, Sept. 22, Oct. 6, 1911; Los Angeles Central Labor Council, *Minutes 1911–1912*, meetings of June 9, July 7, Sept. 1, 1911.

[77] *Citizen*, May 26, June 23, Aug. 4, Oct. 13, 20, 27, 1911; *Times*, June 11, Aug. 13, 1911; *Labor Clarion*, June 30, 1911; Los Angeles Central Labor Council, *Minutes 1911–1912*, meetings of June 2, 16, 30, July 7, 14, 28, Aug. 4, 11, 18, 25, Sept. 1, 8, 15, 22, 29, Oct. 13, 27, Nov. 3, 17, 24, Dec. 1, 17, 1911.

[78] *Citizen*, June 16, 30, Aug. 11, Sept. 1, Oct. 20, Nov. 3, 1911; *Labor Clarion*, Aug. 4, 1911; *Times*, Aug. 30, 1911.

[79] *Times*, July 4, 1911; *Citizen*, July 14, Sept. 15, 1911; *Labor Clarion*, Sept. 22, 1911; *American Federationist*, Aug., 1911, p. 627; *Proceedings of the California State Federation of Labor, 1911*, p. 68; *Proceedings of the American Federation of Labor, 1911*, p. 129.

[80] *Citizen*, Mar. 24, July 21, Sept. 22, Oct. 13, 27, Nov. 3, 17, 24, Dec. 1, 8, 22, 1911; Feb. 2, 1912; *Times*, Sept. 30, Oct. 26, Nov. 7, 17, 1911; *Labor Clarion*, Oct. 20, Nov. 17, 1911; Los Angeles Central Labor Council, *Minutes 1911–1912*, meetings of Oct. 6, 20, 23, Nov. 3, 17, 24, Dec. 17, 29, 1911; *Minutes 1912*, meetings of Feb. 3, 26, Mar. 15, 1912; *Minutes 1912–1913*, meetings of July 26, Sept. 20, 1912; LATU, *Minutes 1908–1911*, p. 292; *Proceedings of the California State Federation of Labor, 1911*, p. 44; *Reports of Officers to the Fifty-seventh Annual Session of the International Typographical Union at San Francisco, California, August, 1911* ([Indianapolis: 1911]), p. 8.

[81] *Citizen*, Jan. 6, 20, 27, June 9, 1911; Los Angeles Central Labor Council, *Minutes 1911–1912*, meeting of Feb. 3, 1911; *California Labor's Greatest Victory; Final Report of the General Campaign Strike Committee for the Unionizing of Los Angeles . . .*, p. 7.

[82] *Citizen*, Jan. 6, 27, Feb. 3, Mar. 17, 31, Apr. 14, 21, May 12, June 16, 30, 1911; LATU, *Minutes 1911–1916*, p. 234.

[83] *Citizen*, Apr. 14, 28, May 26, June 16, Oct. 7, 13, 1911; *Times*, May 22, Oct. 14, 1911; *Labor Clarion*, July 14, 1911.

[84] *Citizen*, May 12, 26, June 9, 16, 23, July 14, 28, Aug. 4, 11, 18, 25, Sept. 1, 8, 15, 22, 29, Oct. 6, 20, 27, 1911; *Labor Clarion*, Sept. 22, 1911; Los Angeles Central Labor Council, *Minutes 1911–1912*, meeting of Dec. 1, 1911; LATU, *Minutes 1908–1911*, pp. 262–3, 265, 282, 286.

[85] *Citizen*, June 30, July 7, 14, Sept. 15, 29, 1911; *Times*, Oct. 26–28, 31, 1911; Los Angeles Central Labor Council, *Minutes 1911–1912*, meeting of Sept. 25, 1911.

[86] *Times*, Nov. 1, 2, 1911.

[87] *Ibid.*, Nov. 1, 1911.

[88] *Labor Clarion*, Sept. 15, 1911.

Chapter XXI

THE "CRIME OF THE CENTURY"

[1] *Times*, Oct. 1, 2, 1910; Marion Dixon, "The History of the Los Angeles Central Labor Council" (unpublished M.A. thesis, University of California, Berkeley, 1929), p. 79; *Final Report and Testimony Submitted to Congress by the Commission on Industrial Relations*, U.S. 64th Cong., 1st sess., S. Doc. 415 (Washington: 1916), VI, 5521.

[2] *Personal Sketch [of Harrison Gray Otis]* ([Los Angeles: 1913]), p. 4.

[3] *Times*, Nov. 16, 1911.

[4] *Ibid.*

[5] *Times*, Oct. 2, 1910; *Citizen*, Oct. 7, 1910; Mar. 31, Apr. 14, 21, June 9, 16, 1911; *Labor Clarion* (published in San Francisco), Oct. 14, 28, 1910; *Proceedings of the California State Federation of Labor, 1910*, pp. 94, 98; "The Los Angeles Conspiracy Against Organized Labor," *International Socialist Review*, XI (Nov., 1910), 262–4; Louis Adamic, *Dynamite* (New York: Viking, 1931), pp. 209, 212; Christopher P. Connolly, "Protest by Dynamite," *Colliers*, XLVIII (Jan. 13, 1912), 10; *The True History of the Famous McNamara Case*, speeches by Anton Johannsen, Clarence Darrow, and Mother Jones (Kansas City, Mo.: Carpenters Local No. 61 [1915?]), p. 5.

[6] *Common Sense*, Apr. 4, 1908.

[7] Dixon, *op. cit.*, p. 82, from the notes of Charles Feider.

[8] *Times*, Oct. 1, 1910.

[9] *Pacific Outlook*, Dec. 3, 1910, p. 21.

[10] *Times*, Oct. 13, 1910; *Citizen*, May 19, 1911; Adamic, *op. cit.*, p. 212; Dixon, *op. cit.*, p. 82; *Proceedings of the California State Federation of Labor, 1910*, pp. 91, 94, 97–8; Alfred Cohn and Joe Chisholm, *"Take the Witness!"* (New York: Stokes, 1934), p. 195.

[11] "The Los Angeles Conspiracy Against Organized Labor," pp. 264, 266.

[12] Adamic, *op. cit.*, p. 213.

[13] *Pacific Outlook*, Dec. 3, 1910, p. 2.

[14] *Ibid.*, Oct. 8, 1910, p. 2.

[15] Frederick Palmer, "Otistown of the Open Shop," *Hampton's Magazine*, XXVI (Jan., 1911), 31.

[16] *Times*, Oct. 2, 1910.

[17] "The Los Angeles Crime," *Independent*, VII (May 4, 1911), 967.

[18] *Times*, Oct. 2, 6–8, 1910; *Citizen*, Oct. 7, 21, 1910.

[19] *Citizen*, Oct. 7, 1910.

[20] *Times*, Oct. 2, 1910.

[21] *Ibid.*

[22] *Times*, Oct. 2–4, 1910; *Citizen*, Oct. 7, 14, 21, 1910; *Pacific Outlook*, Oct. 8, 1910, p. 7; *Graphic*, Oct. 15, 1910, p. 1; LATU, *Minutes 1908–1911*, p. 206.

[23] San Francisco *Call*, Oct. 2, 1910; *Times*, Oct. 6, 1910; *Citizen*, Oct. 7, 1910; *Labor Clarion*, Oct. 7, 1910; *Proceedings of the California State Federation of Labor, 1910*, pp. 9, 91, 96; *Mr. Otis and the Los Angeles "Times"* (Los Angeles: Typographical Union No. 174, 1915), p. 23.

[24] *California Labor Notes: Unions and Protective Associations*, letter from Frank Roney to Ira B. Cross, Oct. 9, 1910.

[25] *Times*, Oct. 2, 1910.

[26] Samuel Gompers, "The McNamara Case," *American Federationist*, XVIII (June, 1911), 435.

[27] *Ibid.*, p. 436.

[28] *Times*, Oct. 4, 6, 1910. The quotation is from the issue of October 6, 1910.

[29] *Times*, Oct. 13, 1910; *Citizen*, Oct. 21, 1910; Adamic, *op. cit.*, p. 212; *Reports of Officers to the Fifty-seventh Annual Session of the International Typographical Union at San Francisco, California, August, 1911* ([Indianapolis: 1911]), p. 101.

[30] *Reports of Officers to the Fifty-seventh Annual Session of the International Typographical Union . . .*, pp. 22, 23.

[31] *Graphic*, Oct. 15, 1910, p. 1.

[32] *Times*, Oct. 2, 1910; *Pacific Outlook*, Oct. 8, 1910, p. 1; *Graphic*, Oct. 15, 1910, p. 1.

[33] *Times*, Oct. 1, 2, 1910; *Citizen*, Oct. 7, 14, 28, 1910; *Graphic*, Oct. 15, 1910, p. 1; LATU, *Minutes 1908–1911*, pp. 197–9, 201; *Mr. Otis and the Los Angeles "Times,"* p. 22; Dixon, *op. cit.*, pp. 82, 88.

[34] *Times*, Oct. 4, 1910.

[35] *Ibid.*, Oct. 6, 12, 14, 15, 21, Dec. 20, 1910; *Citizen*, Oct. 14, 21, 1910; *Pacific Outlook*, Oct. 22, 1910, p. 3; *Graphic*, Dec. 10, 1910, p. 5; Dec. 31, 1910, p. 6; Pauline Jacobson, "Otis: 'Jehovah of Industrial Freedom,'" San Francisco *Bulletin*, Dec. 9, 1911.

[36] Dixon, *op. cit.*, p. 81, from the notes of Joseph Phillis.

[37] *Times*, Oct. 9, 1910.

[38] *Citizen*, Sept. 16, 1910; *Mr. Otis and the Los Angeles "Times,"* p. 23; *Proceedings of the California State Federation of Labor, 1910*, p. 8; Adamic, *op. cit.*, pp. 208–9; Charles Yale Harrison, *Clarence Darrow* (New York: Cape & Smith [c. 1931]), pp. 148–9.

[39] *Times*, Sept. 2, 3, 1910; Dixon, *op. cit.*, p. 66.

[40] *Times*, Oct. 3, 1910.

[41] *Ibid.*, Sept. 10, 11, 13, 14, Oct. 11, 29, Nov. 3, 1910; *Citizen*, Sept. 16, 1910; *Record*, Nov. 3, 1910.

[42] *Times*, May 23, 24, 30, June 7, 22, July 4, 22, 27, Aug. 2, 3, 13, 15, Dec. 9, 1911; Jan. 5, 6, 9–13, 16–18, 20, 24, 25, 27, 31, Feb. 1, 3, 4, 6, 15, 16, 20, 27, Apr. 2, 9, 1912; *Citizen*, June 9, 16, July 7, Aug. 4, 1911; Feb. 2, 9, 16, 23, Mar. 1, Apr. 5, 19, 1912; *Labor Clarion*, June 9, July 28, 1911; Mar. 1, 1912; LATU, *Minutes 1911–1916*, p. 31; Los Angeles Central Labor Council, *Minutes 1912*, meeting of May 24, 1912; interview with L. W. Butler, June 19, 1952.

[43] *Times*, Oct. 3, 1910.

[44] *Ibid.*, Oct. 2–4, 1910.

[45] *Ibid.*, Oct. 2, 1910.

[46] *Citizen*, Oct. 7, 1910.

[47] *Times*, Oct. 2, 4, 5, 11, 1910; Adamic, *op. cit.*, p. 213.

[48] *Times*, Sept. 28–30, Oct. 2, 4, 7–9, 20, Nov. 15, 17, 19, 20, Dec. 14–16, 1910; Feb. 2, 8, Apr. 11, May 5, June 16, July 8, 1911; *Citizen*, Oct. 7, 21, 1910; Feb. 10, Aug. 4, Sept. 15, 1911; Los Angeles Central Labor Council, *Minutes 1911–1912*, meeting of Sept. 22, 1911.

[49] *Herald*, Dec. 25, 27, 1910; *Times*, Dec. 26–28, 1910; *Citizen*, Dec. 30, 1910.

[50] *Graphic*, Dec. 31, 1910, p. 6.

[51] *Times*, Oct. 1, 1910.

[52] *Ibid.*, Oct. 1–3, 8, 9, 1910; *Citizen*, Oct. 14, 1910.

⁵³ *Times,* Oct. 9, 1910.

⁵⁴ *Ibid.,* Oct. 5, 13, 1910; *Citizen,* Mar. 17, 1911.

⁵⁵ *Times,* Oct. 5, 1910; *Proceedings of the California State Federation of Labor, 1910,* pp. 9, 36–7, 91–4, 98.

⁵⁶ *Times,* Oct. 2–4, 6, 1910; San Francisco *Call,* Oct. 2, 1910.

⁵⁷ *Times,* Oct. 3, 6, 1910; John R. Commons and Associates, *History of Labor in the United States* (New York: Macmillan, 1921–1935), IV, 320–1; Cohn and Chisholm, *op. cit.,* pp. 195–7; William J. Burns, *The Masked War* (New York: George H. Doran Co., 1913), pp. 44, 46–9, 51–3.

⁵⁸ *Times,* Oct. 4, 6, 8, 1910; Burns, *op. cit.,* pp. 49, 54. The quotation is from page 54.

⁵⁹ *Times,* Oct. 10, 1910; Burns, *op. cit.,* pp. 46, 49; "How Burns Caught the Dynamiters," *McClure's Magazine,* XXXVIII (Jan., 1912), 326.

⁶⁰ Commons and Associates, *op. cit.,* IV, 318–19; Lewis L. Lorwin, *The American Federation of Labor* (Washington: The Brookings Institution, 1933), p. 80; *The National Erectors' Association and the International Association of Bridge and Structural Ironworkers,* by Luke Grant, U.S. Commission on Industrial Relations (Washington: 1915), pp. 6, 8–11, 20–3; Walter V. Woehlke, "Terrorism in America," *Outlook,* 100 (Feb. 17, 1912), 361.

⁶¹ Commons and Associates, *op. cit.,* IV, 319; Lorwin, *op. cit.,* p. 79; *The National Erectors' Association and the International Association of Bridge and Structural Ironworkers,* by Luke Grant, pp. 12–13, 36–7, 40; Clarence E. Bonnett, *Employers' Associations in the United States* (New York: Macmillan, 1922), pp. 137–41; "The Common Welfare," *Survey,* XXVII (Dec. 30, 1911), 1407–8, 1410.

⁶² Commons and Associates, *op. cit.,* IV, 319–20; Samuel Gompers, *Seventy Years of Life and Labor* (new ed.; New York: Dutton [c. 1925]), II, 183; Lorwin, *op. cit.,* pp. 79, 102; Adamic, *op. cit.,* pp. 191, 195–7; Bonnett, *op. cit.,* pp. 141, 143; "The Common Welfare," p. 1409; Woehlke, *op. cit.,* pp. 361–2; *Times,* Apr. 27, 1911; "Review of the World," *Current Literature,* 50 (June, 1911), 569.

⁶³ Adamic, *op. cit.,* p. 197; Bonnett, *op. cit.,* p. 143; Woehlke, *op. cit.,* p. 363.

⁶⁴ Burns, *op. cit.,* pp. 19–21.

⁶⁵ *Ibid.,* pp. 21–30.

⁶⁶ *Ibid.,* pp. 132–3; *The National Erectors' Association and the International Association of Bridge and Structural Ironworkers,* by Luke Grant, pp. 105–6; "Progress of the Dynamite Trial," *Literary Digest,* 45 (Dec. 14, 1912), 1112.

⁶⁷ Burns, *op. cit.,* pp. 11, 45, 49, 54–64; Cohn and Chisholm, *op. cit.,* p. 196; Clarence Darrow, *The Story of My Life* (New York: Scribner's, 1932), p. 173; *Times,* Oct. 3–13, 17–20, 22–25, 28, 1910; *Citizen,* Oct. 7, 1910; *Herald,* Jan. 6, 1911.

⁶⁸ Burns, *op. cit.,* pp. 63–4; *Times,* Oct. 11, 20, 23, 24, 26, 1910.

⁶⁹ *Times,* Oct. 20, 1910.

⁷⁰ *Ibid.,* Oct. 25–29, 1910; Jan. 6, 8, Oct. 14, 1911; *Record,* Nov. 4, 11, 1910; *Citizen,* Dec. 23, 1910; *Herald,* Jan. 6, 1911.

⁷¹ *Citizen,* Feb. 17, 1911.

⁷² Burns, *op. cit.,* pp. 64–5.

⁷³ *Ibid.,* pp. 67–81, 92; *Times,* Nov. 26, 1910; Harvey J. O'Higgins, "The Dynamiters, a Great Case of Detective William J. Burns," *McClure's Magazine,* XXXVII (Aug., 1911), 357.

⁷⁴ Burns, *op. cit.,* pp. 96–7.

⁷⁵ *Ibid.,* pp. 98–113; O'Higgins, *op. cit.,* p. 358.

⁷⁶ Burns, *op. cit.,* pp. 110–27.

⁷⁷ *Ibid.,* pp. 124, 129–36; O'Higgins, *op. cit.,* p. 360.

⁷⁸ Burns, *op. cit.,* pp. 137–41; O'Higgins, *op. cit.,* pp. 360–1; "How Burns Caught the Dynamiters," p. 328; "Burns' Story on the Trail of the Men Higher Up," *McClure's Magazine,* XXXVIII (Feb., 1912), 363–4; *Times,* Apr. 23, 1911; Ortie E. McManigal, *The National Dynamite Plot* (Los Angeles: The Neale Co., 1913), pp. 87–8.

⁷⁹ *Times,* Apr. 23, 24, 1911; Burns, *op. cit.,* pp. 143, 148, 153–5; McManigal, *op. cit.,*

pp. 12–25, 34, 38, 40–53, 58, 61–70, 89; "How Burns Caught the Dynamiters," p. 328; "Burns' Story on the Trail of the Men Higher Up," pp. 364–6; Cohn and Chisholm, *op. cit.*, p. 197.

[80] *Times*, Apr. 24, 26, 1911; McManigal, *op. cit.*, pp. 75–8.

[81] McManigal, *op. cit.*, pp. 79–81.

[82] *Ibid.*, pp. 89–90; Commons and Associates, *op. cit.*, IV, 321; O'Higgins, *op. cit.*, pp. 361–2; "Burns' Story on the Trail of the Men Higher Up," p. 365; *Times*, Apr. 23, 24, 1911.

[83] Burns, *op. cit.*, pp. 147, 315; Commons and Associates, *op. cit.*, IV, 321; Gompers, *Seventy Years of Life and Labor*, II, 185; Adamic, *op. cit.*, p. 215; "Burns' Story on the Trail of the Men Higher Up," p. 366; "Review of the World," pp. 573–4; "The Dynamiters," *Independent*, LXX (May 4, 1911), 923; "A Charge of Wholesale Murder," *Outlook*, 98 (May 6, 1911), 1–2; O'Higgins, *op. cit.*, pp. 361–2, 364; *Reports of Officers to the Fifty-seventh Annual Session of the International Typographical Union . . .*, pp. 33–4; *Times*, Apr. 24–27, 1911; *Citizen*, Apr. 28, May 5, 19, June 9, 23, 30, 1911.

[84] Burns, *op. cit.*, pp. 211, 215–16; McManigal, *op. cit.*, p. 90; "Burns' Story on the Trail of the Men Higher Up," pp. 365–6; *Times*, Apr. 23–25, 1911.

[85] *Times*, Apr. 24, 1911; *California Outlook*, Apr. 29, 1911, p. 2.

[86] Burns, *op. cit.*, pp. 315–16; *Citizen*, July 14, Aug. 25, 1911; *Times*, Aug. 15, 18, 1911; *Graphic*, Sept. 2, 1911, p. 6.

[87] "Burns' Story on the Trail of the Men Higher Up," pp. 365–6; *Times*, May 3, 1911; *Graphic*, Nov. 18, 1911, p. 3.

[88] Burns, *op. cit.*, pp. 211, 216, 260–1, 272–3, 276–7, 281, 284, 286–7, 291, 296; "Burns' Story on the Trail of the Men Higher Up," pp. 368–9; *Proceedings of the American Federation of Labor, 1911*, p. 315; *1912*, pp. 148–9; *Citizen*, May 5, Sept. 22, 1911; *Graphic*, May 6, 1911, p. 7; *Times*, June 18, 1911.

[89] Interview with Matthew Schmidt, Aug. 11, 1952.

[90] *Proceedings of the American Federation of Labor, 1911*, pp. 315–16; O'Higgins, *op. cit.*, p. 363; *Times*, Apr. 24, 1911; *Citizen*, Apr. 28, May 26, 1911; interview with L. W. Butler, June 19, 1952.

[91] Darrow, *op. cit.*, pp. 173–5; "The Dynamiters," p. 923; Gompers, "The McNamara Case," p. 438; "Burns' Story on the Trail of the Men Higher Up," p. 366; *Times*, Apr. 25, 27, 1911.

[92] *Times*, Apr. 26, 28, 30, May 2, 3, 5, 6, 1911; *Graphic*, Apr. 29, 1911, p. 6.

[93] Commons and Associates, *op. cit.*, IV, 321–2; Gompers, *Seventy Years of Life and Labor*, II, 185–6; Lorwin, *op. cit.*, p. 103; Gompers, "The McNamara Case," pp. 438–9; *American Federationist*, June, 1911, pp. 451–2; *Proceedings of the American Federation of Labor, 1911*, p. 72; *Citizen*, May 5, 1911.

[94] Harrison, *op. cit.*, p. 156.

[95] *Ibid.*, p. 156; Darrow, *op. cit.*, pp. 173, 175–6; *Times*, May 25, 27, 28, 1911; *Citizen*, June 2, Sept. 1, Oct. 13, 1911; *Graphic*, June 3, 1911, p. 6.

[96] Commons and Associates, *op. cit.*, IV, 322; Gompers, *Seventy Years of Life and Labor*, II, 186; *American Federationist*, July, 1911, pp. 537–8; Aug., 1911, pp. 622, 715; *Proceedings of the American Federation of Labor, 1911*, pp. 72, 75; *Proceedings of the American Federation of Musicians, 1911*, p. 43; *Times*, Apr. 27, 29, May 1, 16, 1911; *Citizen*, June 9, 1911; Los Angeles Central Labor Council, *Minutes 1911–1912*, meetings of May 15, June 23, 1911; interview with C. L. Bagley, June 30, 1949.

[97] Adamic, *op. cit.*, p. 221; *Citizen*, June 30, July 7, 14, 1911; *Times*, July 7–9, 14, 15, 1911.

[98] Los Angeles Central Labor Council, *Minutes 1911–1912*, meeting of Aug. 11, 1911; LATU, *Minutes 1908–1911*, pp. 270, 282; *Citizen*, Aug. 4, 25, Sept. 8, Oct. 6, 1911; *Labor Clarion*, Sept. 8, 1911; *Graphic*, Sept. 9, 1911, p. 6.

[99] Dixon, *op. cit.*, p. 85, from a letter written by J. W. Buzzell.

[100] Adamic, *op. cit.*, p. 223; Gompers, *Seventy Years of Life and Labor*, II, 187–8; *Proceedings of the California State Federation of Labor, 1911*, pp. 14–15, 30–1; Los Angeles Central Labor Council, *Minutes 1911–1912*, meeting of Oct. 6, 1911; LATU, *Minutes 1908–1911*, p. 292; *Times*, Aug. 17, Sept. 11, 12, 1911; *Citizen*, Sept. 15, 22, 29, Oct. 6, 20, 27, Nov. 3, 10, 24, 1911; *Labor Clarion*, Sept. 29, Oct. 27, Nov. 17, 24, 1911.

[101] Darrow, *op. cit.*, pp. 177, 179; Harrison, *op. cit.*, pp. 156–7; Lincoln Steffens, *The Autobiography of Lincoln Steffens* (New York: Harcourt, Brace [c. 1931]), p. 666; *Times*, Oct. 8, 1911.

[102] Darrow, *op. cit.*, p. 177; *Graphic*, May 6, 1911, p. 7; *Labor Clarion*, Oct. 20, 1911; "Trial by Jury on Trial," *Outlook*, 99 (Dec. 2, 1911), 794–5.

[103] *Times*, Sept. 30, Oct. 10, Nov. 17, 1911; *Labor Clarion*, Oct. 20, 1911.

[104] *Times*, Oct. 12, 1911; *Citizen*, Oct. 13, 1911.

[105] *Times*, Oct. 12, 13, Nov. 16, 25, 1911; "Trial by Jury on Trial," p. 795.

[106] Commons and Associates, *op. cit.*, IV, 322; Adamic, *op. cit.*, p. 223; *Times*, Oct. 17, 19, 25–27, Nov. 2, 8, 9, 16, 18, 19, 22–25, 28–30, 1911; *Citizen*, Oct. 20, 27, Nov. 3, 24, 1911; *Labor Clarion*, Nov. 3, 1911.

[107] Adamic, *op. cit.*, p. 228; *Proceedings of the American Federation of Labor, 1911*, pp. 18, 296–7, 315–16; *Times*, Nov. 5, 10, 17, 1911.

[108] Adamic, *op. cit.*, pp. 220–1, 223, 225–7; Darrow, *op. cit.*, p. 184; Harrison, *op. cit.*, p. 159; Steffens, *op. cit.*, p. 666; *Citizen*, Dec. 1, 1911; *Labor Clarion*, Dec. 1, 1911.

[109] Adamic, *op. cit.*, p. 225; *Citizen*, Sept. 29, 1911; *Times*, Oct. 11, Nov. 3–9, 12, 16–19, 25, 27–29, 1911; *California Outlook*, Nov. 10, 1911, pp. 2, 7–8; *Graphic*, Nov. 18, 1911, p. 2; Nov. 25, 1911, p. 1; Peter Clark Macfarlane, "What Is the Matter with Los Angeles?" *Colliers*, XLVIII (Dec. 2, 1911), 30–1.

[110] Adamic, *op. cit.*, p. 220; Macfarlane, *op. cit.*, p. 30; *Times*, Nov. 3, 8, 14, 16, 18, 19, 22, 29, Dec. 2, 5, 1911; *Citizen*, Nov. 17, Dec. 1, 1911.

[111] Steffens, *op. cit.*, p. 666; Macfarlane, *op. cit.*, p. 31; *Times*, Nov. 10, 11, Dec. 4, 5, 1911; *Graphic*, Nov. 11, 1911, p. 6; *Citizen*, Dec. 1, 1911; *California Outlook*, Dec. 2, 1911, p. 2; interview with Frank E. Wolfe, Feb. 15, 1952; interview with L. W. Butler, June 19, 1952.

[112] *Times*, Nov. 29, 30, 1911.

[113] Adamic, *op. cit.*, p. 227; Cohn and Chisholm, *op. cit.*, p. 204; Darrow, *op. cit.*, p. 183; Harrison, *op. cit.*, p. 167; *Graphic*, Dec. 2, 1911, p. 5.

[114] Steffens, *op. cit.*, p. 684; *Times*, Dec. 2, 1911.

[115] Adamic, *op. cit.*, pp. 230–1, 233; Steffens, *op. cit.*, pp. 685–6; *Citizen*, Dec. 1, 1911; *Times*, Dec. 2, 1911.

[116] Harrison, *op. cit.*, pp. 159–60; Steffens, *op. cit.*, pp. 658–64; *Citizen*, Nov. 17, 1911.

[117] Adamic, *op. cit.*, p. 227; Darrow, *op. cit.*, p. 179; Harrison, *op. cit.*, pp. 156–7; Steffens, *op. cit.*, pp. 664, 666; *Times*, Jan. 31, 1912; "Burns' Story on the Trail of the Men Higher Up," p. 368.

[118] Commons and Associates, *op. cit.*, IV, 322; Darrow, *op. cit.*, p. 181; Harrison, *op. cit.*, pp. 161–2; Steffens, *op. cit.*, pp. 666–72, 676.

[119] Cohn and Chisholm, *op. cit.*, p. 204; Darrow, *op. cit.*, pp. 181–3; Harrison, *op. cit.*, pp. 163–6; Steffens, *op. cit.*, pp. 672–80.

[120] Commons and Associates, *op. cit.*, IV, 323; Darrow, *op. cit.*, pp. 182–3; Harrison, *op. cit.*, p. 168; Steffens, *op. cit.*, p. 680.

[121] Cohn and Chisholm, *op. cit.*, pp. 203–4; Darrow, *op. cit.*, p. 183; Harrison, *op. cit.*, pp. 167–70; Steffens, *op. cit.*, pp. 679–84.

[122] Steffens, *op. cit.*, pp. 686–7; *Times*, Dec. 2. 1911.

[123] Steffens, *op. cit.*, p. 688.

[124] *Ibid.*, pp. 688, 690; *Times*, Dec. 6, 1911; *Citizen*, Dec. 8, 1911.

[125] *Times*, Dec. 10, 11, 1911.

Chapter XXII

REACTIONS AND AFTERMATH

[1] Clarence Darrow, *The Story of My Life* (New York: Scribner's, 1932), p. 185; Lincoln Steffens, *The Autobiography of Lincoln Steffens* (New York: Harcourt, Brace [c. 1931]), pp. 685, 690; Louis Adamic, *Dynamite* (New York: Viking, 1931), pp. 233, 241; Walter V. Woehlke, "The End of the Dynamite Case—'Guilty,'" *Outlook*, 99 (Dec. 16, 1911), 903.

[2] Adamic, *op. cit.*, p. 233; Alfred Cohn and Joe Chisholm, *"Take the Witness!"* (New York: Stokes, 1934), pp. 201–3, 205; Steffens, *op. cit.*, p. 690; Marion Dixon, "The History of the Los Angeles Central Labor Council" (unpublished M.A. thesis, University of California, Berkeley, 1929), p. 87; Christopher P. Connolly, "The Saving of Clarence Darrow," *Colliers*, XLVIII (Dec. 23, 1911), 10; *Times*, Dec. 2, 1911; *Graphic*, Dec. 9, 1911, p. 1.

[3] Interview with L. W. Butler, June 19, 1952.

[4] Darrow, *op. cit.*, p. 184; Steffens, *op. cit.*, p. 690; Dixon, *op. cit.*, p. 87, from the notes of Joseph Phillis; *Times*, Dec. 2, 5–7, 17, 1911; Jan. 5, 1912; *Labor Clarion* (published in San Francisco), Dec. 8, 22, 1911; *Citizen*, Dec. 15, 1911; interview with Frank E. Wolfe, Feb. 15, 1952; interview with L. W. Butler, June 19, 1952.

[5] Adamic, *op. cit.*, p. 233; Cohn and Chisholm, *op. cit.*, pp. 201–3; Charles Yale Harrison, *Clarence Darrow* (New York: Cape & Smith [c. 1931]), pp. 164, 167; Steffens, *op. cit.*, p. 690; Connolly, *op. cit.*, pp. 9–10; *Times*, Dec. 2, 1911; *Graphic*, Dec. 9, 1911, p. 1.

[6] *Times*, Dec. 2, 1911.

[7] *Ibid.*

[8] *California Outlook*, Dec. 9, 1911, p. 3.

[9] Steffens, *op. cit.*, pp. 690, 841; LATU, *Minutes 1911–1916*, p. 7; Los Angeles Central Labor Council, *Minutes 1911–1912*, meetings of Dec. 4, 29, 1911; *California Outlook*, Dec. 9, 1911, p. 13; *Citizen*, Dec. 22, 1911; Jan. 5, Feb. 9, 16, 1912.

[10] Harrison, *op. cit.*, p. 177; *Times*, Nov. 9, Dec. 12–14, 20, 28, 1911; Jan. 3, 4, 11, 14, 18, 31, Feb. 28, Mar. 2, 1912; *Graphic*, Dec. 30, 1911, p. 7.

[11] Cohn and Chisholm, *op. cit.*, pp. 206, 209–12; Darrow, *op. cit.*, pp. 186–8; Harrison, *op. cit.*, pp. 174–5, 177; Steffens, *op. cit.*, p. 700; *Times*, Jan. 30, 31, Feb. 2, 4, Mar. 2, 1912; *Graphic*, Feb. 6, 1912, p. 1; Feb. 27, 1912, p. 1.

[12] Cohn and Chisholm, *op. cit.*, pp. 212–15; Darrow, *op. cit.*, p. 188; *Times*, Mar. 10, May 15, 16, 23, 28, 29, June 1, 4, 1912; *Citizen*, May 17, July 12, Aug. 2, 16, 1912.

[13] Cohn and Chisholm, *op. cit.*, p. 223.

[14] *Ibid.*, p. 222; Harrison, *op. cit.*, pp. 178–81; Steffens, *op. cit.*, pp. 698, 700–1; *Graphic*, Aug. 24, 1912, p. 1; "The Darrow Acquittal," *Literary Digest*, 45 (Aug. 31, 1912), 323; Clarence Darrow, *The Plea of Clarence Darrow in His Own Defense to the Jury at Los Angeles, August, 1912* (Los Angeles: Golden Press, 1912), *passim*.

[15] Cohn and Chisholm, *op. cit.*, p. 223; Darrow, *The Story of My Life*, pp. 188–9; Harrison, *op. cit.*, pp. 195–8; *Citizen*, Aug. 23, Oct. 18, 25, Nov. 22, 1912; *Graphic*, Aug. 24, 1912, p. 1; Sept. 28, 1912, p. 6; Dec. 28, 1912, p. 3; Los Angeles Central Labor Council, *Minutes 1912–1913*, meeting of Sept. 27, 1912.

[16] Adamic, *op. cit.*, pp. 244–5; *Times*, Dec. 6–10, 13, 21, 26, 31, 1911; Jan. 7, 13, 28, 1912; *Citizen*, Dec. 22, 29, 1911; Apr. 5, 1912.

[17] *Times*, Dec. 26, 1911; Jan. 2, 1912; *Citizen*, Feb. 16, 1912; John A. Fitch, "The Dynamite Case," *Survey*, XXIX (Feb. 1, 1913), 607–8.

[18] John R. Commons and Associates, *History of Labor in the United States* (New York: Macmillan, 1921–1935), IV, 324; Ira B. Cross, *A History of the Labor Movement in California* (Berkeley: University of California Press, 1935), p. 284; *Graphic*, Sept. 28, 1912, p. 7; Oct. 12, 1912, p. 2; Oct. 26, 1912, p. 6; Dec. 28, 1912, p. 3; Jan. 4, 1913, p. 2; *Citizen*, Oct. 4, 1912; "The Dynamite 'Plot' Case," *Literary Digest*, 45

(Nov. 2, 1912), 774; "Progress of the Dynamite Trial," *Literary Digest,* 45 (Dec. 14, 1912), 1112–13; "The Dynamite Cases End in Conviction," *Survey,* XXIX (Jan. 4, 1913), 414; Fitch, *op. cit.,* pp. 609–10, 613–14; Huntington Manuscript 1152, *The United States vs. Frank Ryan et al.,* United States District Court, Indiana, *passim.*

[19] Samuel Gompers, *Seventy Years of Life and Labor* (New York: Dutton [c. 1925]), II, 192; *American Federationist,* Mar., 1912, p. 207.

[20] Fitch, *op. cit.,* pp. 615–17; "Government by Dynamite," *Outlook,* 103 (Jan. 11, 1913), 62; Samuel Gompers, "A. F. of L. and Iron Workers," *Survey,* XXIX (Feb. 1, 1913), 622–3; "Labor Comment on the Dynamite Conviction," *Literary Digest,* 46 (Jan. 18, 1913), 117. The quotation is from the last of these sources.

[21] Commons and Associates, *op. cit.,* IV, 324.

[22] Cohn and Chisholm, *op. cit.,* pp. 224–5; Darrow, *The Story of My Life,* pp. 189–91; Harrison, *op. cit.,* pp. 200–1; *Labor Clarion,* Dec. 26, 1913.

[23] Steffens, *op. cit.,* p. 696; "The Last of the Dynamite Suspects Arrested," *Survey,* XXXIII (Feb. 27, 1915), 570; interview with Matthew Schmidt, Aug. 11, 1952.

[24] Interviews with Matthew Schmidt, Jan. 23, 1950; Aug. 11, 1952.

[25] *Labor Clarion,* July 16, Aug. 27, Oct. 1, 8, Dec. 3, 17, 24, 31, 1915; Mar. 24, 1916; *Western Comrade,* Mar., 1917, p. 31; *The True History of the Famous McNamara Case* (Kansas City, Mo.: Carpenters Local No. 61 [1915?]), p. 14; interview with Matthew Schmidt, Aug. 11, 1952.

[26] Matthew A. Schmidt, *"The Fight for Light and Freedom," an Address of M. A. Schmidt before the Court at Los Angeles, January 12, 1916* (n.p. [1916]), *passim.*

[27] *Labor Clarion,* Jan. 7, 1916; *Citizen,* Sept. 1, 1939; interview with Matthew Schmidt, Jan. 23, 1950.

[28] *Times,* Oct. 29, 1916; *Citizen,* Nov. 3, 17, Dec. 8, 15, 22, 29, 1916; Jan. 12, 1917; interview with Matthew Schmidt, Jan. 23, 1950.

[29] Cross, *op. cit.,* p. 283; *Final Report and Testimony Submitted to Congress by the Commission on Industrial Relations,* U.S. 64th Cong., 1st sess., S. Doc. 415 (Washington: 1916), VI, 5732; *Times,* Dec. 2, 24, 1911; Jan. 2, 1912; Feb. 4, 1913; *Graphic,* Oct. 26, 1912, p. 6; *Citizen,* Nov. 17, 1916; *Western Comrade,* Mar., 1917, p. 31; interview with Matthew Schmidt, Aug. 11, 1952.

[30] *Times,* Dec. 2, 5–9, 1911; *Labor Clarion,* Dec. 15, 1911; *American Federationist,* Jan., 1912, pp. 17–23; Mar., 1912, pp. 230, 250; July, 1912, p. 571; *Proceedings of the American Federation of Labor, 1912,* p. 141; Adamic, *op. cit.,* pp. 236–8; Commons and Associates, *op. cit.,* IV, 323; Gompers, *Seventy Years of Life and Labor,* II, 188.

[31] *Times,* Dec. 2, 3, 5, 9, 1911; *Labor Clarion,* Dec. 22, 29, 1911; *Citizen,* Dec. 29, 1911; Los Angeles Central Labor Council, *Minutes 1911–1912,* meeting of Dec. 1, 1911; LATU, *Minutes 1911–1916,* p. 6; *Proceedings of the California State Federation of Labor, 1912,* p. 96.

[32] Commons and Associates, *op. cit.,* IV, 323; *American Federationist,* Jan., 1912, pp. 22–3; *Proceedings of the American Federation of Labor, 1912,* pp. 141–2; "Gompers Speaks for Labor," *McClure's Magazine,* XXXVIII (Feb., 1912), 371, 375.

[33] Quoted in the *Times,* Dec. 13, 1911.

[34] *Times,* Dec. 2, 1911.

[35] Commons and Associates, *op. cit.,* II, 528; Woehlke, *op. cit.,* p. 903; Paul U. Kellogg, "Conservation and Industrial War," *Survey,* XXVII (Dec. 30, 1911), 1412.

[36] Eugene V. Debs, "The McNamara Case and the Labor Movement," *International Socialist Review,* XII (Jan., 1912), 397–401.

[37] "Larger Bearings of the McNamara Case," *Survey,* XXVII (Dec. 30, 1911), 1428.

[38] *Ibid.,* p. 1419.

[39] Clarence Darrow, "Second Plea of Clarence Darrow in His Own Defense at Los Angeles (in the Bain Case), March, 1913," *Everyman,* IX (May, 1913), 9.

[40] *Proceedings of the American Federation of Labor, 1912,* p. 155; *Graphic,* Aug. 24, 1912, p. 7; "The Common Welfare," *Survey,* XXVII (Dec. 30, 1911), 1407; "Petition

to the President for a Federal Commission on Industrial Relations," *Survey*, XXVII (Dec. 30, 1911), 1431; "Sense and Hysteria on the McNamara Affair," *Nation*, 94 (Jan. 11, 1912), 28; John A. Fitch, "Los Angeles, A Militant Anti-Union Citadel," *Survey*, XXXIII (Oct. 3, 1914), 5.

[41] Commons and Associates, *op. cit.*, IV, 164; Foster Rhea Dulles, *Labor in America* (New York: Crowell [c. 1949]), p. 224.

[42] Commons and Associates, *op. cit.*, IV, 325.

Chapter XXIII

LOS ANGELES: CITY OF THE OPEN SHOP

[1] *Labor Clarion* (published in San Francisco), Jan. 5, 1912; interview with A. J. Mooney, May 27, 1952.

[2] *California Labor's Greatest Victory; Final Report of the General Campaign Strike Committee for the Unionizing of Los Angeles, Embracing Receipts and Expenditures June 1, 1910–April 1, 1912* ([San Francisco: 1912]), pp. 3, 12, 32–3, 38.

[3] *Ibid.*, p. 6.

[4] *Citizen*, Mar. 1, 1912; LATU, *Minutes 1911–1916*, p. 24; Los Angeles Central Labor Council, *Minutes 1912*, meeting of Feb. 16, 1912; *Proceedings of the California State Federation of Labor, 1913*, pp. 74–5; *Final Report and Testimony Submitted to Congress by the Commission on Industrial Relations*, U.S. 64th Cong., 1st sess., S. Doc. 415 (Washington: 1916), VI, 5587, 5645.

[5] *Proceedings of the American Federation of Labor, 1912*, p. 20; interview with L. W. Butler, June 19, 1952.

[6] *Graphic*, Mar. 2, 1912, p. 6; *Times*, Mar. 5, 1912; *Citizen*, Apr. 5, 12, May 24, 1912; Mar. 12, 1937; Los Angeles Central Labor Council, *Minutes 1912*, meetings of Apr. 12, 19, May 24, June 7, 1912; *Minutes 1912–1913*, meetings of July 5, Aug. 2, Sept. 27, Dec. 6, 1912; *Proceedings of the American Federation of Labor, 1912*, p. 20; *Proceedings of the California State Federation of Labor, 1913*, pp. 57–8, 75; *Final Report and Testimony Submitted to Congress by the Commission on Industrial Relations*, VI, 5843; J. W. Buzzell, "An Open Shop Citadel Falls," *American Federationist*, XLVIII (Apr., 1941), 6.

[7] *Final Report and Testimony Submitted to Congress by the Commission on Industrial Relations*, VI, 5581–3.

[8] *Citizen*, Mar. 15, 1912

[9] *Ibid.*, Mar. 29, 1912; *Times*, May 19, 1912.

[10] *Citizen*, Feb. 2, Aug. 2, 1912; Feb. 14, 1913.

[11] *Times*, Apr. 2, 1912; *Citizen*, Feb. 14, 1913; Los Angeles Central Labor Council, *Minutes 1912–1913*, meetings of July 5, Aug. 16, Nov. 18, Dec. 6, 13, 1912.

[12] *Times*, April 14, 1912; *Citizen*, May 24, June 7, Oct. 4, 1912; Feb. 4, 1913; Los Angeles Central Labor Council, *Minutes 1912*, meeting of May 13, 1912.

[13] *Citizen*, Feb. 2, Mar. 8, 15, June 14, July 26, 1912; *Labor Clarion*, May 17, 1912; Los Angeles Central Labor Council, *Minutes 1912–1913*, meetings of Sept. 20, 23, 1912.

[14] *Citizen*, Feb. 14, 1913.

[15] *Ibid.*, Jan. 19, 26, 1912.

[16] *Ibid.*, Mar. 22, May 3, 1912.

[17] *Ibid.*, Feb. 16, Apr. 19, May 10, June 21, 1912; *Proceedings of the California State Federation of Labor, 1912*, p. 75.

[18] San Francisco *Bulletin*, Feb. 9, 1912; *Labor Clarion*, Mar. 22, May 24, 1912.

[19] Pauline Jacobson, "Industrial Freedom Versus Feudalism," San Francisco *Bulletin*, Jan. 27, 1912.

[20] *Proceedings of the California State Federation of Labor, 1912*, pp. 74, 76; *1913*, pp. 57–8.

[21] *Times,* Jan. 1, 1912.

[22] Frederick Palmer, "Otistown of the Open Shop," *Hampton's Magazine,* XXVI (Jan., 1911), 30, 44.

[23] Louis Adamic, *Dynamite* (New York: Viking, 1931), p. 243; Frank T. Stockton, *The Closed Shop in American Trade Unions,* Johns Hopkins University Studies in Historical and Political Science, Series 29, no. 3 (Baltimore: Johns Hopkins Press, 1911), p. 56; Edgar Lloyd Hampton, "The Open Shop Movement as an Aid to Prosperity," *Industrial Digest,* Sept., 1928, pp. 11, 13.

[24] *Citizen,* Feb. 2, 1912.

[25] Los Angeles Central Labor Council, *Minutes 1912–1913,* meeting of Nov. 11, 1912.

[26] *Citizen,* Nov. 10, 1916.

[27] Palmer, *op. cit.,* p. 32.

[28] "General Otis, The Storm-Center of the Unpacific Coast," *Current Literature,* 52 (Jan., 1912), 38.

[29] *The Forty-Year War for a Free City; A History of the Open Shop in Los Angeles* (Los Angeles: Times-Mirror Publishing Co., 1929), p. 10.

BIBLIOGRAPHY

BIBLIOGRAPHY

I. Manuscripts

Charles Dwight Willard Letters, 1876–1913. Huntington Library, San Marino, California.

Cross, Ira B. *California Labor Notes, 1847–1885; 1886–1890; 1891–1896; Biography; Unions and Protective Associations; California Labor Newspapers; Miscellaneous Material, Unions and Protective Associations.* Bancroft Library, University of California, Berkeley, California.

Haskell, Burnette G. *Personal Notes; A Collection of Labor Miscellany, 1879–1893*, vols. 1–4, 8–9. Bancroft Library, University of California, Berkeley, California.

Henry H. Markham Papers, 1879–1898. Huntington Library, San Marino, California.

Huntington Manuscript 1152, *The United States vs. Frank Ryan et al.*, United States District Court, Indiana. 66 vols. Huntington Library, San Marino, California.

Letter from Clark B. Hicks, Research Director of International Typographical Union, to author, April 1, 1948.

Los Angeles Central Labor Council, *Minutes, January 29, 1909 to January 31, 1910; Minutes, February 3, 1911 to January 26, 1912; Minutes, February 3, 1912 to June 28, 1912; Minutes, July 5, 1912 to February 3, 1913.* Los Angeles Central Labor Council.

Los Angeles Typographical Union No. 174, *Minutes 1875–1885; 1886–1888; 1888–1890; 1890–1893; 1893–1896; 1896–1898; 1898–1902; 1902–1905; 1905–1908; 1908–1911.* Los Angeles Typographical Union.

II. Labor and Reform Newspapers and Periodicals*

Advocate, April–August, 1886. Incomplete file.

Alliance Farmer, March–December, 1891. Incomplete file.

American Federationist, 1901–1912. Published by the American Federation of Labor.

California Farmer, January, 1892–March, 1893. Continuation of *Alliance Farmer*.

California Federationist, September 15, 1894.

California Nationalist, February–May, 1890. Incomplete file.

The Carpenter, XXXI (March, August, November, 1911). Published by the Brotherhood of Carpenters and Joiners.

The Challenge, December, 1900–June, 1901.

The Citizen, 1907–1912.

Civic Review, March 30, 1895; January–October, 1896. Continuation of *Farmer and Labor Review*.

Coast Seamen's Journal, San Francisco, 1887–1897, 1899–1910.

Common Sense, August, 1904–August, 1909. Continuation of Los Angeles *Socialist*.

Farmer and Labor Review, March–September, 1893. Incomplete file. Amalgamation of *California Farmer* and *Labor Review*.

---

* Unless otherwise indicated, these papers were published in Los Angeles.

The Fraternity, March 5, 1902. Photostatic copy.

Labor Clarion, San Francisco, 1902–1912.

Labor Gleaner, February 11, 1888.

Labor Review, December 3, 1892.

Labor World, April 2, 1896.

Labor World and Silver Champion, January 7, 22, 1898. Continuation of *Labor World.*

Los Angeles *Socialist,* November, 1901–August, 1904.

Organized Labor, San Francisco, September 17, 1910.

Pacific Opinion, May–November, 1888. Incomplete file.

Pacific Union Printer, San Francisco, August, 1895.

The Porcupine, November, 1882–November, 1883; August 23, 1884; June, 1885–November, 1888 (incomplete file); July 27, November 23, 1889; February 22, March 15, May 3, June 21, 1890; March 28, 1891; December 1, 1894.

Southern California Labor Press, October 30, 1925.

Truth, San Francisco, October 6, 1883.

Union Label Bulletin, July, 1910.

Union Labor News, March 28, April 18, November 7, 1902; December 18, 25, 1903; November 10, 1905–February 22, 1907.

Union "Totem," November 19, 1896.

Voice of Labor, San Francisco, April 10, 1897.

Weekly Nationalist, May–November, 1890. Incomplete file. Continuation of *California Nationalist.*

Weekly Slogan, October 18, 1884.

Western Comrade, 1913–1917.

Workman, November, 1890–April, 1892. Incomplete file.

III. OTHER NEWSPAPERS AND PERIODICALS*

The Architect, Builder, and Mechanic of Southern California, July 22, 1887.

Cactus, 1888–1890. Incomplete file.

California Outlook, February 25–December 30, 1911. Continuation of *Pacific Outlook.*

Commercial Bulletin of Southern California, January 28, April 21, 28, May 5, August 4, 1888; January 9, 1892.

Daily Commercial, March 7–September 5, 1882.

Daily News, 1869–1870. Continuation of *Semi-Weekly News.*

Daily Star, 1876; January–June, October–December, 1878.

Democrat, August–October, 1884. Incomplete file.

Evening Express, 1873–1875; July–December, 1876; 1877–1878; 1880–1881; January–March, October–December, 1882; January–February, 1883; August–September, 1890; April–December, 1892; January–March, 1893; 1894–1895; January–July, 1896; October–December, 1897; April–June, October–December, 1898; April–June, 1899; January–February, 1907.

Evening Post, September–November, 1890.

Evening Telegram, August–September, 1882; July 25, December 12, 1887; March 3, 13, April 10, 1888; September–December, 1893 (incomplete file).

Examiner, December, 1903–December, 1906.

Fraternal Reporter, October 21, 1887.

---

* Unless otherwise indicated, these papers were published in Los Angeles.

Free Lance, July 28–August 24, 1883. Incomplete file.
Graphic, August, 1904–December, 1912.
Herald, October–December, 1873; January–March, 1874; August–December, 1877; 1878–1879; November 9–December 31, 1882; 1883–1884; January–September, December, 1885; January–September, 1886; April–December, 1889; 1890–1892; April–December, 1893; July–September, 1895; June–December, 1896; January–November, 1897; January–March, July–September, 1898; January–March, 1899; March 1–April 5, 1907; January, July, 1908.
Los Angeles *Life,* February, 1889–March, 1891. Incomplete file.
Monthly Summary, Business Conditions in Southern California (published by Security-First National Bank of Los Angeles), September 13, 1947.
Pacific Outlook, October 20, 1906–February 18, 1911.
Record, March 4, 19, 1895; May–September, November, 1896; July–December, 1897; 1898; January, March, May, July–December, 1899; 1900–1904; January 1–March 15, 1905.
San Francisco *Bulletin,* October 25, 27, 29, November 6, December 12, 1879; June 19, 1880.
San Pedro *Shipping Gazette,* October, 1883–April, 1884. Incomplete file.
San Pedro *Times,* September, 1891–January 15, 1898. Incomplete file.
Semi-Weekly News, November, 1865–December, 1868. Incomplete file.
Semi-Weekly Southern News, January, 1860–August, 1862.
Times, December 4–31, 1881; January 1–December 3, 1882; March 4–December 2, 1883; October 1–December 31, 1884; 1885–June, 1912.
Tribune, October 4–December 31, 1886; 1887–1888; January–March, 1889.
Weekly Citizen, September, 1890–June, 1893. Incomplete file.
Weekly Star, 1859–1862; April 19–May 24, 1879.

IV. OFFICIAL PUBLICATIONS OF THE STATE OF CALIFORNIA

California. Bureau of Labor Statistics. *First Biennial Report, 1883–1884.* Sacramento: 1884.
———. *Third Biennial Report, 1887–1888.* Sacramento: 1888.
———. *Fifth Biennial Report, 1891–1892.* Sacramento: 1893.
———. *Seventh Biennial Report, 1895–1896.* Sacramento: 1896.
———. *Ninth Biennial Report, 1899–1900.* Sacramento: 1900.
———. *Tenth Biennial Report, 1901–1902.* Sacramento: 1902.
———. *Eleventh Biennial Report, 1903–1904.* Sacramento: 1904.
———. *Twelfth Biennial Report, 1905–1906.* Sacramento: 1906.
———. *Thirteenth Biennial Report, 1907–1908.* Sacramento: 1908.
———. *Fourteenth Biennial Report, 1909–1910.* Sacramento: 1910.
[California. Bureau of Labor Statistics.] *Statistical Report of Unions Represented in the Council of Federated Trades and Labor Organizations on the Pacific Coast, November 1, 1887.* Sacramento: 1887.
California. Legislature. *Journal of the Assembly.* 29th sess. (1891). Sacramento: 1891.
———. *Journal of the Senate.* 29th sess. (1891). Sacramento: 1891.
———. *Journal of the Assembly.* 31st sess. (1895). Sacramento: 1895.
———. ———. 32d sess. (1897). Sacramento: 1897.
———. *Journal of the Senate.* 32d sess. (1897). Sacramento: 1897.
California. Secretary of State. *California Blue Book, 1899.* Sacramento: [1899].

California. Secretary of State—*Continued*
———. *California Blue Book, 1903*. Sacramento: [1903].
———. *California Blue Book, 1913–1915*. Sacramento: 1915.
California. State Relief Administration. *Migratory Labor in California*. [San Francisco]: 1936. 224 pp.

V. OFFICIAL PUBLICATIONS OF THE UNITED STATES GOVERNMENT

U.S. Bureau of Labor. *Free Public Employment Offices in the United States*, by J. E. Connor. Bull. no. 68. Washington: 1907.
———. *Mexican Labor in the United States*, by Victor S. Clark. Bull. no. 78. Washington: 1908.
U.S. Bureau of the Census. *Eighth Census of the United States, 1860*. Vol. I. *Population*.
———. *Ninth Census of the United States, 1870*. Vol. I. *Population*. Vol. III. *Wealth and Industry*.
———. *Tenth Census of the United States, 1880*. Vol. I. *Population*. Vol. II. *Manufactures in the United States*.
———. *Eleventh Census of the United States, 1890*. Vol. I. *Population*. Vol. XI. *Manufacturing Industries in the United States*.
———. *Twelfth Census of the United States, 1900*. Vol. VIII. *Manufactures*.
———. ———. *Manufactures, California*. Bull. no. 136. Washington: 1902.
———. *Thirteenth Census of the United States, 1910. Abstract of the Census with Supplement for California*. Washington: 1913. 727 pp.
———. *Fourteenth Census of the United States, 1920*. Vol. I. *Population*.
U.S. Commission on Industrial Relations. *The National Erectors' Association and the International Association of Bridge and Structural Ironworkers*, by Luke Grant. Washington: 1915. 192 pp.
U.S. Congress. House. *Reports of the Industrial Commission on Labor Organizations, Labor Disputes, and Arbitration, and on Railway Labor*. 57th Cong., 1st sess., H. Doc. 186. Vol. XVII of the Commission's Reports. Washington: 1901. 1172 pp.
———. Senate. *Final Report and Testimony Submitted to Congress by the Commission on Industrial Relations*. 64th Cong., 1st sess., S. Doc. 415. Vol. VI. Washington: 1916. Pp. 5089–5999.
U.S. Department of Labor. *Brotherhood Relief and Insurance of Railway Employees*, by Emory R. Johnson. Bull. no. 17. Washington: 1898.

VI. PUBLICATIONS OF LABOR ORGANIZATIONS

American Federation of Labor. *History, Encyclopedia Reference Book*. Washington: American Federation of Labor, 1919. 515 pp.
———. *Legislative Achievements of the American Federation of Labor*. Washington: American Federation of Labor, 1916.
———. *Reports of Proceedings of the . . . Annual Convention of the American Federation of Labor. . . .* 1896–1904; 1906–1912.
American Federation of Musicians. *Proceedings of the Sixteenth Annual Convention, 1911*.
Anti-Coolie Club No. One of Los Angeles, California. *Constitution and By-Laws*. Los Angeles: Herald Steam Job Printing House, 1876.

California Chinese Exclusion Convention. *Proceedings and List of Delegates, California Chinese Exclusion Convention held at San Francisco, November 21 and 22, 1901.* San Francisco: The Star Press [1901].

California State Council of Carpenters. *Souvenir Program 20th Annual Convention, 1948.* n.p.: [1948]. 48 pp.

California State Federation of Labor. *Proceedings of the ... Annual Convention of the California State Federation of Labor....* 1901; 1903–1913.

General Campaign Strike Committee for the Unionizing of Los Angeles. *California Labor's Greatest Victory; Final Report of General Campaign Strike Committee for the Unionizing of Los Angeles Embracing Receipts and Expenditures June 1, 1910–April 1, 1912.* [San Francisco: 1912].

Grand International Brotherhood of Railway Conductors. *Constitution and By-Laws.* Los Angeles: 1889.

International Typographical Union. *Reports of Officers to the Fifty-seventh Annual Session of the International Typographical Union at San Francisco, California, August, 1911.* [Indianapolis: 1911].

Journeymen Tailors' Protective Union of Los Angeles, California. *Constitution and By-Laws.* Los Angeles: 1888.

Knights of Labor. *Proceedings of the ... Regular Session of the General Assembly of the Knights of Labor....* 1883–1887.

Los Angeles Central Labor Council. *Los Angeles—"A Model Open Shop City."* Los Angeles: 1907. 6 pp.

[Los Angeles Council of Labor and Building Trades Council]. *Official Trades and Labor Souvenir Directory of Los Angeles and Vicinity.* Los Angeles: Council of Labor and Building Trades Council [1896]. 97 pp.

Los Angeles Musical Association. *Constitution and By-Laws.* Los Angeles: 1895.

Los Angeles Musicians Local 47, A. F. of M. *Fiftieth Anniversary, 1894–1944.* Los Angeles: 1944. Unpaged.

Los Angeles Typographical Union No. 174. *Golden Jubilee, 1875–1925.* Los Angeles: Typographical Union No. 174, 1925. 22 unnumbered pages.

———. *Mr. Otis and the Los Angeles "Times."* Los Angeles: Typographical Union No. 174, 1915. 24 pp.

National Printers' Protective Fraternity. *Constitution and By-Laws Adopted March 15, 1886, at Topeka, Kas.* Kansas City, Mo.: Ramsey, Millett & Hudson, 1886. 19 pp.

The Order of Railway Conductors. *Twenty-Sixth Session of the Grand Division, May 11th, 1897, Los Angeles, Cal.* Los Angeles: R. Y. McBride [1897].

State Building Trades Council of California. *Proceedings of the Tenth Annual Convention, 1911.* San Francisco: [1911].

VII. Pamphlets

Barton, C. V. *The Recall.* Unpublished manuscript. Haynes Foundation, Los Angeles, 1905. 7 pp.

Citizens' Industrial Association of America. *Bulletin No. 1.* Indianapolis: 1903. 23 pp.

———. *Proceedings of the Adjourned Session of the First Convention, February 22 and 23, 1904.* Indianapolis: [1904]. 100 pp.

———. *A Statement of Its Character and Purposes.* Indianapolis: n.d. 15 pp.

Darrow, Clarence. *The Plea of Clarence Darrow in His Own Defense to the Jury at Los Angeles, August, 1912.* Los Angeles: Golden Press, 1912. 55 pp.

Haynes, John R. *The Recall of Councilman Davenport.* Unpublished manuscript. Haynes Foundation, Los Angeles, n.d. 15 pp.

Herald Publishing Company. *The Herald Pamphlet for 1876.* Los Angeles: Herald Publishing Co., 1876.

Los Angeles. Board of Trade. *Annual Report, 1888.* Los Angeles: Evening Express Co., 1888.

Los Angeles County Chamber of Commerce. *Los Angeles, "The Magic City and County."* Los Angeles: County Board of Supervisors, 1951. 48 pp.

Los Angeles *Times. The Forty-Year War for a Free City; A History of the Open Shop in Los Angeles.* Los Angeles: Times-Mirror Publishing Co., 1929. 28 pp.

McManigal, Ortie E. *The National Dynamite Plot.* Los Angeles: The Neale Co., 1913. 91 pp.

Merchants and Manufacturers Association of Los Angeles. *Constitution and By-Laws.* Los Angeles: 1896. 26 pp.

————. *Fiftieth Annual Report, 1896–1946.* Los Angeles: [1946]. 55 pp.

National Municipal League. *Proceedings of the 13th Conference for Good City Government and the 11th Annual Meeting of the National Municipal League.* Philadelphia: 1905.

————. *Proceedings of the 17th Conference for Good City Government and the 15th Annual Meeting of the National Municipal League.* Philadelphia: 1909.

Norton, R. H. *The First Recall Campaign.* Unpublished manuscript. Haynes Foundation, Los Angeles, n.d. 7 pp.

Otis, Harrison Gray. *The Los Angeles Times; A Plain Statement of Bed-Rock Facts and Unanswerable Reasons Sustaining the Attitude of the Times and Its Owners toward Labor during the Past Six Years.* Los Angeles: Times-Mirror Publishing Co., 1896. 8 pp.

Park, J. W. *The Adoption of the Recall in Los Angeles.* Unpublished manuscript. Haynes Foundation, Los Angeles, 1909. 10 pp.

Personal Sketch [of Harrison Gray Otis]. [Los Angeles: 1913]. 4 pp.

[Richardson, Thomas, ed.]. *The Industries of Los Angeles, California.* Los Angeles: Industrial Publishing Co., 1888.

Robinson, Aileen W. *A Critical Evaluation of the American Federation of Teachers.* Chicago: American Federation of Teachers [1934]. 60 pp.

Schmidt, Matthew. *"The Fight for Light and Freedom"; An Address of M. A. Schmidt before the Court of Los Angeles, Jan. 12, 1916.* n.p.: [1916].

Schnitzer, L. M. *Truth—Strikes.* [Oakland, Calif.: 1897]. 16 pp.

[Stephens, Bascom A., ed.]. *Resources of Los Angeles County, California.* Los Angeles: Sprague & Rodehauer, 1887.

The True History of the Famous McNamara Case. Speeches by Anton Johannsen, Clarence Darrow, and Mother Jones. Kansas City, Mo.: Carpenters Local No. 61 [1915?]. 32 pp.

VIII. Theses

Crockett, Earl C. "The History of California Labor Legislation, 1910–1930." Unpublished Ph.D. dissertation. University of California, Berkeley, 1931.

Dixon, Marion. "The History of the Los Angeles Central Labor Council." Unpublished M.A. thesis. University of California, Berkeley, 1929.

Flannery, Helen. "The Labor Movement in Los Angeles, 1880–1903." Unpublished M.A. thesis. University of California, Berkeley, 1929.

Lopez, Espiridion B. "The History of the California State Federation of Labor." Unpublished M.A. thesis. University of California, Berkeley, 1932.

Morgans, Robert DeWitt. "A History of Organized Labor in Long Beach, California." Unpublished M.A. thesis. University of California, Berkeley, 1939.

Weintraub, Hyman. "The I. W. W. in California, 1905–1931." Unpublished M.A. thesis. University of California, Los Angeles, 1947.

IX. ARTICLES

Bacon, Thomas R. "The Railroad Strike in California," *Yale Review*, III (Nov., 1894), 241–50.

Baker, John C. "Birth and Demise of the P. P. F.," *Typographical Journal*, CXI (July, 1947), 25–7.

Baker, Ray Stannard. "Organized Capital Challenges Organized Labor," *McClure's Magazine*, XXIII (July, 1904), 279–92.

"Bliss, William Dwight Porter," *Encyclopedia of Social Reform*, ed. by W. D. P. Bliss (1897), p. 179.

"Burns' Story on the Trail of the Men Higher Up," *McClure's Magazine*, XXXVIII (Feb., 1912), 363–71.

Buzzell, J. W. "An Open Shop Citadel Falls," *American Federationist*, XLVIII (Apr., 1941), 6–7, 30–6.

"A Charge of Wholesale Murder," *Outlook*, 98 (May 6, 1911), 1–2.

Coates, James A. "The Printers' Protective Fraternity," *Kansas Labor Weekly*, Aug. 28, 1947. Unpaged.

Colver, Frank B. "Los Angeles Labor Council," San Francisco *Call*, May 4, 1896.

"The Common Welfare," *Survey*, XXVII (Dec. 30, 1911), 1407–12.

Connolly, Christopher P. "Protest by Dynamite," *Colliers*, XLVIII (Jan. 13, 1912), 9–10, 23.

———. "The Saving of Clarence Darrow," *Colliers*, XLVIII (Dec. 23, 1911), 9–10, 22.

"The Darrow Acquittal," *Literary Digest*, 45 (Aug. 31, 1912), 323.

Darrow, Clarence. "Second Plea of Clarence Darrow in His Own Defense at Los Angeles (in the Bain Case), March 1913," *Everyman*, IX (May, 1913), 3–24.

Debs, Eugene V. "The McNamara Case and the Labor Movement," *International Socialist Review*, XII (Jan., 1912), 397–401.

Drake, Francis. "Board of Publishers of the Organized Labor Movement," *Official Year Book and Reference Manual of the Organized Labor Movement of Los Angeles* (1922), pp. 49–50.

"The Dynamite Cases End in Conviction," *Survey*, XXIX (Jan. 4, 1913), 414–15.

"The Dynamite 'Plot' Case," *Literary Digest*, 45 (Nov. 2, 1912), 773–4.

"The Dynamiters," *Independent*, LXX (May 4, 1911), 923.

"Employers at Last Awake," *The Review* (Oct., 1910), 27–8.

"The End of Two Strikes," *Outlook*, 87 (Nov. 16, 1907), 552.

Fitch, George Hamlin. "Races and Labor Problems in California," *Chatauquan*, XXIV (Jan., 1897), 427–32.

Fitch, John A. "The Dynamite Case," *Survey,* XXIX (Feb. 1, 1913), 607–17.

———. "Los Angeles, A Militant Anti-Union Citadel," *Survey,* XXXIII (Oct. 3, 1914), 4–6.

Frank, H. W. "The Merchants' and Manufacturers' Association," *Land of Sunshine,* VI (Apr., 1897), 212–17.

Gallagher, Andrew J. "Something Doing in Los Angeles," *International Socialist Review,* XI (Sept., 1910), 166–7.

"General Otis, the Storm-Center of the Unpacific Coast," *Current Literature,* 52 (Jan., 1912), 35–8.

Gompers, Samuel. "A. F. of L. and Iron Workers," *Survey,* XXIX (Feb. 1, 1913), 621–3.

———. "The McNamara Case," *American Federationist,* XVIII (June, 1911), 433–50.

"Gompers Speaks for Labor," *McClure's Magazine,* XXXVIII (Feb., 1912), 371–6.

"Government by Dynamite," *Outlook,* 103 (Jan. 11, 1913), 62–5.

Guinn, James M. "Great Real Estate Boom of 1887," *Annual Publications of the Historical Society of Southern California,* I (1890).

Hampton, Edgar Lloyd. "The Open Shop Movement as an Aid to Prosperity," *Industrial Digest* (Sept., 1928).

"Harriman, Job," *Who's Who in America,* X (1918–1919), 1194.

Hertzler, J. O. "Edward Bellamy," *Encyclopedia of the Social Sciences,* II (1930), 504.

Hicks, Clark B. "The Printers' Protective Fraternity," *Typographical Journal,* CX (Feb., 1947), 80–2.

Hilbert, F. W. "Employers' Associations in the United States," *in* Jacob H. Hollander and George E. Barnett, eds., *Studies in American Trade Unionism.* London: Hodder and Stroughton, 1906. Pp. 183–217.

"The House-Cleaning in Los Angeles," *Outlook,* 91 (Apr. 3, 1909), 757–8.

"How Burns Caught the Dynamiters," *McClure's Magazine,* XXXVIII (Jan., 1912), 325–9.

Hoxie, Robert F. "The Failure of the Telegraphers' Strike," *Journal of Political Economy,* XV (Nov., 1907), 545–7.

[Jackson, Helen Hunt]. "Outdoor Industries in Southern California," *Century Magazine,* XXVI (Oct., 1883), 803–20.

Jacobson, Pauline. "Otis: 'Jehovah of Industrial Freedom,'" San Francisco *Bulletin,* Dec. 9, 1911.

———. "The 'M. and M.' and the Struggle of Labor," San Francisco *Bulletin,* Dec. 16, 1911.

———. "Los Angeles and the Piece System," San Francisco *Bulletin,* Dec. 30, 1911.

———. "Industrial Freedom Versus Feudalism," San Francisco *Bulletin,* Jan. 27, 1912.

Kellogg, Paul U. "Conservation and Industrial War," *Survey,* XXVII (Dec. 30, 1911), 1412.

King, W. L. Mackenzie. "The International Typographical Union," *Journal of Political Economy,* V (Sept., 1897), 458–84.

"Labor Comment on the Dynamite Conviction," *Literary Digest,* 46 (Jan. 18, 1913), 117.

"The Labor Exchange," *Encyclopedia of Social Reform,* ed. by W. D. P. Bliss (1897), p. 786.

"Larger Bearings of the McNamara Case," *Survey,* XXVII (Dec. 30, 1911), 1413–29.

"The Last of the Dynamite Suspects Arrested," *Survey,* XXXIII (Feb. 27, 1915), 570.

Layne, J. Gregg. "The Lincoln-Roosevelt League, Its Origins and Accomplishments," *Historical Society of Southern California Quarterly* (Sept., 1943).

Lewis, Austin. "The Drift in California," *International Socialist Review,* XII (Nov., 1911), 272–4.

Los Angeles Brotherhood of Locomotive Firemen. Contributed notice, *Firemen's Magazine,* VII (Jan., 1883), 47.

———. Contributed notice, *Firemen's Magazine,* VII (July, 1883), 320.

"The Los Angeles Conspiracy against Organized Labor," *International Socialist Review,* XI (Nov., 1910), 262–6.

"The Los Angeles Crime," *Independent,* VII (May 4, 1911), 967–8.

McCorkle, Julia Norton. "A History of Los Angeles Journalism," *Annual Publications of the Historical Society of Southern California,* X (1915–1916).

Macfarlane, Peter Clark. "What Is the Matter with Los Angeles?" *Colliers,* XLVIII (Dec. 2, 1911), 28–31.

McWilliams, Carey. "The City That Wanted the Truth," *Pacific Spectator,* III (Spring, 1949), 177–88.

"The Municipal Reform in Los Angeles," *Outlook,* 91 (Mar. 13, 1909), 570–1.

"A Notable Triumph for Free Speech in Los Angeles," *Arena,* XL (Oct., 1908), 350–1.

O'Higgins, Harvey J. "The Dynamiters, A Great Case of Detective William Burns," *McClure's Magazine,* XXXVII (Aug., 1911), 346–64.

Otis, Harrison Gray. "A Long, Winning Fight against the 'Closed Shop': An Account of a Seventeen-Years' Conflict between the Los Angeles 'Times' and the Typographical Union," *World's Work,* XV (Dec., 1907), 9675–9.

———. "Los Angeles—A Sketch," *Sunset,* XXIV (Jan., 1910), 12–16.

Palmer, Frederick. "Otistown of the Open Shop," *Hampton's Magazine,* XXVI (Jan., 1911), 29–44.

"Petition to the President for a Federal Commission on Industrial Relations," *Survey,* XXVII (Dec. 30, 1911), 1430–1.

Phillis, Joseph. " 'Labor Agitators' I Have Known," Los Angeles *Citizen,* Jan.–June, 1911, *passim.*

Plehn, Carl. "Labor in California," *Yale Review,* IV (Feb., 1896), 409–25.

Pomeroy, Eltweed. "The First Discharge of a Public Servant," *Independent,* LVIII (Jan. 12, 1905), 69–71.

———. "Really Masters," *Arena,* XXXIII (Jan., 1905), 51–2.

"Progress of the Dynamite Trial," *Literary Digest,* 45 (Dec. 14, 1912), 1112–13.

"Review of the World," *Current Literature,* 50 (June, 1911), 569–75.

Rolle, Andrew F. "Futile Filibustering in Baja California, 1888–1890," *Pacific Historical Review,* XX (May, 1951), 159–66.

"Sense and Hysteria in the McNamara Affair," *Nation,* 94 (Jan. 11, 1912), 28–9.

"A Senseless Strike," *Outlook,* 86 (Aug. 17, 1907), 794–5.

"The Situation in California," *Nation,* LIX (July 12, 1894), 23.

"Southern California and the Strike," *Land of Sunshine,* I (Aug., 1894), 59.

Splitter, Henry Winfred. "Concerning Vinette's Los Angeles Regiment of Coxey's Army," *Pacific Historical Review,* XXVII (Feb., 1948), 29–36.

Stafford, W. V. "Child Labor in California," *Transactions of the Commonwealth Club of California,* II (Jan., 1906), 104–15.

"The Strike of Telegraphers," *Outlook,* 86 (Aug. 24, 1907), 841.

Taylor, Graham. "The Industrial Viewpoint," *Charities and the Commons,* XVIII (Sept. 7, 1907), 696–700.

Taylor, Paul S. "Foundations of California Rural Society," *California Historical Society Quarterly,* XXIV (Sept., 1945).

"Trial by Jury on Trial," *Outlook,* 99 (Dec. 2, 1911), 794–5.

Vassault, F. I. "Nationalism in California," *Overland Monthly,* 2d Series, XV (June, 1890), 659–61.

Wilkins, M. W. "The California Situation," *International Socialist Review,* III (Jan., 1903), 416–19.

Woehlke, Walter V. "The End of the Dynamite Case—'Guilty,'" *Outlook,* 99 (Dec. 16, 1911), 903–8.

———. "Terrorism in America," *Outlook,* 100 (Feb. 17, 1912), 359–67.

Works, John D. "A City's Struggle for Political and Moral Freedom," *Arena,* XLI (Mar., 1909), 353–7.

X. Books

Adamic, Louis. *Dynamite.* New York: The Viking Press, 1931. xviii, 452 pp.

Ayers, James J. *Gold and Sunshine, Reminiscences of Early California.* Boston: Richard G. Badger [c. 1922]. 359 pp.

Barnett, George E. *The Printers.* American Economic Association Publications, Third Series, Vol. X, no. 3. Cambridge, Mass.: American Economic Association, 1909. 387 pp.

Bates, Joseph Clement, ed. *History of the Bench and Bar of California.* San Francisco: Bench and Bar Publishing Co., 1912. 572 pp.

Bean, Walton. *Boss Ruef's San Francisco.* Berkeley: University of California Press, 1952. 325 pp.

Bonnett, Clarence E. *Employers' Associations in the United States.* New York: The Macmillan Co., 1922. 594 pp.

Brissenden, Paul F. *The I. W. W.* New York: Columbia University Press, 1919. 438 pp.

Bryce, James. *The American Commonwealth.* 2d ed. rev. New York: Commonwealth Publishing Co., 1908. 2 vols.

Buck, Solon J. *The Agrarian Crusade.* Chronicles of America Series, vol. 45. New Haven: Yale University Press, 1921. 215 pp.

———. *The Granger Movement.* Harvard Historical Series, vol. 19. Cambridge, Mass.: Harvard University Press, 1913. 384 pp.

Burns, William J. *The Masked War.* New York: George H. Doran Co. [c. 1913]. 328 pp.

Carr, Ezra Slocum. *The Patrons of Husbandry on the Pacific Coast.* San Francisco: A. L. Bancroft & Co., 1875. 461 pp.

Cleland, Robert Glass. *California in Our Time.* New York: Alfred A. Knopf, 1947. 320 pp.

———. *The Cattle on a Thousand Hills.* San Marino, Calif.: The Huntington Library, 1941. 327 pp.

Cleland, Robert Glass, and Osgood Hardy. *March of Industry*. Los Angeles: Powell Publishing Co. [c. 1929]. 322 pp.

Cohn, Alfred, and Joe Chisholm. *"Take the Witness!"* New York: Frederick A. Stokes Co., 1934. 315 pp.

Coleman, McAlister. *Eugene V. Debs*. New York: Greenberg [c. 1930]. ix, 345 pp.

Commons, John R., and Associates. *History of Labor in the United States*. New York: The Macmillan Co., 1921–1935. 4 vols.

Coolidge, Mary. *Chinese Immigration*. New York: Henry Holt and Co., 1909. 531 pp.

Cross, Ira B. *A History of the Labor Movement in California*. Berkeley: University of California Press, 1935. 354 pp.

Darrow, Clarence. *The Story of My Life*. New York: Charles Scribner's Sons, 1932. 495 pp.

Dulles, Foster Rhea. *Labor in America*. New York: Thomas Y. Crowell Co. [c. 1949]. 402 pp.

Dumke, Glenn S. *The Boom of the Eighties in Southern California*. San Marino, Calif.: The Huntington Library, 1944. 313 pp.

Eaves, Lucile. *A History of California Labor Legislation*. Berkeley: The University Press [c. 1910]. 461 pp.

Faulkner, Harold U. *The Quest for Social Justice, 1898–1914*. History of American Life Series, Vol. XI. New York: The Macmillan Co. [c. 1931]. 390 pp.

Fine, Nathan. *Labor and Farmer Parties in the United States, 1828–1928*. New York: Rand School of Social Science [c. 1928]. 445 pp.

Foner, Philip S. *History of the Labor Movement in the United States*. New York: International Publishers [c. 1947]. 576 pp.

Gilman, Charlotte Perkins. *The Living of Charlotte Perkins Gilman*. New York: Appleton-Century Publishing Co., 1935. 341 pp.

Gompers, Samuel. *Seventy Years of Life and Labor*. New ed. New York: E. P. Dutton and Co. [c. 1925]. 2 vols.

Harrison, Charles Yale. *Clarence Darrow*. New York: Cape & Smith [c. 1931]. 380 pp.

Hichborn, Franklin. *Story of the Session of the California Legislature of 1909*. San Francisco: James H. Barry Co., 1909. 296, xxxiii pp.

———. *Story of the Session of the California Legislature of 1911*. San Francisco: James H. Barry Co., 1911. 348, lxvii pp.

Hicks, John D. *The Populist Revolt*. Minneapolis: The University of Minnesota Press [c. 1931]. 473 pp.

Hill, Laurance L. *La Reina—Los Angeles in Three Centuries*. Los Angeles: Security Trust and Savings Bank [c. 1929]. 208 pp.

Hillquit, Morris. *History of Socialism in the United States*. New York: Funk & Wagnalls Co., 1903. 371 pp.

Hittell, John S. *The Commerce and Industries of the Pacific Coast of North America*. San Francisco: A. L. Bancroft & Co., 1882. 819 pp.

[Kilner, William H. B.]. *Arthur Letts, 1862–1923*. [Los Angeles: Privately printed, 1927.] 273 pp.

Laidler, Harry W. *Social-Economic Movements*. New York: Thomas Y. Crowell Co. [c. 1944]. 828 pp.

Lindley, Walter, and J. P. Widney. *California of the South*. New York: Appleton & Co., 1888. 377 pp.

Lindsey, Almont. *The Pullman Strike*. Chicago: University of Chicago Press [c. 1942]. 385 pp.

Lloyd, Caroline Augusta. *Henry Demarest Lloyd, 1847–1903*. New York: G. P. Putnam's Sons, 1912. 2 vols.

Lorwin, Lewis L. *The American Federation of Labor*. Washington: The Brookings Institution, 1933. 573 pp.

McIsaac, Archibald M. *The Order of Railroad Telegraphers*. Princeton: Princeton University Press, 1933. 284 pp.

McMurry, Donald L. *Coxey's Army: A Study of the Industrial Army Movement of 1894*. Boston: Little, Brown and Co., 1929. 331 pp.

McNeill, George E. *The Labor Movement: The Problem of To-day*. Boston: Bridgman, 1887. 615 pp.

Millis, Harry A., and Royal E. Montgomery. *Organized Labor*. New York: McGraw-Hill Book Co., 1945. 930 pp.

Mowry, George E. *The California Progressives*. Berkeley: University of California Press, 1951. 349 pp.

Newmark, Harris. *Sixty Years in Southern California, 1853–1913*. New York: Knickerbocker Press, 1916. 688 pp.

Perlman, Selig. *A History of Trade Unionism in the United States*. New York: The Macmillan Co., 1922. 313 pp.

Powderly, T. V. *Thirty Years of Labor, 1859–1889*. Rev. and corr. ed. Philadelphia: [c. 1890]. 372 pp.

Robbins, Edwin C. *Railway Conductors: A Study in Organized Labor*. Columbia University Studies in History, Economics, and Public Law, vol. 61. New York: Columbia University Press, 1914. 183 pp.

Rochester, Anna. *The Populist Movement in the United States*. New York: International Publishers [c. 1943]. 128 pp.

Sandmeyer, Elmer Clarence. *The Anti-Chinese Movement in California*. Urbana, Ill.: University of Illinois Press, 1939. 127 pp.

Schlesinger, Arthur M. *The Rise of the City, 1878–1898*. History of American Life Series, Vol. X. New York: The Macmillan Co., 1933. 494 pp.

Spalding, William A., comp. *History and Reminiscences, Los Angeles City and County, California*. Los Angeles: J. R. Finnell & Sons Publishing Co. [1931]. 3 vols.

Spedden, E. R. *The Trade Union Label*. Johns Hopkins University Studies in Historical and Political Science, Series 28, no. 2. Baltimore: Johns Hopkins Press, 1910. vii, 100 pp.

Stedman, J. C., and R. A. Leonard. *The Workingmen's Party of California*. San Francisco: Bacon & Co., 1878.

Steffens, Lincoln. *The Autobiography of Lincoln Steffens*. New York: Harcourt, Brace & Co. [c. 1931]. xi, 884 pp.

Stockton, Frank T. *The Closed Shop in American Trade Unions*. Johns Hopkins University Studies in Historical and Political Science, Series 29, no. 3. Baltimore: Johns Hopkins Press, 1911. 187 pp.

Stowell, Charles Jacob. *Studies in Trade Unionism in the Custom Tailoring Trade*. Bloomington, Ill.: Journeymen Tailors Union of America, 1913. 166 pp.

Taylor, Paul S. *The Sailors' Union of the Pacific*. New York: Ronald Press Co., 1923. 188 pp.

Tracy, George A., comp. *History of the Typographical Union.* [Indianapolis]: International Typographical Union, 1913. 1165 pp.

Vincent, Henry. *The Story of the Commonweal.* Chicago: W. B. Conkey Co., 1894. 247 pp.

Waldron, D. G., and T. J. Vivian, eds. *Biographical Sketches of the Delegates to the Convention to Frame a New Constitution for the State of California, 1878.* San Francisco: Francis & Valentine, 1878. 176 pp.

Ware, Norman J. *The Labor Movement in the United States, 1860–1895.* New York: D. Appleton & Co., 1929. xviii, 409 pp.

Warner, J. J., Benjamin Hayes, and J. P. Widney. *An Historical Sketch of Los Angeles County, California, from the Spanish Occupancy, by the Founding of the Mission San Gabriel Archangel, September 8, 1771, to July 4, 1876.* Los Angeles: Louis Lewin & Co., 1876. 88 pp.

Webb, Sidney and Beatrice. *The History of Trade Unionism.* Rev. ed., extended to 1920. London: Longmans, Green and Co., 1935. 784 pp.

Willard, Charles Dwight. *History of Los Angeles City.* Los Angeles: Kingsley-Barnes and Neuner Co., 1901. 365 pp.

[Wilson, John Albert]. *History of Los Angeles County, California.* Oakland, Calif.: Thompson and West, 1880. 192 pp.

Woehlke, Walter V. *Union Labor in Peace and War.* San Francisco: Sunset Publishing House [c. 1918]. 141 pp.

Wolman, Leo. *The Boycott in American Trade Unions.* Johns Hopkins University Studies in Historical and Political Science, Series 34, no. 1. Baltimore: Johns Hopkins Press, 1916. 148 pp.

INDEX

INDEX

Adams, Robert, 85

Alexander, George: elected mayor, 324–325; reëlection, 364, 398–400, 407; on picketing, 342–344; and *Times* bombing, 348, 371, 372, 377–379, 380, 384, 385, 390; and metal trades strike, 349, 352

American Federation of Labor: policies and objectives, 2, 141, 178, 197, 200, 295, 304, 336; formation and growth, 67, 93, 195–198; and eight-hour day, 96, 101, 135, 192; relations with Los Angeles labor, 122, 149, 178, 194, 195, 206, 207–208, 230–231, 238, 248, 254, 271, 276, 290, 312–314, 316, 319–320, 327–329, 333–334, 350, 352, 422, 430; on open shop, 136, 257; affiliation of Los Angeles labor, 141, 151, 171; and San Francisco labor, 142; and Coxey's Army, 155; and railroad unions, 161; and Chinese issue, 217; and socialism, 218–219, 230–231, 234–235; and *Times* bombing, 370, 393–394, 398, 403–404, 412, 415–416, 419

American Railway Union, 120, 127, 160, 161, 164–171, 173, 179, 219, 222

Anheuser-Busch, 338

Anti-Chinese Non-Partisan Association, 65

Anti-Chinese Union, 31, 49, 62–64

Anti-Citizens' Alliance, 300, 305–306, 309

Anti-Coolie Club No. 1, 11–13

Antimonopolism, 7–9, 16, 19, 26, 27

Arbitration of labor disputes: as objective of labor, 113, 173, 191, 244, 249, 275, 276, 352, 355; proposed by management, 169; printers vs. *Herald,* 239; in contracts, 240, 259, 260

Asiatic Exclusion League, 337

Atwood, H. J. L., 277, 309

Ayers, James J., 105, 106, 110, 121

Bagley, C. L., 394

Bailey, Jonathan D.: background, 56–57; philosophy, 57, 79, 91, 102; anti-Chinese activity, 65; political activities, 92, 98, 143–145, 150, 151, 194, 218; aid to unorganized workers, 94

Bailey, William H., 91

Bailie, William N., 251

Bain, Robert, 409, 411

Baker, E. J., 335

Baker, Fred L., 72, 264, 343, 404

Baker Iron Works, 72, 88, 246, 263, 341, 342, 354, 388

Bakers, 89, 90, 97, 100, 123, 124, 133, 135, 167, 202, 238, 425; first organization, 75; strikes and boycotts, 75, 96, 138, 186, 301–302, 355, 359

Bakers' Association, Master, 256, 302

Barbers, 100, 124, 125, 126, 127, 138, 187, 191, 239, 269, 290; first organization, 97

Barbers' Protective Association, Master, 239

Bartenders, 289, 425

Batchelor, B. W., 146, 150

Beaudry, Prudent, 9

Beck, S. J., 24

Behm, George, 391

Bellamy, Edward, 98

Bellman, P. R., 143, 144

Bender, F. Ira, 374

Biddle, Lemuel D.: background, 98; philosophy, 98–99, 102; political activities, 99, 101, 194, 218, 219, 220, 221, 224, 225, 227, 228, 232, 233, 305–307; union activities 165, 205, 207, 208, 249, 250, 267, 287, 300–301

Bill posters, 332

Black-listing, 96, 111, 119, 134, 165, 178, 247, 256, 289, 293

Blacksmiths, 125; strikes, 72, 340–345, 422

Bliss, W. D. P., 223, 224

Board of Supervisors, Los Angeles County, 129, 155, 178, 191, 375, 377, 384, 390

Boilermakers, 126, 127, 188; first organization, 125; strikes, 263, 303, 340–345, 422

Bonfilio, J., 245

Bookbinders, 202, 264, 425; first organization, 183; strike, 268

Bordwell, Walter, 392, 395, 397, 404–405, 407, 408

Bowen, J. B., 334

Boyce, H. H., 41, 64, 73, 105

Boycotts, 40, 76, 89, 90, 96, 132, 139, 163, 165–166, 189, 239, 243, 245, 259, 262, 266, 268–269, 297, 298, 302, 308, 310, 332, 339, 351, 355, 359, 361; against Chinese, 60, 64–66; against *Times,* 110–115, 117–122, 177, 181, 249–255, 270–271; against People's Store, 114, 250–255, 270, 277–280

Brandeis, Louis D., 418

Brass workers, 340–345

Date Due